Navajo Places

NAVAJO PLACES

HISTORY, LEGEND, LANDSCAPE

A Narrative of Important Places on and near the Navajo Reservation,

with Notes on Their Significance to Navajo Culture and History

Laurance D. Linford

Laurance D. Linford

THE UNIVERSITY OF UTAH PRESS

Salt Lake City

LIBRARY OF CONGRESS CATALOGING-IN-PUBLICATION DATA

Linford, Laurance D.
    Navajo places : history, legend, landscape / Laurance D. Linford.
        p. cm.
    "A narrative of important places on and near the Navajo Reservation, with notes on
their significance to Navajo culture and history."
    Includes bibliographical references and index.
    ISBN 0-87480-623-2 (cloth : alk. paper)—ISBN 0-87480-624-0 (pbk. : alk. paper)
        1. Names, Navajo-Guidebooks.   2. Names, Geographical —Southwest,
New-Guidebooks.   3. Navajo mythology.   4. Navajo Indians—History.   I. Title.

E99.N3 L645 2000
979'.004972—dc21

                                                                        99-053553

To Karen,
who knows the
many reasons why

Contents

List of Maps — viii

List of Tables — viii

List of Abbreviations — viii

Preface — xiii

1. INTRODUCTION — 1
Physiography — 1
The People — 3
Before the Navajos:
10,000 B.C.–A.D. 1600 — 3
The Navajos: Pre-1600 to Present — 3
The Archaeological/Historical
Perspective — 3
The Traditional Navajo Perspective — 4
Intrusion of the Spaniards:
A.D. 1541–1821 — 4
Explorations — 4
Colonization — 5
The Wars — 5
The Mexicans: 1821–1846 — 6
The Americans: 1846–Present — 7
The Early Years — 7
The Navajos Capitulate — 12
The Long Walk — 12
The Reservation Years: 1868–Present — 13
Navajo Social Organization — 13
Political Organization — 14
Chapters — 15

2. THE ROLE OF MYTHOLOGY IN
NAVAJO PLACE NAME ORIGINS — 17
The Practice — 18
The Ceremonies — 18
Holyway Ceremonies — 19
Shooting Chant — 19
Mountain Chant — 19
God Impersonators — 19
Wind Chant — 20
Hand-Trembling Chant — 20
Eagle Trapping — 20
Uncertain Affiliation — 20
Evilway Ceremonies — 20
Lifeway Ceremonies — 20
Ceremonialism and Navajo Place Names — 21

3. THE TRADING POSTS — 23

4. ARIZONA LOCATIONS — 33

5. COLORADO LOCATIONS — 153

6. NEW MEXICO LOCATIONS — 169

7. UTAH LOCATIONS — 285

References — 305

Maps

The Navajo Reservation and
Surrounding Area ix
Arizona x
New Mexico xi
Colorado xii
Utah xii

Tables

1. The Three Major Physiographic
Provinces of Navajoland 1
2. Navajoland Indigenous Cultural History 2
3. Major Spanish Military Expeditions
into Navajoland 7
4. Major Mexican Military Expeditions
into Navajoland 8
5. Major American Expeditions into
Navajoland Prior to 1860 9

Abbreviations

AAA   Southern California Automobile Club
      Indian Country Map
AP   *Will C. Barnes' Arizona Place Names*
      by Byrd H. Granger
AT&SF   Atchison, Topeka and Santa Fe
      Railway
BIA   Bureau of Indian Affairs
BLM   Bureau of Land Management
BNSF   Burlington Northern Santa Fe Railway
DB   *Diné Bikéyah*
      by Richard F. Van Valkenburgh
NMPN   *New Mexico Place Names*
      by T. M. Pearce
USDA   U.S. Department of Agriculture
USDI   U.S. Department of the Interior
USGS   U.S. Geological Survey
USGS-2   U.S. Geological Survey Series 2
USIIS   U.S. Indian Irrigation Service
USIS   U.S. Indian Service

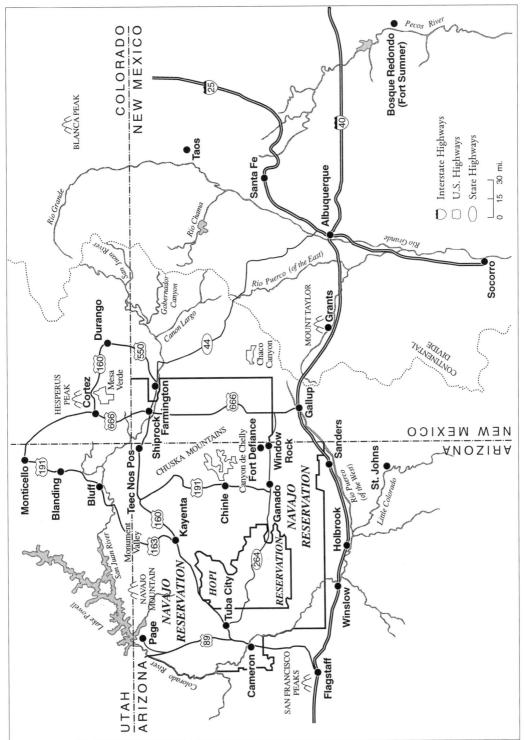

THE NAVAJO RESERVATION AND SURROUNDING AREA

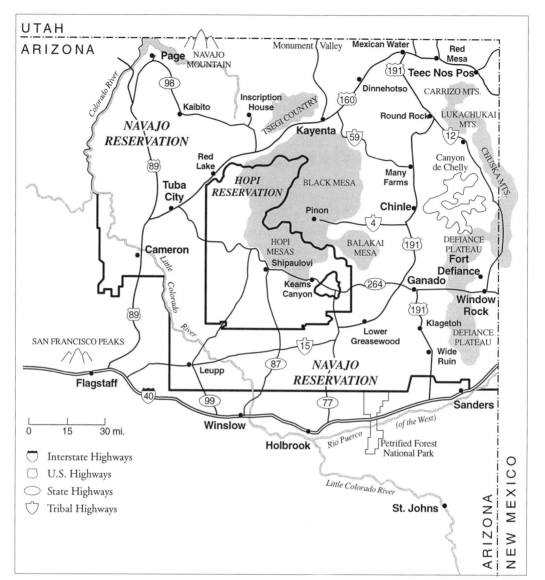

UTAH

ARIZONA

Colorado River

Page
NAVAJO MOUNTAIN

Monument Valley

Mexican Water

Red Mesa

191 Teec Nos Pos

Dinnehotso

CARRIZO MTS.

Kaibito

Inscription House

TSEGI COUNTRY

160

Round Rock

LUKACHUKAI MTS.

NAVAJO RESERVATION

Kayenta

59

12

89

Red Lake

HOPI RESERVATION

BLACK MESA

Many Farms

Canyon de Chelly

CHUSKA MTS.

Tuba City

Pinon

4

Chinle

Cameron

Little Colorado River

HOPI MESAS

Shipaulovi

BALAKAI MESA

191

DEFIANCE PLATEAU

Fort Defiance

Keams Canyon

264

Ganado

Window Rock

89

SAN FRANCISCO PEAKS

River

15

Lower Greasewood

191

Klagetoh

DEFIANCE PLATEAU

Wide Ruin

Leupp

87

NAVAJO RESERVATION

Flagstaff

40

99

77

Sanders

Winslow

Rio Puerco

(of the West)

Holbrook

Petrified Forest National Park

Little Colorado River

St. Johns

0   15   30 mi.

Interstate Highways
U.S. Highways
State Highways
Tribal Highways

ARIZONA

NEW MEXICO

ARIZONA

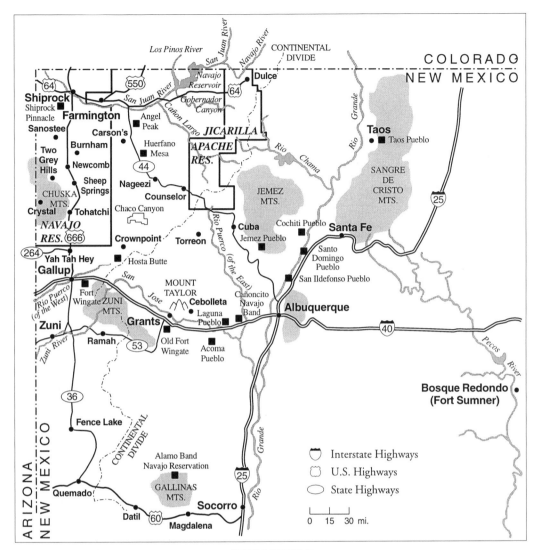

NEW MEXICO

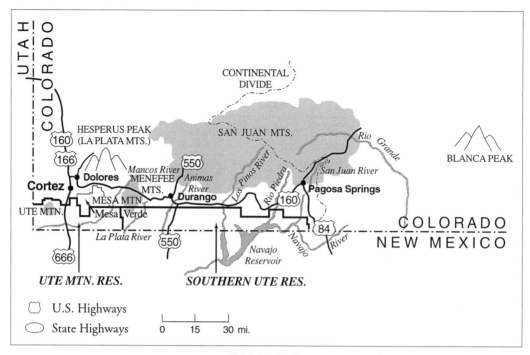

COLORADO

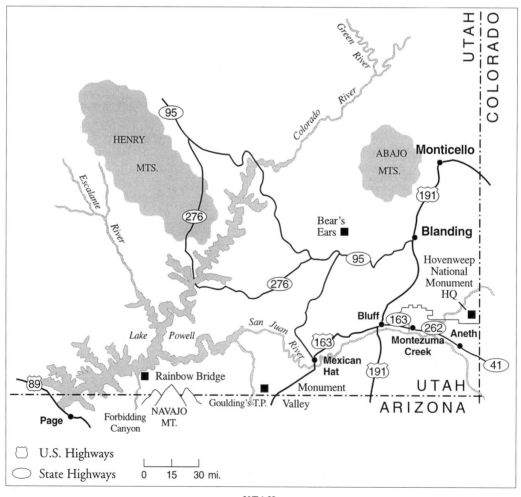

UTAH

Preface

.

This book represents work in progress. It will probably never be finished.

What began as a simple attempt to update a 50-year-old government document gradually—almost secretively—grew into an eight-year effort that roughly tripled the content of that original document. And there was still more information remaining to be collected and included. But the day finally arrived when energy began to flag and an arbitrary time out was called. It was time to show the results of the work to date.

GENESIS

The seeds for this project were planted in 1941, when a team of United States Indian Service (later known as Bureau of Indian Affairs) employees produced a document entitled *Diné Bikéyah* ("Navajo Land"). Richard F. Van Valkenburgh, anthropologist, Research Assistant with the Navajo Service, and a long-time resident of Navajo country, guided the endeavor that seems to have been spurred by the state visitors' guides being produced by the federally funded WPA Writers' Projects at about the same time—but with two critical differences.

First, in *Diné Bikéyah*, the story of the Navajo people (the *Diné)* was presented from the point of view of the Navajos themselves—apparently for the first time. And, second, this volume included the Navajo names for the places, along with their English translations—which rarely bear any resemblance to the English names assigned. (For instance, Na'nízhoozhí, the Navajo name for Gallup, New Mexico, does not mean "Gallup"; it means "Spanned Across.")

Like the WPA guides, Van Valkenburgh's delivery brought the culture and history to life

through short vignettes on 411 isolated places, including little-known details that were important to each location but that would prove boring, tedious, and even irrelevant in a broader historical overview. In the microcosm of individual locations, however, such minutiae become not merely important, but critical. They demonstrate that history is like a grand tapestry. Myriads of tiny fibers merge their colors and textures to create the overall image, but under the microscope, each fiber displays important, distinctive characteristics.

Diné Bikéyah was produced only in typed form. Today it is impossible to guess how many copies were produced by the Navajo Service, but the number is best estimated in tens or possibly dozens. It was never formally published nor copyrighted, and its distribution was limited.

EVOLUTION

In April 1978, I went to work as an archaeologist for the Navajo Nation, in the fledgling Cultural Resource Management Program (CRMP). One of the biggest surprises I encountered was the fact that so many places on the reservation are known almost solely by their English names. The relatively few Navajo names used are generally reduced to English spellings that often render the names senseless gibberish. My curiosity was piqued, for instance, by such names as Washington Pass (which I erroneously assumed was named for the father of our country), Dinnehotso (which I thought might be a Navajo surname), and Azonsosi Mesa, Arizona, which bears little resemblance to the Navajo "Asdzą́ą́ts'ósí," meaning "Slim Woman."

Shortly after I began working on the reservation, someone in the CRMP discovered a copy of

Diné Bikéyah in the Window Rock Library. It was a yellow-paged, dog-eared first- or second-generation photocopy of a carbon copy of an original. Its blurry, smudged content was more than a quarter of a century old, but it quickly answered many questions we had (and many we had not yet even thought) about Navajo history and geography, and it became a sort of "field Bible." It enabled us to document elusive Navajo cultural significance for—and thereby provide protection for—four hundred locations within and beyond the the reservation boundaries.

But, for all its value, *Diné Bikéyah* had its shortcomings. First, it was too brief. Van Valkenburgh himself wrote that "but a fraction of the Navajo place names have been listed, those given have been selected as most important to government employees, students and travelers." And, second, it was nearly 40 years old and therefore largely out of date.

In 1982, when I left my job on the reservation to go work as Executive Director of the Inter-Tribal Indian Ceremonial Association, I took with me a copy of *Diné Bikéyah,* with the intent of bringing Van Valkenburgh's entries up to date. As often happens with best intentions, it gathered dust on a bookshelf for 10 years before I began to work on it. I had no idea that my work would continue for nearly a decade, or that Van Valkenburgh's would be expanded two hundred percent.

The ties between Navajos and their land are deep and profound, so in producing such a volume as this, one must walk a tightrope. I had to temper my zeal to record and disseminate information that I knew could be sensitive to traditional Navajos. And such sensitivities can be fleeting or very deep-rooted. Information one Navajo might find perfectly all right to print might prove objectionable to another. I decided, therefore, to limit this listing primarily to those places already discussed in the literature.

I scoured scores of books, periodicals, journals, monographs, and manuscripts, compiling diverse information on a single location from as many as a dozen sources. When necessary, I augmented these data with personal interviews or questions to acquaintances and their relatives and friends. But when told that certain information was not for distribution (as in the case of Diné College's sacred-place-names project), I did not include that information in this work.

Then, in order to assure that profoundly sensitive information already in the literature was also excluded from this volume, I had it reviewed early on by a consultant to the Navajo Nation Historic Preservation Office and by employees of the Navajo Nation Archaeology Department.

Volumes of primary importance in my research, in addition to *Diné Bikeyah,* were Granger's *Will C. Barnes' Arizona Place Names* (University of Arizona Press, 1960), Van Cott's *Utah Place Names* (University of Utah, 1990) and Pearce's *New Mexico Place Names* (University of New Mexico, 1965). All proved valuable, but each was lacking in two areas critical to this work: the inclusion of the Navajo names and/or discussions of significance to the Navajo people. Two other books that had raised my hopes for new information added little to this work. Wilson's *Navajo Place Names: An Observer's Guide* (Audio Forum, 1995) contained little information beyond that in *Diné Bikéyah,* and Julyan's *Place Names of New Mexico* (University of New Mexico Press, 1996) avoided Navajo names and significance entirely.

An Ethnologic Dictionary of the Navajo Language (The Franciscan Friars, 1910) and the enormous *The Navajo Language: A Grammar and Colloquial Dictionary* (University of New Mexico Press, 1987), by Robert Young and William Morgan, Sr., proved profoundly helpful in identifying and interpreting names.

The original *Diné Bikéyah* has been wholly incorporated into the present volume. However, with the voluminous corrections, updated information, and additions (over a thousand total entries), the resulting volume bears little resemblance to the original. I therefore decided to apply a new title and claim authorship—with kudos to Van Valkenburgh. To insure credit where it is due, all entries derived from *Diné Bikéyah* are preceded by "[DB]" (the initials DB enclosed in brackets). Other initials in brackets indicate either the first or the primary source for an entry.

This project evolved through several stages,

even while the data collection was being carried out. While the basic organization of the volume was determined early on, one of the most difficult decisions was in defining the audience the project would address—and thereby determining the format of the work and the range of information to be included. The choices of audience ranged from scholars to tourists, with professionals, government employees, teachers, and students in between. Possible formats ranged from glove-compartment travel guide to grand coffee-table tome. Eventually, I deferred to Van Valkenburgh's "jack of all trades" style and intent, and targeted all of the above audiences.

The region encompassed by this volume is roughly rectangular, measuring 360 miles east-west (from Flagstaff, Arizona, to Albuquerque, New Mexico), and 230 miles north-south (from Dolores, Colorado, to Socorro, New Mexico).

NAVAJO PLACE NAMES
Perhaps the single most important feature of *Diné Bikéyah* was its extensive compilation of Navajo place names.

> For untold centuries, Native Americans have passed their unique legacy to successive generations through an ancient but fragile chain of oral tradition . . . [a] largely undocumented knowledge base containing the expertise and wisdom of the Native American experience, [which] must be recorded and preserved . . . before traditions and customs disappear from historical memory. The dislocation of Native peoples has exacerbated these difficulties . . . there is . . . an urgent national need to record and preserve the heritage, traditions, achievements and wisdom of Native Americans. (U.S. National Commission on Libraries and Information Service, December 1992)

Like other Native American languages, Navajo continues to experience decline in use. In 1930, 71 percent of Navajos spoke no English—compared to an average of 17 percent for all Indian tribes combined. Yet, by 1980, 7.2 percent spoke *only* English, and within the next decade that

figure had doubled to 15 percent. The Navajo Nation government claims this trend is reversing itself thanks to programs such as Head Start, in which pre-school Navajo children are instructed in Navajo, the federally mandated bilingual education programs in grade school and high school, and Navajo literacy courses at the various branches of Navajo Community College. My personal experience with the children and teachers of the Gallup-McKinley County School district tells me otherwise.

The portion of the Navajo language that has fallen into more disuse than any other is that of place names. Informal banter between Navajo individuals and official communications alike have fallen victim to the overwhelming pressure brought about by assimilation. A century of educating Navajos in an English-based system has resulted in their adoption of the English names used in books, on maps, and on road signs.

Place names are simply a vehicle for conveying information about a location from one person to another. The names generally describe the physical appearance of the location, and rarely give an indication of the importance of the place or its ties to history or religion. Kelley and Francis (1994, 94–95) concur with earlier researchers (Carroll 1982 and 1983) that prioritizing locations' significance can be difficult at best, and a dangerous precedent. But they note (1994, 38) that a listing of just those places with sacred significance could number tens or hundreds of thousands of entries if every individual Navajo were to be consulted.

With all this emphasis on Navajo names and presenting the story of the Diné from their own point of view, why then are the places herein listed by their English names? The answer is simple: the overwhelming majority of these places are represented by their English names on maps (even those produced by the Navajo Nation) and throughout the literature. Therefore, most readers seeking information on them will be seeking by the English name.

NAVAJO PRONUNCIATION

This volume includes proper Navajo spellings for names (place and proper), and makes use of the phonetic diacritical marks. The following information will assist the novice in the correct pronunciation of these special symbols and letters. While it may take a measure of practice to speak like a native, this guide will at least give the reader a notion of what the words are supposed to sound like. And sound is critical in Navajo, as slight variations in pronunciation can drastically alter the meaning of a word.

This simplified pronunciation directory is derived from similar presentations in Van Valkenburgh (1941, ii–v), Correll and Watson (1974, 18), Young and Morgan (1987, xii–xv), and Wilson (1995, xv–xvii).

VOWELS

Letter	Navajo	Meaning	English Sound Approximation
a	gad	juniper	father
e	ké	shoe	met
i	sis	belt	sit
o	tó	water	go

Vowel sounds may be elongated in duration, indicated by doubling the vowel. It is important to distinguish this pronunciation from the English. The double "e" in "jeeh" is pronounced like a drawn-out "e" in "met," as though the word were being pronounced in slow motion. It is not the double "e" in the English "meet." Likewise, "tooh" is pronounced as an elongated "toe," not "too."

Vowels with a "hook" beneath the letter are nasalized, with some breath passing through the nose during pronunciation. All vowels following the letter "n" are nasalized, and are not marked.

Letter	Navajo	Meaning	English Sound Approximation
ąą	tsinaabąąs	wagon	No real equivalent
įį	sįįl	stream	

GLOTTAL STOPS AND RELEASES

Any letter followed immediately by an apostrophe (') will end abruptly as the throat above the vocal cords is "snapped" shut:

Letter	Navajo	Meaning	English Sound Approximation
k'	k'ad	now	No real equivalent
a'	annaa'	enemy, war	

Likewise, any word preceded by an apostrophe will begin abruptly, as the throat is "snapped" open:

Letter	Navajo	Meaning
'a	'azee'	medicine

TONE

Tone refers to the ending of a vowel sound, which may end low (regular) or high (as with a question mark in English). Two words spelled the same can have entirely unrelated meanings depending on tone.

Letter	Navajo	Meaning
ee	'azee'	medicine
éé	'azéé'	mouth

DIPHTHONGS

There are four diphthongs in the Navajo language:

Letter	Navajo	Meaning	English Sound Approximation
ai	hai	winter	aisle
ao	ao'	yes	no real equivalent
ei	séí	sand	weigh
oi	'ayoi	very	Joey

Van Valkenburgh points out that the diphthong "oi," as in "Joey," will often be heard as "ui," as in the English word "dewy." All diphthongs can occur with and without glottal stops, and all can be subjected to tonal differences.

CONSONANTS

Letter	Navajo	Meaning	English Sound Approximation
b	bá	for him	papa
ch'	ch'osh	bug	"ch'osen" ("chosen" with a glottal release)
d	díí	this	tie
dl	beeldléí	blanket	paddling
dz	dziil	mountain	adze
g	gah	rabbit	keep
gh	hooghan	hogan	no real equivalent; like "get" with a gargled "g"
h	háadi	where	jailai (slightly fricative)
hw	hwaáh	whew!	when
j	jádí	antelope	jewel
k	ké	shoe	kick
kw	kwe'é	here	queen
k'	k'os	clouds	"k'ick" ("kick" with a glottal release)
l	laanaa	would that	let
ł	łid	smoke	"tlid," sometimes interpreted as "klid"
m	mósí	cat	man
n	naadą́ą́	corn	not
s	sis	belt	sew
sh	shash	bear	show
t	tó	water	too
t'	t'iis	cottonwood	"t'oo" ("too" with a glottal release)
tł	tła	grease	rattling
tł'	tł'oh	grass	"rattl'ing" ("rattling" with a glottal release)
w	'awéé'	baby	wet
y	ya	sky	you
z	zas	snow	zoo
zh	'ázhi'	name	azure

ACKNOWLEDGMENTS

In addition to Richard F. Van Valkenburgh, to whom this volume owes its very existence, a number of peole played a key role in the production of the manuscript. Miranda Warburton, of the Navajo Nation Archaeology Department, reviewed one of the first drafts. Larry Benally, assistant director of that office, provided assistance in several place names over the years. Tony Klesert, director of that same office, provided advice, resources, moral support, and a sense of humor when it was needed most.

Lu Evans and Eloise "Dewey" Foster, my secretaries at the Inter-Tribal Indian Ceremonial Association, listened to me ramble on about the project for years, and provided insights into Navajo culture and ceremonialism. Dennis Clah, Bureau of Indian Affairs Branch of Roads, was instrumental with road maps of the reservation and anecdotal and language information pertaining to place names. Kay Bennett, Navajo singer and writer, provided information on several place names in the Gallup area. Throughout much of this project, Martin Link, former Navajo Tribal Archaeologist and now publisher of the *Indian Trader Newspaper*, provided bits and pieces of information, lots of encouragement, and a wealth of advice on the project.

Klara Kelley, a consultant to the Navajo Nation Office of Historic Preservation, reviewed a substantially completed draft in 1994. She was consistently encouraging and was of immense help in minimizing the culturally sensitive materials. She also researched and provided several dozen Navajo place names—a substantial contribution.

Clay Slate and Lydia Fasthorse Begay, both with the Navajo Place Names Project at Diné College, Shiprock, New Mexico, supplied a few names and more advice on avoiding the dispensing of sensitive information.

Robert Young, Professor Emeritus, University of New Mexico, thoroughly reviewed what I considered to be the final draft of the manuscript in 1995. His boundless knowledge of the history and culture of the Navajos, coupled with his matchless knowledge of the written Navajo language, were invaluable to the accuracy of both in this volume. It is solely due to his insistence that the correct and proper phonetic spellings of all Navajo words are included in the book.

Stephen C. Jett, Professor, University of California at Davis, and long-time geographer of Navajo country, generously provided unlimited use of an unpublished manuscript on Navajo place names in Canyon de Chelly. Further, conversations with Steve were enjoyable and informative, as were his comments on the draft submitted to the University of Utah Press.

David M. Brugge, retired National Park Service archaeologist and authority on things Navajo, reviewed most of yet another draft of the manuscript in 1996. His extensive knowledge of Southwestern (and Navajo) history and his sharp eye for error provided a critique that vastly improved this volume.

Paul Zolbrod reviewed the draft submitted to the University of Utah Press, and his critical comments and unbridled enthusiasm were most refreshing and appreciated.

And no list would be complete without acknowledging the sacrifice made by my wife, Karen, and my sons, J.D. and Micah. They put up with an often-absentee husband and father as I melded myself to my word processor weekend after weekend and night after night in dereliction of domestic duties. They also suffered in relative silence as we bounced down myriads of back roads and jeep paths in the most remote parts of the reservation. To them go my deepest thanks and appreciation.

FUTURE CONTRIBUTIONS

I have stated that this work is incomplete because the places herein represent a small percentage of locations for which Navajo names and stories must exist. I expect some readers may be surprised that certain places well known to them have not been included. I hope my work spurs readers who know of such places to share their knowledge. I invite those readers willing to share such information to forward it in writing to me through the University of Utah Press (1795 E. South Campus Drive, Salt Lake City, UT 84112-9402) for inclusion in any future revision of this book (with appropriate recognition given to the contributors).

I

INTRODUCTION

Navajoland is the heart and soul of the American Southwest. The Navajo Reservation, officially designated home to some 220,000 Navajos, measures roughly 16,000,000 acres—not counting the smaller Hopi Reservation lying entirely within it. Incorporating portions of Arizona, New Mexico, and Utah (with some disputed territory in Colorado), this reservation is so large that the states of Massachusetts, New Hampshire, and Vermont could all nestle inside its borders. Yet the reservation land is only about half the traditional homeland of the *Diné* ("The People," in their own language), and it is this larger region that is the focus of this study. In one way or another, nearly all of it is sacred to them.

PHYSIOGRAPHY

Sitting atop the enormous physiographic province known as the Colorado Plateau, most of the spectacular landforms that personify Navajo country are the result of five million years of erosion (Miksa 1992, 393–404). Elevations within Navajoland range from 4000 ft (near the east end of the Grand Canyon) to over 14,000 ft in Colorado's San Juan Mountains.

Most of this territory is drained by two tributary watersheds of the Colorado River: the San Juan River on the north, and the Little Colorado River in the west-central region. A small part of the westernmost reaches drains directly into the deep canyons of the Colorado River, which in turn empties into the Gulf of California—and ultimately the Pacific Ocean. The eastern portions of Navajoland lie in the Rio Grande watershed, which flows into the Gulf of Mexico and finally into the Atlantic Ocean.

Anyone who has not spent time in Navajoland will find the climate surprisingly diverse, supporting a broad range of vegetation. Only 5 percent of the reservation (some 1,300 square miles) is classified as "barren" (due to bare rock or extremely inhospitable soil conditions). Yet, the natural monuments and canyons of the barren country have proven so photogenic through the years that relatively few people are aware that there are actually three physiographic provinces in Navajoland (see table 1).

There are five principal mountainous regions in Navajoland. The Zuni Mountains roughly parallel I-40 between Grants and Gallup, New Mexico. The Chuska Range (including the Chuska,

TABLE 1. THE THREE MAJOR PHYSIOGRAPHIC PROVINCES OF NAVAJOLAND
(From "The Navajo Yearbook," vol. VIII: 1961)

Province	Elevation	Precipitation	Temperatures	Area	Predominant Vegetation
Mountains	7500–10,000'	16–27 inches	70–80 in summer	2000 sq. miles (8% of reserve)	Ponderosa pine, other evergreens
Mesas	6000–8000'	12–16 inches	100+ in summer	9000 sq. miles (36% of reserve)	Piñon and juniper
Deserts	4500–7000'	7–11 inches	110+ in summer	14,000 sq. miles (55% of reserve)	Sage, greasewood, grasses

TABLE 2. NAVAJOLAND INDIGENOUS CULTURAL HISTORY
(From Cordell 1984)

Culture	Dates	Lifestyle	Archaeological Evidence
Paleo-Indian	12,000–5,000 B.C.	Nomadic big game hunters	Chipped stone tools
Archaic Tradition	5,500–100 B.C.	Semi-nomadic, hunting smaller game, domesticating plants	Chipped and ground stone tools, with higher incidence of the latter
Anasazi			
Basketmaker	100 B.C.–A.D. 750	Hunting and gathering, increased sedentism	Baskets, sandals and other woven goods, chipped and ground stone tools, pithouses, first pottery (graywares)
Pueblo I	A.D. 750–900	Increased horticulture	More pottery (neck-banded and red wares), aboveground "jacal" structures, pithouses possibly evolving into kivas
Pueblo II	A.D. 900–1100	Additional horticulture	Multi-room, multi-storied structures, great kivas, corrugated pottery, and increased occurrence of painted and red wares
Pueblo III	A.D. 1100–1300	Even further dependence on horticulture, water and soil control measures, population shifts	Multiple plazas, negative-painted pottery designs, aboveground kivas in roomblocks, canals
Pueblo IV	A.D. 1300–1600	Pueblos grow along major water sources (rivers)	Red-slipped and glaze-decorated pottery, kiva murals, carved bone tools, villages of hundreds or even thousands of rooms
Pueblo V	A.D. 1600–Present	Destruction and decline of Pueblo culture; population decimation	Euro-American artifacts
Navajo	Pre-A.D. 1600 to Present	Semi-nomadic, raiding, animal husbandry, some horticulture	Hogan domicile; sheep, weavings, smithing, Euro-American artifacts

Tunicha, Lukachukai, and Carrizo mountains) stretches between Shiprock and Gallup along the New Mexico-Arizona line, peaking at 9784 ft at Roof Butte. Near the center of the reservation, Black Mesa is an extensive "island prominence" with a circumference of 250 miles and elevations as high as 8210 ft. Navajo Mountain, with a summit of 10,416 ft, is located on the Arizona-Utah line east of Lake Powell. The San Juan Mountains, by far the highest in Navajoland, rise to over 14,000' in Southwest Colorado.

The mesa country includes the lower reaches of Black Mesa, the higher portions of the Chaco and Chinle plains, the Skeleton/Tsegi Mesa territory, and the Defiance Plateau.

The combined upland and lowland deserts embrace the San Juan Basin, the majority of the Chinle Valley, the Painted Desert, Monument Valley, and the valley of the Rio Puerco of the West. The meager precipitation of this zone falls on fewer than 50 days per year; nearly half the moisture arrives as torrential rain in August and September. Though the deserts are scorching hot in summer, winter temperatures of 50 degrees below zero have been recorded.

Since the time of human arrival into the region, the climate has continued to grow more arid. Yet much of the stark, unavailing landscape in the desert zone was caused by humans. Historical accounts suggest that a substantial portion of the deep, gorge-like arroyos slashing across the flats and vast expanses of vegetationless, wind-blown sand seen across parts of the region today were produced by severe wind and water erosion advanced by critical overgrazing—particularly by sheep and goats—during the first seven decades after the Navajos returned from the Bosque Redondo.

THE PEOPLE

BEFORE THE NAVAJOS:
10,000 B.C.–A.D. 1600 (APPROXIMATELY)

In the human chronicle, the chapter on the American Southwest is a relatively short one. (See table 2.) The earliest evidence of people in the region is barely 12,000 years old—beginning with the hunter tradition of the paleolithic Clovis Culture. Since that time, this region has never been unoccupied.

THE NAVAJOS: PRE-1600 TO PRESENT

Euro-American historians and archaeologists have argued for decades with Navajo historians and cultural experts over just when the Navajos first entered the southwestern United States. A case can be made for various points of view, depending on how one interprets the data.

The Archaeological/Historical Perspective

Archaeologists are quick to note that the present-day pueblo structures bear more than a passing resemblance to the prehistoric ruins dotting the southwestern landscape. Architectural styles, building materials and technologies, the presence and situation of kivas, the orientation of the structures, and the artifact assemblages of the past have parallels in historic puebloan society. Furthermore, the ample archaeological record is continuous in portions of the Southwest, illustrating an unbroken evolution from Basketmaker II to the present pueblos. Since Navajo material culture and architecture bear little resemblance to this continuum, archaeologists and historians consider the Diné recent immigrants rather than descendants of the prehistoric occupants of the Southwest.

Drawing the same conclusion, linguistic anthropologists point out that the Navajo language belongs to the Athabaskan family, while all the Pueblos are of other linguistic stocks (UtoAztecan, Keresan, Kiowa-Tanoan, and Zuni). Other Athabaskan groups (the Apaches are the only others to reach the Southwest) were nomadic or semi-nomadic peoples, a bold contrast to the sedentary puebloans. Archaeologists speculate that the Athabaskans arrived in North America about 10,000 years ago. Their journey south was not a headlong race completed within a generation or two, but more like a flooding body of water, expanding to fill in voids and spilling over obstacles as population pressure and resources dictated—reaching the northern periphery of the Southwest by about A.D. 1300.

Some historians (McNitt 1972:3–5) suggest that the nomadic "Querechos" encountered by Francisco Vásquez de Coronado during his 1541 Spanish incursion into the Southwest were early Apacheans, possibly including Navajos. ("Querechos" is a Spanish term derived from the practice of these people trading with the Keres—spelled "Queres" in Spanish—pueblos on the Rio Grande, much like later Apaches and Navajos.) But their location and some of their material culture and customs (buffalo-hide tepees and the use of dogs as beasts of burden) suggest these were Southern Plains Indians, probably Kiowa or Comanche or both.

Antonio de Espejo used the term "Querecho" 40 years later to describe "mountain Indians" encountered near the Hopi Mesas and near Cebolleta (in present-day New Mexico) in 1582, and these were almost certainly Navajos.

Archaeologically, the earliest dates recognized for undisputedly Navajo sites cluster in the early 1600s, with carbon 14 dates suggesting the Navajos were in the Southwest possibly as early as 1500 (Brugge p.c. 1996). These earliest sites are found in the "Dinétah," the Navajo homeland, centering along Gobernador and Largo canyons and the Rio Chama, and especially around the confluence of the San Juan and Los Piños Rivers (a highly sacred location to the Navajos, now inundated by the waters of Navajo Reservoir). The earliest reports of a Diné presence in north-central Arizona came with the first Spanish incursions into the region in the 1770s. Though dates are ambiguous, it appears the Navajos did not spread into southern Utah until the 1850s (as they fled the relentless U.S. Army), and when they arrived they met with resistance from the Numic-speaking Utes and Paiutes, who had been in the region since about A.D. 900–1200 (Reed 1992, 25–26).

The Traditional Navajo Perspective

While Euro-American archaeologists draw upon the measurable physical evidence of the past and historians study written records, Navajo historians and cultural experts rely on oral tradition—stories passed down through the ages.

Conclusions drawn by academic archaeologists and historians are admittedly subject to individual bias and revisionist interpretation, but oral tradition is typically the least reliable of documentary evidence. Studies of nonliterate cultures have repeatedly shown that an unwritten story is never told twice in exactly the same way—even by a single storyteller. While the gist or main idea of the story may remain relatively pristine from one telling to the next, minor word substitutions, changes in inflection, and even circumstances under which a telling takes place can effect significant changes over even short periods of time—let alone over hundreds of years.

Yet, certain aspects of Diné tradition deserve closer examination. For instance, the Navajo creation myth has Navajos emerging from four underworlds directly into the Southwest, referring to specific landmarks that are still sacred to them (the sacred mountains). The Diné have a strong tradition of oneness with the land, and fully believe they have been in the Southwest as long or longer than anyone else. (Many Navajos are aware of their relationship to Athabascans far to the north in Canada, but legends suggest these people are descendants of Diné who left the main Navajo tribe and moved north many generations ago.)

Furthermore, many Diné clans identify different locations of origin, including Huerfano Mesa, Kiogi Pueblo (near Jemez), Red House (possibly Kin Lichee), and Deer Springs. Some clans are also thought to have incorporated people from other cultures through the years, including Mohaves, Utes, Apaches, Zunis, and Mexicans. Some clans are known to have metamorphosed from pueblo (particularly Jemez Pueblo) groups migrating into Navajo territory in historic times. It seems entirely logical, if not likely, that similar groups were assimilated in earlier times, and that at least a portion of the Navajo culture evolved in place.

All that is certain is that within a short time of the Spaniards' arrival in the Southwest, the Navajos were making their presence unmistakably clear.

INTRUSION OF THE SPANIARDS: A.D. 1541–1821

It is difficult to imagine anything in the natural order that could have wrought the crushing changes experienced by the native peoples following the arrival of the Europeans in the Southwest. Within just a few generations, the universe as the Indians had known it ceased to exist. And Native Americans have been unable to return to their former glory and lifeways.

Explorations

The first European explorers in the Southwest were Spaniards, enticed by a quartet shipwrecked on the Texan Gulf Coast (following an abortive expedition to western Florida) in 1528. Alvar Nuñez Cabeza de Vaca and three companions—including Estebanico, a Moorish or black slave—returned to civilization in 1536 after being hopelessly lost in the region for eight years. Their tales stirred the imagination of the Viceroy of New Spain, who, after the plunder of the splendors of the Aztec world, dreamed of even more riches in the New World.

Governor Antonio de Mendoza organized the first explorative expedition into this region—and coincidentally into Navajoland. Led by the Moor, Estebanico, and Fray Marcos de Niza, the expedition departed in March 1539.

This journey was noteworthy as the initial probe of the region destined to become the American Southwest. And even though it met with disaster at the Pueblo of Zuni (with the death of Estabanico) less than three months after leaving Culiacan, Fray Marcos carried back to the Mexican authorities blatant lies about nonexistent riches that ensured further exploration.

Francisco Vásquez de Coronado's expedition of 1540–42, guided by the imaginative Fray Marcos, was far more extensive and intensive than the friar's preceding journey. Coronado, or members of his party, visited Zuni, the Hopi villages, the Grand Canyon, El Morro, and Tiguex, Taos, and Pecos pueblos before traveling all the way to what is today known as Kansas. But Coronado never found his cities of gold.

So disheartened were the Spaniards that it was 40 years after Coronado's return to civilization before Antonio de Espejo led a small party of 15 up the Rio Grande and then west to the region of the Hopi Mesas (ostensibly to rescue two priests left with the pueblos by Captain Francisco Sanchez Chamuscado the year before). Here, and in the vicinity of Cebolletta, New Mexico, they encountered "Querechos" who were arguably Navajos (Hammond and Rey 1966, 189). They also visited Zuni and were defeated in a battle against a combined force of Acomas and Querechos at the foot of Mount Taylor. This expedition also marks the beginning of Navajo slaves being acquired by the Spaniards, as the expedition was given a Querecho woman by the Hopis.

Colonization

By this time, land seemed an acceptable prize where gold was once sought, and efforts to colonize were mobilized in the final decade of the sixteenth century. Discounting Gaspar Castaño de Sosa's aborted attempt to settle the upper Rio Grande in 1590–91, the first Spanish foothold in New Mexico is generally considered the colony of San Gabriel del Yunque, established by Don Juan de Oñate in 1598. It was built on the site of a previously existing pueblo called Yunque Yunque (McNitt 1972, 10), on the west bank of the Rio Grande across from San Juan Pueblo.

During this period, the center of Navajoland appears to have been the vicinity of Huerfano Butte (south of Farmington), with Diné territory extending east to the Rio Grande and west to the Chinle Valley, though much of this territory was hunting and raiding range only. The Navajos apparently took a dim view of the Spanish presence on "their" side of the Rio Grande, for their continuous raids and harassment forced the Spaniards to abandon the location. In 1610 the colony was moved to the present site of Santa Fe.

The next 20 years were marked by repeated Spanish slave raids into Navajoland. A decade of relative peace, during which the settlers conducted trade with the Navajos (usually through Pueblo intermediaries) was followed by increased unrest. By the 1640s, Navajo raids were increasing, partly to avenge Spanish and Pueblo raids on them, and partly for livestock acquisition. During this period, the pueblos alternately allied themselves with the Spanish against the Navajos, and vice versa, and from this point on, the interrelationships of the various players became quite unpredictable and very muddled.

Spaniards and their Pueblo auxiliaries launched major attacks on the Navajo "Casafuerte" ("stronghold"), in 1669 and again in 1675. The first expedition failed because the Pueblo auxiliaries deserted in droves as they approached the Navajos; the second defeated the Navajos in battle.

Five years later, the Spanish were routed from all of New Mexico in the great Pueblo Revolt of 1680. This had an unexpected impact on the Navajos, for, attempting to distance themselves from the inevitable return of the vengeful Spaniards, some puebloans fled west beyond the outskirts of their known world and into the eastern fringe of Navajo territory. Here the two cultures mingled and blended, allowing the Navajos, according to some scholars, to adopt such puebloan traits as masonry architecture, pottery, weaving, and, possibly, farming.

When Don Diego de Vargas led the Spanish back into New Mexico in 1692, they came to stay. Fragmented resistance from the pueblos was quickly and thoroughly overwhelmed, driving even more refugees into Navajo territory, further increasing the Pueblo—and unavoidably, some Spanish—influence on the Navajos. The Spanish and Pueblos resumed their forays into Navajo country for the sole purpose of capturing slaves, and the Navajos struck back with redoubled raids along the outskirts of Spanish territory. Thus, an enmity was rekindled between Navajos and European descendants that lasted well into the American period.

The Wars

The first decade of the eighteenth century was marked by several Spanish strikes into Navajoland. However, the next 50 years became an unprecedented period of peace, during which diminished Navajo raids avoided Spanish settlements, striking only Pueblos. Historians attribute this peace to a combination of Spanish punitive raids in 1705, 1708, and 1709, and the fact that Navajo attention was diverted toward traditional enemies: the Utes and Comanches (McNitt 1972, 21–25).

During this period, the Navajo enclave at Cebolleta maintained relatively peaceful relations with nearby Laguna and Acoma pueblos, and some Diné were even being baptized. The Spanish encouraged colonists to settle in the same vicinity by awarding land grants beginning in 1753. Nineteen years later, however, the Navajos and Apaches allied and forced the settlers out.

Governor Pedro Fermin de Mendinueta's subsequent pair of expeditions in 1774 brought about a decade of peace, during which time the Franciscan Fathers Atanasio Dominguez and Silvestre Velez de Escalante conducted a 157-day journey of over 2,000 miles in 1776–77. They were the first Euro-Americans to visit much of what was to become northwestern New Mexico, southwestern Colorado, southeastern Utah, and northeastern Arizona, and many of the names they applied to features they saw are still in use today.

The Navajos allied with the Spanish and Pueblos against the Apaches and fought the Battle of Sierra Azul on June 16, 1785, killing 40 Apaches. Three years later, Navajos joined another expedition against the Gila and Mimbres Apaches.

In March 1786, the Spanish initiated what would prove to be a costly precedent for future Spanish, Mexican, and American dealings with the Diné: they insisted this tribe of disjointed, loosely affiliated bands deal through a central leader (and, moreover, one of Spanish choosing). Governor Juan Bautista de Anza then arrogantly heightened his folly by appointing Don Carlos and Don Joseph Antonio, sons of an older Navajo who had previously cooperated with the Spaniards, as the leaders of choice. In so doing, de Anza completely ignored Antonio El Pinto, the man who was most trusted by the majority of Navajos and who might have served as their spokesman.

But to expect all Navajos to follow the instructions of a single leader—especially one of an enemy's choosing—was tantamount to expecting all the pueblos to obey the headman at Taos or Zuni. Commitments the Antonio brothers made

to the Spanish went unheeded by the majority of Navajos.

In 1796, after a four-year alliance with the Utes in a war against the Comanches, the Navajos, stronger than ever, renewed their affiliation with the Apaches. The two began raiding the Spanish once again, ushering in 65 years of nearly continuous warfare.

One of the most significant events of this period occurred on July 20, 1818, when a Navajo headman named Joaquin warned the alcalde at Cebolleta that a significant gathering of Navajos in the Carrizo Mountains planned an unprecedented attack on the Spanish. Joaquin was convinced that the Navajos would ultimately suffer bitter defeat and wanted no part of the inevitable retaliation. A small body of his followers settled at Cebolleta in a permanent peace with the Spanish. Henceforward, the Diné at Cebolleta were known by other Navajos as "Diné 'Ana'í," or "Enemy Navajos."

THE MEXICANS: 1821–1846

In 1821 the Spanish were finally evicted from Navajoland, but not by the Navajos. The crown's loss in the Mexican revolution ejected them from the New World altogether.

Mexico's success in her War of Independence was of little import to the Diné, though. Their adversaries took orders from a president in Mexico City rather than from the king in Spain, but they still spoke Spanish—and they still warred with the Diné. The Mexican government's abrupt acceptance of commerce with Anglo-American traders did, however, affect the Navajos. It opened the door for a flood of improved equipment—especially firearms—giving the Mexican militia a new advantage in their slave raids.

The period's most ambitious mission against the Diné took place in 1823, when José Antonio Vizcarra led fifteen hundred troops and two regiments of militia on a 74-day expedition across much of the land that would later comprise the Navajo Reservation. Though it was at best a draw militarily, it was one of the most extensive explorations of Navajo country to date. It also marked the first time that the Diné Ana'í took the field against mainstream Navajos.

Despite the obvious dangers, Mexicans settled

TABLE 3. MAJOR SPANISH MILITARY EXPEDITIONS INTO NAVAJOLAND
(From McNitt 1972)

Date	Expedition Leader	Route	Results
1675	Juan Dominguez de Mendoza	Zia Pueblo to "Casafuerte"	15 Navajos killed, 35 captured; corn crops destroyed
1678	Juan Dominguez de Mendoza	Chama Valley	"A number" of Navajos killed, 50 captured; crops burned
1705	Roque de Madrid	Taos, San Juan River, San Juan Mountains, Topicito Arroyo, Canada Larga	39+ Navajos killed, "a number" captured; Navajos sue for peace
1709	7 separate campaigns	Various locations	50 years of relative peace between Navajos and Spaniards (though attacks continued on Pueblos)
1714	Roque Madrid	San Juan Valley by way of Chama Valley	30 Navajos killed, 7 captured; 200 fanegas of corn and 110 sheep seized
1716	Cristobal de la Serna	Jemez Pueblo to "Los Peñalitos"	6 Navajos killed
1774	Gov. Pedro Fermin de Mendinueta	2 expeditions, exact destinations unknown	21 Navajos killed, 46 captured
1800	Gov. Fernando Chacon	Chuska Valley	Council with Navajos; no hostile confrontations
1805	Lt. Col. Antonio de Narbona	Chuska Valley, Canyon de Chelly	Bloodbath at Massacre Cave in Canyon de Chelly

the old colony at Cubero, near Cebolleta, in 1833. And, predictably, Navajo raids increased.

Even a force of six thousand men led by Col. Antonio Perez during the winter of 1836–37 failed to pacify the Diné. Although a peace treaty was signed in July 1839, hostilities were in full swing again by the following September.

For the remainder of the Mexican period, the Navajos alternated between returning stolen livestock and captives in an effort to prove their sincere desire for peace, and attacking villages to replenish their dwindling herds. By 1846 a general state of war existed along the entire Navajo frontier, and may explain in part Governor Armijo's failure to resist the American invasion (McNitt 1972, 91).

THE AMERICANS: 1846–PRESENT

The Early Years

Whether it was dictated policy or simply the personality of Stephen Kearny, the first military governor of the New Mexico Territory, the Americans entered New Mexico in a relatively peaceful frame of mind. They seemed genuinely intent on making friends of the local Hispanic populace, and many scholars believe the Americans intended to treat the Navajos differently than had the Spanish and Mexicans. However, Kearny immediately ordered a total of five companies of mounted volunteers to garrison the villages of Cebolleta and Abiquiu (both long considered the outposts against Navajo incursions), and dispatched several columns of soldiers and local militia into Navajo country. One of these pursued a band of thieves who had snatched six thousand sheep from a single rancho near Valencia.

Most early reports described the Navajo leaders as sincerely desirous of peace. When some of the American columns merged at Ojo del Oso in Wingate Valley, they encountered a party of five hundred Diné led by Zarcillos Largos, known to the Navajos as Naat'áanii Náádleeł, or "Becomes Chief Again" (Hoffman and Johnson 1970, 70). The American commander, Colonel Alexander W. Doniphan, threatened the Navajos with war if they continued their raids on the pueblo and Mexican settlements. Largos rose to the occasion and claimed that his people had good reason to

TABLE 4. MAJOR MEXICAN MILITARY EXPEDITIONS INTO NAVAJOLAND
(From McNitt 1972)

Date	Expedition Leader	Route	Results
1823	Jose Antonio Vizcarra	Rio Puerco, Chacra Mesa, Chuska Valley, Canyon de Chelly, Hopi Mesas, Black Mesa, Blue Canyon, Marsh Pass, Dinnehotso, San Juan River, Valle Grande	33 Navajos killed, 30 captured; 801 sheep and goats, 87 cattle, and 23 horses taken
1835	Blas de Hinojos	Santa Fe to Narbona Pass	Ambushed by Navajos, Hinojos killed, column routed
1836–37	Col. Antonio Perez	El Morro, Pescado Spr., Zuni, Ojo del Oso, Calites Canyon, Chuska Mountains	50 Navajos killed, 20 captured; 8,837 sheep and 206 horses seized
1839	Gov. Manuel Armijo	Jemez Pueblo to Northern Chuska Valley, south to Gila River	78 Navajos killed, 56 captured; 2060 sheep and 226 horses taken
1839–40	Two expeditions	Chuska Valley, Canyon de Chelly, Black Mesa	16 Navajos killed, 2 captured; 10,000 sheep and 145 horses rounded up

war on the New Mexicans. He went so far as to accuse the United States of interfering in a war that should remain between the Navajos and the New Mexicans (McNitt 1972, 118).

Nevertheless, the first Navajo-American peace treaty was signed at Ojo del Oso on November 21, 1846. It called for lasting peace, mutual trade, and return of stolen property—from both sides. It was signed by Colonel Doniphan and such Navajo headmen as Zarcillos Largos, Caballada Mucha, Alexandro, Cayetanito (known to the Diné as K'áák'eh, "Wounded") and his brother Manuelito (called either Nabaahí Jilt'aa, "Warrior Grabbed Enemy," or Hastiin Ch'il Haajiní, "Man of the Black Plants Extend up out Place," and several other names by his people), Jose Largo, Narbona (later known as Hastiin Ke' Ntsaa, "Mr. Big Foot"), Segundo, Pedro Jose, Tapio, and Archuleta Juanico. Sandoval and Savoietta signed for the Diné Ana'í. (Navajo names from Frink 1968; Hoffman and Johnson 1970; Franciscan Fathers 1910.)

This treaty failed five days later, when, in a skirmish south of Socorro, two Missouri Volunteers (Privates James Stewart and Robert Spears) became the first American soldiers considered casualties of the Navajos (Hughes 1962, 156). And thus began a war of skirmishes that would last until 1864. (See Table 5.)

In 1847, close on the heels of the Taos Uprising (in which New Mexico Governor Charles Bent was killed), Major Robert Walker led an expedition into the heart of Navajoland intending to defeat the Navajos once and for all. The column accomplished little more than to improve the Army's knowledge of the lay of Navajo country. However, the American pressure may have been the motivation for a Navajo delegation's trip to Santa Fe to sue for peace, and it may also have led to Diné acceptance of a treaty signed at Beautiful Mountain in May of 1848 by Navajo leaders Jose Largo, Narbona, Zarcillos Largos, and five lesser headmen (Chapitone, Archuleta, Juan Lucero, Segundo, and Pablo Pino) and Colonel Edward W. B. Newby. This treaty was poorly understood by both sides, and hostilities continued (McNitt 1972, 130).

Colonel John Washington, new military governor of New Mexico, led three hundred men west from Fort Marcy in the summer of 1849. On August 31, while camped at a pass in the Chuska Mountains, Washington met with a large contingent of Narbona's followers. Near the conclusion of the peaceful talks, a New Mexican abruptly identified a Navajo's horse as one stolen from him seven months before. When Colonel Washington demanded the horse's immediate return, the Navajos balked and tried to leave the area. On Washington's orders, the Americans opened fire with small arms and a battery of mountain

TABLE 5. MAJOR AMERICAN EXPEDITIONS INTO NAVAJOLAND PRIOR TO 1860
(From McNitt 1972)

Date	Expedition Leader	Route	Results
1846	Col. Alexander W. Doniphan	Santa Fe, Rio Grande Valley, Cubero, Wingate Valley, Narbona Pass, Ojo del Oso	No battles; councils held. Capt. John W. Reid met with Diné headman Narbona and a large party of Navajos in the Chuska Mountains. Doniphan forged the first treaty between the Navajos and the U.S., signed at Ojo del Oso.
	Maj. William Gilpin (as part of Doniphan's force)	Abiquiu, San Juan River up Chama River to the Chuska Mountains and Canyon de Chelly	
1847	Maj. Robert Walker	Santa Fe, Albuquerque, Ojo del Oso, Cienega Amarilla, Red Lake across Defiance Plateau, Canyon de Chelly, Zuni	1 Navajo killed.
1849	Col. John Washington	Santa Fe, Jemez Pueblo, Torreon, Chaco Canyon, Chuska Valley, Two Grey Hills, Narbona Pass, Canyon de Chelly	Battle at Narbona Pass, 7 Navajos (including headman Narbona) killed.
1851	Col. Edwin Vose Sumner	Santa Fe, Santo Domingo, Canyon Bonito, penetrated Canyon de Chelly	Established Fort Defiance, was forced to withdraw from de Chelly by constant Navajo skirmishes.
1858	Lt. Edward S. Beale	Santa Fe to California	Crossed southern Navajoland with famous "Camel Brigade;" surveyed route later followed by AT&SF RR, U.S. Highway 66, and I-40.
1858	Major Electus Backus	Ft. Defiance, Cove Spr., Peña Blanca Creek, Beautiful Mountain (Cogswell's column), Salt Creek, Red Rock, Red Wash, Carrizo Mtns, Canyon de Chelly, Walker (Gothic) Creek, Many Farms, over Defiance Plateau, Ft. Defiance	12 Navajos killed; 40 horses and 300 sheep seized.
1859	Captain John G. Walker	Ft. Defiance, Wheatfield, Canyon de Chelly, San Juan River, back to Ft Defiance via Chuska foothills	Surveyed countryside, found Navajos desiring peace.
	Captain John G. Walker	Second expedition took column from Ft. Defiance to Steamboat Canyon, Black Mesa, Klethla Valley, Marsh Pass, Chinle Valley, Many Farms, over Defiance Plateau to Ft. Defiance	Surveyed countryside, found Navajos generally desirous of peace.

howitzers. Seven Navajos were killed, including Narbona—possibly the one man who could have enforced a peace with the Americans. Unaware of—or not caring about—the impact of Narbona's death, Washington then headed to Canyon de Chelly, where he foisted a treaty on the Navajos there.

(A secondary impact of this expedition, the effects of which are still manifest today, was triggered by First Lieutenant James H. Simpson of the Topographical Engineers. His journal, sketches, and maps described in detail, and applied English and Spanish names to, many features in Navajo country of eastern and central Arizona.)

The Navajos were learning quickly not to trust the Americans. On December 1 of the year Narbona died, Company K, Second Dragoons, reoccupied the first American military post established in Navajo country at Cebolleta (though this post was not officially established until September 1850). Later, on June 15, 1851, San Juan Navajo headman Chapitone was waylaid by New Mexicans near Cebolleta while on his way to talk peace in Santa Fe. Once his party was disarmed under promises of protection, Chapitone and two of his companions were murdered.

Three months later, on September 18, Colonel Edwin Vose Sumner (namesake of the post later erected at the Bosque Redondo) led a column from Santa Fe through Santo Domingo Pueblo and established Fort Defiance at Cañoncito Bonito, a deep dell in Black Creek Valley, right in the heart of Navajo country. (Sumner showed his contempt for the Diné when, after two local headmen declined his invitation to the fort to parley, he issued orders to shoot Navajos on sight.)

A rare positive step was taken late in 1853, when the second Navajo agent, Henry Lafayette Dodge (replacing Spruce Baird, who held the position slightly more than a year) moved his Navajo agency from Chupadero, New Mexico, to the eastern approach to Narbona (Washington) Pass. Under the guiding hand of this agent, who married a kinswoman of headman Zarcillos Largos (McNitt 1972, 243), relative peace prevailed for two years.

On July 17, 1855, a council was called at Laguna Negra, north of Fort Defiance, for the purpose of signing a treaty that called for establishment of a Navajo reserve of seven thousand square miles—less than a third of the 25,000 square miles the Navajos then occupied. In return, the United States would pay a total of $102,000 in annuities over the next 20 years. The United States would dictate how the annuities would be disbursed and how they would be used by the Diné. Several Navajo leaders spoke eloquently against the treaty, yet 27 headmen—representing every division of the tribe except for the Diné Ana'í—signed it. Incredibly, the Navajos narrowly averted disaster when the U.S. Senate failed to ratify this terribly one-sided treaty.

A year later, though, fate struck another blow against the Navajos when, on or about December 1, 1856, Agent Henry Dodge was kidnapped and killed, apparently by Apaches, on Haashk'aan Silá Mesa south of Zuni. The agents who replaced Dodge did not have his easy, comfortable way with the Navajos, and though some may have been sympathetic to their needs, a measure of distrust festered between the Anglos and the Diné.

And still fortune frowned on the Navajos. They were not consulted when, two years later, Lieutenant Edward S. Beale and his "Camel Brigade" surveyed a road to California across the southern portion of their range. Curiously, Beale's caravan, with its peculiar, humpbacked animals, apparently drew little attention from the Navajos, even though the expedition visited Fort Defiance in the heart of Navajo territory (Van Valkenburgh 1938, 13). Yet this expedition had profound future effect on the Navajos, for it surveyed the approximate route later taken through Navajoland by the Atchison, Topeka and Santa Fe Railway—and still later by Route 66 and Interstate 40. Next, in May 1858, the military's distrust of the influential Navajo headman Manuelito led to his humiliation and alienation when he was stripped of his grazing rights at Laguna Negra by a particularly obtuse commandant of Fort Defiance, Major William T. Brooks. Possibly in retribution, a Navajo murdered the major's black servant, Jim, on July 12.

Brooks treated this event as a major affront to the military, and pressured the Diné to produce the killer. On September 8, the Navajos brought to Fort Defiance the body of the man they said had killed Jim. The man had ostensibly been killed by other Navajos in resisting his fate. An autopsy, however, showed the body to be that of a teen-aged New Mexican captive, rather than the tall, middle-aged Navajo witnesses saw slay Jim; that same day, in Santa Fe, Lieutenant Colonel Dixon Stansbury Miles declared war on the Navajos, to "atone for the insult to our flag."

After a couple of months and several ineffective, ill-advised excursions into various Navajo stronghold areas, the Army, seemingly content to call the action a draw, ended the war with an armistice signed by Zarcillos Largos in November 1858.

The war ended, but the warring did not. Navajos continued to acquire sheep by raiding Zuni, Jemez, the Hopi Pueblos, Laguna, Acoma, and Abiquiu (McNitt 1972, 364). And the U.S. Army initiated another series of campaigns in 1859, two of note being led by Captain John G. Walker.

Walker's report from his first expedition noted nothing but friendly behavior and an earnest desire for peace on the part of the Navajos. His commander, Major John Smith Simonson, asked his own superiors to treat the Navajos fairly, warning that otherwise they would have no choice but to retaliate. In response to this plea, Colonel Benjamin Bonneville ordered all-out attacks on the Diné from Fort Defiance on October 22. This imprudence was compounded when shortly thereafter, with the fort all but besieged by hostile Indians, Colonel Thomas Fauntleroy ordered the fort reduced to less than half its normal garrison. Quick to size up the situation, the Navajos launched a series of attacks on work parties from the fort, culminating in a thousand-warrior assault on the fort itself on April 30, 1860. Sheer force of numbers was not enough to take the fort, however, and the post's complement repulsed the attack.

The summer of 1860 began an eight-year period of fear, starving, and exile the Navajos call Ndahonidzood ("Fleeing From Danger Time" or "Being Chased Time"). It began even before the establishment and garrisoning of Fort Fauntleroy, later known as (New) Fort Wingate, at Ojo del Oso on the last day of August, and ended only with the final return of the Diné from Bosque Redondo in June 1868.

Navajo woes continued that fateful year of 1860 when Zarcillos Largos, possibly the most peaceful of the Diné leaders, died in mid-September in a battle with a large party of New Mexican "volunteers" (a euphemism for slave traders) and Jemez Indians on the Pueblo Colorado near the future village of Ganado.

Another treaty was signed by 49 Navajo headmen at a council at Fort Fauntleroy on February 18, 1861. It demanded that all the Navajos move west of that fort. In effect, they were giving up a third of their land—including two of their four sacred mountains—and agreed to return all captives and livestock taken from New Mexican settlements. The Navajos appeared ready to comply, but, even as they began rounding up livestock, several expeditions were launched from the settlements by the erstwhile New Mexican "volunteers."

Because of the imminent outbreak of North-South hostilities and the need for troops in the eastern United States, Fort Defiance was ordered closed less than a week after the treaty of February 18. By the following summer, nearly all regular troops had been withdrawn from New Mexico Territory (which included Arizona). They were replaced by seasoned volunteers—in many cases the very men who had been raiding Navajo country for slaves and plunder.

All-out war with the Navajos was finally assured by the Fort Fauntleroy Massacre. On September 22, 1861, hundreds of Navajos gathered at Fort Fauntleroy for rations promised in the treaty of February 18. They were also to meet the new Navajo agent, Ramon Luna, and the new post commandant, Major Manuel Chavez. In the midst of a carnival atmosphere, in which liquor flowed freely, a horse race erupted into discord when Navajos discovered White soldiers had tampered with a Navajo's saddle, causing him to lose. In the one-sided melee that followed, over a dozen Navajos were killed with rifles, pistols, and even cannon. Major Chavez, who already had established quite a reputation for hating Navajos, was accused of encouraging the massacre, but he was never taken to trial. Any trust the Navajos had had for the Whites was now gone, and the next two years saw an increase in deaths on both sides.

The Navajos Capitulate

On June 15, 1863, Brigadier General George Carleton, military commander of New Mexico for nearly two years, issued General Order Number 15, commanding a reluctant Colonel Christopher "Kit" Carson to move against the Navajos on July 1. The goal was the total subjugation or extermination of the Diné. Historians generally agree that Carson, formerly a hunter, trapper, frontier scout, and Indian agent, was disinclined to make war on the Diné (and the Mescalero Apaches he vanquished immediately before them). He apparently believed they could be brought to terms by other means.

But under Carleton's orders, Carson employed a "scorched earth" policy in which he decimated the Navajos' ability to live through the winter by destroying all their crops, homes, herds, and flocks—especially in the vicinity of Canyon de Chelly. Three hundred Navajo deaths came mostly at the hands of New Mexican "volunteers" and opportunistic Indian auxiliaries accompanying the troops. Fort Defiance was reopened by Carson under its new name of Fort Canby in August. The "war" was essentially over by the end of January 1864, as the Army retired from the field and simply waited for the starving, freezing Indians to surrender.

The Long Walk

Most yielding Navajos had no idea what awaited them as they gave themselves up to the overwhelming odds. They were gathered at Fort Canby and Old Fort Wingate, until large groups could be convoyed on foot to the Bosque Redondo (Fort Sumner) on the Pecos River in southeastern New Mexico. Between February 26, 1864, and March 1865, a total of 9,022 Navajos were interned at the Bosque, nearly twice the number of Navajos General Carleton had estimated existed. And by no means did all the

Navajos surrender. It has been estimated that several thousand more stayed behind during the Fort Sumner period, fleeing to isolated strongholds near Black Mesa, the Grand Canyon, Navajo Mountain, and points north in Utah, far from any White intruders. Recent archaeological evidence indicates that some even managed to stay in the Canyon de Chelly region. Life was severe, for they had to lie low, dwell in places barely accessible, live off the land, and keep a constant guard against White intruders. Yet, despite the years of deprivation, these Diné were the lucky ones.

The Bosque Redondo experience was a nightmare by any definition of the word. Navajos tell tales passed down from ancestors reminiscent of the Bataan Death March and Nazi concentration camps of World War II. No one knows exactly how many Diné left the reservation bound for the Bosque, but it is known that many died or disappeared along the route. One convoy suffered more than 10 percent mortality, with 323 deaths before reaching the Bosque. Starvation, exposure, malnutrition, and disease decimated the Navajos and several hundred Apaches who were crowded onto the same reservation. Complaints of illness or exhaustion—or even childbirth—resulted in execution. Stragglers and escapees were fair game for gangs of New Mexicans that hounded the convoys.

Once they were at the Bosque, their treatment by the military remained harsh. The Navajos were crowded onto the small reservation along with four hundred Apaches. Promised supplies were always short and of dubious quality. Firewood was an even scarcer commodity, and the individual family farming plots were so poor that even the tenacious Navajos could grow little, and what they did grow was subject to insect infestations. In addition to the elements and their less-than-fair handling by the Whites, the interned Navajos had to deal with continued bad blood between their own people and the ever-present Comanches and Utes (Thompson 1976, 145). After resorting to digging mesquite roots all winter for firewood, one spring the rag-clad Navajos were set upon by raiding Comanches as the Army stood idly by. While doing little to protect the Diné, the post commander was ordered by

Carleton to kill any Navajos caught outside the reservation without a pass. A curfew made it a serious offense for a Navajo simply to be outside his home after dark, even on the reservation.

Fate finally began to look more favorably upon the Diné in the final month of 1865, when a small but vocal cluster of Whites who saw the inhumanity of the situation influenced the Department of the Interior to investigate the Bosque reservation. On September 19, 1866, Carleton was removed as commander of the Department of New Mexico. The following January, control over the Navajos was taken from the Army and turned over to the Indian Service in the Department of the Interior. And finally, on June 1, 1868, a new treaty was negotiated, and signed by Barboncito (Bidághaa'í, "Bearded One," or Hashk Yich'į', "Who Hurries Off to War" or "Toward a Warrior"), Armijo (Gish Díílidíní', "the Late Burnt Cane"), Delgado, Manuelito, Largo (Bigod Bijaa', "Ears in His Knees"), Herrero, Chiquito (Ch'ah Łá'ní, or "Many Hats"), Muerto de Hombre (Dichin Biiłhéhé, "Dying of Hunger"), Hombre, Narbono, Ganado Mucho (Hastiin Totsohnii, "Man of the Big Water") and Narbono Segundo (Frink 1968, 83–4; Navajo names from Franciscan Fathers 1910, 125–6; and Hoffman and Johnson 1970, 113).

Less than three weeks later a military escort led some seven thousand jubilant Diné in a ten-mile-long column back to a portion of their homeland. They arrived at Fort Wingate on July 23, 1868.

The road home was not without peril, and a few Navajos died on the journey after surviving the brutal conditions of the internment (Thompson 1976, 157). Their new 3,414,528-acre reservation was

> . . . bounded on the north by the 37th degree of north latitude, south by an east-west line passing through Fort Defiance, . . . east by the parallel of longitude which, if extended would pass through old Fort Lyon, . . . and west by a parallel of longitude . . . [which] embraces the outlet of Canyon de Chilly [sic], which canyon is to be all included in this reservation. . . . (Correll and Dehiya 1978, 3)

It was less than 10 percent of their former range, but the Navajos were home.

The Reservation Years: 1868 to Present

The history of the Navajos since their return from the Bosque Redondo is an illustration of triumph in the face of adversity. Their reservation has grown over the years, through presidential executive orders and acts of Congress, to its present size of nearly 16,000,000 acres. Three "satellite" reservations—Cañoncito, Ramah, and Alamo—contain another 1,974,391 acres, and another two million acres have been set aside for tribal use through tribal, private, or U.S. government ownership (Correll and Dehiya 1978).

Continued conflict with Anglos (and the Pueblos) led Agent Thomas Keam, in August 1872, to form the "Navajo Cavalry." This body, led by headman Manuelito, intercepted Navajo raiders returning to the reservation and confiscated and returned stolen property (mostly livestock) for nearly a year. A formal Navajo Police force of 15 officers was finally established in 1884, but skirmishes with non-Navajos continued through the remainder of the nineteenth century. More disputes were settled by judges rather than by rifles, but the outcome nearly always favored the Anglos and/or the U.S. government (Bailey and Bailey 1986, 31–35, 73–77).

Yet the Diné more than simply survived in the face of enormous obstacles; they have grown in number and in stature, becoming the second most populous tribe in the United States.

NAVAJO SOCIAL ORGANIZATION

Navajo social structure is built around the clan. Anthropologists since Reichard in the 1930s postulate a vague figure of "60 or more" such clans. The clans are matrilineal and matrilocal, tracing lineage and settling about the mother of an extended family (Witherspoon 1983a, 524–26). However, the father's clan is also important. Navajos introduce themselves as being of the mother's clan, born for the father's (Kluckhohn and Leighton 1962, 112). Most are named for the geographic origin of the people within the clan, and some are even named for other tribes or pueblos. (For an extensive listing of the clans, see Young and Morgan 1987, 433.)

The main function of the clan has been to establish relationships among the Diné. Even today, all marriages are determined by clan, as marrying someone from either their own mother's or father's clan is decidedly incestuous and sure to drive one insane. Traditionally, a Navajo will go to greater lengths to aid a clan relative than a non-relative, even if the clan relative is a total stranger.

The clan is also an economic unit. Extended families, called residence units, are the fundamental unit of the Navajo social organization. They are structured about a "head mother," and include members of her own clan by blood or marriage. These units form the basis for grazing and farming rights (Witherspoon 1983a, 528–29).

POLITICAL ORGANIZATION

The Navajos traditionally recognized no clearly defined group larger than the "residence unit" (Witherspoon 1983a, 525–31). Prior to this century, these units were organized loosely into bands with a local headman (called *naat'áanii)*. These headmen annually would gather in a *naa'chid* ceremony, giving a kind of tribal organization, but the headmen could speak for no one outside their own band.

This posed innumerable problems for the Europeans who tried to make the tribe fit the mold of centralized leadership. Often the early Spanish authorities would negotiate treaties with headmen they assumed to be tribal leaders, only to discover that the headmen represented only a small fraction of the tribe. But the Spanish—and later the Mexicans and Americans—seemed incapable of recognizing this. When Navajo raiders would violate a newly signed treaty, the Euro-Americans ignored the possibility that the raiders simply owed no allegiance to the signer(s) of the treaty, and therefore were not compelled to comply with it (*if* they even knew about it). Admittedly, the fallacy may have been perpetuated by Diné who deliberately misled the Spanish into assuming they had more authority than they really did. On the other hand, since headmen ruled only by persuasion, they sometimes signed a treaty in good faith only to discover they were unable to get their followers to adhere to the terms.

This misunderstanding resulted in many more bloody confrontations between the Navajos and Whites than were necessary. The Euro-Americans generally judged acts of treaty non-compliance to be deliberate and deceitful violations, and this propagated their view of the entire tribe as untrustworthy and dishonest.

During the American period this misconception was raised to new heights as military officials believed they could dictate who would serve as Navajo leaders. They invariably chose men who seemed cooperative and compliant—regardless of leadership qualities or the respect of other Diné. The war of 1863–64 might have been averted if the Army had not spurned Manuelito in favor of lesser leaders, or if the Americans had addressed the many regional headmen (McNitt 1972, 320, 325–26).

During the Bosque Redondo period, the Navajos and Whites both became accustomed to dealing through a council of 12 Navajo spokespersons (called Naat'áanii), each representing loosely affiliated groups of extended families (sometimes called bands), who were empowered only to deal with outsiders. This system may have evolved from a traditional Navajo "council" of 12 peace chiefs and 12 war chiefs who gathered once a year for a ceremony known as the "naachid." The last of these was probably held in the middle of the nineteenth century (Witherspoon 1983a, 532–33). Or it may be coincidence that the Army and the Diné agreed to a council of 11 subchiefs (Armijo, Delgado, Manuelito, Largo, Herrero, Chiqueto, Muerto del Hombre, Hombro, Ganado Mucho, Narbono, and Narbono Segundo) and Barboncito, a principal chief. These chiefs signed the Treaty of 1868 (Correll and Dehiya 1978, 6), and governed the tribe in the years immediately following their return to Navajoland.

In 1870, two of these chiefs, Manuelito and Narbono, enforced the Treaty of 1868 by confiscating stolen livestock from raiders returning to the reservation. This marked the first time chiefs tried to force compliance with the terms of a treaty (Bailey and Bailey 1986, 30).

This council of chiefs may have enabled the Navajos to embrace the concept of the later Navajo Tribal Council, which first convened at Toadlena on July 7, 1923, and represented the Navajos' first centralized government system.

The structure was forced on the Navajos by a Bureau of Indian Affairs directive under pressure from outside interests who wished to strike deals with the tribe as a whole. Like the council of chiefs, the first Tribal Council was composed of 12 elected and/or federally appointed delegates from the reservation's federally recognized jurisdictions. The council elected Chee Dodge as its first chairman, and its first order of business was to sign oil leases. Within the first five years, however, this small group exceeded U.S. government expectations as they condemned the use of federally held tribal moneys for the construction of Marble Canyon Bridge, and they forced the passage of the Indian Oil Act of 1927. The chairman of the Tribal Council, also elected by the masses, became known as the leader of the tribe, and was often referred to simply as the Tribal Chairman.

CHAPTERS

Chapters today comprise the political subdivisions of the reservation. The result of a 1922 effort by the Bureau of Indian Affairs to establish chapters of farm clubs on Indian reservations, they were first known as "Chapters of a Livestock Association." The first Navajo chapter was established by Agent John Hunter in 1927 at Leupp in order to work on land and grazing problems (Young 1972, 167–238).

The Navajo term for "chapter" is Táá' Naaznilí, meaning "Group of Three," reflecting the three officers (president, secretary, and treasurer). By 1933, the concept of chapters had spread across the reservation and numbered nearly a hundred. At first there was no formal connection between the chapters and the council or its delegates, but the Navajos were quick to adopt the system and the chapters became conduits for expressions of discontent. The Indian Service withheld operating funds and other support when the chapters became hotbeds of resistance to the stock reduction, and by 1945 their number had declined to 30. In the next decade, the chapters began to recover, and there were 40 operating in 1955 when the Tribal Council decided that its delegates would represent chapters, although chapters with smaller populations share council delegates. Tribal aid came to the assistance of the chapters in 1959, and by the 1980s 105 had been formed.

In 1991, this system was altered by a new Tribal constitution to more closely resemble the U.S. government structure. The Chairman of the Tribal Council was shifted to a newly defined Navajo Nation Presidency, and the old Tribal Council is now the Navajo Nation Council, presided over by a speaker rather than the old chairman.

2

THE ROLE OF MYTHOLOGY IN NAVAJO PLACE NAME ORIGINS

When anthropologist Clyde Kluckhohn (1944, 5) observed that "Thousands of pages have been published on Navajo ceremonials," he could not have foreseen that those pages would increase a hundredfold or more in the next half century. The intricate system of symbolism that is traditional Navajo religion has been studied extensively over the last 70 years. Like most religions, that of the Navajos is comprised of numerous ceremonies, and most have been surveyed, scrutinized, pondered, analyzed, and categorized scores of times (Father Berard Haile 1938a and 1938b; Leland C. Wyman and Clyde Kluckhohn 1938; Gladys Reichard 1974). These studies, however, often reach contradictory conclusions (Zolbrod 1984, 9–12), probably due in large part to reliance on different informants (to whom the legends and ceremonies vary with the individualism that results from having no standard "manual"). Few, if any, have studied the link between the Navajos' religion and the land in which they live.

Perhaps this is due to the enigmatic relationship between places and ceremonialism. For instance, places named conspicuously after Navajo ceremonial figures or events are even more rare than those named after important Navajo persons—if there are any at all. There are no "Listening Woman Peaks" or "Twin War Gods' Canyons." Instead, a location's religious significance is more obscure, usually ascribed through its association with, or mention in, one or more of the stories that are the foundation of Navajo ceremonials. Often, this reference is simply as one of a string of places visited by a character in a story such as the Prostitutionway Chant Legend:

> Then they started to walking from there towards the west to Hole In The Ground. They kept walk-ing to Swallow's Nest. While they were walking toward that place they saw water rising up again in one direction. From there to Cool Water. Then Green In The Mountain. From there to Horse Falls In The Arroyo. Then to House Under The Rock Spreads Out. Then to Mistletoe Hangs. Then Dead Tree Stands Up. Then to Possessing Fish. Then to Red House. Then to Lake With Weeds On Surface. Then to Rock For Making Paper Bread. Then to Rock Points Toward the Valley. Then Wide Reeds. Then In the Middle White Top. Then Hill Where Water Cuts In. Then from there to Water Comes Together. The Water Afraid. [Here the narrator said he had forgotten some names.] Then Big Willow Juts Out And Droops. Then to Keams Canyon. Then to Walpi. (Kluckhohn 1944, 160)

This paragraph in one legend of a single ceremonial refers to more than twenty places, with no apparent purpose. The characters conduct no activity at any of the mentioned places: they gather no food or supplies, they meet no one, and it is unclear whether they stopped at any of the places or merely passed by. They simply visited each while traveling a prescribed route—which was hardly a straight line—in getting from point A to point B, and, since the list can change from one telling to the next, the choice seems utterly arbitrary.

A few places, however, are more important than others. Hosta Butte ('Ak'iih Nást'ání), for instance, is said to be the home of Mirage Stone Boy (Hadahonighe'ashkii) and Mirage Stone Girl (Hadhomighe' 'At'ee) (Apache and Jim 1982, 6). Yet the true significance of such associations can really be perceived only by those who still hold to traditional Navajo values, for they fully understand the role and importance of the stories in their religion.

And that religion is one of many stories. With no Bible, no Koran, no standardized "handbook," the tales and legends verbally carry the basic world view of the Navajo people from ceremony to ceremony, from generation to generation. They may vary from one narrator to another, but these stories are inextricably a part of Navajo history and culture.

THE PRACTICE

Traditional Navajos find their religion is neither complicated nor intricate, but a very orderly system. Unlike most religions best understood by non-Navajos, however, the dogma had no written text (prior to recent recountings published by anthropologists), and was solely in the hands of the practitioners of the religion: the Medicine Men.

These specialists, more appropriately called "singers" (Aberle 1982, 45), train for years as apprentices to practicing singers, usually paternal kinsmen. Validation as a singer usually comes after many years, when the apprentice proves his ability by conducting a full ceremony on his teacher. (Most but not all are male.)

Ceremonies normally take place at the patient's home, and require payment of a fee— often including an exchange of goods. Since tradition requires that they be conducted in a traditional hogan, a majority of Navajos living in modern "ranch-style" dwellings also maintain an octagonal or hexagonal hogan adjacent to the home.

Major ceremonies are "multi-night" affairs. The Blessingway, for instance, is a two-night affair, while the Night Chant will run nine nights. Each 24-hour period is filled with different activities, including the recitation of sequential chants and legends, culminating in the cure of the patient. Rarely is the ceremony strictly a "doctor/patient" affair. The patient's family, friends, and relatives normally attend and observe, often receiving curative benefit of their own simply by association. Even strangers may take advantage of this residual curing.

THE CEREMONIES

The numerous ceremonies of traditional Navajo religion are curative rites. Most require an ailing patient, and a practitioner trained for the ceremony. The religion is based on reciprocity: favor for favor, gift for gift. For instance, gods gave the people the land, water, livestock, etc., so people must reciprocate by caring for these gifts and performing prescribed rituals. Misfortune occurs when gods are offended or injured through someone's carelessness, through offending supernaturally potent animals (such as snakes, bears, or ants) or through contagion (usually by a person's inadvertent and unknown contact with the dead or with the spirit of a dead person). Illness can also be precipitated by disrespectful treatment of human beings and contact with outsiders.

Navajo ceremonies are concerned with restoring proper relations with the supernatural beings (called the Holy People, or Diyin Dine'e, they are powerful and dangerous and can cause illness or injury), the exorcism of ghosts, and the cure of witchcraft. Precisely performed ceremonies require the gods to reciprocate by setting things back to rights. Recovery is through sympathetic magic, with health restored as the supernaturals restore things to their natural order (Aberle 1982, 48–50).

Each ceremony is a grouping of songs interspersed with prayers and periods of no activity. The songs are generally renditions of the Navajo legends. Sandpaintings, also known as "dry paintings," are also an important part of the process. The medicine man produces renderings of important portions of relevant legends on a smooth bed of sand, using sands and finely crushed rock of myriad colors to help summon the aid of the supernaturals. Other activities include offerings to the gods, sweatbaths, bathing and shampoos, herbal medicines, brushing with feathers, body painting, smoking, and incense burning.

The Navajo ceremonial system . . . is sanctioned and explained in a large body of mythology . . . [which] consists of two major parts, the general origin myth including the story of the Emergence from the underworld, and the origin legends of the separate ceremonials, which branch off the origin myth at various points. . . .

The legends generally relate the misadventures of a hero or heroine who, through intentional or unintentional misbehavior, gets into a series of predicaments requiring supernatural assistance and causing injury or illness calling for ritual restoration. The hero thus acquires the ceremonial knowledge and power for establishing a chantway and teaches it to his people. (Wyman 1983, 556)

The term "chant" can refer to a group of ceremonies commonly comprising a "way" (Blessingway, Evilway), or it can be interchangeable with that term. The chant is a recapitulation of scenes in the myth drama whose function is commemoration. Events in the lower world are remembered and certain episodes are acted out or represented in symbols to preserve the timelessness of power.

> For instance, a sick Navajo identifies himself with the rejuvenation of Changing Woman when he recapitulates in the Shooting Chant the place, the circumstances and the ritualistic details she experienced when she was restored to youth and beauty. (Reichard 1974, 116)

There are at least 24 Navajo ceremonials, about half of which, though used in the last century, are today rare, obsolete, or extinct (Wyman 1957, 13; 1983, 545). Those that are extinct or extremely rare are identified below by asterisks. Some can be conducted year-round, others are seasonal. Some ceremonies are intended to benefit strictly the individual patient, while others are conducted for the benefit of the "tribe" (Reichard 1974, 322–23).

Holyway Ceremonies
(from Wyman 1983, 545)

Holyways are generally performed for the attraction of good and the restoration of harmony. They are conducted by one of two subrituals, the Peacefulway or the Injuryway (also known as Angryway, Fightingway, Weaponway). They are considered Peacefulway unless otherwise identified. The Injuryways are held when the patient is affected by natural circumstances beyond his control (snake bite, lightning strike, etc.).

1. Shooting Chant
1a. Hailway (Ńlóee)*: Used for people harmed by water, snow, frost, hail. Extinct.

1b. Waterway (Tłóee)*: Same as 1a. Obsolete.

1c. Shootingway (Na'at'oyee): Used for troubles caused by lightning and thunder or by earthly symbols thereof (snakes, arrows); usually lung and gastrointestinal problems.

1d. Red Antway (Wóláchii'ji): Used for problems caused by ants, horned toads, and (secondarily) by lightning and bears. Primarily genitourinary, chest, and gastrointestinal ailments, skin disorders, sore throat, or rheumatism. May be caused by urinating on an anthill, accidentally swallowing an ant, or an ant bite.

1e. Big Starway (Sǫ'tsohjí) Originally a Holyway, now done according to Evilway ritual and used to treat illness caused by native ghosts and witches.

1f. Flintway (Béshee) The fundamental Lifeway Chant; may actually be part of the Shootingway.

2. Mountain Chant
2a. Mountain Way (Dziłk'ijí): Cure for "bear disease," but also for illnesses caused by any mountain animals (porcupines, weasels, skunks, badgers, even chipmunks and squirrels, and at least one fowl: the wild turkey). Bears are usually associated with arthritis and mental illness. Other distresses caused by different animals include gastrointestinal, kidney, and bladder illnesses (porcupine), nasal discomfort or coughing (squirrels), itching, pimples, and skin irritations (turkey), deafness and eye troubles (mountain sheep).

2b. Beautyway (Hoozhónee): Sister to Mountainway Chant, is concerned with snakes, so firmly that some Navajos call it the "snake chant" in English. It is used to cure such ailments as rheumatism, sore throat, stomach trouble, kidney and bladder trouble, skin sores, or "just about any human misery."

2c. Excessway ('Ajiłee)*: Closely related to the Mothway and possibly the Coyoteway (under God Impersonators below). These ceremonies were all cures for "breaking ceremonial restrictions," recklessness (such as sexual excess), incest, and any sexual irregularities.

2d. Mothway ('Iichąhjí)*: See Excessway above.

3. God Impersonators (Yé'ii Hóló̜ní)
In this group of ceremonies, masked impersonators of the Holy People, called "Yeis," appear in the public portion of the final night.

3a. Nightway (Tl'éé'jí): Used for all types of head ailments, from eye and ear infections to mental illness.

3b. Big Godway (Haashch'éétsohee)*: Closely related to the Nightway; in fact, may have been a branch of that ceremony rather than a separate chantway.

3c. Plumeway ('Ats'osee): Also called Featherway or Downway, this ceremony is used for diseases of the head, like Nightway, but also for rheumatism and other ailments caused by animals (especially deer).

3d. Coyoteway (Ma'iijí)*: See Excessway above.

3e. Dogway (Łééchąą'íjí)*: Extinct, purpose not known.

3f. Ravenway (Gáagiijí)*: Extinct; purpose not known, though may have been related to Coyoteway, used in cases of incest.

4. Wind Chant (Nílch'ijí)

Both branches are closely related, and used for ailments caused by winds (especially whirlwinds), snakes (or lightning and thunder), cactus, the sun, and the moon.

4a. Navajo Windway (Diné Biních'ijí): Has male branch (Injuryway subritual called Striped Windway) and female branch.

4b. Chiricahua Windway (Chíshí Binílch'ijí): This is one of the briefest and most popular of Navajo ceremonies, and appears to be of fairly recent origin, possibly picked up during the Fort Sumner internment.

5. Hand-Trembling Chant

5a. Hand-Tremblingway (N'dilniihjí): Used to diagnose almost any ailment, from over-practicing hand-trembling divination or star-gazing to nervous or mental disruptions, paralysis, vision problems, and chest discomforts.

6. Eagle Trapping

Both of the branches of this chant might be better grouped with the Gameway (hunting) traditions or with the Holyway rites.

6a. Eagleway ('Atsáájí)*: Used to treat specific "eagle infections," such as earache, itching, boils, and sores, sore throat.

6b. Beadway (Yoo'ee)*: Extinct; was closely related to Eagleway above.

7. Uncertain Affiliation

All three of these branches are extinct and have been for some time. The purposes are no longer understood, and the Reared in Earthway is conjectural. (It may not have existed at all.)

7a. Awlway (Tsahaa)*

7b. Earthway (Ni'jí)*

7c. Reared in Earthway (Ni' Honeeyą́ą́jí)*

EVILWAY CEREMONIES

Most of the Holyway Ceremonies have a counterpart that is directed toward exorcising evil rather than attracting good. These are called Evilway Ceremonies, and have different specific chants and procedures, such as brushing the patient with a native grass broom dipped in ashes (Wyman 1983, 553).

A fundamental Evilway ceremony was the extinct Upward Reachingway; Enemyway was also an Evilway chant. The Big Starway and Hand-Tremblingway are more common in their Evilway forms than in the Holyway.

LIFEWAY CEREMONIES

This class includes versions of the Shootingway and formerly the Hand-Tremblingway, and a Flintway. The ceremonies are specifically for treating accidental injuries (Wyman 1983, 542).

No ceremony is regarded as minor (Reichard 1974, 319), but the hózhǫ́ǫ́ji is considered the most universally understood ceremony, and is comprised of the Emergence narrative. Commonly referred to as the Blessingway (Reichard 1974, 328–29; Farella 1984, 20; Wyman 1983, 537), this ceremony unites and controls all others. It is the backbone of Navajo religion and all other rituals derive from it. The Blessingway is concerned with assuring peace, harmony, and all things good in life, and every ceremonial chant, including those of the Evilway group, includes a Blessingway song (Wyman 1983, 539–40).

There are many versions of the Blessingway, but each contains two basic elements: The journey ascending through several worlds below the present one (thus the epithet "Emergence"); and the "cosmic ordering process" of earth once this world was attained (Gill 1983, 502–5). The number of underworlds can vary from two to 14, but all are normally inhabited by insect beings—usually ant people—or animal beings (though all beings supposedly derive from First Man's medicine bundle). This narrative provides a good introduction to nearly all the Navajo legends, because many characters from the Blessingway appear in numerous other narratives. This version is one published by the Navajo tribe:

In the First World, the Black World [or Red, according to Zolbrod 1984, 39] First Man ('Átsé Hastiin) and First Woman ('Atsé 'Asdzáá) are formed. Due to quarrels, they move upward into the Second (Blue) World, populated by animal and insect beings. Again quarreling brings suffering and the beings move to the Third (Yellow) World.

This world has six mountains. Here live Turquoise Boy (Dootł'izhii 'Ashkii) and White Shell Woman (Yoolgai 'Asdzáá). Coyote (Mą'íí), who has come to this world with First Man and First Woman, causes a flood by stealing the child [or two babies, according to Zolbrod 1984, 72] of Water Monster (Tééhoołtsódii). Escape to the Fourth World is accomplished by crawling up a female reed planted by First Man.

Fourth World is the Glittering World. Here First Man and First Woman form the four sacred mountains: North (Hesperus Peak, Colorado), South (Mount Taylor, New Mexico), East (Blanca Peak, Colorado), and West (San Francisco Peaks, Arizona). Talking God (Haashch'ééłti'í) teaches them to make the first hogan. [Some accounts say First Man and First Woman were actually created on this world—Zolbrod 1984, 51]. The stars are placed in the sky, and the sun and moon are formed (from turquoise and white shell, respectively), and day and night are created. Adultery leads to a separation of men and women, but this proves harmful to all, and they are reunited. The world is beset with numerous "monsters."

A baby, Changing Woman ('Asdzáá Nádleehé), is found by First Man and First Woman near Gobernador Knob (New Mexico). After she is grown and undergoes the first Kinaalda (puberty ceremony), the Sun impregnates her in her sleep.

She gives birth to twin sons, Monster Slayer (Naayéé' Neizghání) and Child Born of Water (Tó Bájíshchíní). Spider Woman (Na'ashjé'ii 'Asdzáá) tells them how to reach their father, who provides them with weapons to slay the monsters: the older brother receives Lightning that Strikes Crooked ('Atsiniltłi shk'aa') and the younger receives Lightning that Flashes Straight ('Atsoolaghałk'aa', Sheet Lightning Arrow).

One of the monsters killed is Lone Walking Giant (Yé'iitsoh Łáa'ii Naagháii), whose plentiful blood congeals into the El Malpais Lava Flow at the foot of Mount Taylor. Sun is angered, because many of the monsters were his children. He causes a great flood to cover the earth, though the Holy People save pairs of all animals, including a man and woman. The first Squaw Dance ceremony is held for Monster Slayer, who is adversely affected by the losses caused by the flood. (Yazzie 1971)

The Emergence story continues with the creation of the first four clans by Changing Woman and wandering of the people. Groups break off and become the Paiutes, Chiricahua Apaches, Mescalero Apaches, and Jicarilla Apaches. Finally the Holy People decide to have The People (Diné) settle between the four sacred mountains.

The Emergence story defines meaningful relationships among members of the Navajo community and between that community and the cosmos. Such relationships are still very real and very important among traditional Navajos, providing a measure of ethnic identity (Zolbrod 1984, 25). The personages who people the creation narrative figure in many of the other Navajo legends, as do their relatives and offspring.

CEREMONIALISM AND NAVAJO PLACE NAMES

Navajo chantway myths describe the origin of the associated ceremony. Typically, the hero experiences a series of misfortunes in which he is assisted by supernaturals. He then travels freely among the supernaturals—increasing his power with each misadventure until he has sufficient power to return home without further aid from the supernaturals. He then teaches his people the ceremony he has learned (Spencer 1957, 18–19). But many anthropologists and ethnohistorians believe the tales serve another purpose. Many of the Navajo chantway myths include as integral parts "sky visits," travels to underworld realms, or journeys in the physical world of Earth-surface men, with the latter being the most common. For instance, in the Claus Chee Sonny version of the Navajo Deer Huntingway described by Luckert, the hero completes two journeys that roughly circumnavigate Navajoland—first via a northerly route, then via a southern route, naming many of the same places visited on both trips. Luckert suggests that this repetitiveness helped "the Athabascan hunter lay claim to the southwestern homeland into which the Navajos had relocated from points north—and the northern geography having faded from their conscious memory" (Luckert 1975, 193–200).

Places have the highest possible meaning to Native Americans (Basso 1996, 37). Franz Boaz (1901–02) suggested that investigating their geographical nomenclatures is one of the most effective methods of exploring the mental life of Indian peoples. Even the most minute of occurrences are described by Navajos in close conjunction with their physical settings, suggesting that unless narrated events are spatially anchored their significance is somehow reduced and cannot be properly assessed (Basso 1996, 45, quoting a 1973 personal communication from Harry Hoijer). And when places are actively sensed, through repetitive mention, the physical landscape becomes wedded to the landscape of the mind. Familiar places become inherently meaningful, their significance and value residing in the form and arrangement of their observable characteristics (Basso 1996, 107–8).

Beyond the ceremonial and ethnohistorical importance, places and their names have proven valuable to the Navajo people at another level. Because the ceremonies are considered to be as old as Navajo culture itself, ceremonial significance of a location has been offered as substantiation of the antiquity of Navajo occupation in land claims cases (Indian Claims Commission n.d.).

3

THE TRADING POSTS

Nearly every aspect of modern Navajo life has been affected by the 145-year presence of the Indian trader. The Navajo word for trading post is Naalyéhé bá hooghan, "home for merchandise" (Young and Morgan 1987, 583), and the trader is naalyéhé yá sidáhí, or "he who sits for the sake of the merchandise" (W. Roberts 1987, 30). A mainstay of the Navajo economy from the time the Navajos returned from the Bosque Redondo, this form of commerce proliferated and survived by imposing itself into the most remote reaches of the Navajo domain. The three hundred trading posts included in this volume account for 25 percent of the total toponymic listings.

A trading post, by definition, barters goods for goods. Navajos, whose economy has left them continually short of hard currency, have traded raw wool, finished rugs, jewelry and other crafts, and agricultural crops, to the trader for food staples, dry goods, and more. In addition, nearly every post has conducted a lively trade in livestock, providing the Navajos with an outlet for surplus animals or beasts ready for slaughter in exchange for new breeding stock.

The trading posts flourished because the trader connected the Navajos to the world beyond their borders when the Diné were so isolated that a trip to the nearest town often meant a week or more on horseback. The traders brought to the Navajos products that would otherwise have been denied them, such as canned foods, fuel oils, manufactured clothing, firearms and ammunition, metal pots, pans, and utensils, processed flour and sugar, over-the-counter medicines, and the raw materials, tools, and supplies for art and crafts trades. The posts also served as the Navajos' only connection to outside markets for their wool, livestock, and crafts—which provided the

Diné with the wherewithal for purchasing the modern goods the trader offered. The trader acted as banker, auto mechanic, doctor, pharmacist, talent agent, financier, and financial adviser.

Despite opposition by the federal government, a major component of the trading industry—pawn—was in vogue by 1887 (W. Roberts 1987, 47). An ancient and worldwide phenomenon, the pawn system quickly developed into a unique alternative banking system for the Navajos. Typical trading posts contain large walk-in vaults to hold the valuables left by Navajos as collateral against a credit line or small loans (Noe 1993, 31). Interest rates have remained high for this service (as much as 10 percent per month), but the default rate is also high, and the system allows the Navajos access to credit they might otherwise not be able to obtain.

In addition to providing quick, if expensive, cash and/or credit for the individual Navajo, the system provides a convenient "safety deposit" strategy, for pawned jewelry, rugs, baskets, tack, weapons, etc. are better protected in the trader's vault than in the typical isolated Navajo home. Traders have even been known to lend a pawned item back to an individual for use during a ceremony, even though the loan has not been paid off (Noe 1993, 33). Today horse trailers, tractors, and even automobiles are taken as pawn.

Though the post sutler at Fort Defiance had engaged in trading since the fort's construction in 1851 (Kelley 1985, 19), the first federal license to trade on the Navajo Reservation was issued to Lehman Spiegelburg at the fort in 1868 (McNitt 1962, 109). By 1870 a man named "Charley" was traveling the northern Navajo Reservation trading guns and ammunition for livestock stolen from Mormon settlers. He drove the animals to

Albuquerque for resale (McPherson 1988, 63–64). A small trading post at Ganado in the early 1870s was a precursor to Lorenzo Hubbell's famed post in the same vicinity (W. Roberts 1987, 16).

Traders in Fruitland, Hogback, and Gap all opened for business off-reservation in 1880, the same year Naschitti Trading Post was established. A year later, the post at Tonalea (Arizona) first opened. Thomas Keams opened the famous Keams Canyon Trading Post in 1882, in Keams Canyon, on the Hopi Reservation (W. Roberts 1987, 17). Sam Day was trading in Chinle in 1886, and Tohatchi Trading Post started in 1890. Two of the most revered Navajo blanket sources, Two Grey Hills and Crystal Trading Posts, were founded in 1897.

But not many posts boasted longevity. In 1885, at least seven trading posts existed along the San Juan River in the 35-mile stretch between Bluff, Utah, and the Four Corners. By 1895, only Four Corners Trading Post (Owen E. Noland) remained (McPherson 1988, 65).

The number of reservation posts remained relatively low until early in this century, though posts beyond the reservation boundaries kept pace (Kelly 1977, 151–56). By 1885 there were fewer than 25 within the reservation (Kelly 1977, 153), but by 1939 there were 93, and the number had climbed to 138 by 1960 (Bailey and Bailey 1986, 147, 269), and remained static for a decade and a half (Correll and Watson 1974, 99).

Over the following two decades, however, the trading post began to disappear. Sociocultural factors, such as the rising availability of cash from widespread wage-labor and the increased availability of the automobile (most commonly the ubiquitous pickup truck), coupled with the improved quality of roads throughout the reservation, improved the opportunities for Navajos to visit the nearby border towns, commercial centers offering more variety and lower prices than the trading posts could offer. Some posts withered under accusations of profiteering and other unfair trade practices; others sold out to off-reservation retail corporations and were converted to convenience stores (Guterson 1994, 76–83).

The first on-reservation shopping center, featuring primarily outlets of off-reservation concerns, opened in Window Rock in the late 1960s. Twenty years later, the Navajo government began an aggressive program of constructing shopping centers featuring primarily Navajo-owned businesses across the reservation. Shiprock, Crownpoint, Window Rock, Kayenta, Chinle, and Tuba City all have their own modern stores, providing the Navajos with an alternative both to the trading post and to shopping in the border towns.

Today there are probably no more than a dozen bona fide trading posts on and around the reservation. The exact number is difficult to determine due to the fact that on-reservation licenses list some convenience stores as trading posts (a fine line now separates the trading post from the ever-increasing "7-Eleven"), and the off-reservation posts are not registered at all.

In establishing a post, the trader first determined where a concentrated group of customers was living and then sought permission from their leaders to build a post. In addition to this permission, the trader was also required to acquire a license from the federal government. (This was supposed to insure the trader's moral and financial stability.) Even though the building and goods belonged to the trader, the land that the posts were built on remained Navajo property (Moore 1987, 1).

Life as a trader was not idyllic. In 1913, Albert Starr had to haul water for his Starr Lake Trading Post from Bob Smith's Ojo Encino post nine miles to the north. Mail came from Cabezon, a settlement 35 miles southeast (W. Roberts 1987, 21). Long periods of isolation plagued the early merchants. Not only were they separated from their own culture, even the widely scattered Navajos visited the posts primarily in times of need. And when the two cultures did converge, the interaction was sometimes volatile. At Tuckers Trading Post near Starr Lake, an 18-year-old employee named Pat Smith was killed and the post burned down on July 18, 1918, while the Tuckers were in Albuquerque purchasing a new automobile. Ed Doonan, trader at Chaco Canyon Trading Post, was shot and killed through the window of his post a few months later (W. Roberts 1987, 31–32), and there are many more examples. The long hours, grueling conditions, and low pay took their toll, and the posts opened and closed or changed hands with remarkable speed. Crystal Trading Post, for instance, has experienced a typical ownership schedule:

Romolo Martinez	1873
Ben Hyatt	1882
Stephen Adrich and Elias Clark	1884
Elias Clark and Charles Hubbell	1885
Walter Fales	1885
Michael Donovan	1886
Perry Williams	1887
Joe Reitz	1894
John B. Moore	1896
Jesse A. Molohon	1911
C. C. Manning	1919
Charlie Newcomb	1936
Jim Collyer	1946
Don Jenson	1981

Traders who were also Navajo have been few and far between. Little Mustache and his older brother, Arroyo, built a post on Black Mesa in about 1912–14 (Kelly 1985, 29). In 1945, a Navajo named H. T. Donald purchased the lease for the Tsegi Trading Post in Marsh Pass, halfway between Shonto and Kayenta. Navajos have rarely been successful as traders, largely because of extreme pressure to be generous in a Navajo community, which is counter to sound business. Refusal of credit—even to high-risk clients— often would bring criticism and a boycott. Worse still, success could bring witchcraft (W. Roberts, 1987, 119).

The trading posts often gave rise to Navajo communities. Kelly (1977) demonstrated that the "central place theory" did not account for posts' locations. Rather, savvy traders took possession of scarce water sources, natural destinations for the denizens of this arid land. As schools, wage-labor, utilities, and transportation factors gradually coaxed the widely dispersed Navajos to begin congregating into larger groups, the posts became population magnets. Virtually every Navajo community large enough to show up on a map today, with the exception of a few "government towns" (Window Rock, Fort Defiance, Crownpoint, and Shiprock), sprang from a lonely trading post. Traders sometimes aided this trend,

such as when Stokes Carson donated two acres behind Carson's Trading Post for the Huerfano Chapter House in 1931 (W. Roberts 1987, 87).

The Navajo trader was neither a saint nor a devil. Stories persist of dishonest traders bilking their customers by controlling their government checks (for they also usually served as postmaster), cheating them in business deals, selling contraband liquor, and deliberately providing poor advice inducing further indebtedness to the traders. Proof of these activities lies in government records showing that numerous military leaders and Indian agents tried to throw perpetrators off the reservation—and sometimes succeeded.

Most traders have been honest, hardworking entrepreneurs who stayed on the reservation because they enjoyed working with the Navajo people. Their stores served as post-office, chapter house, clinic, general store, and bank, and often passed from one generation to another. But complaints of inordinately high prices and other perceived abuses led to an investigation by the Federal Trade Commission in 1972, and the traders' laid-back, lackadaisical record-keeping was viewed as their attempt to cover up their wrongdoings and led to their chastisement by the government. As a result, many traders left the reservation, and places like Wide Ruins, Mariano Lake, and Lukachukai were boarded up.

NAVAJO TRADING POSTS

An exhaustive study of virtually all literature concerning Navajo trading posts resulted in a list of some 315 posts that existed at some time in Navajo country. This list includes those posts for which additional information is provided in the following chapters as well as those for which the study revealed no substantive information (beyond name and possibly general location).

Ackmen: Montezuma County, CO.

Algert, C. H., Trading Co.: Fruitland, NM (McNitt 1962, 298–302).

Allentown: Apache County, AZ (Lupton).

Aneth Trading Post: San Juan County, UT (Aneth). Also Riverview, Hayes, and Ames & Scott Trading Posts.

Antelope Springs Trading Post: Navajo County, AZ (Jeddito).

Arnold, Albert, Trading Post: McKinley County, NM (Tohatchi).

Ashcroft Trading Post: McKinley County, NM (Ramah).

B & B Trading Post: San Juan County, NM (Shiprock).

Babbitt's: Navajo County, AZ (Kayenta).

Baby Rocks: Navajo County, AZ (near Kayenta).

Bacon Springs Trading Post: McKinley County, NM (Coolidge).

Balcomb, Spencer, Trader: Apache County, AZ (Sanders).

Ballard Trading Co.: Location uncertain; probably Penistaja, NM.

Becenti Springs: Exact location uncertain, possibly near Becenti, NM.

Beclabito Trading Post: San Juan County, NM (Beclabito).

Bell Trading Post: Coconino County, AZ (Tuba City).

Bennet-Turner Trading Post, Apache County, AZ (near Black Rock).

Bernard, Bruce M., Trading Post: San Juan County, NM (Shiprock).

Betatakin Trading Post: See Shonto Trading Post.

Bibo: Cibola County, NM (south of Cebolleta).

Bickel's Trading Post, Apache County, AZ (near Black Rock).

Bidahochi: Navajo County, AZ (south of White Cone).

Big Mountain Trading Post: Navajo County, AZ (on Black Mesa).

Bisti Trading Post: San Juan County, NM (in the Bisti Badlands).

Bitter Springs Trading Post: Coconino County, AZ.

Bitterweed Springs Trading Post: Navajo County, AZ (at Chilchinbito).

Black Falls Trading Post: Coconino County, AZ (near the Black Falls of the Little Colorado River).

Black Mesa Trading Post: Coconino(?) County, AZ.

Black Mountain Trading Post: Apache County, AZ (also known as Black Mountain Store).

Black Rock: Location uncertain, but probably south of Fort Defiance, AZ. Location of Bennet-Turner, Bickel, and Roberts' trading operations.

Black Salt Trading Post: Apache County, AZ (Black Salt Valley, west of Crystal Trading Post).

Blanco Trading Post: San Juan County, NM (Blanco).

Blue Canyon Trading Post: Coconino County, AZ (12 to 15 miles east of Tuba City).

Bluff: San Juan County, UT (convergence of Cottonwood Wash and the San Juan River).

Boehm's Trading Post: See Hubbell and Cotton Trading Post, Chinle.

Bond Brothers Trading Post: Cibola County, NM (Ramah).

Bond Trading Company: San Juan County, NM (Shiprock).

Borderlands Trading Post: Navajo County, AZ (13 miles north of Winslow).

Borrego Pass Trading Post: McKinley County, NM.

Boyle's Trading Post: See Hubbell and Cotton Trading Post, Chinle.

Brimhall Trading Post: McKinley County, NM (also Brimhall Wash Trading Post, Brimhall).

Buck Trading: McKinley County, NM (White Horse).

Buffalo Springs Trading Post: Location uncertain, but possibly at Iyanbito, NM, east of Gallup.

Burnham's Trading Post: San Juan County, NM (Burnham, later at Sanders, AZ).

Burnt Water: Apache County, AZ.

Cahone: Dolores County, CO (Cahone).

Cameron Trading Post: Coconino County, AZ (Cameron).

Canyon Diablo Trading Post: Coconino County, AZ.

Carson Trading Post: San Juan County, NM (Carson).

Carson Trading Post: McKinley County, NM (near Church Rock).

Castle Butte: Navajo County, AZ (25 miles northeast of Winslow).

Cedar Point: Location uncertain.

Cedar Ridge Trading Post: Coconino County, AZ (seven miles north of Gap).

Cedar Springs Trading Post: Navajo County, AZ (Hopi Buttes region south of the Hopi Mesas).

Chambers Trading Post: Apache County, AZ (I-40, between Gallup and Holbrook).

Chavez Trading Post: Location uncertain.

Cheechilgeetho Trading Post: McKinley County, NM (between Gallup and Zuni, at Chichiltah).

Chilchinbito Trading Post: Navajo County, AZ (Chilchinbito).

China Springs Trading Post: McKinley County, NM
(six miles north of Gallup).

Chinle Valley Trading Post: Apache County, AZ
(exact location uncertain, but probably north of
Chinle).

Chuska Trading Post: McKinley County, NM
(Tohatchi).

Cienega Amarilla: Apache County, AZ (St.
Michaels).

Coal Mine Mesa: Coconino County, AZ.

Conley, Favella and Sharp Trading Post: Location
uncertain.

Continental Divide Trading Post: McKinley County,
NM (25 miles east of Gallup).

Coolidge-Perea: McKinley County, NM. Four posts
in Coolidge between 1890 and 1930.

Coon, A. C., Trading Post: Apache County, AZ
(Sanders).

Coppermine: Coconino County, AZ (25 miles north
of Gap).

Cornfields Trading Post: Apache County, AZ
(Cornfields).

Cottonwood: Apache County, AZ (Cottonwood).

Counselors Trading Post: Sandoval County, NM
(Counselors).

Cousins Trading Post: McKinley County, NM
(Whitewater).

Cove: Apache County, AZ (10 miles west of Red
Valley, on Arizona-New Mexico state line).

Cow Springs Trading Post: Coconino County, AZ
(Cow Springs).

Coyote Canyon Trading Post: McKinley County, NM
(Coyote Canyon).

Crane's Station: See Coolidge, NM.

Cronmeyer, Hoske, Trading Post: Apache County,
AZ (Sanders).

Cross Canyon Trading Post: Apache County, AZ
(Cross Canyon).

Crownpoint: McKinley County, NM (two trading
posts operating nonconcurrently between 1905
and 1915).

Crozier Trading Post: See Newcomb Trading Post.

Crystal Trading Post: San Juan County, NM
(Crystal).

Dalton Pass Trading Post: McKinley County, NM
(five miles north of Mariano Lake).

Danoffville: McKinley County, NM (two miles west
of Pinehaven).

Day's Chinle Trading Post: Apache County, AZ
(Chinle).

Sam Day's Trading Post: Apache County, AZ
(St. Michaels).

Defiance Station Trading Post: McKinley County,
NM (six miles west of Gallup).

Dilcon Trading Post: Navajo County, AZ (Dilcon).

Dinnebito Trading Post: Navajo County, AZ
(Dinnebito).

Dinnehotso Trading Post: Apache County, AZ
(Dinnehotso).

Divide Trading Post: McKinley County, NM (just
east of Window Rock, AZ).

Donovan's Trading Post: Apache County, AZ
(Chinle). See Hubbell and Cotton Trading Post.

Drolet's Trading Post: See Newcomb Trading Post.

Dunn Mercantile Trading Company: Apache County,
AZ (Fort Defiance).

Dunn's Trading Post: San Juan County, UT (on
Navajo Mountain, near Rainbow Bridge.

Echo Trading Post: Exact location uncertain.
Coconino County, AZ (north of Cameron).

Eighteen Miles Spring Trading Post: (?) County,
AZ.

El Morro: Cibola County, NM (El Morro National
Monument).

Escavada: McKinley or San Juan County, NM (exact
location uncertain; in Chaco Canyon vicinity).

Escrito: Rio Arriba County, NM (Lybrook).

Estrella: See Star Lake Trading Post.

Fort Defiance: Apache County, AZ.

Fort Wingate Trading Post: McKinley County, NM
(Fort Wingate; two separate posts).

Forty Four: Location uncertain.

Four Corners Trading Post: Convergence of the four
states.

Frazier's Trading Post: Apache County, AZ (two
posts, one at St. Michaels, one at Many Farms).

Fruitland Trading Post: San Juan County, NM
(Fruitland).

Gallegos Trading Post: San Juan County, NM
(10 miles southeast of Farmington).

Ganado Trading Post: Apache County, AZ (Ganado).

Gap Trading Post: Coconino County, AZ (36 miles
north of Cameron).

Garcia's Trading Post: Apache County, AZ (Chinle).

Gobernador Store: Rio Arriba County, NM (Gobernador).

Gouldings Trading Post: San Juan County, UT (Gouldings).

Graham's: McKinley County, NM (Zuni Pueblo).

Gray Mountain Trading Post: Coconino County, AZ (near Cameron).

Greasewood Trading Post: Apache County, AZ (Lower Greasewood).

Griswold's: McKinley County, NM (Tsé Bonito; moved from Navajo, NM, in 1989).

Hatch Trading Post: San Juan County, UT (confluence of Montezuma Canyon and Alkali Canyon).

Haynes: Rio Arriba County, NM (also Haynes Ranch; five miles north of Counselors).

Heart Butte Post: McKinley County, NM (exact location uncertain, but presumably near Heart Rock, seven miles east of Crownpoint).

Heller Trading Post: Sandoval County, NM (at Cabezon).

Hogback Trading Post: San Juan County, NM (two miles west of Waterflow.).

Houck Trading Post: Apache County, AZ (Houck).

Hubbell and Cotton Trading Post: Apache County, AZ (Chinle).

Hubbell's Chinle Trading Post: Apache County, AZ (Chinle).

Hubbell Trading Post: Apache County, AZ (Ganado).

Huerfano Trading Post: San Juan County, NM (25 miles south of Bloomfield).

Hunters Point Trading Post: Apache County, AZ (Hunter's Point).

Hyatt Trading Post: Apache County, AZ (Fort Defiance).

Indian Wells Trading Post: Navajo County, AZ (Indian Wells).

Inscription House Trading Post: Coconino County, AZ.

Ismay Trading Post: Montezuma County, CO (at the confluence of Yellow Jacket and Bridge Canyons with McElmo Creek).

Jeddito Trading Post: Navajo County, AZ (five miles east of Keams Canyon, one mile north of Arizona Highway 264).

Jones Ranch: McKinley County, NM (11 miles south of Gallup on Navajo Route 7048).

Kaibito Trading Post: Coconino County, AZ (Kaibito).

Karigan's Trading Post: Apache County, AZ (just north of St. Michaels).

Keams Canyon Trading Post: Apache County, AZ (Keams Canyon).

Kerley's Trading Posts: Coconino County, AZ (two posts, one at Tuba City, the other at Kayenta).

Kimbeto Trading Post: San Juan County, NM (also Kimbito, Kinbeto, Kinbito, Kinnebito; junction of New Mexico Highways 44 and 56, four miles southeast of Nageezi).

Kinlichee Trading Post: Apache County, AZ (Kinlichee).

Klagetoh Trading Post: Apache County, AZ (Klagetoh).

Kuhn Trading Post: Apache County, AZ (St. Michaels).

Laguna Pueblo Trading Post: Cibola County, NM (Laguna Pueblo).

Lambson Trading Post: McKinley County, NM (Ramah).

Lee's Ferry: Coconino County, AZ (Lee's Ferry).

Leupp Trading Post: Coconino County, AZ (Leupp).

Lewis Trading: McKinley County, NM (Thoreau).

Lindrith: Rio Arriba County, NM (Lindrith).

Lingle, Washington P. and Thomas J., Trading Post: See Hubbell and Cotton Trading Post, Chinle.

Little Mustache's Trading Post: Navajo County, AZ (on Black Mesa).

Little Water Trading Post: See Sansotee Trading Post.

Lower Greasewood Trading Post: Apache County, AZ.

Low Mountain Trading Post: Navajo County, AZ (west of Low Mountain).

Lukachukai Trading Post: Apache County, AZ (Lukachukai).

Lybrooks Trading Post: Rio Arriba County, NM (Lybrooks).

Madison & McCoy Trading Post: McKinley County, NM (Crownpoint vicinity).

Mancos Creek Trading Post: Montezuma County, CO (foot of Tanner Mesa).

Manning Brothers Trading Company: San Juan
County, NM (Shiprock).

Manuelito Springs Trading Post: McKinley County,
NM (14 miles east of Tohatchi).

Manuelito Trading Post: McKinley County, NM
(12 miles west of Gallup).

Many Farms: Apache County, AZ (Many Farms).

Marble Canyon Trading Post: Coconino County, AZ
(Marble Canyon).

Mariano Lake Trading Post: McKinley County, NM
(Mariano Lake).

Mariano's Store: McKinley County, NM (near
Pueblo Pintado).

McCrary, Charles, Trading Post: Apache County, AZ
(Ganado Lake).

McElmo Trading Post: Montezuma County, CO.

McMahon Trading Post: Apache County, AZ
(St. Michaels).

Mexican Hat Trading Post: San Juan County, UT;
also known as Neville's (Mexican Hat).

Mexican Springs Trading Post: McKinley County,
NM (Mexican Springs).

Mexican Water Trading Post: Apache County, AZ
(Mexican Water).

Montezuma Creek Trading Post: San Juan County,
UT (Montezuma Creek).

Mooney, Bernard J., Trading Post: See Hubbell and
Cotton Trading Post, Chinle.

Naahtee Canyon Trading Post: Navajo County, AZ
(Naahtee Canyon).

Nageezi Trading Post: San Juan County, NM
(Nageezi).

Naschitti Trading Post: McKinley County, NM
(Naschiti).

Navajo Church Trading Post: McKinley County, NM
(east of Gallup).

Navajo Mountain Trading Post: San Juan County, UT
(Navajo Mountain).

Navajo Springs: Apache County, AZ (west of
Holbrook).

Navajo Trails: Coconino County, AZ (Tuba City).

Navata: McKinley County, NM (four miles north of
Gallup).

Nazlini Trading Post: Apache County, AZ (opened
by Lorenzo Hubbell between 1886 and 1900).

Neal and Damon's: Apache County, AZ (Fort
Defiance).

Nelson's Trading Post: See Newcomb Trading Post.

Neville Trading Post: Listed by Van Valkenburgh
(1942, 97) as being on the north side of the San
Juan River at Mexican Hat in 1942.

Newcomb Trading Post: San Juan County, NM; also
Nelson's, Nava, Drolet's, and Blue Mesa or Blue
Point.

New Oraibi: Navajo County, AZ (Hopi Second
Mesa).

Noland's Four Corners Store (Trading Post):
Montezuma County, CO.

Ojo Alamo Trading Post: San Juan County, NM.

Ojo Encino: San Juan County, NM.

Olio Trading Post: San Juan County, NM, near
Kirtland.

Oljeto (Trading Post): San Juan County, UT;
also Oljaytoh, Moonlight.

Oraibi Trading Post: Navajo County, AZ.

Osborne & Walker: Apache County, AZ
(St. Michaels).

Otis, E. E.: Location uncertain; possibly the same as
Otis Trading Post.

Otis Trading Post: San Juan County, NM. Exact
location uncertain.

Outlaw Trading Post: McKinley County, NM, near
Church Rock, NM, and now part of Red Rock
State Park.

Penistaja: Sandoval County, NM (east of Cuba).

Perea Trading Posts: McKinley County, NM (four
trading posts from early 1890s to late 1920s at
Coolidge).

Pinedale Trading Post: McKinley County, NM.

Pinehaven Trading Post: McKinley County, NM.

Pine Springs: Apache County, AZ.

Piñon Springs Trading Post: McKinley County, NM
(between Gallup and Zuni).

Piñon Trading Post: Navajo County, AZ (Piñon).

Polacca: Navajo County, NM (between Hopi First
and Second Mesas).

Prewitt: McKinley County, NM (Prewitt).

Pueblo Alto Trading Post: McKinley County, NM
(14 miles northeast of Chaco Canyon).

Pueblo Bonito Trading Post: San Juan County, NM
(against the north wall of Pueblo Bonito ruin).

Pueblo Pintado Trading Post: McKinley County, NM
(Pueblo Pintado).

Querino Canyon Trading Post: Apache County, AZ (between Houck and Sanders).

Rabbit Mesa Trading Post: Coconino County, AZ (five miles north of Tuba City).

Rainbow Lodge: San Juan County, UT (Navajo Mountain).

Ramah Trading Post: Cibola County, NM.

Rangel Trading: McKinley County, NM (White Horse).

Raton Springs Trading Post: McKinley County, NM (Chaco Canyon).

Rattlesnake Trading Post: San Juan County, NM (eight miles south of Shiprock Pinnacle).

Red and White Trading Post: Cibola County, NM (Ramah).

Red Arrow Trading Post: McKinley County, NM (Thoreau).

Red Lake Trading Post: Coconino County, AZ (Tonalea).

Red Lake Trading Post: McKinley County, NM (northeast of Fort Defiance, AZ).

Red Mesa Trading Post: San Juan County, UT (Red Mesa).

Red Rock Trading Post: Apache County, AZ (Red Rock, NM).

Rimmy Jim's: Coconino County, AZ.

Riverview Trading Post: San Juan County, UT (Aneth).

Roberts' Trading Post, Apache County, AZ (near Black Rock).

Rock Point Trading Post: Apache County, AZ (Rock Point).

Rock Springs Trading Post: McKinley County, NM (northwest of Gallup).

Rocky Point (Trading Post): McKinley County, NM (nine miles west of Gallup).

Rough Rock: Apache County, AZ (Rough Rock).

Round House: McKinley County, NM (18 miles south of Gallup).

Round Rock Trading Post: Apache County, AZ.

Round Top Trading Post: Apache County, AZ (Ganado).

Rudeau, A. C., Trading Company: Apache County, AZ (Fort Defiance).

Sacred Mountain: Coconino County, AZ (between Flagstaff and Cameron on U.S. Highway 89).

Salina Springs Trading Post: Apache County, AZ (Salina).

Sanders Trading Post: Apache County, AZ (two posts, one opening in 1882, the other in the late 1960s).

Sand Springs Trading Post: Coconino County, AZ (south of Hopi Mesas).

Sandoval Trading Company: McKinley County, NM (Thoreau).

Sanostee Trading Post: San Juan County, NM.

Sawmill Trading Post: Apache County, AZ.

Schielingburo Trading Post: McKinley County, NM (six miles northwest of Crownpoint).

Sehili Trading Post: See Tsaile, AZ.

Setzer's Store: See Pueblo Alto Trading Post.

Seven Lakes Trading Post: McKinley County, NM (17 miles northeast of Crownpoint).

Sheep Springs Trading Post: San Juan County, NM.

Shiprock Trading Post: San Juan County, NM (Shiprock).

Shonto Trading Post: Navajo County, AZ.

Smith Lake Trading Post: McKinley County, NM (Smith Lake, south of Crownpoint).

Smoke Signal Trading Post: Navajo County, AZ (near Low Mountain, 15 miles northeast of Keams Canyon).

Spiegelberg Trading Post: Apache County, AZ (Fort Defiance).

Springstead Trading Post: McKinley County, NM (five miles north of Church Rock).

Staggs, W. M., Trading Co.: Apache County, AZ (Fort Defiance).

Stallings, Walter, Trading Post: San Juan County, NM (Waterflow).

Standing Rock Trading Post: McKinley County, NM.

Star Lake Trading Post: McKinley County, NM.

Stateline Trading Post: Apache County, AZ (Lupton).

Steamboat Canyon Trading Post: Apache County, AZ.

Stewart-Weid: Apache County, AZ (St. Michaels).

Stover-Hubbell Trading Post: Apache County, AZ (Ganado).

Sulphur Springs Trading Post: San Juan County, NM (near Ford Butte).

Sunrise Springs Trading Post: Coconino County, AZ (two posts, upper and lower, three miles northwest of Leupp).

Sunrise Trading Post: Apache County, AZ. Exact location uncertain.

Sweetwater Trading Post: Apache County, AZ; also, Tolacon (18 miles northeast of Rock Point).

T & R Market: McKinley County, NM (halfway between Gallup and Ya Tah Hey).

Tanner Lake Trading Post: San Juan County, NM; also Tanner (30 miles downstream from Star Lake Trading Post on De Na Zin Wash, also called Coal Mine Wash).

Taylor Trading Post: San Juan County, NM (Sheep Springs).

Teec Nos Pos Trading Post: Apache County, AZ.

Teec Tso Secad Trading Post: See Burnham's Trading Post.

Tees Toh: Navajo County, AZ; also Teas Toh (three miles east of Arizona 87, 22 miles south of that road's junction with Arizona 264).

Tekapo: McKinley County, NM (six miles west of Zuni Pueblo).

Thoreau Mercantile: McKinley County, NM (Thoreau).

Tinian Trading Post: Location uncertain.

Tis Nes Iah: Apache County, AZ (five miles west of Mexican Water).

Tisyaakin: Location uncertain.

Tiz Na Tzin Trading Post: San Juan County, NM (on Coal Creek Wash between Tsaya and Bisti).

Toadlena Trading Post: San Juan County, NM.

Tocito Trading Post: San Juan County, NM (10 miles north of Newcomb).

Tohatchi Trading Post: McKinley County, NM.

Tohgaii Trading Post: See Tuye Springs Trading Post.

Tolakai: McKinley County, NM; also Tohlakai, Toh La Kai (nine miles north of Gallup).

Tolani Trading: See Red Lake, AZ.

Tolchaco Trading Post: Coconino County, AZ (two posts, Wolf and Walker).

Tonalea Trading Post: See Red Lake Trading Post, Coconino County, AZ.

Torreon: Sandoval County, NM (Torreon).

Trubey's: Rio Arriba County, NM (on Cibola Mesa).

Tsaile Trading Post: Apache County, AZ.

Tsaya Trading Post: San Juan County, NM (10 miles north of Crownpoint).

Tsé Bonito Trading Post: McKinley County, NM.

Tsegi Trading Post: Location uncertain, but probably near Shonto and Inscription House.

Tuba Trading Company: Coconino County, AZ (Tuba City).

Tucker's Store: See Pueblo Alto Trading Post.

Turley Trading Post: San Juan County, NM.

Tuye Springs Trading Post: McKinley County, NM.

Twin Lakes Trading Post: McKinley County, NM.

Two Grey Hills Trading Post: San Juan County, NM.

Two Story Trading Post: Apache County, AZ (a few miles west of St. Michaels).

Two Wells: Location uncertain.

Upper Greasewood Trading Post: Apache County, AZ (south of Lukachukai).

Ute Trading Company: Montezuma County, CO (east of Towaoc).

Valley Trading Post: San Juan County, NM (Waterflow).

Vanderwagen: McKinley County, NM (two posts, 19 miles south of Gallup, and Zuni Pueblo).

Volz Trading Post: Coconino County, AZ (at Canyon Diablo).

Wallace, C. G., Trading Post: McKinley County, NM (Zuni Pueblo).

Wallace, Sabin-R.: McKinley County, NM (Zuni Pueblo).

Warren Trading Post: Navajo County, AZ.

Warren Trading Post: San Juan County, NM (Waterflow).

Weidemeyer's: Fort Defiance, AZ.

Westbrook, Dee, Trading Post: McKinley County, NM (Mariano Lake).

Western Navajo Trading Post: Coconino County, AZ.

Wetherill Trading Post: Navajo County, AZ (Kayenta, AZ).

Wetherill and Coleville Trading Post: Navajo County, AZ (Kayenta, AZ).

White Cone Trading Post: Navajo County, AZ (White Cone, AZ).

White Rock: Location uncertain.

White Rock Trading Post: San Juan County, NM (White Rock [Stoney Butte]).

White Water Trading Post: McKinley County, NM (20 miles south of Gallup).

White Mesa Trading Post: Coconino County, AZ (just north of Kayenta).

Wide Ruin Trading Post: Apache County, AZ (Wide Ruin).

Wildcat Trading Post: McKinley County, NM (the Zuni area).

Wilkin-Wyatt: Apache County, AZ (St. Michaels).

Willow Springs Trading Post: Coconino County, AZ (Willow Springs).

Wingate Trading Post: See Fort Wingate Trading Post.

Wolf Trading Post: Coconino or Navajo County, AZ.

Woodspring: Location uncertain.

Ya Tah Hey: McKinley County, NM (eight miles north of Gallup on U.S. Highway 666, at the junction with New Mexico 264).

Zuni Mountain Trading Post: McKinley County, NM (Prewitt).

4

ARIZONA LOCATIONS

ADAHCHIJIYAHI CANYON: (6200–5400 ft) Navajo County, AZ. Navajo: 'Adah Ch'íjíyáhí, "Where She Fell from the Cliff" (Gillmore and Wetherill 1934, 145), or, more correctly, "Where a Person Walked over the Cliff" (Young p.c. 1995)—though it did happen to be a woman. Deep, curving canyon on the northwest margin of Tyende Mesa, flowing into El Capitan Flat and partially cut by the headwaters of Oljeto Wash.

AGATE HOUSE RUIN: (5450 ft) Navajo County, AZ. Navajo: Uncertain, probably generic Kits'iilí, "Shattered House." Prehistoric Anasazi ruin constructed of petrified wood and dating to the fourteenth century A.D. Located a mile southeast of the southern entrance to Petrified Forest National Park.

AGATHLA PEAK: [DB] (6098 ft) Navajo County, AZ. Also El Capitan, "The Captain," Cerro Elevado, "Soaring Hill" (McNitt 1972, 61). Navajo: 'Aghaałá, "Much Wool" or "Much Fur." A sheer, 1500-ft-high volcanic pinnacle at the southern end of Monument Valley (eight miles north of Kayenta and east of U.S. Highway 163). Commanding a view of the entire Kayenta–Monument Valley region, the pinnacle is of ceremonial significance to the Navajos and is named in the Bead Chant stories of clan wanderings as the place where the Tó Baazhní'ázhí (Two Came For Water) clan joined the Western Water clans on their eastward trek (McPherson 1992, 30–31). Some sources, including Scott Preston, Navajo medicine man from Tuba City (Young p.c. 1995), state that the name "Much Fur" refers to the custom of scraping deer hides

on the coarse basalt that eventually piled up the hair or "wool" along the sides. Interestingly, some Navajos consider Agathla Peak a "wool spinner" in the hand of the anthropomorphic Pollen Mountain of Navajo mythology. Others identify Agathla Peak and Tuba Butte as her breasts (McPherson 1992, 21).

Pollen Mountain is a figure of gigantic proportions, incorporating Navajo Mountain as her head, Black Mesa her body, Balakai Mesa her feet, and Comb Ridge one of her arms (McPherson 1992, 21). A Navajo legend tells that when the animals traveled from Navajo Mountain (when the land was still soft and animals spoke), Big Snake decided to stay here and is coiled about the base, which explains the presence of snake skins in the area (McPherson 1992, 30–31).

The first recorded White incursion into the Agathla area was by Colonel Francisco Salazar, of Governor Jose Antonio Vizcarra's 1823 campaign (McNitt 1972, 61). It is shown as Lana Negra (Spanish: "Black Wool") on McComb's map of 1860. Colonel Christopher "Kit" Carson is credited with applying the name El Capitan to this spire (Klinck 1984, 40). Anglo prospector Samuel Walcott was killed here by Navajos in 1883.

AGUA SAL CREEK: (7000–5500 ft) Apache County, AZ. Navajo: Tó Dík'ǫ́ǫzh, "Saline Water" (Kelley p.c. 1994) or "Bitter Water" (Young p.c. 1995). 25-mile-long creek heading in small streams immediately north of Tsaile Creek near the community of Tsaile. It flows northwest to enter Lukachukai Wash just north of Navajo Route 12, 10 miles upstream (southeast) of

Lukachukai's confluence with Chinle Wash. The name Agua Sal (Spanish meaning "Salt Water") was applied by USGS hydrologist Herbert Gregory in 1915 (Granger 1960, 3).

ALLENTOWN: (6150 ft) Apache County, AZ. Navajo: Dleesh Ndigaií, "White Clay Point." A trading post south of I-40 and the Rio Puerco of the West, about four miles downstream (southwest) of Lupton, at the site of an Atchison, Topeka and Santa Fe Railroad shipping point established in 1900 and named for Allen Johnson, an early settler who raised cattle (Granger 1960, 3).

ALLENTOWN RUIN: (7902 ft) Apache County, AZ. Navajo: Uncertain, probably the generic Kits'iilí, "Shattered House." A Chacoan great-house community about five miles southeast of Houck, and associated with a prehistoric road segment (Gabriel 1991, 278).

ANDERSON MESA (AND POINT): (6830 ft) Coconino County, AZ. Navajo: Hosh Dik'ání, "Beveled Cactus" (U.S. Indian Claims Commission n.d., vol. VI, viii). Five-mile-long mesa some 20 miles southeast of Flagstaff. Named for Jim Anderson, a California immigrant bringing livestock into Flagstaff. According to informants to the U.S. Indian Claims Commission, Navajos lived in this area prior to the Bosque Redondo Period of 1863–68.

ANTELOPE PASS: (6533 ft) Coconino County, AZ. Navajo: Jádí Habitiin, "Antelope Ascending Trail" (Kelley p.c. 1994). The pass through which U.S. Highway 89 cuts through the Echo Cliffs between Cornfield Valley and Page.

ANTELOPE SPRINGS TRADING POST: (6475 ft) Navajo County, AZ. Navajo: Jádító, "Antelope Spring." Located at Jeddito, this post was also known as Babbitt and Roberts Trading Post, one of the many owned by the Babbitts over the years (McNitt 1962, 266).

ARIZONA: Navajo: Béégashii Nit'ání, "Where the Cows Grow Up" (Young and Morgan 1987, 160).

AZANSOSI MESA: [DB] (6600 ft) Navajo County, AZ. Navajo: 'Asdzą́ą́ts'ósí, "Slim Woman," Navajo nickname for Louisa Wetherill (Gregory 1915, 149), wife of trader John Wetherill. The name is applied to the mesa immediately north of Tyende Mesa, separated from the latter by Adahchijiyahi Canyon on the south and Tseye Tsozi Canyon on the east.

BABY ROCKS: [DB] (5500 ft) Navajo County, AZ. Navajo: Tsé 'Awéé, "Baby Rocks" (Van Valkenburgh 1941, 51). A low mesa of fragmented sandstone two miles south of U.S. Highway 160, 11 miles east of Kayenta. The name derives from the unusual appearance of the sandstone, which appears to be composed of myriad small rocks rather than continuous layers of sediment. Baby Rocks Trading Post opened in the early 1960s (Kelley 1977, 155).

Settlers came here from Kayenta to farm, but the floods of 1912 destroyed the natural earth dams in the Segi or upper Laguna Creek and released tremendous heads of water, cutting the channel of lower Laguna Creek down to bedrock, rendering diversion of water for irrigation impossible. Old Crank, who had been the leader of the Baby Rocks colony, now led a movement to establish Dinnehotso about 10 miles upstream, where there was a shallower channel and a natural dam site. Old Crank's earthen dam, reinforced with brush and tree branches, was replaced prior to 1941 with a modern reinforced concrete diversion dam, which irrigated 793 acres of excellent agricultural land.

BALAKAI MESA: (7000–7460 ft) Apache and Navajo Counties, AZ. Also Salahkai, Balukai. Navajo: Báálók'aa'í, "Reeds Under the Rim" (Van Valkenburgh 1974, 11), or Tsélgai, "White Rock" (Young and Morgan 1987, 730). A mesa off the southeastern corner of Black Mesa, associated with the Navajo Blessingway tradition. Also in Navajo mythology, it is considered the feet of Pollen Mountain, a gigantic female anthropomorphic figure that incorporates Navajo Mountain, Black Mesa, Comb Ridge, Tuba Butte, and Agathla Peak (McPherson 1992, 21). The extreme southeastern projection of the mesa, looming some 900 ft above the valley of Chinle Wash, is called Balakai Point.

BEAR SPRINGS: [DB] (6550 ft) Apache County, AZ. Navajo: Shash Bitoo, "Bear Springs" (Van Valkenburgh 1941, 8). Improved springs located in a small, barren, rocky cove, three miles north of Steamboat Canyon on the east side of Steamboat Canyon Wash. An Anasazi ruin sits atop the rim above the spring.

According to Van Valkenburgh, this region abounded with antelope many years ago, and old antelope corrals used for trapping the beasts for the Corral Ceremony were still found in the region in the 1940s. These were usually circular, with very high fences constructed of juniper branches and with small openings flanked by long, expanding wings through which the antelope were driven into the corral.

This spring is an important watering place for the local Navajos and was improved by the Indian Emergency Conservation Works in 1933. It should not be confused with the Bear Springs along present-day I-40 between Petrified Forest National Park and Holbrook.

BEGASHIBITO WASH: (7500–5700 ft) Navajo and Coconino counties, AZ. Navajo: Béégashii Bito', "Cow's Water," béégashii coming from the Spanish "vaca," meaning "cow" (Young and Morgan 1987, 159). A 46-mile-long tributary of Moenkopi Wash, heading in the broken country of the Kaibito Plateau east of Navajo Creek and south of Zilnez Mesa. Merges with Moenkopi Wash five miles northeast of Tonalea. Watering place for cattle.

BEKIHATSO LAKE: [DB] (5800 ft) Apache County, AZ. Also Big Lake, Groaning Lake. Navajo: Be'ek'id Hatsoh, "Big Water Place," or Be'ek'id Di'níní, "Groaning Lake" (Young and Morgan 1987, 152). The name refers to a series of sinks that collect spring runoff and summer rains between Chinle and Balakai Mesa, near the intersection of U.S. Highway 191 and Navajo Route 4 to Piñon. The sinks were augmented in 1934 by a dam.

The Navajo water monster, Tééhooltsódíí, is said to have appeared in this lake, and traditional

Navajos feared the lake because "the water would make a groaning sound at times."

Nearby in 1853, Manuelito, Navajo chieftain (see Manuelito Springs) received a wound from the Mexicans that left a great scar on his right breast (Van Valkenburgh 1941, 8).

BEKIHATSO WASH: (6050–3000 ft) Coconino County, AZ. Navajo: See Bekihatso Lake. This 15-mile-long tributary of the Little Colorado River enters the latter from the north through Salt Trail Canyon.

BIDAHOCHI: (5500 ft) Navajo County, AZ. Also Bitahoii. Navajo: Bidahóóchii', "Red Streaks Going Up" (Van Valkenburgh 1974, 11), "Red Rock Slide" (Gregory 1915, 149). A trading post on Arizona Highway 77, 15 miles south of White Cone. The post was established by Julius Wetzler in 1880; the name refers to red streaks on the nearby cliff face (Granger 1960, 235).

BIG MOUNTAIN: (7000–7100 ft) Navajo County, AZ. Navajo: Dził Ntsaaí, "Extensive Mountain" (Ellis 1974, 465). Rugged rolling uplift atop central Black Mesa, about 20 miles northwest of Piñon and 15 miles southeast of Klethla Valley. Granger (1960, 254) refers to Big Mountain as Ziltahjini Mesa, but that name (actually Dziłłátahzhiní, or "Black Mountain Peak" [Young p.c. 1995]) applies to Little Black Spot Mountain (or Black Speck Mountain, depending on the map), a feature 15 miles southwest of Big Mountain (Young and Morgan 1987, 360).

This locale was the scene of considerable civil unrest in the late 1970s and early 1980s when the region, part of the heretofore Navajo-Hopi Joint Use Area, was divided and fenced, the land split between the two tribes. Many families—mostly Navajo—were forcibly relocated from lands occupied for generations because they suddenly were on the "wrong" side of the new fences.

BIG MOUNTAIN TRADING POST: (7100 ft) Navajo County, AZ. Navajo: Uncertain, probably the same as Big Mountain (above). This post, on Black Mesa, was once owned by Lorenzo Hubbell.

BI'KEESH WASH: (6600–5750 ft) Apache County, AZ. Navajo: Despite its apparent Navajo name, its etymology is uncertain. A dry stream rising on the west flank of Ganado Mesa in a series of convergent arroyos. The stream comes to the west side of U.S. Highway 191 and flows north 15 miles to merge with Pine Springs Wash on its way to Nazlini Creek.

BILL WILLIAMS MOUNTAIN: (9264 ft) Coconino County, AZ. Navajo: Tsin Béel'áhí, "Trees Extended in a Line Up Its Side (slope)" (Young p.c. 1995). This range east of Flagstaff figures prominently in the Blessingway Chant (Van Valkenburgh 1974, 77–78).

BIRD SPRINGS: [DB] (4900 ft) Navajo County, AZ. Navajo: Tsídiito'í, "Bird Spring." A small community on Navajo Route 15, situated on the Coconino–Navajo County line, some 15 miles east of Leupp. Before the development of water wells by the U.S. Indian Service, Bird Springs was one of the most important watering places for the Navajos between the Hopi (Moki) Butte country and Leupp. The community now serves as a chapter seat.

BIS'II AH WASH: (6800–5800 ft) Apache County, AZ. Navajo: Bis 'Íí'á, "Adobe Spire" (Young p.c. 1995). A tributary of Nazlini Wash rising on the west foot of the Defiance Plateau, five miles south of the community of Nazlini. It flows southwest seven miles to the north edge of Ganado Mesa, then turns north for another 15 miles, merging with Nazlini Wash two miles east of U.S. Highway 191 some 20 miles north of Arizona Highway 264.

BITSIHUITSOS: (6000 ft) Apache County, AZ. Navajo: Bitsíjh Hwiits'os, "At the Base of a Cliff," or "Area Tapers at the Base" (Young p.c. 1995). This name is applied to the flat expanse sitting 200 ft above the Chinle Valley at the northeast foot of Yale Point (Gregory 1915).

BITTER SPRINGS: (5000 ft) Coconino County, AZ. Navajo: Uncertain, probably Dích'íító, "Bitter Spring." Bitter Springs Trading Post opened here at the junction of U.S. 89 and Alternate 89 south of Navajo Bridge in the early 1920s.

BLACK CANYON: (6600–7000 ft) Navajo County, AZ. Navajo: Uncertain. This canyon south of Heber has been identified as a traditional Navajo hunting ground (U.S. Indian Claims Commission n.d., vol. IV, 528–30), though those records mistakenly describe the canyon as north of Heber.

BLACK CREEK: [DB] (7200–6000 ft) Apache County, AZ. Navajo: Be'ek'id Halehu Dee, "Flows from Red Lake" (Granger 1960, 5), though Young (p.c. 1995) says it is more likely Be'ek'id Halchíídéé', with the same interpretation. This 50-mile-long stream flows south from Black Lake (north of Fort Defiance), and merges with the Rio Puerco of the West a half-mile south of Houck. A segment of the same watercourse east of Black Lake is called Crystal Creek. Into the 1940s, the ephemeral Black Creek had many dams to feed the Navajo farms along its length. Spencer and Jett (1971, 160) list Red Lake as the head of the creek.

BLACK CREEK CANYON: (7000–6400 ft) Apache County, AZ. Also known as Calites Canyon and Cañon Chennele (Van Valkenburgh 1941, 108 and Lupton map). Navajo: Tsétł'áán Ndíshchí'í, "Ponderosa Rock Rim Crescent" (Kelley p.c. 1994). This canyon of Black Creek is cut through the Defiance Plateau's eastern scarp, where Black Creek turns from its southerly course to almost due west. The mouth of the canyon is seven miles northwest of Lupton, on Navajo Route 12.

The name Calites Canyon comes from the Spanish "Quelites," which means "greens," usually referring to wild plants such as amaranth or goosefoot (Brugge p.c. 1996). The vicinity was penetrated in 1836 by two hundred Spaniards under Fernandez Aragon, of Governor Antonio Perez's campaign (McNitt 1972, 152). American expeditions led by Colonel John Washington (1849), Major Henry L. Kendrick (1856–57) and Captain Lafayette McLaws (1860) passed through the canyon as well (McNitt 1972, 276, 292, 406–7).

Another location by the name of Quelites is at the confluence of the Rio Puerco (of the East) and Rio San Jose in New Mexico (Brugge 1965, 16–17).

BLACK CREEK VALLEY: (7200–6862 ft) Apache County, AZ. Navajo: Uncertain, probably the same as Black Creek Canyon. This is the 12-mile stretch of the Black Creek drainage that lies between Red Lake (north) and Fort Defiance (south). Captain James H. Simpson noted the striking features of this valley in 1850 (Granger 1960, 5) or possibly 1849 (Brugge p.c. 1996).

BLACK FALLS: [DB] (4650 ft) Coconino County, AZ. Navajo: Tsézhin 'Adahiilínígíí, or "Lava Rock Water Fall" (Young p.c. 1995). The U.S. Indian Claims Commission (n.d., vol. VI, xx) refers to the place as Tsézhin Dahiilínígíí, "Rock Crossing," and Van Valkenburgh (1941, 10) suggests the translation of "Black Rock Waterfall." Located about 10 miles downstream from the better-known Grand Falls, water in the Little Colorado River falls over a low lava dike that projects into the river northeast of the Wupatki Basin (and Wupatki National Monument). This was an important crossing of the Little Colorado and rendezvous for early Navajos. In the vicinity are a number of Anasazi ruins, the most significant of which is the Crack-in-the-Rock Ruin.

BLACK FALLS TRADING POST: (4650 ft) Coconino County, AZ. Navajo: Uncertain, probably the same as Black Falls. This trading post near the Black Falls of the Little Colorado River was opened for business in 1885 by Sam Preston, a Kentuckian who came west with a government pack train traveling through the area (McNitt 1962, 267). Preston became one of the Babbitt Brothers manager-partners at Red Lake Trading Post sometime prior to 1894, and the Black Falls post was closed by 1936, when another post was opened (Kelley 1977, 251; 1985, 28).

The new post was on the west bank, built after construction of a diversion dam. Babbitt (1986, 7) credits Emmett Kellam with building the post. It was sold in 1952 to B. B. Bonner. In 1956, the post included a store, house, garage, storage

shed, privy, and storage cellar. It was abandoned in 1964 (Kelley 1985, 28).

BLACKHORSE WASH: (6000–5450 ft) Apache and Navajo counties, AZ. Navajo: Łizhin Bikooh, "Black Creek." This 10-mile-long tributary of Tyende Creek heads on the flats on the northeast flank of Black Mesa near Chilchinbito, and flows through Chilchinbito Canyon. It joins Tyende Creek eight miles northeast of the village of Chilchinbito. Another Blackhorse Creek in the Chaco Valley of New Mexico was said by Gregory (1915, 149) to be named for a Navajo chief, but the origin of the name of the Arizona wash remains problematic.

BLACK LAKE: (7550 ft) Apache County, AZ. Also Laguna Negra, Salitre Negro or "Black Saltpeter," and Cieneguilla Chiquita (Granger 1960, 5). Navajo: Be'ek'id Halzhiní, "Black Lake" (Kelley p.c. 1994). This small lake nestled between the Chuska Mountains and the Defiance Plateau lies in Black Salt Valley, eight miles north of Red Lake. The Spanish called this location Cienega Negra, and they called Crystal Creek (which feeds it) Rio Negro (McNitt 1972, 147). Black Lake is the source of Black Creek, which runs south all the way to the Rio Puerco of the West.

Two miles south of the lake was Ewell's Hay Camp, a grazing area made available for Fort Defiance by Navajo headman Manuelito in 1857 (McNitt 1972, 304). It was named for Captain Richard S. Ewell, a member of the first garrison of Fort Defiance (McNitt 1972, 198). The Army's grazing here was contested by armed Navajos in 1857 and 1858. A Navajo was captured, disarmed, and executed here by a Zuni guide (known only as José) to Colonel Dixon Stansbury Miles, on September 14, 1858 (McNitt 1972, 342).

Lieutenant Simpson noted that when he first saw this pool in 1849, it "appeared" almost black (Van Valkenburgh and Walker 1946).

This was the location of the July 6, 1855, meeting between American troops (New Mexico Governor David Meriweather, Brigadier General John Garland, and W. W. Davis) with Navajo headmen Zarcillos Largos and Manuelito and Navajo Agent Henry L. Dodge (Frink 1968,

35–38). The meeting led to the Treaty of Laguna Negra (or the Treaty of 1855). This potentially incredibly damaging treaty called for a Navajo "reserve" of seven thousand square miles, less than half their domain. However, Congress failed to ratify the treaty.

BLACK MESA OR "BLACK STREAK MOUNTAIN": [DB as Black Mountain] (6000–8000 ft) Navajo and Apache Counties, AZ. Also Black Mountain. Navajo: Dziłíjiin, "Mountain which Appears Black," or "Mountain that Extends Black" (Young p.c. 1995). This immense upland west of Chinle and south of Kayenta is best described as a raised shallow bowl tilting to the south. It measures 75 miles east-west and 50 miles north-south. It is the heart of the Navajo Reservation, and it includes much of the Hopi Reservation.

The terrain consists largely of broad, gently sloping valleys and steep canyons, rolling hills, and abrupt mesas and buttes. It has four major, though ephemeral, drainages: (from west to east) Moenkopi, Dinnebito, Oraibi, and Polacca washes, all tributary to the Little Colorado River (though Polacca Wash merges with Jeddito Wash to form Corn Creek Wash just before merging with the Little Colorado).

The region is perhaps best visualized as a broad, roughly handshaped formation, the wrist consisting of a pine-covered rim generally 8000 ft in elevation. The "fingers" extend to the southwest and form the Hopi Mesas along Polacca, Wepo, Oraibi, and Dinnebito drainages. It is apparently the greatest watershed, in both size and capacity, in the entire Navajo country. Springs fed by seepage in porous sandstones provided the early Hopi villages a permanent water supply. Except for the Navajo Mountain region, this great mesa contains the most remote area in the Navajo Reservation. Most was inaccessible to automobiles as late as the 1960s. Until 1982, Navajo Route 4 was the only all-weather road into the region, extending from U.S. Highway 191 (in the vicinity of Chinle) to Piñon, the location of a trading post, day school, and chapter house.

There are many coal beds in the mesa formations, and several small mines (some dating back to prehistoric times) predate the massive strip-mines Peabody Coal opened in the region south of Marsh Pass during the late 1960s and early 1970s.

Navajos used to say that bears crossing over to this mesa from the Chuska-Tunicha-Lukachukai ranges on the east would bring bad luck. They would go to considerable effort to stop any bear that appeared to be on such a journey westward across the intervening Chinle valley. It is also associated with Blessingway traditions as the body of Female Pollen Range. (See also Navajo Mountain, Balakai Mesa, Agathla Peak, and Comb Ridge for more information on Pollen Mountain; see Navajo Mountain for ceremonial relationships of Black Mesa.) Black Mesa is also the site of much witchcraft (McPherson 1992, 32).

The mesa was first traversed by Whites when Vizcarra visited in 1823. It was referred to as Mesa de las Vacas by Ramon Luna in 1850 (McNitt 1972, 167), and that name was used by Captain John Walker in a report to the War Department in 1858, and is similarly shown on McComb's map of 1860. A single Navajo was killed on the mesa by a U.S. Army detachment under Captain George McLane in October 1858, and other expeditions traversed the mesa in 1859 and 1860 (McNitt 1972, 347). McLane was later killed by Navajos at Black Pinnacle.

During the Navajo Wars of 1863–65, remote reaches of the mesa served as a refuge for many Navajos fleeing Kit Carson's invading army, including Old Man Hat, the father of the subject of Walter Dyk's 1938 autobiographical study, *Son of Old Man Hat* (Ellis 1974, 458). Ute Indians raided Caballado Mucho's band of Navajos on the mesa in January 1866, causing Caballado Mucho to surrender at Fort Wingate for subsequent transfer to the Bosque Redondo (Reeve 1974, 84).

The mesa has been the scene of considerable controversy over the mining of coal. In 1964 the Navajo Tribe was told that their fossil fuel reserves would soon be worthless, so they sold the rights to the coal atop Black Mesa to Peabody Coal for a mere two million dollars per year royalties (Iverson 1981, 105). (This was not renegotiated until the 1990s.) Many Navajos fought the mining, calling it the rape of the Earth Mother. The boundaries of the coal leases also became a focal issue in the settlement of the Navajo-Hopi Land Dispute in the Joint Use Area. A special electric railroad was constructed to haul Black Mesa coal to the Navajo Power Plant at Page, 50 miles to the northwest.

Because of the National Environmental Policy Act and other laws governing the disturbance of federally owned or overseen lands, the mining and road development on the mesa has made Black Mesa one of the best studied regions of the Navajo Nation archaeologically and historically (Gumerman 1970; Gumerman, Westfall, and Weed 1972; Klesert 1979; Linford 1982; Spurr 1993).

Black Mesa Trading Post opened at the foot of the north slope of the mesa in the early 1970s (Kelley 1977, 265) and is still operating.

BLACK MOUNTAIN: (7500 ft) Apache County, AZ. Navajo: Dził́jiin, "Black Mountain" (Kelley p.c. 1994), though some mention another name (etymology unknown), "Back of Deer." A small promontory between Lohali Point (at the far eastern edge of Black Mesa) and Balakai Mesa. The name has also been used for present-day Black Mesa. It figures prominently in the Navajo Coyoteway (Luckert 1979), and is mentioned in the hero's search for his family in the Rounded Man Red Antway Myth (Wyman 1965).

BLACK MOUNTAIN TRADING POST: [DB] (6400 ft) Apache County, AZ. Also known as Black Mountain Store. Navajo: Tók'i Hazbí'í, "Hogan Built over Water," or "Covered Well." This trading post, opened by Lorenzo Hubbell after 1880–81, is located at the southeastern break of Black Mesa, between Hodzhgani Wash (west) and Lohali Point (east). The fortresslike post was later operated by Win Wetherill, Joe Lee, and Miles Hedrick (McNitt 1962,204; Van Valkenburgh 1941, 11).

Ten miles to the west, on the southern slope of Burnt Corn Wash, an underground (shaft) coal mine (discovered by Louis Meyer of Gallup) supplied coal for the various government agencies at Chinle and in the Chinle Valley. Situated on a rounded hill south of Hodzhgani Wash, this was the only shaft mine in the region.

BLACK PINNACLE: [DB] (7850 ft) Apache County, AZ. Navajo: Shash Dits'iní, "Where the Bear Lived," Chézhiní, "Black Rock," and/or Tsé Deez'á, "Standing Rock" (Granger 1960, 5; Eickemeyer 1900, 227). Young (p.c. 1995) notes that Shash Dits'iní is an odd name, dits'iní meaning "hard (like a bone)." He further notes that the literal translation for Tsé Deez'á is "Jutting Rock—It Extends out to a Point." A ragged volcanic cone rising above a ponderosa pine forest one-half mile east of Navajo Route 12, about three miles south of Tsaile, it may well be the Chézhin Deez'áhí (Lava Butte) of Navajo hunting tradition (Luckert 1975, 34; see also Tsaile Peak).

Because of an excellent view west to Black Mesa and south to Fluted Rock, a fire lookout tower is situated atop the pinnacle. In October 1860, Captain George McLane, of Colonel Edward S. Canby's command, was killed by Navajos in this vicinity (McNitt 1972, 400).

BLACK POINT: [DB] (4915 ft) Coconino County, AZ. Navajo: Tsézhin Deez'áhí, "Traprock Pointing Out" (Van Valkenburgh 1974, 11), or "Traprock Jutting Out" (Young p.c. 1995). Volcanic monocline (Thybony 1987, 3)—actually a Walapai tongue of the San Francisco Mountains—standing some 600 ft above the Painted Desert and Little Colorado River to the east, approximately 20 miles upstream (southeast) from Cameron. Navajo traditions give this as a stopping place of the Western Clans on their migration to Navajo Mountain (see Oak Creek Canyon).

In the winter of 1893, R. H. Cameron, then sheriff of Coconino County, assisted by range-hungry stockmen, enforced a questionable cancellation of Navajo allotments on the west side of the Little Colorado. He forcibly ejected Béésh Łigai Atsidii and his people from their hogans, forcing them to cross over to the eastern bank of the Little Colorado. The river was carrying a great deal of ice; many sheep were lost and the Navajos suffered greatly from exposure. Herbert Walsh of the Indian Rights Association took up the cause of the Navajos, but because the Navajo superintendent at Tuba City had failed to notify interested Navajos in time to act on acquiring the lands, cancellation of Indian allotments in the vicinity of Black Point and White Mesa was ultimately upheld.

BLACK ROCK: [DB] (6800 ft) Apache County, AZ. Navajo: Chézhiní or Tsézhiní (alternate forms of the same word), "Traprock." Volcanic dike (actually, a pair of curved monoliths forming a crescent open to the south) about a mile downstream (south) from Fort Defiance at the confluence of Black Creek with Bonito Creek.

In the Navajo Windway Ceremony, this rock is referred to as Tł'iishtsoh Bighan, "Big Snake's House," and is indeed occupied by the mythical Big Snake.

An old military trail used between 1851 and 1864 passed along the east side of the rock, and Van Valkenburgh (1938, 23) identified Black Rock as a favorite place from which the Navajos launched attacks on military columns heading to Fort Canby (Defiance). The presence of plentiful grass and Tsézhin Bii' Tó, "Spring in the Traprock," on the west side of the rock, made this a favorite pasture of the government "corral" during the military days of Fort Defiance as well as a watering place on the trail. Prior to 1864, the Navajos repeatedly raided military cattle and horse herds here, and Black Rock was the site of a pitched battle in 1864, between a military supply transport and Navajo warriors.

Trading posts in this vicinity have included Bennet-Turner (late 1890s to late 1920s), Bickel's (turn of the century to early 1920s), and Roberts (last half of the first decade of the twentieth century) (Kelley 1977, 252–54).

This location is not to be confused with the Black Rock some 200 ft high two miles east of the Little Colorado River Gorge, six miles south of Waterhold Canyon.

ALSO: (7618 ft) Apache County, AZ. Navajo: Chézhiní, or Tsézhiní, "Black Rock" (Young and Morgan 1987, 271). Also called Black Rock Butte. A black volcanic plug, rising 300 ft above Black Rock Plateau (the mesa that separates Canyon de Chelly and Black Rock Canyon),

some three miles south of the head of Black Rock Canyon. It is visible from most of the canyon overlooks in Canyon de Chelly National Monument.

Tsézhini has great ceremonial significance and plays an important part in the Navajo Night Chant and Blessing Chant. The story of the Night Chant (Dog Side) tells that Talking God and House God placed an unidentified bird (about the size of an eagle with a white upper part body) on Tsézhini to keep strangers away while they were building and decorating the White House down in Canyon de Chelly. The gods from Blanco Peak decided to see what was happening in Canyon de Chelly and came down as far as Tsézhini. The guard was sleepy and when he looked around, he did not see the gods. From there they moved to Wide Mesa, and then to the south rim of Canyon de Chelly, across from White House (Van Valkenburgh 1941, 38).

In the Navajo Beautyway Chant, this is where Younger Sister took refuge with the Mountain Sheep People (Benally et al. 1982).

BLACK SALT TRADING POST: (approx. 7200 ft) Apache County, AZ. Navajo: Uncertain, probably the same as Black Salt Valley (below). This post was located in Black Salt Valley, five miles due west of Crystal Trading Post. It was started by Stephen E. Aldrich and Elias T. Clark in 1882 or 1883, just two or three years before they built the Sehili (Tsaile) Trading Post in 1885 (McNitt 1962, 279).

BLACK SALT VALLEY: (7600–7400 ft) Apache County, AZ. Navajo: 'Áshįįshzhiin, "Black Salt" (Kelley p.c. 1994). An eight-mile-long valley just north of Red Valley, between the Chuska Mountains (east) and the northern end of the Defiance Plateau. Contains Black Lake, fed by Crystal Creek.

BLACK SOIL WASH: (8000–6800 ft) Navajo: Uncertain, possibly Łeezh Łizhin Bitó, "Black Soil Water." A 10-mile-long tributary of Kinlichee Wash on western Defiance Plateau, merging with Kinlichee a mile downstream (west) of the mouth of Scattered Willow Wash and Bear Canyon, three miles north of Arizona Highway

264 and four miles north of the original Cross Canyon.

The vicinity of Black Soil is mentioned in the hero's search for his family in the Navajo Rounded Man Red Antway Myth (Wyman 1965).

BLUE CANYON: [DB] (6000–4000 ft) Coconino and Navajo counties, AZ. Also Dot Klish (actually Dootł'izh) Canyon and Algert (after an early trader) (Granger 1960, 64). Navajo: Bikooh Hodootłizh, "Blue Canyon." A wide, high-walled canyon cut through level terrain by Moenkopi Wash, this channel serves as that body's outlet from the southwest margin of Black Mesa, approximately 14 miles northeast of Tonalea. Continues into the flats roughly five miles west of Ha Ho No Geh and Coal Mine Canyons.

The men of Jose Antonio Vizcarra's column were the first White men to visit Blue Canyon, in July 1823 (McNitt 1972, 61). Blue Canyon Trading Post, opening in the early 1880s, was one of the earliest on the reservation, and lasted about 25 years. The first Indian Service school on the Navajo Reservation was established here in 1884 (Bailey and Bailey 1986, 107) by Major Constant Williams, acting Navajo agent, and was originally under the jurisdiction of the Hopi Agency at Keams Canyon. The school moved to Tuba City in 1903, after the relocation of the Mormons under the new Western Navajo Agency in 1902. The land for its site was purchased from the Williams brothers, early traders. Upon erection of the old Tuba City plant in 1904, the school was discontinued. After the first Blue Canyon Trading Post closed in 1889, a second post opened about a decade later (Kelley 1977).

BLUE CANYON TRADING POST: (approx. 5000 ft) Coconino County, AZ. Navajo: Uncertain, probably the same as Blue Canyon (above). Apparently located about 12 to 15 miles east of Tuba City (although McNitt places it 25 miles east by wagon road), this post was opened in 1882 by Jonathon Paul Williams, a frustrated prospector turned trader. By McNitt's map of trading posts, it appears to be almost midway between Tuba City and the great northward turn of Moenkopi Wash, southwest of Red Lake (Tonalea). Williams left in 1889, and the Indian

Service took it over in 1899, with the creation of the Western Navajo extension. An agency and a school were opened in the old post buildings in 1900. C. H. Algert, already operating a post in Tuba City, built an extension on the government buildings, but abandoned this venture after a few years. In 1903, a year after the western boundary of the Navajo Reservation was extended, the government purchased all the Mormon holdings in Tuba City (since they were now inside the reservation) and moved the agency and the school there. The buildings were in disrepair when Hubert Richardson took the post over in 1914; he operated it until 1921, when he finally locked the doors (McNitt 1962, 269, 274–75).

BLUE GAP: (6500 ft) Apache County, AZ. Navajo: Bis Dootł'izh Ndeeshgiizh, "Blue Adobe Gap" (Kelley p.c. 1994). This small mission and school community is situated in the Polacca Wash Valley on Aspen Wash, on the southeast margin of Black Mesa. It sits on Navajo Route 29, halfway between Navajo Route 4 and Tachee.

BODAWAY MESA: [DB] (6000 ft) Coconino County, AZ. Navajo: Ba'ádíwei (Young and Morgan 1987, 145), a Paiute chief's name as pronounced by the Navajos. It refers to a triangular region of rolling country northeast of the junction of Marble Canyon and the Little Colorado River Gorge, along the eastern periphery of Blue Moon Bench. It is also a chapter community.

This region was first entered by Ba Adowe, the Strip Paiute chief and his band around 1840–50. The Navajos later entered and developed great flocks of sheep on the excellent range, some of which still remain today. One of the most inspiring views in the Navajo country is to be found at the junction of the Colorado and Little Colorado Rivers, where 3000-ft cliffs drop down to the rivers. The Navajos refer to the junction of the two rivers as Dził Łibáí Bikooh, "Gray Mountain Wash." Even today, however, poor roads make visiting this site a hazardous trip.

BONITO CANYON: (7600–6700 ft) Apache County, AZ. Navajo: Tséhootsooí, "Green Place Between the Rocks" (Frink 1968, 21–22). This canyon, named Canyoncito Bonito by Captain James H. Simpson in 1849, is almost certainly present-day Quartzite Canyon, a tributary of Black Creek just north of Fort Defiance, drained by Bonito Creek.

A battle between mounted soldiers and Navajos took place here on October 17, 1858. The soldiers referred to the location as "Hell's Gate" (Granger 1960, 6). The mouth of the canyon is called Tsehootsooí Ch'ínílí, "Meadow between the Rocks Flows Out" (Young and Morgan 1987, 729), or, more accurately, "Rock Meadow Outflow" (Young p.c. 1995)

BUELL PARK: [DB] (7000–7800 ft) Apache County, AZ. Also Bule Park, La Joya (Jett 1974, 374). Navajo: Ni' Haldzis, "Earth Hollow" (Young and Morgan 1987, 638). Also Tsé Zhin Hadooklizh, "Black Rock in a Blue Area" (Van Valkenburgh 1974, 11) or Tsézhin Hdootł'izh, "Blue Area in the Lava Flow or Traprock" (Young p.c. 1995). This broad, flat, scenic valley on the eastern shoulder of central Defiance Plateau stretches from Sawmill south to the mouth of Quartzite Canyon and is drained by Bonito Creek. The English name is for Army Major Buell (Gregory 1915, 150).

The Navajos consider this a sacred place due to a feature on the eastern periphery, a cone-shaped hill called Ni'haldizis Dahisk'id, "Hill Above a Basin," or Ni'Haldzis, "Earth Hollow Hill" or "Basin Hill" (Young p.c. 1995). This hill is the starting point of the story of the Diné Binitch'ijí, the Navajo Wind Ceremony. Deposits of garnets are also found here.

BURNT CORN WASH: (7000–6150 ft) Navajo County, AZ. Navajo: Naadą́ą́' Díílid, "Burnt Corn" (Young and Morgan 1987, 754). The upper reaches are also known as Ch'óyaató Bikooh, "Fir Tree Spring Canyon" (U.S. Indian Claims Commission n.d., vol. VI, iv; correct spelling from Young [p.c. 1995]). This 11-mile-long tributary of Polacca Wash heads on the southeast flank of central Black Mesa north of Donkey Spring Canyon. It flows south, passing west of Whippoorwill Springs Mesa before converging with Polacca Wash.

BURNT WATER: (6000 ft) Apache County, AZ. Navajo: Tó Díílidí, "Burnt Water" (U.S. Indian Claims Commission n.d., vol. VI, xvii; spelling corrected by Young [p.c. 1995]). The name of this post a few miles northeast of Sandero, AZ, derives from a burned ramada that collapsed into the well of a post established by Burris N. Barnes sometime between 1915 and 1920 (Kelley 1977, 254). Ashes and timbers fell into the water, giving the post its Navajo name.

Stanley Smith operated this post in the 1930s. Don Jacobs, Sr., ran it from 1957 to 1974, and E. Brady ran it until 1983. The post closed in 1983 (James 1988, 77).

BURRO SPRINGS: (5400 ft) Coconino County, AZ. Navajo: Télii Bito', "Burro Spring" (U.S. Indian Claims Commission n.d., vol. VI, xiv). This spring is located on Oraibi Wash, 15 miles south of Kykotsmovi (Old Oraibi), and about a mile east of Navajo Route 2. Though Granger (1960, 236) erroneously places this spring in Navajo County, she refers to the historical significance of this spring, being a reliable source of water on "the Winslow to Oraibi road" (currently Navajo Route 2, replaced by Arizona Highway 77 as the primary route between the two communities).

CAMERON TRADING POST: [DB] (4200 ft) (Population: 493) Coconino County, AZ. Navajo: Na'ní'á Hayázhí, "Little Span Across." A community on U.S. Highway 89, where it crosses the Little Colorado River.

Bill Kona Sani (Bilagáana Sani, "Old Anglo") conducted the first trading here by pack train, as early as 1850. The first trading post was erected by S. S. Preston, a Navajo, during the construction of "Government Bridge," the suspension bridge across the Little Colorado River Gorge in 1910–11 (Van Valkenburgh 1941, 16), and this date is generally accepted as the beginning of the community. A longer-lived post was built in 1914 by Hubert Richardson, who was then operating the Blue Canyon Trading Post (Richardson 1986, 136; McNitt 1962, 275).

The community was named for Senator Ralph H. Cameron, the last territorial delegate from

Arizona to the U.S. Congress, formerly sheriff of Coconino County in the 1880s and 1890s, and noted entrepreneur of the Grand Canyon's resources. Prior to the construction of the first bridge, the main crossing of the Little Colorado had been Tanner's Crossing, three miles upstream (south), but it was dangerous due to quicksand. The bridge was purportedly built at Senator Cameron's urging, with moneys taken from the Navajo Tribe's Trust Funds—without tribal consent. It was replaced with a wider bridge in 1958 (Granger 1960, 65; McNitt 1962, 275).

Tourism was the main impetus for construction of the bridges and is the mainstay of the community. An early auto camp and the Klo-A-Chee-Kin Hotel catered to the tourists as well as Navajos.

Arizona Highway 64 reaching from Cameron west to the Grand Canyon was originally constructed by the Fred Harvey Company in 1923–24 for the benefit of the company's world-renowned "Indian Detours." It dropped three thousand feet in 35 miles. Cameron received a post office in 1917; today it is a Navajo chapter seat and hosts a large trading concern—complete with motel, restaurant, trailer park, and RV campground.

CANYON DE CHELLY (NATIONAL MONUMENT): [DB] (Rim: 7000–6000 ft; Floor: 6400–5800 ft) Apache County, AZ. (De Chelly is pronounced "de-shay"). Navajo: Tséyi', "Canyon," or Tséyi' Etso, "Big Canyon." Gillmore and Wetherill (1934, 124) suggest this name meant "Big Canyon among the Rocks." In 1849 Señor Danaciano Vigil, Secretary of the Province of New Mexico, told Lieutenant James H. Simpson that the word "chay-e" was the Spanish pronunciation of the Navajo "tseyi" (Farmer 1954, 124–25), and is actually as close as the Spanish language could come in phonetic spelling of tséyi', a Navajo word combining tsé, meaning "rock," and -yi', meaning "inside." Tséyi' is used for any rock canyon, and particularly for Canyon de Chelly (Young p.c. 1995). This extensive, steep-walled canyon system drains the northwest portion of the Defiance Plateau, emptying into Chinle Wash at Chinle. Headwaters for the system begin in the Lukachukai, Tunicha, and Chuska mountains, 40 miles to the east.

Canyon de Chelly appears on the Dominguez-Escalante map of 1776–77. Navajos were likely in the area by the middle 1700s. Spanish expeditions probed the canyons by 1805, but it was not extensively scientifically surveyed until the Wheeler Expedition in 1873. The canyon became a national monument encompassing 83,000 acres on February 14, 1931.

The first Anglo settlers in the vicinity were Lorenzo Hubbell and C. S. Cotton, who set up trading concerns in Chinle in 1886. The numerous prehistoric ruins in the canyon system have been subjected to extensive and intensive scientific excavations, beginning with Mummy Cave, Sliding Rock, White House, and Antelope House from 1923 to 1929. Mummy House was stabilized in 1924 to prevent further erosion (Lister and Lister 1983, 89–108).

Geologically, the canyon cuts through or into four layers of sandstone. The Supai Formation lies at the bottom—exposed only here and there beneath the sandy river beds—and dates to the Permian age (about 250 to 280 million years old). Above this is the massive layer of De Chelly sandstone, which makes up the bulk of the canyon walls. This layer was deposited about 200 million years ago. Between this layer and the next higher one, the Shinarump Conglomerate, is the "Unconformity," a gap of about 30 million years. The Shinarump Conglomerate was laid down about 170 million years ago, during the Triassic period, and yielded the first uranium strikes in the region (though not in the canyon). The topmost and youngest layer is the Chinle Formation, which has been eroded away from most of the rim, but is visible near the National Park Service Visitor Center.

Early Spanish explorers regarded this vast canyon system as an impregnable stronghold of the Navajos. Few Spanish expeditions dared to enter the upper canyons with their sheer walls 1000 ft high or more. Though Antonio de Narbona traversed the northern branch (Canyon del Muerto), the first full exploration by non-Indians did not occur until the winter of 1863–64, when Captain A. F. Pfeiffer and Captain Asa B. Carey of the First New Mexico Volunteers swept the entire canyon system of its Navajo occupants, killing 22 in their ruthless campaign.

Since the early Navajo lifestyle did not leave behind the kinds of tangible evidence left by the ancestors of the pueblos, determining their time of arrival in the canyon is conjectural. Spanish documentaion suggests that they were in the canyons by the 1720s, in villages of up to 10 "forked-stick hogans" on the north rim of Canyon del Muerto. Anasazi remains, on the other hand, suggest human occupation in the canyons by the Basketmaker II era, or between 200 B.C. and A.D. 400. These predecessors of the Pueblo Indians stayed until the later decades of the thirteenth century. In the early 1700s, residents of the Hopi Mesas to the west and Jemez Pueblo (near the Rio Grande) in the east fled the Spanish reconquest of New Spain (following the Pueblo Revolt of 1680) and came to the region for permanent water after a drought in their own country, bringing peach trees to the Navajos. They merged with the Navajo population to become Mą'ii Deeshgizhnii, "Jemez Clan" (Van Valkenburgh 1941, 17).

Valuable crops of corn, melons, squash, and peaches grow in the many alluvial flats and small rincons of the canyons, where in 1941 nearly four hundred people farmed in the Canyon de Chelly proper and in the tributary Canyon del Muerto. During the winter, people traditionally camped on the wooded canyon rim owing to a lack of fuel in the canyon bottoms, but this has changed with the availability of propane.

According to Faris (1990), much of the history of the Nightway Chant centers in the Canyon de Chelly area (along with the lower Chama River and San Juan drainage regions of New Mexico), and a great many of the individual geological and archaeological features within the canyon have considerable historical and/or ceremonial significance to the Navajos.

Except where noted, the body of historical and descriptive material comprising the individual feature descriptions below has been compiled primarily from the following sources: Van Valkenburgh 1941; Bradley 1973; James 1976; McDonald 1976: Fall, McDonald, and Magers 1981; Southwest Parks and Monuments 1989 and 1991, and Jett n.d. The author offers special thanks to Steven Jett for sharing his extensive explorations of the canyons for this volume.

The canyon system is most easily and most commonly entered via the mouth at the west end, near the community of Chinle, Arizona. The following entries are listed in the order in which they are encountered by one moving east from the mouth.

✦ CANYON DE CHELLY: The southern of the two major forks of the canyon network. The rim of the canyon is 5500 ft elevation at the lower western end (in the vicinity of Chinle) and rises to roughly 7000 ft 22 miles to the east, atop the Defiance Plateau. The depth of the canyon ranges from less than 50 ft in the vicinity of the National Monument Headquarters to over 1000 ft near the Spider Rock overlook, about 10 miles upstream. From here the depth diminishes upstream as the slope of the floor becomes steeper.

There are three substantial tributaries to this canyon: Wild Cherry, Bat, and Monument canyons, all branching to the south. Approximately two miles from the eastern end, the canyon splits into North (Wheatfields Creek) and South (Whiskey Creek) Forks. The merging of these two creeks formed the Rio de Chelly, which eroded the main body of the canyon.

The canyon network figures into many Navajo ceremonies, such as the Coyoteway (Luckert 1979).

» CHINLE: [DB] Navajo: Ch'ínílį́, "Water Outlet," referring to the mouth of the canyon, though it later came to be applied to the government community at the mouth of the canyon. Here, at the mouth, the canyon walls are only about 50 ft high, and the canyon is crossed by Del Muerto Bridge, which carries Navajo Route 64 off to the northeast, parallelling the rim of Canyon del Muerto. Adjacent to the mouth, on the south rim, is National Monument Headquarters.

» THINGS FLOW AROUND THE STONE: Navajo: Tsé Biná'áz'éí, "Rock Around Which Floating Took Place" (Jett n.d., 18). This cottonwood-lined island, sitting just upstream from the Del Muerto Bridge, splits the flow of Chinle Creek.

Jett believes it may be the "Water Washes Around the Rock" mentioned in the obsolete Excessway myth, the Tsébina'azalí ("Things Flow Around the Stone") in the Nightway myth, and/or the Tsé Biná'áz'élí mentioned in the Upward Reachingway.

» CONGOLOMERATE WASH: Navajo: Tsé Ch'nl, "Pebble Outflow"; also Mą'iilso Ch'nl, "Yellow Coyote Wash" (Jett n.d., 19). A third of a mile upstream from Things Flow Around Stone, Tsé Ch'nl refers to the Shinarump Conglomerate that caps the rim of the canyon. The origin of the second name is unknown.

» POURING DOWN ROCK: Navajo: Tsébąąh Náálíní, "At Flows Repeatedly Rockside" (Jett n.d., 20). The name refers to a waterfall that forms at the mouth of Conglomerate Wash during or after heavy rainstorms. One of Jett's informants reported a pond at this location, from which Navajos obtained water even before the Bosque Redondo hiatus.

» FLUTE PLAYER CAVE: Navajo: Chooyíní Sitání, "Menstrual-Blood-One (Hunchback) is Lying Down" (Jett n.d., 20). This cave is named for an Anasazi petroglyph of a reclining Kokopelli, the hunchback flute player. The Navajo name refers to the belief that one who is contaminated by menstrual blood will become deformed, usually with a hunchback. This site may be related to Hunchback Rock, listed below.

» ADULTERY DUNE: Navajo: Séí 'Adiléhé, "Adultery Sand" (Jett n.d., 20). A long, low, tree-lined dune near the canyon's left-hand wall. Jett's informants noted the dune was a secluded place en route home from the trading posts at Chinle, which afforded an opportunity for men and women to get away with adultery.

» HUNCHBACK ROCK: Navajo: Chooyíní Dah Sidáhí, "Menstrual-Blood-One (Hunchback) Sitting at an Elevation" (Jett n.d., 21). A stone near the canyon's right-hand wall named for a resemblance to the bowed back of Kokopelli, the hunchbacked flute player. (See Flute Player Cave, above.)

» COTTONWOOD CANYON: Navajo: T'iis Nanít'i'í, "Cove Where Cottonwoods Stretch Across In a Line" (Jett n.d., 21). A tributary of the canyon's right face two and a half miles upstream from the del Muerto Bridge. It is named for the cottonwoods obscuring its mouth. These trees were notable in earlier days, as they were among the first cottonwoods in the canyon.

» PETROGLYPH ROCK: Navajo: Tsé 'Íí'áhí, "Standing Rock" (Jett n.d., 23). This feature, also known as "Scorpion Rock" (after a petroglyph) is on the upstream side of the mouth of Cottonwood Canyon. Note that several other features in the canyon are named Tsé Íí'áhí.

» CROW TRAIL: Navajo: Gáagii Haayáhí, "(Where) the Crow Ascended" (Jett n.d., 23). According to Jett, this trail, on the right face of the canyon behind Petroglyph Rock, is named after one of two events. In the first, the patient of an Enemyway ceremony prior to the Bosque Redondo period fled up the trail to avoid a Ute war party. He wore paraphernalia of the ceremony, including parts of a raven.

The second concerns a post–Fort Sumner Enemyway, at which a man, after arguing with his wife, climbed the trail with crows' feet about his neck.

» TUNNEL TRAIL: Navajo: Tséghájí'nahí, "Rock that People Crawl Through Trail Up Out" (Jett n.d., 25). This trail, though of some antiquity, appears to have been improved with cribbing for the filming of a movie—either *Desert Song* (1942) or *The Trial of Billy Jack* (1970s)—and was originally named for a stretch covered by a fallen sandstone slab that formed a "tunnel". It has been mistaken for Windpipe Trail (Tsé'ázoołyi'í, "Windpipe Rock Interior"), a nearby older trail it supplanted. In 1971, the Park Sevice installed a steel stairway at the head of this trail to provide visitor access to Newspaper Rock and Sleeping Duck Ruin.

Two tributary trails are Rockside Trail (Tsébąąhatiiní, "Trail Alongside Rock") and Gap Trail (Tséghá'atiiní, "Trail Through the Rock").

» SLEEPING DUCK ROCK: Navajo: Tsé Naal'ęęłí, Sitíní, "Lying Down Duck Rock" (Jett n.d., 26). A large rock (actually a continuation of the canyon's south wall) that resembles a duck lying on its stomach. An Anasazi ruin lies nearby.

» TUNNEL CANYON: Navajo: Tséghá'atiin Tséyi', "Trail Through the Rock Within Rock (Rock Canyon)"; also Séí Heeyołí, or Neheyołí Nástł'ah, "Cove Where Sand is Repeatedly Blown" (Jett n.d., 27). Located a half-mile upstream and on the opposite wall from Tunnel Trail and its canyon.

» BLADE ROCK: Navajo: Tsééhdikadí, "Thin Flat One (Extends) Into Rock (Canyon)"; 'E'é'ni' Be'adáád, "Late Game Trap (Obstacle)"; and occasionally Gaaní Bikéyah, "Damaged-Arm's Land" (Jett n:d., 28). A long, thin, slightly curved wall of sandstone reaching into the canyon from Antelope Point on the north rim.

The top of the "blade" forms the beginning of an "escape" trail out of the canyon, known as Tsédáá Na'atiin, "Trail Across Rock Rim." At the tip of the blade is Where the Rock is Marked (Tsé Bik'e'eshchíní, "The Rock's Writing," named for some historic period inscriptions in the rock).

» ZIG ZAG CAVE: Navajo: Tsénii Noǫtl'iizhíí, "Zigzag Rock Niche"; also "Wall with Lightning" (Jett n.d., 30). This rock shelter on the left side of the canyon is the "Rock in the Middle Crooked" mentioned in the obsolete Excessway myth, and appears in the Coyoteway myth as well. The location is named for a white lightning-bolt pictograph accompanied by other figures, apparently of Anasazi origin.

» ROCK LYING OUT: Navajo: Tsé Naa (Dah) Sitání, "Sideways Rock Lies Elongated (at an Elevation)" (Jett n.d., 30). This long finger of rock extends into the first bend in the canyon upstream from Blade Rock.

» MOTHER COTTONWOOD: Navajo: Hama, "Mother Area" (Jett n.d., 30). The name commemorates a large cottonwood tree (still standing by the north wall of the canyon as of 1992) in which two women hid from Spanish or Mexican invaders as their menfolk fled up a trail on the south face.

» FIRST RUIN: [DB] Navajo: Tsé Nááh Sitání Bikits'iilílíí, "Sideways Rock Lies Elongated's Ruin"; also 'Atsé Hooghan ("First Home Place"); Kiníí Dah Shijaa' ("Middle House Sits at an Elevation") (Jett n.d., 31). Some four miles up the canyon on the north wall is First Ruin, clinging inside a rocky "cave," or rock shelter. This ruin contains 10 rooms and two kivas, and was occupied between the late 1000s and the late 1200s. Just up the canyon is the juncture with Canyon del Muerto, heading northeast.

First Ruin was named by Cosmos Mindeleff in 1882 as the first ruin he examined.

» BIGHORN CAVE RUIN: Navajo: Dibéntsaa Tsétah, "Bighorn Sheep Among the Rocks" (Jett n.d., 31). This small Anasazi ruin sits in a rock shelter containing pictographs of bighorn sheep.

» BAD TRAIL COVE: Navajo: Hóchxǫ'í Ha'atiin Nástł'ah, "Ugly Trail Up Out Canyon" (Jett n.d., 32). This small north-side tributary of de Chelly is named for a trail (Hóchxǫ'í Ha'atiin, "Ugly Trail") that was a particularly bad means of exiting the canyon. Later the name was transferred to a second trail in the same vicinity.

» WHERE THE YEI WENT UP: Navajo: Yé'ii Hadeeyáhí, "The Yei Went Up and Out" (Jett n.d., 32). This hand- and toehold outlet from the canyon probabaly predates the Bosque Redondo hiatus, and has religious associations.

» DOG ROCK: Also Junction Rock. Navajo: Tsé Lééchąą'í, "Dog Rock"; also Tsé Dah Sitłé'é, "Rock Sits Spread Out at an Elevation"; Tsé Náhidéétéél, "Flattened Rock"; and Tsé 'Íí'áhí 'Ahidiidlíní, "Confluence Up Extending Rock" (Jett n.d., 32). This sandstone butte at the junction of Canyon de Chelly and Canyon del Muerto resembles the silhouette of a St. Bernard dog. According to Jett, trader Leon "Cozy" McSparron applied its canine name in the 1930s, but the traditional name seems to be Tsé Dah Sitłé'é. Young and Morgan have provided different possible interpretations to this name, having to do with a mushy texture and feces on top of the rock (Jett n.d., 33). Jett notes that the rock served as a refuge, but when and from whom is not specified.

» JUNCTION RUIN: Navajo: Tsédáhí Kits'iilí, "Rock Edge Ruin" (Jett n.d., 91). A half-mile upstream from First Ruin, and on the same cliff, is Junction Ruin, so called because it lies at the juncture of Canyon de Chelly with Canyon del Muerto. It is comprised of 15 rooms and a single kiva, and was roughly contemporary with First Ruin.

» WHITE HOUSE RUIN: [DB] Navajo: Kiníí' Na'ígai, "House with White Stripe Across" (Young and Morgan 1987, 495); also "White Stripe Across its Middle" (Young p.c. 1995). It is two miles upstream from the juncture with Canyon del Muerto. White House is named in the Night Chant as a home to Navajo deities, and as late as the 1940s, only medicine men would enter the site. The yellowish-white room perched 30 ft above the canyon floor gives rise to the English name.

White House was occupied by the Anasazi between A.D. 1060 and 1275, reaching its peak about 1200. The lower section contained about 60 rooms and four kivas, and was multi-storied, providing access to the 20-room complex in the cave above. As many as one hundred people lived here. This ruin was visited in 1849 by First Lieutenant James Simpson and sketched by Edward M. Kern, artist of Brevet Colonel Washington's expedition to Chinle. The first scientific excavations of the site were made in 1893 by Cosmos Mindeleff, archaeologist for the Smithsonian Institution, who called the ruin Casa Blanca following Simpson's notes. Some 30 years later Earl Morris of the Carnegie Institute carried on further excavations. The ruin contains "Chacoan" core-and-veneer masonry and a possible tower kiva (Flint and Flint 1989, 83–85), though many archaeologists argue that such architecture is not necessarily indicative of Chacoan influence.

» WHITE HOUSE TRAIL: Navajo: Tséghá'íldoní, "Blasted through Rock"; also 'Ada'ooldoní, "Blasted Out Downward" (from a height); and Ha'asdoní, "Blasted Away Upward" (Jett n.d., 40). Across the canyon from White House Ruin and along the south wall there winds an excellent trail up to the rim. Parts were cut into the sandstone by the Indian Emergency Conservation Works in 1933, and portions have since been paved by the National Park Service. However, it generally follows an older Navajo trail, called 'Asdzání Habitiin, meaning "Woman's Trail Up" (Young p.c. 1995). It has long been a means of transferring sheep and horses into and out of the canyon. As late as the 1940s, this marked the end of canyon-bottom motor tours, though the more intrepid visitor could proceed by foot or horseback.

Author's Note: Jett (n.d., 33-41) has identified no fewer than eleven trails in the vicinity of White House Ruin. In addition to White House Trail, there is Dah Dą'ąstséłí, "Trail Hacked Out [Notched] Downward at an Elevation"; 'Asdzání Habitiin, "Woman's Trail"; Hastóí Habitiin, "Elderly Man's Trail Up Out"; Yeibichai Trail (Yé'ii 'Adáájé'é'ii or Yé'ii Bicheii Habitiin, "Where Yeis Came Running Down" or "Yeibichai's Trail Up Out"); an unnamed foot trail; Parking Lot Trail (Bigháá Hááda'alwo'ó Ha'atiin, "Vehicles Run To Its Top Trail Up Out"); Coyote Trail (Mą'ii Bikee Ha'atiin, "Coyote's Tracks Trail Up Out"); Walnut Trail (Ha'ałtsédii Íí'áhí Ha'atiin, "Standing Walnut Tree Trail Up Out"); Woman's Trail (2) (Kiníí' Na'ígai Ha'atiin, "There Is a White Stripe Across the Middle House Trail Up Out"); and Yellow Clay Reservoir Trail (Łeetsoii Bii'tó Ha'aatiin, "Yellow Dirt [Ochre] Water Inside Trail Up Out"). Jett has noted that several intersect one another and/or have been mistaken for one another by more than one researcher/informant. It's very confusing, and readers interested in the trails per se are referred to Jett's document.

» MEAT ROCK: Navajo: Tsé 'Atsj', "Meat Rock," or Tsénteel, "Rock Is Flat" (Jett n.d., 41). A large peninsula of sandstone projecting from the north rim said to be striated to the point of resembling sliced meat. Other possible explanations for this name include a story that a goat was trapped atop the rock and became "meat for vultures," and the suggestion that the rock resembles the conchoidal striations on a sheep's intestines.

» TSE TA'A RUIN: (Also called CDC 86.) Navajo: Tsé Táá'á, "Rock Extending into Water" (Jett n.d., 45), named for a low-lying point of rock projecting from a cliff on the canyon's north side. Sitting on the north cliff, a mile and a half upstream from White House, this ruin was excavated in the mid-1960s (Steen 1966). It contains at least two Basketmaker pithouses and a Pueblo component dating through the Pueblo III Stage (A.D. 1100–1300). This latter contains some 30 rectangular rooms and six kivas. (It should be noted that there is another Tse Ta'a Ruin in Canyon del Muerto.)

» MANY PEACHES CANYON: Navajo: Didzé Łání Nástłah, "Many Big Berries (Peaches) Cove" (Jett n.d., 42). Just over a mile upstream from White House Ruin, this narrow canyon houses extensive, possibly old, peach orchards. Many of the trees are now dead.

» SHOOTING ARROWS IN THE ROCK: Navajo: Tsé Né'élzhíhí, "Archery Rock"; or Tsé Né'eltoho, "Shooting Arrows Into the Rock" (Jett n.d., 42). Named for the practice of Navajo men competing for baskets, horses, and even women's favors, by trying to lodge arrows in a pair of narrow fissures in the cliff wall. Navajo archery duels often involved shooting arrows over the rims and out of canyons, or aiming at the tops of spires (such as Cleopatra's Needle in Todilto Park in New Mexico).

» REFUGE ROCK: [DB] Navajo: Tsé'láá Ndzíts'o'í, "Rock Tip (Where) They Repeatedly 'Rubber Neck'" (Jett n.d., 43). This red sandstone monument stands isolated from the canyon walls, and in times past it provided Navajos with sanctuary from Ute, Spanish, and other raiders. Its flat top was accessible only by hand- and footholds scraped out of the rock and by long Douglas fir poles laid across particularly unscalable places.

» SITTING ROCK: [DB] Navajo: Tsé Si'ání, "Rock Sits (In Place)" (Jett n.d., 44). A nondescript name for a nondescript "lumplike" knob of de Chelly sandstone.

» SITTING GOD: Navajo: Yé'íí Dah Sidáí, "The Yei Sits at an Elevation" (Jett n.d., 45). Beyond Refuge Rock, and low in a shallow alcove in the face of the south wall of the canyon can be seen the painting of a Navajo deity. The Navajos regard this place as sacred and call it Yé'ii Dah Sidáhí, "Where the God Sits."

» STREAKED ROCK: Navajo: Tséndíłkéhí, "Streaked Rock" (Jett n.d., 45). This red cliff face, just upstream from Sitting God, is dramatically streaked with black "desert varnish."

» HOOP AND POLE GAME ROCK: [DB] Navajo: Tséyaa Nda'azhǫǫshí, "Rock under which the Hoop and Pole Game is Played" (Young and Morgan 1987, 732). The exact location of this rock is unclear, as Van Valkenburgh gave at least two locations and two names (the second being "Loop Stick Game Rock"). Navajos tell that it was once a favorite place for playing na'azhǫǫsh, (the "Hoop and Pole Game"). In the morning they would play on the cool west side, going around in the afternoon to seek shade on the east.

» SLIDING OFF ROCK: Navajo: Tsé Naashzhoojí, "Sliding Off Rock" (Jett n.d., 47). This spot marks the location of a ceremonial hogan pushed off the talus slope on which it sat and destroyed by a rock slide.

» ROUND CAVE: Navajo: Tsé Bó'oos'ni'í, "Lightning Struck Rock Cave" (Jett n.d., 47). This cave is in a small knob of sandstone just below the base of Rock Struck by Lightning. In it is a small Anasazi ruin, and the walls of the cave are decorated with Navajo star pictographs. (There is also a Round Cave Ruin in Canyon del Muerto.)

» ROCK STRUCK BY LIGHTNING: [DB] Navajo: Tsé Bí'oos'ní'í "Rock Struck by Lightning." Two miles upstream from White House Ruin, on the north side of the canyon. According to Navajo tradition, a lightning strike many years ago left charred streaks down the sides of this reddish rock.

» WILD CHERRY RUIN: Navajo: Łeeyi'Kiní, "Subterranean House" (Jett n.d., 47). This ruin, also known as Spring Canyon Ruin, is at the entrance to Spring Canyon. The walls are largely buried by the sandy canyon floor. Nearby is a pictograph of a leaping deer. Jett notes confusion of this site with another on the opposite side of the canyon, but this is the correct Wild Cherry Ruin. The name apparently derives from the mistaken belief that the canyon next to the ruin was Wild Cherry Canyon (see Spring Canyon).

» SPRING CANYON: [DB, as "Canyon Across from Rock Struck by Lightning"] Navajo: Tsé Bó'oos'ni'í, "The Lightning Struck Rock Cove" (Jett n.d., 48). In the canyon is a "dangerous" trail Van Valkenburgh refers to as Haaz'áí Habitiin, "Ladder Trail" (see Spring Canyon Trail), which is of historical significance.

This canyon has at least once been mistaken for Wild Cherry Canyon on USGS maps, which Jett credits for the name of Wild Cherry Ruin at the entrance to the canyon. Jett notes a petroglyph site in the canyon, but does not identify it as Navajo or Anasazi. The canyon is named for Bubbling Spring (Tó Háálíní, "Bubbling Water [Spring])" (Jett n.d., 48), which sits in one of the small branches that form the head of Spring Canyon. One informant told Jett that the spring is a place for Holy People.

» SPRING CANYON TRAIL: Navajo: Tsé Bó'oos'ni'í Ha'atiin, "Rock Struck by Lightning Trail Up Out" or Tsé Hadoolkǫ Ha'atiin, "Smooth Area Rock Trail Up Out" (Jett n.d., 49); Haaz'áí Habitiin, "Ladder Trail" (see Spring Canyon Trail) (Van Valkenburgh 1941, 20). It was at the head of this trail that a number of Navajos were massacred by troops under Captains Asa B. Carey and A. F. Pfeiffer of Colonel Carson's command in the winter of 1864. Navajos say that the troops trailed them through heavy snow from their winter camps near Nazlini to the rim of this

canyon. They had just started down the trail when the soldiers spied them from the opposite side of the canyon and started firing into them. They made an excellent target and many were killed. (This massacre is not to be confused with the Massacre Cave slaughter of 1805 in Canyon del Muerto).

» SLIDING ROCK RUIN: [DB, as Sliding Ruin] Also Sliding House Ruin. Navajo: Kin Náázhoozhí, "Building that Gradually Slid Down" (Young and Morgan 1987, 495). Less than a mile above Spring Canyon, this ruin sits in a rock shelter 40 ft up in the north face of the canyon. It contains 30 to 50 rooms, and was constructed around the middle A.D. 900s, according to tree-ring samples collected in 1923. A short distance down the canyon a large red and white mural depicts antelopes, very similar to the mural above Antelope House in Canyon del Muerto.

» ZUNI TRAIL: [DB] Navajo: Naasht'ézhí Haayáhí, "Where the Zuni Went Up" (Young and Morgan 1987, 599) is what the Navajos call a precarious trail up the south wall of the canyon between "The Canyon Across from the Rock Struck by Lightning" (also called by the common Navajo descriptive term Tsékooh, "Rock Canyon") and "Canyon Below Wild Cherry Spring." It is named for a Zuni slave who escaped up the trail after four years of captivity in the canyon.

» ROUND ROCK STICKS UP: Navajo: Tsé Náhaaztání, "Round Rock Extending Up Out Rock"; or Tsé 'Íí'áhí, "Up Extending (Standing) Rock" (Jett n.d., 52). Jett considers this feature likely to be the Round Rock Sticks Up mentioned in the obsolete Excessway myth.

» WILD CHERRY CANYON: [DB, as "Canyon Below Wild Cherry Spring"] Navajo: Didzé Sikaad Nástłah, "Chokecherry (Bush) Is Standing Spread Out Cove" (Jett n.d., 52), apparently in reference to a wild-cherry tree near a spring (called Didzé Sikaad Tó, "Chokecherry [Bush] Is Spread Out Spring") at the head of the canyon.

Also called "Canyon Below Wild Cherry Spring"; Tsékooh, a simple generic term meaning "Rock Canyon"; and Didzé Sikaad, "Wild Cherry Tree Sits." This canyon is located about a mile upstream from Spring Canyon (or "Canyon Across from Rock Struck by Lightning"), also on the south side of de Chelly. A number of trails come down the walls of the canyon, the most important one being Sháá Ha'atiin, "Sunshine Trail Up Out."

» SUNSHINE TRAIL: Navajo: Sháá' Ha'atiin, "Sunnyside Trail Up Out" (Van Valkenburgh 1941, 20). The Navajos say that when it snows on this trail it melts quickly because the sun shines directly on the greater part of it.

» SQUIRREL ROCK: Navajo: Hazéi Łání, "Many Squirrels" (Jett n.d, 54). Opposite the mouth of Wild Cherry Canyon, this standing rock is named for the numerous chipmunks that flourished around it. It is also known as Seven Figures Rock, for seven white anthropomorphic pictographs in a cave adjacent to the rock.

» GAP ROCK: Navajo: Tsé Ńdeshgizh, "Rock Gap" (Jett n.d., 54). This spire near the north face of the canyon, about three quarters of a mile upstream from Wild Cherry Canyon, is named for the narrow gap between it and the cliff face.

» BEEHIVE RUIN: [DB] Navajo: Kin Naadzíí, "Beehive House." An Anasazi ruin located five miles upstream from White House Ruin, and one mile downstream from The Window, situated on the north side of the river.

» THE WINDOW: [DB] Navajo: Tséghá-hoodzání, "The Perforated Rock" (Jett n.d., 56). Also called Window Arch. Hole eroded through a large sandstone monument on the north cliff five miles upstream from White House Ruin, and about a mile up from the mouth of Wild Cherry Canyon.

» TRAIL WHERE THE ENEMY WALKED UP SINGING: [DB, as "Trail Where the Enemy Walked Up"] Navajo: 'Anaa' Sin Yił Haayáhí, "Where the Enemy (a Hopi woman) Walked Up Singing." Upstream from The Window, on the north side of the canyon over a heavy talus slide at the head of a small canyon. The Utes used this trail in raiding the Navajos in the canyon in the 1840s, and it is the main Navajo horse trail up onto Black Mesa (separating Canyon de Chelly and Canyon del Muerto). Jett (n.d., 55) labeled this as Beehive Trail (Naadzįįł Haayáhí, "Slave Went Up There Quick"), and refers to it as the most important horse trail on the north side of the canyon. This may be the trail up which Navajo captives were taken by Captain Asa B. Carey during Carson's pillage of the canyon, giving rise to Jett's Navajo name.

» FROG ROCK: Navajo: Ch'al Sitá, "Frog Sits" (Jett n.d., 57). Located in the first cove encountered on the north side upstream from The Window.

» HORSE ROCK: Navajo: Tsé Łįįlí, "Horse Rock" (Jett n.d., 57). A medium-sized boulder upstream from The Window on the right-hand bank, which looks like the silhouette of a running horse.

» SUNSHINE SPRING: [DB, as Sha'thohih Spring] Also Ha'thohih Spring. Navajo: Sháá'tóhí, "Sunshine Water," or "Spring on the Sunny Side" (Young p.c. 1995). Upstream from The Window, on the north side of the canyon, is a spring in the bottom of a small alcove immediately above the canyon floor; and the water that collects in the natural catch-basin drops from the mossy sandstone roof of the alcove. (It is also called Jiłháli Bito', "Always Beaten Up's Spring," after a man called Jiłháłli, "Always Beaten Up").

» HOUSE IN THE ROCK RUIN: [DB] Navajo: Tséyi'kiní Yit'eezh, "Line of Rock-Niche Houses" (Jett n.d., 59). An Anasazi ruin consisting of a line of rooms in a crack in the cliff face right above Sháá'tóhí Spring. Jett believes this to be the House in Middle of Rock mentioned in the obsolescent Excessway myth (Kluckhohn 1967, 166).

» FACE ROCK: [DB] Navajo: Tsé Binii'í, "Rock with a Face" (Jett n.d., 59). Also called "Speaking Rock." A 500-foot rock pillar breaking away from the north canyon wall, three quarters of a mile northwest of and across from Spider Rock. In silhouette, this rock resembles a face with open mouth. Jett identifies it as one of the monoliths known in the nineteenth century as "The Captains" or "The Monuments." (The other is Spider Rock.)

» BUNCHED FEATHERS: [DB] Navajos tell that long ago at this place on the south cliff opposite Speaking Rock, there was a place called T'ánáánééł, loosely translated as "Feathers Bunched." Young (p.c. 1995) notes that T'á means "feathers," but Náásééł means "It (a crowd) is returning," which more correctly translated means "A Crowd is returning with Feathers." An old woman called Tsé hadook'íhí, "Overlapping Rock Layers" (Young p.c. 1995), wanted to get down from the canyon rim. She stuck a bunch of eagle feathers into a small spruce tree and rode it down into the canyon. (It is here that Monument Canyon enters Canyon de Chelly from the south. The features in this tributary are inventoried separately below.)

» SPIDER ROCK: [DB, as "The Monument"] Navajo: Tsé Na'ashjé'ii, "Spider Rock" (Bailey 1964b, 40). At a point eight miles upstream from White House Ruin, after passing Shą́ą́'tóhí Spring, Monument Canyon branches off to the south of Canyon de Chelly. At the mouth of Monument Canyon stands a sheer sandstone pillar some 800 ft high. It is sacred to the Navajos as the home of Spider Woman, an important figure in Navajo mythology who taught the Navajos the art of weaving, and who is said once to have woven her web over the rock.

Modern tales relate that she still lives there, coming down at night to steal away unruly children, whose names are told her by Face Rock. She devours them, and their bones litter the top of the spire. Jett (n.d., 59, 61) identifies Spider Rock and Face Rock as two monuments known as "The Captains" or "The Monuments" during the nineteenth century, and one of his informants identified Spider Rock as one of the two most sacred features in the entire canyon complex (the other being White House Ruin).

» WIDE ROCK: [DB] Navajo: Tsénteel, "Rock is Broad (Flat)" (Jett n.d., 63). This isolated mesa, some 600 ft high, sits between Spider Rock and the plateau at the juncture of de Chelly and Monument Canyon. Sheer-walled for many feet below the rim, long talus slopes form the remainder of its sides to the canyon floor. On the north face in the main body of the rock is a long vertical fissure that the Navajos say is a door for certain holy people who live in the rock. Two large snakes in Navajo mythology are also said to have lived here, and it is also mentioned as an important place in the Dog Side of the Night Chant. It also figures in the Nightway and Beautyway myths, as well as the Coyoteway, Female Mountaintopway, and Upward Reachingway myths. Moreover, local Navajos state that Bá Hózhoónii, "Goodfellow," a famous medicine man of the last century, used this place to make prayers and deposit kethans, or prayer sticks. As late as the 1940s, no Navajo would enter this place unless in possession of proper medicine.

✤ UPPER CANYON DE CHELLY: The main branch of Canyon de Chelly continues east another 20 miles from its juncture with Monument Canyon, to its headwaters, Wheatfields. Whiskey and Coyote Creeks join to drop into the main canyon. Navajo tradition relates the origin of the whole canyon system:

Before there was the Canyon de Chelly, Tsézhini, "Black Rock," stood above the plain. A great fire set the world blazing. This great fire was started when Coyote asked for fire and the people did not want him to have it as he was a mischief maker. He begged so hard that they finally let him have it. He tried to make fire, and finally threw one flint rock against another [and] made a spark, starting the blaze. Coyote ran away. The fire burned so fiercely that the earth cracked. Tó Neinilí, "The Water Pourer," poured water on the fire, and the water started cutting these cracks deeper and deeper until the canyons reached their present depth.

If you look at the canyon today, you can see

how both sides of the canyon fit together. (Van Valkenburgh 1941, 22)

» WINDY ROCK (West): Navajo: Tsé Bináyołí, "Rock Around Which the Wind Blows" (Jett n.d., 64). This spire stands among others, but is located at the lower side of the mouth of Black Rock Trail Canyon.

» BLACK ROCK TRAIL CANYON: Navajo: Tsézhíní Ha'atiin Nástłah, "Black Rock Trail Up Out Cove" (Jett n.d., 64). The second north-side tributary of de Chelly north of Face Rock, named for a trail within it. Jett suggests it may also be known as "Bear Canyon." This is likely the Black Rock Rincon Older Sister went into in the Female Mountaintopway.

» BLACK ROCK TRAIL: Navajo: Tsézhin Ha'atiin, "Black Rock Trail Up Out" (Jett n.d., 64). This trail is navigable on horseback, and reaches the rim near the head of Black Rock Trail Canyon, a little less than two miles from Black Rock butte. The canyon is a "wind canyon," being windy even when the wind is not blowing elsewhere in the canyons. Navajo werewolves, who inhabited Black Rock, were said to have flown to First Mesa of the Hopi via this wind.

» HEAD ROCK: Navajo: Tsébitsii'í, "Rock's Head" (Jett n.d., 65). Also Tsé Sitłé'é, "Rock Sits Spread Out." About a mile and a third above Black Rock Trail Canyon, this spire rises from the talus slope of the north wall of Canyon de Chelly. The knobby top resembles a head. Jett takes care to point out that this is *not* the formation known as "Father Rock" due to its resemblance to a priest. (See Father Rock, below.)

» RED ROCK POINT: Navajo: Łichíí Táá'á, "Red Extends Into Water" (Jett n.d., 66). A "stepped" red sandstone outcrop on the north side of the canyon, lined with significant standing red rocks. It is important as the home of the Holy People in the Nightway myth.

» FATHER ROCK: Navajo: 'Azhei, "Father," or Tsé Bazhei ("Rock's Father") (Jett n.d., 66). One

of the rocks near Red Rock Point, this one looks like a priest in a long robe.

» RED CLAY CANYON: Navajo: Chííh Hajíítseełí Nástłah, "Hack Out Red Ochre Place Cove" (Jett n.d., 67). This tributary is named for Red Clay Cave situated within it.

» RED CLAY CAVE: Navajo: Chííh Hajíítseełí, "Hack Out Red Ochre Place" (Jett n.d., 67). This recess in the cliff wall once housed an outcropping of red ochre, mined for face painting, that has now dissipated. It is likely the "Place Where Red Ochre is Gathered" mentioned in the obsolete Excessway myth.

» MULE CANYON: Navajo: Dzaanééz Habitiin Nástł'ah, "Long Ear's (Mule's) Trail Up Out Cove" (Jett n.d., 67). A southside tributary named for a trail within it.

» MULE TRAIL: Navajo: Dzaanééz Habitin, "Long Ear's (Mule's) Trail Up Out" (Jett n.d., 67). This trail in the canyon's left-hand branch was so rocky, only mules could climb it. It was utilized by archaeological expeditions in the 1920s.

» ASPEN CANYON: Navajo: T'iisbáí Bikooh, "Gray Cottonwood Wash" (Jett n.d., 68). The first northside tributary above Red Clay Canyon, it was named for the aspens growing in it. It houses two trails, Aspen Trail (T'iisbáí Ha'atiin, "Aspen Trail Up Out") and Red Ochre Trail (Chíí'a Ha'atiin, "Red Ochre Trail Up Out").

» WINDY ROCK (EAST): Navajo: Tsé K'ééyoł, "Wind-Swept Rock" (Jett n.d., 68). This largest standing rock in this part of the canyon resembles a stove-pipe, possibly located at the lower side of Cave Ruins. This may be one of two "talking rocks" in the canyon.

» TWIN ROCKS: Navajo: Tsé 'Ahéskéhé, "Two Rocks Sit Together" (Jett n.d., 69). Two columns of rock, side by side, two miles above the mouth of Aspen Canyon. The Navajo name actually implies a marriage between the rocks.

» CHOKE CHERRIES SPREAD OUT CANYON:
Navajo: Didzé Sikaad Bikooh, "Chokecherry
(Bushes) Are Standing Spread Out Wash" (Jett
n.d., 70). Two miles above Aspen Canyon, this
tributary is named for a patch of wild cherry
bushes in the upper canyon. It is possibly the
same patch mentioned in the Beautyway myth
and the obsolete Excessway.

» WHITE RESERVOIR CANYON: Navajo:
Be'ek'id Halgaa, "White Area Pond" (Jett n.d.,
70). A sizable tributary about two and a half
miles above Aspen Canyon. It is named for the
small reservoir impounded by White Dam.

» WHEATFIELDS CANYON: Navajo: Tó Dzís'á
Bikooh, "Strip of Water Extending Into Distance's Wash" (Jett n.d., 71). The uppermost extension of Canyon de Chelly, this canyon is
formed by the juncture of Wheatfields and
Whiskey creeks. (These two features are discussed under their own headings.) Young and
Morgan (1987, 572) give the name Nát'oste'
'Álíní, "Place Where Stone Pipes are Made," but
this most likely refers to a specific locale in the
canyon, Pipe Caves.

This upper canyon is apparently used by Navajos today for gathering medicinal plants.

» WHISKEY CREEK CANYON: Navajo: Tó Diłhił
Bikooh, "Water is Dark Colored Wash" (Jett n.d.,
73). Right-hand tributary joining Wheatfields
Canyon about five miles below its head. The
English name denotes a dual meaning of the
Navajo word Diłhił, which can also mean
"causes dizziness." (See also Whiskey Creek
under separate listing.)

» COYOTE WASH CANYON: Navajo: Tsé Dáá
Bikooh, "Rock Edge Wash" (Jett n.d., 73). This
major right-hand branch of Whiskey Creek
Canyon joins the latter about a mile downstream
from its head. The Navajo name derives from
Rock Edge (Tsé Dáá, "Rock Edge"), a truck
trail that crosses the wash about a mile above
the canyon's mouth, near a bare rock slope (or
edge).

Jett considers the location of this canyon com-
patible with the Coyote Box Canyon mentioned
in the obsolete Excessway myth.

» GREEN COTTONWOOD CANYON: Navajo: T'iis
Ndiitsoí Nástł'ah, "Yellow-green Cottonwoods
Extending Downward (In A Line) Cove" (Jett
n.d., 75). Half a mile up Coyote Wash Canyon
from its mouth is a right-bank canyon from
which cottonwood trees poke above the rim.

» PIPE CAVES: Navajo: Nát'ostse' 'Álíigi,
"Where Smoked Stones (Pipes) Are Made" (Jett
n.d., 75). Jett notes some confusion over the location of this feature, including possibilities in
Wheatfields Canyon. He equates the feature with
the Makes Hunting Pipes mentioned in the obsolete Excessway myth.

» MONUMENT CANYON: Navajo: Tsénteel
Bikooh, "Wide Rock's Wash" (Jett n.d., 76);
Tsíhidzo Biihílį', "Flow of the Fluted Rock"
(Franciscan Friars 1910, 134) (though Young [p.c.
1995] questions the meaning or even the existence of the word "Tsíhidzo"); and Tsįįh Hidzoh
Bikooh, "Log Place Wash" (Jett n.d., 76). This
tributary of de Chelly, opening in the latter's
south wall near Spider Rock, is second only to
del Muerto in size. The canyon is 12 miles long
and forms a major fork of de Chelly. Captain
John G. Walker, in the 1858 report of his exploration of Canyon de Chelly, referred to this
canyon as "Alsada Canyon," which was a Mexican translation of the Navajo name, and reportedly meant "Canyon of High Rock" (Bailey
1964b, 40). Alzada is Spanish for "Raised."

The name of the canyon apparently derives
from a number of upright stone pinnacles within
it. (See Rock that People Turned Into, below.)

» ROCK THAT PEOPLE TURNED INTO: [DB]
Navajo: Tsé Ná'áz'élí, which Van Valkenburgh
(1941, 21) translated as "Rock They (the people)
Turned Into" (hence the English name), but is ac-
tually "Rock that Water Flows Around" (Young
and Morgan 1987, 730). Also Tséneeyséél
("Many Rock Pinnacles"); Tsé Dah Seeshzhaaí
("The Spikey Rock At An Elevation"); Ghą́ą́'
'Ask'idii ("Hunchback [God]" or "Camel"); Tsé

Náhoolyélí ("Turning [Changing] Rock"); Tsé Ńdadzisdlí'í ("Rock that People Turned Into"); Tsé Ha'ałchíní ("Family Members Rock"); Tsé Ná'áz'élí (another spelling for "Rock that Water Flows Around"); and Tsé Biná'ázélí ("Things Flow Around the Stone") (Jett n.d., 80).

This tight mass of sandstone pinnacles a mile upstream in Monument Canyon resembles a group of people. One legend has it that they had once been people who worshipped Spider Woman. However, she didn't want this adoration, and so turned them into stone. Another, related by Van Valkenburgh (1941, 21) relates that

. . . long ago, the old people were not allowed by the Gods to have any farms or hogans in this vicinity. Some Navajos made their first farms here. They harvested their crop and piled the corn into this isolated rock that stands in the middle of the canyon. The Holy People who were living in Wide Rock found them and turned them and the piled corn into this isolated rock that stands in the middle of the canyon.

» GOPHER WATER RUIN: [DB] Navajo: Na'azízí Tó, "Gopher Spring" (Young p.c. 1995). One mile upstream in Monument Canyon from Rock That People Turned Into. This place was once the field of a woman named 'Asdzą́ą́ Yázhí, "Little Woman" (Young p.c. 1995), and above it is a good-sized Anasazi ruin. Two important trails connect the canyon floor to the rim in this vicinity, Łį́į' Habitiin ("Horsetrail Going Up") on the east wall and heading near White Clay; and Dibé Habitiin ("Sheep Trail Going Up") on the west wall of the canyon, across from Horse Trail.

» BAT CANYON: [DB] Navajo: Jaa'baní Bikooh, "Buckskin Ears (Bat) Wash" (Jett n.d., 77). This three-mile-long spur of Monument Canyon enters from the southwest approximately a mile upstream from the de Chelly–Monument Canyon juncture. The name stems from Bat Rock, Tsé Jaa'abaní ("Buckskin Ears [Bat] Rock"), which in turn was named for an infestation of bats behind a nearby slab of stone, which has since fallen to the ground. The canyon houses a trail called Jaa'abaní Habitiin ("Buckskin Ears [Bat] Trail"), which was one of the main trails by which the Navajos moved live-stock between the canyon floor and the rim. At the head of this spruce-lined canyon is a Navajo Tséniijih ("Putting On Rocks," or "Rocks are Customarily Placed") (Young p.c. 1995), an offering cairn of stones and twigs, where passing travelers leave an offering and a rock. Halfway down the trail is a petroglyph of a horse's head, said by the Navajos to have been pecked in the rock in 1864 by Captain Pfeiffer's men (see Chinle, Canyon Across From the Rock Struck By Lightning). At the point where the trail begins to flatten out is Tséjaa'abaní ("Bat Rock"), from which the canyon gets its name. The rock is said to be infested with bats. A short distance north of Bat Rock is an old stone Navajo eagle cage. As with all the canyons in this vicinity, Bat Canyon contains numerous Anasazi ruins.

» MANY WATERS CANYON: Navajo: Tó Łání, "Many Waters (Springs)" (Jett n.d., 79). This *may* be the name of the easterly fork of Bat Canyon. However, Jett notes that other names have been suggested for this minor canyon, such as Tsé Bitłą́áh Hachíí' ("Red Area Rock Underside") and Ch'ó Łání ("Many Douglas Firs"), and Savino or Sabina (Spanish for "Red" or "Juniper") Canyon. It has been suggested that the real Many Waters Canyon is nearer to Fluted Rock, and is not part of Canyon de Chelly at all.

» GOPHER CANYON: Navajo: Na'azísí Nástł'ah, "Pockets About (Gopher) Cove" (Jett n.d., 83). A minor right-side canyon, named after nearby Gopher Spring, Na'azísí Tóhí ("Pockets About [Gopher] Spring"). This spring, located in Monument Canyon a mile upsteam from Rock that People Turned Into, is named for an abundance of gophers in the area.

» TWIN LADDER HOUSE: Navajo: Haaz'éí Nahíítání, "Dangling Ladder"; or Haaz'éí Dah Hidétání Kit'siil, "Hanging Ladder Fragmented House" (Jett n.d., 84). This Anasazi ruin lies in the first left-bank tributary above Gopher Spring. It occupies two levels of the rock shelter, and is reached by a pair of (steel axe) notched ladders.

» SMALL TWIN TRAILS CANYON: Navajo: Mą'ii Bikooh, "Coyote Canyon" (Jett n.d., 84). This may be the Coyote Box Canyon mentioned in the obsolete Excessway myth. An alternative location for the canyon of the myth, however, is Coyote Wash Canyon (above). The more recent (English) name comes from the presence of Small Twin Trails, 'Áłnaashii Ha'atiin Hayázhí, "Small Trails Up Out Opposite Each Other." Only one of these is currently evident, and there is some speculation on Jett's part that descriptions of the southernmost one actually refer to a path known as Coyote Trail (Mą'ii Ha'atiin, "Coyote Trail Up Out") that is also situated in Small Twin Trails Canyon. The northern Twin trail cuts through the first "significant" right-bank tributary above Gopher Canyon.

» BIG COTTONWOOD CANYON: T'iis Nitsxaaz Sikaad Nástłah, "Huge Cottonwood Spreads Cove" (Jett n.d., 86). The next right-bank tributary canyon above Small Twin Trail Canyon, named for a sizable cottonwood tree, the stump of which is "still there." The canyon houses an easy footpath, Big Cottonwood Trail, T'iis Nitsxaaz Ha'atiin ("Huge Cottonwood Trail Up Out").

✤ CANYON DEL MUERTO: [DB] Navajo: 'Ane'étséyi', "Back Of In Between The Rocks," or, more simply, "Back Canyon." De Muerto is Spanish for "the Dead Man." This main tributary of Canyon de Chelly enters from the northeast some four miles upstream from Chinle. At this point, del Muerto rims are roughly 6000 ft in elevation, rising to 7200 ft at the headwaters of the canyon some 20 miles upstream. This is the northernmost of the two main channels of the Canyon de Chelly system, and it is drained by Rio del Muerto, which emanates from Tsaile Lake, a man-made reservoir on Tsaile Creek, formerly called Spruce Creek.

Del Muerto has three significant tributaries: Black Rock and Twin Trail Canyons, branching off to the east, and Middle Trail Canyon, branching to the north where del Muerto turns sharply to the east.

Captain John G. Walker, in his 1858 exploration of the canyon system, referred to del Muerto as "Cañon Trigo," or "Wheat Canyon" (Bailey 1964b, 41; Bailey 1970, 45).

Some say Canyon del Muerto took its Spanish name (Canyon of the Dead Man) from the massacre of Navajos by Lieutenant Chacon's Spanish and Zunis in 1805 (see Massacre Cave, below). However, it is also said that the name was bestowed in the 1880s by Colonel Stephenson, following his excavation of mummy burials at Mummy Cave.

Like de Chelly, del Muerto is characterized by high, sheer red sandstone cliffs. The peninsula of land separating the two canyons is appropriately named 'Ata'adeez'á ("Point Between the Canyons"). There are a number of small ruins before the first significant place in Canyon del Muerto is reached. As far as can be ascertained these ruins have no names.

» THE JUNCTION: Navajo: 'Ahidiidlíní, "The Confluence" (Jett n.d., 89). The confluence of Canyon de Chelly with Canyon del Muerto is marked by a small ruin, named Tsédáhí Kits'iilí ("Rock Edge Ruin") (Jett n.d., 91) (see listing under Canyon de Chelly).

» LADY WHITE TRAIL: Navajo: 'Asdzą́ą́ Łigaaí Habitiin, "Lady Is White's Trail Up Out" (Jett n.d., 91). Also known as Junction Trail, this path ascends del Muerto's left side to the Black Rock Peninsula just above the Junction. The name is for a member of the Tó Dích'íí'nii ("Bitter Water") clan named Lady White, who probably lived in the area shortly after the Bosque Redondo hiatus.

» WHITE LADY FORTRESS: Navajo: Uncertain, possibly 'Asdzą́ą́ Łigaaí Kits'iilí, "Woman Is White's Ruin." This Navajo defensive site is located on an isolated projection above the junction of Canyon del Muerto and Canyon de Chelly. The site is comprised of defensive walls and possible masonry storage structures (Fall, McDonald, and Magers 1981, 209).

» ECHO CAVE: Navajo: Tséyaa Hodiits'a'í, "Rock Under Which There Is an Echo" (Jett n.d., 92). One bend above the Junction is an area that echoes sound. The Park Service has applied the name to a ruin on the north side of the canyon, but Jett's informants related that the name applies to the whole area.

» BALANCED ROCK: Navajo: Tsé Si'ání, "Rock Sits" (Jett n.d., 92). One bend upstream from Echo Cave a boulder sits on the talus on the right-hand side of the canyon.

» SPRING WATER: Navajo: Tséyaa Tóhí, "Under Rock (Cave) Water," or Habídí Bito'í, "Mourning Dove's Spring" (Jett n.d., 93). In the early morning, mourning doves gather at this spring, across and slightly upstream from Balanced Rock.

» BARE ROCK TRAIL: [DB, as "Stepped Rock Trail"] Navajo: Tsé Hadeesk'ihí, "Overlapping Layers" (Young p.c. 1995), mistranslated by Van Valkenburgh (1941, 23). Unmaintained horse trail named for the unevenly eroded beds of sandstone near its base. The trail predates the Bosque Redondo hiatus, and Utes once hurled rocks down on Navajos below in this vicinity.

» ROUND CAVE RUIN: Navajo: Tłízí Tsé Yaa Kin, "House Under Goat Rock" (Jett n.d., 93). This ruin is in a small rock shelter above the canyon floor below Bare Trail. One of Jett's informants related that a goat entered the ruin and never came out.

» BABY PEE(D) TRAIL: Navajo: 'Awéé Haazhilizhí, "Where a Baby Urinated on the Way Up" (Jett n.d., 94). This foot trail with pole ladders is on the left side of a small tributary canyon across from Bare Rock Trail. The two trails were used in sequence to get from the north rim of the canyon to Black Rock Peninsula. This was also an alternate route out of the canyon used when Utes would throw rocks down on Bare Rock Trail. It was during one such flight that a young woman's baby urinated about halfway up the climb. In 1983 some steps were carved in the trail, and steel rails have been added in places.

» CAT FACE: Navajo: Mósí Bitsiits'iin, "Cat's Head" (Jett n.d., 94). A projection on the end of the spur on which Baby Peed Trail lies resembles a cat's head.

» ROCK THEY RAN INTO: [DB] Navajo: Tsé Biih Ńjíjahí, "Where People Repeatedly Run Into the Rock (Cave?)" (Jett n.d., 94). On the southeast wall of the canyon, nearly opposite Stepped Rock Trail, is a crack in the cliff face, visible only from a certain angle, that Navajos used as a refuge from enemies. Here a trail— sometimes consisting only of hand- and footholds cut into the sandstone—leads up the canyon wall, following a narrow ledge, until it enters a deep crevice. The crevice is visible from only one angle from the canyon floor, and it served as a Navajo refuge when the Spanish or other enemies were in the canyon.

» BUTTERFLY CAVE: This rock shelter is of major religious significance to the Navajos (Jett n.d., 95). The Navajo name is withheld, as are specifics about its location and certain descriptive information that would make it easier to identify. Legend has it that the concavity hides a tunnel that leads to a ruin in Canyon de Chelly.

» LEDGE RUIN: Navajo: Tsé'níí' Kin Yít'eezhí, "Line of Houses Ledge" (Jett n.d., 96). A mile and a half upstream from the convergence of Canyon del Muerto with Canyon de Chelly, a moderate Anasazi ruin sits on a narrow ledge 100 ft above the canyon floor in the north wall of the canyon. Ledge Ruin is ceramically dated to between A.D. 1050 and 1275. Surface remains suggest the presence of 29 storage rooms and a two-story habitation structure of as many as 29 rectangular rooms and two kivas.

» UTE FIGHT MURAL: [DB] Navajo: Nóódá'a Łii' Bił Yikahigi, "More than Three Utes Which Ride Along on Horses" (Jett n.d., 96). Some three miles upstream from the junction with Canyon de Chelly, Ute Fight Mural is located on the west wall of Canyon del Muerto under a deep ledge. A Navajo named Philip Draper had fields here in the 1940s. This painted mural depicts a Ute raid into Canyon del Muerto under Tsiiłigai ("White Hair") in the 1840s. White Hair was the Navajos' most important enemy of that period, and was later killed in a Navajo reprisal raid into the Los Pinos River region of southern Colorado.

Two trails pass between Rock They Ran Into and Ute Fight Mural. The first, on the west wall, is 'Ak'ehal'í ("Refused to Follow") (Van Valkenburgh, 1941 23), named after some Navajos refused to ascend the trail. Young (p.c. 1995) says the name is more likely Doo 'Ak'eh hół'íida, "He Doesn't Obey." Jett (n.d., 98) suggests that this is the trail also known as Antelope Trail (Jádí Habitiin, "Swift One's Trail Up Out"), which he describes as a horse trail on the south wall of the canyon.

The second, Baby Trail, 'Awéé Hajiloh ("Baby is Customarily Hoisted Up [with a rope]") is on the east wall, and includes a difficult climb of 10 feet of sheer wall at the bottom. If a Navajo woman had a baby with her, a rope was used to hoist the baby up over this section (Van Valkenburgh 1941, 23). Jett (n.d., 96) also mentions Ute Raid Trail, 'Anaasází Habitiin ("Anasazi's Trail") in the same vicinity, ascending a north-side spur just below Far Spiral Canyon.

» FAR SPIRAL CANYON: Navajo: Nízaa'-aliwozh Nástłah, "Far Spiral Cove" (Jett n.d., 96). This right-side canyon is five and a quarter miles upstream from the junction of del Muerto with de Chelly. It is said to house a spiral-shaped hole in one of its walls, "just like in your ear."

» BRIDGE TRAIL: Navajo: Na'iiníjé'é, "Bridge Across Parallel Place" (Jett n.d., 97). This trail, which seems to predate the Bosque Redondo hiatus, is named for a bridge of parallel logs that once spanned a crevice along its route. The logs are no longer there, and travelers now must leap the crack.

» TOMB OF THE WEAVER: Navajo: Hastiin Tl'ó Bitséyaa, "Mister Weaver's Under Rock (Cave)" (Jett n.d., 100). This Anasazi burial was found in an alcove in the southeast wall, on the downstream side of the juncture of Canyon del Muerto and Black Rock Canyon—the most prominent eastern tributary of del Muerto. The grave was against the cliff, inside a curved stone wall. The mummified body was wrapped in a blanket made of golden eagle down feathers, and lay on two cotton blankets, which in turn lay on a reed mat covering the floor of the grave. Accompanying the body were five pottery jars and four yucca-leaf baskets filled with cornmeal, husked corn, piñon nuts, beans, and salt. Also found was a stout wooden bow and a single arrow. But most unusual was the presence of skeins of cotton yarn that totaled more than two miles in length. A wooden spindle—a weaving tool—lay on the yarn.

» ANTELOPE HOUSE: [DB] Navajo: Jádí Deí-jeehí Kits'iilí, "Where Swift Ones (Antelope) Run Along Ruin" (Jett n.d., 99). Van Valkenburgh (1941, 23) gave the name 'Asgą' Dah Sitáni, "Dry Hide Hanging Up," but Jett asserts this name belongs to a feature just below Fir Tree Canyon. At the base of the northwest wall of the canyon, across from the mouth of Black Rock Canyon, is one of the largest Anasazi ruins in the Canyon de Chelly system. Named for red and white paintings of antelopes high on the canyon wall above the site, the ruin contains Basketmaker III through Pueblo III components, dating A.D. 700 to 1270. The pictographs are known as Jádí Deíjeehí ("Where Swift Ones Run Along.") The site contains two Basketmaker structures and, in the later Pueblo occupations, two distinct roomblocks with at least 23 rectangular rooms and three to five kivas, along with numerous small storage rooms. Local Navajos attribute the antelope paintings to Dibé Yázhí, "Little Sheep," a famed Navajo pictorialist of the middle nineteenth century. On the same wall, a number of glyphs of Anasazi origin can be seen (Van Valkenburgh 1941, 24).

Antelope House was partially excavated by Dr. Frank Palmer and Charles Lummis in an expedition of the Southwest Museum in 1907. The most interesting material collected consisted of a number of large corrugated pottery vessels containing infant burials. Earl Morris also did some work in this ruin for the Carnegie Institute, and Don P. Morris conducted extensive investigations in 1970–73.

» BLACK ROCK CANYON: [DB] Navajo: Tsézhiní Yistł'ah (Tsézhiní Nástłah), translated as "Curved Traprock" by Van Valkenburgh (1941,

23) and "Black Rock Cove" by Jett (n.d., 100), but literally "Inside Corner of the Traprock" (Young p.c. 1995). Some five and a half miles upstream from the Junction, this southside tributary of del Muerto is some eight miles long, with headwaters just north of Black Rock butte. A trail the Navajos call Haaz'áí Łání ("Many Step Ladders [trail]") comes down into the canyon from the south about a mile upstream from the mouth (Van Valkenburgh 1941, 23).

» LITTLE MIDDLE MESA: Navajo: 'Ata'deez'á Hayázhí, "Little Area Point Between" (Jett n.d., 91). This is the small peninsula of land between Black Rock Canyon and Canyon del Muerto. Also known as "The Peninsula."

» NAVAJO FORTRESS: (Also Black Rock Navajo Fortress and Fortress Rock.) Navajo: Tséláá, Nteel, "Wide Rock-Tip" (Jett n.d., 101), or possibly Tségháá', "Top of the Rock" (Young p.c. 1995). This site rests atop the isolated sandstone butte at the juncture of Canyon de Chelly and Black Rock Canyon. The site is accessible by Navajo Fortress Trail, Tséláá Ha'atiin ("Rock Trail Up"), a path that begins in the cleft separating the butte from the southeast rim, zigzags up the eastern face, and includes 11 pole ladders plus steps cut into the stone walls. The trip is quite precarious, involving narrow ledges and notched-log ladders. The site is fairly large, covering more than four square kilometers, and contains the ruins of 49 stone hogans and 22 defensive wall segments, all concentrated on the southeast corner of the butte.

According to Navajo tradition, three hundred Navajos evaded Kit Carson's 1864 round-up by seeking refuge here, pulling up the log ladders behind them and manning rifle pits along the trail. They are said to have lived on the rock from October of that year until March of 1865 (Fall, McDonald, and Magers 1981, 209–12).

» NAVAJO FORTRESS GAP: Navajo: Tséláá Ndeshgizh, "Rock-Tip Gap" (Jett n.d., 102). This name refers to the saddle between Navajo Fortress and Little Middle Mesa, the peninsula between Black Rock Canyon and Canyon del Muerto.

» STANDING COW RUIN: [DB] Navajo: Béégashii Sizíní Kits'iil, "Standing Cow Ruin." This ruin is a mile and a half up Canyon del Muerto from Antelope House at the foot of the north wall of the canyon. The site is named for Standing Cow Pictograph, Béégashii Sizíní ("Standing Cow") (Jett n.d., 105), a large painting on the canyon wall above the ruin, executed in grayish-black. This is considered one of the largest Anasazi sites in the canyon system, though not much remains visible today. When it was described by Cosmos Mindeleff from the Smithsonian Institution in 1883, nearly four hundred feet of masonry walls could be traced along the base of the canyon walls, and 55 rooms and three kivas were visible.

By 1939, this ruin appeared as a high mound against the canyon wall, topped by a large Navajo summer camp. Some of the old Anasazi walls have been augmented and used by the Navajos for storing corn and melons. The Standing Cow, apparently resembling the Mexican cattle, is reputed to have been painted by Dibé Yázhí, "Little Sheep," in the 1830s.

Nearby is Standing Cow Trail, also known as Crack in Rock Trail, which the Navajos call Tsék'iz Ha'atiin ("Rock Fissure Trail Up Out") (Jett n.d., 104). This path climbs the north cliff to the north rim of the canyon.

» SPANISH EXPEDITION MURAL: [DB] Navajo: Uncertain. Some two hundred yards downstream from Standing Cow Ruin, and high on the canyon wall, is a mural known as the Spanish Expedition Mural. In 1941, local Navajos stated that it was painted "three old men's lives ago" (literally thrice old age has killed), or some 250 years ago, about A.D. 1700 (Van Valkenburgh 1941, 24). However, Young (p.c. 1995) notes that the Navajo term "old age kills" refers to 104 years, and that the term Táade Sá Náoogáádáá', "Three Times Old Age Killed Ago," would equal 312 years, placing the date at closer to A.D. 1630. Like Standing Cow Pictograph, this painting is attributed to Dibé Yázhí.

The mural appears to record the first Spanish expedition seen in the Navajo country. The central figure is mounted, wearing a black cassock with a white cross. Surrounding him is a group of horsemen with flintlock rifles. The mural can be reached over a narrow, dangerous ledge trail.

» STANDING ROCK AND FLAT ROCK REFUGE: [DB] Navajo: Tsé 'Íí'áhí, "Standing Rock" (Jett n.d., 105), or Tsénteel, "Wide Rock" (Granger 1960, 11). Around the bend of the canyon upstream from Standing Cow Ruin sits Flat Rock Refuge—an isolated, high red sandstone butte that was once an important Navajo refuge from raiders. This may be the Navajo "fort" referred to in Spanish and early American documents, and which apparently has not been used since the Carson campaign of 1864. A number of old hogans sit atop the mound, reached by a series of notched poles.

Some Navajos attribute the masonry walls atop the butte to Hopis who intermarried with Navajos (Jett n.d., 106).

» MANY CHERRY CANYON: Navajo: Didzé Łání Nástl'ah, "Many Berries Cove" (Jett n.d., 106). Two and a half miles above the mouth of Black Rock Canyon, this minor tributary of del Muerto is named for wild cherry trees growing there.

Many Cherry Trail (Didzé Łání Ha'atiin, "Many Berries Trail Up Out") (Jett n.d., 107) ascends the head of Many Cherry Canyon.

» ROCK EXTENDING INTO WATER: Navajo: Tsé Táá'á, "Rock Extending Into Water" (Jett n.d., 107). This tail of rock is on the right side of del Muerto, above Many Cherry Canyon. There is another Rock Extending Into Water in Canyon de Chelly.

» BLUE CAVE PICTOGRAPH: Navajo: Dóola Dootl'izh Sizínígí, "Blue Bull that Stands" (Jett n.d., 107). This large Navajo pictograph is in a right-side crevice just downstream from Twin Trail Canyon. Roughly across the canyon is Turkey Trail (Tazhii Habitiin, "Turkey's Trail Up Out") (Jett n.d., 107), a foot trail that turkeys supposedly used.

» TWIN TRAIL CANYON: [DB, as "Cross Canyon Trail"] Navajo: 'Alnaashii Ha'atiin,

"Trails Up Out Opposite Each Other (or On Opposite Sides)" (Jett n.d., 108), translated as "Trails Up on Both Sides" by Young (p.c. 1995). Also, Tséyí Naakií Habitiin ("Twin Trail Canyon"). Located four miles upstream from the juncture with Black Rock Canyon, a pair of tributaries enter del Muerto from opposite sides. The two trails combine to form the route most commonly used in the past for Navajos to travel between the north rim and Black Rock Plateau (the mesa between Canyon de Chelly and Canyon del Muerto). Jett notes that the left-side trail (in Twin Trail Canyon) has largely fallen into disuse, but the trail from the north rim has been improved by the Park Service and is the second most heavily used access to del Muerto's interior (second only to the mouth of the Canyon).

The trail up the east side may be the one Van Valkenburgh referred to as Ch'ódáá'haazt'i' ("Trail Where the Fir Trees Reach the Canyon Rim") (Young p.c. 1995). It is used mostly for livestock. Jett notes that the twin trails are distinguished by specifying "eastward trail" (ha'a'aahjígo ha'atiiní) or "westward trail" ('e'e'aahjígo ha'atiiniigí).

Jett also identifies another trail in Twin Trail Canyon, Sunnyside Trail. Sháá' Ha'atiin ("Sunnyside Trail Up Out") is on the right (northeastern) wall of the canyon.

High on the right-hand wall of Twin Trail Canyon, near its mouth, is Twin Trail Ruin.

» STANDING ROCK: Navajo: Tsé 'Íí'áhí, "Up-Extending (Standing) Rock" (Jett n.d., 108). This monolith of red sandstone in the middle of Twin Trail Canyon is about a third of the way upstream from its mouth.

» BIG CAVE: [DB] Navajo: Tsé'áántsoh, "Big Space Under Rock (Cave)," erroneously named Tsétsoh, "Big Rock" by Van Valkenburgh (1941, 25). High up in the northwest wall of a rounded rincon some two miles up del Muerto from the mouth of Twin Trail Canyon, this is one of the largest caves in the canyon system. It contains Anasazi ruins subjected to early and intensive excavations, beginning with Earl Morris's excavations in the 1920s. The site dates to A.D. 331–835, and included three fascinating interments.

One contained the remains of an old man whose shins had been broken and remarkably well set and mended before death. Another held the remains of 14 infants in a slab-lined cyst that previously had functioned as a storage bin. These overlay the skeletons of four children in a large basket. The third interment has been titled "Burial of the Hands," for, though apparently undisturbed through the centuries, it contained only a pair of lower arms, hands still attached. A large basket covered this burial; and three abalone shell pendant necklaces were wrapped about the wrists. A pair of fine unworn sandals, a small basket of white shell beads, and a cache of mallard and parrot feathers accompanied the hands.

Jett (n.d., 109) lists "Screen Cave" (because it is "screened" by a curving arm of sandsone projecting from the rim) and "Royal Arch" (refering to the shape of the cave or rock-shelter) as names also applied to this feature.

» BIG CAVE GAP: Navajo: Tséyaahatsoh Ndeeshgizh, "Big Space Under Rock Gap" (Jett n.d., 109). At the end of the narrow point of sandstone screening Big Cave is a "gunsight" formed by two pinnacles separated by a deep notch. This is Big Cave Gap.

» DRY HIDE HANGING UP: Navajo: Asga Dah Sitání, "Stiff Dried Hide Lying Up at an Elevation" (Jett n.d., 110). This name, which Van Valkenburgh erroneously applied to Antelope House Ruin, actually refers to a whitish water-stain pattern on the left wall of del Muerto just below the mouth of Fir Tree Canyon. The stain resembles a buckskin left hanging over a line to dry, with its head, legs, and tail pointing down.

» FORK ROCK: Navajo: Dooyá Ndeeshgizh, "Not-go (Forbidden?) Gap" (Jett n.d., 10). This two-pronged sandstone monument stands at the end of a point of rock in the next right-side cove upstream from Big Cave.

» FIR TREE CANYON: Navajo: Nástl'ah, "Cove (Where) Douglas Firs Extend Up Out in a Line (to the Rim)" (Jett n.d., 110). This left-side canyon is named for its vegetation. Jett connects the trees in the canyon to Ch'ó Haazt'i' ("Dou-

glas Firs Extend Up Out in a Line"), a myth of the Coyoteway, in which the leader of the Yellow Corn People jumped from a cliff in Fir Tree Canyon and left footprints in the floor of the canyon, from which Douglas firs sprang up.

Fir Tree Trail, Ch'ódáá Haazt'i' Ha'atiin, "Trail Went Up Out (where the Douglas Fir Trees Extend Up Out In a Line [to the Rim])" (Jett n.d., 111), a horse trail, climbs the head of Fir Tree Canyon. It has also been called Fir Line Trail.

» GIANT TRACK CANYON: Navajo: Yé'iitsoh Bikooh, "Big Yei's Wash" (Jett n.d., 111). This tributary of Fir Tree Canyon is named for giant tracks near the head of the canyon. The tracks apparently resemble dinosaur footprints, and are attributed to Big Yei (Yéiitsoh).

A trail in the canyon is named Yé'iitshoh Haayáhí ("Big Yei Went Up and Out") (Jett n.d., 111).

» FIR TREE ALCOVE: Navajo: Tséyaa Ch'ó 'Íí'áhí, "Under Rock Standing Douglas Fir" (Jett n.d., 112). This large rock shelter (shallow cave) is on the sloping foot of del Muerto's left wall, upstream from the mouth of Fir Tree Canyon. For decades, a fir tree in this alcove was the source of boughs for the ruffs of yeibichai dancers. The tree died sometime prior to 1984.

» SHEEP POINT CANYON: Navajo: Dibé Dáád Nástlah, "Bighorn Sheep Ambush Cove" (Jett n.d., 112). Situated on the left side of del Muerto about a half-mile upstream from Fir Tree Canyon, this canyon is named for Sheep Point.

» SHEEP POINT: Navajo: Dibé Dáád, "Bighorn Sheep Ambush" (Jett n.d., 112). This point of sandstone forms the north wall of Sheep Point Canyon. In the old days, it was a prime bighorn trap.

» HANGING (POLE) LADDER TRAIL: Navajo: Haaz'éí Dah Hidédlo'í Ha'atiin, "Dangling Ladder Trail Up Out," or Haazéí Hidétání, "Hanging Ladders Trail Up Out" (Jett n.d., 113). A foot trail ascending the head of Hanging Ladder Canyon, just up from Sheep Point Canyon. Log ladders in a fissure are secured in place with ropes. This trail has also been called Many Ladders Trail. Jett found no name for the canyon itself.

» TSEH YA KIN CANYON: Navajo: Tséyaakiní Nástl'ah, "Under Rock (Cave) House Cove" (Jett n.d., 113). Nearly a mile upstream from Sheep Point is a left-side tributary, which bears the Navajo name of Mummy Cave Ruins. Location of an unmaintained horse trail, Tséyaakiní Ha'atiin ("Under Rock (Cave) House Trail Up Out."

» MUMMY CAVE: [DB] Navajo: Tséyaakin, "House Under the Rock." (This name is applied to other ruins in Navajoland, such as Poncho House on lower Chinle Wash.) Fifteen miles from the mouth of Canyon del Muerto, the canyon breaks up with a number of deep rincons coming in from all sides. The streambed turns rocky, and spruce trees dot the landscape, even to the canyon floor. Here, at the end of a long peninsula projecting from the east wall of the canyon, sits a pair of large caves or alcoves, several hundred feet above the canyon floor, known collectively as Mummy Cave. The name is sometimes applied as well to Mummy House, an Anasazi ruin constructed in the pair of adjacent alcoves. This ruin is one of the largest in the del Muerto system, and contains evidence of occupation from the earliest dates of human presence in the canyon—about A.D. 300—all the way to the abandonment of the canyons as permanent habitations by the Anasazi.

The two large caves are joined by a narrow ledge. The eastern portion contains 55 rectangular rooms and four kivas; the western alcove holds 20 rooms. Seven rooms—including a three-story tower—were constructed on the central ledge, but this structure postdates the other buildings (dating to A.D. 1284), and contains Mesa Verdean–style masonry. Throughout the ruin vestiges of painted plaster remain.

The English name is derived from the discovery, during an archaeological expedition of the late 1880s, of two mummified skeletons weathering out of cysts in the high, steep talus slope below the ruin. It is also written that the leader of that expedition, Colonel Stevenson, gave the canyon itself its name, "Canyon del Muertos," Spanish for "Canyon of the Dead People," later shortened to "del Muerto," "Dead Man."

A large roofless rectangular structure may have served as a great kiva in the Chaco tradition, as did a similar structure at Fire Temple Ruin on Mesa Verde (Colorado). This structure at Mummy Cave had strong Mesa Verdean characteristics (Ferguson and Rohn 1987, 176).

» MASSACRE CAVE: [DB] Navajo: 'Adah 'Ahodoonilí, "Where People Were Pushed Away Downward (from a Height)," or Naakaii Hojííghání, "Spaniards Massacred" (Jett n.d., 114). Also called Cave of the Bones. Two miles upstream from Mummy Cave, where the canyon bends sharply eastward, Massacre Cave sits atop a steep talus in a long rock shelter lying at the foot of the north cliff of the canyon.

In 1805 a raiding party composed of Spaniards, Opata Indians (from Mexico), and Zunis under Lieutenant Colonel Antonio Narbona coolly massacred some 70 Navajo women and children in the cave by shooting from a nearby peninsula of the rim. The able-bodied Navajo men were in the Lukachukai Mountains hunting, and the women, children, and old people, after spotting a party of Spaniards at the mouth of Canyon de Chelly, fled to the cave. The Spaniards gave chase, following the west rim of Canyon del Muerto as far as the head of Trail The Mexican Came Down Canyon, where they split their force. One party descended into the canyon, while the other party stayed up on the rim to cover the descent into and movements within the canyon. Upon reaching the base of the talus slide, the canyon party of Spanish and Zunis attacked, but they were driven back by the Navajos' stones and arrows.

The party on top could not locate the Navajos until an old woman, not realizing that enemies remained on the rocks above, screamed curses at the attackers below. The rim party then opened fire, their heavy musket balls striking directly or, more often, ricocheting into the huddled Navajos. The marks of these balls may still be seen on the sandstone walls of the cave, and a confused jumble of human skeletal material lies on the floor. It is interesting to note, however, that Narbona's records do not agree with Navajo tradition placing this battle in Massacre Cave (McNitt 1972, 43–44).

Above the cave is a place called Naa'azhníídee'é ("Where Two Fell Down"), where a Navajo woman is said to have climbed from Massacre Cave and wrestled with a Spanish soldier, pulling him with her as she fell off the cliff. (Jett n.d., 115).

Massacre Cave Trail (Hazneest'í'í, "Where They Sneaked Up") is a path followed by two Navajo men who tried to reach the cave to check for survivors. Fearing for their own safety, however, they never reached the cave. This trail is "taboo" for Navajos (Jett n.d., 115).

» GOAT LEDGE: Navajo: Tłízhí Nínílganí, "Goat Became Emaciated" (Jett n.d., 116). About a half-mile upstream from Massacre Cave, there is a high point on the south cliff on which a goat starved to death.

» BAD TRAIL: [DB] Navajo: Hóchxǫ́ Ha'atiin, "Bad Trail Up." Two miles above Massacre Cave and on the same side of the canyon is a trail used as a shortcut down into the canyon from the north rim. The trail was found and used by a man who escaped the Long Walk to the Bosque Redondo in 1864. Van Valkenburgh noted that it had fallen into disuse by 1939 (due to the slipping of certain sections and removal of old poles over bad sections), but Jett suspects it has since been refurbished.

» PINE TREE CANYON: Navajo: Ndíshchíí Haazt'i' Nástl'ah, "Ponderosa Pines Extending Up Out In a Line Cove" (Jett n.d., 117). A right-side tributary about a mile and a half upstream from Massacre Cave. It is named for pines on its slopes and rims.

In del Muerto near the mouth of Pine Tree Canyon is Narrow Canyon Trail ('Atíin Honítzaa), and the canyon houses Pine Tree Trail, Ndíshchíí Haazt'i Ha'atiin ("Ponderosa Pines Extend Up Out In a Line Trail Up Out"), mostly along the eastern wall, near the canyon's head.

» MIDDLE TRAIL CANYON: Navajo: 'Ata' Ha'atiin Nástl'ah, "Trail Up Out Between Cove," and Nínánízaadí Ha'atiin Nástlah, "Long Trail Across Up Out Cove" (Jett n.d., 118). This is a significant right-hand tributary of del Muerto above Pine Tree Canyon.

A trail up the first right-hand branch of this canyon is known as Middle Trail ('Ata' Ha'atiin, "Trail Up Out Between"). It is also referred to as Slab Rock Trail, and Jett suggests it is most likely the trail that a detachment of Spanish soldiers used after the incident at Massacre Cave. Interestingly, the name Middle Trail is also applied to another, easier, but longer path that ascends the entire length of Middle Trail Canyon. This one is more commonly called Long Trail (Nízaad Ha'atiin, "Long Trail Up Out").

Jett (n.d., 122) has determined that Middle Trail is the Trail Mexicans Came Down (see below).

» CHARCOAL CLIFF: Navajo: Tsék'i Na'asht'ézhí, "Charcoal Mark on Rock" (Jett n.d., 119). On the north wall of del Muerto, slightly upstream from Middle Trail Canyon, a slightly overhanging cliff protects a number of Navajo charcoal drawings.

A trail ascending a small side canyon above the cliff is known as Windy Trail (Hol Hahayólí, "With People Pushed Upward By Wind," or Hatsxil Háayolí, "Wind-swept Vulva"), named for the propensity of the wind to blow up women's skirts (Jett n.d., 120).

» WHIRLWIND CAVE: Navajo: Tséyaa Hahwiiyoolí, "Where the Wind Eddies Under Rock" (Jett n.d., 119). This minor rock shelter is on the canyon's south face, upstream from Charcoal Cliff, and is named for the wind that swirls sand in the alcove.

» BIG FLOW CANYON: Navajo: Náálí Hatsoh Nástl'ah, "Big It Flows Downward Area Cove" (Jett n.d., 120). This southside tributary of del Muerto is named for a large quantity of water that runs down the canyon. "Náá-" refers to a straight-down flow, and there is a waterfall about three quarters of a mile up the canyon.

Náálí Hatsoh Ha'atiin, "Big It Flows Downward Area Trail Up Out" (Jett n.d., 121) is a footpath acsending the head of the canyon.

» SPANISH TRAIL: Navajo: Naakaii 'Adáánání Ha'atiin, "Where Spaniards Descended Trail Up Out" (Jett n.d., 121). Though carrying the same name Van Valkenburgh applied to Trail the Mexicans Came Down (see Middle Trail Canyon), this steep horse trail travels up the talus in a shallow south-side cove a short distance up del Muerto from Big Flow Canyon.

» TRAIL THE MEXICANS CAME DOWN CANYON: [DB] Navajo: Naakaii 'Adáánání, "Trail the Mexicans Came Down" (Young and Morgan 1987, 576) or Naakaii Habitiin, "Mexican Trail Leading Up and Out" (Van Valkenburgh 1941, 26). A mile above Bad Trail is the mouth of a two-mile-long canyon that enters the main channel from the northeast.

A horse trail from the rim to the floor (Young and Morgan 1987, 576) of this canyon is the one utilized by Lieutenant Colonel Narbona's men in the attack upon Massacre Cave in 1805. There is a good-sized Anasazi ruin in this canyon called Canyon Ruin.

By Van Valkenburgh's description, this canyon seems to be the same as that labeled "Middle Trail Canyon" on modern maps. It is the single most conspicuous branch off del Muerto to the left as one travels upstream. It leads generally north while the main channel swings to the east.

» POISON IVY CANYON: Navajo: 'Ashíshjíízh Sikaad Nástl'ah, "Poison Ivy Stands Spread Out Cove" (Jett n.d., 123). This canyon, housing an Anasazi ruin and a trail ('Ashíshjíízh Sikaad Ha'atiin, "Poison Ivy Stands Spread Out Trail Up Out"), is two and a half miles upstream from Big Flow Canyon.

» BIRD HEAD ROCK: Navajo: Tsídii Binii'í, "Bird's Face" (Jett n.d., 124). This rock, projecting from the north rim of del Muerto, resembles a bird's head in profile. Below it is a trail, Tsídii Binii'í Ha'atiin (Bird's Face Trail Up Out) that

has fallen into disuse due to the collapse of a cliff wall.

Cotton was introduced to Canyon de Chelly during the Basketmaker periods, but did not appear in textiles until the early Pueblo era (Bohrer 1972, 3). The peach trees so plentiful today spread from the Hopi Mesas, where the Spanish introduced them in the seventeenth century. Cottonwood and willow trees were introduced as erosion control by the National Park Service in the 1930s (Ambrose 1975).

There are more than five hundred Anasazi sites in the monument (McDonald 1976, 6). The earliest evidence of Navajo occupation in the region is at Tsé Ta'á Ruin, dating no earlier than A.D. 1700 (about the time they were pushed from the Dinétah by the Utes). The canyon figures in the Zuni migration narrative and is important to their Sword Swallower Society, as are Chaco Canyon and Mesa Verde (Ferguson and Hart 1985, 126).

CANYON DIABLO: [DB] (5500–4700 ft) Coconino County, AZ. Navajo: Kin Łigaaí, "White House," referring to old Volz Trading Post (see Canyon Diablo Trading Post) on the Atlantic and Pacific Railroad (presently the Burlington Northern Santa Fe). This 30-mile-long string of canyons heads in the region southwest of Meteor Crater, cutting through the Kaibab Sandstone. It flows north and intersects I-40 at Two Guns before continuing north and northeast to join the Little Colorado River at Leupp.

The first known White men to cross Canyon Diablo were Lieutenant A. W. Whipple's survey party on December 10, 1863. One of the early trading posts in the Navajo country was opened here by F. W. Volz in the 1890s. In 1898 dissent between White stockmen and Navajos near the canyon resulted in the killing of two Whites. After some delay, the Navajos implicated in the melee were brought to trial at Flagstaff. They pleaded self-defense, and surprisingly, given the usual outcome of such legal proceedings, they received little or no punishment.

New reservation boundaries prescribed in President Theodore Roosevelt's Executive Order of November 14, 1901, placed this area within the

Leupp jurisdiction of the reservation, and between 1929 and 1934, additional lands in this region were added to the Navajo Reservation by purchase of railroad and private property.

An old stage station and Wilson Pueblo (an Anasazi ruin dating to about A.D. 1050, excavated by the Museum of Northern Arizona) lie near Two Guns on I-40, three miles north of the site of the old Canyon Diablo Trading Post.

This canyon figures in the Zuni migration narrative (Ferguson and Hart 1985, 127).

CANYON DIABLO TRADING POST: (5200 ft) Coconino County, AZ. Navajo: Uncertain, but likely the same as Diablo Canyon. One of the earliest posts in the region, established in 1882, when Pennsylvanian Charles H. Algert set up shop in an abandoned boxcar as the railroad bridge was constructed spanning the canyon. Later, the business shifted to Indian clientele, and was sold to Frederick W. Volz between 1897 and 1899. Volz, backed by Lorenzo Hubbell, had previously been trading at Red Lake (Cow Springs) in competition with the Babbitt Brothers. His post in Canyon Diablo was just north of the Atlantic and Pacific Railroad (now the Burlington Northern Santa Fe) crossing, and its construction coincided with a range war between the Navajos and White ranchers.

In 1902 President Theodore Roosevelt established the Leupp jurisdiction, extending the reservation westward by 24 square miles and subjecting Volz to Indian Service regulation. He was soon in disagreement with the local Indian agent, Joseph E. Maxwell, and his license was not renewed after 1904, though he continued to trade for some years thereafter (McNitt 1962, 270). Volz sold his business to Babbitt Brothers in 1912, and they moved it several miles south to U.S. Highway 66 (now I-40) in 1922 (Babbitt 1986, 4).

When the railroad moved, a new post was opened by Joe Stiles in 1934 (Richardson 1986, 136).

CANYON PADRE: [DB] (6600–5200 ft) Coconino County, AZ. Navajo: Gadtah Dahisk'id Bikooh, "Hill among Cedars Canyon" (U.S.

Indian Claims Commission n.d., vol. VI, vii; spelling corrected by Young, p.c. 1995). This deep, rugged, 20-mile-long canyon is tributary to Canyon Diablo. It heads approximately seven miles south of I-40, two miles east of Deep and Potato lakes (both ephemeral) between Mormon and Anderson Canyons. It flows north and northeast, turning southeast for the final five miles, entering Canyon Diablo 10 miles upstream from that channel's confluence with the Little Colorado River.

CARRIZO MOUNTAINS: [DB] (9412 ft) Apache County, AZ. Navajo: Dził Náhoozłii, erroneously interpreted as "Circular Mountains" by Van Valkenburgh (1941, 27), is actually "Mountain that Gropes Around" (McPherson 1992, 22). The Spanish "Carrizo" means "Reed Grass" (Gregory 1915, 150). The large, isolated pine- and spruce-covered range is located in the extreme northern end of the Chuska, Lukachukai, Carrizo chain. Pastora Peak is the highest point. The Carrizos lie south of U.S. Highway 160 and Teec Nos Pos, with the eastern slope touching the New Mexico state line. These mountains were also known as the Polonta Mountains (Correll 1976, vol. 1, 481), presumably Spanish, but translation unknown.

These mountains are separated from the Lukachukais by the Red Rock country. They were shown as the Sierra de Chegui on the Dominguez-Escalante map of 1776 (though Dave Brugge suggests that this referred to the entire Lukachukai-Tunicha-Chuska range), and as the Sierra de Carriso on the J. F. McComb map of 1850. Major J. S. Simpson passed over a trail along the southern flank in 1858.

Many Navajo traditions refer to these mountains, which constitute the lower extremities of the mythological Yódídziil, Goods of Value Range, of which Chuska Peak is the head. (Beautiful Mountain is his feet and Shiprock is a bow or medicine pouch he carries.) This figure is the male counterpart of the female anthropomorphic figure, Pollen Mountain, made up of Black Mesa, Navajo Mountain, Balakai Mesa, and other features.

Some medicine men state that certain Navajo

clans took their names from places in this range. In the Navajo creation myth, Shásh Na'ałkaahí (Tracking Bear) was killed by the Twin War Gods in these mountains (Benally et al. 1982, 17). This may be the range alluded to as "Dziłyi'" in Powell's (1887, 385) discourse on the Mountain Chant.

Until the 1920s and 1930s, this was the habitat of a small number of grizzly bears. Beaver and muskrat still inhabit the upper elevations. Anasazi ruins dot the lower slopes. Rumors of silver and other ore deposits in the Carrizos resulted in many encroachments by White prospectors, and great holes visible on the slopes were created by prospectors who roamed over the mountains from the 1880s until the 1940s.

In the 1880s a prospector named Swift was killed in the Carrizos by Niche, a Navajo. Niche was caught, tried, and convicted, and was sent to the penitentiary two years later. One rush lasting from 1889 to 1892 led to a confrontation with the Diné that was dispelled only by cavalry intervention. In March 1890, Agent C. E. Vandever (called Bináá Dootł'izhí, "Blue Eyes") learned that a party of 50 prospectors had illegally entered the Carrizos. Accompanied by Chee Dodge, Ben Whittick (well-known photographer of the 1880s and 1890s), and two troops of cavalry from Fort Wingate, he rescued 15 miners holding out against infuriated Navajos, and promptly escorted them off the reservation.

Despite fantastic stories, no appreciable amounts of any minerals have been taken from this area. The Navajo Commission examined the mountains in 1892, but found no minerals, and so allowed the Navajos to keep their mountain (McPherson 1988, 87–89). More rumors led to 640 acres of land being leased to George F. Hull at the turn of the century. He employed six Navajos at five dollars per day, but came up dry. In the 1940s, however, vanadium was discovered and mined (Leighton and Kluckhohn 1974, 122).

CASTLE BUTTE: (6000 ft) Navajo County, AZ. Navajo: Uncertain. This 650-ft-high butte is two miles east of Arizona Highway 87, ten miles south of Tees Toh (see Dilcon). Castle Butte

Trading Post opened here between 1906 and 1910 (Kelley 1977, 253).

CEDAR RIDGE: (6200 ft) Coconino County, AZ. Navajo: Yaaniilk'id, "Hill Slopes Down and Ends"; also Ndeelk'id, "Ridge" (Young and Morgan 1987, 605). This name is applied to the eastern end of Bodaway Mesa, where a high sandstone ridge parallels Hamblin Creek and U.S. Highway 89, two miles southwest of the community of Cedar Ridge, and some 40 miles north of Cameron. In the first half of this century, this was a favorite camping place for the small band of Strip Paiutes who are remnants of Padawa's old band.

CEDAR RIDGE TRADING POST: [DB] (5900 ft) Coconino County, AZ. Navajo: K'iishzhinii, "Black Alder" (Young and Morgan 1987, 511). This trading post is located on U.S. Highway 89, about seven miles north of the Gap, and named for the geologic formation two miles to the southwest. The post was established in a partnership between John P. Kerley and the Babbitt Brothers prior to 1920 (McNitt 1962, 266–67; Kelley 1977, 254). According to Hegeman (1963, 61), the original post was east of the highway; it was later moved to its present location adjacent to the road.

CEDAR SPRINGS TRADING POST: [DB] (6300 ft) Navajo County, AZ. Navajo: Uncertain. This post is situated near a well-known small but permanent spring in the Hopi Buttes region south of the Hopi Mesas. Located three miles east of present-day Arizona Highway 87, four miles southeast of Tees Toh, this post, established by Jake Tobin prior to 1885 (McNitt 1962, 204; Kelley 1977, 251), was the first in the Hopi Buttes region. Long (1992) says the post was owned by Lorenzo Hubbell in 1910. The government stockman's headquarters located at Castle Butte was transferred to Cedar Springs in 1920 when the Indian Department purchased the land on which the spring is located. In the 1930s fine grasses—known as among the best horse ranges in the Navajo country—were the norm in the now barren Hopi Buttes region.

Part of the Cedar Springs region was added to the Navajo Reservation between 1910 and 1929 by purchase, and the Boundary Bill of 1934 included all of the Cedar Springs area south of the Hopi Reservation to the present reservation line. This location was headquarters for Land Management District No. 7, and included the district supervisor's residence and other buildings. Seba Dalkai Day School is six miles northwest. Coal mines in Giant's Chair (not to be confused with the Giant's Chair on Polacca Wash) were called Black Chief and American Coal Company Mines.

CHAISTLA BUTTE: (6098 ft) Navajo County, AZ. Navajo: Chaa'istł'ah, "Beaver Rincon" (Gregory 1915, 150). This sandstone butte is a mile east of U.S. Highway 163 and five miles north of U.S. Highway 160, in the Little Capitan Valley, southeast of Monument Valley.

CHAMBERS: [DB] (5750 ft) Apache County, AZ. Navajo: Ch'izhóó, "Sand sage (Artemesia frigida)." A small trading community at the junction of I-40 and northbound U.S. Highway 191, some 49 miles east of Holbrook. In the 1940s, there was a bentonite mine (Filtro Company of California) four miles northeast of this crossroads. The trading post opened in the late 1870s (Kelley 1977), and was run at some point by L. J. Cassidy. The Anglo name was for a man associated with the Atchison, Topeka and Santa Fe Railroad, although a man named Chambers was associated with the Chichiltah Trading Post of the same era some 30 miles to the east in New Mexico (Van Valkenburgh 1941, 37). Its proximity to Taylor Spring, called 'Asdzání Taah Yíyá ("Woman Went into Water") by the Navajos a mile and a half to the west, originally made the location important to the Navajos. This spring was once the property of a Navajo called Tsénáséyá, "I Walked Around the Rock."

According to Van Valkenburgh (1941, 36), the Navajo name for the spring derives from a story that many years ago a woman of the Tsi'naajinii clan left her home near present Crownpoint and went to the White River Apache country where she married an Apache and had a daughter. When the girl grew to womanhood her mother sent her

back to her own people. The girl stopped at Taylor Spring and went into it. This was taboo, and gave the spring its Navajo name.

CHAMBERS RUIN: (5750 ft) Apache County, AZ. Navajo: Uncertain, possibly the generic Kits'iilí ("Shattered House") used for so many ruins on the reservation. This Chacoan greathouse community on the Rio Puerco of the West, near Chambers, is associated with three prehistoric road segments (Gabriel 1991, 277–78).

CHARLEY DAY SPRING: [DB] (4950 ft) Coconino County, AZ. Navajo: Séí Haha'eeł, "Sand Floats Up Out" (Young and Morgan 1987, 684). A spring, and an archaeological and paleontological site located in northeast Tuba City. This spring was developed in 1928 by C. L. Walker, superintendent of the old Western Navajo Jurisdiction. In the course of excavations, the teeth of extinct species of horse, bison, camel, and elephant were encountered, in association with dart points and other evidences of early man.

The Anglo name for the spring came from Charley Day, a blind old Navajo scout who served in the Army during the Apache campaigns of 1885, whose hogan was at this spring.

CHAVES PASS RUIN: [DB] (approx. 6600 ft) Coconino County, AZ. Navajo: Uncertain. Hopi: Chópkwitsáłaa, "Place of the Antelope Notch." Late thirteenth- and fourteenth-century Anasazi ruins located in Chaves Pass, some 35 miles southwest of Winslow.

The large ruin, rectangular in layout and built of traprock, is believed to have been named after an old Spaniard who was killed in the pass by the Apaches. Some, however, say that it was named after Lieutenant Colonel J. Francisco Chaves, builder of old Fort Wingate (see San Rafael, New Mexico) and who guided the first gubernatorial party to Arizona in 1863 (see Navajo Springs) (Van Valkenburgh 1941, 37).

Indians and exploring parties, and later the old Albuquerque–Fort Whipple Star Mail Route, went through Chaves Pass, over the old trail from the Little Colorado River country to the Verde River and southern Arizona.

Van Valkenburgh quotes Navajo mythology in telling of 12 sacred antelope who migrated from the Carrizo Mountains to Rock Point on the Chinle Wash, to Be'ek'id Hatsoh, "Big Lake" (west of Chinle), on to the gap between Ganado and Steamboat Canyon, and then to Chaves Pass. After the trip all but two died, the male antelope taking the upper butte and the female taking the lower.

CHEVLON BUTTE: (6800 ft) Coconino County, AZ. Navajo: Jadi Bukiikaad, probably a misspelling of Jadí Bik'iilkaad ("Covered Antelope"). This conical butte sits seven miles southeast of Sunset Mountain, approximately midway between Chevlon Creek and Clear Creek. According to informants of the U.S. Indian Claims Commission, Navajos occupied this region prior to their removal to the Bosque Redondo in 1863–64 (U.S. Indian Claims Commission n.d., vol. IV, 729).

CHILCHINBITO: [DB] (6000 ft) Navajo County, AZ. Navajo: Chiiłchin Bii'Tó or Tsiiłchin Bii'Tó, "Spring in the Sumacs (Rhus trilebata)" (Young and Morgan 1987, 272), "Scented Reed Water" (Gillmore and Wetherill 1934, 92). Also Bitterweed Springs, after the trading post. A trading post, chapter seat, and school on the northeast flank of Black Mesa, a mile and a half southwest of Navajo Route 59, 14 miles south of the junction of that road with U.S. Highway 160. In the 1940s, a Soil Conservation Service Demonstration Area (of 16,586 acres) was here. The community is situated in a wooded cove and badly broken country below the northeastern rim of Black Mountain some 25 miles south of Kayenta.

According to Van Valkenburgh, Navajos tell that once the Paiutes chased a Navajo from Kayenta to Chilchinbito, where other Navajos ambushed the Paiutes. The Paiutes' bones were used as late as the 1940s by local medicine men in the 'Ana'í Ndaa', the Enemyway Chant, commonly called the Squaw Dance (and formerly called the War Dance). Tsiiłchin, or sumac, growing around this spring was favored by Navajo women for use in making basketry.

CHILCHINBITO TRADING POST: (6000 ft) Navajo County, AZ. Navajo: See Chilchinbito. This trading post was operated by George Washington Sampson (known locally as Hastiin Báí, "Gray Man") as early as 1902, and certainly by 1911 (McNitt 1962, 214–15). It is unclear whether this is the post identified by Van Valkenburgh as "Bitterweed Springs."

CHINDE MESA: (6000 ft) Apache County, AZ. Navajo: Ch'įįdii: "Ghost (or Spirit) Mesa." A small, irregular mesa on the northern boundary of Petrified Forest National Park. Its name supposedly derived from an incident in which USGS topographic engineers startled local Navajos by emerging from a "chinde hogan" on the mesa in 1936.

Author's Note: Traditional Navajos have a healthy respect for the spirits of the dead. So much so, that they will not use a hogan (or any other structure) in which an individual has died, for fear of being harassed by the "ghost" or "chinde" of the deceased. Thus, any hogan in which a person has died is abandoned after the destruction of its north wall—to provide the chinde an avenue of departure. In this incident, if it is true, the topographers were mistaken for ghosts.

CHINLE: [DB] (5058 ft) (Population: 5,590) Apache County, AZ. Also Chinlee, Chin Lee, Tsinlee. Navajo: Ch'ínílį́, "Water Outlet," referring to the mouth of Canyon de Chelly. This thriving community (at the junction of U.S. Highway 191 and Navajo Route 7) began as a government settlement, along the south bank of the de Chelly fork of Chinle Wash, a mile west of the mouth of Canyon de Chelly. The community is the gateway to Canyon de Chelly National Monument, the boundaries of which now abut Chinle's eastern margins. One of the largest and fastest growing towns on the reservation, Chinle is now a major trading center and tourism destination, with motels (most notably the Thunderbird Lodge, formerly a guest ranch—see Day's Chinle Trading Post) and multiple trading posts and galleries. A major school complex (Arizona Public Schools) is situated in Chinle, along with many multi-family housing units, swelling the population of the community in a short time.

In 1910 the fifth boarding school on the reservation was located here. In the 1930s and 1940s, the U.S. Indian Irrigation Service located a maintenance camp here. The Indian Service Irrigation District included 771 acres of excellent agricultural land serviced by a diversion dam, and ran from Chinle down the valley to the vicinity of Many Farms (formerly the Chinle Valley Store), 10 miles north.

Historically, the town has included such traders as Lorenzo Hubbell, C. N. Cotton, C. Garcia, L. McSparron, and Wallace Gorman. The Franciscan Fathers and the Presbyterians both hosted missions in Chinle.

The vicinity has been known to Whites for nearly two centuries. Spanish and New Mexican expeditions of war and trade came here until the beginning of the American occupation. The first visit to the locality by American military forces occurred in the fall of 1849, under the command of Lieutenant Colonel John Washington, accompanied by the territorial governor, James S. Calhoun, Captain Henry Lafayette Dodge, Lieutenant James H. Simpson, artist Edward Kern, and other members of Washington's command.

On the small knoll some one hundred yards north of the Thunderbird Lodge, they held a council with Navajo chiefs Mariano Chavez, Zarcillos Largos, and Chapiton. The council led to the signing of the Treaty of 1848, and the troops moved on through the pass along the southeast rim of Canyon de Chelly and across the Defiance Plateau along approximately the same route as the later Chinle to Fort Defiance Road (Navajo Route 7).

During the winter of 1864, at the location of the historic council, Colonel Christopher Carson, Captain Francis McCabe, and Captain Albert Pfeiffer accepted the surrender of about 50 de Chelly Navajos under Hastiin Chooyiní (Mr. Humpback) and the Navajo woman chief, K'íníbaa', "She Made a Discovery While on the Warpath."

The first trading post was established at Chinle in 1882 (at a site later occupied by Dick Dunnaway) by a Mexican, Naakaii Yázhí, "Little Mexican." This trader operated from a tent, and was ejected the following year by Dennis M. Rior-

dan, the Navajo agent. Samuel E. Day and Anson C. Damon established a small trading camp here in 1885, and Michael Donovan took over that post. In 1887, C. N. Cotton succeeded Donovan and in 1888–89, the Lingle Brothers ran a store at Chinle. Many others have followed these early traders.

The Franciscan Fathers established their first Navajo mission here in 1904, under the guidance of Father Leopold Osterman. In 1906, Navajo Agent Ruben Perry, while attempting to force Navajo children into school at Fort Defiance, was overpowered and held captive by Doo Yáłti'í, "Silent One," and his followers for two days. Soldiers later captured the rebels, who were sent for a year to Alcatraz Prison in San Francisco Bay before being transferred to Fort Huachuca, in extreme southern Arizona.

In the Emergence story of the Navajo creation legend, a ceremony was held near Chinle to celebrate the "nubility" of Asdzą́ą́nádleehí, or Changing Woman (Matthews 1897, 104, 134, 234, spelling corrected by Young, p.c. 1995).

CHINLE WASH: (5058–4200 ft) Apache County, AZ, San Juan County, Utah. Navajo: Same as for community of Chinle. This stream is formed by the confluence of De Chelly and Del Muerto Washes at the mouth of the Canyon de Chelly system, just east of the community of Chinle. From here it turns north and travels some 85 miles through Many Farms and Rock Point to empty into the San Juan River in Utah, approximately midway between Bluff and Mexican Hat. Along the way, it is fed by the major tributaries of Nazlini Wash, Black Mountain Wash, Lukachukai Wash, Laguna Creek, and Walker Creek.

Troops under Major Henry L. Kendrick called the wash Rio de Chelly (or Rio de Cheille or Rio de Chella) in 1853, since it came forth from the mouth of the canyon complex (McNitt 1972, 235).

CHOAL CANYON: (4600–4300 ft) Coconino County, AZ. Also Chaol. Navajo: Chá'oł, "Piñon" (Gregory 1915, 150). This 1000-ft-deep canyon is tributary to Navajo Canyon approximately 18 miles upstream (east) of the larger channel's confluence with Lake Powell. When the lake is at its peak holding capacity, it actually encroaches so deeply into Navajo Canyon that Chaol Canyon can be said to empty directly into Lake Powell.

CIÉNEGA AMARILLA: (7000 ft) Apache County, AZ. Navajo: Ts'íhootso, "Meadow Extends Out Horizontally" (Young and Morgan 1987, 742). This broad, grassy region lies between present-day Window Rock and St. Michaels. The Spanish explorers named it Ciénaga Amarilla ("Yellow Marsh") in apparent reference to a multitude of sunflowers that grew here.

A trading post was first opened here sometime before 1890 by a Defiance trader named Caddy Stewart. About 1890, Stewart sold the post to William Weidemeyer, who in turn sold it a Missourian, John Wyant, who took Joe Wilkin—an erstwhile freighter—as a partner until Wilkin sold his share to William A. "Billy" Meadows. Anson Damon was the first recorded settler in the Cienega, coming in 1875. In 1882, Sam Day (II?) settled the lower end of the valley, trading and farming until he sold this property to the Catholic Church for St. Michaels Mission and Day School. (Day moved to a new trading post at Chinle the next year.)

On January 17, 1860, an estimated 250 to 300 Navajos led by headman Huero and a former interpreter, Juan Anaya, hoped to drive the Whites out of a weakened Fort Defiance once and for all. They attacked the grazing camp at Ciénega Amarilla, first striking a wagon party leaving the camp. Three of four soldiers in the party were killed with a total of 130 arrows. The Diné then besieged the herd guard and attacked a lumber detail three miles away (wounding a teamster and killing one soldier). Infantry from the fort dispersed the Navajos, who suffered two casualties.

Three weeks later, another attack on the grazing area—this time involving an estimated five hundred warriors—was dispersed by a mountain howitzer unit from the fort, with Major Oliver Sheperd reporting 10 slain and/or wounded Navajos carried off by their comrades (McNitt 1972, 380–81).

COAL MINE CANYON: [DB] (6500–5000 ft) Coconino County, AZ. Navajo: Honoojí, "Jagged Area," or Hááhonoojí, "Rough Spot" (Young and Morgan 1987, 425, 458). The names describe erosion forming the canyon. A nine-mile-long tributary of what maps list as Ha Ho No Geh (Nahoneeshjéél, "Rough Rocky Canyon") (U.S. Indian Claims Commission n.d., vol. VI, viii), converging with the latter two miles upstream (south) of Ha Ho No Geh's merging with Moenkopi Wash (some 17 miles southeast of Tuba City).

This deep, varicolored canyon is cut into the Mesa Verde and Mancos shales of Coal Mine Mesa, with scenery similar to Bryce Canyon National Park in Utah. Tuba City Coal Mine is located at the head of one of the west forks of the canyon. The fine, many-hued sands and shales are greatly favored by Navajo medicine men for sand paintings. Van Valkenburgh notes an abundance of fossil shells to be found along the rim of the canyon.

COAL MINE MESA: (6650 ft) Coconino County, AZ. Navajo: Łeejin Haageed, "Coal Mine" (Kelley p.c. 1994). A small chapter seat community on Arizona Highway 264 five miles west of the southern tip of Howell Mesa (which lies some five miles west of Hopi Third Mesa). The Coal Mine Mesa Trading Post closed in 1968 (James 1988, 80)

COCONINO POINT and PLATEAU: (approx. 7500 ft) Coconino County, AZ. Also Gray Mountain. Navajo: Dził Łibáí, "Gray Mountain." This name refers to that vast highland plateau that comprises the South Rim of the Grand Canyon and gives rise to the San Francisco Peaks. Formerly Havasupai territory, this plateau was first entered by Navajos about the middle of the nineteenth century, according to Béésh Łigaii Atsidí ("Silversmith"), who stated that his father and other Navajos from the Piñon region lived with the Havasupai on Gray Mountain over one hundred years ago.

During the 1850s, Coconino Point was the scene of a fight between Navajos and a band of Mexican horse thieves and slave raiders. The Mexicans were all killed, except for two who escaped to Oraibi and, with the help of the Hopis, eventually made it to the Rio Grande.

Traditionally, many Little Colorado River Navajos would leave the treeless barrens of the river valley for the abundance of winter fuel growing on the plateau. A presidential executive order of 1918 and the additional purchases by the Indian Department gave the Navajos title to certain springs on the south side of the highland over which there had been a great deal of trouble between Navajos and White stockmen.

COLD SPRING: (7400 ft) Apache County, AZ. Navajo: Tó Sik'az Háálíní, "Cold Water Flows Up" (Young and Morgan 1987, 708). This spring is on the eastern slope of the Defiance Plateau, about five miles northwest of Fort Defiance.

COLORADO RIVER: (12,000–0 ft) Grand, Eagle, Garfield, and Mesa counties, CO; Grand, San Juan, Garfield, and Kane counties, UT; and Coconino and Mohave counties, AZ; and forming the Arizona-Nevada and Arizona-California state lines. Navajo: Tónits' 'Osíkooh (Austin and Lynch 1983, 24; actually Tó Nts'ósíkooh, "Slim Water Canyon"). Another name meant "Life Without End" in English (McPherson 1992, 49).

The Colorado is female, mounted by the male San Juan River at what is now Lake Powell (McPherson 1992, 49). Originally, the river was called the Colorado only below the confluence of the Green and Grand rivers in eastern Utah. The Colorado legislature changed the name of the Grand to the Colorado, in order to gain a claim on the massive amount of water this 1,440-mile-long river dumped into the Gulf of California. Along this journey, the river takes in such tributaries as the Gunnison, Green, San Juan, Little Colorado, Paria, Escalante, Virgin, Williams, and Gila rivers. It has been dammed at Glen Canyon (to form Lake Powell), Black Canyon (forming Lake Mead), and Davis (for Lake Havasu). During the 1960s, the Department of the Interior even planned dams in Marble Canyon and the Grand Canyon, but these were thwarted by environmentalists.

This river is in serious danger today. During the 1960s, with the completion of Glen Canyon Dam and the intensive irrigation projects in southern California and Arizona, the water's salinity at the Mexican border went from 200 parts per million to 1,500 parts per million, rendering the water unusable. With the OPEC oil embargo of the 1970s, however, when Americans began eyeing perceived Mexican oil reserves, the United States constructed the Yuma River Desalinization Plant, which now purifies water at $300.00 per acre-foot (irrigators along the river pay only $3.50 per acre-foot of water used) (Martin 1989).

COMA'A SPRING: [DB] (5680 ft) Navajo County, AZ. Navajo pronunciation of the Ute word "Goma'a," meaning "rabbit" (Brugge p.c. 1996). On USGS maps, listed as Comar Spring. Granger (1960, 237) tells that in the 1880s, Hopis settled here at the urging of their White agent, to prevent the Navajos "from taking over the Hopi Reservation." According to Granger, Navajos attacked and drove the Hopis out, and then burned the settlement. (Brugge doubts this version of events.)

COMB RIDGE: (5945 ft) Navajo and Apache Counties, AZ, and San Juan County, UT. Navajo: Tsé Yík'áán, "Rock Extends in the Form of a Narrow Edge." This major sandstone uplift runs northeast to southwest for fifty-five miles between Chaistla Butte and Cane Valley. It forms the southern boundary of the Little Capitan Valley (south of Monument Valley) approximately four miles north of U.S. Highway 160.

This formation is important in Navajo mythology. It is considered one of the arms of a female anthropomorphic figure known as Pollen Mountain. (Navajo Mountain is her head, Black Mesa her body, Balakai Mesa her feet, and Tuba Butte and Agathla Peak her breasts) (McPherson 1992, 21). It is also the edge of a massive furrow dug by the youngest brother in the Changing Bear Maiden legend of the Upward Reachingway chant of the Evilway Ceremony. It is the sharp edge of one of four arrowheads used to form the earth during the creative period, and it is considered the spine of the world, encircling the earth underground from its prominence in Arizona and Utah (McPherson 1992, 30, 34–37).

CONCHO: (6000 ft) Apache County, AZ. Navajo: Tóts'ózí, "Slim Water." Mexican settlement of the late 1860s, in a shell-like basin near St. Johns. Mormons arrived in 1879, naming their ward Erastus (for Erastus Snow, later of Snowflake). The Mormons adopted the name Concho on March 21, 1890. The Zunis used to maintain farms in this area (Ferguson and Hart 1985, 129).

COPPERMINE: [DB] (6100 ft) Coconino County, AZ. Also Keams District. Navajo: Tsinaabáás Habitiin, "Ascending Wagon Road." Located on the Red Mesa portion of the Kaibito Plateau 25 miles north of the Gap, this tiny chapter seat and trading community is 10 miles due east of Bitter Springs and the junction of U.S. Highway 89 and Alternate 89 along the Echo Cliffs. Coppermine Trading Post opened in the early 1930s (Kelley 1977, 254).

Thomas Varker Keam (of Keams Canyon) and associates prospected and located copper here in the 1880s. In 1915, the Pittsburgh Copper and Mining Company worked the mines and in 1917 the Navajo Copper Company reopened the 1882 diggings. The Arizona Copper and Chemical Company followed. In the 1940s, there was considerable activity mining and manufacturing copper sulphate. During that time 15 to 20 Navajos were employed. The surrounding region is good stock country, and a small band of antelope still roamed the plateau in the forties.

Two sets of three-toed, bipedal dinosaur tracks are known in the Navajo and Wingate sandstones of the Kaibito Plateau, one a half mile north of Coppermine, the other two miles north (Brady 1960, 81–82).

CORNFIELDS: [DB] (6050 ft) Apache County, AZ. Navajo: K'iiłtsoiitah, "Among the Rabbit Brush" (Chrysothamnus naneosus var. graveolens). This small chapter and day school community is located in the wide valley of the Pueblo Colorado Wash, some eight miles southwest of Ganado, and 12 miles northwest of Sunrise Springs, on Navajo Route 15. The English name is for Navajo cornfields plentiful in the region (Granger 1960, 9).

CORNFIELDS TRADING POST: (6050 ft) Apache County, AZ. Navajo: Uncertain, likely the same as the community. A trading post operated by Lorenzo Hubbell in 1896–97 in the region now known as Cornfields.

COTTONWOOD TANK: [DB] (approx. 5400 ft) Coconino County, AZ. Navajo: T'iis Sitání, "Cottonwood Tree Lying Down." A natural, ephemeral reservoir situated a mile west of U.S. Highway 89, three miles south of the Gap on Roundy Creek. Located on the old Mormon trail laid out by Jacob Hamblin from southern Utah to Arizona, Cottonwood Tank is now used as a watering place by the Navajos.

COTTONWOOD WASH: (7400–5450 ft) Apache County, AZ. Navajo: T'iisbáí Bii' Tó, "Spring in the Quaking Aspens." A 35-mile-long ephemeral wash heading on the western ridge of Black Mesa, approximately midway between Yale Point (north) and Lohali Point (south). It flows due south, passing to the east of Black Mountain before turning west to join Nazlini Wash just south of Chinle.

COVE: (6500 ft) Apache County, AZ. Navajo: K'aabizhii, a species of cactus (Biznauga sp.). Also K'aabizhiistł'ah, "A Corner Where a Small Stubby Cactus with Interlocking Thorns Grows" (Young and Morgan 1987, 501). This tiny trading community is centered around Cove Trading Post, 10 miles west of Red Valley, on the northeast slope of the Lukachukai Mountains. In addition to the post, the community hosts a day school, and the Cove Soil and Conservation Service Demonstration area was located in a large cove in the red sandstone country between the Lukachukai and Carrizo Mountains. Broken by many blind and hidden canyons and coves among the forests of the Lukachukai Mountains, this remote region was an excellent, defendable hiding place and served as a Navajo rendezvous.

Van Valkenburgh (1941, 45) relates a Navajo tradition involving a sheer rock in Mexican Canyon prior to the removal of the Navajos to Fort Sumner in 1864:

A long time ago in the time of our grandfathers, the Navajos had a citadel on top of Tsénikání

("Round Rock"). In times of trouble they moved up there to live in security until the enemies left. Once the Mexicans came, but they could not climb the sides of the rock so they camped below and tried to starve the Navajos out. After a few days the Navajos knew they had to do something and held a meeting.

Among them was a man who was supposed to be a witch and they asked him to try his power on the Mexican captain. That night he made evil medicine. In the morning, when the Navajos were all together again, the witch said, "I killed the Mexican captain." They looked down and the captain lay dead and the Mexicans were moving out.

American military parties first entered the region in the 1850s. In 1859, Captain John Walker led the first American military party to cross the Lukachukai Mountains, marching around the eastern flanks of the Carrizos, crossing Cove Mesa, and passing over the Lukachukais near the head of Tsaile Creek or Spruce Creek. That same year, Major J. S. Simpson also crossed the mesa, and Lieutenant W. O. Brown visited the vicinity in 1892. Brown noted a small mud spring four and a half miles northeast of Shiprock Pinnacle near Mitten Rock, a name he apparently applied. Brown described the Cove region as an area with "good agricultural possibilities," needing only good irrigation. He remarked that the locality was the finest he had observed and that not a wagon or plow had been used in the entire valley. At this time the Cove was under the control of a local Navajo headman named Black Horse. (See Round Rock for more information on this leader.)

The red sandstone country between the Carrizo and Lukachukai Mountains is rich in Anasazi ruins and old Navajo sites. During the 1930s, Earl Morris of the Carnegie Institute investigated this region, considered at the time one of the most untouched archaeological areas left in the Navajo country. The antiquities were protected by the U.S. Indian Service and a "Roving Field Ranger" of the National Park Service.

The Soil Conservation Service Demonstration area was established in 1934 upon invitation from Old Policeman and Jimmy the Boatman (who used to run the ferry across the San Juan River at Shiprock), who wanted their community to have the benefits of range conservation and agricultural and timber development. A USIS irrigation project on the Cove fork of the Red Rock Wash with a reinforced concrete dam and two masonry diversion dams served 144 acres of agricultural land.

COVE MESA: (7000 ft) Apache County, AZ. Navajo: Chooh Dínéeshzheé (Austin and Lynch 1983, 36), "Fringed with Roses." This mesa sits between the Lukachukai and Carrizo Mountains, north of Mexican Cry Mesa.

COW SPRINGS TRADING POST: [DB] (5800 ft) Coconino County, AZ. Navajo: Béégashii Bito', "Cow Spring" (Austin and Lynch 1983, 24; Young p.c. 1995). This trading post on U.S. Highway 160, some nine miles northeast of Tonalea, was established as a summer and fall post by George McAdams in 1882. It was run as a William and Babbitt post by 1895 (Kelley 1977, 252). Cow Springs Wash was encountered by men of Vizcarra's campaign of 1823, who called it "Arroyo de los Pilares," apparently in reference to the nearby Elephant's Feet pillars (Brugge 1965, 16–17).

CROSS CANYON: (7000–6800 ft) Apache County, AZ. Navajo: 'Ah Ba Deel Hadisa, "Creek Connection" (U.S. Indian Claims Commission n.d., vol. VI, i); also Béésh Dich'ízhii, "Rough Flintstone" (Young and Morgan 1987, 167). A canyon at the head of Fish Wash, five miles south of the last Cross Canyon Trading Post on Arizona Highway 264. In the 1940s a collection of hogans here was called Burnt Piñon (Van Valkenburgh 1941, 173). The English name comes from a Navajo trail crossing the canyon (Granger 1960, 9).

CROSS CANYON TRADING POST: (7000 ft) Apache County, AZ. Navajo: See Cross Canyon. Trading post on Arizona Highway 264 on the west slope of the Defiance Plateau, about 10 miles east of Ganado. The original post was built south of the present highway (Brugge p.c. 1996) by C. C. Manning of Gallup at the turn of the century (Kelley 1977, 252). According to Van Valkenburgh, some considerable Navajo-White violence occurred here between 1915 and 1922.

CROWN ROCK: [DB] Exact location uncertain. Navajo County, AZ. Navajo: Háásita', "Its Back" (literally "Area in one's back between the shoulder blades") (Young and Morgan 1987, 430). Van Valkenburgh described this feature as a roughly rectangular sandstone crag lying between the southern point of Balakai Mesa and the rolling, broken canyon country six miles southwest of Steamboat Canyon. The only notable feature in this vicinity on current or historic maps is Eagle Crag, just north of Steamboat Canyon. The feature was noted for a fourteenth-century Anasazi ruin atop the rock, and also served as a Navajo shrine.

DAY'S CHINLE TRADING POST: (5058 ft) Apache County, AZ. Navajo: Uncertain. Large, log trading post built in 1902 by Sam Day, Sr., formerly of Ciénega Amarilla (later known as St. Michaels). The post was purchased by the partnership of Camille Garcia, Leon H. "Cozy" McSparron, and Hartley T. Seymour in 1923, and later became the landmark "Thunderbird Ranch." Day had previously settled at the lower end of the Cienega Amarilla around 1882, bringing his wife and son to Coolidge by rail, then to the Cienega by ox team (McNitt 1962, 247).

DEADMAN FLAT: (6400 ft) Coconino County, AZ. Navajo: Naakaii Jííghání, "Mexicans Were Massacred" (U.S. Indian Claims Commission n.d., vol. VI, xii; Young p.c. 1995). The broad, flat expanse north and east of the San Francisco Peaks, stretching toward Wupatki National Monument.

Granger (1960, 68) notes several legends about White men meeting their demise here, but only one might pertain to Mexicans being killed, that being a dateless story of a party driving horses from California to Colorado being attacked by Indians.

DEAD WASH: (6200–5200 ft) Apache County, AZ. Navajo: Uncertain. Heading in several

washes in the Painted Desert between Wide Ruin Wash and I-40 (north of Navajo, Arizona), this dry stream flows southwest 25 miles. It joins the Rio Puerco of the West in Petrified Forest National Park. Granger (1960, 10) tells the story of an "Old Man Lynn" who died in this vicinity. One of his two none-too-bright daughters wandered into Adamana for help, not knowing the man had been dead several days.

DEBEBIKID LAKE: (7200 ft) Navajo County, AZ. Also Teyebaakit Lake. Navajo: Dibé Be'ek'id, "Sheep Lake" (Gregory 1915, 150) An ephemeral sink on the East Fork Dinnebito Wash, approximately two miles down from that stream's headwaters.

DEFIANCE PLATEAU: (8304 ft at Fluted Rock, its highest point) Apache County, AZ. Navajo: Uncertain, but generically referred to as Dził, "Mountain." A massive upland plateau west of the Chuska Mountains and east of the Painted Desert and Chinle Valley. It extends from the Rio Puerco of the West (near Houck) in the south 75 miles north to the vicinity of Lukachukai. From St. Michaels, in the east, it reaches west to Ganado. In all, it covers some 1,875 square miles. This is the body from which nature excavated Canyon de Chelly. The English name is for Fort Defiance (Gregory 1915, 50), situated at its eastern foot in the vicinity of today's community of the same name.

This upland is heavily forested in ponderosa pine, and has seen many episodes of logging prior to the moratorium placed on such extractive activities in the late 1980s. The village of Sawmill, once the site of the Navajos' own sawmill, sits high on the eastern slope of the plateau near Fluted Rock.

DESERT VIEWPOINT: (7000 ft) Coconino County, AZ. Navajo: Yaa'íí'áhí, "Standing Tower." Small point of the South Rim of the Grand Canyon juts northward, forming a fine overlook about three miles north of Cedar Mountain, at the hairpin curve of Arizona Highway 64. A Mountain Top Chant was held here in 1861 (Van Valkenburgh 1974, 12).

DESHGISH BUTTE: (6300 ft) Navajo County, AZ. Navajo: Deeshgizh, "Gapped Butte" (Young and Morgan 1987, 311). A low, broad mesa in the northeast periphery of the Hopi Buttes, located adjacent to and immediately east of Arizona Highway 87, some five miles south of White Cone.

DIAMOND FIELDS: (approx. 5000 ft) Apache County, AZ. This name is mistakenly applied to an area near the Little Colorado River south of the Hopi Mesas; the exact location is unknown. It is named for the great "Arizona Diamond Swindle," even though the land salted with low-grade diamonds was actually in southwestern Colorado (Granger 1960, 10).

DILCON: [DB] (5962 ft) Navajo County, AZ. Also spelled Dilkon. Navajo: Tsézhin Dilkǫǫh, "Smooth Lava Rock," or Chézhin Dikǫǫhí, "Smooth Rock" (Young and Morgan 1987, 732, 271). A chapter community located in the high smooth plains and volcanic buttes of the Hopi (Moqui) Butte country, at the juncture of Navajo Routes 15 and 60, six miles east of Arizona Highway 87 and 15 miles north of the southern boundary of the Navajo Reservation (about 35 miles northeast of Winslow).

A trading post was built here in 1919 by J. W. Bush, just south and west of Tsézhin Dilkooh. Bush dropped the first part of the compounded Navajo word and in 1920 was allowed by the Post Office Department to use the name Dilcon, an Anglicized version of the last part of the Navajo name. According to Granger (1960, 238), the earliest English name for this community was Castle Butte, for the formation six miles to the southwest.

Today, the community is comprised of several detached clusters spread over a large area. The school is now a day school, and Bureau of Indian Affairs district offices occupy buildings in the same complex, along with teacher housing. At least three units of modern subsidized housing surround the school complex. Across Navajo Route 15, a new convenience store/hardware store sells gas, and, farther north, toward Tees Toh, lie an El Paso Natural Gas plant and a Navajo Utility Authority district office.

DILCON TRADING POST: (7000 ft) Navajo County, AZ. Navajo: Tsézhin Dilkǫǫh (same as Dilkon community) (Van Valkenburgh 1941, 50). Van Valkenburgh says the post was built in 1919 by J. W. Bush, but Kelley (1977, 253) asserts that it was opened between 1911 and 1915.

DINNEBITO: [DB] (6100 ft) Navajo County, AZ. Navajo: Diné Bito', "Navajo's Spring." Small trading community located in the sparsely vegetated Valley of the Dinnebito Wash on Navajo Route 62, nine miles north of Arizona Highway 264, on the Navajo-Hopi boundary and Dinnebito Wash. Some 15 miles east is Masipa or Shato Spring (not to be confused with the Shanto Springs in the Marsh Pass, Canyon de Chelly, and Pueblo Colorado regions).

Ten miles down the wash is the region once controlled by Hastiin Naat'aánii, a Navajo leader who constructed many diversion dams and ditches for placating the alkaline waters of the Dinnebito. None lasted long, however, being washed out by the heavy spring or summer flash floods that rush down the long drainage that heads on Black Mesa above Chilchinbito. In 1937 the Indian Irrigation Service constructed a reinforced concrete diversion dam of the counterfoot type, which provided for the irrigation of some 230 acres. The dam is called Tse' De Ninít'i', "Rock that Extends Outward and Ends" (Young and Morgan 1987, 729).

DINNEBITO TRADING POST: (5923 ft) Navajo County, AZ. Navajo: See Dinnebito. Built on the sandy side of the south slope of the Dinnebito Wash between 1911 and 1915 (Kelley 1977, 253), this post was a center for the Navajos living along Dinnebito Wash. It was once owned by Lorenzo Hubbell, Jr.

DINNEBITO WASH: (7200–4400 ft) Navajo and Coconino Counties, AZ. (See also East Fork Dinnebito Wash.) Navajo: See Dinnebito. This 96-mile-long tributary of the Little Colorado River is one of the four major drainages of Black Mesa (the other three are Moenkopi, Oraibi, and Polacca Washes). It heads on the northeast escarpment of the mesa and flows southwest through that portion of the Hopi Reservation northwest of Third Mesa. It merges with the Little Colorado River five miles northwest of Grand Falls—nine miles east of Wupatki Ruins.

A portion of this wash was scouted by (Governor) Colonel Jose Antonio Vizcarra in July 1823 (McNitt 1972, 60).

The upper reaches of this drainage are referred to by the Navajos as Hooghan Bijáád Łání, "Many Legged Hogan (home)." This refers to an unusual construction style common to hogans in the region, incorporating circular walls of stockaded logs planted vertically in the ground.

DINNEHOTSO: [DB] (5000 ft) (Population: 616) Navajo County, AZ. Also Dennehotso and Dennehatso. Navajo: Denihootso, "Upper Ending of the Meadow," or, more literally, "Yellowgreen Streak that Extends Up and Ends" (Young p.c. 1995). Small chapter community described by Granger (1960, 10) and Van Valkenburgh (1941, 51) as a summer camp for five hundred Navajo families. It is situated in a shallow sandy valley called Dennehotso Canyon (of Laguna Creek), covered in places with growths of chico or black greasewood. It is located on U.S. Highway 160, some 15 miles west of the junction of that road with U.S. Highway 191. The community hosts a day school and trading post.

On the north side of the valley is Comb Ridge and on the south a rolling country that slopes east into Chinle Wash, which Van Valkenburgh calls a "concentrated agricultural area," with little timber for winter firewood.

Previous farming operations in the lower valley of the Laguna Creek were at Tsé 'Awe' ("Baby Rocks") some 15 miles west of Dinnehotso by settlers who came there from the Kayenta region. The floods of 1912, which destroyed the natural earth dams in the Segi or upper Laguna Creek and released tremendous heads of water, cut the channel of the lower Laguna Creek down to bedrock and made it impossible for the farm colony at Baby Rock to divert water from the deep streambed. Old Crank, who had been the leader of the Baby Rocks colony, now led a movement to establish Dinnehotso where there was a shallower channel and a natural dam site. Old Crank's earthen dam, reinforced with brush and tree branches, was

replaced prior to 1941 with a modern reinforced concrete diversion dam, which irrigated 793 acres of excellent agricultural land.

DINNEHOTSO CANYON: (5000–4800 ft) Apache County, AZ. Also Dennehotso. Navajo: See Dinnehotso. Seven-mile-long canyon drained by Laguna Creek, and stretching between Dennehotso and Chinle Wash.

DINNEHOTSO TRADING POST: (6000 ft) Apache County, AZ. Navajo: See Dinnehotso. Opened between 1911 and 1915 (Kelley 1977, 253), one of some 20 in New Mexico, Arizona, and Utah owned early by the Foutz Brothers (Junius, Alma, Hugh, Jess, Leroy, and Luff) (McNitt 1962, 205n). Van Valkenburgh lists the trader in 1941 as Charles Ashcroft.

DINOSAUR CANYON: [DB] (5400–4350 ft) Coconino County, AZ. Navajo: Tsé Ndoolzhaaí, "Upward Projecting Rocks Strewn Along" (Van Valkenburgh 1941, 51), or "Jagged Rock Extending Upward" (Young and Morgan 1987, 731). A tributary of the Little Colorado River cut through the reddish Wingate sandstone at the base of a great Navajo sandstone escarpment of Ward Terrace some 14 miles southeast of Cameron. It flows west 15 miles to join the Little Colorado River opposite Black Point. Here, on a slab of white calcarious sandstone, dozens of three-million-year-old three-toed biped dinosaur footprints were found by Hubert Richardson in 1928. They were authenticated a year later by an expedition of the American Museum of Natural History.

Navajos call these tracks tsidii nabitiin (bird's tracks).

DO HA HI BITON: (4700 ft) Navajo County, AZ. Navajo: probably Doo Hahí Bito', "Slow Man's Water" (Young p.c. 1995). A small tributary of the Little Colorado River, five miles east of Leupp.

DONEY MOUNTAIN: [DB] (7740 ft) Coconino County, AZ. Navajo: Dził Łichíí', "Red Mountain." The largest and southernmost of a chain of four volcanic cones rising above the cinder-covered mesa and volcanic escarpment country at the northern end of Deadmans Flat (also known as Doney Park). Situated three miles west of U.S. Highway 89 at a point five miles south of the junction of that highway with the Sunset Crater/Wupatki road.

The mountain was named after the renowned pioneer and prospector of the San Francisco Peaks country, Ben Doney. It is important to the Navajos because they capture eagles nesting in its crevices and use their feathers for ceremonial purposes. Small house ruins of the Anasazi are found on the mountain.

DOWOSHIEBITO CANYON: (7000–6300 ft) Navajo County, AZ. Navajo: Díwózhii Bii'Tó, "Spring in the Greasewood" (Kelley p.c. 1994). Ten-mile-long canyon with numerous tributaries cutting into Skeleton Mesa from the southwest. It intersects Tsegi Canyon five miles upstream from Marsh Pass (the sharp cleft) between Skeleton and Black Mesas.

DUNN MERCANTILE TRADING COMPANY: (4489 ft) Apache County, AZ. This enterprise is listed by Van Valkenburgh (1941, 57) as one of three at Fort Defiance (the others being A. C. Rudeau Trading Company and W. M. Staggs Trading Company).

DZIŁ DASHZHINII: (7220 ft) Navajo County, AZ. Navajo for "The Black Mountain" (Young and Morgan 1987, 360). This feature sits atop the northern end of Big Mountain, itself a feature on southern Black Mesa, between Moenkopi and Dinnebito Washes.

EAGLE CRAG: [DB] (approx. 6600 ft) Apache County, AZ. Navajo: Tsé Łigai Dah' 'Azkání, "White Rock Mesa." Isolated crag four miles northwest of Steamboat Canyon, according to Van Valkenburgh (1941, 52). It is topped by Anasazi ruins, and is a nesting place for eagles—because of which ownership (custodianship) was hotly contested between the Navajos and Hopis.

EAST FORK DINNEBITO WASH: (7400–6500 ft) Navajo County, AZ. Navajo: At least part is referred to as Mą́'ii' 'Aztł'iídi,

"Where Coyote Farted" (U.S. Indian Claims Commission n.d., vol. VI, x). This 15-mile-long tributary of Dinnebito Wash lies between the latter and Oraibi Wash. It heads on east-central Black Mesa, near Debebikid Lake, entering Dinnebito Wash five miles east of Big Mountain.

ECHO CLIFFS: (6600 ft) Coconino County, AZ. Navajo: Tsé Yík'áán, "Hogback" (Kelley p.c. 1994). A 40-mile-long, 1000-ft-high ridge of red sandstone cliffs adjacent to and east of U.S. Highway 89. Forms the east boundary of Cornfield Valley, running from a point 10 miles north of the U.S. Highway 89/160 junction to the Echo Peaks on the east bank of the Colorado River. The portion of the cliffs south of the community of Gap is also referred to as Hamblin Ridge.

John Wesley Powell's men named the cliffs after reverberations of a gunshot fired by one of the party (Granger 1960, 69).

ECHO TRADING POST: Exact location uncertain. Coconino County, AZ. Navajo: Uncertain. A Babbitt Brothers post north of Cameron (McNitt 1962, 266).

EGLOFFSTEIN BUTTE: (6600 ft) Navajo County, AZ. Navajo: Uncertain. This 800-ft-high butte is on the northwest periphery of the Hopi Buttes region, and is located four miles north of Tees Toh and two miles east of Arizona Highway 87. Named for Frederick F. W. von Egloffstein of the Ives Expedition of 1858 (named by Gregory 1915, 151).

EIGHTEEN MILES SPRING TRADING POST: Exact location uncertain. Navajo: Uncertain. This post was started by Freeman H. Hathorn in 1896, and sold to Edwin Marty of Gallup in 1908 (McNitt 1962, 274n).

ELEPHANT FEET (LEGS): (5500 ft) Coconino County, AZ. Also Elephant Legs. Remarkable sandstone formation located on U.S. Highway 160, across the highway from Tonalea (Red Lake Trading Post). Early explorers referred to these twin pillars simply as Los Pilares, "The Pillars" (Brugge 1965, 16–17).

EMIGRANT SPRINGS: (5900 ft) Apache County, AZ. Navajo: Chiihtó, "Red Clay Springs." The location of this spring, important as a camping spot for westbound emigrants of the late 1800s, seems to coincide with that of present-day Pine Springs, some two miles south of Sanders.

ESCUDILLA MOUNTAIN: (10,877 ft) Apache County, AZ. Navajo: Uncertain. Mountain range south of Springerville is said to have been occupied by Navajos prior to their 1863–64 removal to the Bosque Redondo (U.S. Indian Claims Commission n.d., vol. IV, 526–27).

THE FINGERS: (7600–6800 ft) Navajo County, AZ. Navajo: Tsé 'Ií Ahí, "Standing Rock" (Austin and Lynch 1983, 24). A series of fingerlike crags on the east flank of Black Mesa immediately west of Chilchinbito.

Sam Day II told Van Valkenburgh that the Navajos who killed prospector Samuel Wolcott near El Capitan in 1884 trailed his partner, James McNally, to a canyon near The Fingers (a sandstone projection standing apart from the northeast rim of Black Mesa southeast of Chilchinbito), and killed him there (see Monument Valley).

FLAGSTAFF: [DB] (6905 ft) (Population: 45,857) Coconino County, AZ. Navajo: Kin Łání Dook'o'oosłííd Biyaagi, "Many Houses Below San Francisco Mountains." Several towns are named Kin Łání, so Flagstaff is differentiated by describing its location in relation to the mountains. This is northern Arizona's largest city. It is located near the east-west center of the state on the Burlington Northern Santa Fe Railway and I-40, at its junction with I-17, nestled in the southern shadow of the San Francisco Peaks.

Flagstaff for many years has been the wholesale trade center for the Hopi and western Navajo reservations, and is a stock and lumber shipping point. It serves as a tourist center and home of Northern Arizona University (formerly Arizona Teachers' College) and the world-class Museum of Northern Arizona. This venerable institution hosts three annual exhibitions for Zuni, Hopi, and Navajo artisans. (Previously, a junior art show and an Arizona art and artisan show were held in May and August.) Until the early 1980s, Flagstaff also hosted the annual Southwest Indian Powwow held over the Fourth of July. In the nearby San Francisco Peaks is Lowell Observatory.

The first settler in the Flagstaff region was Edward Whipple, operator of the Texas Star saloon near Flagstaff Spring in 1871. Edwin Beale, however, of "Uncle Sam's Camels," is known to have camped near Le Roux and Eldon Springs in September 1857.

In 1876, a party of eastern settlers known as the "Boston Party" attempted to settle in the Little Colorado River valley near the Mormon town of St. Joseph (present Joseph City) east of Flagstaff. Suspicious of the Mormons and discouraged with the country, they moved west to Prescott (founded 12 years earlier). That Fourth of July, a party of them camped at Antelope Park a short distance southwest of present Flagstaff. They celebrated their Fourth by hoisting a flag on a pole made by stripping the boughs from a large pine tree. When the Atlantic and Pacific Railroad reached Flagstaff in 1882, the pine was still standing. This natural flagpole gave the name to the City of Flagstaff. Opinions differ and sources are obscure concerning the exact time and details of the incident.

The arrival of the railroad and the creation of a sawmill by E. E. Ayer marked the beginning of extensive settlement. On February 4, 1886, a fire practically wiped out the town, destroying more than 20 buildings. Within 10 months, 60 buildings replaced those burned, but on a new site. This was called New Town to distinguish it from the original town, which was appropriately called Old Town. Flagstaff was incorporated as a town on July 4, 1894, and as a city in 1929.

FLUTED ROCK: [DB] (8304 ft) Apache County, AZ. Also Dzil Tusyan Butte (USGS) Navajo: Dził Dah Si'ání, "Mountain that Sits up on an Elevation" (Young and Morgan 1987, 359). Traprock plug atop the Defiance Plateau 18 miles northwest of Fort Defiance. It is the highest point on the plateau. Its sides are "fluted" vertical columns, giving rise to the name.

Van Valkenburgh suggests that during the

Navajo Wars of 1863–64, the U.S. Army used Fluted Rock as a heliograph station from which signals could be flashed on clear days to as far away as Navajo Mountain (125 miles to the northwest). However, this story must be considered approcryphal, since the heliograph was not invented until August 27, 1880 (Oxford University 1989, 114–15). In 1880, Captain Frank T. Bennett established a small sawmill five miles east of the rock for cutting and rough finishing the abundant ponderosa pine that blankets the level top of the plateau.

Fluted Rock has many Navajo stories. Van Valkenburgh (1941, 56) offered one from the Blessing Chant:

> Fluted Rock had Hadahoniye' 'Ashkii, ("Mirage Stone Boy"—aragonite), and Hadahoniy' 'At'ééd, ("Mirage Stone Girl"). There is a big hole in the side of the rock and very few Navajos have gone in it for any distance. Long ago there was a lad named 'Ashkii Chilí ("Little Boy"), whose grandmother was living on the Defiance Plateau. Her name was 'Asdzání Na'ashjé'ii. She carried a basket and lived on deer meat. She always carried this basket and when deer meat was scarce she turned into an antelope, and went into this hole in Fluted Rock. She still lives in there. When the Navajos can't grow crops and food is scarce, they go to Fluted Rock and pray for food. They also do this when they are in need of sheep and horses. They usually pray from the west end of the mountain.

Fluted Rock is also mentioned at the end of the hero's search for his family in the Navajo Rounded Man Red Antway Myth, and is the home of the Bear People in the Gun Shooter Red Antway Myth (Wyman 1965). It is a location of prayer for the starving and hungry (Van Valkenburgh 1974, 164–78).

FOREST LAKE: (6600 ft) Navajo County, AZ. Navajo: Dibé Bighanteelí, "Wide Sheep Corral," and Dibé Be'ek'id, "Sheep Lake" (U.S. Indian Claims Commission n.d., vol. VI, v), and Tsiyi'í Be'ek'id, "Forest Lake" (U.S. Indian Claims Commission n.d., vol. VI, xxiii). A chapter house on Black Mesa, where Navajo Route 41 crosses the East Fork Dinnebito Wash.

FORT DEFIANCE: [DB] (6892 ft) (Population: 4,489) Apache County, AZ. Navajo: Tséhootsooí, "Meadow in Between the Rocks." Located in Black Creek Valley at the mouth of Cañon Bonito and six miles north of Window Rock, this community is called simply "Fort" by most Navajos.

Fort Defiance began as an isolated military post, but was converted to the Navajo Agency in 1868 after the Diné returned from the Bosque Redondo. Today it houses a chapter seat, schools, and Public Health Service Hospital (formerly a U.S. Indian Service Tuberculosis Sanatorium). After its transformation from a military post, Good Shepherd (Episcopal), Presbyterian, and Franciscan missions settled around the establishment in an effort to induct the sizable numbers of Navajos visiting the Navajo Agency.

Traders serving the agency have included Lehman Spiegelberg (whose July 1868 license was the first issued for trading on the reservation—though others traded in the vicinity prior to the establishment of the reservation), Neal and Damon (1870s), Hyatt (1880s), Weidemeyer (1890s–1960s), Dunn Mercantile, W. M. Staggs, and A. C. Rudeau.

The steep-walled basin at the eastern foot of the Defiance Plateau, in which the fort was constructed, was first named Cañon Bonito ("Beautiful Canyon," not to be confused with nearby Tsé Bonito) by the Spanish, and was a favored Navajo rendezvous in the pre-American era. Medicine men here collected herbs known as Łe'éze' (Horse Medicine), and the bubbling springs were shrines into which white shell and turquoise were thrown as payment for blessings received or pleas for further blessings. A small reinforced concrete dam in Cañon Bonito irrigated all of 25 acres in 1941. The community early on boasted fire service, radio and patrol, and the District Supervisor of USIS District 18.

The first known visit by Americans to the site of Fort Defiance was in the fall of 1849, when the expedition led by Colonel John Washington stopped to rest by the lush cienega on the return journey to the Rio Grande after concluding the Treaty of 1849 with the Navajo chiefs at Chinle.

Fort Defiance was established under its present name by order of Colonel Edwin V. Sumner in the fall of 1851. It was not a true fortress, but rather a collection of adobe or log buildings. Captain Electus Backus laid out the buildings around a rectangular parade ground with a sally port opening to the south. It was first garrisoned by the Third Infantry, called the "Buff Sticks" (Frink 1968, 21–22), quickly supported by one artillery company and four companies of cavalry (Broder 1990, 125). The soldiers nicknamed the post "Hell's Gate" or "Hell's Hollow," largely because of its distance from civilization and the poor location that gave the Navajos the high ground above the fort.

Between 1856 and 1863, the Navajos subjected the Army to continual guerilla warfare. In April 1860, Fort Defiance was attacked by a reported one to two thousand Navajos. They were driven off by the garrison of 150 soldiers of the First U.S. Infantry under Captain O. L. Shepherd. A single private, Sylvester Johnson, was killed and three other soldiers wounded. At least 20 Navajos, including a chief from Canyon de Chelly, were killed. Private Johnson's grave is marked by a tombstone in the old Fort Defiance Post Cemetery.

Author's Note: The reported number of Navajos might be a tactical exaggeration. Gatherings of this many Navajo warriors were rare, and a surprise night attack on the unwalled post with attackers outnumbering defenders nearly ten to one seems likely to have had a different outcome. Inflating the number of attackers would have improved the defenders' valor on paper, and would also have supported pleas to increase the garrison's size.

On April 25, 1861, at the beginning of the Civil War, Fort Defiance was abandoned in favor of Fort Fauntleroy (later named Fort Lyon and, still later, Fort Wingate), built a year later and 40 miles to the southeast at Bear Springs in New Mexico. But the continued depredations of the Navajos led General Carleton to send Kit Carson and a group of Army officers from Fort Union (near Mora, New Mexico) into the Navajo country in the summer of 1863 to establish a military post on Pueblo Colorado Wash on the western slope of the Defiance Plateau (near present-day Ganado). After a survey of possible post locations, the party recommended the reestablishment of old Fort Defiance. That fall Carson led companies of New Mexico Volunteers, a few regular Army officers, and Ute, Zuni, and New Mexico Irregulars, to reoccupy the fort, which was temporarily renamed Fort Canby. Throughout the winter, the troops pursued and captured Navajos, and the fort served as a concentration point for captive Navajos prior to shipping them to the Bosque Redondo at Fort Sumner. Many of the prisoners died from exposure and from eating food to which they were not accustomed.

In the spring of 1864 the so-called Navajo War ended, and the Navajos were marched off on the Long Walk to Fort Sumner at the Bosque Redondo, three hundred miles away on the Pecos River. The fort was again deserted on October 20, 1864 (Kelly 1967, 59), and roaming bands who had eluded the troops and scouts of Carson burned the cane and timbered sections of the fort, leaving only the thick sod and rubble walls.

Upon the signing of the Treaty of 1868 at Fort Sumner, which allowed the Navajos to return to a portion of their own country, Fort Defiance was selected as the site of the Navajo Agency. The treaty required the government to build a warehouse, an agency headquarters, carpenter and blacksmith shops, a school, and a chapel. Because no troops were to be housed within the reservation boundaries, the closest military presence was at Fort Wingate near Gallup—some 30 miles to the southeast. Most of the old buildings were repaired and Major Theodore Dodd, called Na'azísí Yázhí, "Little Gopher," by the Navajos, became the civil agent. On his death shortly after his appointment, he was succeeded by Captain Frank T. Bennett, whom the Navajos called Chąąt sohi, "Big Belly" (Van Valkenburgh 1941, 58). (The name is actually interpreted as either "Big Beaver" or "Big Excrement" [Young and Morgan 1987, 270].) In the fall of 1869, Bennett issued the sheep and goats stipulated in the Treaty of 1868. Over thirteen thousand ewes and three hundred rams (purchased from Vicente Romero, a large operator in the vicinity of Fort Union, New Mexico) as well as nine hundred female and one hundred male goats, were distributed, forming the basis of the present flocks. The erstwhile military post slowly developed into an Indian agency.

Article 6 of the Treaty of 1868 called for the U.S. government to provide for the education of Navajo children with a schoolhouse and teacher for every 30 children. But it also dictated that the Navajos would send all children between the ages of 6 and 16 to those schools, and therein lay the dilemma. This was not fully understood nor accepted—nor even desired—by the average Navajo, and the provision provoked many bitter confrontations between the Diné and their white overseers.

The government first introduced schools by contracting with various missionary societies and churches. The first established was a Presbyterian school at Fort Defiance in December 1869 (Bailey and Bailey 1986, 64–65). The first school was a mission school, opened by the Foreign Board of the Presbyterian Church (John Roberts, missionary, and Charity Gaston, teacher) in 1869. No students attended, and the school failed in less than a year. The same year the school failed, Missionary Roberts was "removed" for having performed a "mixed marriage" (Bailey and Bailey 1986, 63–64). This was followed by the second mission established by John Menaul in 1871, which also failed. A new school was constructed between 1879 and 1881. The Fort Defiance School became the reservation's first boarding school in 1880 (Young 1961, 8). At first the Navajos sent only sickly children until the Navajo police began to enforce attendance in 1887. Still, by 1892, fewer than one hundred students were enrolled in all reservation schools (Johnston 1982, 362). Regular medical service did not begin until 1880, and a 140-bed hospital was built in 1938.

Until 1899, Fort Defiance continued as the agency for all Navajos and Hopis, but in that year a separate Hopi agency was established at Keams Canyon, and in the next 10 years four other Navajo agencies were organized to deal with this large reserve. In 1936 these were again centralized, by Commissioner Collier, and the new agency established at Window Rock, less than five miles southeast of Fort Defiance.

The Episcopal Church sent medical missionar-

ies to the fort in the 1890s, along with Miss Eliza Thackara, a nurse (Stirling 1961). They were kept very busy, and started a tradition lasting through the present. In 1941, Fort Defiance was the Navajo medical center, its 294-bed base hospital, and tuberculosis sanatorium, completed in 1938, serving all parts of Navajoland. Since then, hospitals have been established at other communities, the largest (larger even than the one in Fort Defiance) in Gallup. The boarding school had a capacity of three hundred students in 1941, but eventually gave way to day school preferences and was eventually replaced with Window Rock High School and Arizona public school.

Fort Defiance also served as headquarters of Land Management District 18, which included some 5,300 Navajos. (This governmental agency eventually became the Forestry Department of the Bureau of Indian Affairs.)

FORT WHIPPLE: (5200 ft) Yavapai County, AZ. Navajo: Uncertain. Military post established in the vicinity of "Postle's Ranch," (near Prescott) in the new Military District of Northern Arizona, on December 23, 1863. The site, first known as Whipple Barracks, was the seat of the first Arizona Territorial Government, though this was quickly moved to a new community known as Prescott, and a new Whipple Barracks (or Camp Whipple) was erected in the vicinity on May 18, 1864.

According to Barnes (Granger 1960, 362–63), the post was named for General Amiel Weeks Whipple, who died of wounds received in the Civil War battle of Chancellorsville. Whipple was an instrumental member of survey parties exploring the Colorado and Gila drainages, international boundaries, and a possible railroad route to the Pacific Ocean from 1849 to 1856.

The post was described as "ramshackle [and] tumble-down . . . constructed of unseasoned, unpainted pine planks . . ." by Lieutenant John G. Bourke, yet it became the headquarters for the Department of Arizona, comprised of the entire state (including the Navajo Reservation), southern California, and, for a short time, all of New Mexico. It was abandoned in 1898 but regarrisoned four years later for a period of eight years before the duties and garrison were permanently removed to Los Angeles. Today a Veterans' Hospital occupies the original buildings.

FRAZIER'S TRADING POST: (7000 ft) Apache County, AZ. Van Valkenburgh (1941, 129) listed the post as one of three at St. Michaels in 1941. The others were Kuhn Trading Post and McMahon Trading Post.

FRENCH BUTTE: (approx. 6450 ft) Navajo County, AZ. Navajo: Uncertain. Small butte on the southwest periphery of the Hopi Buttes, located four miles east of Arizona Highway 87, two miles southwest of Castle Butte.

French Butte was named for Franklin French, later husband of one of John D. Lee's nine widows, who lived at Hardy Station, 24 miles west of Holbrook (see Lee's Ferry) (Granger 1960, 239).

GANADO: [DB] (6400 ft) (Population: 1,257) Apache County, AZ. Navajo: Lók'aahnteel, "Wide Band of Reeds up at an Elevation" (Young and Morgan 1987, 514). This substantial chapter, school, mission, and trading settlement lies on Arizona Highway 264 and Pueblo Colorado Wash, 29 miles west of Window Rock and 40 miles north of Chambers, on I-40. It is the home of Hubbell Trading Post National Historic Site, Sage Memorial Hospital, and a branch of Diné College, formerly Navajo Community College (NCC), formerly the Presbyterian College of Ganado.

The Soil Conservation Demonstration Area with 7,899 acres was located a mile north, watered by Ganado Lake, a natural sink later augmented with a dam. Traders have included Stover-Hubbell, opened in the early 1870s (Kelley 1977, 251); Hubbell Trading Post, also opened in the early 1870s, and now a National Historic Site; Round Top Trading Post; and Ganado Trading Post, opened in the late 1920s. The Stover-Hubbell post opened about the same time as Hubbell's first post, but only Hubbell's remains today, operated by the National Park Service and the Southwest Parks and Monuments Association.

The settlement is named after Ganado Mucho (Spanish meaning "Much Livestock"), the last

peace chief of the Navajos and the twelfth signer of the Treaty of 1868. Called Tótsohnii Hastiin, "Mr. Big Water," by the Navajos, Ganado Mucho was the head chief of the western division of the Navajos until his death in 1892.

The Ganado vicinity was sometimes labeled Pueblo Colorado on early maps, after the nearby stream, which in turn was named for a pueblo ruin the Navajos called Kin Dah Lichí'í (Red House in the Distance), located some 10 miles northeast of Ganado near Kin Lichee.

Ganado was one of the earliest centers of American activities to be developed on the reservation. In 1871, Charles Crary settled at Ganado Lake and started a small trading post. A short time later William ("Old Man") Leonard opened a post on the site of the present Hubbell Ranch and Trading Post, and in 1878 was bought out by Juan Lorenzo Hubbell, known to the Navajos both as Nák'ee Sinilí, "Eye Glasses," and Naakaii Sání, "Old Mexican." In 1884 Hubbell formed a partnership with Clinton N. Cotton, a former telegraph operator on the Atlantic and Pacific Railroad. Hubbell, conversant with Indian life after 10 years of wandering among the Paiutes, Hopis, and Navajos, handled the Ganado end of the business, while Cotton mostly managed the affairs from Gallup—though he lived at the Hubbell post for some time and was sole owner from 1884 to the early 1900s. Cotton later went into banking in Gallup while Hubbell divided his interests between Ganado and St. Johns, until the time of his death in 1930.

Cotton, while a telegrapher at Wingate Station, had become interested in silver craft as a commercial possibility for Navajos, and in the mid-1880s he and Hubbell brought Naakaii Dáádiil ("Thick Lipped Mexican") from Cubero, New Mexico, and other Mexican silversmiths to Ganado. Introducing the more easily worked Mexican pesos or silver dollars, they taught the craft to local Navajos who had already started rudimentary work in silver. By 1890, the value of the silver craft products in the hands of Navajos was estimated by their agent as some $300,000.

For many years the Hubbell home at Ganado was the center of Navajo activities in the western part of the reservation, and the gathering place for many White writers and artists. Burbank, prolific artist of Indian life, did much of his best work while visiting with the Hubbells.

A Presbyterian mission was established at Ganado in 1901, and a school and hospital started, forerunners of the Ganado Mission, with its high school, and the 164-bed Sage Memorial Hospital.

GANADO LAKE: [DB] (6650 ft) Apache County, AZ. Navajo: Tséttaak'ą́ą́gi Dá'deestł'-inígíí, "Dam at the Place Where the Rock Slants into the Water" (Van Valkenburgh 1941, 65; Young p.c. 1995); Tsé Tééh Yik'ání, "Rock Slants into Deep Water" (Young and Morgan 1987, 731)—referring to the dam itself; or Be'ek'id Halchíí', "Red Lake" (Young and Morgan 1987, 152). Once a small, murky, ephemeral lake on Kinlichee Wash, three miles upstream (northeast) of Ganado, held in place by an Indian Irrigation Service (USIS) dam.

The site of the first trading post operated by Charles Crary in 1871 is situated near this lake. Navajos tell that in 1878 Manuelito and Ganado Mucho led an effort to exterminate "ladrones" (Spanish for "thieves") and suspected witches, killing some 20. One of these met his death in the doorway of the post, making it necessary to burn the building. Some historians have identified the site of the old store as Fort Canby (see Fort Defiance), which was actually a reoccupation of the erstwhile Fort Defiance on the east side of the Defiance Plateau. There may, however, have been a military outpost camp some seven miles east of Ganado, at Kin Lichee.

Ganado Lake, held in check by a dam since 1890, was once a permanent pond or sink that rarely went dry. The dam, repaired and remodeled during the 1930s by the Indian Irrigation Service, served 602 acres in the vicinity of Ganado. By 1992, the dam was nonfunctional, the lake bed filled with silt and grown over with vegetation.

However, in the mid-1990s the lake bed was dredged and the lake once again serves as a favorite fishing spot.

GANADO TRADING POST: (6400 ft) Apache County, AZ. Navajo: Uncertain. One of three posts listed at Ganado by Van Valkenburgh (1941, 64), along with Hubbell's and Round Top Trading Posts.

GANADO WASH: (6700–5200 ft) Apache County, AZ. Navajo: Lók'aaniteel Ch'ínílí, "Reeds at Elevation Water Outlet" (Austin and Lynch 1983, 24). According to USGS maps, this name refers to Pueblo Colorado Wash and its tributary, Kinleechee Creek.

GAP (TRADING POST): [DB] (approx. 5900 ft) Coconino County, AZ. Navajo: Yaaniilk'id, "Sloping Down" (Van Valkenburgh 1941, 65), or Tisnaabąąs Habitiin, "Wagon Trail Up Out" (Young and Morgan 1987, 737). A natural gap was discovered in the Echo Cliffs northwest of Tuba City, 36 miles north of Cameron on U.S. Highway 89. Being the only passage past the cliffs (the crest of which is known as Hamblin Ridge) onto the Kaibito Plateau for a dozen miles north, this was a natural location for a trading post. Such a post was first operated by Joseph Lee (son of John Doyle Lee of Lee's Ferry) sometime between 1876 and 1880 (McNitt 1962, 265; Kelley 1977, 251). The post is located at the base of the Echo Cliffs, and faces south, at a point where a natural gap in the cliffs granted access to central Kaibito Plateau. (In 1941, Joe Lee was the oldest living Navajo trader, then located at Black Mountain Store.)

Hamblin Creek, named after Jacob Hamblin, the Mormon missionary and explorer, passes by Gap Trading Post. A partially graveled road, Navajo Route 20, runs northeast through the Gap to Coppermine. Another, even poorer road leads to the west across Bodoway Mesa toward the junction of the Little Colorado and Colorado rivers.

In addition to Navajos, a small contingent of Paiutes (numbering 28 in 1941) range in the vicinity, led by Nomutz in the 1940s.

GARCES MESA: (5000 ft) Coconino County, AZ. Navajo: Uncertain. Flat highland south of Padilla Mesa—of the Hopi Mesas—between Dinnebito and Oraibi Washes. Named by Gregory (1915, 151) for Francisco Garces, the noted missionary who came to the Southwest in 1768 and was killed by Indians in 1781.

GARCIA'S TRADING POST: (5058 ft) Apache County, AZ. Navajo: Uncertain, possibly the same as Chinle. Built around 1900 by Lorenzo Hubbell and sold to C. N. Cotton in 1917, this post was purchased by the partnership of Camille Garcia, Leon H. "Cozy" McSparron, and Hartley T. Seymour in 1923. Garcia died in a plane crash with his son Abel in 1963. The business continued to operate until the late 1970s, and is often misidentified as the one started by Hubbell and Cotton in 1886—or even more often as the post that later became Cozy McSparron's Thunderbird Lodge. (The latter actually started as Sam Day's Trading Post.)

GLEN CANYON: (4000–3000 ft) Coconino County, AZ. Navajo: Uncertain, but probably Tséyi', the generic term for "canyon." Currently this name applies to that stretch of 1000-ft-deep Colorado River Canyon lying between Lake Powell (north) and Lee's Ferry (south). The true length of this canyon extends an additional curvilinear one hundred miles northeast of Glen Canyon Dam, but this portion of the geological feature is now beneath the waters of Lake Powell. The first water was retained behind the dam in 1964.

Named by explorer John Wesley Powell in 1869 (Powell 1895, 232–35), the lake was made a National Recreation Area by act of Congress in 1972. (See also Page and Glen Canyon Dam, Arizona, and Lake Powell, Utah.)

Cass Hite mined in the canyon in the 1880s and 1890s. Navajos called him Beesh Łigaii ("Mr. Silver") (Crampton 1983, 125).

GLEN CANYON DAM: (3715 ft) Coconino County, AZ. Navajo: Dá'deestł'in, "Dam." Concrete dam across the Colorado River at the narrows of Glen Canyon. Authorized by Congress in 1956 as part of the Colorado River Storage Project. Construction was initiated by the Bureau of Reclamation in 1959 and completed in 1964. First water was held on March 13, 1963, after diversion tunnels were closed. The first power generated

by Glen Canyon Generating Unit No. 1 began around midnight, September 4, 1964. Now 30,000 cubic feet of water pass through penstocks. (See also Glen Canyon and Page, Arizona, and Lake Powell, Utah.)

GRAND CANYON: [DB] (8300 ft North Rim–2800 ft floor) Coconino County, AZ. Navajo: Bidáá' Ha'azt'i', "Railroad Ends" (Van Valkenburgh 1941, 67), more literally translated as "Something (the Railroad) Extends in a Line to Its Brink" (Young p.c. 1995); Bikooh Ntsaa Ahkee, "Deep Canyon" (U.S. Indian Claims Commission n.d., vol. VI, iii); Tsékoo Hatso, "Big Canyon" (Young and Morgan 1987, 730). Vast canyon located west of the Navajo Reservation, north of the San Francisco Peaks. This is the most extensive canyon system cut by the Colorado River, lying just downstream (southwest) of Marble Canyon and the juncture of the Colorado and Little Colorado Rivers. The region on either side of the canyon is now a national park.

Here the waters of the Colorado River have cut a winding channel a mile deep through limestone, sandstone, shale, and igneous, Precambrian rock. Grand Canyon Village (formerly "El Tovar") (Van Valkenburgh 1941, 67), with complete tourist accommodations and its own school for Park employees, is located on the south rim of the canyon.

So great a natural phenomenon could not be unknown to the Indians who roamed the Southwest, and it would be interesting to know what the name was prior to the arrival of the railroad. Many legends center about the canyon, which was first discovered by Whites in 1540, when a detachment of Spaniards under Don Pedro de Tovar of the Coronado Expedition of 1540 dispatched Don Lopez de Cardenas to investigate the Hopi tales of a great chasm.

A Paiute legend relates that the canyon came into existence when Umbah, a chieftain, grieved at the door of his house over the loss of his wife. Taavotz, a god, appeared to him and told Umbah that his wife was in another land and offered to lead him there. Before taking him, the god made Umbah promise that he would never mourn again after his return. Umbah agreed and Taavotz led him as he cut a trail through the mountain that guarded the western spirit land. Umbah saw his wife and was happy. After they returned through the great gorge cut by Taavotz, the god told the chief to tell no one of the spirit land or its great beauty. Then Taavotz rolled the river into the gorge that he had made, and that is the raging torrent that flows through the Grand Canyon today. Traditional Paiutes believed that the river swallowed anyone attempting to follow it west. Little has been identified as relating to the Grand Canyon in Navajo folklore, but it is important to both Zuni and Hopi mythology. Both tribes believe that certain kachinas dwell in the canyon in the wintertime.

Even before the exile to Fort Sumner, the canyon's South Rim, though Havasupai territory, was occupied at times by the Navajos as far west as present-day Grand Canyon Village. The tribes were usually friendly and the region was a favored camping place in the fall and when the piñon crop was good. Béésh Łigaii 'Atsidii ("Silver Smith"—born near Cameron, Arizona; died in 1939), told of a Navajo Dził'ijí Bi'áádjí (Female Mountain Top Ceremony) that was held near Desert View in 1862.

The Navajos also are known to have crossed the Colorado River at the Crossing of the Fathers upstream from the mouth of Navajo Canyon, traveling southwestward to hunt deer and wild horses along the north rim of the Grand Canyon, on Kaibab Plateau, in a region known to them as Nát'oh Dził, "Tobacco Mountain."

In the winter of 1863–64, great numbers of Navajos, fleeing Kit Carson's New Mexico Volunteers and raiding Utes, traveled west, taking refuge in the canyon. One group is known to have gone down the Tanner Trail from the canyon rim near present Desert View Tower (formerly Hopi Tower), some 30 miles east of Grand Canyon Village. When the refugees got halfway down the sheer walls of the canyon they stopped to rest and camp on a wide shelf. Here they were attacked by a band of Navajo renegades. After considerable fighting, the renegades were ambushed and killed.

The refugees then moved deeper into the canyon and stayed there until Round Moccasin, a Navajo emissary of Carson's, followed their trail and offered them food and protection. Most of the Navajos accepted the offer, and they left the canyon to go to Fort Sumner. A few decided not to surrender and stayed in the canyon, eventually ascending what is now Bright Angel Trail. They had to hoist their sheep up over the steep places with yucca-fiber ropes.

GRAND FALLS: [DB] (4600 ft) Coconino County, AZ. Navajo: 'Adahiilí, "Water Dropping Down" ('Adahiilíní, according to Young and Morgan 1987, 388.) These spectacular, 18-ft falls of the Little Colorado River are located some 20 miles downstream (northwest) of Leupp. They are usually dry, except after rains or the melting of snow.

In 1851, Lieutenant Sitgreaves embarked on a survey of the Little Colorado and Zuni rivers to see if they were navigable to the Pacific Ocean. He followed the Little Colorado River downstream to the Grand Falls, where he realized the futility of the scheme and cut west to the San Francisco Mountains through the Wupatki Basin. On Lieutenant J. F. McComb's map of 1860 the falls are shown as the Cascades.

The falls are in the main channel of the Little Colorado River and are made by a lava tongue (deposited by eruption of Merriam Crater) projecting through Moenkopi sandstone from the west. This throws the river channel into an east hairpin before it goes over the falls. During the flood season the Little Colorado is so filled with suspended mud that a damp red dust rises from the churning falls. There is a Hopi shrine in the vicinity, and the Museum of Northern Arizona has excavated some Anasazi pit houses near the falls.

Author's Note: To protect the shrine, an imprecise location is deliberately given here.

GRAY MOUNTAIN: (7000 ft) Coconino County, AZ. Navajo: Dził Łibáí, "Gray Mountain," though this designation also refers to Coconino Rim and Coconino Plateau (Young and Morgan 1987, 360). That mountainous region immediately south (uphill) of the Coconino Rim, some two to four miles south of Arizona Highway 64 and six miles west of U.S. Highway 89.

This name was also applied by the Navajos to the entire Coconino Plateau. Important location in Navajo Coyoteway (Luckert 1979, 194) and the Navajo hunter tradition (Luckert 1975, 149).

ALSO: (5040 ft) Coconino County, AZ. Navajo Dził Łibáí, "Gray Mountain." This tiny community on U.S. Highway 89 lies eight miles south of Cameron. It consists of several motels, Gray Mountain Trading Post (opened during the late 1930s) (Kelley 1977, 254), gas stations, and a giant Arizona Department of Transportation maintenance yard.

GRAY MOUNTAIN CANYON: (3000 ft, floor) Coconino County, AZ. Navajo: Dził Łibáí Bikooh, "Gray Mountain Canyon." Refers to the junction of the Grand Canyon and Little Colorado River Canyon.

GREASEWOOD (LOWER): [DB] (5900 ft) (Population: 196) Apache County, AZ. Navajo: Díwózhii Bíí'Tó, "Spring in the Greasewood." A trading post, opened prior to 1915 (Kelley 1977, 253), and a school located near Greasewood Spring in the wide, barren valley of the Pueblo Colorado Wash, some 20 miles south of Ganado. (Not to be confused with Greasewood Trading Post near Lukachukai.)

GREASEWOOD (UPPER) TRADING POST: (7200 ft) Apache County, AZ. Díwózhíí Bíí'tó, "Water in the Greasewood" (Austin and Lynch 1983, 36). This post, opened about 1900 (Kelley 1977, 252), was four miles south of Lukachukai on Navajo Route 12. It no longer exists. Kluckhohn (1927, 154) referred to this area as Greasewood Springs.

HA HO NO GEH CANYON: (6200–5000 ft) Coconino County, AZ. Navajo: Nahoneeshjéél, "Rough Rocky Canyon" (U.S. Indian Claims Commission n.d., vol. VI, viii). A 20-mile-long canyon running north-south in extremely rough country between Howell Mesa (south) and Moenkopi Wash (north). This ephemeral water course heads on Howell Mesa some 12 miles due west of Hotevilla, and flows north into Moenkopi Wash five miles south of a feature known as

Middle Mesa (not to be confused with Hopi Second Mesa).

HAMBLIN RIDGE: (5983 ft) Coconino County, AZ. Navajo: "Sa Kahn" (meaning uncertain). That portion of the Echo Cliffs running south from Gap, parallelling Hamblin Wash. Both were named for Jacob Hamblin, the Mormon missionary in charge of the Latter Day Saints' early Arizona colonization (Granger 1960, 72).

HARD ROCK: (6000 ft) Navajo County, AZ. Navajo: Tsé Dildǫ'í, "Booming Rock" (Kelley p.c. 1994). A small chapter community on central Black Mesa, six miles west of Little Black Spot Mountain on Oraibi Wash.

HASBIDITO CREEK: (6800–5150 ft) Apache County, AZ. Navajo: Hasbídí Tó, "Turtle Dove Spring" (Gregory 1915, 151). This body heads on the northwest slope of Mexican Cry Mesa, between the Lukachukai Mountains (on the north) and Cove Mesa. It flows northwest and southwest 20 miles into Lukachukai Wash seven miles downstream (northwest) of Round Rock.

Early Spanish explorers named this channel Arroyo del Carrizo (Brugge 1965, 16–17), for the mountains to the east, from which the spring rises.

HAVASUPAI INDIAN RESERVATION: [DB] Coconino County, AZ. Also Supai, Coconino. Navajo: Góóhníinii, from a Hopi word of obscure etymology. Havasupai: Havasuwaipaa, "Blue (or green) Water People." Hopi: Komina, of obscure origin. Indian reservation along the south rim of the Grand Canyon, between the Kaibab National Forest (east) and the Hualapai Indian Reservation (west). In 1941, this tribe numbered only two hundred people, living mostly in Cataract or Havasupai Canyon, a southern tributary of the Grand Canyon and the Colorado River. The administrative agency is at Truxten Canyon, Valentine. The Havasupai are of Yuman linguistic stock.

The Havasupai may have had contact with the Spaniards as early as 1540 (Schwartz 1983, 14–15), and a Spanish mission may have been established in the Moenkopi area as early as 1665 (Brugge p.c. 1996). However, European influence on the Havasupai was minimal until after 1776, when Father Francisco Garcés was guided to their Cataract Canyon by Walapais. A century and a quarter ago they held the lower Moenkopi Wash (shown on McComb's map in 1869 as Cosonino Wash), the Gap country, and Coconino Point (Gray Mountain), as well as the northwestern slopes of the San Francisco Peaks. In the early American period they picked piñons on Gray Mountain with the Navajos, and traded fine-quality tanned deer hides in exchange for Navajo blankets. They were alternately friendly and hostile toward their neighbors as territory disputes developed in the 1840s.

Though primarily a hunting people, the Supai carried on a certain amount of agriculture in favorable locations. One of their farms was formerly at Willow Spring Oasis some 15 miles northwest of Tuba City.

The Havasupai carry on much the same existence today, raising corn, beans, squash, sunflowers, figs, and peaches, gathering numerous wild foods—piñons, prickly pears, mesquite beans, mescal and juniper berries—and hunting deer, mountain sheep, small animals, and birds. In winter they live on the mesas above their deep canyon, herding cattle and sheep, and in summer move down into the canyon where all their farming is concentrated. They make a great variety of basketry and excellent tanned buckskin, and formerly made utilitarian pottery, but this has been almost completely replaced by metal utensils.

HA WHI YALIN WASH: (6200–5900 ft) Navajo County, AZ. Navajo: Hahoyílíní, "Up Well Flow" (Kelley p.c. 1994). This wash heads on the southern slopes of Star Mountain, and flows east approximately 10 miles before terminating in an alluvial sink some five miles west of White Cone.

THE HAYSTACKS: (6755 ft) Apache County, AZ. Navajo: Tséta' Ch'ééch'í, "Breezes Blow Out from Between the Rocks" (Young and Morgan 1987, 731) and Tseyt', "Between the Rocks." (Not to be confused with Haystack Butte near Dilkon.) A series of abrupt sandstone monu-

ments about 100 ft high in Tsé Bonito Tribal Park (established October 1, 1963), on the north side of Arizona Highway 264 in Window Rock, nearly abutting the New Mexico state line. This park serves as home to the Navajo Nation Zoo and other offices.

This locale was the first stopping place for four thousand Navajos on the Long Walk (from Fort Defiance, Arizona, to Fort Sumner, New Mexico, in 1864. (See also Tsé Bonito, New Mexico.)

HOGANSAANI WASH: (6050–5500 ft) Coconino County, AZ. Navajo: Hooghansáanii, "Lone House in the Desert" (Gregory 1915, 151). According to Young (p.c. 1995) this makes no sense, and the name is probably Sahdii Hooghaní, "Lone Hogan." A seven-mile-long tributary of Shinumo Wash, this normally dry riverbed heads on Limestone Ridge and flows west into Shinumo Wash approximately two miles upstream of the head of Twentynine Mile Canyon.

HOLBROOK: [DB] (5245 ft) (Population: 4,686) Navajo County, AZ. Navajo: T'iisyaa Kin, "House Under the Cottonwoods." A small city on the Santa Fe Railroad and the Rio Puerco of the West 26 miles west of Petrified Forest National Park. Here Arizona Highway 77 intersects I-40. The population in 1941 was only 1,200. It once was an important cattle and lumber shipping point, now mostly a tourist center, as the entry to Hopi, Navajo, and White Mountain Apache country. It also serves as a commerce center for members of all these tribes. Petrified Forest National Park is only 18 miles to the east, reached by either U.S. Highway 260 or I-40.

The first settler in the Holbrook vicinity was Juan Padilla, who in the 1870s opened a saloon just east of the famous Horsehead Crossing immediately above the junction of the Little Colorado and Rio Puerco of the West. Bill Haywood operated a government post here serving the Star Mail Route between Fort Wingate and Fort Whipple. In 1881, the Atlantic and Pacific Railroad head-of-track reached the settlement, and the new station was named for a locating engineer, H. R. Holbrook (Granger 1960, 240). In

1882 the town site was moved to the new railroad station, and when Apache County was divided in 1895, Holbrook was made county seat of the new Navajo County. It was known in the early days as one of the most lawless towns in the Southwest and was frequented by many notorious characters.

Navajos tell of a fight with the Utes between Holbrook and Joseph City, around 1855. In the 1880s and 1890s, with the influx of settlers, Holbrook became the center of many difficulties between Whites and Navajos over cattle stealing, land, and water rights (Van Valkenburgh 1941, 72).

A feature known as Riverward Knoll, a few miles southwest of Holbrook, is important to the Navajo Mothway myth (Haile 1978, 83).

HOMOLOVI: [DB, AP] (4900 ft) Navajo County, AZ. Also Homolobi. Navajo: Uncertain. Hopi: Homolovi, of obscure meaning. A well-defined mound enclosing a Pueblo IV Hopi ruin occupied from A.D. 1300 to 1540 on the east bank of the Little Colorado River, three miles northeast of Winslow (on I-40).

The Hopis believe that several of their clans lived in Homolovi and other nearby pueblos during the fourteenth century, and moved from the region owing to a mosquito plague and waterlogged soil.

J. Walter Fewkes of the Smithsonian Institution excavated the Homolovi sites in the 1890s.

HOPI BUTTES: [DB (as Moqui Buttes)] (5400–6740 ft) Navajo County, AZ. Also Moqui Buttes, Blue Peaks, Rabbit Ear Mountain, and Moki Buttes. Navajo: Dibé Dah Sitíní, "Mountain Sheep Lying Down Up at an Elevation," though Florence Ellis (1974, 423) recorded the name as Dibehn Jikahn, the meaning of which is uncertain. Hopi: Each of the buttes has its own name. Hopis call Breast Butte "Pi tukwi," Saddle Butte "Yatkuatukwi," etc. This rough, broken, and barren country lies between the Hopi Mesas (north) and I-40 (south). The area is dotted with many small and moderate-sized volcanic plugs in the form of buttes and mesas between 800 and 1000 ft high (Egloffstein Butte, Nipple Butte, Montezuma's Chair, Castle Butte, Chimney

Butte, Star Butte, Badger Butte, Round Top, Elephant Butte, Janice Peak, Five Buttes, Flying Butte, Stephen Butte, Teshim Butte, Deshgish Butte, French Butte, Haystack Butte, Smith Butte, Mitten Peak, Hennesey Buttes, etc.) The region is the scene of early summer eagle harvesting by Hopis (Granger 1960, 240).

This picturesque region, visible for miles from the south and west, was shown on McComb's map of 1860 as Blue Peaks, and until about 1915 was known as Johnson's Extension. Parts of the region were acquired for the Navajos by successive executive orders and acts of Congress, the latest action being in 1934.

Van Valkenburgh (1974) describes "Moqui Butte" (Navajo: Tsézhin Ch'ínít'i, "A Line of Lava Extends Horizontally Outward") as important to the western clans' eastern migration stories.

HOPI RESERVATION: [DB] (4650–7220 ft) Navajo and Coconino Counties, AZ. Also Moqui or Moki, a word believed to be derived from the Zuni or Hopi spelling of an archaic word, "mókwi." This term was commonly used after 1598, but was changed to Hopi, a more modern term used by the Hopi themselves, because the English pronunciation of the older term was offensive to the Hopi as it was too similar to their word móki, meaning "dies, or is dead" (Harrington 1945, 177–78; Connelly 1979, 551). Navajo: 'Ayahkinii, "Underground People" (Young p.c. 1995). Calling themselves Sinome, this pueblo tribe lives in 13 villages located on the 2,472,320-acre Hopi Reservation in north-central Arizona. The population in 1939 was 3,248; in 1990 it had reached 11,173. The villages are mostly located on the southwestern fingers of Black Mesa, with an agency at Keams Canyon. The language falls into the Shoshonean family of the Uto-Aztecan stock.

This reservation is entirely contained within the larger Navajo Reservation, and incorporates a portion of southern Black Mesa in the north, and the barren Painted Desert region to the south. The southern—and lowest—portion of this parcel of desert land is some of the most desolate country in the United States, yet the Hopi Indians have lived for centuries in numerous small villages situated among three peninsular mesas projecting from the southern margin of Black Mesa. Although the region is dotted with sporadic small streams, it has no permanent rivers. The predominant ephemeral channels are Moenkopi, Dinnebito, Wepo, Oraibi, and Jeddito Washes.

The historically traditional Hopi homes were pueblos of the classical style, and these are still in evidence atop the three mesas. Between the mesas, however, many individual family units have sprung up, both incorporated in villages—like Polacca—and as isolated farmsteads.

The Hopis are the oldest continuous inhabitants of northern Arizona; some of their ancestors may have lived in the region as early as A.D. 700. The ample and permanent springs fed from seepages carried along non-filterable strata from Black Mesa have had a great deal to do with their stability. Tradition relates that some of their early ancestors were immigrants from the Tsegi and Canyon de Chelly Anasazi ruins. Later groups came from Chaves Pass, Homolovi, and other southern pueblos, joined still later by Tewas and Keres from the Rio Grande region in New Mexico.

The first Europeans to visit the Hopis were Don Pedro de Tovar and Father Juan Padilla in 1542 on a side exploration from the Coronado Expedition. At that time all the pueblos, with the exception of Oraibi, were located on the foothills below the mesas and on the lower terraces. The Spaniards called the general Hopi region "Province of Tusayan."

The Franciscans established the first mission among the Hopis in 1629 and introduced peaches and other domesticated plants, as well as domesticated animals. Most of the missions were destroyed and their priests killed in the Pueblo Revolt of 1680. Seeking refuge from the possible reprisals during the reconquest of New Mexico, and from increasing Ute and Navajo raids, the Hopis moved from the foothills and terraces to the more defensible positions on the mesa rims, leaving only Oraibi occupying its original site. Soon after the Spanish Reconquest, groups of Tewa from the Rio Grande moved in and established themselves among the Hopis.

Until 1906, there were seven main villages and the farming village of Moenkopi, an offshoot of Oraibi located some 40 miles westward near Tuba City. The Hopis had been in difficulty with the government since 1880, for refusal to send children to school or allow the introduction of modern sanitation and medical methods necessitated by epidemics of smallpox. In 1904 the Hopi Indian agent was attacked at Shungopovi over the forced schooling issue, and a number of Hopis were sent to Alcatraz Prison for a year. Oraibi had split into two factions in the 1890s, the "Unfriendlies," or Conservatives, and the "Friendlies," or Non-conservatives, the terms indicating their attitude toward the government.

The final outcome was the migration of the Conservatives to establish the present village of Hotevilla. With them went certain ceremonials, including the Snake Dance. A lowering of the water table and loss of agricultural lands through floods led to a further decline of Old Oraibi, until there are now fewer than one hundred inhabitants, the remainder having moved off the mesa and settled at Kykotsmovi (known until about 1982 as New Oraibi).

The economic basis of Hopi life rests upon an extremely specialized form of agriculture. No permanent streams flow through the Hopi country. Rainfall annually averages less than 12 inches and comes almost solely in the summer months. There is little snow in winter.

The majority of the farm lands lie along washes, where temporary dams of brush, earth, or stone divert the flood waters over the fields. These are usually bordered or "diked" following the natural contour of the land in an effort to conserve all the moisture. On the mesa tops as well as on the plains below them, the Hopi farmer constructs brush barriers of any shrub or tree available in order to accumulate the wind-blown sand for mulch.

Hopi agricultural products include corn of the flint type, a quick-growing and hardy species commonly known as "Indian corn," over 20 varieties of beans, melons, and squash, as well as fruit trees, particularly peach tees, which are planted on sand and talus slopes near springs and sub-irrigated places. This delicious, small fruit of today's peach tree was introduced hundreds of years ago by the Spanish, probably the Franciscan Fathers of the seventeenth century. In the past, some native cotton was raised, but little if any is now grown. Some families also own cattle and sheep.

Hopi women manufacture decorated and undecorated pottery. All of the decorated pottery was made on First Mesa until the 1970s. The men weave blankets and engage in silversmithing, painting, and woodcarving. Basketry is made on Second and Third Mesas. In the section following, see also Hano, Hotevilla, Kykotsmovi (formerly New Oraibi), Mishongnovi, Oraibi (Old Oraibi), Shipaulovi, Shungopovi, Sichomavi, Sikyatki, and Walpi.

✤ AWATOVI: [DB] (6200 ft) Navajo County, AZ. (Also Awatobi) Navajo: Táala Hooghan, "Flat-Topped Hogan" (Young p.c. 1995). Hopi: Awatovi, "Place of the Bow." Ruins (Pueblo III through historic periods) of Hopi, a village located on the extreme western point of juniper-covered Antelope Mesa south of Keams Canyon, and north of Jeddito Valley. This village was the first point of Hopi contact by Pedro de Tovar in 1540, by Antonio de Espejo in 1583, and by Oñate in 1598. The village was Christianized by the Spanish Franciscans in 1629, but Father Figueroa was murdered and the mission destroyed in the Pueblo Revolt of 1680. Awatovi was the only Hopi village to return to Christianity following the Spanish Reconquest. It was sacked and burned by Hopis from the villages of Walpi and Mishongnovi in the winter of 1700–1701. All adult male villagers were killed, and women and children were carried off. Hopi traditionalists explain the massacre was carried out because "The town was filled with 'singing men' (Christians) whom the other Hopis did not like."

Test excavations were conducted at Awatovi and its cemetery by Dr. J. Walter Fewkes in the 1890s, with more extensive excavations by the Peabody Museum of Harvard University in the 1940s. The latter produced a tentative founding date of about A.D. 1100 for the village.

This site is mentioned in the Navajo Windway Ceremony (Van Valkenburgh 1974, 11), and is home of the hero and his grandmother in the Navajo Man Red Antway Myth (Wyman 1965).

✤ FIRST MESA: (6000–6400 ft) Navajo County, AZ. Easternmost of three "fingerlike" peninsulas projecting from the southern edge of Black Mesa (see also Second Mesa and Third Mesas). Some 10 miles long and a half mile to four miles wide, this mesa is the site of the Hopi villages of Walpi, Sichomovi, and Hano. First Mesa is bounded on the west by Wepo Wash and on the east by Polacca Wash.

» HANO: [DB] (6200 ft) Apache County, AZ. Also called Tewa. Navajo: Naashashí, "Bear People," or, more literally, "Enemy Bears," the name deriving from the bear sandpaintings of the Tewas at Hano. The same name is applied to Santa Clara Pueblo in New Mexico (Young p.c. 1995). Hopi: "Hanu," from the Hopi language, referring to the "ha" commonly heard in the Tewa language, and which has come to mean "Tewa" in Hopi. A Tewa (language) village on Hopi First Mesa, settled by refugees from the Rio Grande pueblos fleeing the Spanish reconquest of the territory in 1692 following the great Pueblo Revolt of 1680. This is the northeastern-most village on First Mesa (see also Sichomavi and Walpi). The village had a population of 285 in 1939. Located on the Hopi Indian Reservation on top of East or First Mesa.

Around the year 1700, a portion of the population of the village of Tsewaii (or San Cristobal), in the Galisteo Basin southwest of Santa Fe, New Mexico, left their homes to establish the new pueblo of Hano in the Hopi country (Schroeder 1979a, 247–48). They came at the invitation of Hopi emissaries who promised them attractive lands in return for help in fighting the Utes and Navajos. They first settled near Coyote Spring, but after a battle in which they defeated a Ute war party that had attacked Walpi, they were invited to settle atop First Mesa (James 1990, 11).

Although they lived in close proximity with, and even intermarried with, the Hopis, they have never been fully absorbed into that tribe, and still retain the Tewa language of the Rio Grande villages. Once famous warriors, they became the policemen for the Hopi Reservation.

The Navajo Rounded Man Red Antway Myth mentions this community in the hero's search for his family (Wyman 1965).

» POLACCA: [DB] (6000 ft) (Population: 1,108) Navajo County, AZ. Navajo: Uncertain. Hopi: Polakaka, "Butterfly," after Tom Polacca (James 1990, 11). A Hopi village, located at the foot of the southeast point of First Mesa, on Arizona Highway 264, eight miles east of the junction with Arizona Highway 87. In 1990 the population of 200 was more than the census total for all Hopi villages combined in 1940. A Baptist mission is found in the village, along with a Hopi-run trading post and a model high school. The first trading post was established in the early 1890s (Kelley 1977, 252).

Tom Polacca, a Tewa from Hano, moved down from the mesa top in 1890 and established the village of Polacca. In 1891, the U.S. government, wishing to induce the Hopis and Tewas to come down from the mesa-top villages considered unsanitary, began extensive building operations at Polacca, and by 1900 over one hundred stone houses had been built. Ten years later, less than half of the buildings were occupied. Doors, windows, and floors had been removed and transported to the top of the mesa. In 1935 only 7 percent of the people of First Mesa were to be found in Polacca.

Two miles north of Polacca lie the 10-to-15-acre ruins of Sikyatki (Yellow House), destroyed by the people of Walpi in the sixteenth century, after some years of bitter animosity between the people of the two villages (James 1974, 26).

» SICHOMAVI: [DB] (6200 ft) Navajo County, AZ. Also Sichomovi. Navajo: 'Ayahkin, "Underground House." Hopi: Shichomovi, "Place of the Wild Currant Mound." Also known as Middle Village, this community lies between Walpi and Hano villages.

Members of the Potki, Lizard, Wild Mustard, and Badger clans from Walpi built this village (James 1990, 10) about 1750. Later, a Tanoan clan from the Rio Grande Valley is said to have joined the village after having been invited to help fight the Utes, and these are said to be the ancestors of the present Asa Clan.

This village is also reputed to have been the stopping place of certain Jemez groups fleeing the Rio Grande in the last decade of the seventeenth century. They later joined the Navajos in Canyon de Chelly and became affiliated with others to form the Ma'ii' Deeshgizhnii ("Coyote Pass People") clan of the Navajo.

The village was once decimated by smallpox, and the survivors fled to Tsegi Canyon, Monument Valley, and Zuni. They later returned and rebuilt the village (James 1990, 10). The population of Sichomavi in 1941 was 406. Traders at that time were Charley Naha and Robert Satala.

» WALPI: [DB] (6225 ft) Navajo County, AZ. Navajo: Deez'áajj', "Up to the Point (of the Mesa)" (Young p.c. 1995); also Niiyahkinii, "People of the Kiva" (Franciscan Fathers 1910, 135), or, more literally, "Underground Houses" (Young p.c. 1995). Hopi: Walpi, "Place of the Gap," referring to a "notch" in the mesa north of Walpi (James 1990, 10). This stone pueblo is located at the extremely rocky southernmost tip of First Mesa on the Hopi Reservation, where its nearest neighbors are Sichomovi and Hano (Tewa).

Walpi was constructed prior to A.D. 1700. Its protective location across "the Gap" from the other First Mesa villages may have offered protection from the reconquering Spaniards following the Pueblo Revolt of 1680, as well as from Ute and Navajo raiders. Tully Rock, on the trail up the south side of the mesa, is engraved with the record of Navajos, Apaches, and Utes killed by residents of First Mesa.

Because of Hopi conservatism concerning archaeologists and anthropologists, the exact beginning of human occupation of First Mesa remains uncertain. Pithouses on the slopes of the mesa date to about the time of Christ, and shortly after A.D. 1300, the Anasazi ancestors of the Hopis built a pueblo called Walpi below the present village bearing the name, on a ledge called Quchaptuvela (Gray Slope).

The first documented European contact with Walpi appears to have been the arrival of Espejo in 1583. In 1629, when the first Franciscan missionaries established themselves in Hopi territory, Walpi was not important enough to house a mission, though a visita was constructed on the ledge at the tip of the mesa. Many Hopis from Quchaptuvela settled around the visita, bringing with them the name Walpi. After the Pueblo Revolt of 1680, the population moved from the ledge to the top of the mesa. Thereafter, the site they abandoned on the ledge was called Ki-isa'ovi (Ladder House).

Modern Walpi can be reached by a paved road from Polacca, on the desert floor, though as late as the 1950s the road was unpaved, more winding, and far more precarious. Walpi hosted the Hopi Snake Dance in odd years, during which time the road was closed and visitors had to hike to the top of the mesa.

» SIKYATKI: [DB] (approx. 6000 ft) Navajo County, AZ. Also spelled Sitkyatki. Navajo: Uncertain. Hopi: Sikyatki, "Yellow House of the Firewood People" (Van Valkenburgh 1941, 147), though more likely "Cut-Off/Divided Valley" (Lomatuway'ma, Lomatuway'ma, and Namingha 1993, 118). A Hopi ruin on the eastern foot of First Mesa, two miles north of Polacca, this village was destroyed by other Hopis in the fifteenth century.

The village's demise is attributed to inter-village strife between Sikyatki and Walpi (Fewkes 1895, 576; Mindeleff 1891, 24–25; and James 1917, 93) or between Sikyatki and a village known as Qöötsaptuvela (Curtis 1922, 189–90; Courlander 1982, 39–40). However, it is also said that the village met its end due to intra-village strife (Waters 1963, 97–102; Lomatuway'ma, Lomatuway'ma, and Namingha 1993, 123–47). In the latter version, two men vying for the love of a young maiden staged a foot race for the right to marry her. One resorted to witchcraft but still lost and was subsequently killed by the other. Bad blood led to growing animosities within the village, and its chief finally appealed to a neighboring chief to attack the village and destroy it. This was done, with nearly all the Sikyatki villagers killed, including the scheming chief. This nearly obliterated the Coyote Clan (Lomatuway'ma, Lomatuway'ma, and Namingha 1993, 147).

Pottery with a rich yellow slip and beautiful geometric and animorphic designs recovered in the 1895 excavations inspired noted potter Nampeyo, the Hopi wife of one of the workmen, to use old techniques and designs.

This led to the renaissance of First Mesa decorated pottery, which is known as the Sitkyatki Revival. Nampeyo's name has been for 80 years synonymous with First Mesa pottery. Nampeyo lost her vision before her death, and her daughter, Fanny Polacca, carried on the tradition. Until recently, all decorated Hopi pottery has been made on First Mesa, with the other mesas manufacturing plainware for utilitarian purposes. Painted pottery has now spread beyond First Mesa.

✤ KAWAIOUKUH: (6000 ft) Navajo County, AZ. Navajo: Uncertain. An abandoned Hopi village on Balakai Mesa, three miles southeast of Awatovi. In July 1540, Spaniard Don Pedro de Tovar attacked and destroyed this habitat. It was reoccupied sometime prior to 1582, but had been abandoned for good by 1598 (Granger 1960, 243)

✤ SECOND MESA: (6200–6450 ft) (Population: 929) Navajo County, AZ. Navajo: Uncertain. Intermediate of the three "fingerlike" mesas projecting southwest from the southern edge of Black Mesa, known collectively as the "Hopi Mesas." Second Mesa is 20 miles long, and two to 10 miles wide, splitting into two peninsulas. It houses the Hopi villages of Shungopovi, Mishongnovi, and Shipolovi. It is bounded on the west by Oraibi Wash, and on the east by Wepo Wash.

» MISHONGNOVI: [DB] (5750 ft) Navajo County, AZ. Also known as Second Mesa. Navajo: Tsétsohk'id, "Big Boulder Hill." Hopi: Moshangnovi, "Place of the Black Man" (Van Valkenburgh 1941, 99); a less accepted name means "the other of two sandstone columns remains standing" (Granger 1960, 244), referring to the fact that one of two (James [1990, 12–13] says three of four) sandstone pillars several hundred yards from the village had collapsed. This Hopi village sits on the eastern rim of Second Mesa, located a mile south of Shipaulovi, at the junction of Arizona Highway 264 at Arizona Highway 87. The town had a population of only 227 in 1939.

An older village of the same name was established in the thirteenth century, then abandoned sometime prior to 1680. Its ruins sit on the first terrace below and south of the present village.

Van Valkenburgh adheres to Colton's (1947) suggestion that the name is said to refer to a chief, Mosahng, or Mishong, a member of the Crow Clan who led his people to the Hopi towns from the San Francisco Mountains sometime before the thirteenth century. The people of old Shungopovi refused to allow them to settle in their village because they had performed no service. Finally, they were given permission to build a town near Corn Rock on condition that they protect the rock, which was a shrine for the people of Walpi.

Another story of the founding, though not as plausible as that put forth by Colton (James 1974, 12) is that the village was originally founded by female survivors of the massacre at Awatovi in 1700.

The Franciscan mission of San Buenaventura, established at the old village in 1629, was destroyed during the Pueblo Revolt of 1680, and the villagers fled to the top of the mesa where they established the present town.

The Snake Dance is held here at the same time as at Walpi in odd years; while Shungopovi, Hotevilla, and Shipaulovi hold theirs in even years.

» SHIPAULOVI: [DB] (6050 ft) Navajo County, AZ. Also Shipolovi, Sipaulovi. Navajo: Tsétsohk'id, "Big Boulder Hill." [*Author's Note:* This name also applies to Mishongnovi, and a variant to Toreva. It appears to refer to Second Mesa itself rather than individual communities. Hopi: Shopaulovi, "Place of the Mosquitos."] One of three Hopi villages atop Second Mesa (see also Mishongnovi and Shungopovi). Shipaulovi and Mishungnovi are located at the distal end of the easternmost peninsula of the mesa, with Shipaulovi the more northerly of the two. This village was founded about 1750, with beams from the old mission at Shungopovi, indicating that at least some of the population came from that village. The Hopi name of the village, "Place of the Mosquitos," actually refers to the village of Homolovi, from whence the population was forced by a plague of mosquitos. These people settled at Shipaulovi, and currently comprise the largest clan there (Van Valkenburgh 1941, 143; Granger 1960, 250).

However, Colton (1939) states that the presence of mission beams, or vigas, suggests that Shipaulovi was settled by people from old Shungopovi (rather than Homolovi), abandoned in the early part of the eighteenth century. Its erstwhile inhabitants are said to have established Shungopovi and Shipaulovi.

In 1940 the population was 130 persons, and two traders were present (Secakuku and David Talawittima), both Hopi.

» TOREVA: [DB] Navajo County, AZ. (5900 ft) Navajo: Tsétsehk'id, "Big Rock Hill." See author's note for Shipaulovi. This village was founded in the late 1800s at the southwest base of Second Mesa, and was the site of a USIS day school. The Sunlight Baptist Mission was founded in the 1890s by the "Misses Watkins and Collins."

» SHUNGOPOVI: [DB] (6440 ft) (Population: 730) Navajo County, AZ. Also New Shungopovi, Shongopavi, Shongopovi, Shungopavi, Chimopovy. Navajo: Kin Názt'i', "Houses Strung in a Circle." Hopi: Shung-o-hu Pa Ovi, "Place by the Spring where the Tall Reeds Grow." James (1990, 11) notes that there are at least 57 spellings for the name of this village, one of three on Second Mesa (see also Shipaulovi and Mishungnovi). Shungopovi is located on the southwestern projection of the mesa.

The Hopis refer to the village as the oldest Hopi settlement, but they are referring to Old Shungopovi, whose ruins are found on the hills below the present town. It is estimated to be about as old as Oraibi, established during the fourteenth century according to tree-ring data. The Mission of San Bartolome was established at Old Shungopovi in 1629. It has been estimated that at that time the population was two thousand persons. In the Pueblo Rebellion of 1680 the mission was destroyed and the friars killed. The remains of the mission still stand on the south side of the road leading up to Shungopovi. According to the Shungopovi traditions, only seven village families escaped the reprisals of the Spaniards in the reconquest of 1692. They fled from Old Shungopovi to the site of their present village in 1629 (James 1990, 12). In 1941, the population was estimated at 353. Four traders (Peter Nuvamsa, Paul Saufkia, Sammy's Store, Archie Quamala) operated at that time. A day school (USIS) was opened on the lower bench of the mesa. In 1898, during a smallpox epidemic, military from Fort Wingate were obliged to arrest and remove Hopi priests, tear down houses, and vaccinate the villagers (Van Valkenburgh 1941, 146).

This village is often regarded as the most traditional (conservative) of all Hopi enclaves. In a bitter dispute between the "conservatives" and the "progressives" at Oraibi in 1906, a contingent from Shungopovi joined the conservative leader, Chief Youkeoma. They were evicted and went with Youkeoma to found Hotevilla. A couple of months later, however, cavalry troops visted Hotevilla and forced the Shungopovi residents to return home. Youkeoma and 26 others were arrested and imprisoned at Fort Wingate (James 1974, 133–39).

Shungopa Spring failed in 1870 when the slumping of the rim above created a minor earthquake. Masipa or Gray Spring, nearby, now supplies Shungopovi with water for drinking. Shungopovi hosts the Snake Dance in even years.

✤ THIRD MESA: (6000–6450 ft) Navajo and Coconino Counties, AZ. The westernmost of three "fingerlike" peninsulas projecting southwest from the southern edge of Black Mesa. This mesa is 15 miles long (northeast to southwest) and varies from a half-mile to five miles across. On it are situated the Hopi villages of Hotevilla, Bacavi, and Oraibi (actually on the eastern flank). It is bounded on the west by Dinnebito Wash and on the east by Oraibi Wash.

» BACAVI: [DB] (6583 ft) Navajo County, AZ. Also Bacabi, Bakabi. Navajo: Tł'ohchintó Biyáázh, "Offspring of Wild Onion Spring" (referring to Hotevilla). Hopi: Baakavii, "Place of the Jointed Reed." A Hopi village on the eastern flank of Third Mesa, on Arizona Highway 264 eight miles north of Kykotsmovi. Founded in 1907 (James 1974, 15). Van Valkenburgh described this village as the newest Hopi village. The population was 184 in 1939 (Van Valkenburgh 1941, 7).

This village was populated originally by "Conservatives" or "Hostiles" under the leadership of Lomahongyoma, who, after being forcibly evicted from Oraibi in 1906, helped found the village of Hotevilla. Shortly after, Lomahongyoma led a more moderate contingent back to Oraibi, but found they were not welcome, so left once again to found Bacavi in 1907 (James 1974, 142). The town was laid out by Hopi agent Lee Crane, with houses built separately to allow for filling in as the population increased. Bacavi's school was constructed in 1910.

» HOTEVILLA: [DB] (6000 ft) (Population: 869) Navajo County, AZ. Also Hotevilla. Navajo: Tł'ochintó, "Wild Onion Spring." Hopi: Hitaveli, "Skinned Back" (James 1990, 114). This Hopi village lies on the west flank of Third Mesa, and is off Arizona Highway 264. The 1939 population was 507.

The name Hitaveli was taken from a spring that was located in a low cave, so that one entering to get water often skinned his back. This spring was visited by Colonel (Governor) Jose Antonio Vizcarra in 1823 (McNitt 1972, 61; Brugge 1964, 235).

This village was born as a result of strife in the "mother" village, Oraibi, between 1905 and 1906. The population was sharply divided into two factions, the Conservatives (or Hostiles), and the Progressives (or Friendlies). After a confrontation, the former group, under the leadership of Youkeoma, left Oraibi in 1906 and established the village of Hotevilla. (Youkeoma and a couple dozen others were arrested and imprisoned at Fort Wingate shortly after the fracas at Oraibi.) A further split at Hotevilla in 1907 led to the founding of the village of Bacabi one mile to the east.

For two decades Hotevilla refused to send children to school, and on one occasion the U.S. Cavalry was called out to round up the children hidden in the houses. The people also refused to allow their sheep to be dipped, and for this Youkeoma was banished to California. Today, Hotevilla is one of the most conservative of the Hopi pueblos, producing high-quality baskets and textiles. It hosts the Snake Dance every even-numbered year.

Navajos from the Dinnebito region carry on considerable trade in Hotevilla.

» KYKOTSMOVI: (5770 ft) (Population: 773) Navajo County, AZ. Formerly New Oraibi or Lower Oraibi. Navajo: Uncertain, possibly Oozéí Biyázhí, "Offspring of Eagle Traps" (Young p.c. 1995), referring to Oraibi. Hopi: Kiakochomovi, "Place of the Hills of Ruins." This relatively new community—founded in 1906—is the seat of Hopi tribal government. It is on Arizona Highway 264 and Oraibi Wash, at the east base of Third Mesa.

The 1941 population was 495 (listed under Oraibi). This community includes Hopi High School, several traders (formerly including Lorenzo Hubbell), and the Evangelization Movement mission. The first trading post was opened in the late 1880s (Kelley 1977, 252).

This town was composed of Progressives from Old Oraibi led by Chief Tewaquaptewa, who settled around the school, mission, and trading store in 1906, and established a community politically independent from Old Oraibi. The school was started by missionary cooperation in 1890, and the major part of the population moved off the mesa in 1894. In 1937 a new Hopi High School was completed. Previously most Hopi high school students had gone to Phoenix.

» ORAIBI: [DB] (6050 ft) Navajo County, AZ. Also Old Oraibi. Navajo: 'Oozéí Biyashi, from 'Odzai, "Many Eagle Nests" (Franciscan Fathers 1910, 135); though Young (p.c. 1995) asserts it is simply 'Oazéí, "Eagle Traps." Hopi: Oraivi, "Place of a Rock Called Orai." A Hopi village on the southeast tip of Third Mesa, a mile or so west of Oraibi Wash on Arizona Highway 264.

The population in 1941 was only seventy-five persons. The village contains the ruins of an old Mennonite mission built by H. R. Voth in 1901 and destroyed by lightning in 1942. A trading post operated by Hopi Howard Sekestewa was situated five miles to the northwest.

Though its age has not been adequately studied, Oraibi shares Acoma Pueblo's (New Mexico) claim to be the oldest continuously occupied community in the United States. Tree-ring data

indicate that certain beams used in Oraibi buildings were growing between A.D. 1260 and 1344. According to Hopi tradition, these beams were hauled from the San Francisco Mountains almost one hundred miles to the west. The Franciscan Mission of San Fernando, established here in 1629, was destroyed during the Pueblo Revolt of 1680.

The village was visited in 1823 by troops of Vizcarra's expedition (Benally et al. 1982, 95). In 1837, Oraibi was almost destroyed by the Navajos. Until his death in 1957, Navajo medicine men used to visit a Hopi priest named Na'ashja' for certain medicines. Navajos regarded Oraibi as a favorite place to obtain ló K'aatsoh ba'ádí, a large cane used in the manufacture of certain types of Navajo k'eet'áán, or prayer sticks.

Unrest was common at Oraibi during the last decade of the nineteenth century, between Hostiles (conservatives) and Progressives, which led to 19 Hostiles, led by Chief Lomahongyoma, being arrested and incarcerated at Alcatraz on January 3, 1895. They were released August 7 of the same year, having exhibited good behavior (James 1990, 114–16; and Dockstaader 1979, 527). Internal dissension continued to simmer. In 1906 Chief Tewaquaptewa forced out all villagers who were Christian or intended to become Christian. They founded the village of New Oraibi (see Kykotsmovi). Then, on September 8, 1906, the Hostiles were forced to leave the village, and they established Hotevilla. (A subsequent rift at Hotevilla sent the most conservative element to establish the village of Bacavi in 1908.)

Oraibi's population, which numbered in the thousands in the seventeenth century, declined to fewer than a hundred by the middle of the twentieth century. Van Valkenburgh (1941, 110) cites smallpox epidemics in 1760, 1840, and 1898, though other sources (Dockstaader 1979, 525) mention only one in 1853–54, followed by a devastating drought, as causes of the heavy population losses. Van Valkenburgh also cites additional droughts between 1890 and 1904, when the Hopi country was visited by alternate drought and torrential rains, clan lands were swept away, and Oraibi Wash was cut to bedrock, seriously lowering the water table.

Arrows for the Navajo Male Branch of Shoot-ingway were made from reeds obtained at either Oraibi or Taos, New Mexico (Haile 1947, 18).

As evidenced in many of the above entries, the Hopis and Navajos have long been traditional enemies. In particular, the Navajos would raid the Hopis for slaves, taking young boys and girls capable of riding horses (Ellis 1974, 113). Some-times they were adopted into families, other times they were ransomed or traded into more distant slavery with the Utes, Comanches, or Spaniards. Yet the record seems to suggest a more fearful attitude on the part of the Hopis toward the Utes, and Brugge (p.c. 1996) notes that far more Hopi captives were carried off by New Mexican Hispanics than by Navajos; and the Hopis suffered less than the Utes, Apaches, Paiutes, and Navajos in this respect.

It sometimes appears that the enmity between the Hopis and Navajos has been exacerbated by the tribal governments and non-Indian advo-cates of Hopi causes, such as in the case of the Navajo-Hopi land dispute. The relationship has also been one of such amicable activities as visiting and trading, with a generous amount of intermarriage. The land problems have been especially hard on the intertribal couples and their half-Hopi, half-Navajo children (Brugge p.c. 1996).

HOPI SALT MINE: [DB, in description of Wil-low Spring] (approx. 4050 ft) Coconino County, AZ. Navajo: 'Áshįįh, "Salt" (Van Valkenburgh 1974). This source of salt is in the mouth of a large cave in the Little Colorado River Canyon, two miles downstream from Hopi Trail Canyon, in which salt crystals hang from the 50-ft ceiling like stalactites. Nearby is the little-known Blue Spring, said to be the most voluminous spring in Navajo country. Strangely, the water of this spring is indigo blue. Its stream is said to be three feet deep.

Traditionally, only Hopis from Third Mesa en-tered the salt mine, while residents of First and Second Mesas obtained their salt from Zuni. The salt from the mine was used on food and for cer-emonial purposes (Eiseman 1959, 25–32).

HOSKININNI MESA: (7000–6000 ft) Navajo County, AZ., and San Juan County, UT. Navajo: Hashké Neiniihí, "He distributed them with Angry Insistence," referring to Navajo Headman Hoskinini's giving sheep to returning tribesmen after the Bosque Redondo (Young and Morgan 1987, 418), "Giving Out Anger" (McPherson 1988, 9), also translated as "Angry One" and "Angry Warrior," again referring to Hoskinini (Gregory 1915, 151), who lived in the vicinity until his death in 1909 (Granger 1960, 242), when he was succeeded by his son Hashké Neiniihi Biye', who died in 1958. The upland west of El Capitan Flat in the Monument Valley region, south of the San Juan River. The mesa stretches eight miles north-south, five miles in Arizona, three in Utah. Author Samuel Moon (1992, 68) once saw a device against the coyote here, in the form of goats dressed in old cast-off sweaters and shirts, "scarecrow like."

The region of Hoskininni Mesa was visited by Colonel (Governor) Jose Antonio Vizcarra in 1823 (McNitt 1972, 63). Hashké Neiniihí led his people in a resistance of the U.S. Army in the canyons of this region during the Kit Carson and Bosque Redondo years, as did K'aayélii ("Quiver Man") near the Bears Ears (in Utah), Dáhgaa' Sikaad ("Tufted Mustache") on the Kaibito Plateau, and Spane Shank near Navajo Mountain (McPherson 1988, 9; Young p.c. 1995).

HOT NA NA WASH: (5400–3050 ft) Coconino County, AZ. Navajo: Ha'naa Na'ní'á, "Bridge Across," (Kelley p.c. 1994, Young p.c. 1995). A 10-mile-long tributary of the Colorado River, entering Marble Canyon from the south about a mile upstream (north) of House Rock Rapids.

HOUCK: [DB] (6000 ft) Apache County, AZ. Navajo: Mą'iito'í, "Coyote Spring." This small community is located on the northern edge of the Valley of the Rio Puerco of the West, near the mouth of Black Creek. On present-day I-40, Houck is roughly 10 miles west of Lupton, and 13 miles west of the New Mexico state line. The community hosts the Franciscan Catherine Tekakwitha Mission and school and several small trading concerns (including the former White Mound Trading Post).

Houck was named after James D. Houck, an early settler in the Valley of the Rio Puerco of the West. The Navajo farmers in this vicinity mostly live on Indian allotments and leased lands. According to Adolph F. Bandelier (Lange and Riley 1970, 30), the location was better known as "Bennett's" in 1883, and Granger (1960, 13) misidentifies it as the scene of the "murder" of William Walker and William Smith by Indians in 1880. (See Houck Trading Post.)

HOUCK TRADING POST: (6000 ft) Apache County, AZ. Navajo: Same as the community. This post was built by James Houck, and was known as Houck's Tank until 1881, when the Atchison, Topeka and Santa Fe Railroad (now the Burlington Northern Santa Fe) passed close by. In 1885, Houck moved on to the Mogollon Mountains to the south. The Houck trading post was off-reservation, and thus not subject to Indian Service controls, and, like many such posts, saw its share of Indian-White conflicts. In 1887, two White men and a Navajo were killed in a shooting incident near here. On June 25, 1915, two employees from Houck found the bodies of two traders at Cronenmeyer's Trading Post (near Zuni), after receiving a rare phone call from that post announcing that the owner and an employee had been shot. (Cronenmeyer's was sometimes spelled Kronemeyer or Kronemayer)

HOWELL MESA: (6400 ft) Coconino County, AZ. Navajo: Tsin Bił Dah 'Azkání, "Flattop (Mesa) with Trees" (Young and Morgan 1987, 737; Kelley p.c. 1994; U.S. Indian Claims Commission n.d., vol. VI, xxiii). A 400- to 600-ft mesa above the Moenkopi Plateau, some 10 miles due west of Third Mesa, and traversed by Arizona Highway 264. The English name is for E. E. Howell, geologist of the Wheeler Survey (Gregory 1915, 151).

HUBBELL TRADING POST: (6400 ft) Ganado, Apache County, AZ. Navajo: Lók'aahnteel (Malone p.c. 1997), "Wide Band of Reeds up at an Elevation." Possibly also Nák'ee Sinilí, ("Eye Glasses") or Naakaii Sání ("Old Mexi-

can"), names by which the Navajos knew Lorenzo Hubbell. Since the earliest posts in the Ganado vicinity predated the reservation extension to this locale, and since Lorenzo Hubbell cared little for dates, the early history of this national historical site is shrouded in educated guesses. McNitt (1962, 200–202) notes that a man named Charles Crary was known to be trading at present-day Ganado by 1871 or 1872, but he was gone within five years, evidently selling to William ("Old Man") Leonard. Meanwhile, working for John Wetherill at Chaco Canyon, Lorenzo Hubbell had likely invested in a post run by his brother Charles south of Ganado Lake.

When local witchcraft violence apparently doomed that post in 1878, Lorenzo purchased Leonard's buildings in the Valley of the Red House for a post of his own (Brugge 1993, 24–25), and Leonard moved to Fort Defiance. In 1879, Hubbell married Lina Rubi, daughter of Cruz and Tafoya Reyes Rubi, of Cebolleta, New Mexico. A presidential executive order of January 6, 1880, expanded the western boundary of the Navajo Reservation, and Hubbell found his property engulfed and labeled "reservation," and his trader's license in danger of suspension. He began a long battle to get this ruling reversed, as property occupied prior to a reservation expansion was normally "exempted" if not purchased from the owner.

Hubbell was elected sheriff of Navajo County, and in 1884 he found himself in need of a partner to manage the trading post. This partner was Clinton (C. N.) Cotton of Gallup, who bought out Hubbell's share a year later.

An act of Congress in 1902 declared the trading post private property, and it was probably about this time that Cotton sold the post back to Hubbell (Williams 1989, 16–17), though Brugge (1993, 31) suggests this happened as early as 1895. In any case, Cotton moved to Gallup to open his other soon-to-be-famous concern, C. N. Cotton Trading Company, and if the Ganado post had not been sold back to Hubbell prior to that time, he certainly managed it for Cotton. It was not until 1917, however, that a patent for homestead was issued to Hubbell for the Ganado property (McNitt 1962, 216–17).

When Lorenzo Hubbell died on November 12, 1930, the post was taken over by his son Roman, who ran it until his death on October 14, 1957. His widow, Dorothy, kept the post under family management until the National Park Service purchased the property on April 3, 1967. Under a management agreement with the Southwest Parks and Monuments Association, the post has continued as a living exhibit, under the management of Bill Young (1967–79), Al Grieve (1979–82) and Bill Malone (1982–present) (James 1988, 63–69).

Though sometimes described as "fortress-like," the structure at Ganado—built in a square enclosing a small courtyard—was the result of separately erected buildings being joined after 1900 (Brugge p.c. 1996). Some Navajos say Hubbell mortgaged his post to Chee Dodge for $30,000 to pay off costs of a failed U.S. Senate bid, and that he never fully repaid this debt. At least one report has the trading post made of stones from a nearby Anasazi ruin—but Hubbell was too smart for that (Blue 1986, 12–13), as this would have summarily killed his Navajo business if it had been discovered by the ghost-fearing Diné.

Lorenzo Hubbell, Sr. (also called Don Lorenzo), also owned, at one time or another, posts at Chinle, Black Mountain, Nazlini, Oraibi, and Cedar Springs in Arizona, and Piñon Springs (south of Gallup) and in Gallup, New Mexico. His son, Lorenzo, Jr., owned posts at Keams Canyon, Piñon, Big Mountain, Dinnebito, Na-ah-tee, Sand Springs, and Marble Canyon, all in Arizona. Post ownership by this father and son duo is often confused (Brugge 1993).

HUBBELL AND COTTON TRADING POST:

(5058 ft) Apache County, AZ. Navajo: Uncertain. In 1886 Lorenzo Hubbell of Ganado and C. N. Cotton of Gallup were granted the first license to trade at Chinle, in an old abandoned hogan to which they added three stone rooms in a "fortress" style. They operated the post for less than a year, though Hubbell opened a new post in 1900, which survived to become Camille Garcia's post, which closed in the 1970s. In the interim, the building was likely occupied by a host of erstwhile traders licensed for the area, including Michael Donovan (1886), Washington P. and

Thomas J. Lingle (1888), Bernard J. Mooney and James F. Boyle (1889), and John Boehm (1889).

HUBBELL'S CHINLE TRADING POST:

(5058 ft) Apache County, AZ. Navajo: Uncertain. Around 1900, Lorenzo Hubbell entered into his second trading venture in Chinle with the opening of the most impressive trading post on the Navajo Reservation. Built in the "fortress" style for which he was known, the second story of this building measured 107 by 35 feet, and housed ample guest facilities. It was situated atop the low hill that later was the site of a post office, and on which still later the Chinle Navajo Police Headquarters was located.

The post never paid for itself, and in 1917 Hubbell sold it to C. N. Cotton of Gallup. Cotton kept the post going until he sold out to the partnership of Leon H. "Cozy" McSparron, Hartley T. Seymour, and Camille Garcia in 1923. This partnership purchased the other two extant trading posts in Chinle at the same time, and closed down the old Hubbell Post.

HUNTERS POINT: [DB] (6800 ft) Apache County, AZ. Navajo: Tsé Naachii', "Red Rock Coming Down," and Tsé Náshchii', "Red Rock Going Around in a Circle" (Young and Morgan 1987, 730). The names refer to the physical feature, a long, high, wooded point projecting eastward from Defiance Plateau seven miles south of St. Michaels, as well as to a trading/BIA boarding-school community on the eastern foot of the Defiance Plateau on the west bank of Black Creek and Navajo Route 12. A mile north of the community is an El Paso Natural Gas pumping station situated two miles west of the highway.

This point is covered with thick vegetation on the east while the west side exposes alternate layers of red and buff sandstone, and was named after John G. Hunter, former agent of the Southern Navajo jurisdiction. A Navajo tséninájihí (a rock pile shrine), is located near the tip of the point and a number of small unit-type Anasazi houses have been found between the point and Black Creek (Van Valkenburgh 1941, 77).

A small battle took place in this vicinity in November 1860, when troops of Captain Lafayette McLaws killed four Navajo men and captured four women, including a niece of headman Armijo (McNitt 1972, 406).

HUNTERS POINT TRADING POST: (6800 ft) Apache County, AZ. Navajo: Uncertain, but probably the same as Hunters Point community. Opened by 1916 (Kelley 1977, 253). At some time in its past, it was owned by one or more of the Foutz brothers (McNitt 1962, 300n).

INDIAN WELLS: [DB] (5800 ft) Navajo County, AZ. Navajo: Tó Hahadleeh, "Where Water is Drawn out One Quantity after Another" (Young and Morgan 1987, 706). This small trading post, chapter, and Presbyterian mission community is located under the southeast rim of a volcanic mesa a mile west of Arizona Highway 77 on Tesbito Wash, some 15 miles south of White Cone. The Twin Buttes lie four miles east, in this area that Van Valkenburgh called a high grassland plateau in 1941, but that is now a desert.

Indian Wells Trading Post is the focus of the community, while Bitahoochee Trading Post and Bitahoochee Butte are merely a mile and a half to the east.

The Indian Wells Mission was founded in 1912 by the Rev. W. R. Johnston, previously of Tolchaco. Johnston, well known by Indians and Whites for his stalwart defense of Indian land rights, was instrumental in the creation of the former Leupp jurisdiction and the return of the Paiute Strip (near Monument Valley) to Navajo tribal ownership (Van Valkenburgh 1941, 75–77). A later pastor of the mission was Roger Davis, Sr., a Navajo who was prominent in the Navajo Tribal Council. The trading post was built at the location eventually to adopt the post's name by Hubert Richardson and Edwin Jacob Marty shortly after 1908.

This vicinity (along with nearby Sunrise Springs and White Cone) is the home of various Ant People in the Rounded Man Red Antway Myth (Wyman 1965).

INSCRIPTION HOUSE (TRADING POST): [DB] (6850 ft) Coconino County, AZ. Navajo: Ts'ah Bii' Kin, "House in the Sage." This old trading location (and formerly a tourist lodge)

was opened in the early 1920s (Kelley 1977, 254). It is situated on the Shonto Plateau, east of the head of Navajo Canyon, on Navajo Route 16, five and a half miles north of Arizona Highway 98, 49 miles northeast of Tuba City. In 1954, S. J. Richardson sold this post to Stokes Carson, who operated it until his death in 1974. Carson's daughters inherited the lease, and granddaughter Wy and her husband Al Townsend operated it until the lease expired in 1990 (Brugge p.c. 1996; James 1988, 88–90). Al Grieve took over management briefly in 1991 with intent to purchase, but this deal fell through. The location is also a chapter seat.

The name comes from the nearby Inscription House ruin, a famed Anasazi ruin, with an almost illegible wall inscription interpreted by some to read, "Carlos Arnais 1661," or "S-haperio Ano Dom 1661." More recent investigations show it probably dates to the late nineteenth century, probably 1881. This ruin, a component of the Navajo National Monument but normally closed to the public, contains some 48 rooms, and is reached by a horse trail from the post to Navajo Canyon and the ruins (Van Valkenburgh 1941, 78).

IVES MESA: (5500 ft) Navajo County, AZ. Navajo: Uncertain. The name applies to an extremely rough highland region lying between the Hopi Buttes (north) and the Painted Desert (south). It sweeps northwest to southeast, between Marcou Mesa (east) and Tovar Mesa (northwest). About 20 miles north of I-40, its eastern end is traversed by Arizona Highway 87. Named by Gregory (1915, 151) for Lieutenant Joseph C. Ives, who led a party through the region in May 1858.

JACOB'S WELL: [DB] (approx. 5700 ft) Apache County, AZ. Navajo: 'Ahoyoolts'ił, "Crumbling Well," so named due to the sides of the well continually falling away, making the hole bigger and bigger (Young p.c. 1995). This important watering hole on the military trails between the Rio Grande and the Colorado River is situated some 12 miles southwest of Sanders, though the exact location remains undetermined.

The well was located by Lieutenant Amiel W.

Whipple's survey party in 1853 (Granger 1960, 13). Lieutenant Edwin F. Beale watered Uncle Sam's camels here in 1857 and his journal gives an excellent description of the place at that time. Later, it was an important stop between Zuni and Navajo Springs on the military and emigrant trail between Fort Wingate (see San Rafael, New Mexico) and Fort Whipple near present Prescott.

Navajos say that 70 years ago Jacob's Well was three saddle ropes or 90 feet across and some 90 feet deep. In 1941, the depth was 10 feet and the circumference one-quarter mile (Van Valkenburgh 1941, 13).

JEDDITO: (6475 ft); Navajo County, AZ. Navajo: Jádító, "Antelope Spring." Also called Jedito and Jadito. This trading community sits two miles north of Arizona Highway 264 on Jeddito Wash. The community includes a chapter house, and lies at the northern boundary of a small island of Navajo Reservation enclosed within the Hopi Reservation. The trading post opened in the first decade of the twentieth century, closing in the later 1960s (Kelley 1977, 253, 255).

JEDDITO MESA: (7485 ft) Navajo County, AZ. Named for the spring (see Jeddito above). The Navajos call the southwestern tip of this mesa Tse Łitso, "Yellow Rock" (U.S. Indian Claims Commission n.d., vol. VI, xx). Extensive, relatively low upland southeast of Polacca Wash, drained by Jeddito Wash.

JEDDITO WASH: (7485–4900 ft) Navajo County, AZ. Also Jedito Wash, Jadito Wash. Navajo: See Jeddito. A 65-mile-long wash draining Balakai Mesa, flowing southwest across the Hopi Reservation. Jeddito Wash merges with Polacca Wash to form Corn Creek Wash, which then flows another eight miles into the Little Colorado River.

This region was first visited by Europeans in the person of Pedro de Tovar of Coronado's expedition of 1541 (Granger 1960, 242).

JOINT USE AREA: (approx. 5000–7000 ft) Navajo: Uncetain. This "buffer zone" surrounding the Hopi Indian Reservation was intended "for the use of the Moqui [Hopi] and such other Indians as the Secretary of the Interior may see fit to settle thereon [Navajo]" (Executive Order of December 16, 1882). Many attempts have been made over the years to divide the land equitably between the two tribes, but technicalities and each tribe's desire to retain its perceived share of a wealth of resources in the region stymied all such attemps until 1974. Actual compliance with this agreement led to the forced resettlement (relocation) of 26 Hopi families and over 3,600 Navajo families. Delays in the relocation continue to the publication date of this volume.

JOSEPH CITY: [DB] (5000 ft) Navajo County, AZ. Navajo: Náyaaseęsí, "Wart Under the Eye." Also Todiiniishii, "Stream of Water" (according to U.S. Indian Claims Commission n.d., vol. VI, xvi, though Young was unfamiliar with this word). This small Mormon village on I-40 10 miles west of Holbrook was settled as an agricultural and dairying community on March 24, 1876; the nearby Arizona Public Service Company Cholla power plant was constructed in the 1970s.

William Allen and a company of about 50 Mormon men and their families came to the area to settle the town, which was first given the name of Allen's Camp in honor of their captain. This "camp" was erected on the south bank of the Little Colorado River at a cost of $5,000 and 960 days, but it was washed out with the first flood, whereupon it was moved to the north bank (WPA 1940a, 314). The name was changed to St. Joseph on January 27, 1878. However, to avoid confusion with St. Joseph in Missouri, the name was later changed to Joseph City. It is the oldest community in Navajo County.

Other Mormon villages of this vicinity along the Little Colorado River were Brigham, Sunset, Old Taylor, and Obed. Difficulties in maintaining diversion dams and poor, saline land drove the early settlers of these communities to other locations up the river or entirely out of the valley of the Little Colorado.

Navajos are said to have lived in this region prior to their 1863–64 removal to the Bosque Redondo (U.S. Indian Claims Commission n.d., vol. IV, 526–27).

JUNIPER RIDGE: (6600 ft) Navajo County, AZ. Navajo: Gad Bił Naalk'id, "Juniper Slope" (Young p.c. 1995). This east-west canyon near the mouth of Keams Canyon is important to some Blessingway rites (Van Valkenburgh 1974, 183).

KAIBAB PLATEAU: (9000–7800 ft) Coconino County, AZ. Navajo: Nát'oh Dził, "Tobacco Mountain" (U.S. Indian Claims Commission n.d., vol. VI, xii). This upland comprises the North Rim of the Grand Canyon, west of House Rock Valley. It is nearly a thousand feet higher than the south rim, and is heavily forested with ponderosa, fir, and even aspen groves. In years past, it was referred to as the Buckskin Mountains (Wetherill 1987, 241). Tobacco Mountain is said to be important to the Navajo hunter tradition (Luckert 1975, 46).

KAIBITO: [DB] (6070 ft) (Population: 641) Coconino County, AZ. Navajo: K'ai' Bii' Tó, "Spring in the Willows" (Van Valkenburgh 1941, 83). This small trading, chapter, and school community lies in the upper canyon of the Kaibito, the southern branch of Navajo Canyon on the Kaibito Plateau, about half a mile south of Arizona Highway 98 and 30 miles northwest of the junction of that road with U.S. Highway 160. This location places it between the northern extremities of Mormon Ridge (west) and White Mesa (east).

This region was a stronghold for Navajo refugees of the war and Bosque Redondo years of the 1860s, under headman Dághaa' Sikaad (McPherson 1988, 9).

KAIBITO PLATEAU: (5800–8000 ft) Navajo and Coconino Counties, AZ. Navajo: See Kaibito. A huge upland expanse lying between the Colorado and San Juan Rivers (north) and Marsh Pass and Klethla Valley (south), and between the Echo Cliffs (west) and Skeleton Mesa (east). Incorporated into this vast region are such other features as the Rainbow Plateau, the Gray Hills, White Mesa, Zilnez Mesa, Tsegi Canyon, etc.

KAIBITO TRADING POST: (6070 ft) Coconino County, AZ. Navajo: See Kaibito. This post, constructed in 1914, was built at the foot of

White Horse Mesa by C. D. Richardson. In 1916, Navajo outlaw Taddytin (Tádídíín, "Pollen") (Young p.c. 1995) was killed near here. Tuba City Indian Agent Walter Runke and Ashley Wilson, chief of the Navajo Police, were later charged with his murder (Richardson 1986, 111–13).

KANA'A CREEK: (7000–4350 ft) Coconino County, AZ. Navajo: Uncertain. This normally dry wash heads just west of Sunset Crater and flows approximately 20 miles to the northeast through the Kana'a Valley, before entering the Little Colorado River about a mile upstream (southeast) of the mouth of Deadman's Wash. It is named for the Hopi Kana'a Kachina (Granger 1960, 74).

KARIGAN'S TRADING POST: (approx. 7000 ft) Navajo: Uncertain, probably the same as St. Michaels. This post was located just north of St. Michaels, during the 1960s (McNitt 1962, 325–26), but details of its origin remain uncertain.

KAYENTA: [DB] (5800 ft) (Population: 4,372) Navajo County, AZ. Navajo: Tó Dínéeshzhee', "Fringed Water" or "Fingers of Water" (Young and Morgan 1987, 706). Granger (1960, 243), suggests that "Kayenta" is an English rendering of "Téé'ndééh," which referred to a deep boghole (literally, "Animals fall into Deep Water" (Young p.c. 1995); Kluckhohn (1927, 180) asserted that it means "Three Springs Come out of the Side of a Hill"). This chapter community lies south of Monument Valley at the foot of a small bench a short distance from Laguna Creek, at the junction of U.S. Highways 160 and 163.

An early day school was established here, along with a USIS tuberculosis sanatorium, now a Public Health Service hospital. Trading posts have included Wetherill and Colville Trading Company (opened prior to 1910); Babbitt Trading Company (opened prior to 1915); and Joe Kerley. The Wetherills even had a ranch in the vicinity, and USIS helped establish Navajo agricultural work in the area. By 1941, there were some 150 acres of land under irrigation, served by an Indian Irrigation Service concrete dam on Laguna Creek.

U.S. Army Captain John Walker and his Mounted Rifles (see Black Mountain) named the place Laguna in 1860, due to the pools and lush vegetation then found along the creek. Navajos call a place one mile downstream from the old Indian Irrigation Service dam (and at a fall in the creek bed) Tééh'ndééh.

The first White visitor in 1823, Colonel Francisco Salazar, traveled north from the Hopi Mesas, east to Chinle Valley to rejoin the main body of Vizcarra's Navajo expedition. During the Kit Carson campaign of 1863–64, Hashké Neiniihí led his people into deep canyons of the region, waiting out the return of the bulk of the Navajos from the Bosque Redondo. Hashké Neiniihí died in 1909 (see also Hoskininni Mesa).

The first traders to settle here were John and Louisa Wetherill in 1910 (having moved from their Oljeto, Utah, post, which they had founded in 1906). The Wetherills advertised their post office as the most distant from a railroad in the United States. The community served as a base for numerous archaeological and exploratory expeditions into the great wild country that spreads northward like a fan.

KEAMS CANYON: [DB] (6400 ft) (Population: 393) Navajo County, AZ. Navajo: Lók'a'deeshjin, "Reeds Extend in a Black Line" (Young p.c. 1995). Some interpret it as "Black Reeds in the Distance." Hopi: Pongsikvi, "Government Community." This community is located in a deep canyon of buff Mesa Verde sandstone that runs west to join the Polacca Wash near Polacca, some 80 miles north of Holbrook. The Hopi Indian Agency is located here, with a hospital, boarding school (USIS), missions of the Franciscan Fathers and Rainbow Baptists, and a post office.

Originally a Hopi farming area, this site was called Peach Orchard Spring at the opening of the American era, when Billy Dodd—brother of Navajo Agent Major Theodore Dodd—opened a trading post in the canyon in the 1860s. The settlement received its present name from Thomas Varker Keam, an Englishman who fought under Kit Carson, and later acted as agent and inspector for the Navajos. Keam moved to present

Keams Canyon in 1880 and established a trading post and ranch, and was instrumental in opening the first Hopi school in 1881. When a separate Hopi agency was opened in 1899, Keams Ranch was selected as the site, but in 1902 the agency was moved down the canyon to its present site.

On the canyon walls near the ruins of Keam's old ranch is an inscription made during the Navajo Wars bearing the name "C. Carson-63." Carson passed through the Hopi country in 1863 while on a sortie against the fleeing Navajo "ricos" as far west as the Little Colorado River (Van Valkenburgh 1941, 83).

ALSO: (6790–5575 ft) Navajo County, AZ. A stream and its deep, steep-sided channel heading on Balakai Mesa at ephemeral Bighams Lake some four miles south of Low Mountain. It flows southwest through the community of Keams Canyon (10 miles downstream) then turns west to flow into Polacca Wash 15 miles farther downstream. This canyon is mentioned in the hero's search for his family in the Navajo Rounded Man Red Antway Myth (Wyman 1965).

KEAMS CANYON TRADING POST: (6400 ft) Navajo County, AZ. Navajo: See Keams Canyon (community). This post was constructed by Thomas and William Keam on August 31, 1875, in the canyon that eventually took on their name. The original site was upstream from the present location. When the government purchased the original land and buildings for a school in 1887, Keam rebuilt at the present site.

Exactly when Keam sold the post to Lorenzo Hubbell, Jr., is problematic, but Hubbell sold it to Joseph Schmedding in 1914 (Schmedding 1974, vi, 313–15). Schmedding sold the post to E. P. Halderman in 1924, following a nasty fight to keep it after tarnished Secretary of the Interior Albert B. Fall tried unsuccessfully to strip him of his license (Schmedding 1974, 349–62). McNitt (1962, 274) also names Freeman H. Hathorn as a trader at Keams Canyon after 1908.

KEET SEEL CANYON: (7000–6400 ft) Navajo County, AZ. Navajo: Łeets'aats'iil, "Broken Pottery House" (Gregory 1915, 152; Young p.c. 1995), or Kits'iilí, "Shattered House" (Young and Morgan 1987, 496), which Granger (1960, 243) erroneously interprets as "Empty Houses." This 600-ft-deep canyon cuts six miles into the west rim of Skeleton Mesa. Keel Seel is tributary to Dowozhiebito Canyon, which is in turn tributary to Tsegi Canyon. Keet Seel Ruins are located in the canyon. (See Navajo National Monument.)

KENDRICK PEAK: (10,418 ft) Coconino County, AZ. Navajo: Dził Ba'áádi, "Female Mountain" (U.S. Indian Claims Commission n.d., vol. VI, vi). Formed by lava flows, this feature received its English name from Lieutenant Whipple in honor of Major Henry Lane Kendrick, Second U.S. Cavalry. Kendrick was commander of the escort for the Sitgreaves Expedition in 1851, and later commanding officer of Fort Defiance (Granger 1960, 74).

KERLEY'S TRADING POSTS: [DB (map 6)] Navajo: Uncertain, various. There were actually at least two posts operated by John P. Kerley in the northwest region of the reservation. One was in Tuba City, located in a canyon beside the road between the community and U.S. Highway 160, back before the community stretched all the way to the highway. The other post was in Kayenta. Little historical information is available on either. Kerley was also a partner in the Cedar Ridge Trading Post with the Babbitt Brothers.

KIDZIIBAHI: (9000–7000 ft) Apache County, AZ. Navajo: "Gray Streak Mountain." The Navajos consider this westernmost slope of the Tunicha Mountains above Lukachukai to have been the Holy People's home before humans were created (Luckert 1975, 11, 22–23)

KINLICHEE: [DB] (6600 ft) Apache County, AZ. Also Kin Lichee. Navajo: Kin dah'lichi'i, "Red House in the Distance," named for an Anasazi ruin in the vicinity, now a Navajo Nation park. A BIA boarding school located two miles north of Arizona Highway 264 on Navajo Route 39, eight miles east of Ganado, closed in 1979–80. The school was situated along the deeply eroded Sage House Wash. In the 1940s,

the USIS had 130 acres under irrigation here. A trading post opened here between 1881 and 1885 (Kelley 1977, 251), and closed within 15 years.

The Anasazi ruin was formerly commonly known as Pueblo Colorado (Spanish for "Red Town"). During the Navajo War of 1863–64, U.S. Army Camp Florilla, an outpost and remount camp, was located here by a large spring. Robert Young (p.c. 1995) suggests the Navajo name for the ruin is Táala Hodijool, "Flat-Topped Round Area," erroneously interpreted by Frink (1968, 45) as "Round Place Where a Sing was Held." However, Brugge (p.c. 1996) places Táala Hodijool, consisting of an Anasazi structure and several Navajo hogans dating to the 1760s, north-west of Ganado and not in the vicinity of Kinlichee.

KIT SILI WASH: (6000–5200 ft) Apache County, AZ. Navajo: Kits'iili, "Shattered House" (Young and Morgan 1887, 496), erroneously interpreted as "Broken Pottery" by Gregory (1915, 152). A tributary of Sweetwater Creek, south of Toh Atin Mesa. It heads on the northwest flank of Toh Chin Lini Mesa (on the west flank of the Carrizo Mountains) and flows 10 miles west past Totacon, to join the Sweetwater some three miles upstream (northeast) of its convergence with Walker Creek.

KLAGETOH (TRADING POST): [DB] (6200 ft) Apache County, AZ. Navajo: Łeeyi'tó, "Water in the Ground." This post, located in a small basin on U.S. Highway 191, 13 miles south of Ganado and 10 miles north of Wide Ruins, was opened in the early 1920s (Kelley 1977, 254). The post has closed, but there is now a chapter house and several homes in the area, along with a day school.

At Sagebrush Spring south of here, Navajo headman Zarcillos Largos was killed by New Mexican militia and Pueblo auxiliaries in October 1860.

The Soil Conservation Service established a Demonstration Area here, with 179 acres under irrigation in 1941. A twelfth-century Anasazi ruin is also present (Van Valkenburgh 1941, 84).

During the 1920s, this post was run by artist

Nils Hagner and his Navajo wife, Teeklee (Hegeman 1963, 204), and Wheeler ran it during the 1960s and 1970s.

KLETHLA VALLEY: (6600–5900 ft) Navajo County, AZ. Also Klethlana Valley. Navajo: Łį́į́ Łani, "Many Horses" (probably, according to Kelley p.c. 1994). This 10-mile-long valley lies between Black Mesa (south) and the Shonto Plateau (north). It heads at the mouth of Long House Valley and the headwaters of Laguna Creek on the northeast, and runs southwest to approximately the point where the Shonto Wash exits the Shonto Plateau.

KUHN TRADING POST: [DB, under St. Michaels, AZ] Location uncertain. Navajo: Uncertain. Van Valkenburgh lists this as one of three posts in the St. Michaels area in 1941. The other two are Frazier's Trading Post and McMahon Trading Post (Van Valkenburgh 1941, 129).

LAGUNA CREEK: (6700–4800 ft) Navajo and Apache Counties, AZ. Navajo: Possibly the same as Marsh Pass. Covering some 50 miles east to west, Laguna flows between Black Mesa (south) and the Shonto Plateau (north). With headwaters at the west end of Long House Valley, the stream flows east to converge with Chinle Wash through Dinnehotso Canyon, some six miles southwest of the junction of U.S. Highways 160 and 191.

See Marsh Pass and Kayenta for more information.

LECHE'E: (4200 ft) Coconino County, AZ. Navajo: Łíchíí, "Red." Navajo chapter-house community on the southern outskirts of Page.

LECHE'E ROCK: (5900 ft) Coconino County, AZ. Navajo: Uncertain, most likely Tsélchíí, "Red Rock," or Tsélchíí Íí'áhí, "Red Rock Spire" (Young p.c. 1995). A 900-ft-high butte atop the Kaibito Plateau, two miles east of Arizona Highway 98 and about five miles west of the juncture of Navajo and Kaibito Creeks.

LECHE'E WASH: (6200–4000 ft) Coconino County, AZ. Navajo: See Leche'e. A 10-mile-long tributary of Tatahatso (Tát'a Hatso, "Big Rock Ledge") Wash on Blue Moon Bench east of Marble Canyon. Heads near the western edge of Bodaway Mesa, and flows west into Tatahatso Wash two miles east (upstream) of the juncture of that channel and the Colorado River.

LEE'S FERRY: (3170 ft) Coconino County, AZ. Navajo: Tsinaa'eeł Dah Si'á, "At the Boat" or "Where the Boat Sits up at an Elevation" (U.S. Indian Claims Commission n.d., vol. VI, xxii), probably referring to a rock formation (Young p.c. 1995). This historical crossing of the Colorado River is located at the downstream terminus of Glen Canyon, at the confluence of the Colorado and Paria rivers, a northern tributary. The ferry was initiated by Mormon John D. Lee in 1871, with his seventeenth wife, Rachel Andora. The crossing was known to Jacob Hamblin as Lonely Dell. Hamblin helped Lee reach the dell, as Lee was a fugitive, having taken part in the "Mountain Meadows Massacre."

In this infamous episode, the Fancher party, a wagon train of immigrants from Arkansas and Missouri, was set upon about 30 miles southeast of Cedar City, Utah, in September 1857. They made no secret of their disdain for Mormons, some even claiming to have taken part in the rousting of the Mormons from the midwest. A band of Paiutes were induced by the Mormons to attack the train. The travelers were convinced by the Mormons to surrender—under promise of safe passage. When the party was disarmed, 115 to 120 of them were slaughtered by the Mormons. The only survivors were 16 or 17 children under the age of seven who were spared. This act of mercy proved to be the perpetrators' downfall, as a number of the children served as witnesses in the eventual disclosure of the story and identification of the Mormon leaders, inlcuding Lee.

Lee and his small party arrived at the dell in December 1871. Only two days later he helped a group of 15 Navajos cross the Colorado. From then on, Paiutes, Navajos, Hopis, and Utes came to Lonely Dell to cross the river. Lee also traded handily with his clients, Indian and White—though the former greatly outnumbered the latter. Once the ferry was established, Navajos came to the site to trade blankets for horses; they called the place Tsinaa'eeł Dah Si'ání ("Where the Boat Sits"). Prior to this they had referred to the location as Tó Ha'naant'eetiin, "Where they Crossed Against the Current" (Van Valkenburgh 1941, 103), and used it to cross when on trading trips to Paiutes. Young (p.c. 1995) suggests this name is more correctly Tódáá' N'deetiin, "Trail across at the Brink of the Water," and refers to the Crossing of the Fathers, not Lee's Ferry.

In 1879, the Mormon Church built a fort at Lee's Ferry for its protection. In the same year Major John Wesley Powell of the U.S. Geological Survey stopped at Lee's Ferry while on the first exploration of the full length of the Colorado River. He left two boats, one of which was discovered in the spring of 1939 by Leo Weaver, then owner of Paradise Valley Ranch, built on the site of Lee's Ferry.

Lee was eventually captured, tried, and sentenced to death for his role in the Mountain Meadows Massacre. He was shot while sitting on his coffin on March 23, 1877, at the Mountain Meadows site of the massacre (Granger 1960, 75).

His successors operated a trading post at this location until about 1910 (Kelley 1977, 253). The ferry wasted away in 1928, just a few months prior to the completion of the Marble Canyon Bridge. Northern Arizona was virtually isolated (Hegemann 1963, 61) until its completion.

LEROUX WASH: (5560–5075 ft) Navajo County, AZ. Navajo: Uncertain. Twenty-mile-long tributary of the Little Colorado River, formed in the Painted Desert region—north of the Petrified Forest National Park—by the convergence of Wide Ruin Wash and Sabito Wash. It flows southwest past Mitten Peak to join the Little Colorado immediately west of Holbrook. It was named Leroux Fork by Lieutenant Whipple in 1856, for Antoine Leroux, the guide for his expedition across Arizona.

LEUPP: [DB] (4714 ft) Coconino County, AZ. Navajo: Tsiizizí, "Scalps." Also referred to as Tó Naneesdizi, "Tangled Water" (literally "Place

of the Water Rivulets"). This vicinity is important in the Navajo Coyoteway Ceremony (Luckert 1979).

This small village began as a government settlement, and sits on the north bank of a treeless bottom of the Little Colorado River at the junction of Arizona Highway 99 and Navajo Route 15. (Old Leupp was located two miles to the southeast; the current settlement grew around the old Sunrise Trading Post, and includes a chapter seat.) It was named for Indian Bureau Commissioner Francis E. Leupp, who served from 1905 to 1908 (Richardson 1986, 128). The USIS operated a hospital here.

The Navajo name is said by some Navajos to be derived from the story of a fight between the Navajos and the Walapai Indians, or Dilzhí'í (Small Jay Bird), near Sunrise Trading Post. In this fight the Navajos took three Walapai scalps. A less exciting explanation is that the name came from the fact that a former agent, named Maxwell, was bald-headed and wore a wig. The Leupp Jurisdictional Agency was founded in 1908, and located on a bar or islet in the river bottom. The shifting of the river channel made it necessary to erect high dikes, but it was practically inundated in the spring floods of 1937. In 1909, the reservation's fourth boarding school opened at Leupp.

Traders have included Leupp Trading Company (formerly Lower Sunrise Springs, opened in the first decade of this century) and Upper Sunrise Trading Post (opened a mile to the north in the early 1890s) (Kelley 1977, 252–53). The first Navajo Business Council (one of the earliest steps toward self-government) was established in Leupp in 1904. It consisted of two Navajo Court judges and three "elected" headmen (Bailey and Bailey 1986, 109–10). A prisoner of war camp was located here during World War II (Moon 1992, 169).

LEUPP TRADING POST: (4714 ft) Coconino County, AZ. Navajo: Uncertain, probably the same as the community. As early as 1911, this post was operated by John G. Walker, a half-Navajo who moved here from Tolcheco, northwest of Canyon Diablo. Prior to 1905, he had been a partner of Thomas Osborne in St. Michaels (McNitt 1962, 250, 266).

LIMESTONE TANKS: [DB] (6000 ft) Coconino County, AZ. Navajo: Tsinyaa Ńt'i'í (U.S. Indian Claims Commission n.d., vol. VI, xxiii), "Under Trees Extending (as in a line)" (Young and Morgan 1987, 678, 738). Natural and/or improved catch-basins in which rain or snow runoff is accumulated, located one mile west of U.S. Highway 89, six miles north of Cedar Ridge Trading Post.

The old Mormon trail laid out by Jacob Hamblin from southern Utah to Arizona passed by this oasis, and it remains today a watering place for the Navajos.

LITTLE BLACK SPOT MOUNTAIN: (7001 ft) Navajo County, AZ. Also Little Black Speck Mountain. Navajo: Dził Dah Zhin, "Black Speck Mountain" (Young and Morgan 1987, 360). Steep-sided mesa on south-central Black Mesa, five miles southwest of Piñon. The Navajo name also has been applied to Big Mountain, 15 miles to the northeast (Granger 1960, 254), but that feature is more properly known as Dził Ntsaá, "Extension Mountain" (Ellis 1974, 465).

LITTLE COLORADO RIVER: (approx. 8000–4200 ft) Apache, Navajo, and Coconino Counties, AZ. Navajo: Tółchí'íkooh, "Red Water Canyon" (Franciscan Fathers 1910, 132; Kelley p.c. 1994). This 275-mile-long river heads near Nutrioso (on U.S. Highway 666 south of Eager) and flows north to Zion Reservoir. Exiting the reservoir, the stream flows northwest through Holbrook and Winslow, on I-40, before snaking through the Painted Desert to Cameron. It joins the Colorado River at the south end of Marble Canyon (where the Grand Canyon begins).

The Spanish and Mexicans had named this stream the "Rio Colorado Chiquito" (Little Red River), a variant of which found its way into the July 17, 1855, Treaty of Laguna Negra (McNitt 1972, 437).

Early Spanish explorers often referred to a Rio del Lino (Flax River) while in the vicinity of the Little Colorado, and Lieutenant Whipple labeled it Flax River in 1854, though common usage was already accepting Chiquito Colorado ("Little Red") (Granger 1960, 244).

In the Navajo creation myth, this channel worked with the Colorado River to protect Changing Woman during Creative Time. It was turned red and salty by the blood of Changing Woman's first menstruation (which was also the first among the Diné) (McPherson 1992, 49).

Captain Lafayette McLaws, U.S. Army, led three companies of infantry from Fort Defiance to the Little Colorado country on November 18, 1860, in search of Navajos Colonel Canby thought were congregating there. They struck the river near present-day Holbrook (McNitt 1972, 405–6).

LITTLE MUSTACHE'S TRADING POST: (approx. 6500 ft) Navajo County, AZ. Navajo: Uncertain. Very small trading post on Black Mesa, opened around 1912 by two Navajos, Little Mustache and his brother, Arroyo. (Even today, Navajo ownership of a trading post is a rarity; in 1912, it was remarkable.) One of the buildings at the post was constructed of palisaded logs, a style called "many legs" by Navajos. The two traders lived on a homestead less than a mile from the post, and there is speculation that Little Mustache acquired his trade goods from larger posts nearby, rather than from such trade centers as Holbrook or Gallup, New Mexico. The post was open only a few years before a family quarrel forced Little Mustache to move away; Arroyo subsequently set up a store of his own elsewhere (Kelley 1985, 29).

LITTLE ROUND ROCK: (6000 ft) Apache County, AZ. Navajo: Possibly Tsé Nikání Yázhí, "Little Round Rock." A small rounded sandstone plug a mile north of the larger Round Rock, between Chinle Wash and Agua Sal Creek, four miles northwest of the junction of U.S. Highway 191 and Navajo Route 12.

LITTLE SALT CANYON: (7000–6600 ft) Coconino County, AZ. Navajo: Possibly 'Áshįįh Bikooh Yázhí, "Little Salt Canyon." A four-mile-long canyon on the Shonto Plateau, formed by the headwaters of Shonto Wash, just a couple of miles southeast of Tsegi Canyon and Betatakin Ruin (Navajo National Monument).

LITTLE WHITE HOUSE CANYON: [DB] (6800–5550 ft) Apache County, AZ. Navajo: Tséyi' Hats'ósí, "Narrow Canyon," or Tsé Hons'ózí, "Narrow Rock Canyon" (Young and Morgan 1987, 729, 732). Deep sandstone canyon two miles south of—and running parallel to—Canyon de Chelly. This cleft is some 400 ft deep and 10 miles long. It is tributary to Nazlini Wash three miles south of Chinle.

There is a small twelfth-century Anasazi ruin in this canyon, somewhat resembling the White House Ruin in Canyon de Chelly. This canyon formerly entered Chinle Wash at the mouth of Canyon de Chelly, but it broke through to its present course directly west to Nazlini Wash some years prior to 1941.

LOHALI POINT: (7400 ft) Apache County, AZ. Navajo: Łóó' Háálí, "Fish Spring" (Gregory 1915, 152), or "Fish Flow Out" (Young p.c. 1995), also called Fish Point on some older maps. This is the southeastern tip of Black Mesa, five miles north of Navajo Route 4 and Cottonwood Wash, 15 miles west of Chinle, AZ.

LOLOMAI POINT: (8050 ft) Navajo County, AZ. (Also Lolami Point) Navajo: Uncertain. Hopi: "Good," name of Oraibi headman (Gregory 1915, 152) Northernmost projection of the north rim of Black Mesa, above Kayenta.

LONE MOUNTAIN: Location uncertain. Navajo: T'áá Sahdii Dah 'Azkání, "Mesa Apart" (Young and Morgan 1987, 722). While this feature is named in some legends and its Navajo name is deciphered by Young and Morgan, no trace of it could be found on any maps available to the author. One possibility is that this is 5510-ft Lonely Mountain, located just off Cement Trough Canyon on the Fort Apache Reservation in east-central Arizona.

LONG HOUSE: (approx. 6500 ft) Navajo County, AZ. Navajo: Uncertain, possibly Kits'-iilí, "Shattered House," a generic Navajo term for

Anasazi ruins. Also known as "Ruin A," it sits four miles south of Marsh Pass in Long House Valley. This Pueblo III Anasazi ruin was first described by Whites on Captain John G. Walker's September 1857 expedition. Two of his men, Lieutenants Walker and Nell, left inscriptions on wall blocks (McNitt 1972, 371).

LONG HOUSE VALLEY: [DB (map 3)] (6600–6300 ft) Navajo County, AZ. Navajo: Uncertain. Short, narrow valley between Marsh Pass (northeast) and the Klethla Valley (southwest), separating Black Mesa (south) and the Shonto Plateau (north). The southwestern terminus is also the headwaters of Laguna Creek.

Long House Ruin in this vicinity was visited by troops under Captain John G. Walker in September 1859. Lieutenants Thomas W. Walker and William H. Bell left inscriptions on the walls (McNitt 1972, 371).

LOS GIGANTES BUTTES: (6460–6490 ft) Apache County, AZ. Navajo: Tsé Ch'ídeelzhah, "Rocks Jut Out" (Young and Morgan 1987, 729). Sandstone buttes located five miles west of Mexican Cry Mesa, and two miles south of Hasbidito Creek.

LOW MOUNTAIN: (6760 ft) Navajo County, AZ. Navajo: T'áásahdii Dah 'Azkání (U.S. Indian Claims Commission n.d., vol. VI, xiv), or Jeeh Deez'áhí, "Pitch Point" (Kelley p.c. 1994). A broad, low mound situated between the root of First Mesa and Balakai Mesa. It is flanked by Polacca Wash (north) and Tsé Chizi (Tséch'ízhí) Wash (east, south, and west). Schmedding Trading Post opened here in the early 1950s (Kelley 1977, 255).

ALSO: (6200 ft) Navajo County, AZ. Navajo: Same as the land form. A small community and chapter house on Tsé Chizzi (Tséch'ízhí) Wash, on the south flank of Low Mountain. A few miles to the east of the community is Smoke Signal Trading Post, opened in the late 1960s (Kelley 1977, 255).

LUKACHUKAI: [DB] (6433 ft) (Population: 113) Apache County, AZ. Navajo: Lók'a'jígai,

"Reeds Extend White" or Lók'a'ch'égai, "White Streak of Reeds Extends Horizontally Out" (Young and Morgan 1987, 514). A small chapter and school community located in a large cove on the west foot of the Lukachukai Mountains near the base of Lukachukai Pass, four miles northeast of the junction of U.S. Highway 191 and Navajo Route 64 (James 1988, 37–38). The community hosts a day school and used to host an annual fair in September. A new housing development has expanded the community to the junction of Highway 191 with the lesser Navajo Route 13.

The first trading post was established here in 1892 by George N. Barker. In 1916, St. Isabel Mission, established by (Franciscan) Father Berard Haile, operated a school that was taken over by the government in 1933.

This prosperous agricultural area of some three hundred acres is furrowed by Tótsoh (Big Water), Tł'ézhiitóhí ("Horsefly Creek"), Na'ashǫ́'iito'í ("Big Lizard Creek"), and Díwózhii Bii' Tó ("Greasewood Creek"). A diversion dam on Totsoh Creek supplies water for irrigation.

LUKACHUKAI MOUNTAINS: [DB] (9460 ft) Apache County, AZ. Navajo: Shį́į́k'eh, "Summer Place" (James 1988, 37–38). Narrow strip of rugged mountains forming a northern extension of the Chuska Mountains, lying between the Chuskas and the Carrizo Mountains. These mountains are mentioned in the Navajo Coyoteway (Luckert 1979).

The first uranium mining on the reservation was at the Vanadium Corporation of America mine in the Lukachukais, during World War II. There were other mines later at Monument Valley, Tuba City, Mexican Hat, and Shiprock (Moon 1992, 175–85), and near Grants and Gallup.

LUKACHUKAI TRADING POST: (6433 ft) Apache County, AZ. Navajo: Chéh'ilyaa, "Under the Oaks" (Van Valkenburgh 1941, 88). The first post opened in this region was owned by George N. Barker in 1892. George Washington Sampson—known to the Navajos as Hastiin Báí or "Gray Man"—operated the post at the turn of the

century. Rico Menapace is mentioned in some records and may have managed it between Sampson and the next confirmed owner, W. R. Cassidy, who is known to have sold the post to Earl Kennedy in October 1928. Following Earl's death in 1971, his son Kenneth took over the post. It was closed in 1979, and only the foundations of the old buildings remain, seen just north of Navajo Route 13, a mile east of U.S. Highway 191. Trading is now conducted at Totsoh Trading Post, operated by Bradley and Victoria Blair just east of the original post. (McNitt 1962, 251; James 1988, 37–38).

LUKACHUKAI WASH: (6400–5100 ft) Apache County, AZ. Navajo: See Lukachukai. This 25-mile-long tributary of Chinle Wash is formed near the village of Lukachukai by the confluence of several smaller streams exiting the Lukachukai and Tunicha mountains to the east. It passes through some of the driest, most desolate land of the Navajo Reservation, including the community of Round Rock, before entering Chinle Wash about six miles south of Rough Rock.

This is probably the stream referred to as Arroyo del Carrizo when visited by a column led by Major Electus Backus in 1853 (McNitt 1972, 348–49).

LULULONGTURKUI: (approx. 6000 ft) Navajo County, AZ. Navajo: Uncertain. Hopi "Bullsnake Point." This is the location of Peacock Ruin, a prehistoric Hopi ruin excavated in 1901. It is situated on the east side of Jeddito Valley (Granger 1960, 244).

LUPTON: [DB] (6165 ft) Apache County, AZ. Navajo: Tsé Dijoolí, "Round Rock"; also Tsé Si'ání, "Sitting Rock." A chapter community on I-40 at Navajo Route 12, on the north bank of the Rio Puerco of the West, some 28 miles west of Gallup, New Mexico. The English name is for G. W. Lupton, trainmaster at Winslow in 1905 (Granger 1960, 14).

The route traveled in 1849 by Colonel John Washington's column crossed the Rio Puerco near Lupton, swinging southeast across the Zuni Mountains to Zuni Pueblo, roughly following an old Zuni and Mexican trading trail (providing access into the Fort Defiance region of the Navajo country). A later military trail struck the Puerco near Lupton and swung westward.

The deep canyon running between Lupton and Manuelito and bounded by scenic red Wingate sandstone cliffs was called Helena Canyon in the 1880s. It forms a natural pass from the Gallup region into eastern Arizona, and the Burlington Northern Santa Fe Railroad and I-40 follow this route.

The first trading post in Lupton was opened around 1905 (Kelley 1977, 253). The old State Line Trading Post, complete with hotel and restaurant, was operated in 1941 by J. W. Bennett, one of the oldest traders in the Navajo country, who had started trading at Houck in 1882. Now the community hosts Shirley Trading Post.

MANY FARMS: [DB] (5304 ft) (Population: 1,294) Apache County, AZ. Navajo: (recent name) Dá'ák'eh Halání, "Many Fields" (Young and Morgan 1987, 302); old name was Tó Naneesdizí, "Water Stringing Out in Rivulets" (Van Valkenburgh 1941, 92; Young p.c. 1995). A small farming, trading, and chapter community in the alluvial flats of Chinle Valley, at the juncture of U.S. Highway 191 and Navajo Route 59, 14 miles north of Chinle. In 1940, there were about 650 acres under irrigation here. The region was formerly the site of Many Farms Lake, a small ephemeral sink on the east margin of the village of Many Farms. It is fed by Sheep Dip Wash. Navajo farms were seen in the vicinity by the first Spanish expeditions, who called the area La Labor, "The Tillage" (Brugge 1965, 16–17).

The vicinity was visited by Captain John G. Walker's 1858 expedition, at which time Walker noted "a succession of fields growing corn, some of them containing from forty to sixty acres" (Bailey 1964b, 47).

Many Farms was started by Navajo initiative some 80 years ago, about the same time the first trading post opened there (Kelley 1977, 254). In 1937 the subjugation of five hundred acres was undertaken. The headworks of this project, a loose rock-weir diversion dam and concrete headworks feeding into the irrigation ditch, were located three miles north of Frazier's Trading Post.

In 1941, Many Farms was the site of the Navajo Tribal Slaughter House and Cannery, which supplied fresh and canned meat from livestock purchased from Navajos for school and hospital use on the reservation.

MANY SHEEP VALLEY: (6800–6200 ft) Navajo County, AZ. Navajo: Possibly Dibé Łání, "Many Sheep Valley." Tributary of Dinnebito Wash on Black Mesa, some seven miles downstream from the mouth of East Fork Dinnebito Wash.

MARBLE CANYON: (5200–2800 ft) Coconino County, AZ. Navajo: Na'ní'á Hatsoh, "Big Bridge" (Young p.c. 1995). The gateway to the Grand Canyon, this 55-mile-long chasm of the Colorado River ranges from 1000 ft to over 2400 ft deep along its course between Lee's Ferry (upstream) and the confluence with the Little Colorado River (downstream). It was named by the John Wesley Powell expedition of 1867, members of which noted the change from sandstone to marble in the cliff walls (Granger 1960, 150; Martin 1989, 261; Powell 1895, 241).

MARBLE CANYON TRADING POST: (approx. 5200 ft) Coconino County, AZ. Navajo: Uncertain, most likely the same name as the canyon itself. McNitt (1962, 205n) lists this post as one of at least eight posts owned at one time by Lorenzo Hubbell, Jr. Others owned included Keams Canyon, Oraibi, Big Mountain, Dinnebito, and Na-ah-tah Canyon. The post was opened around 1929 (Kelley 1977, 256).

MARSH PASS: [DB] (6000–6300 ft) Navajo County, AZ. Navajo: Tsé Yík'áán, "Hogback"; Bitát'ah Dzígai, "White Streak on the Ledge" (Young and Morgan 1987, 247, 732); "Rocks in a Row" (Van Valkenburgh 1941, 93). Narrow, steep-walled pass between Black Mesa (south) and the Shonto Plateau (north), connecting Long House Valley and Laguna Valley. It follows the course of Laguna Creek for a distance of about two miles east and two miles west of the mouth of Tsegi Canyon. The canyon offered access from the east to the coal mine on Black Mesa.

Colonel (Governor) Jose Antonio Vizcarra visited the pass in 1823, and the Spaniards named it Puerta de las Lemitas, after the three-leafed sumac, a small, red, intensely acid berry (valuable as an antiscorbic), plentiful in the vicinity (Bailey 1964b, 85). Captain Walker and his Mounted Rifles passed through here in 1859, applying the name Puerta Limita, as shown on McComb's map of 1860. Puerta Limita, or "Narrow Gate," although descriptive of the pass, is a misinterpretation of the Spanish (Correll and Watson 1974, 144). There are numerous Anasazi ruins in the vicinity, the best known being Swallow's Nest in the Segi Canyon, near its juncture with Marsh Pass. Inscriptions discovered in Long House Ruin at the north end of Long House Valley were made by members of Walker's expedition. Colonel Edwin S. Canby led another expedition through the pass in 1860 (McNitt 1972, 392).

In April 1897, a party led by John Wetherill was relieved of its sponsor, George Bowks (Bailey and Bailey 1986, 167), a wealthy Harvard student, and his tutor, C. E. Whitmore, by Navajo or Paiute raiders at night. The two were held for a ransom of $300, paid by Wetherill with money raised in Bluff. This affair is highly unusual (McNitt 1966, 155–62), and smells of conspiracy, as the kidnappers seemed to have prior knowledge that the party would split and rejoin more than once during the expedition, and the victims were conveniently selected from the party.

An irrigation project (USIS) of 145 acres located in Long House Valley was fed by a diversion dam on the south fork of the Laguna Creek. John Wetherill stated that in 1910 they were able to drive their wagons in the bed of the Laguna where today there is a deep wash. Kayenta Coal Mine, supplying the Kayenta Hospital and day school and the Dinnehotso day school, is located on Black Mesa, some five miles south of the pass. Near the point where the coal mine road departs south from the main Tuba City–Kayenta Road, there is the north turn-off to the headquarters of the Navajo National Monument, seven miles north over rough road. Marsh Pass Board-

ing School, the eighth on the reservation, was opened in 1914.

Granger (1960, 245) notes some speculation that the English name for the pass honors a Professor Marsh of Yale University, but then suggests it is more likely descriptive, asserting that marshes were common before the deep arroyo cutting resulting from overgrazing.

MATTHEWS PEAK: (9512 ft) Apache County, AZ. Navajo: Chézhín Náshjiní, "Lava with Black Band Around It," or Tsé Binááyołí, "Rock Around Which the Wind Blows" (Young and Morgan 1987, 271, 729). The second highest peak in the Tunicha Mountains, north of the headwaters of Tsaile Creek. The English name was applied by USGS cartographer Gregory in honor of Washington Matthews, the physician from Fort Wingate whose ethnographic studies were among the first scholarly studies of the Navajos (see Matthews' *Navajo Legends*) (Granger 1960, 15).

McCLELLAN TANK: [DB] (5800 ft) Coconino County, AZ. Navajo: Uncertain. A watering hole located a mile west of U.S. Highway 89, 12 miles north of Cedar Ridge Trading Post, on Jacob Hamblin's old Mormon Trail from southern Utah to Arizona. This watering place has been heavily used by Navajos. The name is likely for William C. McClellan, a member of the Mormon Battalion of 1846, or John McClellan, an early rancher (Granger 1960, 97).

McMAHON TRADING POST: (approx. 7000 ft) Apache County, AZ. Navajo: Uncertain, possibly the same as for St. Michaels. Van Valkenburgh lists this post as one of three operating in St. Michaels in 1941. The others were Kuhn Trading Post and Frazier's Trading Post.

MESA REDONDA: (6830 ft) Apache County, AZ. Navajo: Dził Bii'Haldzisí, "Mountain with a Basin in it." Dome-shaped mesa rising 800 ft above surrounding plain about 12 miles southwest of Concho. It is associated with the Navajo Blessingway rites. Navajo tradition holds that ancient Pueblo people in this vicinity were destroyed by wind and fire (Van Valkenburgh 1974, 84). Navajos are said to have lived in the region prior to their 1863–64 removal to the Bosque Redondo (U.S. Indian Claims Commission n.d., vol. IV, 526–27).

METEOR CRATER: [DB] (5500 ft rim–5050 ft floor) Coconino County, AZ. Also Coon Butte or Coon Mountain, and Barringer Crater. Navajo: 'Adah Hosh Łání, "Many Cacti (Coming) Down from a Height." A gigantic crater a mile in diameter, created by the impact of a meteor striking the earth about 49,000 years ago. The crater is located seven miles north of Interstate 40, some 20 miles west of Winslow. At the interstate exit is a tourist stop once called Rimmy Jims, where there used to be a "meteor observatory."

The first White report of Meteor Crater was in 1871 (by a member of the Wheeler survey party then searching for a railroad route to the Pacific Ocean), when it was thought to be just another volcanic crater. When viewed today from a distance, the crater appears as a low, jagged hill, though Van Valkenburgh notes that in 1941 the hill looked rounded. Within, however, is a slightly oval depression over 4000 ft in diameter and 570 feet deep.

Thanks to the work of Dr. Daniel Moreau Barringer, a Philadelphia mining engineer who explored the crater from 1902 to 1929, geologists now believe that a meteor—or tight cluster of small meteors—about 80 to one hundred feet in diameter plunged into the earth's crust here, throwing up earth and rocks on every side. The meteor is thought to have been traveling toward the southeast at 43,000 miles per hour.

Dr. Barringer and subsequent explorers searched for the main body of the meteor, hoping to capitalize on the rich deposits of iron and nickel they expected to find, but scientists now believe that up to 80 percent of the meteor vaporized on impact. The property, still owned by the Barringer family, was designated a natural landmark by the Department of the Interior in 1968. The crater is the first and largest definitely identified (on the basis of meteorites in and around it), and is the best preserved impact crater on earth. It was the site of Apollo astronaut training in the 1960s.

The Barringer family have constructed a sizable visitor center on the north rim, complete with an Astronaut Hall of Fame and Museum of Astrogeology. An admission fee is charged.

MEXICAN CRY MESA: (7000–7600 ft) Apache County, AZ. Navajo: Uncertain. Mesa at the northern end of the Lukachukai Mountains, due west of Red Rock Valley (in New Mexico), and south of Cove Mesa. The English name is intriguing, but its origin is unknown. Luckert (1975, 43) describes White Ash Streak Mountain, mentioned in the Navajo hunter tradition, as lying between Lukachukai and Cove—the location of Mexican Cry Mesa.

MEXICAN WATER: [DB] (4800 ft) Apache County, AZ. Navajo: Naakaii Tó, "Mexican Water." An older name is Naakaii Tó Hadayiiznilí, "Mexicans Dug Shallow Wells" (Granger 1960, 15). A small community with a trading post and a chapter house north of U.S. Highway 160, west of U.S. Highway 191, on Walker Creek a mile south of the Utah state line.

It is situated at a steep rocky crossing of the boxed Chinle Wash some 21 miles east of Dinnehotso. Boundary Butte, so called after the northwestern corner of the Treaty Reservation of 1868, is located some 10 miles southeast of Mexican Water (though Van Valkenburgh placed it northeast of that hamlet).

In this rough country the soil covering is generally quite thin and "baldy," with small wind-blown hillocks scattered over tracts of bare rock. Before the paving of U.S. Highways 160 and 190, the roads were marked in places only with piles of rocks.

Until July 1939, the crossing of Chinle Wash, some three miles west of Mexican Water Trading Post, was made over a treacherous 30-degree grade dropping down to the bedrock of the channel, skirting the flash floods. Mexican Water Bridge, a 250-foot steel bridge, replaced the old crossing on July 1, 1939. This bridge, in turn, was replaced about 20 years later. Numerous Anasazi ruins are found in the region.

Granger (1960, 15) notes one source that suggests the name came from the trading post, which was so named because this portion of Walker Creek used to be called Mexican Water.

MEXICAN WATER TRADING POST: (5000 ft) Apache County, AZ. Navajo: Same as Mexican Water community. Built by Hamblin Noel in 1907, two years after he had opened Teec Nos Pos Trading Post, and about seven years after he and brother Henry took over Two Grey Hills Trading Post from another brother, Frank Noel. (McNitt 1962, 259, 343)

MITTEN PEAK: (5800 ft) Navajo County, AZ. Also Rabbit Mountain. Navajo: Bidahóóchii', "Red Streak Running Down." Small, isolated butte towering above the Leroux Wash floodplain in the Painted Desert, about a mile east of Arizona Highway 77, and five miles north of the point where Highway 77 crosses Leroux Wash.

According to local Navajos, the mountain is home to a monster:

> Many years ago numbers of species of deer went into a cave in Rabbit Mountain. This was a favored place to hunt. Once a hunter went into a small canyon running almost to the summit from the east side of the mountain. A deer ran into a narrow opening in the rock. It was winter and the hunter followed his tracks into the opening. It grew darker the farther in he went. Presently he saw ahead of him a shaft of light coming down from the top. He went farther in, and it grew darker again. He heard a great roar and ran out as fast as he could. There is said to be a monster in there and that was the roar the hunter heard. (Van Valkenburgh 1941, 119)

MOENAVE: [DB] (5000 ft) Coconino County, AZ. Also Moe Ave. Navajo: Kin Łigaaí, "White House." Hopi: Moenave (Van Valkenburgh 1941, 100). Mormon community founded at Moe Ave Springs by Jacob Hamblin in 1879. By 1900 there were only three families still living there. The community was located six miles west of Tuba City on the road now labeled Navajo Route 23. However, the Mormons sold the land to the Bureau of Indian Affairs in 1903 and moved out lock, stock, and barrel.

In this green oasis nestled in the coves of the same sandy mesa upon which Tuba City is built,

Father Garcés rested on his visit to the Havasupai in 1776. John Doyle Lee is reputed to have hidden here in the 1860s following his accusation as a participant in the Mountain Meadows Massacre; and Jacob Hamblin founded a Mormon missionary colony here in 1871 under the present name. (See Navajo Bridge.)

In 1934, the Soil Conservation Service established a 10,500-acre demonstration area here under agreement with the local Indians. Between 1935 and 1938, a 32-acre irrigation project (USIS) was developed and supplied from the springs of the oasis.

MOENKOPI: [DB] (4750 ft) (Population: 924) Coconino County, AZ. Also Moencopi. Navajo: 'Oozéí Hayázhí, "Little Oraibi." Hopi: Moncapi, "Place of Running Water." A scattered Hopi farming village founded on the north bank of Moenkopi Wash by "Tuvi" (also Tlvi, Tivi, Toobi, etc.), a chief from the Hopi village of Oraibi, during the 1870s. (Tuvi is the chief for whom Tuba City—two miles northeast–is named.) Originally about a half mile south of Arizona Highway 264 at its juncture with U.S. Highway 160, the village has grown to the intersection itself. In 1941, the population was 416.

Situated on the sloping north terrace of the Moenkopi Wash, which the Navajos call Naak'a' K'éédílyéhé ("Where Cotton is Cultivated"), and which is actually the lower course of Blue Canyon, the wash runs westward through a flat, silty valley bottom between Shinarump and Chinle sandstone cliffs and grotesque formations. Early Spanish documents refer to this region as Los Algodones, "The Cotton Fields" (Brugge 1965, 16–17).

Juan de Oñate visited this site, formerly occupied by a fifteenth-century Anasazi pueblo, in 1604 and called it Rancheria de Gandules. It was part of the old Havasupai habitat and is shown on the Dominguez-Escalante map of 1776 as a point of the Cosoninas trail to the Colorado River from Cosoninas Wash, which became known as Moenkopi Wash in 1870. (Cosoninas was derived from the Hopi name for the Havasupai, Kohninih, of obscure origin.) Father Garcés visited the Havasupai village here in 1776.

Tuvi was friendly with the Mormons, and

made a trip to Salt Lake City with other Hopis while certain Mormons stayed with the Hopis as hostages. It was through his friendship that the first Mormon colony on the Navajo Reservation was established at Moenkopi.

In 1870, John W. Young, a son of Brigham Young, built a woolen mill at Moenkopi, with 192 spindles to be operated by Indian labor. The mill, still standing in 1941, was not successful and was soon abandoned. On the outskirts of the present Hopi village is the old Mormon cemetery with many headstones bearing names familiar in the Navajo country today. Lot Smith, the founder of Sunset, was killed in 1894 by Chách'osh, a Navajo, in a fracas over pasture and water at Spring Canyon, three miles north of Moenkopi. The Mormon settlement at Moenkopi was abandoned after the sale of the region to the Indian department in 1903 (see Tuba City), as the community was within 1,575,369 acres added to the reservation by executive order on January 18, 1900 (McPherson 1988, 34–38).

The village became a refuge for polygamists in 1880, as did the Bluff, Utah, region. Mormons shipped 1,400 pounds of wool from Moenkopi to Provo in 1883, the same year Navajos and Hopis there raised 5,000 bushels of grain.

MOENKOPI WASH: (7400–4200 ft) Navajo and Coconino Counties, AZ. Navajo: Naak'a' K'éé'dílyéhé, "Where Cotton is Cultivated." Ninety miles in length, Moenkopi Wash is one of the major tributaries of the Little Colorado River. The stream heads on northeastern Black Mesa, near Lolomai Point. It is one of the four major drainages of the mesa (see also Dinnebito, Oraibi, and Polacca Washes), though all are ephemeral. The wash exits Black Mesa through Blue Canyon (called Bikooh Dootł'ish Canyon, "Blue Canyon," by Victor Mindeleff in 1891). This canyon takes the channel west to the village of Moenkopi, after which the wash turns south for 25 miles before it joins the Little Colorado River a couple of miles west of Cameron.

This wash was traversed by Colonel (Governor) Jose Antonio Vizcarra's expedition of 1823 (McNitt 1972). Early Spanish explorers called this wash Arroyo de los Algodones, "Stream of the Cotton Fields" (Brugge 1964), an apparent reference to the crops of native agriculture practiced in the region.

MOGOLLON RIM: (7292 ft) Apache, Navajo, and Coconino Counties, AZ. Navajo: Tsii' Dził (U.S. Indian Claims Commission n.d., vol. VI, xxii), "Head Mountain." The elevation changes roughly two thousand feet from the bottom (south side) of this precipitous ridge running nearly two hundred miles east to west, to the top (north side). It stretches from the vicinity of the Little Colorado River's headwaters, near Nutrioso on U.S. Highway 666, westward to a point some 60 miles south of the San Francisco Peaks.

MONTEZUMA'S CHAIR: (6710 ft) Navajo County, AZ. Also Giant's Chair. Navajo: Kits'-iilí, "Shattered House" (naming an Anasazi ruin in the vicinity) (Young and Morgan 1987, 496), though sometimes interpreted as "Pottery Sherds," which is actually Ásaats'iil or Łeets'-aats'iil. Hopi: Hoyapi, "Big Hopi House." One of a pair of high, sheer, volcanic plugs springing from the same footing on the western periphery of the Hopi Buttes. They are located six miles east of Jeddito Wash, five miles west of Arizona Highway 87.

Montezuma's Chair rises some 150 ft above the plain, and is located on the north bank of the Polacca Wash some 10 miles southwest of Shungopovi. A fourteenth-century Hopi ruin lies at the foot of the plug's south talus slope.

This is a favorite place for the Hopis to catch eagles for their Niman Kachina dance. Burro and Coyote Springs in the immediate vicinity have been the scenes of friction between the Hopis and Navajos over range and water.

MOQUI BUTTES: [DB] See Hopi Buttes; some scholars suggest "Moqui" may be an attempt at Hispanicizing "Hopi," though this seems unlikely. Granger (1960, 79) asserts that the term is a misspelling of a Navajo term, "mogi," which is supposed to mean "dead," as a derogatory term for the peaceful Hopi Indians, and James (1974, xiii) says Hopis consider it a term of derision, a notion possibly derived from

Foreman (1941, 156). Young (p.c. 1995), however, emphatically points out that there is no such word in Navajo.

Instead, the word apparently derives from either the Zuni or the Hopi spelling of an earlier term, "mó kwi," with which the Hopis labeled themselves (Harrington 1945, 177–78), and which was commonly used from at least 1598. However, early in the twentieth century anthropologists discovered that the typical Spanish and English mispronunciation was offensive to the Hopis because it was too close to their móki, meaning "dies," or "is dead." Jesse Fewkes recommended adopting the name "Hopi," taken from a more modern name, and in 1923 the name of their reservation was officially changed to Hopi, and the term Moqui was stricken from government use (Connelly 1979, 551).

MORMON LAKE: (7107 ft) Coconino County, AZ. Navajo: Be'ek'id Hoteel, "Wide Lake" (U.S. Indian Claims Commission n.d., vol. VI, iii; Kelley p.c. 1994). Seven miles southeast of Flagstaff, and four miles south of Walnut Canyon National Monument. Named for proximity to a Mormon dairy on the west side of the lake (Granger 1960, 79–80).

Informants to the U.S. Indian Claims Commission (n.d., vol. IV, 526–27), suggest that Navajos were living in this vicinity prior to their 1863–64 removal to the Bosque Redondo. If so, this is likely the most southwesterly extent of Navajo occupation prior to the Bosque Redondo period.

NAAHTEE CANYON: (6150 ft) Navajo County, AZ. Also Na-ah-tee. Navajo: Náá'á Dįįh, "Without Eyes," refers to "Locoweed," according to the U.S. Indian Claims Commission (n.d., vol. VI, x). The name actually means "toadstool," with a literal meaning of "Eyes Become None" (Young and Morgan 1987, 578). A small community located in the Hopi Buttes region, four miles west of Arizona Highway 77, 10 miles south of White Cone.

NAAHTEE CANYON TRADING POST: (approx. 6150 ft) Navajo County, AZ. Navajo: Uncertain, probably the same as the canyon. This is one of several owned at one time by Lorenzo Hubbell (McNitt 1962, 205n), though spelled "Na-ah-tah." The post was opened about 1900, and closed during the mid-1920s (Kelley 1977, 252, 254).

NASHBITO: (approx. 6600 ft) Apache County, AZ. Navajo: Na'ashǫ́'iito'í, "Lizard Spring" in Chinle Valley (Gregory 1916, 151). This spring is located about 10 miles west of Ganado (Young and Morgan 1987, 937).

NATURAL BRIDGE: [DB] (approx. 7000 ft) Apache County, AZ. Navajo: Tsé Naní'áhí, "Rock Span Across" (Young and Morgan 1987, 730). Low sandstone bridge located at the mouth of Natural Bridge Canyon that cuts west into a spur of the Defiance Plateau some four miles southwest of the community of Fort Defiance. The bridge is quite substantial, able to support a man on horseback, and seven or eight riders abreast could easily pass beneath it. The canyon carries a permanent spring-fed stream of water. In the 1930s, a small irrigation project was initiated where Natural Bridge Canyon enters Black Creek with a diversion of Black Creek serving some 80 acres of agricultural land.

Near the bridge lie the remains of the stone house in which Chee Dodge lived with his adopted father, Perry H. Williams, and his father's Navajo wife. There are small Anasazi remains in Natural Bridge Canyon and in the next canyon west are found some small unit houses of undetermined age.

NATURAL BRIDGE CANYON: [DB (map 11)] (7800–6900 ft) Apache County, AZ. Navajo: Uncertain. A tributary of Black Creek, four miles southwest of Fort Defiance. It flows off the eastern edge of the Defiance Plateau, and harbors a natural bridge at the mouth of the canyon, several small Anasazi ruins, and the house in which Chee Dodge lived with his adopted father, Perry H. Williams, and his wife.

NAVAJO ARMY DEPOT: (7100 ft) Navajo County, AZ. Also Navajo Ordnance Depot. Navajo: Uncertain. Located at Bellemont. Within weeks after Pearl Harbor, eight hundred Navajos were working on construction of this munitions depot. By 1945, the Indian Service estimated 10,000 Navajos were employed by the war effort (Moon 1992, 167).

Bellemont was named in September 1882, for Belle Smith, daughter of the General Superintendent of the Atlantic and Pacific Railroad, F. W. Smith. It was earlier called "Volunteer" because of campsites of volunteers in 1863, and was one of the largest munitions depots for the Pacific theater of World War II (Trimble 1986, 274). The depot now serves as an Army National Guard camp.

NAVAJO BRIDGE: [DB] (3603 ft) Coconino County, AZ. Also Lee's Ferry Bridge, Marble Canyon Bridge. Navajo: Na'ní'á Hatsoh, "Big Span." This bridge on Alternate U.S. Highway 89 crosses Marble Canyon and the Colorado River approximately four miles downstream from Lees Ferry. The bridge is 834 feet long and 467 feet above the river (Granger 1960, 80). In the immediate vicinity are Marble Canyon Trading Post, a post office, and Marble Canyon Lodge.

Jacob Hamblin was the first White person known to have attempted crossing the precipitous gorge of the Colorado. Unsuccessful in the 1850s, he made the crossing on a raft in 1864 at a point six miles above the present Navajo Bridge. In December 1871, John Doyle Lee secured rights to operate a ferry about three miles above where the bridge is now located (see Lee's Ferry).

In 1929 the Navajo Bridge was opened, then the highest highway bridge in the United States.

NAVAJO CANYON: [DB] (6800–4300 ft) Coconino County, AZ. Also Navajo Creek, Kaibito Canyon. Navajo: No general Navajo name other than the general descriptive terms, Tsékooh ("Lesser Rock Canyon") or Tséyí' ("Deep Rock Canyon"). The Upper Crossing is Gishí Bikéyah ("Mr. Cane's Field"); the Middle Crossing, 'Ałtíí Jik'áshí ("Bow Smoother," referring to a shrub that grows at the crossing). The lower (and main) crossing between Kaibito and Navajo Mountain is Ch'áyaí ("Armpit," a person's nickname). A

crossing five miles up canyon from the Colorado River (believed locally to be the Crossing of the Fathers, across which Fray Escalante followed an old Cosoninas trail in 1776) is referred to as 'Ahidiidlí ("Where They Flow Together").

This 32-mile-long creek winds through a deeply cut canyon in the Kaibito Plateau. Heading in the White Mesa region near the Inscription House Ruins (Navajo National Monument), it merges with Lake Powell approximately 10 miles upstream (northeast) of Glen Canyon Dam. However, when the lake is at its peak holding capacity, the waters back up into Navajo Canyon to the mouth of Chaol (Cha'oł) Canyon. The name Navajo Creek was applied by John Wesley Powell (Granger 1960, 80).

An agricultural area is located in the canyon between Navajo Mountain and Inscription House Trading Post. Inscription House Ruin, a part of Navajo National Monument, is located some five miles west of Inscription House Trading Post. A pictograph in the canyon depicting a crescent moon was suggested to be astronomical in nature as early as 1955, along with a similar depiction on White Mesa (Miller 1955, 6–12).

NAVAJO NATIONAL MONUMENT: (7286–5800 ft) Coconino and Navajo counties, AZ. Navajo: Bitát'ahkin (Austin and Lynch 1983, 36), "House on a Rock Ledge," referring to Betatakin Ruin in the monument. During the winter of 1895, Richard Wetherill and Charlie Mason spent four months in the Monument Valley, Marsh Pass, and the Tsegi Canyon Region of the Shonto Plateau, discovering Keet Seel (Kits'iil) Ruin in the canyon. Wetherill became the first superintendent of Navajo National Monument in 1909. The monument is a series of isolated islands of territory around three major ruin complexes. Construction of all three ruins is attributed to the Kayenta branch of the Anasazi, with occupation of the region beginning during the Basketmaker II period, about the time of Christ. Although the Kayenta Anasazi graduated from pithouses to aboveground dwellings as early as A.D. 600, construction of the multi-storied, many-roomed structures at these three ruins did not begin until about A.D. 1250—after the abandonment of the larger villages at Chaco

Canyon to the east. The Navajo National Monument villages seem to have peaked about A.D. 1290, and were largely abandoned within the next decade.

Tsegi Canyon and its numerous side canyons and rincons house hundreds of prehistoric Anasazi ruins, but the best known are Betatakin, Keet Seel, and Inscription House. Other important ruins are Rubbish Ruin (A.D. 1257), Turkey Cave, Bat Woman, Twin Caves, and Swallow's Nest.

Dinosaur tracks are also known in the sandstone of the monument (Brady 1960, 81–82). Snake House, a minor, 19-room pueblo, is located near the larger Inscription House.

✦ BETATAKIN RUIN: (7000 ft) Navajo County, AZ. Navajo: Bitát'ahkin, "House on a Rock Ledge" (Young and Morgan 1987, 247), or "Side Hill House" (Gregory 1915, 149). Also Kin Łaní (Many Houses). The most accessible ruin of the Navajo National Monument group, Betatakin is located near the head of Betatakin Canyon, a two-mile-long southern branch of Tsegi Canyon, joining the latter six miles northwest of the juncture of that canyon with Marsh Pass. The overhanging red sandstone cliff rises 500 ft above the 135-room ruin (Lister and Lister 1983, 149), situated at the base of the north wall of the canyon. Discovered in 1909 (14 years after the discovery of Keet Seel) by John and Richard Wetherill, the ruin was stabilized by Neil M. Judd in 1917. Betatakin is the second largest cliff dwelling in the Tsegi region, and dates to A.D. 1260–77. This ruin is open to the public via scheduled three-hour tours of no more than 20 persons.

✦ INSCRIPTION HOUSE: (5800 ft) Coconino County, AZ. Navajo: Ts'ah Biis Kin, "House in the Sagebrush" (Young and Morgan 1987, 742). This 74-room ruin with granaries and a kiva (Lister and Lister 1983, 149) is located on the north side of the mouth of a branch of Nitsin Canyon, on the east bank of Navajo Creek, approximately five miles downstream (north) of that channel's headwaters, and some four miles northwest of historic Inscription House Trading Post. The ruin was recorded by Byron Cummings in 1909, just a few days before Betatakin Ruins were discov-

ered (Lister and Lister 1983, 149). The English name results from a non-decipherable inscription noted on the cliff wall. In 1909, John Wetherill interpreted what was then visible as the letters "CHOS" and the date "1661 A d n." This cryptic, partial message has been interpreted by others as "Carlos Arnais 1661" or "S-haperio Ano Dom 1661" (Van Valkenburgh 1941, 78). Though the inscription is generally attributed to Spanish explorers, it must be pointed out that the date may indeed be 1861. This ruin is closed to the public indefinitely, pending desperately needed stabilization.

✦ KEET SIEL: (7200 ft) Navajo County, AZ. Also Kiet Siel. Navajo: Kits'iil, "Shattered House" (Young and Morgan 1987, 496). (Granger [1987, 152], suggests a more widely used—if erroneous—translation: "Broken Pottery," or Kiits'illi.) Also called Kin Yits'ill, "Empty House." Yet another interpretation refers to a large spruce log lying across a retaining wall. The ruin was first called Long House (McNitt 1966, 79–80). In 1895, Keet Siel was the first of the Navajo National Monument ruins to be discovered, as Richard Wetherill searched for his wayward mule, "Neephi." Situated in Keet Siel Canyon, it is the largest cliff dwelling in Arizona, with 160 rooms and five or six kivas. Keet Siel was constructed between A.D. 1274 and 1286. Visitation to the site is limited to 20 persons per day, and 1,500 annually, and visitors must register with the Park headquarters. Some overnight camping is allowed during the summer.

NAVAJO SPRINGS: [DB] (5600 ft) Apache County, AZ. Navajo: Tó Sido or "Hot Spring"; also Kin Łigaaí, "White House" (a previous name for an abandoned settlement off I-40, on the north side of the Rio Puerco, 42 miles east of Holbrook, now commonly called Navajo); and 'Ahoyoolts'ił, "Hole Spreading as its Sides Continuously Crumble and Fall Away," which is also the name for Jacob's Well (Young p.c. 1995). The springs are located three miles southeast of Navajo, across the Rio Puerco of the West. As many as five possible Chacoan prehistoric road segments have been identified in this region (Gabriel 1991, 277–78).

The territorial organization of the present state of Arizona took place at Navajo Springs on December 29, 1863, while Governor John Goodwin and party were en route from Old Fort Wingate (see San Rafael, New Mexico) to Fort Whipple near present Prescott, Arizona.

Navajo Springs was a main point on the Whipple Railroad Survey of 1853 between Jacob's Well and Lithodendron Wash, and an important resting place on the military and emigrant trail between Old Fort Wingate and Fort Whipple. Major G. B. Willis, First Infantry of California Volunteers, laid out the route as an official trail in 1863. In his notes, as published in the Rio Abajo News, he states that the site had good water and grass.

The valley of the Rio Puerco of the West was the center of many Navajo-White difficulties in the 1880s, brought about by land grant to the Atlantic and Pacific Railroad (now the Burlington Northern Santa Fe). When White homesteaders and ranchers purchased railroad land, or settled under the Homestead Act, they ejected Navajos from favored ranges and water. The trouble eventually resulted in the murder of Tsinadjinih Begay by C. P. Owen on March 15, 1884. Only the prompt action of Navajo Agent Dennis Riordan prevented the wholesale massacre of all the Whites in the vicinity. Troops under Lieutenant Lockett had to be sent from Fort Wingate to quell further disorders. Owen, after some gestures of the courts at trying him, was set free.

A trading post was erected here between 1881 and 1885, and closed in the late 1950s (Kelley 1977, 251, 255).

ALSO: [DB] (5300 ft) Coconino County, AZ. Navajo: Uncertain. A spring located at the foot of the Echo Cliffs, a mile east of Alternate U.S. Highway 89, approximately five miles southeast of Navajo Bridge. This was a watering place and campsite along Jacob Hamblin's old Mormon Trail in the 1850s (Granger 1960, 80). At present it is used by the Navajos.

NAZLINI: [DB] (6300 ft) Apache County, AZ. Navajo: Názlíní, "Makes a Turn Flowing" (a bend in a river) (Young p.c. 1995). A small chap-

ter and trading community (Nazlini Trading Post) and school on Navajo Route 27, 17 highway miles north of Ganado, on Nazlini Creek at the western foot of Rock Mesa, in the upper Beautiful Valley (actually the upper end of the Chinle Valley). Anasazi ruins have been found in Nazlini Canyon, some three miles east and up Nazlini Creek. An abundance of petrified wood is found five miles northwest of Nazlini Trading Post in Beautiful Valley. A USIS Irrigation system was installed at Nazlini.

NAZLINI CANYON: (7000–6400 ft) Apache County, AZ. Navajo: See Nazlini. The canyon of Nazlini Creek, cutting east into Rock Mesa a mile east of Nazlini. Nazlini Canyon, rising in the western flank of the Defiance Plateau, is a deep, rugged red and buff sandstone gorge in which are found many Anasazi sites, and old Navajo campsites and peach orchards. This old-time Navajo rendezvous was deserted some years ago because of the heavy inroads of erosion on their agricultural lands and orchards. There is a concrete diversion dam (USIS) located one mile east of the store on Nazlini Creek that irrigates some 60 acres.

NAZLINI TRADING POST: (6400 ft) Navajo: Uncertain. Opened by Lorenzo Hubbell between 1886 and 1900 (McNitt 1962, 204), and still in operation during the 1970s.

NITSIN CANYON: (6150–5800 ft) Coconino County, AZ. Navajo: possibly Niidzí, possibly "We Stand in a Row," though Young (p.c. 1995) doubts this. This tributary of Navajo Canyon near its headwaters on the Kaibito Plateau (five miles north of Arizona Highway 98) conceals Inscription House Ruin of Navajo National Monument. Three miles northwest of the canyon is Inscription House Trading Post.

OAK CREEK CANYON: [DB] (6900–3200 ft) Coconino and Yavapai Counties, AZ. Navajo: Tsé Nahoot'ood, "Springy Rock" (Young p.c. 1995). This deep, scenic canyon heads on the Coconino Plateau, at the confluence of Oak Creek and Pumphouse Wash, some 10 miles south of Flagstaff, between U.S. Highway 89A (west) and I-17 (east). Flowing generally southwest for approximately 40 miles, the channel exits the plateau near Sedona and flows on to join the Verde River a couple of miles northeast of Arizona Highway 279, about midway between Camp Verde (on I-17) and Cottonwood (on U.S. 89A). The canyon is deepest along its northern half, where U.S. 89A parallels the river on the 1500-ft-deep canyon floor. The southern half is not nearly so deep, but it is extremely tortuous and winding.

The upper part of Oak Creek Canyon is reputed by the Navajos to be the traditional stopping place of the Western Water Clans in the Bead Chant stories. The Tó Dich'íi'nii ("Bitter Water" People), Bit'ahnii ("Arms Folded" People), Hashtłishnii ("Mud" People), Honágháhnii ("He Walks Around One" People), and the Tótsohnii ("Big Water" People) were created at the home of Yoołgaii 'Asdzaan ("White Shell Woman") on a jeweled island in the Pacific Ocean. The five clans migrated east to find their relatives and after years of wandering, joined the nuclear clans on the San Juan River—having passed through Oak Creek Canyon (Van Valkenburgh 1941, 108).

OAK SPRINGS: [DB] (6800 ft) Apache County, AZ. Also Oak Spring. Navajo: Teeł Ch'ínít'i', "Tule Extending Out," or "A Line of Cattails." The name applies to both a spring and a small chapter community that has sprung up around it. The canyon in which the spring and community lie is called Tsétł'áán Ńdíshchí'í, "Pines in a Crescent Around the Canyon's Edge" (Young and Morgan 1987, 731). The community sits on Navajo Route 12 near Hunters Point, where Navajo Route 12 crosses Black Creek. Farm and ranch houses line both sides of the road in this valley.

Some farming is done in the area, which is a large basin bounded on the west by the Defiance Plateau, by the spur of Hunter's Point on the north, and by a red sandstone monocline on the east. A large twelfth-century Anasazi ruin in the basin is named Chéch'il Bii' Kin ("House in the Oaks") (Young p.c. 1995).

The spring was formerly called Willow Springs, as on McComb's map of 1860. This same map (and other old maps) show Black Creek Canyon as Cañon Chennele.

O'LEARY PEAK: (8916 ft) Coconino County, AZ. Navajo: Dził Nééz, "Tall Mountains," or "Tall Mountain" (U.S. Indian Claims Commission n.d., vol. VI, vii). Volcanic plug three miles northwest of Sunset Crater. The English name honors Dan O'Leary, a guide for General George Crook (Granger 1960, 81). This region has been identified by informants as having been a pre–Bosque Redondo (pre-1864) Navajo grazing area (U.S. Indian Claims Commission n.d., vol. IV, 712–15).

ORAIBI TRADING POST: (6050 ft) Navajo County, AZ. Navajo: Uncertain, possibly the same as the community of Oraibi (see Hopi Reservation). This post was built by Lorenzo Hubbell about 1882. It was purchased from the Hubbell family by the Babbitt Brothers in 1955 (McNitt 204, 266).

ORAIBI WASH: (7600–4950 ft) Navajo and Coconino Counties, AZ. Navajo: 'Asdzání 'Ayáásh Bitooh, interpreted as "Lady Behind's Spring" by the U.S. Indian Claims Commission (n.d., vol. VI, i), referring to the upper wash area. Young (p.c. 1995) suggests it is rather 'Asdzání Bitł'aa' Bikooh, "Woman's Derriere Canyon." This 85-mile-long, intermittent stream heads on Black Mesa, near the northeast rim of the mesa, and flows south through the Hopi Reservation, passing a mile east of Oraibi. It joins Polacca Wash a mile east of Red Lake, seven miles upstream of the point where Polacca Wash and Jeddito Wash merge to form Corn Creek Wash.

PADILLA MESA: (6000–6300 ft) Coconino County, AZ. Navajo: Gad Dah Yisk'id, "Juniper Hill," (U.S. Indian Claims Commission n.d., vol. VI, vii) or Tsin Dah Yiskid, "Woody Hill" (U.S. Indian Claims Commission n.d., vol. VI, xxiii). Actually a lower, southwesterly extension of Third Mesa, this feature is some 10 miles long. Named by Gregory (1915, 153) for Fray Juan

Padilla of Coronado's 1540 expedition. Granger (1960, 81) suggests that Padilla was later killed by Hopi Indians, but this cleric was actually killed on the Great Plains by Kiowa or Kansas Indians (Bolton 1951, 340).

This region has been identified by the U.S. Indian Claims Commission studies (vol. IV, 712–15) as being a pre–Bosque Redondo (pre-1864) Navajo grazing area.

PAGE: (4310 ft) (Population: 6,598) Coconino County, AZ. Navajo: Da'deestł'in Hótsaa, "Big Dam" (Young p.c. 1995), or Na'ní'á Hótsaa, "Big Span" (Austin and Lynch 1983, 36). The largest community along a 720-mile stretch of the Colorado River, this town on the south shore of Lake Powell was born of the need for a place to house the massive construction crews building Glen Canyon Dam. On March 22, 1957, a 24.3-acre tract of land on Manson Mesa was deeded to the Bureau of Reclamation from the Navajo Tribe in return for a similar parcel on McCracken Mesa, near Aneth, Utah. The community was first labeled "Page Government Camp." The name honors John C. Page, a commissioner of the Bureau of Reclamation from 1937 to 1943, who died in 1955.

The camp was designed with a park, a school complex, a warehouse district, churches, and three hundred permanent homes and one thousand mobile homes. After several major fluctuations in population following the completion of the dam project, the townspeople incorporated in 1975 (Martin 1989).

This community is also the home of Navajo Generating Station, constructed between April 22, 1970, and June 1976. The plant employs seven hundred, and produces 2.5 million kilowatts. However, it uses 36,000 acre-feet of water per year, which comes out of Arizona's meager 50,000-acre-foot allotment of Colorado River water. The Navajos actually had first rights to this water, but they relinquished them in favor of employment preference at the plant and the privilege of purchasing power from the plant (Iverson 1981, 109–11).

PAINTED DESERT: [DB] (4400–6000 ft) Coconino, Navajo, and Apache Counties, AZ.

Navajo: Halchíítah, "Among the Red Areas" (Young and Morgan 1987, 409), a general descriptive term for this type of country. This huge crescent of badlands—desert flats and sandstone mesas formed of Chinle shale—extends from the northern end of Marble Canyon (northwest) southeast to Winslow and Holbrook, then northeast to the western periphery of the Defiance Plateau near Houck. This swath extends some three hundred miles along the north bank of the Little Colorado River (WPA 1940a, 311), and in places is over 25 miles wide. The name is derived from the variety of hues presented by the various exposed strata of sandstone, clay, volcanic soils, and rock—usually occurring in parallel layers.

One of the most accessible parts lies in the northern portion of Petrified Forest National Park, some 28 miles northeast of Holbrook. Here the Fred Harvey Company once operated the Painted Desert Inn, which housed the well-known Adolph Schuster Indian basketry collection. The inn is now a Park Service facility.

Spanish explorers first came upon this vast region of grotesquely eroded desert in 1540. Its brilliant colors, ever-changing with the intensity of sunlight, led them to name it El Desierto Pintado—the Painted Desert. Wild horses still roam many parts of the area and find drinking water at the old Star Mail Route Station on Lithodendron Wash, which cuts between the inn and Chindi (Ghost) Mesa. The name was officially applied by Lieutenant Ives in 1861 (Gregory 1916, 153).

PARIA PLATEAU: (6000–7300 ft) Coconino County, AZ. Paiute: "Elk Water" (Granger 1960, 81). An uplift, cresting on the east, tilting down toward the west, bounded on the southeast by the Vermillion Cliffs and on the northeast by Paria Canyon.

PETRIFIED FOREST NATIONAL PARK: [DB] Apache County, AZ. Navajo: General area from the north called Sahdii Bisí, "Chunks of Earth Sticking up Alone" (Austin and Lynch 1983, 37). Also Tsé Nástánii, "Stone Logs." The smallest of all American national parks, Petrified Forest straddles I-40, 79 miles east of Gallup, New Mexico. The park measures approximately 25 miles north-south, and varies from one to 12 miles in width. Here a vast area of petrified wood is eroding from a virtually treeless plateau. The "wood" emerging from the clay soil ranges from small chunks and nuggets to entire, horizontal tree trunks tens of feet long.

The first scientific investigations in the park, archaeological in nature, took place under Jesse Fewkes in the late 1800s. The vicinity was proclaimed a national monument as an area of outstanding geological importance by President Theodore Roosevelt in 1906 (Lister and Lister 1983, 159–61) in an effort to stem the constant unchecked removal of the petrified wood from the area.

The region was once the center of a great basin overflowed by running water. Giant fallen trees gradually became waterlogged and were eventually covered by layer upon layer of sand and gravel that washed down from the surrounding elevations. Over the eons, the mineral-laden waters impregnated the trunks with silica, petrifying them for posterity. The earth's crust gradually rose to its present elevation, and wind and water eroded the many layers of stone, breaking them up and grinding them into the loose earth that now yields up the harder stone of the petrified wood.

Several moderate archaeological sites exist within the park, giving prehistorians a glance at the border region where the Anasazi, Mogollon, and Hakataya cultures came together. The park's main content, however, is obviously the fossil remains of plant and animal life dating back to the late Triassic period, about 180 million years ago. Especially numerous are the silicified trunks of Araucarias, Woodworthias, and Schilderias—the trees of ancient forests. The park also contains 2,500 acres of the Painted Desert, purchased in 1932, giving it a total of 93,492 acres. The monument became a national park in 1962, and eight years later an additional 50,000 acres were set aside as wilderness.

In addition to Fewkes's early work, the Laboratory of Anthropology conducted Civil Works Administration surveys and tests in the 1930s, concentrating at Agate House (a Pueblo III hamlet constructed of petrified wood), Puerco and Flattop Ruins (each containing about 125 rooms, and pithouses). In 1941–42, new surveys by the Park Service increased the known archaeological sites in the park to 304.

Evidence of possible "solar markers," indicating archaeoastronomical activities, has been found at ten prehistoric sites in the national park, along with eight others just beyond the park boundaries. Most include sharp wedges of sunlight bisecting or pointing to center markings on petroglyphs at the summer and winter solstices and at the equinox (Preston and Preston 1983). Puerco Ruins date to A.D. 1250–1350 (Schroeder 1961, 93–104). Flattop Ruins date to A.D. 600, and Twin Buttes Site dates to A.D. 600–800 (Wendorf 1951, 77–83).

PINE SPRINGS: (6950 ft) Apache County, AZ. Navajo: T'iis 'Íí'áhí, "Standing Cottonwood" (Young p.c. 1995). Small trading and school community located on southern Defiance Plateau, on Navajo Route 9010, nine miles north of Houck, and nine miles west of Oak Springs (and Black Creek).

Located in rising juniper- and piñon-covered country north of Houck (on I-40), Pine Springs is shown on McComb's map of 1860 as Agua Vibora (Spanish for "Viper Water"). Troops under Major O. S. Shepherd camped here in 1859. There seems to be a measure of likelihood that this is the springs called Emigrant Springs in the 1800s.

The region is famous for the quality of its weaving and silvercraft. Kelley (1977, 254) places the opening of the post prior to 1920, but another source has the post constructed in 1928. The post closed in 1971, one of the 50 that shut their doors during that decade due to stiffer regulations, competition from 7-Eleven stores, and tribal efforts to put more of the posts in Indian hands. Only the front walls remain standing.

PIÑON: [DB] (6315 ft) (Population: 468) Navajo County, AZ. Navajo: Be'ek'id 'Ahoodzání, "Lake that has a Hole in It" (Young p.c. 1995). Chapter village located in the rolling partly wooded mesa country on southeast Black Mesa, at the junction of Navajo Routes 4 and 41, some 41 miles west of Chinle. The Spanish name is for the nut-bearing evergreen.

According to Bailey (1964b), Captain John

Walker and two companies of Mounted Rifles were the first Americans known to have traversed this wild region, traveling northwest from near Salina to Marsh Pass in 1859. Walker described the region as a series of broken hills, mesas, and canyons. Except for the eastern periphery, the area was then uninhabited.

Walker warned that in case of war with the United States, the Navajos could easily conceal themselves in this ". . . labyrinth of hills, valleys and arroyos. Discovering their hiding places would be as difficult as it was to find the Seminoles in the Everglades of Florida." To this day, the region remains relatively isolated, and is populated by extremely conservative Navajos.

An aged Navajo, Béésh Łigaii 'Atsidí (who died in 1939), told the story of a Mexican trading expedition bringing a carreta (a two-wheeled wooden cart) into the Piñon country over the Canyon de Chelly rim trail, across Black Mountain (now Black Mesa) and then down as far as Gray Mountain on the Little Colorado River. According to Van Valkenburgh, the Navajo name refers to a carreta falling into a deep arroyo on the return trip over Black Mesa. Informants from Chinle state that Black Mesa was the habitual winter range of the Chinle Valley people many years ago.

In October 1939, Ramon Hubbell and Evon Vogt found old Spanish inscriptions in this vicinity, near a spring the Navajos called Naakaiitó (Mexican Water). The Navajos thought that the inscriptions had been left there by a party of Spanish or Mexicans who had killed some Navajos near Ganado and then proceeded northwest. A part of the cliff had fallen off, covering the inscriptions, and the explorers lacked the tools for the removal of the rocks.

A new 25,000-square-foot shopping center was completed in Piñon on Sunday, December 12, 1993, replacing 13.1 acres of juniper scrub land in the heart of the Navajo Nation with a grocery store, a video rental outlet, and a pizzeria.

PIÑON TRADING POST: (6315 ft) Navajo County, AZ. Navajo: Uncertain, possibly the same as the community. Remote trading post opened during the first decade of this century

(Kelley 1977, 253). It was owned early—and possibly founded—by Lorenzo Hubbell, Jr. His cousin George Hubbell (and George's wife, Madge) ran it during the 1930s (Brugge p.c. 1996). It was operated at one time by the Foutz brothers, and later by McGee. Bill Malone—later of Hubbell Trading Post—managed it for McGee in the late 1970s.

PIPE SPRING: (5100 ft) Mohave County, AZ. Navajo: Uncertain, though Granger (1960, 220) suggests that "Indians" called this location "Yellow Rock Spring." The name Pipe Spring came from an 1858 incident in which William Hamblin, a member of a Mormon party passing through, shot out the bottom of another man's smoking pipe on a wager (Granger 1960, 220). Mormons settled the area by 1863, along with Short Creek and Moccasin, Arizona, and Kanab, Utah. They relocated Paiutes of the region to locations outside the area to serve as an early warning system against Navajos and Utes. Alexander McIntyre and Dr. J. N. Whitmore were killed near here by a band of 25 Paiutes and Navajos from Navajo Mountain in 1866 (McPherson 1988, 6, 12). The Indians were pursued and nine were killed (Correll 1968, January).

PIUTE: [DB] (approx. 6000–5000 ft) Coconino and Navajo Counties, AZ. Also Paiute, Piute Strip, Paiute Strip. Navajo: Báyóodzin Bikéyah, "Piute Land" (Young and Morgan 1987, 148). Van Valkenburgh locates this entry in the broken country between the Little Colorado River and the Kaibito Plateau. It is the home of a small band (28 members in 1941) of Paiutes who are descended from ancestors brought there from the Coconino Plateau (Gray Mountain) under the leadership of Badawa (namesake of Bodaway Mesa) in 1869. Though they spoke Shoshonean-stock Paiute, they were visually indistinguishable from their Navajo neighbors, having adopted—like the Navajos—White men's clothing, and living in Navajo hogans. This band was even administered for a time through the Central Navajo Agency at Window Rock. They have, though, filed for official federal recognition as a separate tribe, which would presumably give them a separate reservation, most likely land they occupy in the existing Navajo Reservation.

Relatives of these Paiutes live in Piute Canyon and Allen Canyon some 50 miles west of Blanding, Utah. Today, this tiny band is poverty-stricken, having a few sheep and conducting a little farming in the small alluvial fans along Cedar Ridge. In the summer and fall, they live together in open piñon or cedar windbreaks or corrals of the Great Basin type. In winter, they dwell in two or three hogans of the general Navajo type.

Although they have been in continuous contact with the Navajos for over a century, and the two peoples have generally been friendly and closely allied, the Navajos did not readily intermarry with them. However, there is a considerable amount of Paiute blood among the Navajos to the northeast (Van Valkenburgh 1941, 114). The Paiutes call the Navajos Kwatsih ("Friend").

POLACCA WASH: (7200–4900 ft) Navajo County, AZ. Navajo: Uncertain. One of four major drainages of Black Mesa (see also Dinnebito, Oraibi, and Moenkopi Washes). 85-mile-long tributary of Corn Creek Wash, heading 10 miles north of Lohali Point on the easternmost point of the mesa. The wash flows southwest between Whippoorwill Spring Mesa and Balakai Mesa and northwest of Low Mountain. It skirts southeast of Polacca and continues another 45 miles before joining Jeddito Wash to form Corn Creek Wash, which flows another eight miles into the Little Colorado River.

The earliest Spanish maps of this region, dating to the early 1700s, refer to this as Arroyo de Moqui, or Moqui Wash (Brugge 1965, 16–17).

POLLEN MOUNTAIN: Navajo: Tádídíín Dził, "Pollen Mountain," or Ni'go'Asdzáán, "Earth Woman" (Luckert 1977:5). This colossal mythological formation covers much of the central and western Navajo Reservation. A female, anthropomorphic, mythological figure, comprised of Navajo Mountain (her head), Black Mesa (her body), Balakai Mesa (her feet), Comb Ridge (one of her arms) and Tuba Butte and

Agathla Peak (her breasts—although some accounts feature Agathla Peak as a wool spinner in her hand) (McPherson 1992, 21).

PRESTON MESA: (6830 ft) Coconino County, AZ. Navajo: Uncertain. Large mesa on the Kaibito Plateau resting approximately 15 miles east of Gap. It measures four miles east-west, and five miles north-south, rising 1000 ft above the surrounding terrain. It was named for Navajo trader Sam Preston (Granger 1960, 82).

PUEBLO COLORADO WASH: (6700–5200 ft) Also Ganado Wash. Navajo: Uncertain, though Hubbell Trading Post manager Bill Malone (p.c. 1988) believes the traditional name was Lók'aahnteel, "Wide Band of Reeds up at an Elevation"—the same name used for Ganado. Formed by Lone Tule, Sage House Ruin, Kinlichee, and Fish Washes, which converge near Ganado Lake, this stream is tributary to Cottonwood Wash approximately 25 miles upstream (northeast) of the confluence of the latter with the Little Colorado River. The name's first "official" use was by Lieutenant Ives in 1858. Brugge (p.c. 1996) notes that it appears on maps of the Mexican period, particularly on the Mira y Pacheco maps of the 1770s. The name Cumaa appears to be at a crossing of this wash.

In September 1847, 15 soldiers under Lieutenant Thomas H. Coats, of Major Robert Walker's command, were fired upon by Navajos near the head of this creek. They charged and killed one Navajo (McNitt 1972, 272). Lieutenant Colonel Dixon Stansbury Miles's Third Infantry from Fort Defiance attacked Manuelito's camp on this wash near Kinlichee in October 1855 (Frink 1968:45). Three years later, a column led by Miles was forced to withdraw from Canyon de Chelly along this streambed. In the vicinity of Ganado, on October 7, 1860, troops under Brevet Major Henry Sibley were fired upon from the mesas overlooking the wash (McNitt 1972, 272, 341, 395). (This is the same Henry Sibley who resigned his general's commission in 1861 to command the Confederate forces in the Southwest.)

During the spring of 1863, at the height of the Navajo wars, Kit Carson was instructed by General Carleton to establish a post in the vicinity of Miles's attack on Manuelito, but after surveying the site, Carson decided instead to reoccupy the structures of old Fort Defiance, which had been abandoned two years earlier. The resurrected post was named Fort Canby (Frink 1968, 79–80).

RABBIT MESA TRADING POST: Coconino County, AZ. Navajo: Uncertain. George W. McAdams built this post around 1876, about five miles north of Tuba City (Richardson 1986).

RAINBOW TRAIL: (6000–6450 ft) Coconino County, AZ. The name refers to the road to Navajo Mountain Trading Post and Rainbow Lodge. The road was built in 1924 by Gladwell Richardson and John Daw (a Navajo), amid threats and raids by Kayenta Navajos stirred up by other Whites in the region who did not want to see the road completed (Richardson 1986).

RED LAKE: [DB] (7000 ft) Apache County, AZ. Navajo: Be'ek'id Halchíí, "Red Lake." Named for its reddish color (created by silt), this small, semi-artificial lake sits at the north end of Black Creek Valley, north of Fort Defiance, between the Chuska Mountains (east) and the Defiance Plateau (west). Fed by ephemeral streams—mostly originating on the western slopes of the Chuska Mountains and flowing through Todilto (Tó Dildǫ' "Popping Water") Park in New Mexico—the lake is held in check by a dam constructed by the Indian Service to replace an earlier one built by the Navajos at the south and waters 128 acres of farm land below it in Black Creek Valley. Black Creek flows south from this lake through Black Lake and points south.

A jagged lava plug called Tsézhiní ("Traprock") by the locals (also called Church Rock and Buell Mountain) rises abruptly out of the flats west of the south end of the lake. Dził Ditł'oí ("Fuzzy Mountain"), a high rounded mountain, stands to the southeast. This formation is also called Shash Bighan ("Bear House"). A chapter house has been constructed in the vicinity.

Red Lake is important in the Navajo Sǫ'tsohjí

("Big Star" Ceremony). The volcanic plugs near Red Lake are reputed to have once been ant hills, and the long white ridge running along the east side of the lake from the base of Fuzzy Mountain and cut by Todilto Wash was once the home of a big snake.

ALSO: [DB] (as Tolani Lake)] (5000 ft) Coconino County, AZ. Also Tolani Lakes. Navajo: Tó Łání, "Much Water," or Tó Nehelį́įh, "Water Flows and Collects" (Young and Morgan 1987, 707). This extensive delta of Oraibi Wash gave rise to a USIS day school and trading post approximately 15 miles northwest of Leupp, at the junction of Navajo Routes 6810, 6812, and 6820. The name Tolani Lakes (plural) used to apply to a collection of catch basins approximately five miles to the northwest. Hopis claim that this was actually once the property of certain Hopi clans from Oraibi and Shungopovi, who were displaced in the 1870s by Navajos moving in from the north. The Hopis had farming camps here, but not permanent villages. There is now a Navajo chapter house in the vicinity.

RED LAKE TRADING POST: (5500 ft) Coconino County, AZ. Also Tonalea. Navajo: Tó Nehelį́įh "Water Flows and Collects" (Kelley p.c. 1994). George Washington McAdams founded this post at the location later to become known as Tonalea around 1878 (Van Valkenburgh 1941). In 1881, it was run by Joseph M. Lee (son of John D. Lee of Lee's Ferry) as a canvas-topped shack that occupied two locations. In 1885, George McManus moved the store back to its original location, and sold out to "Ditt" Dittenhoffer, who was killed in a lover's quarrel at the post in 1890. Babbitt Brothers moved the post to its present location and built the two-story structure.

Subsequent managers were Sam Preston (1891–97), H. K. Warren (1897–1905), Earl Boyer (1905–18), Johnny O'Farrell (1918–35), Floyd Boyle (1935–53), Coit Patterson (1953–55), Harold Lockhart (1955–73), and Jerry Norris (1973–87) (James 1988, 84–85). Red Lake Trading Post became famous for storm-pattern Navajo rugs, and its businesses eventually gave rise to a chapter community.

RED MESA: (5500 ft) Apache County, AZ. Navajo: Tsé Łichii Dah' 'Azkání, "Red Rock" (Austin and Lynch 1983, 38) (actually "Red Rock Mesa"). Located three miles north of U.S. Highway 160, about 15 miles west of Teec Nos Pos. In Navajo mythology, Monster Slayer killed Déégééd here, staining the sand red with the monster's blood (McPherson 1992, 33).

RED POINT: (approx. 6500 ft) Apache County, AZ. Navajo: Uncertain. This red sandstone formation northwest of Ganado, west of Kinlichee, is important to the Navajo hunter tradition (Luckert 1978, 71–72).

RED ROCK TRADING POST: (5800 ft) Apache County, AZ. Navajo: See Red Valley. Van Valkenburgh states that the first trading post at Red Rock was built in 1900 by James Walker and Walter Whitecroft. However, McNitt (1962, 353n) attributes the founding of the post to Olin C. Walker, around 1908, and Granger (1960, 20) says 1906.

The walls were 18 inches thick, constructed by the unusual method of pouring a mixture of adobe and stone into forms made of wood placed directly on the wall. In 1918, the post was purchased by Willis Martin, who hired as manager Roswell Nelson, son of Charlie Nelson of Newcomb Trading Post (McNitt 1962, 353n).

RED VALLEY: (6200–5600 ft) Apache County, AZ, and San Juan County, NM. Also Red Rock Valley. Navajo: Tsé Łichíí Dah 'Azkání, "Red Rock Mesa" (Kelley p.c. 1994), the same name applied to Red Mesa. This broad, flat valley is bounded on the southeast by the Lukachukai Mountains, on the northeast by the Carrizo Mountains, and on the south by the Chuska Mountains. The far western portion is called Kah Bihghi Valley (also spelled Kah Bizhi or Koh Bizhi). A tall red spire in the valley, known as Chi'idi, is mentioned in the Navajo Coyoteway myth (Luckert 1979).

Captain John G. Walker referred to this vicinity as "Mesa Colorado" during his 1858 explorations (Bailey 1964b, 51). Vanadium and later uranium were mined in this region, and many

miners suffered physically from the effects of employment in these mines. The valley is sometimes referred to as "Valley of the Widows" (Brugge p.c. 1996).

ALSO: [DB] (5800 ft) Apache County, AZ. Navajo: Same as above. A small trading, chapter, and school community on the New Mexico state line, situated on Red Wash in Red Rock Valley, the broken red sandstone country between the Lukachukai and Carrizo Mountains (and 21 miles west of U.S. Highway 666).

In 1892, Lieutenant W. C. Brown, First U.S. Cavalry, detailed to make a water survey of the Navajo Reservation, inspected the Red Rock country and reported that springs were abundant and no special work was needed to develop them. He found a number of Indian farms in Black Horse's district (see Round Rock) watered by a running stream. The first trading post at Red Rock was established in 1900 by James Walker and Walter Whitecroft.

Indian Service irrigation projects were established before 1941 in the Red Rock Unit near the day school, watering 165 acres from Red Rock Wash. In the Red Rock Valley Unit, 81 acres were irrigated, and some six miles north, in the Zilbetod district, another 20 acres were watered.

ALSO: (6000–5700 ft) Coconino County, AZ. Navajo: Uncertain. This is the 30-mile-long valley that lies west of Inscription House Trading Post on the Kaibito Plateau.

ROCK MESA: (6500 ft) Apache County, AZ. Navajo: Uncertain, possibly Tsé Dah 'Askán, "Rock Mesa." South of Chinle, this shelf of the Defiance Plateau is two miles northeast of Nazlini. It is drained by upper Nazlini Creek. It is the burial place of Navajo Chief Narbona, killed at Narbona Pass (formerly Washington Pass) by troops of Colonel John Washington on August 31, 1849 (Newcomb 1966, 41).

ROCK POINT: [DB] (5000 ft) Apache County, AZ. Navajo: Tsé Łichíí' Deez'áhí, "Red Rock Extending Out to a Point," or Tsé Ntsaa Deez'áhí, "Big Rock Point" (Young and Morgan

1987, 730). A small trading and day school community on the west bank of Chinle Wash and U.S. Highway 191, 15 miles south of Mexican Water. This community also houses the Rock Point Chapter House and a sizable assemblage of new government housing.

At Rock Point, Chinle Wash starts to "box" between high sandstone walls, and Rock Point is found in the sandy alluvial deposits of the wash, where the USIS established an agricultural area in the 1930s.

Two miles south of the day school there are two red sandstone crags that the Navajos call Tse'asdzáán ("Woman Rock"). They tell that a man coming from the west met a woman coming from the east at this point. While talking, they turned to stone. The woman was carrying a babe, and the hump on the east crag is the child.

One mile farther south is a high rock called Tsédaa'tóhí ("Spring on the Edge of the Rock"). The Navajos used to show their prowess as archers by shooting arrows over this high rock. (Van Valkenburgh 1941, 124).

A large rock diversion dam with a concrete heading on the Chinle Wash irrigates some seven hundred acres of agricultural land at Rock Point. Some four hundred acres of this land was developed under the "Bolsa System": When Chinle Wash is running, the waters are diverted into large checks or rectangles with two-foot dikes. The water soaks deeply into the earth, assuring the farmer adequate moisture during dry seasons. Two miles upstream on the Lukachukai Wash is the Upper Rock Point agricultural area, with some 70 acres under irrigation.

ROCK POINT TRADING POST: (5000 ft) Apache County, AZ. Navajo: Uncertain. This post, opened between 1906 and 1910 (Kelley 1977, 253), sits on the west side of Navajo Route 12 at the community of Rock Point. It also served as a post office from 1926 to 1930 (Granger 1960, 20).

ROCKY POINT: Location Uncertain. Navajo: Tsélchíít'aah, "Close to the Red Rock" (Young and Morgan 1987, 730).

ROOF BUTTE: [DB] (9784 ft) Apache County, AZ. Navajo: Dził Dah Neezłínii, "Mountain that

Lay Down" (Young and Morgan 1987, 359). (Van Valkenburgh translates as "Where the Mountain Went Out on Top.") Also 'Adáá Dik'á, "Slanted (roof-shaped) Rim" (Young and Morgan 1987, 11). This remarkable, majestic butte—the highest point in the Lukachukai Mountains—is located 10 miles northeast of Lukachukai. Though the butte is sacred to the Navajos, it serves as a BIA Forestry lookout.

The name Roof Butte was first applied to another high elevation near Dził Dah Neezłínii, by Professor Sin, a school teacher and farmer at Lukachukai. This is called 'Adáá'dilkóóh (Smooth on Edge), and rises to 9340 ft. Yet another peak named Roof Butte rises in the White Mountains of west-central Arizona.

The Navajo medicine men tell of Dził Dah Neezłínii:

> Tsé Nináhálééh ("Picking Up Feathers"), a big bird that lived on top of Shiprock Pinnacle came to Dzł Dah Neezłínii to get men. Never Women. He went there every day. He is not here any more, but lives in the Sun's house. He was the child of the Sun and Changing Woman. This is told in the Naayée'ee Hatáál. (Van Valkenburgh 1941, 127)

ROUGH ROCK: (6500 ft) (Population: 523) Apache County, AZ. Navajo: Tséch'ízhí, "Rough Rock" (U.S. Indian Claims Commission n.d., vol. VI, iv). A trading point and chapter house on Navajo Route 59, at the foot of the eastern scarp of Black Mesa. It is 13 miles northwest of Many Farms and 16 miles southeast of Chilchinbito. The first trading post was opened here in the late 1920s (Kelley 1977, 254).

After an abortive effort at Lukachukai, the Navajo Nation's first operative community school, called a "demonstration school," was opened at Rough Rock in 1966 (Iverson 1981, 115). It showed that the Navajo communities could govern their own schools, taking the responsibility from the Bureau of Indian Affairs.

ROUND ROCK: [DB] (6020 ft) Apache County, AZ. Navajo: Tsé Nikání, "Round Flat-Topped Rock." A high, rounded, sandstone butte some 600 ft high, midway between Chinle Wash (on the west) and Agua Sal Creek, two miles north of U.S. Highway 191.

According to Bailey (1964b, 49), Round Rock is likely the "Piedra Rodilla," possibly "Knee Rock" (Young p.c. 1995) explored by Captain John G. Walker's 1858 expedition.

Traditional Navajos will not climb the precipitous sides of this sacred rock for fear of punishment by lightning, snakes, whirlwinds, or bears. They tell the following tradition of the rock:

> It was during the time when the Navajos were at war with the Utes. The Navajos made two arrows with eyes. As they were going down the Chinle Valley, the Navajos saw the Utes coming from the north. As soon as the Utes got behind Round Rock, the Navajos shot one of the arrows and clipped off the top of the mesa. The sliding rock killed most of the Utes and the rest ran off because they were outnumbered. (Van Valkenburgh 1941, 127)

East of Round Rock and beyond the trading post, there is a Navajo shrine called Yé'ii Shijéé' ("Ye'iis Lying Down"). A visit to this shrine by Sam Day II and Ramon Hubbell in the summer of 1938 was greatly publicized, but the exact location is withheld from this volume, in deference to its sacredness. This place was first found around 1840 by Washington Matthews' great informant, Hataałii Nééz. The Navajos tell that he went to sleep in the cave that is across the canyon from an Anasazi ruin. He heard singing in the cave where the shrine is, and in the morning went up and saw sculptured figures. These are nearly 18 inches high, and Navajos question whether they are of Navajo or Anasazi origin. Offerings of turquoise are made to them.

ROUND ROCK TRADING POST: (5600 ft) Apache County, AZ. Navajo: Bis Dootł'izhí Deez'áhí, "Blue Clay Point" (Young and Morgan 1987, 245). Some 25 miles north of Chinle on Lukachukai Wash at the junction of U.S. Highway 191 and Navajo Route 12, about six miles east of the Round Rock butte. This post, cited by Van Valkenburgh as the first in the region, was established by Stephen Aldrich of Manuelito, a former cavalryman and veteran of the Apache campaigns in 1885. It was managed by Chee Dodge. It was visited by Benjamin Alfred Wetherill and Baron Gustof Nordenskiöld of the Stockholm Museum as the former guided the latter through the Chinle Valley in November 1891 (Wetherill 1987, 220). C. N. Cotton purchased it from Aldrich in 1911.

Combative Navajo Agent Henry F. Shipley took shelter in this post in October 1892 after an abortive meeting with Navajo headman Black Horse and his followers, who were resisting the taking of Indian children to the distant boarding schools. The badly beaten Shipley, already suffering a broken nose and bruises, was dragged into the trading post by Chee Dodge and others, saving his life. They were besieged in the post for 36 hours, during which time Black Horse's followers continuously jeered them and threatened to kill them. A Navajo policeman accompanying Shipley escaped unseen and returned with a contingent of 11 soldiers, breaking up the siege. Shipley returned to Fort Defiance without any children from the Round Rock area. Interestingly, Black Horse apparently was not resisting the forced education, but was protesting the crowded conditions of the boarding schools, the rampant illnesses among their students, and the poor food (McNitt 1962, 278–81).

A small community, including a chapter house and a school, grew up around the trading post. A USIS agricultural area was established in the 1930s eight miles to the east on Lukachukai Wash.

ROUND TOP TRADING POST: (approx. 6400 ft) Apache County, AZ. Navajo: Uncertain. This is one of three trading posts Van Valkenburgh listed as doing business in Ganado in 1941. (The others were Hubbell Trading Post and Ganado Trading Post.) In the early 1990s it was operated by Norman Gorman, Navajo.

A. C. RUDEAU TRADING COMPANY: (approx. 6892 ft) Apache County, AZ. One of three posts listed by Van Valkenburgh (1941, 57) present in Fort Defiance in 1941 (the others being Dunn Mercantile and W. M. Staggs Trading Company).

ST. JOHNS: [DB, AP] (5733 ft) (Population: 3360) Apache County, AZ. Navajo: Tsézhin Deez'áhí, "Ridge that Runs Out to a Point," or

Chézhin Deez'áhí, "Lava Point" (Young and Morgan 1987, 271, 732). Mormon farming and livestock community situated on the Little Colorado River at the junction of U.S. Highways 666 and 180. This community, having grown from a 1940 population of 1,500, has been county seat of Apache County since 1879.

Early Spanish explorers named this vicinity El Vadito del Rio Chiquito Colorado ("Little Crossing of the Little Colorado River"). The location was later called San Juan ("Saint John"), possibly after the Feast of San Juan (held June 24), or after a woman named Senora Maria San Juan Baca de Padilla (Granger 1960, 21).

In 1863, U.S. troops attacked Navajos in this vicinity (Ferguson and Hart 1985, 61). In 1866, W. R. Milligan, one of the first White settlers in Apache County, located in a valley near the future St. Johns (though he later moved to Round Valley). Four years later, Frank Walker, a mail and express carrier between Fort Wingate, New Mexico, and Fort Apache, Arizona (and father of the Frank Walker who served as an interpreter at St. Michaels), built a shack at The Meadows, a crossing of the Little Colorado River some five miles north of the present site of St. Johns. In 1871 a few Spanish-Americans gathered in the vicinity, and in the spring of 1872 established an agricultural settlement at St. Johns.

Solomon Barth and his brothers, Nathan and Morris, began farming activities in 1873. In 1879, a Mormon named Ammon M. Tenney bought out Barth's activities. In 1880, Wilford Woodruff, President of the Mormon Church, picked a spot about a mile north of St. Johns for a Mormon settlement, but later moved it to higher ground adjoining the Spanish-American settlement. By 1884, there were 586 Mormons living at St. Johns. The first newspaper was published by C. A. Franklin in July 1882.

In addition to being a major Mormon stronghold (Jacob Hamblin, famed Mormon missionary and Indian agent, is buried at Alpine, a village some 60 miles south of St. Johns), this rough, remote region was a favorite haunt for many notorious bad men, and was used as a base and hideout for operations in southern Arizona.

The location is mentioned prominently in the Navajo Mothway myth (Haile 1978, 79). The

U.S. Indian Claims Commission studies (vol. IV, 528–30) assert that Navajos have traditionally gathered nuts and berries in this region, and between 1870 and 1890, Navajos did considerable business in St. Johns. The region is also a traditional grazing area for Zunis (Ferguson and Hart 1985, 128).

ST. MICHAELS: [DB] (7000 ft) (Population: 1,119) Apache County, AZ. Navajo: Ts'íhootso, "Yellow Meadow" or "Area that Extends Out Yellow and Green." Catholic (Franciscan) mission and school and chapter community on the eastern slope of the Defiance Plateau, situated on Arizona Highway 264 three miles west of Window Rock. Early Spanish documents called this locale Cienega Amarilla ("Yellow Meadow"). In 1850, in the first English mention of the place, Lieutenant J. H. Simpson called it Cienega de Maria (almost certainly a misnomer for Amarilla).

The mission is located above a well watered, wooded, and verdant meadow on the west slopes of Black Creek Valley. Traders in the region have included Stewart-Weid (opened in the early 1880s and closed about 1900); Wilkin-Wyatt (opened in the late 1880s); Sam Day (opened shortly after 1900); Osborne and Walker (opened in 1902); and Frazier's, Kuhn, and McMahon Trading Posts (Kelley 1977, 251–56; Van Valkenburgh 1941, 129).

In the 1850s the hillside near St. Michaels was the scene of a planned ambush by the Mexicans on the Navajos. It was frustrated by Chách'oshnééz ("Tall Syphilis") of the Diné 'Ana'í ("Enemy Navajos"—see Cebolleta, New Mexico), who accompanied the Mexicans from Cebolleta. While the Navajos and Mexicans were making arrangements to exchange slaves, the Mexicans planted a cannon in a hidden spot, planning to fire it into the Navajos when they were all assembled. Chách'oshnééz went to the Navajo camp and warned them. They invited him to join them. He accepted and was later one of the signers of the Treaty of 1868 under the name of Delgadito.

The Franciscan mission and school was established in 1898 by Father Juvenal Schnorbus with Father Anselm Weber as assistant. The site was donated by the Reverend Mother Katherine

Drexel, head of the Sisters of the Blessed Heart of Philadelphia. The mission was for many years the headquarters of Father Weber's fight for protection of Navajo lands. Stirling (1961) suggests that these missionaries were the first to reduce the Navajo language to writing, but Young (p.c. 1995) notes that the first extensive writing of Navajo was actually by Captain J. H. Eaton at Fort Defiance in 1852. Eaton's extensive word lists were published in Henry Roe Schoolcraft's 1856 "History, Condition and Prospects of the Indian Tribes of the United States."

The Franciscans operate from here in general field work with the Navajos. The Sisters of the Blessed Sacrament manage the boarding school.

SACRED MOUNTAIN TRADING POST: (6600 ft) Coconino County, AZ. Navajo: Uncertain. This trading post on U.S. Highway 89 three miles north of the southern entrance to Sunset Crater National Monument was opened in the early 1920s (Kelley 1977, 254), and is still in operation, owned for some years by William ("Bill") Beaver.

SALINA: [DB] (6600 ft) Apache County, AZ. Also Salina Springs. Navajo: Tsé Łání, "Many Rocks" (Young and Morgan 1987, 730); also Tsigai Deez'áhí, "White Rock Point" (Austin and Lynch 1983, 38). Small trading settlement located in sloping foothill country with scant vegetation on the east side of Balakai Mesa, six miles south of Cottonwood (and Navajo Route 4), some 19 miles west of Chinle. This is the site of Tselani Chapter House.

The Presbyterian Church established the Child's Community Center here, along with the Tselani Health Center, which closed in 1962 (Allen 1963, xiii). Salina Springs Trading Post sits here.

Balakai Mesa, which dominates the whole horizon west of Salina, is some 20 miles long from north to south and averages 10 miles wide. The northern end is separated from Black Mountain by Burnt Corn Wash, a headwater of Polacca Wash. This mesa is the summer range for the Salina Navajos and is ceremonially important as the lower extremities of the female figure called Pollen Mountain of the Blessing Side Ceremony.

SALINA SPRINGS TRADING POST: (6600 ft) Apache County, AZ. Navajo: Uncertain, probably the same as for the community. This post was opened in Salina about 1910 (Kelley 1977, 253), and has sometimes been referred to as "Cottonwood."

SALT SPRINGS: [DB] Location: Uncertain. Navajo: Uncertain. This locale is listed by Van Valkenburgh as being at the confluence of Cottonwood Wash and the Little Colorado River, which is seven miles south of the southern boundary of Petrified Forest National Park. Lieutenant A. W. Whipple used this as a stopping place in 1853. Later it became a regular stopping place on the road between old Fort Wingate and Fort Whipple.

SALT TRAIL CANYON: [USGS] (5800–3000 ft) Coconino County, AZ. Navajo: 'Ashííh Nabitiin, "Salt Trail." (U.S. Indian Claims Commission n.d., vol. VI, ii) Cut by Bekihatso Wash, this two-mile-long tributary of the Little Colorado River Gorge enters from the north just a quarter mile downstream from the gorge's junction with Big Canyon.

SANDERS: [DB, AP] (5800 ft) Apache County, AZ. Navajo: Łichíí' Deez'áhí, "Horizontal Red Point," a name that is said to refer to the autumn color of the deer populating this region, rather than the color of the local sandstone mesas (Luckert 1975, 36). An old name was Chííh Tó ("Red Ochre Water") (Young and Morgan 1987, 272). This small settlement on the Rio Puerco of the West sits some 42 miles west of Gallup, New Mexico, at the junction of I-40 and U.S. Highway 666 (formerly Arizona Highway 61).

Traders have operated in the area since at least 1882 (Kelley 1977, 256) and have included Spencer Balcomb, A. C. Coon, and Hoske Cronmeyer Trading Posts. In the 1940s, Sanders was a shipping point for clay on the Atchison, Topeka and Santa Fe. Currently the community supports several merchants, including Burnham's Trading Post, established in the late 1920s (Kelley 1977, 254). This post was instrumental in developing the New Lands Navajo rug design, a mixture of the Western Reservation styles (Raised Outline and Coalmine Mesa) with Wide Ruins tones, beginning in the late 1960s (James 1988, 80). The name of the rug style derives from a large tract of land in the vicinity purchased by the Navajo Nation for the resettlement of five hundred families from the old Navajo-Hopi Joint Use Area in the early 1980s (James 1988, 80).

Granger (1960, 22) contends that the English name derives either from C. W. Sanders, office engineer of the AT&SF, or as a corruption of Saunders, for trader Art Saunders. To avoid confusion with another Sanders on the AT&SF, the railroad changed the name of its station here to Chato, but locals continued to call it Sanders.

SANDERS RUIN: Apache County, AZ. Navajo: Uncertain, possibly Kits'iil, "Shattered House." A Chacoan great-house community, with a possible prehistoric road segment heading northeast, up the Rio Puerco of the West drainage.

SANDERS TRADING POST: (5000 ft) Apache County, AZ. Navajo: Uncertain, probably the same as Sanders. George Washington Sampson built his first post at this remote location on the Rio Puerco of the West in 1883. At one time or another, he also operated posts at Cienega Amarilla (St. Michaels), Chilchinbito and Lukachukai, Arizona, and at Coyote Canyon and Rock Springs in New Mexico.

SAND SPRINGS: (5200 ft) Coconino County, AZ. Also Whippoorwill. Navajo: Sáí Biis Tóhí, "Spring in the Sand" (Young and Morgan 1987, 684). A tiny community on Dinnebito Wash, in the barren flats of the Painted Desert of the Hopi Reservation, 15 miles west of Navajo Route 2 and 20 miles south of Coal Mine Mesa.

A trading post was opened here prior to 1910, and closed before 1925 (Kelley 1977, 253–54). It was a business outpost of Lorenzo Hubbell, Jr., operated by a Navajo manager. Carl F. Steckel also traded here (Brugge p.c. 1996).

SANENEHECK ROCK: [AP] (6656 ft) Navajo County, AZ. Navajo: Tsé 'Ani'įįhí, "Thief Rock." (U.S. Indian Claims Commission n.d., vol. VI, xx) A small cone of sandstone on the Shonto Plateau, four miles south of Shonto, and over-looking the Klethla Valley to the east. Saneneheck is an English corruption of the Navajo name.

SAN FRANCISCO PEAKS: [DB, AP] (6000–12,633 ft) Coconino County, AZ. Navajo: Dook'o'osłííd, "Never Thaws on Top" (Van Valkenburgh 1974, 5). Sacred Navajo name: Diichiłí Dziil, "Abalone Shell Mountain." Hopi: Nuvatekiaqui, "Place of Snow on the Very Top." Havasupan: Hvehasahpatch, "Big Rock Mountain" (Van Valkenburgh 1941, 134). Another Navajo name is Dził Ghá'niłts'įįlii, "Faultless Mountain" (Young and Morgan 1987, 351). This cluster of volcanic mountains north of Flagstaff comprises the tallest peaks in the state. The three main peaks are Humphreys Peak (12,633 ft), Agassiz Peak (12,340 ft), and Fremont Peak (11,940 ft). These mountains may have been more than 15,000 ft high before they collapsed into an empty magma chamber 500,000 years ago (Thybony 1987, 5).

The name San Francisco was probably applied by Father Marcos de Niza in 1539. The mountains are shown as Sierra Sinagua by Fanforan and Quesada in 1598, and in 1776, Father Garcés called them the Sierra Napoc. They are also known as Corn Mountain and Jewel Mountain, mentioned in Navajo Coyoteway (Luckert 1979, 193).

The peaks comprise the Navajo sacred mountain of the west, believed by traditional Navajos to mark the tribe's rightful western boundary. According to Navajo creation mythology, First Man adorned them with diichiłí (abalone shell), yellow clouds, male rain, and all animals, and fastened them to the sky with sunbeams. They are also the home of Haashch'ééłti'í (Talking God), Naadą́'áłgaii 'Ashkii (White Corn Boy) and Naadą́'áłtsoii 'At'ééd (Yellow Corn Girl). Their symbolic color is yellow (McPherson 1992, 15). The Navajos consider these peaks and Blanca Peak, Colorado (sacred mountain of the east), to be male, while Mount Taylor, New Mexico, and Hesperus Peak, Colorado, are female (Luckert 1977, 51). Two additional peaks, Gobernador Knob and Huerfano Mesa, in New Mexico, are sacred mountains internal to Navajoland.

The San Francisco Peaks are remarkable for

their variety of vegetation. One passes through flora characteristic of arid zones and to the meager herbage of arctic regions. They are a favored place for the Navajo collection of herbs and medicine, and among traditional Navajos, only those bound to obtain medicine ascend the mountains.

The Navajos are not the only tribe to lay claim to the peaks. To the Hopis, the peaks are the mythological home of the Kachina People and they are looked upon with awe and reverence, and the northwestern slopes were formerly Havasupai habitat. They also figure in the Zuni migration narrative (Ferguson and Hart 1985, 126).

O'Leary Peak, 12,340 ft, named for Dan O'Leary, a guide for General Crook during the Indian wars, erupted 230,000 years ago (Thybony 1987, 9). Humphreys Peak, 12,794 ft, was named by geologist G. K. Gilbert for his superior, Corps of Engineers Brigadier General A. A. Humphreys. Fremont Peak, 12,000 ft, was named for John C. Fremont, famous explorer (Colton and Baxter 1932, 85–86). Agassiz Peak, named in the late 1860s for Jean Louis Rodolphe Agassiz (a Swiss geologist who surveyed in the region between 1855 and 1860), was the original San Francisco Mountain (Granger 1960, 61).

SASTANHA MESA: (7210 ft) Navajo County, AZ. Navajo: Despite the name's apparent Navajo origins, its etymology is uncertain. A long, narrow mesa running northeast to southwest, south of Black Mesa, and between Burnt Corn Wash (on the west) and Polacca Wash. It is north of Whippoorwill Spring Mesa.

SAWMILL: [DB] (7600 ft) (Population: 507) Apache County, AZ. Also Nehiagee Post Office. Navajo: Ni'iijíhi, "Sawery." Also called Ni'iijíhí or Ni'iijíhí Hasání ("Old Sawmill"). A small chapter community located on the eastern slope of the Defiance Plateau on Navajo Route 7 some 12 miles north of Fort Defiance. The village boasts a day school (USIS) and a Sawmill Trading Post and Post Office. The sawmill was established in 1907 (Granger 1960, 22).

This sawmill, property of the Navajo Tribe, cut and milled up to 40,000 board feet daily of ponderosa pine, an excellent building timber cut

from 140,893 acres of Navajo forests. The mill included the most modern of methods and equipment and employed one hundred Navajos. The mill and timber operations were initiated as part of the Navajo Service management of tribal resources, with the tribe's million-dollar timber resource (1940s value) being properly liquidated by the Division of Forestry.

The community virtually shut down in 1962, with the opening of the new, updated sawmill at Navajo, New Mexico, some eight miles to the east in Black Creek Valley (see Navajo, New Mexico).

SAWMILL TRADING POST: (7600 ft) Apache County, AZ. Navajo: Uncertain, possibly the same as the community. This post, which opened about 1910 (Kelley 1977, 253), was once owned by the Foutz brothers (McNitt 1962, 300n.)

SEBA DELKAI: (5000 ft) Navajo County, AZ. Navajo: 'Azee' Dích'íí', "Bitter Medicine Butte" (U.S. Indian Claims Commission n.d., vol. VI, ii); Séí Bídaagai (Young and Morgan 1987, 1001), "Sand Piled against the Ridge" (Clah p.c. 1994). Small community a mile west of Arizona Highway 87, some 22 miles south of that road's intersection with Arizona Highway 264.

SEGETOA SPRING: (7800 ft) Apache County, AZ. Also Tsegito. Navajo: Tsiyi'tóhí, "Spring in the Forest" (Young and Morgan 1987, 741). A spring on the Defiance Plateau, three miles west of Fluted Rock.

SEGIHOTSOSI CANYON: [DB] (6200–5400 ft) Navajo County, AZ. Navajo: Tséyi' Hats'ózí, "Slender Canyon." A steep, narrow canyon rising in the slick Navajo sandstone on Skeleton Mesa and running northeast between the northern end of Tyende and Azonsosi mesas, breaking out into the sandy, rolling country of western Monument Valley.

This deep canyon was once thought of as a possible mining area, and several prospectors who dared Navajo resentment at their encroachments lost their lives here. Some years prior to 1940, trader Sam Day II and his brother Charley found the remains of a prospector and his equipment on a small rise in the upper part of the canyon. In the 1930s some 20 acres were put under irrigation in the canyon with the help of a USIS diversion dam.

SEGI MESAS: (7,790 ft) Navajo County, AZ. Also spelled Tsegi. Navajo: Tséyí', generic term for "canyon." This name refers collectively to the 1000-ft mesas (Ellis 1974, 197) in the vicinity of Tsegi Canyon, including Skeleton (the highest), Hoskinnini, Azonsosi, and Tyende.

SEI DEELZHA: (6600 ft) Apache County, AZ. Navajo for "Jagged Sand Dune" (Young and Morgan 1987, 684). This feature lies just west of Klagetoh.

SEKLAGIDSA CANYON: [DB (map 3)] (7000–5600 ft) Apache County, AZ. Navajo: Uncertain, but translate as "Prominent White Cliffs," as named by Emery (Gregory 1915, 153). This is the north fork of Walker Creek, rising on the west slope of the Carrizo Mountains, five miles southwest of Pastora Peak (the highest point). It flows southwest seven miles to join Alcove Canyon to form Walker Creek.

SHADOW MOUNTAIN: (5422 ft) Coconino County, AZ. Navajo: Dził Diłhił, "Dark Mountain" (Kelley p.c. 1994). A roughly circular peak situated three miles west of U.S. Highway 89, at a point seven miles north of Cameron. Home of Navajo leader Big Horse for a time (Bennett 1990).

SHEEP HILL: [DB] (7415 ft) Coconino County, AZ. Navajo: Dibé Dah Shijé'é, "Where Sheep Lie up at an Elevation" (Young and Morgan 1987, 312). This small, pine-covered, conical butte is located a mile east of Mount Elden (north of Flagstaff and immediately east of U.S. Highway 89).

This was a traditional camping place of the Navajo Western Water Clans on their eastward migration. Three hundred feet across old Highway 66, north of the hill, is the site of Elden Pueblo, excavated in 1926, and roughly contemporaneous with Wupatki, Keet Siel (see Tsegi Canyon), and Cliff Palace (Mesa Verde).

Elden Spring, located about a mile to the west, was named San Francisco Spring in 1850 and was a stopping place on the trail laid out by Major G. B. Willis in 1852. Mount Elden, a volcanic pile of some 9000 ft, forms a southeast spur of the San Francisco Peaks.

Three miles northeast of Elden Pueblo is Old Caves Hill, the south face of which is covered by an Anasazi ruin, peculiar because each room has an underground room or cellar. It dates from between A.D. 1100 and 1300.

SHONTO: [DB] (6500 ft) (Population: 710) Navajo County, AZ. Also Shato, Shanto. Navajo: Sháá'tóhí, "Spring on the Sunny Side" (Young and Morgan 1987, 691), also interpreted as "Sunshine Water" (Van Valkenburgh 1974, 15) This same name is applied to Sunrise Spring. Located at the end of Arizona Highway 98, this isolated trading and chapter center sits on Shonto Wash some 20 miles upstream of the confluence of Shonto and Begashibito Washes.

Sháá'tóhí is located a mile and a half up-canyon from the Shonto Trading Post. For years, Navajos in the vicinity have used wells at the trading post. The Navajos were led into this canyon from Black Mountain some time before they went to Fort Sumner by Tséyi' Sizíní and Hashké'. Navajos state that the soldiers of Colonel Kit Carson were in the canyon in 1864. In 1915 John Wetherill and Joe Lee started a trading post here and later sold out to Harry Rorick. Once, Shonto was a lush meadow with many small lakes like the Segi Canyon, but in 1912 floods broke the natural earth dams and released the impounded waters. Many Anasazi ruins, mostly open pueblos, are found along the floor of the canyon.

In Navajo traditions, one arm of Corn Pollen Woman mountain of the Blessingway lies in this vicinity. See also Navajo Mountain, Comb Ridge, Black Mesa, and Balakai Mesa (Van Valkenburgh 1974, 184).

SHONTO SPRING: [DB] (5400 ft) Navajo County, AZ. Also Shanto Spring. Navajo: Sháá'tóhí, "Sunshine Water." Hopi: Masipaa. An excellent spring located on Dinnebito Wash and Navajo Route 2, some 15 miles southwest of Oraibi, and nearly on the Coconino County line.

Both Hopis and Navajos have made good use of the abundant waters of this spring, which flow into a catch basin and trough in a sandy cove. The surrounding sand dunes and knolls are covered with Anasazi pottery sherds.

SHONTO TRADING POST: (6500 ft) Navajo County, AZ. Navajo: Uncertain, probably the same as the spring. Joe D. Lee established this post in 1914, in partnership with John Wetherill and Clyde Coleville (Richardson 1986, 75). Joe Lee developed the post in 1914, working out of a one-room stone building (James 1988, 89). C. D. Richardson purchased it later that same year, erecting the first stone building. In the early years, the post was known as Betatakin Trading Post.

A day school and a community center were constructed here in 1933–34. A boarding school was added in 1961 (Hegemann 1963, 383).

SHONTO WASH: (7000–5700 ft) Coconino County, AZ. Navajo: Shą́ą́a'tóhí, "Sunshine Water." This ephemeral stream heads in Little Salt Canyon five miles upstream of Shonto, traveling 25 miles south and southwest, passing the community of Shonto, and entering Begashibito Wash in the vicinity of Cow Springs in the Klethla Valley.

It passes through a short, deep canyon cut through the Navajo sandstone heading in the Little Salt and John Smith canyons. A long-standing Navajo agricultural area exists along the canyon bottom.

SHOW LOW: (6331 ft) Navajo County, AZ. Navajo: Uncertain. During the winter of 1864–65, Peshlakai Etsidi's (also spelled Etsiddi, Etsitty, Edcitty, Etcitty) family spent time here while fleeing the U.S. Army's roundup of Navajos for deportation to the Bosque Redondo. According to Peshlakai, ". . . hunting was good and we gathered nuts and berries" (Ellis 1974, 467).

SKELETON MESA: (7650–8100 ft) Navajo County, AZ. Navajo: Tsin Kíikaad, "Scattered Bones" (Austin and Lynch 1983, 24). Comprised of several long, narrow fingers (peninsulas) of flat highland south of—and above—Hoskinnini Mesa, north of Marsh Pass, across from Black Mesa. Cut from the west by deep and rugged canyons: Long, Keet Seel, and Dowoshiebito, all flowing northeast to southwest.

SMOKE SIGNAL: (6400 ft) Navajo County, AZ. Navajo: Łid Néigahí (Austin and Lynch 1983, 24), "White Smoke Marks." A trading post on Tse Skizzi Wash, a couple of miles east of Low Mountain, established in the late 1950s (Kelley 1977, 255).

SNOWFLAKE: [DB] Navajo County, AZ. Navajo: Tó Diłhił Biih Yílį (spelling corrected by Young and Morgan 1987), "Where It Flows Into the Dark Water." This village started out as a Mormon farming community on a cottonwood-studded mesa, on the east bank of Silver Creek, 27 miles south of Holbrook.

James Stinson established this farming community in 1873. In the same year, William J. Flake and others bought the site from Stinson and started the Mormon community. A new name was coined in honor of both Flake and Erastus Snow, a dignitary in the Mormon Church.

The Navajos did a great deal of trading here in the 1880s and 1890s. They used the village as a stopping place on their way to the White Mountain Apache country where they traded blankets for deer hides.

In the general vicinity of Snowflake are a number of other Mormon-initiated villages, including Showlow (established in 1870), Forestdale (1878), Taylor (1878), Lone Pine (1878), Shumway (1875), Linden (1878), Pinedale (1879), Joppe—or Aripine—(1883), and Pinetop (1886, founded by a soldier from Fort Apache).

SONSOLA BUTTES: [DB] (8733 ft and 9000 ft) Apache County, AZ. Also Sonsala Buttes. Navajo: Sǫ Silá, "Stars Lying Down." Two truncated volcanic buttes 10 miles west of Chuska

Range, and five miles northwest of Crystal, New Mexico. The ranch of Chee Dodge, first Navajo Tribal Council Chairman, lay on the south slope of the buttes, and was operated by his son Ben Dodge (Young p.c. 1995) following his death. There is an old horse trail passing through the gap between the buttes.

The buttes were once sacred to the Navajos, and are said to be located where there were eight round stones, graduating in size and iridescent at night. The vicinity figures in the Navajo Gun Shooter Red Antway Myth, and in the hero's search for his family in the Rounded Man Red Antway Myth (Wyman 1965). It is also important to the Navajo hunter tradition (Luckert 1975, 33).

SPRINGERVILLE: (7052 ft) Apache County, AZ. Navajo: Tsé Noodǫ́ǫ́z (U.S. Indian Claims Commission n.d., vol. VI, xxi), "Striped Rock." This community on the Little Colorado River was first established as Springer's Store in 1875 by Harry Springer with goods brought from Albuquerque, and serving the Mormon communities of Omer and Amity, along with Mexican settlers and outlaws. A year later, the brothers Julius and Gustav Becker opened a store in the same vicinity, which they stocked from Belen, New Mexico, with ox trains that took 60 days to complete a round trip (Granger 1960, 23).

Springerville is the location of an unusual prehistoric ruin called Casa Malpais, "House of the Badlands." This ruin is attributed to the Mogollon culture of southeastern Arizona and southwestern New Mexico, and the site dates to A.D. 1250–1450. The ruin was first reported on in 1911, and was listed as a historic landmark by Edward B. Danson of the Museum of Northern Arizona in 1948. The site's most unusual feature is the presence of some 200–300 burials stored in a series of walled crevices turned into subterranean catacombs up to 50 feet deep. This is unique to Southwestern prehistory (Morse 1992, 34–37).

According to the U.S. Indian Claims Commission studies (vol. IV, 528–30), Navajos have traditionally gathered nuts and berries in this region on a seasonal basis.

SQUARE BUTTE: (6300 ft) Coconino County, AZ. Also Segeke Butte. Navajo: Tsé Dik'ání,

"Square Rock." (Gregory 1915, 153) This extensive table land is located on the Kaibito Plateau, eight miles east of Kaibito, and east of Navajo Creek in the vicinity of the Inscription House section of Navajo National Monument.

W. M. STAGGS TRADING CO.: (6892 ft) Apache County, AZ. Navajo: Uncertain, possibly the same as Fort Defiance. This is the third trading post listed by Van Valkenburgh as operating at Fort Defiance in 1941 (the others being Dunn Mercantile Trading Company and A. C. Rudeau Trading Company).

STANDING RED ROCKS: (approx. 5,500 ft) Apache County, AZ. Navajo: Tsé Łichii 'Ííá'ahí, "(Two) Standing Red Rocks." Lying between Round Rock and Rock Point, these formations are said to have once been a man and a woman (Luckert 1975, 44), and are important to the Navajo hunter tradition. From Luckert's description, they may well be the formations shown on USGS maps as Round Rock and Little Round Rock.

STAR MOUNTAIN: (6400 ft) Navajo County, AZ. Navajo: Sǫ'tso Lá, "Big Stars Strung Out," though Young (p.c. 1995) notes that "Lá" makes no sense in this context. A cone-shaped butte on Windswept Terrace, five miles west of Stephen Butte between Jeddito and the Hopi Buttes. Associated with the hunting portion of the Blessingway rite (Van Valkenburgh 1974, 71–72).

STATELINE TRADING POST: (6200 ft) Apache County, AZ. Listed by Van Valkenburgh (1941, 89) as being in business in Lupton in 1941. It was run by J. W. Bennett, "one of the oldest traders in Navajo country," who had previously traded at Houck, 11 miles to the west.

STEAMBOAT CANYON: [DB] (6300 ft) Apache and Navajo Counties, AZ. Navajo: Tóyéé', "Scarce Water," or Hóyéé', "Terrible" (Young and Morgan 1987, 459), which Van Valkenburgh translated as "Fear." Traversed by Arizona Highway 264, 27 miles east of Keams Canyon, this canyon is the site of a sizable chapter and day school community, including two subdivisions of Navajo housing. It was labeled White Spring on McComb's map of 1850.

The present English name derives from a ship-like sandstone crag, which is about a mile east of the day school. Gregory (1915, 164) calls this crag an "erosion remnant." The Navajo name stems from a spring called Hóyéé, located about a mile upstream (north) of the trading post—where the sandstone walls are covered with Anasazi and Navajo petroglyphs as well as inscriptions in English and Spanish. One of the inscriptions bears the date 1869, while another, in Spanish, is reputed to be "A20 Abril 20, Año de 1665. Po de Mondoya." Yet another inscription bearing the date 1839 shows two clasped hands; and another has a flag above an arrow, and reads "Thy Small Drink. St. John—Colyer."

There are many Anasazi ruins in the area dating as far back as the Basketmaker period, and a Hopi and Zuni shrine "of great age" lies about a half mile east of the trading post "under a sandstone crag resembling an eagle with outspread wings" (Van Valkenburgh 1941, 152).

The Navajos first settled this area shortly before their exile to Bosque Redondo at Fort Sumner, though they had used it intermittently during the previous one hundred years. In this century, the region was a Soil Conservation Service Demonstration Area, and a USIS sheep dip was built here for the local flocks.

STEAMBOAT CANYON TRADING POST: (6300 ft) Apache County, AZ. Navajo: Uncertain; possibly the same as the spring. This post opened between 1906 and 1910 (Kelley 1977, 253), and was listed by Van Valkenburgh as being in business in 1941, but it has since been transformed into a convenience store. A chapter house has been built in the vicinity.

SUNRISE SPRINGS: (6200 ft) Apache County, AZ. Navajo: Sháá' Tóhí, "Sunnyside Spring" (Kelley p.c. 1994). A small community (occupied as early as 1907) on Pueblo Colorado Wash, eight miles northeast of Lower Greasewood, 16 miles south of Steamboat Canyon. A possible Chacoan prehistoric road has been identified in this vicinity (Gabriel 1991, 277).

This locale (along with nearby White Cone and Indian Wells) is the home of various Ant People in the Navajo Rounded Man Red Antway Myth (Wyman 1965).

SUNRISE SPRINGS TRADING POST: (4700 ft) Coconino County, AZ. Navajo: Séí' Ndeeshgizh, "Sand Gap" (Kelley p.c. 1994). Trading location three miles northwest of Leupp, at the confluence of Canyon Diablo and the Little Colorado River. (Not to be confused with Sunrise Springs on the Pueblo Colorado Wash between Greasewood and Ganado.)

According to Richardson (1986, 127–28), this post was built about 1905 by the Babbitt Brothers, across the stream from Tolchecko Mission. When the mission burned in 1913, the post almost went bankrupt. Manager Nebby Smith stayed on, serving "traveling" Indians, and secretly building a newer, larger post closer to Leupp (across the road from an older post—name uncertain—that had been established in 1904 and was still standing but apparently abandoned). When the Babbitts discovered this construction, they put a halt to it, and it was some time before Smith talked them into completing the building and moving into it, which apparently took place about 1920 (Kelley 1977, 251–53). C. D. Richardson acquired this newer post from the Babbitts in 1928 (Richardson 1986, 128).

SUNRISE TRADING POST: (6200 ft) Apache County, AZ. Navajo: Uncertain, probably the same as Sunrise Springs (on which it was located). Most of what is known about this post is gleaned from McNitt (1962, 273–74).

This post was located about eight miles southwest of Ganado, and was established by J. H. McAdams and E. J. Marty in 1907. Lorenzo Hubbell was furious at this encroachment into his perceived territory, and his threats apparently caused Marty to abandon the post almost immediately. McAdams held on, and in 1909 sold the post to his nephew, Hubert Richardson, who had been working for McAdams at the post.

Hubert sold the post to the William Bickel Company in the 1920s. Ownership was transferred to Albert Hugh Lee and Clarence A. Wheeler when they purchased the Bickel Company in 1929.

SUNSET: [DB] (approx. 5000 ft) Navajo County, AZ. Navajo: Uncertain. The exact location of this abandoned community is not shown on current maps, but it was located on the east bank of the Little Colorado River, three miles north of Winslow (across Little Colorado River from Brigham City).

SUNSET CRATER NATIONAL MONUMENT: [DB] (8000 ft) Coconino County, AZ. Navajo: Dził Bílátah Łitsooí, "Yellow Topped Mountain" (Van Valkenburgh 1974, 15). Six miles east of San Francisco Peaks, 17 miles northeast of Flagstaff. The focus of the monument is on Sunset Crater, a volcanic cone. The crater was an important stopping place for the Western Water Clans on their eastward migration (Van Valkenburgh 1974, 98). The crater rises 1070 ft, to an elevation of 8030 ft. It is the youngest of four hundred craters in the vicinity.

Ash from Sunset's eruptions was blown over eight hundred square miles starting between September 1064 and June 1065 and lasting until roughly 1220. The national monument was originated by Presidential Proclamation 1721 on December 9, 1924, though the first superintendent was not appointed until 10 years later (A. Roberts 1987, 29–31). The Museum of Northern Arizona's first Navajo Craftsman Exhibition was held at the monument in June 1936, aiding in a special relationship between Anglos and the Wupatki Navajos (A. Roberts 1987, 32).

However, this region was fraught with strife between Anglos and Navajos in the 1890s. Whites considered Navajos in the region to be off-reservation intruders. Coconino County officials levied a tax of $5 per 100 head on Navajo sheep in the area, and dislocated any families unable to pay. The reservation boundaries were extended by Teddy Roosevelt thanks to the efforts of Peshlakai Etsidi (also spelled Etsiddi, Etsitty, Edcitty, Etcitty) and the Rev. Philip Johnston (A. Roberts 1987, 30–31).

Hopis believe Kana'a spirits (kachinas) live on Sunset Crater; Wind God Yapancha is said to live in a fissure at the base, sealed by Twin War Gods. A small vent opened later lets out just enough wind. The crater is a Hopi shrine (Thybony 1987, 21).

SUNSET MOUNTAINS: (6595 ft) Coconino County, AZ. Navajo: Jádí Bí'h iikááł, "Antelope Refuge." Located 16 miles southwest of Winslow, this pair of steep-sided mounds (labeled West Sunset Mountain and East Sunset Mountain) rise about 1000 ft above the surrounding plain. Arizona Highway 87 from Winslow to Payson threads the pass separating the mountains.

The mountains are associated with Navajo hunting rites and the Blessingway (U.S. Indian Claims Commission n.d., vol. III, 520). According to Navajo tradition, 12 sacred antelope migrated here from the Carrizo Mountains and became the progenitors of all later antelope in the region.

TA CHEE: (6000 ft) Apache County, AZ. Navajo: Táchii', "Red Streak Running into Water" (Young p.c. 1995). This chapter house is located on Navajo Route 29 on southeast Black Mesa, some 12 miles north of Navajo Route 4 (north of Black Mountain and Blue Gap).

TALAHOGAN WASH: (6400–5700 ft) Navajo County, AZ. Navajo: Táala Hooghan, "Flat-Topped Hogan" (Young p.c. 1995), erroneously interpreted as "House at the Water" by Gregory (1915, 164). A dead-end wash on the southern periphery of Windswept Terrace, heading at Talahogan Spring, five miles south of Keams Canyon. The wash flows southwest for about 10 miles before fading out.

TANNER CROSSING: (approx. 4000 ft) Coconino County, AZ. Also Tanner's Crossing. Navajo: Uncertain. This ford of the Little Colorado River near Cameron was rock-strewn, allowing travelers to avoid the quicksand for which this river has been noted. This crossing was discovered by a Mormon pioneer, Seth B. Tanner of Tuba City, who helped establish the Tanner-French trail into the Grand Canyon.

TANNER SPRINGS: [DB] (approx. 6000 ft) Apache County, AZ. Navajo: K'ai' Si'ání, "Sitting Willow" (Young and Morgan 1987, 501). This spring, shown on McComb's map of 1860 as Jara Spring, is on land once belonging to

Henry Chee Dodge on Wide Ruin Wash, 15 miles northwest of Navajo, and approximately eight miles upstream (northeast) of Wide Ruin's confluence with Leroux Wash.

Navajos and White cowboys fought over land and water rights here in 1884. Ranchers had bought and leased railroad lands and homesteaded other tracts on the adjacent public domain. A Navajo was killed by Whites as he watered his sheep at the springs. Only the intervention of Ganado Mucho, chief of the Western Navajos, and a relative of the murdered Indian, prevented serious Navajo reprisals that could well have escalated into all-out war.

This locale is one of many mentioned in the hero's search for his family in the Navajos' Rounded Man Red Antway Myth (Wyman 1965).

TANNER TRAIL: Navajo: Tse Joshi Si'ani (U.S. Indian Claims Commission n.d., vol. VI, xx). Translation uncertain.

TATHOYSA WASH: (6050–2950 ft) Coconino County, AZ. Navajo: Uncertain; etymology unknown. A 10-mile-long tributary of the Colorado River, this stream heads on Blue Moon Bench and heads north to enter Marble Canyon at President Harding Rapids.

TATOHATSO POINT: (5400 ft) Coconino County, AZ. Navajo: Bidáá Hatsoh, "Big Rim" (Kelley p.c. 1994). A peninsula of the south (or east) rim of Marble Canyon, projecting westward into the canyon at the southern end of the Eminence Break, and north of Blue Moon Bench.

TATOHATSO WASH: (6000–4000 ft) Coconino County, AZ. Navajo: see Tatohatso Point. This 15-mile-long dry stream heads on Blue Moon Bench—east of Marble Canyon—and flows north into the Colorado River north (upstream) of Tatohatso Point.

TEEC NOS POS: [DB] (5450 ft) (Population: 317). Apache County, AZ. Also Tisnasbas. Navajo: T'iis Názbas, "Cottonwoods in a Circle." (Earlier mistranslation: "Warpath Cottonwood.") A small trading, chapter, and school community on T'iisnazbas Creek, at the junction of U.S.

Highways 160 and 64. Originally, this community was situated several miles south of U.S. 64, where the BIA school now sits, but the population has gradually migrated northward to the highway junction.

The Indian Irrigation Service constructed two concrete diversion dams on the creek here in the 1930s, in order to irrigate some four hundred acres of Navajo farmland. On Teshda'astani Creek—about five miles to the southwest—another concrete dam provided irrigation to about one hundred acres. Today this crossroads community is mainly a commercial center.

TEEC NOS POS TRADING POST: (5450 ft) Apache County, AZ. Navajo: Uncertain, probably the same as the community. In 1905, Hamblin Bridger Noel, from Essex County, Virginia, established this post, even though others had tried before him. He calmly demonstrated his proficiency with a high-powered Remington rifle to the local inhabitants, then mounted the rifle above his counter. The Navajos, under the leadership of Black Horse, held a day-long council before voting to let him stay. Bert Dunstin and Al Foutz purchased the post in 1913. Ray Burnham was the manager in 1927, and purchased the post in 1945. In 1959 the post burned down and was rebuilt a few miles to the north at its present location at the intersection of U.S. Highways 64 and 160, the "gateway to the Four Corners Monument."

In the fall of 1907, Noel believed this post was threatened with destruction by the Navajo participants in the Byalille (Ba'álílii) Incident, a near re-enactment of the 1893 Black Horse rebellion at Round Rock (McNitt 1962, 344). However, Ba'álílii was quickly arrested and detained, and no trouble approached Teec Nos Pos. (For more details on the Ba'álílii incident, see Aneth, Utah.)

TEES TOH: (5750 ft) Navajo County, AZ. Also Teas Toh. Navajo: T'iis Tó, "Cottonwood Water." A small trading and chapter community three miles east of Arizona Highway 87, 22 miles south of that road's junction with Arizona Highway 264. Homes are generally scattered, but a couple of government-subsidized clusters of modern houses built in housing-development style have greatly enlarged the community. The chapter house is separate from the majority of the houses, situated at the junction of U.S. Highway 87 and Navajo Route 60.

TESBITO WASH: (6175 ft) Navajo County, AZ. Navajo: T'iis Bitó, "Cottonwood Spring." Heading immediately south of White Cone Peak, this intermittent wash flows south for 20 miles through the eastern portion of the Hopi Buttes region. It passes between Indian Wells and Bidahochi to join Pueblo Colorado Wash just northwest of Five Buttes.

TESHIM BUTTE: (6450 ft) Navajo County, AZ. Navajo: Uncertain; etymology unknown. A broad 400-ft-high mesa immediately west of Arizona Highway 77, five miles south of White Cone.

TES NEZ IHA: (4800 ft) Apache County, AZ. Navajo: T'iis Nééz 'Íí'á, "Tall Cottonwood Stands." This small community on U.S. Highway 160 is situated on the west bank of Chinle Wash, about five miles west of Mexican Water. A trading post was established here in the early 1970s (Kelley 1977, 256).

TES YAHZ ŁANI: (4700 ft) Coconino County, AZ. Navajo: T'iis Yáázh Łání, "Many Little Cottonwoods" (Young p.c. 1995). A feature on the east bank of the Little Colorado River, two miles downstream (northwest) of Leupp.

THREE TURKEY CANYON: (6600–5600 ft) Apache County, AZ. Navajo: Uncertain. A seven-mile-long red sandstone canyon on the west slope of Defiance Plateau, south of Little White House Creek and Canyon de Chelly. The English name denotes the presence of Three Turkey Ruin, an Anasazi ruin, in the canyon. Van Valkenburgh (1941, 157) refers to the canyon in which Three Turkey House is located as "Whitish Red Ochre Canyon."

THREE TURKEY RUIN: [DB] (6400 ft) Apache County, AZ. Also Three Turkey House. Navajo: Tséníí' Kiní, "Rock Niche House";

Tsághii Bikin, "Turkey's House"; and Chííłigai, "White Ochre" (Young and Morgan 1987, 272, 731). An Anasazi ruin at the headwaters of Three Turkey Canyon, six miles south of Canyon de Chelly. (Van Valkenburgh calls this canyon Whitish Red Ochre Canyon.)

This 19-room cliff-dwelling dates to A.D. 1266–76, and was visited by Sam and Charley Day in 1900 under the guidance of Hataałiinééz. It is one of the best preserved cliff dwellings in Navajo country. Three red and white figures identified as turkeys, handprints, or gourds are visible on the plaster of one room. A small permanent stream trickles down the canyon. The canyon also contains many old Navajo hogan sites predating the Long Walk of 1864. At the head of the canyon is an old deposit of ochre, which Navajos use in making the pigments used in sandpaintings.

TODOKAZH SPRING: (approx. 6200 ft) Apache County, AZ. Navajo: Tó Dik'óózh, "Sour Water" (Brugge p.c. 1996). This spring is located 10 miles southeast of Ganado.

TOH ATIN MESA: (6627 ft) Apache County, AZ. Also Gothic Mesa, Dineh Mesa, or Dinne (Diné) Mesa. Navajo: Tó 'Ádin Dah 'Azká, "No Water Mesa" (Young and Morgan 1987, 706). A long, thin mesa seven miles northwest of Black Rock Point of the Carrizo Mountains, five miles south of U.S. Highway 160. The name Gothic appears on McComb's map of 1859.

TOH CHIN LINI CANYON (AND WASH): (8000–5800 ft) Apache County, AZ. Navajo: Tó Ch'ínlíní, "Water Flowing Out." The canyon is a 10-mile-long southern tributary of Toh Chin Lini Wash, merging with the latter three miles upstream of Walker Creek.

TOH CHIN LINI MESA: (6400 ft) Apache County, AZ. Navajo: Unknown, possibly same as Toh Chin Lini Canyon. Located on the western slope of the Carrizo Mountains, immediately south of Black Rock Point.

TOHDENSTANI WASH: [DB] (8800–4600 ft) Apache County, AZ. Also Todastani. Navajo: Tó

Dah Da'aztání, "Blisters of Water here and there at an Elevation" (Young and Morgan 1987, 706). Gillmore and Wetherill (1953, 15) translated this as "Water Comes like Fingers out of a Hill." A tributary of the San Juan River, rising on the north slope of the Carrizo Mountains. It flows northeast about 16 miles, crossing the Utah line to merge with the San Juan River.

TOLACON (TRADING POST): [DB] (6400 ft) Apache County, AZ. Also Sweetwater. Navajo: Tó Łikan, "Sweet Water." This very small community is located on Kit Sili (Keet Seel) Wash, a mile upstream (northeast) of that channel's confluence with Sweetwater Wash, and about five miles south of Toh Atin Mesa. This trading post was opened between 1911 and 1915 (Kelley 1977, 253); Leroy Foutz was once a partner here (McNitt 1962, 302). The community is home to the Sweetwater Chapter House.

TOLCHACO TRADING POST: (approx. 4700 ft) Coconino County, AZ. Navajo: See Tolchico below. McNitt (1962, 250) credits John G. Walker with establishing this post in 1905, but Babbitt (1986, 5–6) asserts the post was actually established in 1900 by YMCA Rev. William H. Johnston. Walker was a half-blood Navajo who had previously traded at Cienega Amarilla (St. Michaels) and later at Leupp, where he was apparently in good stead with the local weavers with his vegetable dyes not fully appreciated by other traders until 20 years later (McNitt 1962, 250). He purchased the post from Johnston.

In 1920, W. H. Smith and the Babbitts built a new post of red sandstone near the new bridge across Canyon Diablo's mouth at Leupp, and called it Sunrise Trading Post. This post put Walker out of business. Another post, Wolf's, had been operating here since the early 1880s, but closed before 1911 (Kelley 1977, 251–53).

TOLCHICO: [DB] (approx. 4700 ft). Coconino County, AZ. Also Wolf's Crossing, Volz Crossing, Tolchaco. Navajo: Tółchí'íkooh, "Red Water Wash." This abandoned trading and mission community sat amid the cottonwoods on the Little Colorado River, some 15 miles northwest of Leupp, and 20 miles north and east of Canyon

Diablo. It no longer shows up on maps (McNitt 1962, 250, 266).

This was once the location of the famous Wolf's Crossing (later known as Volz Crossing) of the Little Colorado River. Nearby is the site of a great 1840s battle between the Navajos and the Utes. Beavers were once trapped in the marshes and swamps that used to exist along the Little Colorado in this vicinity.

A mission was established here by the Rev. W. R. Johnston in 1897. Johnston championed Navajo land claims, and was instrumental in bringing about the January 8, 1900, presidential executive order removing 1,575,367 acres between the Navajo and Hopi reservations and the Colorado River from public domain. Another 425,171 acres were removed by executive order on November 11, 1901 (Bailey and Bailey 1986, 113). The community had a post office started in 1903.

TO NA LIN MESA: [DB] Coconino County, AZ. Navajo: Tó Náálíní, "Water Flows Downward." A small mesa atop the northwest corner of the Moenkopi Plateau, four miles south of U.S. Highway 160, four miles west of Arizona Highway 264 near Moenkopi and Tuba City.

TOVAR MESA: (5500 ft) Navajo County, AZ. Navajo: Uncertain. Broad, relatively flat land to the west of the Hopi Buttes country, south of the Hopi Mesas. Named for Pedro de Tovar, a member of the 1540 expedition led by General Francisco Vasquez de Coronado, who was dispatched by the general with 17 horsemen and three or four footmen from Zuni to the "Tusayan Province," or the Hopi region.

TOWER BUTTE: (5282 ft) Coconino County, AZ. Navajo: Uncertain. This steep sandstone butte rises nearly 1000 ft above the surrounding terrain of Wild Horse Mesa (south of Lake Powell). This promontory is also called Poverty Butte by the Navajos (Richardson 1986).

TOYEI: (approx. 6300 ft) Navajo County, AZ. Navajo: Tóyéé, "Scarce Water," though the name used to be Hóyéé', "Dreadful," due to an eerie sound from the spring in a nearby canyon

(Young and Morgan 1987, 708). Gregory (1915, 155), working for the U.S. Geological Survey, recorded the name as Tuye, meaning "Echo of Thunder." On Arizona Highway 264, midway between the community of Steamboat and the Apache/Navajo County line, Navajo Route 9031 heads due south for three miles. At this end of this road is the community of Toyei.

This community was home of the Navajo Nation Law Enforcement Academy in the early 1990s, training about two dozen cadets a year for the Navajo police force. The buildings of the Academy were those of a closed BIA boarding school (Brugge p.c. 1996).

TSAILE: [DB] (7050 ft) (Population: 1,043). Apache County, AZ. Also Sehili, Tsehili, Tse-a-lee, Tsalee, etc. Navajo: Tsééh Yílí or Tsééhílį, "Where the Water Enters a Box Canyon." Located on Tsaile Creek at the far eastern end of Canyon Del Muerto, a mile east of Navajo Route 12. This chapter community (Tsaile-Wheatfield) is named for the creek of the same name. The community now hosts the main branch of Navajo Community College, established in January 1969 as an alternative for those Navajo students who, prior to its opening, had to leave the reservation for higher education. When opened, this was the first Indian-owned college in the United States (Lavender 1980, 205–6).

The multi-million-dollar facility opened with eight divisions offering associate degrees, including one in bilingual and bicultural education. The college's first graduating class, in June 1970, boasted two students, but by 1981 the enrollment exceeded 2,000, and by 1997 it had reached 4,707 at two main campuses (Tsaile and Shiprock, New Mexico) and six "community" campuses (Chinle, Ganado, Kayenta, Tuba City, and Window Rock, Arizona, and Crownpoint, New Mexico). The Tsaile campus now includes a cultural center, 10 residence halls, a cafeteria, a gymnasium, a student union, a library, classrooms, a post office, a computer center, a museum, a college press, and a bookstore. Tuition is a reasonable $25 per credit hour, and the college offers Associates (two-year) degrees in the arts, sciences, and applied sciences. A bachelor's (four-year) degree is offered in teaching.

In Ganado, Arizona, the college occupies a portion of the campus of the erstwhile College of Ganado, which the Presbyterian Church for financial reasons was forced to abandon in the late 1980s.

TSAILE CREEK: (8800–5750 ft) Apache County, AZ. Also Sehili, Tsehili, Tse-a-lee, Tsalee, Spruce Creek, Brook Creek (Van Valkenburgh 1941, 161). Heads on the western flank of the Chuska Mountains, at the southern foot of Roof Butte. Flows south and west, past Matthews Peak and Tsaile, and into Canyon del Muerto. In all, the creek has traveled some 35 miles by the time it reaches the confluence of Canyon del Muerto and Canyon de Chelly. This channel was once known as Spruce Creek.

TSAILE PEAK: (9000 ft) Apache County, AZ. Also Tsaile Butte, Tsaile Pinnacle. Navajo: Possibly Tsézhin Tsiits'iiní, "Lava Head" (Young p.c. 1995); Chézhin Deez'áhí, "Traprock Point"; Tłiish Bitsoo', "Tongue of the Snake." This peak is on the western scarp of the central Chuska Mountains, about five miles south of Matthews Peak and three miles east of the community of Tsaile.

This sheer, rusty brown pile of igneous rock standing south of the creek is sacred to the Navajos. It may be the "Lava Butte" mentioned by Luckert (1975, 33), as important to the Navajo hunter tradition, and which as late as the 1940s was ascended only by Navajo medicine men seeking herbs and offering prayers. However, Lava Butte may refer to Black Pinnacle instead.

Brugge (p.c. 1996) notes that Tsaile Peak was likely a location of Navajo refuge during the wars of the mid-nineteenth century, as there are hogan remains atop the peak dating to that period.

TSAILE TRADING POST: (7050 ft) Apache County, AZ. Navajo: see Tsaile. This post, known also under the names Sehili, Tsehili, and Tse-a-lee, was opened by Stephen Aldrich of Manuelito and Elias S. Clark in 1885. The structure was built of logs, and was one of only three licensed trading posts on the Navajo Reservation. After a year, Clark sold out his interest in this post and one at Manuelito to Archibald Sweet-land, who became the sole owner in 1889. Sweet-land operated the store only until November 1892, before abandoning it due to deep snows and extreme isolation.

Aldrich and Clark had apparently run a trading operation at Black Salt—five miles west of Crystal, New Mexico—in 1882–83, prior to opening at Tsaile. After selling out to Sweetland at Tsaile, Aldrich opened the trading post at Round Rock (McNitt 1962, 279n).

TSAI SKIZZI ROCK: (6312 ft) Coconino County, AZ. Navajo: Tsé K'izí, ("Rock Cleft)." A 400-ft-high butte above Gray Mesa on the Kaibito Plateau, some two miles south of Navajo Creek.

TSA YA KIN: (approx. 6000 ft) Navajo County, AZ. Navajo: Tséyaa Kin, "House Under the Rock." Cliff dwelling, probably in Monument Valley.

TSE CHIZZI WASH: (6600–6100 ft) Navajo County, AZ. Navajo: Tséch'ízhí, "Rough Rock" (Young p.c., 1995). This 10-mile-long creek heads at Tse Chizzi Spring on Balakai Mesa, three miles southeast of Low Mountain. It flows north, then west, joining Polacca Wash some three miles west of Low Mountain.

TSEDAA HWIIDEZOHI PEAK: [DB] (approx. 8000 ft) Navajo County, AZ. Navajo: Tsédáá Hwiidzohí, "Line on the Canyon's Edge" (Young and Morgan 1987, 729), or "Line Carved into the Rock" (Wilson 1995, 64). Van Valkenburgh translates as "Rock Rim on Which there are Marks (Scratches)." This cone-shaped peak near Yale Point on the east rim of Black Mesa (above Rough Rock) is a landmark of Navajo ceremonial significance. It is connected to the Navajo mythology, being the hogan of a person named Bida', who raised deer. When a cloud settles over the cone, it is believed that rain will come soon. Until the 1940s, only medicine men would climb the peak, and it was generally believed that all the other Navajo sacred mountains could be seen from its summit.

TSEDAATAH CANYON: [DB] (6600–5800 ft) Apache County, AZ. Navajo: Tsédáá'tah, "Among the Cliff Edges" (Young and Morgan 1987, 729). Heading 15 miles southwest of Lukachukai, Tsedaatah Canyon runs northwest into Agua Sal Creek five miles south of Round Rock and the junction of U.S. Highway 191 and Navajo Route 12. In addition to numerous old (eighteenth- and nineteenth-century) Navajo sites, the region abounds in Anasazi ruins covering the later Basketmaker and Pueblo phases. During the Navajo Wars (1863–64), the Navajos used this canyon to hide from the White intruders.

TSEGAHODZANI CANYON: [DB] (approx. 6300 ft) Apache County, AZ. Navajo: Tséghá-hoodzání, "Rock with a Hole in It" (Young and Morgan 1987, 729). This canyon is on the east side of the divide between the Mexican Cry Mesa (south) and the Carrizo Mountains (north). It is west of Red Rock, and contains the natural sandstone arch named Wittick Arch.

TSEGI CANYON: [DB] (7200 ft rim–6100 ft floor, at Marsh Pass) Navajo County, AZ. Also Segi Canyon, Laguna Canyon. Navajo: Tséyi', "In Between the Rocks," or "Inside the Rock," the general descriptive Navajo term for any deep canyon lined with sheer walls. This deep canyon between Skeleton and Zilnez Mesas is tributary to Marsh Pass some 10 miles southeast of its headwaters, about 11 miles northeast of Kayenta. Tributaries of this canyon harbor such cliff dwellings as Keet Seil and Betatakin, parts of Navajo National Monument.

Members of some of the early military expeditions may have entered the canyons, but they left no record. John Wetherill and his brothers, well known archaeological explorers of Mesa Verde and the Navajo country, explored the canyons in the 1880s. Inscriptions in the Long House Ruin at the lower end of Long House Valley and at the opening of Marsh Pass, three miles from where the Tsegi joins Marsh Pass, are dated 1859. (See Navajo National Monument.)

At one time there were many small pools and marshes in the floor of Tsegi Canyon held in check by natural earth dams at the mouth of the main canyon. In the floods of 1912, the dams were washed out and great heads of water gushed out of the canyon into Marsh Pass and dropped eastward, cutting a channel through Laguna Valley down to the sandstone bedrock. Today, Tsegi Canyon, with its slick sandstone run-off, feeds an appreciable amount of water for the Kayenta and Dinnehotso Irrigation projects.

Early Spanish documents referred to the Tsegi Canyon/Skeleton Mesa/Marsh Pass region as Chellecito, apparently a diminutive of "Chelle," the Spanish pronunciation of "tséyi'," which means "canyon" (Brugge 1965, 16–17).

Matthews (1897, 238) identifies a canyon by this name as being a favored home of the Navajo yeis or gods. He locates the canyon north of the San Juan River, "in Colorado or Utah," however, and suggests it corresponds with either Mancos or McElmo Canyons. Yet, unfamiliarity with the geography is evident throughout his study, and he may well have mislocated this feature.

TSEYE HA TSOSI CANYON: [DB] (5400 ft) Apache County, AZ. Navajo: Tséyaa 'Ałts'ózí, "Slim Canyon between the Rocks" (Gillmore and Wetherill 1953, 92), more accurately "Narrow Under the Rocks" (Young p.c. 1995). The narrow pass between Azonsosi Mesa (on the west) and Boot Mesa, on the southwest margin of Monument Valley.

TSIN LANI CREEK: (6200–5300 ft) Apache County, AZ. Navajo: Tsín Łání, "Many Trees" (Young and Morgan 1987, 738). A 10-mile-long tributary of Lukachukai Wash, rising on the southwest flank of Mexican Cry Mesa. It flows west to meet the Lukachukai a mile northwest of Round Rock Trading Post.

TSIN SIKAAD: [DB] (approx. 6400 ft) Apache County, AZ. Navajo: Tsin Sikaad, "Tree Grove." A location in the barren sandstone country and plains that slope west from the Navajo cordillera toward Chinle Valley, some 15 miles northeast of Chinle, a short distance from Navajo Route 64.

The location is of historical importance, for in the spring of 1859 the last Naachid (tribal assembly) was held near here. Van Valkenburgh holds

that it was held for a woman named 'Asdzą́ą́ Nichxó'í (Ugly Woman). Frink (1968, 47) suggests it was held to determine whether or not the Navajos should attack Fort Defiance. Manuelito counseled for war, but Zarcillos Largos recommended peace, predicting his own death if they attacked the fort. The next year the Navajos attacked the fort, and, in a separate incident, Zarcillos Largos was killed.

Naachid refers to a legendary nine-day political-religious ceremony. This was one of the most important and spectacular of all Navajo ceremonials. There has been some question as to its political importance by the few ethnologists who have been able to get any information on it, for it has been extinct for over a century. According to Van Valkenburgh's informants, the entire Navajo tribe came and camped in two divisions, one on the south of the Naachid ceremonial enclosure (and deeply excavated hogan), and the other to the north. These divisions seem to have been Peace and War parties. After months of preparation, the ceremonial would start after harvest and continue at regular intervals until just before spring planting. Should there be an emergency such as an internal tribal matter, the Peace Chiefs would control the meeting. Should the crisis be war or external matters, the War party would control the meeting.

TUBA BUTTE: (5785 ft) Coconino County, AZ. Navajo: Uncertain. This butte is located seven miles northwest of Tuba City, two miles east of U.S. Highway 89. (See Tuba City for origin of name.)

This promontory is considered in Navajo mythology to be one of the breasts of a female anthropomorphic figure known as Pollen Mountain. Navajo Mountain is her head, Black Mesa her body, Balakai Mesa her feet, Comb Ridge one of her arms, and Agathla Peak her other breast (McPherson 1992, 21).

TUBA CITY: [DB] (4950 ft) (Population: 7,327). Coconino County, AZ. Navajo: Tó Naneesdizí, "Place of Water Rivulets" (Young and Morgan 1987, 707; Van Valkenburgh 1941, 163), a historic name referring to the irrigation ditches with which the Mormons irrigated their Moenkopi Wash fields. Old Navajo names: Sei Ha'a'eeł, "(Water) Washing Out Sand"; Nahodits'ǫ, "Bog Hole," referring to Charley Day Spring.

Today one of the largest communities on the Navajo Reservation, Tuba City is located at the foot of the southern escarpment of the Kaibito Plateau, just north of Moenkopi Wash, at the junction of U.S. Highway 160 and Arizona Highway 264. It is a chapter seat, hosts several mainstream fast food restaurants, had for decades the only auto (Chevrolet) dealership on the reservation, and has a great many businesses and homes.

The name "Tuba" is a derivative of "Tuvi" or "Tuve," the name of a Hopi chief who became a strong friend of the early Mormon settlers of this region in the 1870s (McNitt 1962, 95) and even accompanied Jacob Hamblin to Salt Lake City.

Tuba's written history covers only 200 years, but unwritten records date back to the Pleistocene horses, camels, elephants—and possibly humans. During the twelfth and thirteenth centuries A.D., Anasazi inhabitants constructed communal pueblos on the Moenkopi sandstone ledges west of Tuba City; and during the fifteenth century, the Hopis built a pueblo near the present site of Moenkopi.

As with nearly all the Navajo reservation, the first European contact came with Spanish explorers and missionaries in the seventeenth century. Father Garcés reported an agricultural settlement of 50 "Mahave Apaches" (interpreted by Van Valkenburgh as "Havasupai, no doubt") in 1776. During this same period, the Hopis cultivated their fields near the aforementioned pueblo— by then in ruins—on Moenkopi Wash.

The first American to visit the region was the famed Mormon missionary and pathfinder Jacob Hamblin, who passed by on a number of trips to the Hopi villages during the 1850s and 1860s. In 1873, Horton D. Haight led a colony of Mormons to northern Arizona. They stayed in Tuba City for some time, but moved on south to the Little Colorado River in the vicinity of present Holbrook. In 1875 another party of Mormons under James S. Brown arrived at Tuba (then the site of Navajo cornfields), and three years later Erastus Snow (later of Snowflake) laid out the townsite.

While Mormon-Navajo relations were at first friendly, it wasn't long before the inevitable trouble started over land and water rights. In 1894, the strife led to the killing of Mormon Lot Smith by a Navajo, and the tensions increased until federal intervention. In 1900, the Mormon Ward of Moenkopi (they had also changed the name of Escalante's Cosmisas Wash to Moenkopi Wash), of which Tuba City was a part, numbered 150 persons. In 1903, however, the Mormons were forced to relocate when the Navajo Reservation was expanded to its present western boundary. They sold their property and improvements to the U.S. Indian Service for $45,000. Today, the only evidence of the Mormon community at Moenkopi is the old cemetery at Hopi Moenkopi village.

The first evangelistic missionary efforts on the reservation were at Tuba City, initiated by the Gospel Union in 1896 (Stirling 1961). Until 1901, the only Indian school in the Tuba City vicinity was at Blue Canyon, 18 miles to the east. (This was the second built on the reservation.) That year, Blue Canyon School was closed and a boarding school for Hopi and Navajo students was opened at Tuba City a year later. The Western Navajo Agency developed from this school, eventually holding dominion over the entire western half of the reservation until 1936, when jurisdictions were abolished in favor of the Central Navajo Agency at Window Rock.

The Tuba region became a major agricultural center for both Hopi and Navajo farmers. Early USIS irrigation projects of the 1930s included the Lower Moenkopi Project (400 acres), Reservoir Canyon (225 acres), Moenkopi Wash Project (305 acres), and Moenave Spring project (32 acres).

There are at least two known sets of dinosaur tracks near Tuba City. One (badly eroded by vandals) lies eight miles southwest of the town. Another is found beside Arizona Highway 264 east of the town. Other geological features in the vicinity include the Stone Pumpkin Patch on Highway 89 (toward Cameron) and the Elephant's Feet, on U.S. Highway 160 (toward Kayenta).

Uranium mining took place in the Tuba City

vicinity during the 1950s (Moon 1992, 175–85), and a uranium mill is situated about six miles northeast of the community on U.S. Highway 160.

TUBA TRADING COMPANY: (4950 ft) Coconino County, AZ. Navajo: Uncertain. This post was opened by C. H. Algert and was later owned by the Babbitt Brothers (McNitt 1962, 266). The Babbitts conducted extensive remodeling in 1986 (Brundige-Baker 1986, 30). Another post in Tuba City was Navajo Trails, opened in the late 1950s (Kelley 1977, 255).

TUNICHA MOUNTAINS: (9512 ft) Apache County, AZ. Navajo: Tó Ntsaa, "Big Water" (Gregory 1915, 155). These mountains are located on the western fringe of the Chuska Mountain Range, northeast of Tsaile, and four miles east of Lukachukai.

TUNNEL SPRING: [DB] (approx. 6800 ft) Apache County, AZ. Navajo: Tséníí'tóhí, "Spring in the Rock Niche." This spring is five miles northeast of Fort Defiance, in the Fort Defiance monocline of red Wingate sandstone. The spring sits some 20 feet into a narrow fissure, about 50 feet above the floor of an alcove. There are numerous carvings on the wall of the fissure, the earliest being "John Stewart, 1878." Somewhere nearby is a cairn erected in 1884 by Samuel Day, Sr., marking the Arizona-New Mexico state line where it bisected the then Navajo Reservation's southern boundary line.

TWIN BUTTES: (6685 and 6200 ft) Apache County, AZ. Navajo: Uncertain. Granger (1960, 25) applies this name to the Stinking Springs Mountains northwest of St. Johns.

ALSO: (8546 ft) Apache County, AZ. Navajo: Uncertain. A pair of flat-topped, volcanic cones in the southwestern Chuska Mountains, four miles east of Black Creek Valley, 12 miles northeast of Fort Defiance.

ALSO: (5675 ft) Navajo County, AZ. Navajo: Uncertain. Twin sandstone buttes some 200 ft high,

three miles south of the Rio Puerco of the West, four miles west of the Apache County line.

TWO STORY TRADING POST: (7100 ft) Apache County, AZ. Navajo: Ts'íhootso, "Yellow Meadow" (the name for St. Michaels). This trading post is located on Arizona Highway 264 on the eastern slope of the Defiance Plateau, a few miles west of St. Michaels. It was opened in the early 1900s by Sam Day, Sr., and his son, Charles Day, with Charles taking J. P. Peterson as a partner in 1915. Sam Day, Sr., had previously left nearby St. Michaels after selling his property to the Franciscan Friars for a mission school in 1901. He opened a post at Chinle, which he subsequently sold to John Weidemeyer (son of the Fort Defiance trader Charles F. Weidemeyer) in 1905, moving first to Navajo, then to Two Story Trading Post (McNitt 1962, 250–52).

TYENDE CREEK: (6000–900 ft) Apache and Navajo Counties, AZ. Also Tyenda Creek. Navajo: Téé'ndééh, "Things Fall into Deeper Water" (Young and Morgan 1987, 705). Rising on the northeast slope of Black Mesa, near "The Fingers," this normally dry wash flows northeast some 20 miles to merge with Chinle Wash 10 miles downstream (northwest) of Rock Point Trading Post, and 10 miles east of Dinnehotso (on U.S. Highway 160). Granger (1960, 252) identifies this as the longest perennial creek in the vicinity.

TYENDE MESA: [DB] (6496 ft) Navajo County, AZ. Also Tyenda Mesa. Navajo: See Tyende Creek. North of Kayenta, this substantial, very flat elevation lies east of Skeleton Mesa, on the southwest margin of Monument Valley. U.S. Highway 163 swings a wide curve to the east around this mesa as it leaves Kayenta. It is drained by Parish Creek and Cutfoot Wash to the south, and includes Half Dome and Owl Rock on the eastern margin. At the east end of this mesa, some three miles north of Kayenta, are Segeke Butte and Slim Rock. Immediately east of Owl Rock stands the crumbly, greenish-black igneous Chaistla Butte.

VOLUNTEER: See Navajo Army Depot.

VOLZ TRADING POST: (5350 ft) Coconino County, AZ. Navajo: Uncertain. This trading post at Canyon Diablo was once owned by the Babbitt Brothers (McNitt 1962, 266).

WALKER BUTTE: (6000 ft) Apache County, AZ. Also Gothic Butte (a name also applied to Toh Atin Mesa). Navajo: Tséyí' Hóchxǫ'í, "Ugly Canyon" (Young and Morgan 1987, 732). A low, flat butte on a bench above and south of Walker Creek, six miles south of the juncture of Walker Creek and Sweetwater Wash. The English name is for Captain Joseph Walker, U.S. Army, who led a detachment of Mounted Rifles and infantry on a reconnaissance of the region in July 1859 (Gregory 1915, 155).

WALKER CREEK: (6800–4700 ft) Apache County, AZ. Also Gothic Wash. Navajo: Granger (1962, 25) cites Gregory as noting that the Navajos call this channel Ch'íníljí (" Water Outlet") at its source, and Naakai Bito' ("Mexican Water") along its mid-section—in the vicinity of the community of Mexican Water. However, Ch'íníljí is also the name of the larger creek Walker drains into just three miles west of Mexican Water, so there seems a distinct possibility that Gregory (and/or Granger) may have confused the two washes.

This extensive ephemeral wash of the northern Chinle Valley rises in Alcove and Seglagidsa canyons on the west slope of the Carrizo Mountains, and flows northwest some 35 miles to merge with Chinle Wash six miles west of Mexican Water. The English name is for Captain Joseph Walker (see Walker Butte).

WALNUT CANYON (NATIONAL MONUMENT): [DB] (7000 ft rim–6500 ft floor) Coconino County, AZ. Navajo: Kits'iił, "Broken Down House" (U.S. Indian Claims Commission n.d., vol. VI, ix), or "Ruined House" (Young and Morgan 1987, 496). A deep canyon zigzagging through the Coconino National Forest, three miles south of I-40 at Cosnino (seven miles east of Flagstaff). The National Monument preserves prehistoric ruins in the easternmost three miles of the 10-mile-long canyon.

These ruins are mud and stone Anasazi structures (dating to the tenth and eleventh centuries A.D.) sitting on the multiple narrow ledges of the canyon. At least five fortresslike sites were constructed on the rims of the canyon. A trail led down the north wall to the pooled stream on the bottom, where fields were planted with crops. However, when the Arizona Lumber and Timber Company built a dam upstream (some 10 miles south of Flagstaff), the stream ceased flowing in the vicinity of the monument.

This canyon was known to local stockmen for years, but the first scientific studies began with the first visit of James Stevenson of the Smithsonian Institution in the late nineteenth century. National Monument status was bestowed on November 30, 1915. In 1932, Lyndon L. Hargrave of the Museum of Northern Arizona excavated and restored two rooms dated A.D. 1092–96.

WARREN TRADING POST: (5800 ft) Navajo County, AZ. Navajo: Uncertain, most likely the same as the name for Kayenta. This post at Kayenta was once owned by the Babbitt Brothers (McNitt 1962, 266).

WEPO SPRING: (approx. 6000 ft) Navajo County, AZ. Navajo: 'Adeií Tó, "Upper Spring" (U.S. Indian Claims Commission, vol. VI, i). This spring lies on the northwest slope of First Mesa, above Wepo Wash. Granger (1960, 253) identifies this as the starting point of certain Hopi ceremonial races.

WEPO WASH: (7700–5590 ft) Navajo County, AZ. Navajo: Uncertain. This 35-mile-long tributary of Polacca Wash heads near the northeast escarpment of Black Mesa and flows southwest, through Piñon (20 miles downstream), and passes under Arizona Highway 264 midway between Polacca and Shimolovi. It merges with Polacca Wash a mile south of the highway.

It was along this wash that Tewas, seeking the right to settle at Hopi following the Spanish Reconquest of 1692, pursued a band of Utes that had attacked Oraibi, killing eight Hopis. The

Tewas caught the Utes and killed all but one, who was sent home to warn the Utes that Tewa warriors were now living with the Hopis (James 1974, 10–11).

This channel was explored by Colonel (Governor) Jose Antonio Vizcarra's 1823 expedition (McNitt 1972, 60–61).

WESTERN NAVAJO TRADING POST: (4950 ft) Coconino County, AZ. Navajo: Uncertain, possibly the same as the name for Tuba City. This post in Tuba City was once owned by the Babbitt Brothers (McNitt 1962, 266).

WETHERILL AND COLEVILLE TRADING POST: (5800 ft) Navajo County, AZ. Navajo: Uncertain, possibly the same as the name for Kayenta. This post was listed by Van Valkenburgh (1941, 83) as one of two at Kayenta, in 1941. The other is Joe Kerley's Trading Post.

WHEATFIELD LAKE: [DB] (7250 ft) Apache County, AZ. Navajo: Uncertain. Same as Wheatfield community. Located 20 miles south of Lukachukai, this man-made lake is three miles west of the New Mexico state line, a mile north of White Cone Peak.

WHEATFIELDS: [DB] (6300 ft) Apache County, AZ. Navajo: Tó Dzís'á, "Strip of Water Extending Away into the Distance" (Young and Morgan 1987, 706), referring to a series of small lakes. Early Spanish intruders named the region Cañon de Trigo ("Wheatfield Canyon") for the fields of Navajo wheat found growing there, and the U.S. Army used the area (then called Cienega Juanico) in growing grain for Fort Defiance (Jett n.d., 72). Situated 30 miles north of Fort Defiance on Navajo Route 12, this community is nine miles south of that road's junction with Navajo Route 64, where Route 12 crosses Wheatfields Creek. This stream, after passing through farming country, joins Whiskey Creek to form the headwaters of Canyon de Chelly.

Colonel John M. Washington, after traveling westward through Washington Pass, passed through this vicinity in the summer of 1849. Lieutenant James Simpson reported that a great number of Navajo wheatfields were destroyed here, giving rise to the English name. In 1864, Captain Albert Pfeiffer and his command "rounded up" the Navajos of the vicinity while making a circular approach to Canyon de Chelly.

A government irrigation project had been approved by the Commissioner of Indian Affairs in 1886, and work was begun by Agent Samuel Patterson in 1887. In 1892 Lieutenant W. C. Brown recorded the water resources of the vicinity, including the excellent flows of water from Wheatfields and Whiskey Creeks. Today, a modern diversion dam irrigates hundreds of acres of Navajo farm land.

According to Luckert (1975, 33) a small lava hill southeast of the lake is known to the Navajos as Beexh Wahaaldaas ("Falling Flints"), which figures prominently in the Navajo hunter tradition.

WHEATFIELDS CREEK: (8000–800 ft) Apache County, AZ. Navajo: Nát'ostse' 'Ál'íní, "Place where Stone Pipes are Made" (Young and Morgan 1987, 572). A stream rising immediately east of Tsaile Peak in the Chuska Mountains, and flowing south 11 miles into Wheatfields Canyon, the northeast branch of Canyon de Chelly. About nine miles upstream (east) of Spider Rock, it merges with Whiskey Creek and Palisades Creek to form the Rio de Chelly. (For more information, see Wheatfields Canyon listing under Canyon de Chelly.)

Navajos were encountered along this wash by Colonel Dixon Stansbury Miles's column on November 8, 1858, and again by troops under Captain John G. Walker on July 18, 1859 (McNitt 1972, 348, 367). Walker referred to Wheatfields Creek as "Cienega Juanica," probably after Juanico, a Navajo headman in the region during the early to mid 1800s (Jett n.d., 72).

WHISKEY CREEK: (9000–6600 ft) Apache County, AZ., and San Juan County, NM. Navajo: Tó Diłhił, "Dark Water." An extensive stream rising near the eastern escarpment of the Chuska Mountains in New Mexico, a mile south of Toadlena Lake (11 miles north of Washington Pass). It flows southwest and west, crossing into

Arizona where the state line intersects Navajo Route 12. It then flows into the easternmost extension of Canyon de Chelly, merging with Wheatfields Creek and Palisades Creek to form the Rio de Chelly.

The vicinity of the creek was explored by Captain John G. Walker in 1858, though he referred to it as "Rio Estrella" or "Cienega Negra" (Bailey 1964b, 38).

According to Jett (n.d., 73), this is possibly the Black Water mentioned in the obsolete Excessway myth and in the Deer Cathingway myth. A location known as the Tapering Sandhill in the vicinity of this creek is important to the Navajo Mothway myth (Haile 1978, 89). Since Haile did not give the Navajo name for this feature, it is not certain whether he referred here to White Cone or Little White Cone.

WHITE ASH-STREAK MOUNTAIN: Apache County, AZ. Navajo: Uncertain. This feature is said to lie between Lukachukai and Cove, which would place it in the Lukachukai Mountains, possibly Mexican Cry Mesa. It is mentioned in the Navajo hunter tradition (Luckert 1975, 43).

WHITE CLAY WASH: [DB (map 7)] (7800–5900 ft) Apache county, AZ. Navajo: Dleesh Łigai, "White Clay." This stream heads three miles north of Fluted Rock on the Defiance Plateau near Sawmill. It flows north 10 miles into Monument Canyon, a southern tributary of Canyon de Chelly. It then flows another 10 miles to merge with the Rio de Chelly at the mouth of Monument Canyon.

This wash is mentioned in the hero's search for his family in the Navajo Rounded Man Red Antway Myth (Wyman 1965). The general vicinity is also important to the Navajo hunter tradition (Luckert 1975, 35)

WHITE CONE: [DB] (8511 ft) Apache County, AZ. Navajo: Séí Heets'ósí Ba'áád, "Conical Sands Female." A high cone of whitish, friable Chuska sandstone located west of the main scarp of the Tunicha Mountains, and about a mile and a half southeast of Wheatfields Lake.

This is a ceremonial location, where Navajo medicine men come to climb the cone and obtain plant medicine for women who have gone crazy from incest. It is also an important location in the Navajo Coyoteway (Luckert 1979).

ALSO: [DB] (8200 ft) Apache County, AZ. Also Little White Cone. Navajo: Séí Heets'ósí Biką', "Conical Sands Male" (Young and Morgan 1987, 684). This cone is on the south bank of Whiskey Creek about a mile east of Navajo Route 12, and approximately 10 miles northwest of Crystal, New Mexico. As at the White Cone described above, Navajo medicine men visit this peak to obtain medicine for women who have been victimized by incest (Van Valkenburgh 1974, 163–64).

ALSO: [DB] (6050 ft) Navajo County, AZ. Navajo: Possibly Baa'oogeedí, "Where It Was Dug into" (Young and Morgan 1987, 149). This small chapter community is located west of Beshbito Wash, some 12 miles north of Indian Wells (on Arizona Highway 77), and immediately southeast of a geological feature by the same name. The community boasts a new "subdivision" of modern housing about two miles south of the ruins of an older smaller, community. Don Pedro de Tovar of the Coronado Expedition of 1542 passed by this White Cone on the old Hopi-Zuni trail on his way to Awatovi and the Hopi towns.

ALSO: (6420 ft) Navajo County, AZ. Navajo: Hak'eelt'izh, "Head of One's Penis" (Young and Morgan 87, 401), a descriptive name. Peak atop the broad irregular butte that sits adjacent to Arizona Highway 77, about four miles north of Deshgish Butte. This promontory, along with nearby Indian Wells and Sunrise Springs, is home to various Ant People and figures in the hero's search for his family in the Rounded Man Red Antway Myth (Wyman 1965).

WHITE CONE TRADING POST: (6050 ft) Navajo County, AZ. Navajo: Baa'oogeedí (same as the community above). This post was established between 1916 and 1920 (Kelley 1977, 254) at White Cone (near Beshbito Wash).

WHITE MESA: (6500–6700 ft) Coconino County, AZ. Navajo: Łigaii Dah 'Azkání, "White Mesa" (Luckert 1975, 23). A small upland on the southeast perimeter of the Kaibito Plateau.

Colonel (Governor) Jose Antonio Vizcarra's column attacked an Indian camp in this vicinity on August 8, 1823. Four Indian men were killed and seven prisoners taken before it was discovered that these were Paiutes, not Navajos (McNitt 1972, 61–62).

A pictograph here, depicting a crescent moon, may have been astronomical in nature, along with another in Navajo Canyon (Miller 1955, 6–12). According to Granger (1960, 90), this feature was named for James White, who claimed to have rafted the Grand Canyon in 1857 (12 years prior to John Wesley Powell's famed expedition), losing two companions (Captain C. Baker and Henry Strole) in the process.

WHITE MESA TRADING POST: (approx. 6600 ft) Coconino County, AZ. Navajo: Uncertain, but probably Łigaii Dah 'Azkání, "White Mesa." This small trading post north of Kayenta was once owned by the Babbitt Brothers.

WHITE MOUNTAINS: (7,500–11,500 ft) Apache, Navajo, Gila, and Coconino Counties, AZ. Navajo: Na Daxas'ai, "Yucca Range" (Haile 1950, 125); Dzilghą'í Bikéyah, "Mountaintoppers Land," referring to White Mountain Apaches (Kelley p.c. 1994). Brugge (p.c. 1996) asserts that the name Na Daxas'ai is actually Noodah Haas'ei, "Agave Slope," and refers specifically to Mogollon Baldy in the Mogollon Mountains of New Mexico. This extensive, rough, mountainous country of west-central Arizona stretches from Alpine to Showlow.

These mountains figure in the Beautyway story of the Younger Sister and Big Snake Man (Benally et al. 1982), and in the Navajo Ghostway tradition of the Male Branch of Shootingway (Haile 1950, 125). Navajos also hunted in these mountains, and gathered nuts and berries seasonally (U.S. Indian Claims Commission n.d., vol. IV, 526–30).

WIDE RUIN (TRADING POST): [DB] (6200 ft) Apache County, AZ. Navajo: Kinteel, "Wide House" (also spelled Kin Tiel), the Navajo name for any large, open ruin (see also Aztec, Pueblo Pintado, New Mexico). Also, referring only to the "outer sections" of the ruin, Tsin Naajinii, "Black Streak of Wood." Zuni: Heshota Pathlta, "Butterfly Ruin." Located 17 miles north of Chambers on Wide Ruin Wash, this region was not part of the Navajo Reservation until 1880. It was named for nearby Anasazi Indian ruins, which date to the late thirteenth century and contain Chacoan architecture.

The Spanish called this ruin Pueblo Grande ("Large Village"), the name used on McComb's map of 1860. Van Valkenburgh suggests that the Dominguez-Escalante map of 1776 (drawn by Miera Pacheco) shows it as a Navajo settlement and mission station on the trail between the Zuni and Hopi villages, but Brugge (p.c. 1996) notes that the circled crosses on the Pacheco maps show camping spots, not missions. The Zuni name derives from the way the site covers two sand hills suggesting the wings of a butterfly. According to Zuni tradition, this ruin was home to their Le'atakwe People, who took part in a great northward migration of the Bear, Frog, Deer, Yellow Wood, and other ancestral clans long ago. It is also included in Navajo rite-myths and is considered a stopping place in Navajo clan migrations.

It is possible that Tovar and Cardenas of Coronado's 1542 expedition stopped at Wide Ruin. American military parties did stop here, including Major Shepherd's command in 1859. A trade trail between Zuni and Chinle also passed the ruin, and it was on this trail that the great Navajo Peace Chief Zarcillos Largos was ambushed and killed by New Mexicans and Zunis in 1862. It is said that Zarcillos Largos killed three of his attackers before succumbing to his wounds.

Van Valkenburgh describes a pitched battle taking place a few miles south of Wide Ruin in 1805 between Spaniards (and their Zuni allies) and Navajos, following the slaughter of Navajos in Massacre Cave (in Canyon de Chelly). Brugge (p.c. 1996), however, questions this assertion.

The first trading post here was constructed of sandstone slabs (obtained, unfortunately, by pulling down the 12-ft-high walls of the Anasazi ruin), possibly by Sam Day, Sr., as early as 1895.

This structure was fortresslike. A larger stone post was built across Wide Ruin Wash in 1902. It was later owned by Spencer Balcomb, Wallace Sanders, and Per Paquette. Walter and Sallie Lippencott purchased it in October 1938. They sold it to the Navajo Tribe in 1950, but the tribe sold it to Foutz and Sons, under the name of "Progressive Mercantile," a few years later. Jim Collyer—son of a Crystal trader—took over the location in 1957. He was joined by John Rieffer in 1964. Rieffer and his wife, Sharon, purchased it in 1973. The post no longer exists, having fallen into ruins by 1987. (James 1988, 70–75). A chapter house is now the community center.

WILDCAT PEAK: (6805 ft) Coconino County, AZ. Navajo: Náshdóíts'o̱'í, "Wildcat Guts" (Young and Morgan 1987, 569); Gregory (1915, 155), working for the U.S. Geological Survey, recorded the name as "Mountain Lion." This is a sharp promontory on the Kaibito Plateau, seven miles east of Preston Mesa.

WILLOW SPRING: [DB] (4900 ft) Coconino County, AZ. Navajo: Aba'tó, "Waiting Water" (Young and Morgan 1987, 3); Van Valkenburgh (1941, 173) translates as "Lost Spring" or "Last Spring." A famed oasis at the southern end of Hamblin Ridge, located three miles southwest of Tuba Butte and a mile east of U.S. Highway 89.

The spring is tributary to Hamblin Wash, and was once the site of a Havasupai farming village. This locale may have been passed by the Dominguez-Escalante Expedition of 1776. The spring flows from a small canyon, the walls of which are decorated with carved names of hundreds of pioneers and travelers who watered at the spot in the 1870s and 1880s—mostly following the old Mormon Trail, blazed by Jacob Hamblin.

A mile south of the spring lies what Van Valkenburgh (1941, 173) described as "one of the finest and largest series of inscriptions in the Southwest," a grouping of petroglyphs completely covering a number of large, smooth boulders for about 75 feet. They are thought to span the time between the twelfth and twentieth centuries, and until the early 1900s they were used as clan symbols by Hopis traveling to the Hopi Salt Mine in the Little Colorado River Gorge.

This vicinity is one of many mentioned in the hero's search for his family in the Navajo Rounded Man Red Antway Myth (Wyman 1965).

WILLOW SPRINGS TRADING POST: (4900 ft) Coconino County, AZ. Navajo: Uncertain, probably the same as the springs (above). Sam Preston, a native Kentuckian, came to the West with a government pack train and opened the Black Falls Trading Post in the middle 1880s. He was selected by the Babbitt Brothers as the first partner-manager for their firm, working at Red Lake around 1890. In 1894 he struck out on his own again at Willow Springs, perhaps buying a post George McAdams may have built about the time Preston was at Black Falls (McNitt 1962, 266–67; Richardson 1986, 24). Preston traded here until about 1910 (Kelley 1977, 253).

WINDOW ROCK: [DB] (6755 ft) (Population: 3,306) Apache County, AZ. Navajo: Tséghá-hoodzání, "Perforated Rock." At the time the Central Navajo Agency was established, Ni' 'Ałníí'gi, "Earth's Center," was proposed, but never used; Navajos ridiculed it as Ni'ałníí'gó, "Your Middle" (Young p.c. 1995). Originally a couple of miles north of Arizona Highway 264, nestled at the foot of the sandstone formation that gave it its name, the capital of the Navajo Nation has now spread out to include the junction of Highway 264 and Navajo Route 7, virtually straddling the Arizona–New Mexico state line. However, on the New Mexico side of the line, the community takes the name of its "suburb" predecessor, Tse Bonito. Window Rock is the seat of the Navajo government, with many office buildings and the Tribal Council chambers. Also present are BIA regional offices and a growing business community.

Until 1936, Window Rock was simply the site of one of the major scenic wonders of Navajoland. That year Commissioner of Indian Affairs John Collier selected the site for the planned Navajo Central Agency, and the buildings were constructed of locally quarried rust-colored sandstone. White difficulties in pronouncing the original Navajo name, combined with traditional Navajo aversion to profane use of a sacred name, led to the community being officially named Window Rock.

Tséghahoodzání, the natural arch immediately north of the tribal administration complex, is important in Navajo ceremonialism and rite-myths of the Tohee (Waterway Ceremony). It was one of the four places Navajo medicine men went with their basketry water bottles seeking water for the prayer ceremony for abundant rain.

An interesting historical site in the Window Rock vicinity is "The Haystacks" (Tséta' Ch'ééch'i, "Breezes Blow Out from Between the Rocks"; Tséyaatóhí, "Spring Under the Rock"), a mile south of the Window Rock. This small basin dotted with red sandstone monuments (the Haystacks) is now home to the Navajo Nation Zoo and, at the time of this writing, a brand-new cultural center and library that has stood unoccupied and unpaid-for for over a year.

Tséyaatóhí, "Spring Under the Rock," (on present-day Arizona Highway 264 just south of the Haystacks) was the first stopping place out of Fort Defiance when some four hundred Navajos started their "Long Walk" to Fort Sumner in 1864. Captain John Bourke visited Window Rock in 1881 and gave an excellent description of the region.

Archaeological remains in the Window Rock vicinity include both Anasazi (dating to the earliest Puebloan phases) and early Navajo. A ten-room, thirteenth-century Anasazi site sits beneath the Window Rock itself.

WINONA: (6400 ft) Coconino County, AZ. Navajo: Tsin Názbąs, "Round Stick Lying Down" (U.S. Indian Claims Commission n.d., vol. VI, xxii), or "Round Wood" (Young and Morgan 1987, 991). A railroad switching station originally named Walnut. The name was changed to Winona in 1886 because there were 31 other Walnuts in Arizona. The community has existed since 1912 on U.S. Highway 66, just north of I-40. The first tourist camp in the United States was opened here, just 10 miles east of Flagstaff, in 1920 by Billy Adams.

WINSLOW: (4938 ft) (Population: a little over 11,000) Navajo County, AZ. Navajo: Béésh Sinil, "Iron Lying Down," referring to the stacks of rails stored here by the Atlantic and Pacific Railroad (later the Atchison, Topeka and Santa Fe and currently the Burlington Northern Santa Fe Railway). This trading center and former sheep-shipping point is located on I-40, some 56 miles east of Flagstaff. In the first half of this century, the town was home to the Navajo Service Tuberculosis Sanatorium.

The first settler in Winslow is thought to have been an F. G. "Doc" Demerest, a hotel man who lived in (and did business from) a tent in 1880. Shortly thereafter, J. H. Breed, previously trading above Sunset (Leupp) on the Little Colorado River, moved in and constructed the first store building. After the Atlantic and Pacific Railroad arrived in 1882, the town began a rapid growth. A post office was sanctioned on January 10, 1882, with U. L. Taylor as postmaster. Fourteen miles north on Arizona Highway 87, Borderlands Trading Post was opened in the early 1960s (Kelley 1977, 255).

The origin of the name Winslow is problematic. Some state that it honors General Edward Winslow (President of the old St. Louis-San Francisco Railway, one of the companies forming the Atlantic and Pacific), while others suggest that the town was named after Tom Winslow, an early prospector and inhabitant of the town.

WITTICK NATURAL ARCH: [DB] (approx. 6300 ft) Apache County, AZ. Also Royal Natural Bridge, Red Rock Bridge. Navajo: Tséghá-hoodzání, "Perforated Rock," a name applied to nearly any natural arch in Navajoland. This large (30-foot), red sandstone arch is located in Tseghahodzani Canyon, between the southernmost reaches of the Carrizo Mountains (north) and Mexican Cry Mesa (south). The arch is on a spur of the north wall of the canyon, about six miles northwest of the community of Cove and some 10 miles west of Red Rock.

The arch was well known to White traders in the area for many years—and to local Navajos for many more years—but the first report on it was made by Charles L. Bernheimer of the American Museum of Natural History in 1930.

There are a number of Anasazi ruins in Tseghahodzani Canyon (called Prayer Rock

Canyon by Bernheimer). Bernheimer noted the presence of a number of depressions on a ridge of the canyon, said by his Navajo guide to be a place where the Navajos "prayed to the rocks in the east." According to Bernheimer, the Navajos called this "Rock Canyon People Rolled Down." Van Valkenburgh (1941, 175) says this is probably Tse-hada'eemaz, "Rocks Rolled Down.") The name is the result of a battle between Utes and Navajos in the vicinity, in which Navajos scaled the rim and, being pursued by Utes, slid back down; most were killed.

Bernheimer applied the name "Royal Natural Bridge" to the arch, but as no official name had been listed, Van Valkenburgh (1941, 174) named it for the famed western photographer Benjamin Wittick, who roamed Navajo country between 1878 and 1903.

WOLF CROSSING: [DB] (4000 ft) Coconino County, AZ. Also Woolf's Crossing. Navajo: Tólchí'íkooh, "Red Water Wash." A Little Colorado River crossing near Tolchico, 15 miles northwest of Leupp. This famous ford, later known as Volz Crossing, was first named after Herman Wolf (a.k.a. Woolf, Wolff). Wolf was born in Germany about 1810, and his grandfather was a Major General in the German Army. Wolf rode with Kit Carson and other mountain men (including Fred Smith, of the Richardson trading family in Gallup) as early as 1854.

Wolf, called Hastiin Chaa' (Mr. Beaver) by the Navajos, trapped for beaver with Smith, Billy Mitchell, and W. C. Seifert in the 1850s along the cienegas of the Little Colorado River. (This sandy, usually dry river was once a series of pools and grassy meadows a century and a half ago, according to Navajo stories.) This same foursome trapped in the Navajo Canyon country (southwest and west of Navajo Mountain) the next decade, and are believed to have left inscriptions in both Navajo and Piute Canyons.

Sometime around 1870, Wolf returned to the Little Colorado, built a stockade on the south bank of the river, and between beaver-trapping forays ran a one-room trading post. Most of his goods were traded for the beaver pelts the Navajos brought in. His business boomed with the arrival of immigrant trains. He was known to be

extravagant in these final years, importing many indulgences from Germany, including wine. He died in 1899, and was buried in a bronze coffin at Canyon Diablo.

The post was purchased by George McAdams, in partnership with the Babbitt brothers, the year Wolf died (Richardson 1986, 25). In 1903, the post was sold to Leander Smith, who, as a practical joke, placed an excavated human skull in a window—effectively killing his business. The post closed for good within a year (Babbitt 1986, 3).

It was at this location in the late 1890s that S. I. Richardson was able to dissuade about three hundred Navajos from an ill-conceived plan to attack Flagstaff (Richardson 1986, 26).

WOODRUFF BUTTE: [DB] (5595 ft) Navajo County, AZ. Navajo: Toojj' Hwiidzoh, "Line Extends to the River" (Young and Morgan 1987, 708). This small volcanic cone is located on the east bank of the Little Colorado River, some 15 miles southeast of Holbrook. Until the 1940s, a small Mormon community named Woodruff, for a dignitary of the Mormon Church, lay just south of the butte and gave its name to the cone.

The cone and its immediate slopes comprise a Navajo sacred place in the traditions of the Prostitutionway (Van Valkenburgh 1974). Medicine men come from all over Navajo country to collect jimsonweed (Datura stramonium), called ch'il agháni ("plant that kills things") by the Navajos (Young and Morgan 1987, 288). (Van Valkenburgh mistakenly labels jimsonweed ch'óhogilyééh, which is actually locoweed.) Jimsonweed is commonly used by Indians of the Southwest and California in ceremonials as well as for anesthesia. Until the 1940s, the only Navajos climbing Woodruff were medicine men, and they held a "sing" in a natural amphitheater on the east side of the butte before ascending.

In 1876, Lewis P. Cardon, Joseph Richards, James Thurman, and Peter O. Peterson began farming near the butte. Three years later, Luther Martin settled in the region, establishing a ranch two miles south of the later Mormon village, founded in 1880 by Ammon M. Tenney. (For some time the settlement—built around a stockade of rock and adobe—was known as Tenney's

Camp. The name was changed to Woodruff in 1888 after a dignitary of the Mormon Church.)

In the Navajo Red Antway Myth, the hero comes to Woodruff Butte after the first Coyote transformation. The second Coyote transformation may also have taken place here (Wyman 1965). Navajos also traditionally gathered nuts and berries here in season (U.S. Indian Claims Commission n.d., vol. IV, 528–30).

Woodruff Butte is also sacred to the Zunis, figuring in their migration narration (Ferguson and Hart 1985, 18). In recent years, Navajos, Zunis, and Hopis have protested the carrying away of cinders from this cone (Brugge p.c. 1996).

WUPATKI (NATIONAL MONUMENT):
[DB] (4861 ft) Coconino County, AZ. Navajo: 'Anaasází Bikin, "Anasazi House" or "Alien Ancestor's House." Hopi: Wapatkikuh, "Tall House Ruins." This monument lies between U.S. Highway 89 (west) and the Little Colorado River (east), roughly halfway between Flagstaff and Cameron. It features prehistoric ruins of the Sinagua culture, a farming people blending traits of the western Anasazi, the Hohokam to the south, and possibly even the Mogollon culture (Cordell 1984, 81). The name Sinagua was given to the San Francisco Peaks by Farfan and Quesada in 1598.

The earliest vestiges of this culture are characterized by a widely dispersed hunter-gatherer/ farmer population of pithouse dwellers in the vicinity of present-day Flagstaff. Through the following 12 centuries, they seemed to concentrate their farming efforts on the perimeters of the abundant lava fields in the region. Following the eruption of Sunset Crater in the winter of A.D. 1064–65, they moved into the Wupatki Basin, where they were joined by people of the Cohonina and Kayenta Anasazi cultures (from the west and northeast, respectively). Nearby settled people from the more southerly Hohokam and Cibola cultures. The Sinagua quickly adapted to aboveground masonry habitations, giving rise to Wupatki Pueblo. They took the new lifestyle with them to other locations, such as Walnut Canyon, 25 miles to the south. Wukoki, Citadel, and Lamoki were all villages of the dominant Kayenta people, though all residents of the re-

gion appear to have lived in peace. After a little more than a hundred years, the Wupatki Basin was abandoned, with the Sinagua moving—a few at a time—to the Verde Valley. Though the Hopis may have attempted an occupation about 50 years later, the region was largely uninhabited for six hundred years (Noble 1981, 99–103).

The Havasupai, who are known to have dwelt north of the Wupatki region as late as 1850, claim in their traditions that a Puebloan clan that was incorporated into their tribe, long ago built and occupied permanent villages along the Little Colorado River and east of the San Francisco Mountains. The ruins of Wupatki Basin were pointed out to Major J. W. Powell by a Havasupai chief who claimed they were the former homes of his people.

The ruins of Wupatki were vandalized by Ben Doney (see Doney Mountain) in the 1880s. In 1896, excavations were conducted by J. W. Fewkes. Various studies have been conducted in the twentieth century. Ceremonially buried parrots and macaws are among the more unexpected findings, along with copper bells, all of which are presumed to be of Mexican origin. The area is rich in Sinagua rock art, including unusual textile patterns (Schaafsma 1987, 21–27).

Hopis trace several clans from the Chaves Pass region through Wupatki. Nuvakwewtaga is considered home of the Water, Sun Forehead, and Side Corn Clans (Pilles 1987, 11).

For years evidence suggested that Navajos entered the region following their return from the Bosque Redondo (A. Roberts 1987, 29), but more recent studies show they were in the area by 1825 (Roberts 1990, 6.7). Archaeological research began with Lorenzo Sitgreaves' 1851 military expedition down the Little Colorado River, and continued through Anderson's (1987, 18) intensive site surveys of the 1980s to today. Some 2,500 sites have been identified within the monument (Thybony 1987, 38).

Wupatki Basin is inhabited by a few Navajo families once headed by Clyde Peshlakai, who used Wupatki Spring for water, with Park Service blessing. In the 1870s, Béésh Łigaii Yitsidii' or Béésh Łigaiitsidii (also spelled Peshlakai Edsitty, Etsitty, Etsidi, Etsiddi, Etcitty; "Silver Maker") settled in this vicinity. This old leader had taken part in the "Long Walk" of 1864, and traveled to Washington to visit President Theodore Roosevelt to negotiate Navajo allotments in the Wupatki region. He passed away in 1939.

Navajo tradition states that the pueblos of Wupatki were destroyed by rain, lightning, and whirlwinds, brought on by the greed of the Anasazi.

YALE POINT: (8000 ft) Apache County, AZ. Navajo: 'Adáá' Hwiidzoh, "Line on the Rim" (Young p.c. 1995). The English name is for the university. This promontory lies on the western perimeter of Black Mesa, at the point where the rim turns from north-south to northwest-southeast. This is the home of the Navajo deity Black God (Luckert 1975, 23).

At the base of the point is Bitsííh Hwiits'os, "Area Tapers at its Base" (Young and Morgan 1987, 252).

YON DOT MOUNTAINS: (6235 ft) Coconino County, AZ. Navajo: Yaa Ndee'nil, "Series of Hills Going Down" (Young p.c. 1995). These are the low hills midway between Marble Canyon (west) and U.S. Highway 89 (east), approximately three miles southwest of Bodaway Mesa.

ZILBETAD PEAK: (8800 ft) Apache County, AZ. Navajo: Dził Béét'óód, "Bald Mountain"; or Dził Bét'ood, "Balding Mountain" (Gregory 1915, 155). The northeasternmost peak in the Carrizo Mountains, above Beklabito, New Mexico (on New Mexico Highway 504) and Cottonwood Canyon.

ZILLESA MESA: (7700 ft) Navajo County, AZ. Navajo for "Mountain Surrounded by Barren Soil" (Gregory 1915, 155), Dził Deez'á, "Where Mountain Range Begins" (Young and Morgan 1987, 360). A round knob atop eastern Black Mesa, between Oraibi Wash and Wepo Wash.

ZILNEZ MESA: (7620 ft) Navajo County, AZ. Navajo: Dził Nnééz, "Long Mountain" or "Tall Mountain" (Gregory 1915, 155). In the Segi (Tségi) country, this mesa lies west of Skeleton Mesa, separated from it by Long Canyon, and south of Piute Mesa and Nokai Canyon.

This may be the "Dził Nnééz," (also known as "Cerro Alto," Spanish for "High Hill") that the U.S. Indian Claims Commission (n.d., vol. IV, 712–15) assert was a traditional Navajo wild plant gathering location.

5

COLORADO LOCATIONS

ANIMAS CITY: (approx. 6500 ft) La Plata County, CO. Navajo: Uncertain. Located in the Animas Valley, near today's Baker's Bridge in 1860–61, this community was part of the first mining rush into the San Juan Mountains (Smith 1992, 5–6), at the time the northern boundary of Navajoland.

A second townsite by the same name was first settled nearby in the 1870s, officially surveyed in 1876. This farming community had a flour mill by 1879, along with fruit trees, dairy cattle, and a sawmill. However, in 1880, the town failed to "buy into" the Denver & Rio Grande Railroad, so the railroad bypassed the town and founded Durango. Animas was soon overshadowed (Smith 1992, 6–7).

Eleven companies of cavalry and infantry were stationed at Camp Animas just outside Animas City during the aftermath of the Meeker Massacre on September 29, 1879. The troops departed in 1880 (Smith 1990, 7).

BLANCA PEAK: (14,345 ft) Costilla, Alamosa, and Huerfano Counties, CO. Also Sierra Blanca, Sierra Blanco. Navajo: Sisnaajiní, "Descending Black Belt (or Mountain)" (Young p.c. 1995). Ceremonial name: Yoołgaii Dziil, "White Shell Mountain" (Young and Morgan 1987, 804). This peak lies in the Sangre de Cristo Mountains, about 10 miles north of the community of Blanco (some 20 miles east of Alamosa, on U.S. Highway 160).

Sacred to both the Navajos and the Jicarilla Apaches, this is one of several mountains hypothesized to be the Navajo sacred mountain of the east (Haile 1938; McPherson 1992, 15). (Wheeler Peak, Pelado Peak, and Pedernal Mesa, all in New Mexico, have also been sug-

gested as the sacred mountain of the east, but those sources deemed most reliable agree that Blanca Peak is Sisnaajiní.)

Descriptions of the mountain in Navajo mythology suggest the colors of Sisnaajiní shift according to the position of the sun, and that it has an encircling black band. This led Father Berard Haile and others to identify it with the high Sierra Blanca, with its glistening snowfields and clearly visible timber line. The second most popular guess is Pelado Peak in the Jemez Mountains of New Mexico (Matthews 1897; O'Brian 1956).

Generally speaking, there are six Navajo sacred mountains, though other landmarks are also mentioned in the mythology. The four primary sacred mountains mark the four cardinal directions and were once considered boundaries of Navajo range. Besides Blanca Peak, these are Colorado's Hesperus Peak (Díbé Ntsaa, "Big Sheep"), the sacred mountain of the north; New Mexico's Mount Taylor (Tsoodził, "Tongue Mountain" or, ceremonially, Dootł'izhii Dziil, "Turquoise Mountain"), the sacred mountain of the south, and Arizona's San Francisco Peaks (Dook'o'słííd, "Never Thaws on Top"), the sacred mountain of the west. Navajos consider Blanca Peak and Hesperus Peak as female, and Mount Taylor and the San Francisco peaks as male (Luckert 1977, 51).

Gobernador Knob (Ch'óol'į'í, "Spruce Hill," or, ceremonially, Ntł'iz Dziil, "Hard Goods Mountain") and Huerfano Mountain (Dził Ná'oodiłichííí, "People Encircling Mountain"), are two New Mexico promontories internal to Navajoland that are also sacred, having their own places in Navajo mythology (McPherson 1992, 190).

Each sacred mountain houses gods, and upon

these four mountains sit "sky pillars" (Yá Yíyah Niizíinii, "Those Who Stand Under the Sky"), which hold up the sky (McPherson 1992, 23).

According to the Navajo creation myth, Sisnaajiní was the first sacred mountain created by First Man and First Woman in the upper world. Hashch'é'éłti'í (Talking God) and another being called Hozdziłkhe Naat'aanii, which he identifies as "the Crane," brought up mud from the eastern sacred mountain of the Yellow World. From this Sisnaajiní was made. It was then decorated with white shell, the source of the mountain's ceremonial name. It is the property of Hashch'é'éłti'í, and it was he who placed animals, plants, and other things upon it.

Sisnaajiní also figures in Navajo traditions relating to the separation of Athapaskan-speaking peoples. It is told that when the Diné lived between the four sacred mountains (Blanca Peak, Mount Taylor, San Francisco Peaks, and the Hesperus Peak), the different factions of the Diné were always quarreling as to what territory they should occupy. At this time, there was a mountain near Sisnaajini called "Flat Topped Mountain." It was covered with fine stands of flora, including berries and nuts, while Sisnaajini was barren but covered with grass, upon which thrived deer, horses, and other animals. The Navajos told other Diné that they could take their choice between the two mountains. The other Diné could think of nothing except to get food easily and chose Flat Topped Mountain for theirs. As soon as the Diné moved up on the mountain, Naayée' Neizghání (Slayer of Monsters) blew on Flat Topped Mountain and moved it far into the south. This home of the Apaches is in the White Mountains of Arizona and is now called Mount Thomas or Baldy.

BOWDISH CANYON: (5200–5000 ft) Montezuma County, CO. Navajo: Deestsiin Bikooh, "Piñon Canyon" (U.S. Indian Claims Commission n.d., vol. VI, v). A three-mile-long canyon on the northwest flank of Ute Mountain, it is tributary to McElmo Creek from the south some four miles east of the Utah state line.

CHIMNEY ROCK: (7902 ft) Archuleta County, CO. Navajo: Tsé 'Íí'áhí, "Standing Rock." At the foot of this sandstone formation sits a Chacoan great-house community, situated on a high, thin ridge 1200 ft above the valley floor, 18 miles west-southwest of Pagosa Springs (just north of Colorado Highway 151), on the Rio Piedra. This multi-storied ruin contains up to 70 rectangular rooms and two great kivas. The site exhibits the distinctively late P-II (A.D. 1000–1100) Chacoan core-and-veneer architecture, and it dates to A.D. 1076–1093.

Though there are numerous sites of the same period in the vicinity, only this one shows Chacoan great-house architecture (Flint and Flint 1989, 31–33). This is considered the most remote from arable land of all the Chacoan "outlier" sites, and it is one of the earliest, predating others by at least a decade. The building cycles coincide with the lunar standstills of October 1075 and June 1094, which could have been observed from the towers of the main ruin.

The sandstone double spires of this locale dominate more than one hundred Pueblo I and Pueblo II sites (A.D. 925–1125) in the immediate vicinity. The chimneys are considered a shrine to the Twin War Gods of Taos Pueblo (Malville and Putnam 1989, 51), and this is the site where Two Faced God was killed (Van Valkenburgh 1974, 128). (See also Dolores and Mancos Canyon.)

ALSO: (6000 ft) Montezuma County, CO. Navajo: Tsé 'Íí'áhí, "Standing Rock" or "Rock Spire" (Kelley p.c. 1994). This 400-ft-high spire is located at the foot of the far-western tip of the Mesa Verde uplift, four miles northeast of the junction of U.S. Highways 160 and 666, and about three miles north of Jackson's Butte (Wetherill 1987, 93), a high promontory atop the western end of Mesa Verde. This Chimney Rock is some 80 miles due west of the Chacoan outlier Chimney Rock listed above. (Yet a third Chimney Rock appears on the USGS Shiprock 1:250,000 topo map, 10 miles south of the Colorado line on Eagle Nest Arroyo.)

CORTEZ: (6198 ft) (Population: 7,284) Montezuma County, CO. Navajo: Tséyaatóhí, "Water Under the Rock" (Young and Morgan 1987, 732). A farming and stock town in the well-watered McElmo Creek Valley. The Spanish name is for the Spanish explorer Hernan Cortez, applied by the first settlers who founded the town in 1887 (Dawson 1954, 19), by James W. Hanna, who suggested the name. The town was incorporated on November 2, 1902. The town is located on McElmo Creek, the highway junction of U.S. Highways 164 and 666, and is the western entry to Mesa Verde National Park, 11 miles east of the community.

Cortez serves as a commercial center for residents of Colorado's Ute Mountain Ute and Southern Ute reservations, as well as for Navajos of southeastern Utah.

CROW CANYON: (6200–5800 ft) Montezuma County, CO. Navajo: Gáagii Bikooh, "Crow Canyon" (U.S. Indian Claims Commission n.d., vol. VI, vii). Small tributary to McElmo Creek five miles southwest of Cortez, and half a mile west of U.S. Highway 666.

DOLORES: (7000 ft) Montezuma County, CO. Navajo: Hodíílid, "Burned Area" (Van Valkenburgh 1974, 12; Young and Morgan 1987, 453). This small community is located on its namesake river, some eight miles north of Cortez. The vicinity is important in the Navajo traditions of Two-Faced Monster (Van Valkenburgh 1974, 127). (See also Chimney Rock and Mancos Canyon.)

DOLORES RIVER: (approx. 14,159–4500 ft) Dolores, Montezuma, San Miguel, Montrose, and Mesa Counties, CO., and Grand County, UT. Also Rio Dolores. Navajo: Bikooh Hatsoh, "Big Canyon," referring to the deep canyon near the community of Dolores. This extensive, meandering river rises at the north foot of 14,159-ft El Diente Peak of the San Juan Mountains. It flows southwest into Montezuma County near the village of Stoner, and, near the community of Dolores, it turns northwest, flowing into the Colorado River some 30 miles northeast of Moab, Utah. During the 1980s, the river was dammed about eight miles downstream from Dolores, forming McPhee Reservoir, which extends back upstream all the way to Dolores.

The name is Spanish, meaning "sorrows" or sadness, and refers to "Our Lady of Sorrows."

The name was bestowed by the Dominguez Escalante Expedition of 1776 (Dawson 1954, 23). In September 1866, a combined party of Navajos, Weenimuchi Utes, and Paiutes passed along the "Rio Dolores" on the way to their refuge at the Bears Ears (in Utah) following a dispute between the Weeminuchis and Capote Utes over a plan to ambush the same Navajos near Tierra Amarilla, New Mexico (McPherson 1988, 14).

DURANGO: (6,505 ft) (Population: 12,480) La Plata County, CO. Navajo: Kin Łani, "Many Houses." This tourist favorite at the junction of U.S. Highways 160 and 550 sits on the Animas River some 21 miles north of the New Mexico state line. "Durango" comes from a Basque word meaning "watering place," and the name was bestowed in honor of Durango, Mexico (which was in turn named for a city in Spain). Originally "Urango," from "Ur" meaning water, and "Ango" meaning town. The town plays host to the Durango-Silverton Narrow Gauge Railroad, fall hunters, and winter skiers.

Durango was founded in 1880 by the promoters of the Denver & Rio Grande Railroad (in bypassing Animas City), William Bell and Alexander Hunt. Governor Hunt was credited in 1881 with naming the town for its Mexican namesake, where he had traveled on business. However, a mine by the same name had existed by September 1879, and may have lent its name to the town. Navajos have occasionally been hired for menial chores in Durango at low wages (Smith 1992, 92).

Gobernador-phase Navajo pottery has been identified in the region, and Ellis (1974, 321) suggested that Navajos may have collected obsidian nodules from the banks of the Animas River in the vicinity of Durango, but did not actually live there. However, more recent archaeological research indicates that Dinétah-Phase Navajos lived along the nearby La Plata River as early as A.D. 1500 (Brown and Hancock 1992, 88–89; Reed and Reed 1992, 101).

FORT LEWIS: (6610 ft) Montezuma County, CO. Navajo: Tłahchíín, "Collected Tallows" (Kelley p.c. 1994). The fort bearing the name Lewis actually began as an Army camp established near Pagosa Springs, where Indian and military trails crossed the San Juan River. It was first garrisoned in 1878 by about one hundred soldiers (O'Rourke 1980, 52), to enforce the Brunot Treaty, intended to reconcile differences between the Ute Indians and the voracious Colorado miners. (In actuality, the treaty left many questions unanswered and compounded disputes over territorial rights.) According to historian Duane A. Smith (1992, 32), the fort was of far more economic than military importance to the region.

In August 1879, six hundred troops from that Fort Lewis, Fort Wingate, and Fort Lyon converged on the Animas River across from Animas City in reaction to the Ute uprising surrounding the Meeker Massacre. They remained until January 1880, when the Pagosa Springs post was abandoned, and the encampment moved to a location on the right bank of the La Plata River, west and a little south of Durango. This second Fort Lewis was labeled Cantonment La Plata during the construction phase. The name Fort Lewis honored Colonel William H. Lewis of the 19th U.S. Infantry, killed in a battle with the Northern Cheyenne at Punished Woman's Fork, Kansas, in September, 1878 (Ayres 1931, 81–92; Frazer 1972, 38).

The fort was abandoned as a military post in the fall of 1891. In 1892, the facility was turned into an Indian school. Shortly afterward, angry Indian students burned all but two buildings. In 1911, the school reopened, but as the School of Agriculture, Mechanical Arts, and Household Arts, providing free education to Indian students (Ayres 1931, 81–92). The institution evolved into a junior college (still focusing on agriculture and mechanical arts), and in 1957 the campus moved to its present location in Durango. It gained its current status as a four-year college in 1962. According to historian Smith (1992, 172–73) the college has had more of an economic impact on the Durango region than any other single event. Perhaps more important is the number of Navajos (among other Native American students) who were able to attend this institution thanks to their tuition waivers.

GRAND JUNCTION: (4597 ft) Mesa County, CO. Navajo: Uncertain. This community hosted

the first Indian boarding school in the United States (Bailey and Bailey 1986, 168).

HESPERUS PEAK: (13,232 ft) La Plata County, CO. Also Mount Hesperus. Navajo: Dibé Ntsaa, "Big Sheep." Located approximately 11 miles north of Mancos (and U.S. Highway 160), this is the highest point in the La Plata Range of the San Juan Mountains. Its English name commemorates the schooner in Longfellow's poem "The Wreck of the Hesperus."

This is the Navajo northern sacred mountain, and in the Navajo creation myth, First Man impregnated it with jet and covered it with darkness (its symbolic color is black). He fastened it to the sky with a rainbow (McPherson 1992, 16). It is one of the six sacred mountains. Blanca Peak, Mount Hesperus, Mount Taylor, and the San Francisco Peaks mark the four cardinal directions and were once considered boundaries of Navajoland; Gobernador Knob and Huerfano Peak are the two internal to Navajoland. Navajos consider Hesperus Peak and Mount Taylor (sacred mountains of the north and south) to be female, while the San Francisco Peaks and Blanca Peak (sacred mountains of the west and east) are thought of as male.

IGNACIO: [DB] (6432 ft) La Plata County, CO. Navajo: Bíina, derived from the Spanish "pino," meaning "pine tree." This capital of the Southern Ute Reservation and home of the Southern Ute Agency is located on Colorado Highway 172, in the valley of the Rio Los Pinos, approximately 15 miles southwest of Durango and some 10 miles north of the New Mexico state line. The name Ignacio honors the famous subchief under Chief Ouray of the Weminuche Band Utes. He was considered head of the Consolidated Utes after the death of Ouray in 1880, and was designated head chief of the Utes by Congress in 1895. Today's village is actually a merger of a smaller Ute village with an older Hispanic agricultural community.

The Southern Ute Boarding School was founded in 1902, serving Ute and Navajo children previously sent to Fort Lewis School (see Fort Lewis). The Ute agency and school was eventually placed at Ignacio because of the concentration of Utes on allotted lands along the Los Pinos River.

The valley of the Rio Los Pinos (also Los Pinos River) is a fertile agricultural area and is well known to sportsmen for excellent trout fishing and views of the scenic San Juan Mountains that rise to the north. The Los Pinos Dam, some 30 miles upstream from Ignacio, supplies water for irrigation on Ute Indian lands.

ISLAND LAKE: County unknown. Navajo: Hajíínái "Place of Emergence" or Nihoyostsatse "Land Where They Came Up," although Young (p.c. 1995) was unable to confirm this etymology. This location is mentioned often in Navajo myths and songs, but the exact location is not known. Matthews (1897, 218) suggests that it might be the lake called Trout Lake by USGS geologist Whiteman Cross, and San Miguel Lake by Hayden's survey. In Cross's time, the lake was considered sacred by the local Indians, whose name for it translated to "Spirit Lake." Or, offers Matthews, Hajíínái may be Island Lake on a branch of the South Fork of Mineral Creek, three miles south of Ophir. He also notes that Silver Lake, five miles southeast of Silverton, could also be Hajíínái.

The Navajos, led by First Man and First Woman, are said to have emerged from the fourth world into this one at Hajíínái, which has an island near its center and is surrounded by high cliffs (Matthews 1897, 76–77).

ISMAY TRADING POST: (5000 ft) Montezuma County, CO. Navajo: Uncertain. This post is located at the confluence of Yellow Jacket and Bridge canyons with McElmo Creek, on the peninsula separating McElmo Creek from Yellow Jacket Canyon, almost on the Colorado-Utah state line. Founded by Mr. and Mrs. John Ismay, who were running it in 1962 (McNitt 1962, 324n).

LA PLATA MOUNTAINS: [DB] (12,000–13,000 ft) La Plata and Montezuma Counties, CO. Also Sierra de la Plata (Spanish for "Silver Mountains"), a name applied by the Dominguez and Escalante expedition of 1776. Navajo: Dibé Ntsaa, "Big Mountain Sheep." Also Dził Bíni' Hólóonii, "Mountain that Has a Mind" (Young and Morgan 1987, 312). Ceremonial name: Baashzhinii Dziil, "Jet Mountain." The range runs roughly north-south for 50 miles, fading into Mesa Verde at the southern terminus, and reaching Silverton in the north. It includes such noted heights as Snowstorm Peak (12,511 ft), Lewis Mountain (12,720 ft), Parrot Peak (11,857 ft), Madden Peak (11,972 ft), Gibbs Peak (12,286 ft), Spiller Peak (13,123 ft), Mount Moss (13,192 ft), Banded Mountain (13,062 ft), Mount Hesperus (the highest at 13,232 ft), and Sharkstooth (12,462 ft), all with heavily timbered zones and many lakes and streams.

Many gold and silver mines are found in the range; the earliest mentions of "metallic veins and rocks" came during the Dominguez-Escalante Expedition (Velez de Escalante 1976, 13).

This range is the northern sacred elevation of the Navajos. It is said to be fastened to the heavens with a rainbow and decorated with jet, dark mist, and wild animals, and is the home of mythological Tádídíín 'Ashkii (Pollen Boy) and 'Aniłt'ánii 'At'ééd (Corn Beetle Girl). It is also the traditional northern Blessingway boundary mountain (Van Valkenburgh 1974, 136), and is mentioned in the Navajo Mountain Chant (Powell 1887, 410) and the Coyoteway Ceremony (Luckert 1979).

In the northern end of the La Platas, seven miles west of Silverton, a small island sits in the center of Island Lake, surrounded on the four cardinal directions by four high peaks. This is thought to be Hájíínái, the Place of Emergence of the Navajos, where the Diné emerged from the underworld, and where the spirits of the dead pass to the nether world.

MANCOS: (7032 ft) Montezuma County, CO. Navajo: Often same name as Mancos Canyon/ Creek (Kelley p.c. 1994). This small town is on U.S. Highway 160, approximately 17 miles east of Cortez. Named for the nearby river, the name is Spanish for "One-handed," or "Crippled." The community served as the shipping point for the La Plata district mining activities.

MANCOS CANYON: (6400–5600 ft) Montezuma County, CO. Navajo: Tó Hasłeeh,

"Where the Water Comes Up," referring only to that portion of the Mancos River that traverses Mesa Verde (Van Valkenburgh 1941, 90), though it can also be referred to by the name of the entire creek, Tó Nts'ósíkooh, "Slim Water Canyon" (Van Valkenburgh 1974, 13). This deep cleft is a location of considerable ceremonial significance to the Navajo people.

This canyon plays an important role in the Navajo Two-Faced Monster traditions (Van Valkenburgh 1974, 128; see also Dolores and Chimney Rock). The vicinity figures in the conclusion of the Navajo Gun Shooter Red Antway Myth, and is where the Red Ant People moved after the Restoration Rite (Wyman 1965). The canyon is also possibly the "Tseghi" of Navajo mythology, where the gods created the Tséníjíní ("Honeycombed Rock People"), possibly the oldest Navajo clan (McPherson 1992, 82–85), and is important in the traditions of the wanderings of other early Navajo clans.

In 1874, W. H. Jackson became the first known White man to pass through Mancos Canyon as he led a government photographic survey party through it.

MANCOS CREEK: [DB] (10,800–4,800 ft) Montezuma County, CO (and San Juan County, NM). Navajo: Tó Nts'ósíkooh, "Slim Water Canyon" (Van Valkenburgh 1974, 13). The Spanish name "Mancos" means "One-handed" or "Crippled." According to legend, the name was applied by the Dominguez-Escalante expedition of 1776, during which a member of the party fell from his horse while fording the river, injuring his hand. Brugge (p.c. 1996), however, notes that there is no entry in the Escalante Journal to substantiate this story. Escalante was aware of this name, however, although he preferred Rio de San Lázaro (Brugge 1964, 16–17 and p.c. 1996). At its headwaters, this creek is formed by three branches, East, Middle, and West, which drain the La Plata Mountains in the vicinity of Sharks Tooth Mountain. The creek then passes through the Mesa Verde Country, traveling 67 miles before crossing into New Mexico, where it enters the San Juan River approximately five miles farther downstream.

The river forms a long canyon passing southwest from its source in the La Platas through the Mesa Verde region and enters the San Juan River 15 miles downstream from Shiprock, New Mexico. There are many important Anasazi ruins in the canyons and its branches, the most important being those of Mesa Verde National Park.

The point where Mancos Creek and the San Juan River meet is especially powerful, and may be where Navajo warriors prayed for victory in combat (McPherson 1992, 50). The Ant People of the Navajo Antway moved to Mancos Creek after the Restoration Rite (Wyman 1965). It is also mentioned in the Navajo Coyoteway myth (Luckert 1979), and figures heavily in the stories of Monster Slayer and Born for Water, and the teachings of Female Mountainway (McPherson 1992, 50; Wyman 1975, 244).

MANCOS CREEK TRADING POST: (possibly 5100 ft) Montezuma County, CO. Navajo: Uncertain. Kelley (1977, 251) lists this post as opening about 1890, but McNitt (1962, 310) credits Frank Pile with opening this post near the foot of Tanner Mesa around 1920. The exact location of the post is uncertain, but it may coincide with Mancos Trading Post on U.S. Highway 666 where it crosses Mancos Canyon, about two miles north of the New Mexico state line.

MARIANO WASH: (7000–4800 ft) Montezuma County, CO. Navajo: Uncertain. A stream rising on the southwest slope of Sleeping Ute Mountain, flowing southwest and west some 15 miles before converging with Coyote Wash two miles east of that channel's confluence with Marble Wash (a mile east of Colorado Highway 41). Little information is available about the name of this feature, but it was almost certainly named for Mariano, the prominent Navajo headman of the later nineteenth century.

McELMO CREEK: (6000–4700 ft) Montezuma County, CO., and San Juan County, UT. Navajo: Uncertain. This river rises amid a plethora of small creeks and springs southwest of the city of Cortez, in the vicinity of Denny Lake. It flows due west some 30 miles to the Utah state line, passing immediately north of Sleeping Ute Mountain. Just west of the mouth of Yellow Jacket and Bridge Canyons (at the state line), the river turns southwest for another 15 miles before converging with the San Juan River at the community of Aneth, Utah. Benjamin Albert Wetherill (1987, 203) notes that the waters of McElmo Creek were not exactly palatable: "Talk about alkali water! McElmo Creek has any place beaten by miles. You can drink it if it is made into strong coffee or tea, but even then it is villainous stuff." Two pages later, he refers to the water as ". . . the vilest water that humans ever tried to drink."

In June 1885, Utes raided White ranchers along this creek, killing a rancher named Guenther in retaliation for an ambush on Beaver Creek (15 miles south of Dolores), in which several Whites killed a Ute man, his two children, and one of his two wives. (The other wife escaped, raising the alarm among the Utes.) Guenther's wife and two children escaped the attack on their ranch (McNitt 1966, 18).

Navajos have grazed livestock along this creek before and after the Bosque Redondo Period of 1863–68 (U.S. Indian Claims Commission n.d., vol. IV, 712–15).

The name McElmo is problematic. However, in 1892 a small community by the same name was situated on the south side of the San Juan River at its juncture with McElmo Creek (across from the later site of Aneth, Utah) (Crampton 1983, 132).

McELMO TRADING POST: Exact location uncertain. Navajo: Uncertain. Kelley (1977, 251, 253) lists the post as being active from the late 1870s until about 1915.

MENEFEE MOUNTAIN (and Peak): (8135 ft) Montezuma County, CO. Navajo: Ńdíshchíí' 'Ajisht'óóhí, "Shooting Pine," deriving from a tale in which a Navajo shot an arrow into a pine tree after a failed attempt to catch Two-Faced Monster on the mountain (Van Valkenburgh 1974, 13, 141). This mountain is located southeast of the community of Mancos. It is bounded on the west by Weber Canyon and on the south and east by East Canyon. Menefee Peak is the

promontory near the north end of this nine-mile-long north-south range. The English name is for George Menefee, one of the earliest settlers in the Mancos Valley, who arrived prior to the 1890s (McNitt 1966, 19, 48).

MESA MOUNTAIN: (7000 ft) Montezuma County, CO, and San Juan County, NM. Also Tank Mountain. Navajo: 'Azhííh Naachii', "Cedar Bark Descending Red" (Young p.c. 1995). Upland straddling the New Mexico–Colorado line between the Animas and Los Pinos rivers, and traditionally associated with the Navajo Two-Faced Monster stories (Van Valkenburgh 1974, 13, 142).

MESA VERDE: [DB] (approx. 8393–6000 ft) Montezuma County, CO., San Juan County, NM. Navajo: Gad Deelzhah, "Cedars in an Undulating Line" (Young p.c. 1995). Also sometimes erroneously referred to as Nóódá'í Vi' Dziil, by those confusing the uplands with the nearby Ute Mountains; it may also have been called Tó Nts'ósí, "Slim Stream (Canyon)" (Gillmore and Wetherill 1934, 125). The Spanish name, Mesa Verde, means "Green Tableland," so called because the juniper and piñon trees give a verdant tone. This abruptly rising extensive plateau in southwest Colorado is a massive deposit of Cliff House Sandstone, laid down 75 million years ago. Bounded on the north and west by Montezuma Valley, on the east by the La Plata River, and on the south by the Mancos River, the land is cut by an extensive series of steep-walled canyons flowing north and south. Benjamin Albert Wetherill (1987, 99–100) suggests that rather than a free-standing mesa, the landform is actually a continuation of the southern slope away from the La Plata Mountains, but that a good amount of erosion has taken place, forming the Mancos and Montezuma valleys, giving it the appearance of an uplift.

A portion of the mesa has been set aside as a national park eight miles wide and 15 miles long, but the majority of the landform lies within the Southern Ute Indian Reservation. The mesa is best known for its extensive assemblage of prehistoric Anasazi ruins, particularly the dramatic cliff dwellings nestled in eroded alcoves in the vertical walls of the numerous canyons. Except for Moccasin Canyon, which was named by early trappers, virtually all of the canyons, mesas, and ruins on Mesa Verde were named by the Wetherills, a family of ranchers that discovered and explored many of the ruins in the late nineteenth century.

The origin of the Spanish name of the mesa itself is problematic. It has been speculated that it was named by the Dominguez-Escalante expedition of 1776, but their map refers only to the Sierra Datil (Van Valkenburgh 1941, 94), or Sleeping Ute Mountain to the east, and the Mancos River—both tantalizingly close. Bolton (1951, 14) suspects it was known as Mesa Verde even by the time of that expedition. In any case, the name was in common use by 1859, when Dr. J. S. Newberry listed it in his report on the exploration of the San Juan region. Captain J. F. McComb's map of 1860 gives the name Mesa Verde.

Humans have been exploiting the mesa for at least three thousand years. Prehistoric "Desert Culture" inhabitants were growing corn on the mesa by 1000 B.C. The "Anasazi" (generally considered to be ancestral to today's Pueblo Indians of Arizona and New Mexico) were building habitation structures by the Basketmaker I period (so called because of the excellent baskets found with their remains). Basketmaker remains are not as spectacular as those of the Pueblo period, as the inhabitants made open caves their early homes. Later they started building settlements of small houses, constructed over shallow pits covered with head-high superstructures of poles and earth, on mesa tops and in caves, ending about A.D. 550. By the Pueblo I or Developmental Pueblo era, about A.D. 800, subterranean pithouses were giving way to rectangular surface structures constructed in "jacal" style—interwoven branches covered with mud.

Sophistication increased through the Pueblo II period, when dwellings were linked in long rows, and with courts in front of the houses with one or more subterranean chambers that became kivas (men's secret ceremonial rooms). During the twelfth century, a large portion of the population of Mesa Verde moved into the most desir-

able caves and built cliff houses. Typical of these is Cliff Palace (about A.D. 1100–1275). Those remaining on the mesa tops built large communal houses with as many as two hundred rooms, and some reached the height of four stories. Typical of these is Far View House.

Then these sedentary occupants left the mesa around A.D. 1300. The population decline of Mesa Verde seems to have come quickly, and seems to coincide with the beginning of a great drought that struck the region and most of the Colorado Plateau, though there is no proven correlation. In any case, the population apparently drifted southward, and their descendants may be living in the modern Rio Grande, Zuni, and Hopi pueblos.

They were replaced by the Ute Indians, but (historians speculate) not for a hundred years. Historians believe the Navajos arrived later still, though archaeological investigations continue to push back their earliest demonstrable arrival dates.

By the middle 1700s, two centuries after the first Spanish incursions into the American Southwest, rumors of mineral wealth in the San Juan Mountains prompted Governor Juan de Rivera to launch three expeditions to the region from Santa Fe between 1761 and 1765. These probes passed the La Plata Mountains, crossing the Dolores River and reaching the confluence of the Uncompahgre and Gunnison Rivers, where they established trade with the Utes. Fur trappers explored the region "en masse" from 1812 to 1821. Early American explorers ignored the Mexican ban on their presence to search the region for minerals and a passage to the Pacific Ocean for the next decade.

Following the ceding of the territory to the United States as a result of the Mexican-American War, a long-time trapper in the region guided Captain John William Gunnison's first official American expedition into the region in 1853. Gunnison was searching out a railroad route from Leavenworth, Kansas. The expedition was set upon by hostile Paiutes in the valley of the Sevier River in Utah, and Gunnison and all but four of his men were killed. For the next three decades miners, railroaders, ranchers, and soldiers overwhelmed the indigenous Ute Indians of southwestern Colorado. Ferdinand Hayden and William H. Jackson explored the Mesa Verde region for the Department of the Interior in 1874–75, recording the flora, fauna, geologic formations, and the first written descriptions of Indian ruins. A year later, Professor William H. Holmes, later chief of the Bureau of American Ethnology, passed through the Mancos and reported remarkable stone watchtowers.

The White influx into the territory culminated in the White River Agency Uprising (better known by its sensationalist title, "The Meeker Massacre") on September 30, 1879, and the establishment of Fort Lewis on the La Plata River in 1880.

The 50,275-acre national park contains over six hundred Anasazi ruins, 75 percent of which consist of fewer than five rooms. The location (but not the ruins) was first photographed and described in writing by William Jackson (head of the Photographic Division of the U.S. Geological and Geographical Survey of the Territories), who explored Two Story House in 1874. In 1880–81, the Wetherill family—formerly of Leavenworth, Kansas—homesteaded the Alamo Ranch in the Mancos Valley to the east of Mesa Verde, and, owing to a good relationship with the Ute Indians, began running cattle on the mesa. By 1883 the five Wetherill brothers and brother-in-law Charlie Mason were actively exploring the canyons for cliff dwellings, locating a good many of the major ruins.

In 1888, cattlemen Richard Wetherill and Charley Mason discovered a great two-hundred-room cliff dwelling, which they named the Cliff Palace. In the years that followed, the Wetherill brothers discovered hundreds of Anasazi ruins.

Scientific explorations began with the 1891 excavations of Kodak House, Long House, and Step House by the young Swedish archaeologist, Baron Gustof Nordenskiöld of the Stockholm Museum, guided and assisted by the Wetherills. Uncontrolled excavations ravaged the mesa for nearly two decades, leading Edgar L. Hewitt of Santa Fe's School of American Research to lead a drive for the protection of all Indian ruins. The result was the Federal Antiquities Act of 1906—

the same year that Mesa Verde National Park was established on July 29. Mrs. Virginia McClurg of Colorado Springs worked tirelessly for many years toward the establishment of the park.

Navajos hunted on the mesa, and medicine men traveled up Mancos Canyon on their way north to the La Plata Mountains for ceremonial purposes. The cliff houses must have been known to the Navajos, for they are crystallized in Navajo mythology and play important parts in the Ha'neełnéehee (Upward Reachingway), and the Dził k'ijí Ba'áádjí (Mountaintop Way, Female Branch) ceremonies. Some are also mentioned in the Navajo Flintway rites and in traditions of Two-Faced Monster (Van Valkenburgh 1974, 128). Interestingly, very few (if any) of the ruins today retain readily remembered Navajo names.

✤ SUN TEMPLE, atop Chapin Mesa at the tip of the peninsula formed by Cliff Canyon and Fewkes Canyon, is mentioned in Navajo mythology as a home of Navajo deities (McPherson 1992, 83). The ruin dates to A.D. 1200. Present-day Indians identify the features classifying this as a ceremonial structure. The symmetrical D-shape is unusual for Mesa Verde. The wall once stood 11 to 14 feet high, with 23 rectilinear rooms and five kivas—and it was probably never finished. It was excavated in 1916 by Jesse Fewkes, revealing Chacoesque round rooms and veneer masonry. Archaeologists consider it a part of a community that included Cliff Palace, Sunset House, Oak Tree House, and other smaller cliff dwellings (Flint and Flint 1991, 99–101).

Mesa Verde also figures in the Zuni migration narrative and is important to their Sword Swallower Society, as are Chaco Canyon and Canyon de Chelly (Ferguson and Hart 1985, 126).

✤ NAVAJO WATCHTOWER is a ruin with a misleading name, for it was constructed neither by the Navajos nor in defense of them. It is named for the canyon in which it is situated, and in fact was originally called Navajo Canyon Watchtower.

MONTEZUMA VALLEY: (6200 ft) Montezuma County, CO. Navajo: Díwózhii Bikooh

(Roessel, Jr. 1983b), "Greasewood Arroyo" (Kelley p.c. 1994). This valley runs northeast to southwest along the northwestern edge of Mesa Verde. Within in it lies the town of Cortez.

MOQUI CANYON: (6000–5400 ft) Montezuma County, CO. Navajo: Uncertain. A southern tributary of Mancos River rises in the highlands of southern Mesa Verde. It flows northwest five miles to join the Mancos River some nine miles east of the westernmost extension of the mesa (the extension southeast of Mancos Trading Post).

The term "Moqui" derives from either the Zuni or Hopi spelling of an earlier term, "mó kwi," with which the Hopis labeled themselves (Harrington 1945, 177–78). It was commonly used to label the Hopi Indians of northern Arizona from at least 1598 until anthropologists discovered that the typical Spanish and English mispronunciation was offensive to the Hopis, as it is too close to their móki, meaning "dies," or "is dead." Jesse Fewkes recommended adopting the name "Hopi," taken from their name for themselves (Connelly 1979, 551).

NAVAJO CANYON: (6800–5600 ft) Montezuma County, CO. Navajo: 'Anaasází Bikooh, "Pueblo Canyon" (U.S. Indian Claims Commission n.d., vol. VI, i, spelling corrected by Young [p.c. 1995]), referring to numerous ruins. This canyon is formed by the confluence of East Fork and West Fork Navajo Canyon, flowing another 10 miles south before entering the Mancos River.

NAVAJO PEAK: [DB] (11,323 ft) Archuleta County, CO. Navajo: Dził Binii' Łigaii, "White Faced Mountain." A peak in the Summitville Group of the San Juan Mountains. It is near the community of Chrono in south-central Colorado.

To the Navajos, this peak is sacred and is situated in Dinétah (the Old Navajo country). One of the headwaters of the Navajo River rises on this peak. On the Dominguez-Escalante map of 1776 the river is shown as the Rio de Navajoo and on the McComb map of 1860 as the Rio Navajo.

NAVAJO SPRINGS: Exact location uncertain. Montezuma County, CO. Navajo: K'iiłtsoii,

"Rabbit Brush" (Kelley p.c. 1994). Located in the wide valley west of Mesa Verde and near the southern foot of Ute Mountain, this was the site for a new agency following the expansion of the Southern Ute Reservation in 1896–97. The tin-roofed adobe buildings were abandoned almost upon completion, due to a complete lack of water. The agency moved to Towaoc.

This site was visited by ladies of the Colorado Cliff Dwellers Association in 1904, in an attempt to convince the Ute leader, Ignacio, to lease the Mesa Verde cliff dwellings. Their lobbying failed, and in 1906 the Mesa Verde ruins were detached from the Ute Reservation and turned into Mesa Verde National Park (Smith 1992, 87).

NOLAND'S FOUR CORNERS STORE (TRADING POST): (approx. 4800 ft) Montezuma County, CO. Navajo: Uncertain. This post was built on the north bank of the San Juan River by Owen Edgar Noland in the winter of 1884–85. It was "within rifle shot of the Four Corners." It was an L-shaped building of cotton-wood logs, with its back to the river, the front facing north. The long wing was the store, while Noland and his wife, Callie Mitchell Noland, lived in the other. A ware room, constructed of stone, was added later at the west end. The interior walls were plastered white, and each exterior wall had loopholes for defense (which was apparently never needed). Noland later built a second post (in Utah), called Riverview, which later became known as Aneth (McNitt 1962, 308–9).

SAN JUAN MOUNTAINS: [DB] (10,000–14,246 ft) Montezuma, San Juan, La Plata, Archuleta, Rio Grande, San Miguel, and Hindsdale Counties, CO. Navajo: Dził Łigaii, "White Mountains." (The Franciscan Fathers identified this range as Dibé Ntsaa, "Big Sheep." However, most authorities limit that name to Mount Hesperus.) This is the predominant mountain range in south-central and southwestern Colorado and includes the Bend Group, Northeast San Juan, Lake City Group, Courthouse Group, Telluride Group, Sneffles Range, San Miguel Range, Needle Mountains, Rico Mountains, the La Plata Range, and the Southeast San Juan. Lesser formations consist of the

Cochetopa Hills, Ouray Group, West Needle Mountains, Needle Mountains–Vallecito Basin, Uncompahgre Plateau, Southwest Corner, Silverton East Group, Silverton West Group, Southeast San Juan, Piedra Mountains, and the Navajo-Chama Group.

This range, or one slightly to the north, is shown on the Dominguez-Escalante map of 1776 as the Sierra de las Grullas, "Crane Mountains." This name was used by Captain Roque de Madrid, who explored the mountains in 1705 (Hendricks and Wilson 1996), though he probably did not coin the name as suggested by McNitt (1972, 20), because he used it as though it was already well known. The Dominguez-Escalante map indicates it as the source of the Rio Nabajoe, Rio San Juan, Rio de la Piedra Parada (Standing Rock River), and the Rio de los Pinos (Pine River). To the north the map shows the Sierra de la Plata (Silver Mountain), which would lie in the vicinity of present Mount Elous (14,060 ft), and Mount Nebo (13,191 ft.), some 50 miles north of Durango.

To the Navajos (and the Jicarilla Apaches), this is a place of great importance, containing, according to some authorities, the Navajo Place of Emergence (in the La Plata Range). Matthews (1897) suggests Trout Lake is the location. Traditionally Navajo hunting parties avoided the vicinity of this lake, and call it by a name translated as Spirit Lake. On the maps of the Hayden Survey, this sheet of water is called San Miguel Lake and is located near the line of the Denver & Rio Grande Western Railroad, at the head of the south fork of the San Miguel River. However, this lake has no small island in the center as described by the Navajos. A more likely candidate for the Hájíínáí, the Place of Emergence, is Island Lake in the northern end of the La Platas, about seven miles west of Silverton. A small island sits in the center of the lake, surrounded on the four cardinal directions by four high peaks, and it is thought to be where the Diné emerged from the underworld, and where the spirits of the dead pass to the nether world (Van Valkenburgh 1941, 86).

The San Juans are noted for their high scenic mountains, fine streams for fishing, and for deer and elk hunting. Heavy snow in the winter usually closes all mountain passes. Navajos hunted deer and elk all through this country, though it was Ute territory. Hunting parties went into the region as late as 1895, but were eventually excluded from the region by the White population and the game laws.

In 1937, U.S. Highway 160 was rerouted from the roundabout Cumbres Pass on the south to the newly paved Wolf Creek Pass that crosses the mountains from east to west over an elevation of 10,850 ft.

SAN JUAN RIVER: (4800–3400 ft) Montezuma and Mineral Counties, CO., San Juan and Rio Arriba Counties, NM, and San Juan County, UT. Navajo: Commonly called Tooh, "Water" (Young p.c. 1995); numerous other names are discussed below. This is one of the Southwest's major rivers. It heads in the vicinity of Wolf Creek Pass in Mineral County (well beyond the scope of this volume), and flows 80 miles into the northeast corner of man-made Navajo Lake, about two miles north of the New Mexico state line. The river emerges from the south end of the lake and continues its westward course through Bloomfield, Farmington, and Shiprock, New Mexico, before re-entering Colorado about two miles east of the Four Corners, approximately 120 miles after it left Navajo Lake. It travels less than three miles before entering Utah some three miles north of the Four Corners, and continues west another 125 miles. Its waters merge with the Colorado River as they flow into the San Juan River Arm of Lake Powell at Piute Farms north of Nasja Mesa, about 55 miles upstream (northwest) of Glen Canyon Dam.

This river is sacred to the Navajos. According to McPherson (1992, 49), they call it Sá Bitooh (Old Age River), Tooh Bika'í (Male Water) (as opposed to the Colorado, which is female), Bits'iis Nineezí (One with Long Body), and Bits'iis Nteelí (One with Wide Body), Nóóda'í Bito' (Utes' River).

Its junctures with Los Pinos River (a place called Tó 'Aheedlí, "Water Flows in a Circle," now submerged under the waters of Navajo Lake), Mancos Creek, and the Colorado River are among the most sacred of all places in Navajoland. This is probably the most important river to the Navajos, and it figures heavily in Blessingway, Enemyway, and Evilway legends, and, according to Powell (1887, 339), it also figures in the Mountain Chant.

The Navajos alternately describe the river as an older man with hair of white foam (who "mounts" the female Colorado River); as a snake wriggling through the desert (particularly at the Goosenecks in Utah); as a flash of lightning; and as a black club of protection keeping invaders from the Navajos (McPherson 1992, 50). For years the Navajo presence in the area had been thought to have begun in the late 1600s (Sessions and Williams 1979, 202), but more recent evidence documents their presence since about A.D. 1500 (Schaafsma 1996, 43; Brown 1996, 57).

The river's relationship to the Navajos is reflected in the fact that early Spanish maps refer to it as "Rio Navajoo," or "Navajo River" (Miera y Pacheco map of 1778; Reeve 1956, 301). Brugge (p.c. 1996) suggests that the river's importance as a boundary by various tribes is over-emphasized because such boundaries shifted through time.

SENTINEL ROCK: Exact location uncertain. Montezuma County, CO. Navajo: Uncertain, but probably Tsé 'Íí'áhí, "Standing Rock." This spire of rock is located at the southern foot of Ute Mountain.

SODA SPRING: (6400 ft) Montezuma County, CO. Also Sulphur Spring. Navajo: Todkonzh 'Adlii, "Alkaline Water Coming Out." Located near the head of Iron Springs Wash, some five miles east of Redmesa. This is a traditional location of Two-Faced Monster and a source of medicinal water (Van Valkenburgh 1974, 141).

SOUTHERN UTE INDIAN RESERVATION: (7600–6000 ft) Montezuma and Archuleta Counties, CO. Navajo: Nóóda'í. No translation known, probably a shift or corruption (Young p.c. 1995).

The Southern Utes (population 843, 1941 census) are settled on the consolidated Southern Ute Reservation in southern Colorado. The federal agency and the capital of the reservation are at Ignacio. The Ute language is of Shoshonean stock.

The Utes (also called Utahs, Yutas, Yutes, and Ytaws in early accounts) were, together with the Paiutes, the northern neighbors of the Navajos. At one time, they occupied the entire central and western portion of what is now Colorado and the eastern portion of what is now Utah. In the Treaty of February 7, 1879, the Kapot (Capote), Moache, and Wiminche divisions of the tribe ceded their rights to the upper San Juan drainage given them under the earlier Treaty of 1863. In exchange, the government agreed to establish a reservation for them immediately north of the San Juan River in southern Colorado.

Famed chiefs of that time were Ouray, the recognized chief of the confederated bands, who was born in 1820 and died in 1880; Buckskin Charley, called Yo'o'witz (the Fox) by his people, chief of the Moache band living on the Los Pinos River; Severe, born in the Moache band, married into the Kapot band, of which he became chief; and Ignacio, for whom the agency was named, chief of the Wiminche band.

Today the Utes are a quiet people residing along fertile river valleys and grazing their stock on reservation and Indian homesteads and allotments and in the national forests. Prior to American subjugation they were a warlike, nonagricultural people of the Great Basin type of culture with many Great Plains inflections. Their raiding expeditions swept out into the Comanche and Kiowa habitat on the upper Cimarron River in eastern New Mexico and Texas.

They were generally allied and often intermarried with the Jicarilla Apaches, their southeastern neighbors. They were traditional enemies of the Navajos, whom they called Bloody Knives. Ute forays swept the entire Navajo country and beyond the Hopi towns to the eastern slopes of the San Francisco Peaks. The Utes also allied themselves with the Spaniards and later Mexicans against the Navajos, and as late as 1863–64 they acted as spies and guides for Kit Carson's New Mexico Volunteers in the Navajo Wars.

Despite their enmity, the Utes and Navajos also carried on an extensive trade. Navajo trading parties penetrated as far northward as the northern Uncompahgre Utes in northeastern Utah. The Navajos wove special blankets to trade for Ute elk and deer hides. From the Utes are descended the Nóóda'í Dine'é (Ute Clan) and other Navajo clans. Certain parts of the 'Anaa'jí (Enemyway Ceremony) are thought by some ethnologists to come from the Utes.

The Ute chief most belligerent to the Navajos was White Hair ('Atsii' Łigaii, Bitsii' Łigaii, or Tsii' Łigaii), who raided Canyon de Chelly in the 1840s and 1850s. The Navajos finally caught up with him in his own country in the 1850s. The Navajos signed a treaty with the Utes at Fort Wingate in 1868.

TOWAOC: [DB] (5800 ft) Montezuma County, CO. Navajo: Kin Dootł'izhí, "Blue House" or "Green House" (Young and Morgan 1987, 494). Capital of the Ute Mountain Indian Reservation, located three miles west of U.S. Highway 666, at the eastern foot of Ute Mountain, some 29 miles north of Shiprock, New Mexico. This site was chosen for the Ute agency in 1897, following abandonment of the short-lived Navajo Springs agency.

This region—the eastern slope of Ute Mountain—was once the territory of the Mouache (also spelled Maguache, Magache) band and the Capote (also Kapote) branch of the Southern Utes. Towaoc was the site of the Consolidated Southern Ute boarding school before the division of the Ute Reservation into the Southern Ute and Ute Mountain reservations. Some of the students here were Paiutes from Allen Canyon, Utah, 30 miles west of Blanding, at the foot of the Abajo Mountains. These people—Shoshonean linguistic stock—were an isolated division of the Paiutes who once ranged into the Piute Strip and Navajo Mountain region.

These Paiutes make coiled, bowl-shaped baskets with red and black motifs that are known as "Navajo wedding baskets." Such baskets are still carried by many traders on and around the Navajo Reservation, even though few, if any, are made by Navajos. The Diné obtained most of their baskets from the Paiutes, Havasupais, Hopis, and Jicarilla Apaches, though they did weave some themselves in a tradition that most

likely grew from Pueblo roots long before European contact (Brugge p.c. 1996).

TRAIL CANYON: (6400–5600 ft) Montezuma County, CO. Navajo: Didzétsoh Łání Bikooh, "Many Peaches Canyon" (U.S. Indian Claims Commission n.d., vol. VI, xxii; Young and Morgan 1987, 963). Five-mile-long tributary of McElmo Creek immediately west of Alkalai Canyon. Most of its course is southward, turning west for the last mile before its confluence with McElmo.

UNCOMPAHGRE PLATEAU: (9120 ft) San Miguel, Ouray, Montrose, Delta, and Mesa counties, CO. Navajo: Dził Łigaii, "White Mountain" (U.S. Indian Claims Commission n.d., vol. VI, vii). Uncompahgre is Ute for "Hot Water Spring" (Dawson 1954, 66). This 90-mile-long ridge runs from the Dallas Divide in the south to Grand Junction in the north.

UTE MOUNTAIN: [DB] (9977 ft) Montezuma County, CO. Also Sleeping Ute Mountain. Navajo: Dził Naajiní, "Black Mountain Sloping Down." High, isolated mountains towering over the rolling plains and mesa country of the southwest corner of Colorado, immediately south of McElmo Creek and west of U.S. Highway 164. This range, viewed from the south, takes on the appearance of a sleeping person with raised knees to the southwest (8959-ft Hermano Peak is often referred to as "The Knees"), and the head (Ute Peak) to the north. The name comes from the presence of the Moguache Utes, who dwelt along its eastern flanks at the time of European arrival in the vicinity. Hovenweep National Monument lies 15 miles to the west of the range, and Yucca House National Monument (another substantial Anasazi ruin) is some 10 miles east of the northern end of the range. Early Spanish maps of the area labeled these mountains Sierra del Datil, "Date Mountains" (as in the fruit of the palm) (Brugge 1964, 16–17). In the southwestern United States, the datil can also refer to the fruit of the yucca (Brugge p.c. 1996).

According to Navajo medicine men, Ute Mountain is suspended from the sky by a cord of rain, and it is decorated with corn pollen, dark mist, and female (gentle) rain. It is said to be the home of Holy Boy and Holy Girl, who make rough jewels. The mountain is important in the Moving Upward Way, Enemyway, and Flintway rites (Van Valkenburgh 1974, 129).

Medicine men who know the rite-myth of the Beadway Ceremony tell of a deep canyon called Tséyi', the common Navajo descriptive term for a deep rock-walled canyon, which Van Valkenburgh (1941, 167) believed was on Ute Mountain. In this canyon was a ruin called Tséyi' Kin (a house with one black wall, perched in a cave in the wall of the canyon). In this cliff dwelling the yé'ii (gods) found the white and yellow corn cobs used to create a pair of the Tséyi' Kiní. It also plays a role in the Navajo Mountain Chant (Powell 1887, 410).

According to Ute legend, this mountain is a deity who collected all rain clouds in anger. Storms come from clouds that happen to escape his pockets. Ute tradition says he will awaken some day and fight their enemies (McPherson 1992, 22).

Mancos Canyon (called Tó Nts'ósíkooh, "Slim Water Canyon," by the Navajos) passes south and east of Ute Mountain after exiting the Mesa Verde highlands. The "Tseghi" mentioned above may be a side canyon of Mancos, which is itself important in Navajo rite-myth, including the Moving Upward Way, the Enemyway, and others.

Some Navajos joined the Utes in the vicinity of Ute Mountain in 1834, due to miliary pressure from the Mexicans (McNitt 1972, 73).

UTE TRADING COMPANY: Exact location uncertain. Montezuma County, CO. Navajo: Uncertain. This post was established by Bob Bryce in the late 1880s as the first post in the region. It was later bought and named by Louis Ismay of Ismay's Trading Post. It is located on U.S. Highway 666, east of Towaoc.

WETHERILL MESA: (7200–6400 ft) Montezuma County, CO. Navajo: Uncertain, probably the same as Mesa Verde: Gad Deelzhah, "Cedars in an Undulating Line" (Young p.c. 1995). The peninsula of Mesa Verde lying be-

tween Long Canyon (on the east) and Rock Canyon (on the west). It is home to Step House, Badger House Community, Long House, and other prehistoric Anasazi ruins. In 1891, Swedish archaeologist Baron Gustof Nordenskiöld of the Stockholm Museum named the mesa for the Wetherill family, who had explored much of the region for years and served as his guides and excavators on his own expedition to Mesa Verde.

YELLOW JACKET CANYON: (7400–5000 ft) Montezuma County, CO. Navajo: Uncertain. This major canyon network heads approximately five miles northeast of the community of Yellow Jacket. It flows southwest some 30 miles to merge with McElmo Creek at the Utah state line. Its name derives from numerous yellow jacket wasp nests (WPA 1941a).

This canyon was on a major trade route between the Utes and the Navajos. In 1873, Navajos and Paiutes attacked a group of miners near Needle Rock. These were possibly the same Indians who killed three Mormons near Mountain Meadows, Utah, at about the same time (McPherson 1988, 16).

YELLOW JACKET RUIN: (6800 ft) Montezuma County, CO. Navajo: Uncertain. One of eight major ruins in the Montezuma Basin (Lowry Ruin, Sand Canyon Ruin, Goodman Point Ruin, Mud Springs Ruin, Yucca House Ruin, Lancaster Ruin, and Wilson Ruin are the others). Lowry Ruin has 110 kivas, Sand Canyon 90, and Goodman Point 85. Yellow Jacket is possibly the largest known Anasazi Pueblo III–era ruin, with the highest concentration of kivas in the known Anasazi realm—minimally 120, including at least one Great Kiva—a Chaco phenomenon. It has been suggested that the site was solstice-predicting, as the sun rises over distant Lizard Head Peak (13,113 ft) as viewed from the southern part of the ruin 16 days prior to the summer solstice. Stone monoliths in the site may have been sun, moon, and/or star markers. Alignments of features in a great kiva are equivalent to those found in Casa Rinconada at Chaco Canyon (Malville and Putnam 1989, 68–69).

This ruin's layout suggests traffic lanes deliberately planned between the separate buildings arranged into eight distinct "villages." The site is Classic Pueblo III (A.D. 1100–1300) and contemporary with Mesa Verde to the south (Ferguson and Rohn 1987, 123–29). The complex was possibly a town of three thousand people, or a ritual site, or both (Brody 1990, 126).

YUCCA HOUSE (NATIONAL MONUMENT): (5700 ft) Montezuma County, CO. Navajo: Uncertain. The name Yucca House derives from the local Ute name for Ute Mountain, which means "Yucca Mountain" (National Park Service 1926, 67). This Anasazi ruin complex lies two and one-half miles west of U.S. Highway 666, nine miles south of Cortez. Excavations in 1939 showed these ruins to have been occupied by Mesa Verdean Anasazi, and the two roomblocks, about one hundred yards apart, appear to have been constructed of fossiliferous limestone probably quarried from the base of Mesa Verde.

These ruins were first described by Professor William H. Holmes in 1877, who named the two roomblocks Upper House (the most prominent) and Lower House.

The land on which the monument is located was donated to the Park Service by Henry Van Kleek, of Denver.

Near the ruin, at a place called Snider's Well (on a ranch owned by a man named Snider), in a ruin excavated by the Wetherills and the Hyde Expedition, a kiva was found full of skeletons, "thrown into the room in a haphazard manner. All of the skulls saved had each a hole in it such as would be made by striking it with a stone axe" (McNitt 1966, 74). Walls of the kiva were painted, and the Wetherills drew the conclusion that the skeletons were the remains of prisoners or captives killed and thrown in.

6

NEW MEXICO LOCATIONS

ABIQUIU: [DB] (6000 ft) Rio Arriba County, NM. Navajo: Ha'ashgizh, "Cut Upward" (Young and Morgan 1987, 403), also translated as "Long Upgrade Gap" (Van Valkenburgh 1941, 1). Old Hispanic village 23 miles northwest of Española (on New Mexico Highway 84), situated on the northwestern foot of Abiquiu Mesa at the confluence of the swiftly flowing Rio Chama and Abiquiu Creek. Approximately six miles southwest is Abiquiu dam and reservoir, constructed in the 1970s.

This old adobe village was built by the Spaniards upon the site of an old Tewa Indian pueblo in 1747. It was later abandoned, but resettled in 1754. Escalante spoke of a settlement called "Santa Rosa de Abiquiu" in 1776, and there is speculation that the name is possibly a corruption of a Tewa word meaning "timber end town" (Pearce 1965, 1). Throughout the eighteenth century, many Indian captives were brought here, and a number of Hopis settled at the community, probably to escape difficulties at Hopi (Brugge p.c. 1996). Their presence gave rise to another Navajo name meaning "Big Leggings," a reference to the Hopis' buckskin leggings. There was considerable Spanish intermarriage with Indians here.

Abiquiu was one of the early frontier posts established by the Spanish government to deal with predations of the belligerent and semi-nomadic Jicarilla Apaches and Utes in the northern reaches of New Spain. Navajos frequented the vicinity for hunting, raiding, and trading, and conflicts with Navajos were recorded as early as 1702 (Reeve 1958, 214). However, the village was established during a long period of peace between the Spanish and Navajos, and at least one historian believes its founding was more likely

an expansion of the Spanish frontier than to defend against Navajo attacks (Brugge p.c. 1996).

The community later became the starting point of the old Spanish trade route of 1800 to 1846, over which passed New Mexican and Navajo blankets, and sometimes slaves, for exchange in California for mules, horses, and china silks.

After the American conquest of 1846, General Kearny garrisoned a post at Abiquiu with companies of Missouri Mounted Volunteers to control two or three approaches to the Rio Grande settlements used by Navajo, Ute, and Jicarilla raiders (McNitt 1972, 97). From here soldiers also ranged north into Utah to deal with the Utes (McNitt 1972, 106).

Navajos raided the community for horses and mules in the spring of 1850 (McNitt 1972, 162), and eight years later Diné raiders drove off two thousand head of sheep. The village became the Ute agency as well as agency for the Jicarilla Apaches. In 1860, Ute Agent Albert H. Pfieffer led Utes in a slave raid against the Navajos, capturing 19 women and children and killing six men. Then, in May 1863, the village was raided in a concerted uprising of Navajo and Pueblo Indians (McNitt 1972, 162, 310, 366, 379, 398).

Today the mostly Spanish-American population farms the river bottom and cultivates fruit along the rising hills, and a small artist colony has burgeoned in the community. (Renowned artist Georgia O'Keeffe lived for many years at Abiquiu, until her death in 1986.) The village is home to Ghost Ranch Living Desert Museum and the Florence Hawley Ellis Museum of Anthropology.

ACOMA PUEBLO: [DB] (7000 ft) (Population: 2,590) Cibola County, NM. Navajo: Haak'oh,

"Acoma," from the native Keresan name of the pueblo, meaning "People of the White Rock" (New Mexico Office of Cultural Affairs 1991, 2). Also known as "Sky City." A pueblo of Keresan language stock, located 14 miles south of I-40, some 56 miles west of Albuquerque. According to Van Valkenburgh, the community had a population of 1,210 in 1940.

The old pueblo sits atop a 357-ft-high mesa, reached by a single trail before the road was constructed. In 1539, Fray Marcos de Niza referred to it as "the Kingdom of Hacus." Captain Alvarado of the Coronado Expedition described the pueblo in 1540 as having two hundred houses. Some anthropologists believe its people to be related to those of the pueblo of Zia.

Three miles eastward from this mesa is the famed Enchanted Mesa, of traditional importance to the Acomas, and with sheer walls that have been ascended by very few Whites.

Acoma, called by the Spanish "Acus" and, later, "San Estevan de Acoma," was well known for its stalwart unfriendliness to Whites, a condition brought about by the January 22, 1599, attack on the pueblo by Vicente de Zaldivar. Approximately eight hundred Acomas were killed in the attack, and all male captives over 25 years of age were sentenced to have one hand and one foot cut off, and to 20 years "personal service" (slavery). All males between the ages of 12 and 25 were sentenced to 20 years of servitude, as were all females above the age of 12 (Garcia-Mason 1979, 457).

With the exception of very short intervals, the Acoma people have lived for centuries on their mesa, and contest with the Hopi village of Oraibi for the title of the oldest continually occupied settlement in North America. During the time of the seventeenth-century Spanish explorer Espejo, the Acoma people farmed fields to the north of the village, but no permanent settlements were built until the 1863–64 Navajo deportation to Fort Sumner ended Diné raiding. Acomita, San Fidel, and McCarty's all are Acoma colonies.

ACOMITA: [DB] (6250 ft) (Population: 314) Cibola County, NM. Navajo: Tó Łání Biyáázh, "Offspring of Many Bodies of Water" (Young

p.c. 1995), "Many Bodies of Water" referring to Laguna Pueblo. This farming colony of Acoma Pueblo sits on the south bank of Rio San Jose three miles east of McCarty's, two miles south of San Fidel and I-40. It was established around 1870 after the danger of Navajo and Apache raids had passed. The Burlington Northern Santa Fe Railway runs east-west just north of town, and the community is currently the site of an Indian Health Service Hospital to the north, constructed in 1978.

AHSHISLEPAH WASH: (6700–6000 ft) San Juan County, NM. Navajo: 'Áshįįh Łibáhí, "Gray Salt" (Young p.c. 1995). Heading in San Juan Basin, four miles north of Chaco Canyon, this normally dry channel flows southeast into Chaco Wash four miles northeast of Chaco Canyon National Cultural Historical Park.

ALAMO: [DB (as Puertocito)] (6100 ft) (Population: 1,271) Socorro County, NM. Navajo: T'iistsoh, "Big Cottonwood Tree." Also Puertocito, Spanish for "Little Door" or "Little (mountain) Pass," and Field. "Alamo" is Spanish meaning "cottonwood tree." While Alamo and Field refer to a small village on New Mexico Highway 52, some 35 miles northeast of Magdalena, Puertocito usually referred to a small isolated band of Navajos (two hundred people in 1941) situated in the high mesa and lava country of the Alamo Navajo Reservation, 40 miles south of Suanee (a switching station on the AT&SF west of Albuquerque). A trading post was operated here in the 1940s by Nelson A. Field, for whom the first post office (1930–43) was named. (Field was also a cattleman and New Mexico Land Commissioner.) The USIS day school was named Alamo, and this gradually became the name of the community, which today is also the chapter seat.

One of the largest springs in New Mexico is located here in this stock country with intermixed Navajo, Hispanic, and Anglo holdings. Although the Indians are Navajo, they were administered for a number of years by the United Pueblo Agency due to their nearer proximity to the Pueblos than to the main Navajo Reservation.

This small band of Navajos has been isolated

from the main body of the tribe for some one hundred years. Henry Chee Dodge stated: "They were once part of the Diné 'Ana'í ("Enemy Navajos"), and are called by the Navajo proper, Tsé Dei'aałí ("Stone Chewers"), for when they fought, they were reputed to get so angry that they chewed rocks."

Van Valkenburgh (1941, 117) recounted headman Jose Maria Apache's account of the Puertocito Navajo origins:

Long ago, the Mexicans stole a band of Navajos and took them to Socorro as slaves. After a time, three women and two men escaped and headed for the Navajo country. They suffered many hardships before they came to a large spring called Tótsoh ("Big Water"). This is now at Field's place. They decided to stay there and for some years lived on animals, roots, seeds, and grass. The big spring was used to hunt deer. Later, when the Mexican sheep man began coming to the spring, they stole sheep and ate them.

Soon they started to herd for the Mexicans. When the Mexicans started to pay them in hard money, they didn't know what it was and asked for sheep instead. During this time, Chiricahua and Mescalero Apache, as well as Mexican inter-marriages took place. (Van Valkenburgh 1941, 117–18)

Historians, however, believe that the region was populated at least in part by "hideouts" dodging the massive roundup of Navajos in 1863–64 and escapees from the Fort Sumner internment. Navajos tell of an old chief named Viejo, who, with his three sons, fled the main Navajo area in 1863 to avoid Kit Carson's Army then pillaging the region. They went south and settled in the Alamo area. Later, Navajos at Fort Sumner heard of them and, on escaping the Bosque Redondo, sought refuge with Viejo's people (Ellis 1974, 483).

Today, the Puertocito Navajos live on their small reservation, making a living wherever they can. Some have a few sheep and others herd for other stock owners, Indian and non-Indian. A few small fields of corn are planted.

ALBUQUERQUE: (5000 ft) (Population: 384,736) Bernalillo County, NM. Navajo: Bee'eldííldahsinil, "At the Place of the (Bell) Peals" (Young and Morgan 1987, 816). Largest city in New Mexico, located near the geographic center of the state, straddling the Rio Grande at the western foot of the 10,678-ft Sandia Mountains (at the crossroads of Interstate Highways 25 [north-south] and 40 [east-west]).

Albuquerque was founded in 1706 to colonize and promote protection from Indian attacks along the Rio Abajo (lower Rio Grande Valley). Ranches in this vicinity were raided by Navajos as early as March 1786. The city served as headquarters of the 9th Military Department in 1852 (McNitt 1972, 211). Many military expeditions against the Navajos were launched from or marched through Albuquerque. On one such auspicious occasion, Colonel Andrew W. Doniphan led a column from the city on October 26, 1846, intending to impress and contain the Navajos, only to have the Navajos attack the city later the same day (Lavender 1954, 292–94).

Today Albuquerque is home for the Indian Pueblo Cultural Center, University of New Mexico, the Maxwell Museum of Anthropology, the Atomic Museum, the Museum of Albuquerque, and the New Mexico Museum of Natural History, and a good many eastern Navajos conduct business there.

(C. H.) ALGERT TRADING CO.: (approx. 5100 ft) San Juan County, NM. Navajo: Uncertain. Established in Fruitland in 1903 by its namesake, a non-Mormon who followed his Mormon friends to Fruitland when they were displaced from Tuba City. (An expansion of the western boundary of the Navajo Reservation engulfed that community, forcing the mostly Mormon non-Indian residents to vacate.) Algert's was a wholesale enterprise, buying goods from Charles Ilfeld Co. of Gallup and hauling them for six to ten days up to the San Juan for resale. A few years later, Algert sold out to Junius and Al Foutz, who changed the name to Progressive Mercantile. Charles Ilfeld Co. purchased an interest in the venture and later took it over entirely.

ALLEGRO MOUNTAIN: (10,244 ft) Catron County, NM. Navajo: K'ii'aaha, translation uncertain. Also Daadílí, "Thick Lips" (Young, p.c 1995.). Navajos have gathered wild plants on this mountain, some 25 miles due south of Datil (U.S. Indian Claims Commission n.d., vol. IV, 712–15).

AMBROSIA LAKE: (6971 ft) McKinley County, NM. Navajo: Bits'ádi (U.S. Indian Claims Commission n.d., vol. VI, iii), translation uncertain; Young (p.c. 1995) suggests this is only part of a word. A uranium processing plant on New Mexico Highway 509 five miles northeast of its junction with New Mexico Highway 53 and two miles southwest of San Mateo Mesa. The full Spanish name is La Laguna del Difunta Ambrosio, named for a man, killed by arrows, whose body was found in the seasonal lake bed that lies about three miles northwest of the plant. The lake is now dry.

ANGEL PEAK: (6880 ft) San Juan County, NM. Also Angel's Peak. Navajo: Tséłgizhíí, "Rock Pass"; also Ma'ii Dah Siké, "Two Coyotes Seated at an Elevation" (Young and Morgan 1987, 520). This is the chief landmark in the "Garden of Angels," 80 square miles of tortured landscape with formations resembling a group of angels (WPA 1940b, 365).

ANIMAS RIVER: (approx. 12,000–5300 ft) San Juan County, NM, and San Juan and La Plata counties, CO. Navajo: Kinteeldéé' Ńlíní, "Which Flows from the Wide Ruin," referring to Aztec Ruin. This river heads in the La Plata Mountains east of Telluride, Colorado, and flows 50 miles through Colorado and another 20 miles in New Mexico before merging with the San Juan at Farmington. The confluence is called Tó Dootłizhi, "Blue Land Goes Into River," and is a very significant ceremonial location for the Navajos, figuring in the Coyoteway Chant (Luckert 1979). In October 1861, Ute Indian Agent LaFayette Head credited "numerous and implacable" Navajo warriors with forcing the abandonment of the Rio di (*sic*) Animas mining region in Colorado (Correll 1968, October 2).

ANTELOPE LOOKOUT MESA: (6760 ft) McKinley County, NM. Navajo: Jádí Hádít'įįh, "Antelope Lookout." Elevated region traversed by New Mexico Highway 371, some five miles north of its junction with New Mexico Highway 57 (north of Crownpoint). This elevation gives a wide, panoramic view of the lowlands below, and was apparently used by Navajo hunters watching for game.

ANZAC: [DB] (5900 ft) Cibola County, NM. Navajo: Ye'iitsoh Bidił Niníyęęzh, "Where Big Enemy God's Blood Stopped Flowing," a reference to the lava flows in the vicinity. An abandoned train station situated eight miles southeast of Grants on the Burlington Northern Santa Fe, where the Rio San Jose cuts through the lava flow. Named by the railroad from the initials of the Australian and New Zealand Army Corps in World War I (Pearce 1965, 9)—though exactly why remains problematic. Of this location, the Navajo Anaa'jí, or Enemyway Chant, includes the following reference:

> Near San Rafael at Tó Sido (a thermal spring) the Twin War Gods, Naayéé' Neizghání ("Killer of Monsters") and Tóbájíshchíní ("Born for Water") started to fight Ye'iitsoh, Chief of the Enemy Gods. The fight raged northward where the blood of Ye'iitsoh flowed. He was finally vanquished at the foot of the low juniper-covered slope immediately south of Highway 66 (now I-40). The white ash outcroppings are said to have been caused by the heat of the fierce combat; the lava flow that caps the sandstone is the hardened blood of Ye'iitsoh and certain paleontological material reputed to have been found there, are his bones. [See also Cabezon Peak.] If the lava flow separated by the Rio San Jose ever again meets, Ye'iitsoh will live again, and again become the destroyer of mankind. To guard against this, Naayéé Neizghání, the elder brother of the twins, drew a line with a sacred flint along the face of the northern edge of the lava flow. (Van Valkenburgh 1941, 3)

ASAAYI LAKE: (7500 ft) McKinley County, NM. Navajo: 'Ásaayi', "In a bowl" Lake (Correll and Watson 1974, 131). This man-made reservoir lies 11 miles east of Navajo, in the Chuska Mountains, on Bowl Canyon Creek. It is the site of an extensive Boy Scout camp and public campground.

ATARQUE: [DB] (6800 ft) Cibola County, NM. Navajo: 'Adáágíi Łichi'i, "Red Rocks Standing Up" (Van Valkenburgh 1941, 5; Young p.c. 1995). Also Tsé Łichíí Sikaadí, "Red Rock Spreading Out," and Tsé Łichíí, "Red Rock" (Young and Morgan 1987, 730). Spanish-American village located 35 miles south of Zuni Pueblo, in rolling country dotted with numerous volcanic outcroppings and mesas (a mile and a half west of New Mexico Highway 602, six miles north of Fence Lake). "Atarque" is Spanish meaning "diversion dam." A trading center for the Ramah Navajo, the small community was home of the Atarque Trading Co. and Atarque Sheep Co. (Van Valkenburgh mistakenly places this location 10 miles east of Fence Lake.)

The first White settlement in the community was made in 1881 when Mrs. Cecelia Ortega de Garcias, following the murder of her husband by Chiricahua Apaches, moved to the vicinity with her sons and Manuel Landavazo (father of Guillermo, later cattle man and storekeeper at Atarque). At that time a lone Zuni Indian was living in a cave above the main spring raising wheat. In 1885 the Garcias relocated to the present site of Atarque and built an earth dam that extended across the valley, confining a large amount of water. The dam was later washed out by heavy storms.

It was in this region that the Nihoobáanii ("Gray Streak Ends People") Clan of the Navajo were reputed to have lived before joining the tribe. The numerous Anasazi ruins dotting the surrounding country are possibly those of the Province of Marata mentioned in the Relación of Fray Marcos de Niza in 1539 (1559?). About 15 miles east of Atarque (Van Valkenburgh mistakenly says north) the landscape is dominated by a volcanic cone named Cerro Alto (Spanish for "Tall Hill"), which the Navajos call Dził Nééz ("Tall Mountain").

Zunis used to farm this area before the coming of the Whites (Ferguson and Hart 1985, 129). Some 10 miles west of Atarque a bean farming community called Fence Lake was founded in 1932 by Texans and Oklahomans dislocated by the great drought. The name derives from the fenced lake of Sylvestor Mirabel, an early stockman. Until the 1940s, Dyer's Store and Bond and Sargent's Store here served some two thousand people scattered over the area and many Zunis from Ojo Caliente (15 miles north).

There have long been strained relations between the largely Hispanic population of Atarque and the transplanted Anglos of nearby Fence Lake (Vogt and Albert 1970, 57–61).

AZTEC: [DB] (5650 ft) (Population: 5,479) San Juan County, NM. Navajo: Kinteel, "Wide House." An agricultural town at the crossroads of New Mexico Highways 173, 544, and 574, and U.S. Highway 550, 13 miles northeast of Farmington, and eight miles north of Bloomfield. In 1940, the population was only 1,200, and the town was served by the Denver & Rio Grande Railroad, which moved largely livestock. The town is located on the south bank of the Animas River, in the fertile Animas Valley. It is the home of Aztec National Monument, an Anasazi ruin in the form of a Chacoan great house, and source of the town's name. The ruins, partially excavated between 1916 and 1924, figure heavily in Navajo folklore. The structure has been partly reconstructed.

The first settlers were wheat farmers Frank and George Coe in the 1880s, following the reopening of portions of the Jicarilla Apache Reservation in 1876. Aztec became the seat of San Juan County when that body was carved out of Rio Arriba County in 1887 due to political differences (New Mexico Office of Cultural Affairs 1991, 17).

AZTEC RUIN: [DB] (5650 ft) San Juan County, NM. Navajo: Kinteel, "Wide Ruin." Located 15 miles northeast of Farmington (exactly halfway between Chaco and Mesa Verde), this is the third largest known Chacoan great-house community (behind Pueblo Bonito and Chetro Ketl in Chaco Canyon). The main building contains 437 rectilinear rooms and 30 round rooms, organized in a U-shaped structure, portions of which were at least three stories high. It was constructed 50 years after Great North Road (A.D. 1100–1120). The site contains two other large buildings and 90 units surrounding two major prehistoric roads (Gabriel 1991, 275; Flint and Flint 1989, 23–25).

The ruin figures extensively in Navajo folklore (Van Valkenburgh 1974). Members of the Salt Clan say that Anasazi moved from here to Pueblo Bonito in Chaco Canyon (McPherson 1992, 88).

The earliest record of the ruin is on the Miera y Pacheco map of the Dominguez-Escalante expedition of 1776–77, though it is not likely that they visited it. It was visited by Captain John S. Newberry (for whom Newberry Mesa in Arizona was named) in August 1859.

The first scientific investigations and detailed descriptions of the site were in 1878, by anthropologist Lewis Morgan. He recorded rooms with ceilings intact, but noted that as much as 25 percent of the stones had been carried away by recent settlers for construction purposes. The American Museum of Natural History conducted excavations in the latter 1910s, under Earl Morris—who later became the first custodian of the newly established national monument in 1923 (on land donated by the American Museum of Natural History). Later additions brought the site to 27 acres containing six major ruins and seven or eight smaller ones (Lister and Lister 1983, 79–84).

BARBER PEAK: [DB (map 4)] (5600 ft) San Juan County, NM. Navajo: Tsé Naajin, "Black Downward Rock" (Kelley p.c. 1994). Sandstone butte in the San Juan Basin adjacent to the east side of U.S. Highway 666 (directly opposite the much larger Table Mesa) 13 miles south of the town of Shiprock.

BEAUTIFUL MOUNTAIN: [DB] (9400 ft) San Juan County, NM. Navajo: Dziłk'i Hózhónii, "Mountain Beautiful on Top" (Young and Morgan 1987, 360). This large, isolated mountain spur runs northeast from the Tunicha Range on the Arizona state line 24 miles southwest of Shiprock. McComb's map of 1860 shows this mountain as Mesa Cayatano, and it appears as Corona de Geganta on a U.S. Geological Survey map of 1882. The peak of this mountain, reached by only two horse trails, is sacred to the Navajos. This region was most likely the Navajo stronghold referred to as "Casafuerte" ("Fortification")

in Spanish documents as early as 1673 (McNitt 1972, 8).

Governor Antonio Perez visited the region in 1836, and Colonel Edward E. B. Newby followed with 150 men of the 3rd Missouri Mounted Volunteers and 50 Illinois Infantry in May 1848 (McNitt 1972, 128). This latter incursion led to a treaty signed by Navajo headmen Jose Largo, Narbona, Zarcillos Largos, and five others. A year later, Colonel Washington's expedition camped in this vicinity, his jittery men shooting at one another in the dark. White expeditions attacked the region in 1858 (led by Lieutenant Cogswell under Colonel Dixon Stansbury Miles), in May 1859 (Major John Smith Simonson) and in October 1859 (Major Oliver L. Shepherd). A civilian militia expedition marched on the vicinity in 1861 (McNitt 1972, 146, 347, 351–53, 376).

Beautiful Mountain was the home of Navajo medicine man Hostiin Bizhóshí. In September 1913, Bizhóshí's son, ("Little Singer") was sought by Shiprock Navajo Agent W. T. Shelton for bigamy. Although Hataałii Yázhí was not captured, his three wives were taken into custody at Shiprock. Hastiin Bizhóshí and Hataałii Yázhí and nine other men rode into Shiprock and freed the women by force—and then went into hiding.

Shelton, who had been in Durango during this incident, announced upon his return his intention to make examples of these Navajos. Warrants were issued charging 13 men with everything from horse-theft to deadly assault. Hastiin Bizhóshí announced he would not surrender without a fight. Despite the negotiations by Fr. Anselm Weber, Chee Dodge, and the Fort Defiance Agency superintendent, Shelton seethed as the "renegades" camped for three months on Beautiful Mountain, visiting Frank Noel's Sanostee Trading Post almost daily.

On November 18, Troops A, B, C, and D of the U.S. 12th Cavalry (261 men with 300 rounds per man, 256 horses, 40 mules, and a "jackass battery" of Gatling guns) were dispatched from Fort Robinson, Nebraska, to Gallup. General Hugh L. Scott, ordering Shelton to stay away, arrived at Sanostee Trading Post on November 27 (Thanksgiving Day). He conferred with Bizhóshí and his men, who agreed to surrender, thus bringing to an end what appears to be the last use of U.S. Army troops against American Indians.

In Gallup, nearly all charges were dropped. Bizhóshí and two of his sons were sentenced to 10 days in jail; Hataałii Yázhí and another man were sentenced to 39 days. All sentences were served in the McKinley County Jail in Gallup (McNitt 1962, 347–58).

In Navajo mythology, this mountain is the feet of Goods of Value Mountain, a male anthropomorphic figure, the head of which is Chuska Peak, the body the Chuska Mountains, and the feet the Carrizo Mountains. Shiprock is a medicine pouch or bow that he carries (McPherson 1992, 21). (This figure is countered by a female figure known as Pollen Mountain, comprised of Navajo Mountain, Black Mesa, and other features.)

BECENTI: (6800 ft) McKinley County, NM. Navajo: Tł'óo'di Tsin, "Outside Post" (possibly referring to a boundary marker), or Jádí Hádít'ijíh, "Antelope Lookout" (Kelley p.c. 1994; Young p.c. 1995). This community eight miles north of Crownpoint, on New Mexico Highway 371, is little more than a chapter house. Becenti, now a common Navajo surname, was one of the most important Navajos of the Crownpoint area, a progressive who cooperated with the U.S. government all his life. He was the son of Becenti Sani, who met with other Navajo chiefs and U.S. officials at Fort Wingate in 1868 to draw up the boundaries of the new Navajo Reservation (Correll and Watson 1974, 151).

Becenti Springs Trading Post (late 1870s to near 1920) (Kelley 1977, 251, 254) may have been in the vicinity of this community.

BECLABITO: [DB] (5802 ft) San Juan County, NM. Navajo: Bitł'ááh Bit'o, "Spring Underneath" (Young and Morgan 1987, 251), though Gregory (1915, 149), working for the U.S. Geological Survey, listed the translation as "Spring Under a Rock." Also Biklabito. This day school, chapter, and trading-post community is located on the rolling and rocky northeastern slopes of the Carrizo Mountains of extreme northwestern

New Mexico, on U.S. Highway 504, 10 miles east of the Arizona state line. (Van Valkenburgh mistakenly places the location in northeastern Arizona.)

This was one of the five regions explored for uranium in the late 1970s (Iverson 1981, 186). (See also Shiprock, Red Rock, Sanostee, Two Grey Hills.)

BECLABITO TRADING POST: (5802 ft) San Juan County, NM. Navajo: Uncertain, probably the same as the community. Billy Hunter founded this post in 1911, constructing it from wood washed down the San Juan River in flood season. (This may or may not be the same Hunter who built Bisti Trading Post in the early 1900s.) Hunter sold Beclabito to a freighter named Biffle Morris, who in 1924 sold it to Hugh Foutz. Russell Foutz purchased the post in 1953 (McNitt 1962, 302, 304).

BEE BURROW RUIN: (6400 ft) McKinley County, NM. Navajo: Uncertain, but the region is generally referred to as Tsé 'Achíjh, "Nose Rock." A Chacoan great-house community approximately 10 miles south of Chaco Canyon, on Seven Lakes Road. It is situated on the Chacoan South Road, and dates to A.D. 1050–1200, with 11 ground-floor rectangular rooms, and round rooms, and portions that were possibly two stories high.

BENNETT PEAK: [DB] (6471 ft) San Juan County, NM. Navajo: Tsézhin 'Íí'áhí, "Traprock Sticking Up" (Van Valkenburgh 1941, 9) and Tsé Naajiin, "Black Rock Coming Down" (Young and Morgan 1987, 826). This volcanic plug stands immediately west of U.S. Highway 666, 65 miles north of Gallup, across from Ford Butte. It was named for Frank Tracey Bennet, Navajo Indian agent at Fort Wingate 1869–71. Table Mesa Oil Lease (3,200 acres leased by Santa Fe Co.) lay 30 miles to the north in the 1940s.

In 1838, Mexican Capitan Lujan attacked a Navajo rancheria in the Bennett Peak/Ford Butte vicinity, killing three adults and capturing six children (Ward, Abbink, and Stein 1977, 218). The peak was first described by Lieutenant

J. H. Simpson of the Washington Expedition of 1849. The locale was also referred to as "Ojos Calientes," and was home to Navajo headman Armijo's village from 1841 to 1861 (McNitt 1972, 86n, 179, 249). Narbona habitually stationed watchers atop the peak to warn the Navajo rancherias of approaching enemies by smoke signal or signal fires (Newcomb 1964, 17).

Sometime between 1912 and 1936, Arthur Newcomb (of Newcomb Trading Post) unearthed a grave he described as "non-Indian" at the foot of this rock. The skeleton wore copper spurs. Newcomb presumed it to be that of a Spanish explorer (Newcomb 1964, 154).

BERNALILLO: (5100 ft) (Population: 5,968) Sandoval County, NM. Navajo: Kin Noodǫ́ǫ́z, "Striped Houses." Located on Rio Grande, 14 miles north of Albuquerque by U.S. Highway 85. This community was founded after the Spanish Reconquest of 1692. Don Diego de Vargas, hero of the Reconquest, died here in 1704. It is the home of Coronado State Park (Tiwa pueblo of Kuaua, dating to A.D. 1300). The monument was established in 1935 (New Mexico Office of Cultural Affairs 1991, 19).

BIBO: (6400 ft) Cibola County, NM. Navajo: Uncertain. Tiny community south of Cebolleta on New Mexico Highway 279. Trading post founded prior to 1880 to serve Navajo and Laguna Indians, lasting about a decade.

BIG BEAD MESA: (approx. 8000 ft) Sandoval County, NM. Also Cerro Calisto. Navajo: Yoo'tsoh, "Big Bead." Located on the northeast slope of the San Mateo Mountains, this mesa is named after Yoo'tsoh–Big Bead, a rounded peak standing away from the main range to the east (Van Valkenburgh 1941, 70). It contains numerous Navajo ruins, including defensive sites with coursed-stone masonry. One even incorporates a masonry breastwork built across a narrow, sheer ridge joining two sections of the mesa. Behind this breastwork are the remains of some 50 hogans. Archaeological investigation of this site was started in 1939 by Columbia University.

Big Bead was a stopping point in the wandering of the early Navajo clans, as told in the Yoo'

Hataal (Bead Chant). Many other Navajo names of ceremonial importance are found in this region not far east of their present habitat (Van Valkenburgh 1941, 70). It was also the home of Navajo headman El Pinto, who was raided by Apaches in the fall of 1783, in reprisal for an earlier Navajo raid on the Apaches. El Pinto pursued the raiders and was mortally wounded (McNitt 1972, 35).

BIG ROCK HILL: (7020 ft) McKinley County, NM. Navajo: Tsé Teelí, "Wide Rock" (Kelley p.c. 1994). This westerly peninsula of the massive upland comprising Mesa de los Lobos is some five miles northeast of Twin Lakes, a mile or so south of Sheep Spring Hill.

BIG WATER: (6400 ft) Rio Arriba County, NM. Navajo: Tótsoh, "Big Water." A spring located in lower La Jara Canyon some 10 miles southeast of its confluence with the San Juan River. The locale is tied to the traditions of the Navajo Tótsohnii (Big Water People) Clan (Van Valkenburgh 1974, 151).

BISTI (BADLANDS): [DB] (5750 ft) San Juan County, NM. Navajo: Bistahí, "Among the Adobe Formations" (Young and Morgan 1987, 245). An ancient lake bed, now broken badlands and low hills some 30 miles south of Farmington, on New Mexico Highway 371 where it crosses Hunter Wash. See also Bisti Trading Post. ("Bisti" is pronounced bis-tie, and sounds much like the Navajo Bistahi.)

BISTI TRADING POST: (5750 ft) San Juan County, NM. Navajo: Same as the badlands (above). Bistahí, "Among the Adobe Formations." This isolated post in the Bisti Badlands region of the San Juan Basin east of Chaco Canyon was founded in the early 1900s by a man named Hunter. It is possible that this Hunter is Billy Hunter, who established Beclabito Trading Post in 1911 (McNitt 1962, 304n).

BITANI TSOSI WASH: [DB] (7200–6300 ft) San Juan, Sandoval, and Rio Arriba counties, NM. Also Betonnie Tsosie. Navajo: K'aí' Naashchii' Bikooh, "Wending Red Willow

Wash" (Young and Morgan 1987, 501). This twenty-mile-long wash heads in badlands just south of New Mexico Highway 44, a couple of miles southwest of Lybrook, and flows southwest, merging with Escavada Wash some two miles upstream (east) of the mouth of Kimbeto Wash.

Shown as Eduardo Wash on the U.S. Geographical Survey map of 1884, the name Bitani Tsosi is after a wealthy Navajo, Bit'ahniits'ósí ("Slim Bitani"; etymology of Bitani unkown) (Van Valkenburgh 1941, 9). The area is rich in paleontological remains.

BLACK ROCK: (6500 ft) (Population: 958), McKinley County, NM. Navajo: Tséhįįh Deezlį́, "Into the Black Rock it Starts to Flow" (Young and Morgan 1987, 732), and Tsézhiní, "Black Rock" (Van Valkenburgh 1941, 12). Five miles west of the junction of New Mexico Highways 602 and 53. Site of the Indian Health Service Zuni Medical Facility and housing. The first dam on the Zuni Reservation was built at this location in 1904–8, and led to the founding of the village of Tekapo (Ferguson and Hart 1985, 101).

BLANCO: [DB] (5600 ft) San Juan County, NM. Navajo: Taahóóteel, "A Broad Strip of Land (Valley) Extends to the River." A Spanish-American farming village scattered along the north bank of the upper San Juan River at its confluence with Largo Canyon, some 11 miles east of Bloomfield, on U.S. Highway 64. A school and Franciscan mission operated here in the 1940s, and Van Valkenburgh (1941, 12) lists the Blanco Trading Co. as the main mercantile at that time.

U.S. Army Captain J. F. McComb listed this site as Station 44 in his survey of 1859. Major John Simonson also passed here in the same year.

The mouth of the Largo forms a large fan-shaped muddy delta nearly half a mile wide. The Navajos call this Tsííd Bii' Tó, "Spring in the Coals" (Young and Morgan 1987, 740) or Taahóóteel. According to Navajo traditions, this region of broad alluvial flats sloping upward to cobbled river terraces was one of the places where the early clans lived for some years, and

where they learned agriculture and the manufacture of pottery from incoming Puebloan clans. This is a part of the Dinétah—the "homeland," or old habitat of the Navajos—and many Anasazi and Navajo sites are found in the vicinity. Across the river and to the south stands Dził Ntsaa, "Big Mountain," one of the sacred mountains of the Navajos.

BLANCO CANYON (and BLANCO WASH): [DB] (6400–5700 ft) San Juan County, NM. Navajo: T'iistah Diiteelí, "Spread Among the Cottonwoods" (upper canyon) (Young and Morgan 1987, 723); Tó Diłhił Bikooh, "Dark Water" (lower part of canyon); also Tsííd Bii' Tó, "Coal Spring Canyon," and Tsébáálígai, "White Rock-Edge." A wide, sandy canyon (with patches of cottonwood) running some 40 miles south to north between Lybrooks (on New Mexico Highway 55), and Blanco (on New Mexico Highway 64). Heads at 7200 ft on the south edge of Crow Mesa, near Lybrooks, and flows into Largo Canyon from the south at Salt Point, about eight miles upstream from the confluence of Rio Largo and the San Juan River. Blanco Wash exceeds the length of the canyon, which is bounded abruptly on the east by Cibola Mesa and on the west by gently rising plains.

This region is an important Navajo agricultural area, with water in seepages and shallow wells. Some White ranchers also live in the canyon, as this is "checkerboard" land.

In 1941, Van Valkenburgh noted a somewhat isolated group of Navajos living along the lower courses of the Blanco, having entered the region in the late 1800s from the vicinity of present-day Carson's Store. The headman of those Navajos living in the upper reaches of the canyon was named Comanche. These people were linked with the people in the Counselor region.

Archaeologists have identified Navajo "constellation" glyphs in this canyon (Williamson 1987, 173), giving rise to theories of ancient Navajo archaeoastronomy.

BLANCO TRADING POST: (5600 ft) San Juan County, NM. Navajo: Uncertain, likely the same as the community. Founded about 1920, by Wilfred "Tabby" Brimhall and Jim Brimhall

(McNitt 1962, 303). The trading post is still in operation, located at the junction of New Mexico Highways 44 and 57, the northern entry to Chaco Canyon National Historical Cultural Park. New subsidized housing is plentiful, and the community is home to a major Indian Health Service facility and a modern school.

BLOOMFIELD: [DB] (5500 ft) (Population: 5214) San Juan County, NM. Navajo: 'Ahihodiiteel, "Where Two Wide Valleys Come Together." Also 'Anabi'ání or Naabi'ání, "Enemy's Cave" (Young and Morgan 1987, 573). A small community on the north bank of the upper San Juan River, eight miles south of Aztec on New Mexico Highway 44, at that road's junction with New Mexico Highway 64. (These highways were previously New Mexico Highways 55 and 17, respectively.) Oil and gas wells abound in the badlands some 10 miles to the south, in the vicinity of Kutz Wash. In 1941, a trading post here was operated by R. L. Tanner.

At one time, the Office of Indian Affairs considered the feasibility of purchasing some of the fertile river lands in this vicinity for Navajo Indian use.

Early on, Bloomfield was a wild cow town, home of the Stockton Gang, led by Port Stockton (a cattle rustler and stagecoach robber). It was originally settled in 1881 by William B. Haines, an Englishman (WPA 1940b, 364).

BLUE MESA: (5900 ft) San Juan County, NM. Navajo: Uncertain. This name refers to the mesa behind Newcomb Trading Post, and in fact the post was sometimes called Blue Mesa Trading Post (Newcomb 1966).

BLUEWATER: [DB] (6550 ft) Cibola County, NM. Also Agua Azul (Spanish). Navajo: T'iis Ntsaa Ch'ééłí, "Large Cottonwood Tree Where the Water Flows Out." This small White farming community sits in a basin sloping eastward from the Zuni Mountains on I-40 and the Santa Fe Railroad, 11 miles northwest of Grants. Some Navajo trading was done here in the early days.

Agua Azul was stipulated as the southeastern boundary of the Navajos in the Navajo-Spanish Treaty of 1819. In May 1863, Navajos killed two

shepherds here. Bluewater Lake, which irrigates the valley here, is located in the foothills of the Zuni Mountains some 10 miles southwest of Bluewater. Sportsmen come long distances to fish in this artificial lake.

The first dam in Bluewater Canyon (also called Bluewater Creek) was built in 1894, on the Lotta Ranch by the Bluewater Land and Cattle Company. It was washed out in 1904. In 1912, more Mormons (refugees from the Madera Revolution in Mexico) arrived. Bluewater Toltec Irrigation District was organized in 1925. A new dam was built seven miles upstream from the old one (Noe 1992, 10–11). Zunis killed some Navajos here in 1844 and again in 1861 (Ferguson and Hart 1985, 60–61).

BORREGO PASS TRADING POST: (7000 ft) McKinley County, NM. Navajo: Dibé Yázhí Habitiin, "Ascending Lamb Trail" (Austin and Lynch 1983, 36; Young p.c. 1995). This trading post and community is located on Navajo Route 48 some 15 miles southeast of Crownpoint. The post was opened in the early 1930s by Don and Fern Smouse, and has been operated since 1990 by Merle and Rosella Moore (Guterson 1994, 76–77).

BOX S RANCH: [DB] (7000 ft) McKinley County, NM. Navajo: Kin Na'ní'á, "Bridged House" (Young and Morgan 1987, 494), referring to an Anasazi ruin built across the canyon from the ranch. This now-abandoned ranch was located about three miles southeast of Nutria.

The ranch, with nearly 10,000 head of cattle, was established in the 1870s by a group of Army officers from Fort Wingate. They operated under the name of "Box S Land and Cattle Company." After the establishment of various public reserves in the region, the company broke up. By the 1940s, only the walls of the old ranch remained. Captain Clark M. Carr ran the ranch for many years.

Rustlers killed four Zunis here in 1889 (Ferguson and Hart 1985, 61).

BOWL CANYON CREEK: (9000–7200 ft) McKinley County, NM. Navajo: 'Ásaayi', "In the Bowl" (Kelley p.c. 1994). This 11-mile-long stream heads in the Chuska Mountains south of Narbona Pass and flows southwest into Tohildonin (Tó Dildǫ'í) Park.

BREAD SPRINGS: (7100 ft) McKinley County, NM. Navajo: Bááh Háálí, "Bread Flows Up and Out" (Young and Morgan 1987, 148). This chapter house and school community is located on the west slope of the Zuni Mountains, at the end of Navajo Route 74, 11 miles south of Gallup, three miles east of New Mexico Highway 602.

Navajos claim to have been grazing stock in this region as early as 1866 (U.S. Indian Claims Commission n.d., vol. IV, 712–15).

BRIMHALL TRADING POST: (6100 ft) McKinley County, NM. Also Brimhall, Brimhall Wash Trading Post. Navajo: Mą'ii Tééh Yítłizhí, "Coyote Fell into Deep Water" (Young p.c. 1995). Located on Navajo Route 9, 10 miles east of U.S. Highway 666, this post was founded by Alma James Brimhall, who earlier had settled in Fruitland. He was also the father of Wilfred "Tabby" Brimhall and Jim Brimhall, who ran both Blanco and Nageezi trading posts. The post was near the Togay Trail, an early wagon road between Gallup/Fort Wingate and Farmington, and was operated by a man named Walker in the 1920s (Kelley 1985, 26–27).

BURNED DEATH WASH: (6890–6400 ft) McKinley County, NM. Navajo: 'Azéé' Díílid, "Burned Death." A drainage of Defiance Draw between Yah Ta Hey and Tse Bonito. Heads on the southeast slope of the Chuska Mountains some seven miles northwest of Yah Ta Hey, flowing east, south, and southwest.

BURNED WATER CANYON: (7529–6430 ft) McKinley County, NM. Navajo: Tó Díílid, "Burned Water." A tributary of Standing Rock Wash north of Mesa de los Lobos. Lies between Edge Canyon and Narrow Canyon, and intersects with Dog Spring and Running Edge Canyons to form Standing Rock Wash.

BURNHAM: [DB] (5450 ft) San Juan County, NM. Navajo: T'iistsoh Sikaad Tséta', "Big Cottonwood Tree Sitting Between the Two Walls of the Canyon." This tiny chapter community (Burnham's Trading Post and Chapter House) is located in the barren, treeless country of Brimhall Wash, 12 miles east of U.S. Highway 666 on Navajo Route 9. A USIS day school was operated here in the 1940s. Surface coal deposits are in close proximity.

BURNHAM'S TRADING POST: (5450 ft) San Juan County, NM. Navajo: Uncertain, probably the same as the community. Founded about 1927 by Roy Burnham at T'iistsoh Sikaad, "Big Cottonwood Tree Sits" (Young p.c. 1995). This location was about 12 miles east of U.S. Highway 666 on Navajo Route 5.

CABEZON: [DB] (6070 ft) Sandoval County, NM. Navajo: Gaawasóón, the Navajo pronunciation of the Spanish Cabezon, which means "Big-Headed." This abandoned Hispanic farming village was located on the north bank of the Rio Puerco of the East, about four miles north of Cabezon Peak. It is 14 miles south of Torreon, and was a trading center (Dick Heller's Trading Post) from the 1880s to nearly 1950 (Kelley 1977, 251, 255) for the Hoolk'idnii Dine'é (the Rolling Hill Navajos) (Young p.c. 1995) of the Torreon region.

The Cabezon region was once held by the Navajos, and a few families still have their allotments 10 miles north of the village. Old Torreon Navajos state that a few miles south of Cabezon a large rock monument was placed by the Spaniards to mark the tribe's eastern boundary. However, this was destroyed many years ago by New Mexican sheepherders. The region around Cabezon is filled with many old Navajo sacred places and sites, such as Yoo'tsoh ("Big Bead"), Na'azísí ("Gopher"), Mesa Prieta (10 miles south of Cabezon), and Hosh Yishkhíízh, ("Spotted Cactus"; a small mesa just south of Cabezon).

The Hispanic village was known as "La Posita" in the early days when it was a post station on the overland route from the Gallup region via Mount Taylor and Chico Arroyo to Santa Fe. Predating this village, however, the Miera y Pacheco map of 1779 shows two settlements. Porteria sat on the west bank of the Rio Puerco of the East, and El Cabezon de los Montoias was across the river, at the foot of Cabezon Peak. Miera y Pacheco designated both by symbols meaning "Arruinadas por los Enemigos" ("Ruined by the Enemies"), suggesting they were abandoned by 1779 (Adams and Chavez 1956, 2–3, 218). Brugge (p.c. 1996) believes the abandonment came during the Navajo-Spanish war of 1774–75.

CABEZON PEAK: [DB] (7785 ft) Sandoval County, NM. Also El Cabezon, Cerro Cabezon. Navajo: Tsé Naajiin, "Black Rock Coming Down" (Van Valkenburgh 1941, 15). (The same name is applied to Bennett Peak.) A dome-shaped volcanic plug located in the rolling country east of Mount Taylor in the Rio Puerco valley, midway between Mesa Prieta on the south and Mesa San Luis on the north, and two miles south of New Mexico Highway 239 and 11 miles west of New Mexico Highway 44. The abandoned Hispanic villages of Cabezon and Dominguez lay a few miles to the north. Navajos also refer to the peak as "Dropped Out Mountain," where Big Snake lived in the Navajo Rounded Man Red Antway myth (Wyman 1965). Etymologically, it is interesting to note that Navajo legend identifies the peak as the head of the giant Yé'iitsoh (Matthews 1897, 234), and the Spanish "Cabezon" means "large head".

Cabezon and other volcanic plugs in the area are extensions of the northern lava flow of Mount Taylor, the highest peak of the San Mateo (or Cebolleta) Mountains. This feature, visible for many miles, is a Navajo landmark of ceremonial importance. It is associated with the Navajo traditional story of the killing of Yé'iitsoh, the Chief of the Enemy Gods in the Yé'iitsoh Hatáál, the Enemy Chant. The blood of Yé'iitsoh is said to have run from Mount Taylor northward (the lava flow shown on most maps as the Cebolleta Mountains). (See also San Rafael and Anzac.)

Between the peak and the abandoned village of Cabezon is a tsé ninájihí, a rock pile shrine of the Navajos, along with a sacred walled spring in which the Navajos made offerings when on the trail to Jemez and Zia Pueblos. Navajos were living in this vicinity as early as 1800, but their numbers began to dwindle in 1816 (McNitt, 1972, 36, 47).

CACHE MOUNTAIN: Location uncertain. Sandoval County, NM. Navajo: Yisdá Dziil, "Refuge Mountain." Located in the vicinity of La Ventana, near Jemez.

CAMES CANYON: [DB] (6600–6300 ft) San Juan County, NM. Also Kaimes Canyon, Ice Canyon. Navajo: Uncertain. This short, rugged canyon rises in the Carson National Forest and is tributary to Largo Canyon, 10 miles north of Trubey's Store (about 24 miles upstream from Blanco Canyon). The canyon is named for a rancher who lived there. The mesas beyond the canyon abound in old ruins, presumably of an early Navajo phase. Navajo tradition holds that Navajos from the Chaco and Torreon areas took refuge in this region during the Carson "roundup" of 1863–64.

CAÑONCITO: [DB] (6200–5250 ft) (Population: 1,189) Cibola and Bernalillo counties, NM. Navajo: Tó Hajiileehé, "Where Water is Drawn Up Out" (Young p.c. 1995). An island of Navajo Indian Reservation in rolling country west of the Rio Puerco of the East, 28 miles east of Albuquerque and four miles north of I-40.

A small band of Navajos lives here on allotted land, separated by as much as 75 miles from the main body of the tribe, who call this isolated group the Diné 'Ana'í (Enemy Navajos). The Diné 'Ana'í lived in the Cebolleta and Mount Taylor country under headman Sandoval as early as 1858, having remained there when the main tribe pushed westward to Canyon de Chelly. Especially vulnerable to reprisal attacks by the Mexicans and Pueblos, they early allied themselves with these neighbors and acted as spies and guides against the larger body of Navajos. Later, in order to benefit from the proximity of the Mexicans when the rest of the Navajos began to retaliate, they moved to Cañoncito for protection.

According to Van Valkenburgh (1974, 184–85), however, some informants believe that Cañoncito Navajos are descendants of Navajos who escaped the Long Walk to Fort Sumner, while still others consider them a band who stopped there on the way back from the Bosque Redondo in 1868. Jenkins and Minge (1974) note that a pair of Navajos in 1869, and 17 others between 1870 and 1881, wandered into the rugged Cañoncito region west of the Laguna Paguate tract, settled, and later homesteaded (under the Indian Homestead Act of July 4, 1884) lands over which the Lagunas had grazed for many years.

There are no cultural differences between the Cañoncito Navajos and the main body of Navajos, though the "western" Navajos say their witches come from the Cañoncito people.

CANTONMENT BURGWIN: (approx. 6900 ft) Taos County, NM. Also referred to as Fort Fernando de Taos, though the post was never designated a "fort" (Frazer 1972, 96). Navajo: Uncertain, though possibly indistinguishable from the community of Taos. This military post was established on August 14, 1852, to provide protection against Ute and Apache incursions. It was abandoned in 1860. It was named for Captain John H. K. Burgwin, killed in the battle for Taos in 1847 (in which New Mexico Governor Bent was killed by Mexican and Indian insurgents). Expeditions were mounted against the Navajos from Burgwin in 1858 (led by Captain H. B. Schroeder) and 1859 (led by Captain Thomas Dunan) (Murphy 1973, 5–26). The reconstructed facility is now the Fort Burgwin Research Center (Frazer 1972, 96).

CAPTAIN TOM WASH: (9000–5450 ft) San Juan County, NM. Navajo: Tó Ntsaa Bito', "Big Water's Spring" (referring to someone named Tó Ntsaa) (Young p.c. 1995). Newcomb (1964, 66) translated this as "Much Water Creek." Heads in the Chuska Mountains, flowing northeast through Two Grey Hills and Newcomb. Tributary to Chaco Wash about eight miles east of U.S. Highway 666, three miles west of Burnham Trading Post. See Tunsta Wash for additional details.

CARSON TRADING POST: (6200 ft) San Juan County, NM. Also Carsons. Navajo: Hanáádlį́, "It Flows Back Out." Located 18 miles south of Bloomfield, off New Mexico Highway 44, near the head of Gallegos Canyon on the east fork of Gallegos Wash. Site of Huerfano Chapter House and Huerfano School. This post was es-

tablished around 1920 by O. J. Carson (McNitt 1962, 303).

Located some 10 miles outside the eastern boundary of the Navajo Reservation, the numerous Navajos of this vicinity occupy lands granted them in 1909 (and subsequent dates) under the Indian Allotment Act of 1897. As quarter-sections of land were granted to Navajos (generally clustered by family) to protect their traditional use areas from White settlers (mostly big stockmen and their employers), a "checkerboard" pattern occurred, alternating parcels of Navajo land with public domain lands, private White holdings, and state lands. (See Checkerboard Area.)

During the 1930s and 1940s, White stockmen would move large quantities of Colorado sheep to winter ranges in this area.

CASA DEL RIO RUIN: (5980 ft) McKinley County, NM. Navajo: T'iis 'Eejin Ch'íní'lí, "Outflow Where Cottonwoods Extend Away in a Black Line" (Young p.c. 1995), referring to the area in which the ruin lies. This Chacoan greathouse community is near the juncture of Kin Klizhin (Łizhin) Wash and the Chaco River, west of Chaco Canyon. This ruin is an extremely large, L-shaped kiva-less structure (Gabriel 1991, 258).

CASAFUERTE: The exact location of this obscure place is speculative. Navajo: None known. The name is Spanish for "stronghold," and crops up in numerous early Spanish documents. Locations suggested include the Cebolleta Mountains or Chaco Canyon in the east (Reeve 1956, 308–9) and Beautiful Mountain and the Red Rock Valley region to the west (McNitt 1972, 6–8). Historians lean toward Beautiful Mountain as the true Casafuerte option. References to the casafuerte usually were tied to speculation as to the strongest concentration of Navajo warriors, a place the Spanish wanted to avoid.

CASAMERO LAKE: (6700 ft) McKinley County, NM. Navajo: Toh'ko'ozhi (U.S. Indian Claims Commission n.d., vol. VI, xvii), possibly Tó K'óózhí or Tó Dík'óózhí, "Sour Water" (Young and Morgan 1987, 1017). Five miles east of Smith Lake (on New Mexico Highway 371), in the far-eastern end of "Lobo Valley," the valley that runs east-west, along the southern foot of Mesa de los Lobos. A chapter house is situated here.

CEBOLLETA: [DB] (6400 ft) Cibola County, NM. Also Seboyeta, though this spelling usually applies to the modern village four miles to the southeast. Navajo: Tł'ohchin, "Wild Onions," similar to the Spanish "Cebolleta," meaning "Little Onion." This old New Mexican farming village is located at the mouth of a scenic wooded canyon on the east slopes of the Cebolleta Mountains, 11 miles north of Laguna Pueblo at the end of New Mexico Highway 279.

Many old Navajo circular stone hogan foundations are found in the area, and Spanish Governor Cuervo named this vicinity as the eastern boundary of Navajo country in 1706 (McNitt 1972, 37).

In the latter part of the eighteenth century, Antonio el Pinto was known to have been the chief of the region's Diné 'Ana'í ("Enemy Navajos," so named because of their tendency to side with the Mexicans in attacks on the main body of Navajos to the west). The present-day village is on the site of a Franciscan mission that the Spaniards forced the Laguna Indians to build for the Navajos in 1749 (Worcester 1951, 110–11). The mission, probably made of perishable material, operated for a very few years. The Navajos would stay through the winter for the food and clothing, but to the frustration of the missionaries, they would exit the area as soon as summer came; they abandoned the mission altogether in 1750. Later that century, Cebolleta was a frontier outpost and garrison for the Spanish military forces in their operations against the Navajos.

Some thirty stockmen and their families from Albuquerque settled in the vicinity on January 31, 1800, and ran into immediate conflict with the Navajos. On August 3, 1804, a major force reportedly comprised of nine hundred to a thousand Navajos struck the village, causing the Spaniards to flee. However, they were forced to return by order of Governor Chacón (McNitt 1972, 37, 41). This attack led to Lieutenant Antonio Narbona's punitive expedition to Canyon de Chelly and Canyon del Muerto, during which more than one hundred Navajos were killed, including the slaughter at Massacre Cave (Benally et al. 1982, 91). The village was a slave-trade center during the Mexican and American periods (Bailey 1966, 108, 114, 127). American troops were garrisoned here off and on between 1846 and 1851 (McNitt 1972, 97, 157–58).

In 1863, Sandoval and his band of some 50 Diné 'Ana'í were the first contingent of Navajos to be interned on the Fort Sumner Reservation—despite their protests that they were Catholics and loyal to the American government.

The Spanish-Americans at Cebolleta have numerous traditions relating to the Navajo residence in their country and have blended these with their own folklore. Van Valkenburgh described a Catholic shrine (to La Virgen Nuestra Senora de Lourdes, Los Portales) of great beauty under a large rock shelter some three miles up Cebolleta Canyon. Springs seep from the wooded cove in which the shrine is located, and lush vegetation lines the brook that trickles down the canyon floor. The shrine was erected after the male population of the village was reduced to 15, and the remaining colonists journeyed one thousand miles to Chihuahua, Mexico, on foot, "with a request to be sent back to Spain" (WPA 1940b, 318). Brugge (p.c. 1996) notes that since these settlers were most likely New Mexicans who had never been anywhere near Spain, this request sounds fictional, or at best confused. In any event, they were sent back to Cebolleta. The shrine was a pledge of an annual feast to Our Lady of Lourdes as long as the village survived (WPA 1940b, 318).

Spanish land grants (to the Montaños family) were made in this region as early as November 23, 1753.

CEBOLLETITA: (6400 ft) Cibola County, NM. Also Bibo, for a trading family from Laguna and Acoma (McNitt 1972, 156n). Navajo: Uncertain. Three miles south of Cebolleta, three miles north of Paguate. This small community was originally populated by people from Cebolleta.

CEREZA CANYON: [DB, as Campañero Canyon] (7200–5400 ft) San Juan and Rio Arriba counties, NM. Also Carrizo Canyon, Campañero Canyon. Navajo: Uncertain. Deep, high-rimmed, 42-mile-long canyon cut by Arroyo Campenero, heading near the continental divide and New Mexico Highway 537, and running northwest through the Carson National Forest to join Largo Canyon about a mile upstream from the confluence of the latter with Blanco Canyon. A wild mesa/canyon country important in Navajo tradition as part of the Dinétah.

Van Valkenburgh (1941, 16–17) recounts a story by Navajo medicine men concerning the section of this canyon near Gobernador Knob:

Jiní, they tell.

A group of old paralyzed Navajos were inside a hogan when some Utes crawled up on top of the hogan. One fell in. One of the old Navajos caught him and cut his legs off right up to the knees. The other Utes got afraid and ran away.

CERRO BERRO: Exact location uncertain. Valencia County, NM. Navajo: K'aalógii Dził, "Butterfly Mountain"; also Dólii Dził, "Bluebird Mountain." The Spanish name means "Watercress Hill." Near Correo, this hill is associated with the Blessingway traditions and is a source of aragonite (Van Valkenburgh 1974).

CERRILLOS: (5700 ft) Santa Fe County, NM. Navajo: Dólii Dził, "Bluebird Mountain" (Kelley p.c. 1994; Young p.c. 1995). Located some 12 miles south of Santa Fe, in the Ortiz Mountains, this was the site of several important turquoise mines even in prehistoric times. Stones from here were traded as far away as the Valley of Mexico, as well as to the Navajos. A Spanish community (the name means "Little Hills") was founded a few miles south of the mines in 1879, but the earliest settlers were refugees from the Pueblo Revolt of 1680 (New Mexico Office of Cultural Affairs 1991, 22). Stories abound concerning Indians pressed into Spanish slavery at these mines, though recent research has labeled these stories myths (Goodman and Levine, 1990).

CHACO CANYON: [DB] (6100 ft) McKinley and San Juan counties, NM. Navajo: (highly conjectural) Tségai, "White Rock," Hispanicized as "Chaca." "Tségai" can mean "home" to many Navajos, particularly those who trace their ancestry to the Chaco region (Brugge 1986, 1). The Spanish name "Chaca" has been in use over 150 years (Lister and Lister 1983, 110). In ancient Navajo usage different parts of the canyon were known by distinctive names. (Van Valkenburgh 1941, 29). Additional discussion of possible origins of the name follows below.

Chaco is located 70 miles north of Thoreau, and 61 miles south of Aztec. Pearce (1965, 30–31) notes a community on New Mexico Highway 56 and on Chaco North Fork at Pueblo Bonito, with a post office operating from 1936 to 1942. Brugge (p.c. 1996) notes that this community consisted of a trading post, National Park Service personnel, and the surrounding Navajos. A Civilian Conservation Corps camp also operated here, housing at various times young men from the eastern states and Sioux Indians from the Dakotas.

During this period, it was also a campsite for the University of New Mexico Summer Field School, which excavated Pueblo Bonito and other sites. Approximately 21,000 acres in and around the canyon became a National Monument on March 11, 1907. This was expanded to include 33,989 acres on December 19, 1980, with the establishment of Chaco Culture National Historical Park in 1981.

The 12-mile-long "canyon" proper is generally broader than it is deep. Bounded on the south by Chacra Mesa (also called Chaco Mesa), South Mesa, and West Mesa, and on the north by North Mesa, topography rarely varies more than 400 ft from mesa to tops to canyon bottom, stair-stepped in increments of 50 to 100 ft. The canyon floor varies roughly from a quarter-mile (1,320 feet) to a half-mile (2,640 feet) in breadth. The canyon was first described in 1849 by Captain James Simpson.

The source or meaning of the name "Chaco" remains a mystery, despite a considerable body of study on the topic. The name appears on the Dominguez-Escalante Map of 1776, and is shown as a Navajo habitat. In 1796, Lieutenant Colonel Don Antonio Cordero identified Navajo "domiciles of which there are ten, namely Sevolleta, Chacoli, Guadalupe, Cerro-Cabezon, Agua

Salada, Cerro Chato, Chusca, Tunicha, Chelle and Carrizo" (Matson and Schroeder 1957, 356). At least two of these, "Chacoli" and "Cerro Chato," sound suspiciously like "Chaco," and in fact are seemingly equated with Chaco Canyon and Chacra Mesa by McNitt (1972, 36) as "one of four regions of contiguous Navajo occupation."

However, on the Miera y Pacheco map of 1779, Chacoli was actually the name of a minor tributary of the Jemez River (Adams and Chavez 1956, 3), and Vizcarra's journal records "El Chacolin" as a camp nine leagues from Jemez Pueblo and two leagues from the Rio Puerco of the East (Brugge 1964, 227). Cerro Chato was the name of a hill near the Rio Puerco of the East, just south of Salado Creek, about a half mile west of the east boundary of the Cebolleta Grant (Brugge p.c. 1996).

In 1804–5, Lieutenant Vicente Lopez "defeated the foe at Chacra," which, according to McNitt (1972, 42), refers to either Chaco Canyon or Chacra Mesa. The meaning and origins of these words is not explained in the literature, although Pearce (1965, 30) suggests it is regional Spanish for "desert."

At any rate, the name seems ephemeral, as the literature next refers to the area as "Mesa Azul" (Spanish for "Blue Mesa") in an 1824 report by Colonel (Governor) Jose Antonio Vizcarra. He also calls the river through the canyon "La Agua de San Carlos" (McNitt 1972, 57). Apparently, however, the name Chaco was in vogue by the time the region was traversed by Colonel John M. Washington's force (comprised of two companies of the Second Artillery—complete with 12 mountain howitzers, four companies of the Third Infantry, and 197 militia) in 1849. The journal of Lieutenant James H. Simpson of this command provided the first written accounting of the assemblage of massive prehistoric ruins in the canyon (McNitt 1972, 137–41). Pearce (1965, 30–31) suggests that the name *may* derive from a Navajo phrase, "tséyaa chahałeeł Ńlíní," interpreted as "Stream in the Dark Under Rock" or "Darkness Under the Rock Stream" (Young p.c. 1995). Van Valkenburgh (1941, 29) suggests the possibility that the Spanish name Chaco has influenced the Navajo to use the term "tsékooh" for any lesser box canyon.

The main body of the canyon is about a half-mile wide and 10 miles long, and contains 18 major ruins and thousands of smaller units—all Anasazi in origin—the earliest dating back to about A.D. 800. During the next five centuries, the region became a focal point of religious and/or economic activity. The latter half of this period is marked by the intense building activity that resulted in the "Chacoan Great Houses" and "Chacoan Roads" (which may or may not have been roads), both characteristics that quickly spread throughout and beyond the Four Corners region. The term "Chaco Phenomenon" refers to an integrated system of cooperating towns and villages that produced and assembled goods for local consumption and for widespread distribution.

The canyon may have been a turquoise distribution center. Large quantities of finished items and raw turquoise have been found at Pueblo Alto and several small sites excavated by the Chaco Center, as well as in earlier excavations at Pueblo del Arroyo, Una Vida, Kin Kletso, Pueblo Bonito, and other sites (Frazier 1986, 182–84). However, the canyon was largely abandoned by A.D. 1275, with the next occupation being left to the Navajos, who appear to have arrived about A.D. 1720 (Brugge 1986, 13).

A Spanish force under Lieutenant Vicente Lopez attacked Navajos in the vicinity of the canyon in 1804, and Colonel (Governor) Jose Antonio Vizcarra visited the region in 1823 (McNitt 1972, 42, 57). On September 5 or 6, 1849 (shortly after Colonel Washington's incursion into the region), mail carrier Charles Malone and his guide were killed by Navajos at the canyon in retaliation for the death of Narbona at Washington's hands near today's Narbona Pass (formerly Washington Pass) (McNitt 1972, 148). The Navajos were excluded from the canyon in the 1855 Treaty of Laguna Negra, a treaty that inexplicably—but luckily for the Navajos—Congress never ratified.

The first substantive reports on Chaco Canyon were those of Lieutenant James H. Simpson, who recorded many of the larger ruins in 1849. The U.S. Geological and Geographical Survey surveyed the area in 1877. Research in Chaco Canyon began in 1888 with a visit by Charles

Lummis. Shortly thereafter, the first excavations were conducted by the Hyde Expedition for Explorations in the Southwest, under the guidance of Richard Wetherill, who homesteaded in the canyon in 1896. Since that time a number of expeditions have carried on the work of excavation, including the National Geographic Society (1921), the Smithsonian Institution (1929), the Museum of New Mexico and the School of American Research (1930s), the University of New Mexico Field Schools (1930s and 1940s) and the Chaco Center, a joint National Park Service–University of New Mexico research facility (1970s). Intensive stabilization began in 1933. A hundred thousand trees were planted along the Chaco River for erosion control. The Chaco Center surveyed 435 square miles, recording over two thousand sites and identifying roads, irrigation systems, etc.

A trading post at Pueblo Bonito was operated by Richard Wetherill until he was shot dead by a Navajo on June 22, 1910. In 1936, the traders were Colonel Springstead and his wife, who was a member of the Kirk trading family (Young p.c. 1995).

Lately astronomers and archaeologists have become increasingly interested in the possibility of archaeoastronomical observations by the Chacoans. The canyon is one of 12 U.S. sites on the international list of World Heritage Sites (New Mexico Office of Cultural Affairs 1991, 22).

The ruin names used by the Park Service are those found in early exploration records. According to McNitt (1966, 118–19), Rafael Carraval, a Jemez guide from San Ysidro with Washington's 1849 expedition, applied most of the names still used today. Below is a listing of some of the larger sites in the canyon.

✤ CASA CHIQUITA: (6200 ft) Navajo: Uncertain. The Spanish name translates to "Little House." This north bank site dates to A.D. 1100–1130, and its square configuration contains some 54 rectilinear rooms and two kivas. It sits north of the mouth of Cly Canyon, and can be reached only by hiking. Masonry is of the McElmo pattern. The ruin is roughly contemporaneous with the nearby, larger Kin Kletso (Navajo: Kin Łetso). This site was tested in 1927,

providing tree-ring samples, and some stabilization work took place in 1964. In 1849, Lieutenant Simpson recorded this site as No. 9.

✤ CASA RINCONADA: (6150 ft) Navajo: Kin Názbąs, "Circular House," descriptive term coined by the Navajos who live in the Chaco region and have worked for the excavators. The Spanish name translates to "Cornered House." This south bank Great Kiva site is a quarter mile south of Pueblo Bonito, and dates to the last half of the A.D. 1000s, though a remodeling phase took place sometime later, during which the Type III masonry was covered with a McElmo veneer and the floor of the kiva was raised (Flint and Flint 1987, 24). In addition to the single massive round room—traditionally identified as one of six great kivas in the canyon—there are at least five rectinilear rooms. However, the visitor trail from Monument Drive to the site passes several other small villages contemporary with it. The site has been subject to excavations in 1931–32, 1933, and 1955. This is the single largest kiva in the canyon.

The kiva exhibits a complicated series of posts and 28 wall niches. During the summer solstice sunrise, a sunbeam passes through an opening in the northeast wall and strikes a niche on the opposite wall, giving rise to theories of archaeoastronomy. However, the wall in the vicinity of the opening is a reconstruction and the opening is not necessarily the size and shape of the original (Malville and Putnam 1989, 35–36).

It is possible that another feature of the kiva is predictive, as the northeast wall opening also lights up another niche seven weeks prior to the summer solstice (Zeilik 1983, 39).

✤ CHETRO KETL: (6200 ft) Also Rain Pueblo, Chettro Kettl, Cheto Kette, Ketro Kete, Shining Pueblo. Navajo: Tsé Bidádi'ní'ání, "Scaled Rock" (Young p.c. 1995). The meaning and origin of the name Chettro Kettle is problematic.

Located one-quarter mile east of Pueblo Bonito on the north side of Chaco Canyon, this site dates from A.D. 1010–30 until sometime after A.D. 1105, partially predating Pueblo Bonito. The site has at least 337 rectilinear rooms and at least 21 kivas, with some roomblocks three or more stories high. Test excavations on the site's southeast corner took place in 1920–21, and the University of New Mexico Archaeology Field School excavated the ruin from 1929 to 1934. A room with murals was discovered in 1936. Repair and stabilization projects were undertaken in 1948, 1950, and 1964. Masonry Types II, III, and IV dominate between A.D. 1010 and 1059; Type III dominates between 1060 and 1109 (Flint and Flint 1987, 28). Approximately 17,000 beads were recovered from a single feature nicknamed "The Sanctuary" (due to numerous sealed niches). Another interesting feature of this site is the south wall of the north-central roomblock. Called "The Colonnade," this wall originally consisted of 13 or more masonry pillars joined by a low wall. At some later date, the spaces between the pillars were filled in with masonry, resulting in a solid wall.

The "modified D-shape" of the pueblo resulted in an enclosed plaza or courtyard, typical for this period. As with Pueblo Bonito, the rear wall of the pueblo is parallel to the cliff behind it.

Navajos consider Chettro Ketl as a home of some Diné deities (McPherson 1988, 83; Watson 1964, 19).

✦ FAJADA BUTTE: (6450 ft) Also Mesa Fahada, Mesa Fachada, Mesa Fajada. Navajo: Tsé Diyiní, or Tsé Diyilí, both of which mean "Holy Rock" (Brugge 1986, 5).

This 450-ft-high sandstone landmark between South Mesa and Chacra Mesa sits a mile and a half east of Fajada Wash, and an equal distance south of Chaco Wash. In the Navajo Windway, the hero becomes involved with Woman Who Dries People Up and is stranded on a rock that grows through the night, with both of them upon it, explaining the origin of Fajada Butte (Spencer 1957, 176–80).

It is one of the important stopping places in the story of the Male Shooting Chant of the Navajos. In addition, a feature called the "Sun Dagger" near its summit has recently become the focus of a study on prehistoric astronomy. Here, a pair of petroglyph spirals have been discovered on a cliff wall beneath three huge slabs of sandstone leaning against the cliff. A remarkable "dagger" of light is formed by the sun shining through

gaps between the naturally positioned sandstone slabs (Carlson 1983, 83). The entire dagger passes across the spirals at the equinox and summer and winter solstices, as well as at major and minor standstills of the moon (Malville and Putnam 1989, 30–33). It has also been surmised, however, that this is nothing more than a shrine no longer used (Zeilik 1983, 32), and that its equinox and solstice ties are purely coincidental.

Two additional sites with possible astronomical markings have been recorded on the east and west sides of the butte (Sofaer and Sinclair 1983, 44). Medicinal plants are collected here by nearby Navajos.

✦ GALLO CANYON. Also Gio Canyon. Navajo: Ńdíshchíí' Názt'i', "Circle of Pine Trees." This canyon (and arroyo by the same name) enters Chaco Canyon from the north midway between Una Vida and Wijiji Ruins. (Van Valkenburgh notes that the same name was once applied to a wash entering from the north across the canyon from Shabik'eschee Village.) Van Valkenburgh also states that, until a few years prior to 1941, there was a string of ponderosa pine trees in Gallo Canyon.

✦ HUNGO PAVI: (6200 ft) Also Hungopavie, Hopi meaning "Crooked Nose." Navajo: Tsin Łeeh Yí'áhí, "Burned Post" (Van Valkenburgh 1941, 32) or "Post Sticks into the Ground" (Young and Morgan 1987, 738). The name applies to Mocking Bird Canyon, which joins the Chaco Wash at this ruin. The name Hungo Pavi may also be a corruption or shift from the Hopi word Shonopavi. Located a mile and a half east of Chettro Kettle, this ruin sits on the north bank. It dates to A.D. 990–1080, and consisted of at least 143 rectinilear rooms and two kivas. This site has not been excavated. The D-shaped structure shows masonry in the Types II and III (from A.D. 960–1009) and Type IV (from 1060 until abandonment) (Flint and Flint 1987, 32). It appears that the walls of the first building period were partially destroyed and used as a foundation for the later building phase.

A stairway has been carved into the cliff face behind the ruin, leading to the mesa top.

✤ KIN BENYOLA: (6150 ft) Also Kin Benay-ola. Navajo: Kin Binááyołí, "House the Wind Blows Around." Also Kin Bii Naayoli, "Building in which the Wind Blows About" (Young and Morgan 1987, 494).

✤ KIN KLETSO: (6100 ft) Navajo: Kin Łitsooí, "Yellow House." On the north bank, about a mile and a half upstream (southeast) of the mouth of Cly Canyon, and midway between Casa Chiquita and Pueblo Bonito, this site dates to A.D. 1125–1130+. The solid rectangular block contains at least 134 rectilinear rooms and nine kivas, but no apparent plaza or courtyard. It may have risen to three stories on the north side. Excavations have taken place in 1896–99 (the Hyde Exploring Expedition), 1934 (School of American Research), and 1950–51 (National Park Service).

A "tower kiva" in the site was built atop a massive sandstone boulder, reminiscent of many sites in Hovenweep National Monument. The predominant masonry type is McElmo. This site was No. 8 in Lieutenant Simpson's 1850 report.

✤ KIN NASBAS: (6200 ft) Navajo: Kin Názbąs, "Circular House." An isolated great sanctuary a quarter-mile northeast of Una Vida, excavated for the School of American Research in 1935.

✤ KINTEEL: (6300 ft) Navajo: Kinteel, "Wide House." Home of The Gambler, Nááhwíiłbįįhí, known as "One Who Wins People (in Gambling Games)" (McPherson 1988, 87; Young p.c. 1995).

✤ LEYIT KIN: (6350 ft) Navajo: Łeeyi' Kin, "House in the Ground" (Young and Morgan 1987, 517). This ruin lies half a mile east of the old University of New Mexico Field School, which was one hundred yards south of Casa Rinconada. It is a small pueblo with 14 rooms and two kivas exposed, built between A.D. 1035 and 1041. As with Tseh So, this small and unspectacular ruin is important in reconstructing the earlier history of Chaco Canyon.

✤ PEÑASCO BLANCO: (6400 ft) Navajo: Táalakin, "Flat Topped House" (Young and Morgan 1987, 705). The Spanish name translates to "White Rock Crag, Pinnacle or Boulder" (Young

p.c. 1995). This ruin is located on a high point atop the far northwestern tip of West Mesa (on the south bank of Chaco Wash), nearly 10 miles downstream (northwest) of Pueblo Bonito. It dates circa A.D. 900 to circa 1125. The unique, nearly circular structure contains at least 234 rectinilear rooms and nine kivas, all in the north and western quadrants; the other half of the site consists of a row of single rooms encircling the plaza.

The site's excavation history includes early probings by Richard Wetherill in 1896–99 and National Park Service stabilization in 1971–72. It exhibits four separate construction periods, with Type I masonry dominating A.D. 910–959, Type IV from A.D. 1010 to 1059, Types III and IV and McElmo dominating from A.D. 1060 to 1109, and Type III and McElmo predominant from A.D. 1110 to 1159 (Flint and Flint 1987, 44).

Possible archaeoastronomical activity is seen at Penasco Blanco in a nearby pictograph with a handprint, sun, crescent moon, and star. It has been interpreted by some as a record of the Crab Nebula supernova of A.D. 1054, a date that coincides with the occupation of the ruin (Malville and Putnam 1989, 36–38). During the supernova, a star flared to five times greater than the brightest planet, and could be seen in daylight for 23 days. The handprint motif has been interpreted as marking sacred sites among pueblos (Frazier 1986, 201–2).

✤ PUEBLO ALTO: (6450 ft) (Not to be confused with Pueblo Alto Trading Post near Pueblo Pintado.) Navajo: Nááhwíłbiihí Bikin, "Gambler's House" (Wilson 1995, 44). The Spanish name translates to "High Town." This site sits atop the southern slope of North Mesa, approximately two and one-half miles north of Pueblo Bonito. It exhibits a "modified D-shape," with one long and two short roomblocks, and an outwardly curved wall (containing a few rooms) joining the ends of the short roomblocks. There were three construction periods at Alto, dating to A.D. 1010–59 (masonry Types II, III, and IV), 1060–1109 (McElmo facing), and 1110–1159 (McElmo and derivative styles) (Flint and Flint 1987, 48). The site contains at least 137 rectilinear rooms and eighteen kivas, and was tested in 1974 and 1976–79. It has been noted that two older rooms predate the earliest identifiable construction phase, and are perhaps unrelated to the final layout.

According to Van Valkenburgh, the commanding location of this ruin has generated a "great deal of tradition," being generally known as the "House of Nááhwíłbįįhí, the Great Gambler, who won everything—including people" (Young p.c. 1995). Noted turn-of-the-century photographer William Henry Jackson was told by a Navajo named Hosta that the ruin's size and location indicated it was "El Capitan" or "El Jugador" (Spanish for "The Supreme" or "The Player") (McNitt 1966, 121–22).

✤ PUEBLO BONITO: (6200 ft) Navajo: Tsé Bíyah' 'Anii'ahí, "Propped Rock," or, more literally, "Rock Under which Something Extends Supporting It" (Young and Morgan 1987, 729). This refers to a huge detached slab of the mesa cliff that loomed dangerously above the pueblo for centuries. The Anasazi worked to prevent its collapse with a supporting masonry wall. The slab finally gave way and smashed a portion of the ruin in 1941. The Spanish name translates to "Beautiful Town."

This is possibly the most famous ruin in the United States, and has been excavated more than any other Chacoan ruin. The massive site covers two and one-half acres on the north bank of Chaco Wash, about three and one-half miles upstream (southeast) of the mouth of Cly Canyon. This D-shaped pueblo is the "type" site for the Classic Bonito Phase (A.D. 1020–1120). It is often touted as the largest excavated prehistoric site in North America, and contained at least 482 rectilinear rooms and at least 40 or more kivas.

Judd (1964, 22) discovered several pithouses beneath the West Court and under Room 241. These dated to Basketmaker II and Pueblo I (A.D. 500–850). The later pueblo experienced three major building phases. Type I masonry dominated from A.D. 910 to 959; Types II, III, and IV from A.D. 1010 to 1059; and Types III and IV and McElmo were predominant from A.D. 1060 to 1109 (Flint and Flint 1987, 52). These phases were not solely expansionary. Rooms were re-modeled, foundations laid that were never used, walls were torn down. Kivas were built and then filled with soil and rubble; doors were added while others were reduced in size or sealed up. This site was extensively excavated by the Hyde Exploring Expedition of 1896–99; it saw excavations by the Phillips Academy in 1897; and the National Geographic Society excavated some 126 rooms in 1921–27.

Pueblo Bonito is another location of hypothesized archaeoastronomical activity. Corner openings in walls track the sun and could have been used to predict the summer solstice as well as confirm it. However, most archaeologists today believe these openings were in interior walls at the time of occupation. Thus, they were not likely astronomical features unless there were similar openings in the outer walls, which are now collapsed (Malville and Putnam 1989, 35). Zeilik (1983, 31) notes a similarity with the corner doorways of room 228.

Another interesting feature of Pueblo Bonito is its orientation. The pueblo is laid out within 15 minutes of true north, and within eight minutes of true east—very nearly a true north-south orientation (Malville and Putnam 1989, 35).

Members of the Navajo Salt Clan say Anasazi moved here from Aztec lands (McPherson 1988, 88). Navajos say they learned the Hail Ceremony (an autumn healing rite) from the ancients of Pueblo Bonito (Newcomb 1964, 102).

✤ PUEBLO DEL ARROYO: (6100 ft) Navajo: Tábąąkiní, "Shore House" (Young and Morgan 1987, 697). This south bank site is approximately a half mile west of Pueblo Bonito, on the north bank of the Chaco River. The southern walls are partially eroded by the river. Another D-shaped structure, this pueblo contains at least 301 rectilinear rooms and 26 kivas, constructed in two phases. Masonry types II, III, and IV and McElmo predominate from A.D. 1060 to 1109, and Type IV and McElmo are dominant from A.D. 1110 to 1159 (Flint and Flint 1987, 56). This site was first excavated in 1900 (Government Land Office), with subsequent digs in 1923–26 (National Geographic Society), 1950, and 1959 (National Park Service). The site's most unique feature, a circular "tri-walled" structure outside the later phase's linear west wall, was destroyed in prehistoric times. Similar features are seen at Aztec ruins, and atop Chacra Mesa south of the canyon. It is unknown whether they represent variants of kivas.

❖ SHABIK'ESCHEE VILLAGE: (6400 ft) Navajo: Tsé Bik'e'eschí, "Graven Rock." Also Shá Bik'e'eschí, "Sun is Engraved Upon It" (Young and Morgan 1987, 691), referring to a petroglyph on a large boulder in the vicinity. This Basketmaker III pithouse village lies atop the north cliff of Chacra Mesa, a mile and a half upstream (southeast) of Wijiji. It dates to A.D. 700–750, and probably underwent two separate occupations. Nine pithouses and the kiva were constructed during the first phase, while phase two consisted of nine or 10 pithouses and a "proto-kiva." The similar size of the two occupations led Frank H. H. Roberts (1929) to conclude that the original occupants may have left under duress and returned at a later date.

❖ THREATENING ROCK: (See Pueblo Bonito) Also called Leaning Rock. Navajo: Tsébíyah 'Anii'áhí, "Propped Rock." The Navajo name for Pueblo Bonito actually refers to this immense block of Cliffhouse sandstone (Van Valkenburgh says Mesa Verde sandstone), which towered 100 feet high, 150 feet across, and 30 feet thick above Pueblo Bonito. Its base rested on the unstable shale at the foot of the north cliff of the canyon, behind and slightly above the ruin. The slab leaned visibly outward from the cliff, and was tipping slowly, inexorably, farther away—an obvious threat to the pueblo. This led the Anasazi to construct a masonry retaining wall under the rock in the hope of preventing it from toppling. This worked for some eight hundred years.

Movement	Years Required
first foot	1,600
second foot	650
third foot	200
fourth foot	45
fifth foot	6.0
sixth foot	0.2
(from Early 1976, 10)	

On January 22, 1941, at about 10 A.M., the rock toppled, obliterating 23 ground-floor rooms (and the corresponding upper-floor rooms) of the back wall of Pueblo Bonito.

The Navajo name for this rock, in addition to referring to Pueblo Bonito, also referred to Chaco Canyon in general (Apache and Jim 1982, 69).

❖ TSEH SO: Navajo: Tsétsoh, "Big Rock." This ruin is partially excavated from a ruin-mound at the mouth of the first rincon east of the University of New Mexico Field School (near Casa Rinconada). The village had four kivas and twenty-four rooms in the upper structure, or Pueblo II phase, of the Anasazi. The beams from this section of the ruin were cut near A.D. 950. Below the superstructure, excavators found evidence that Tseh So had been built upon a mound of earlier structure. This earlier occupation has been identified as of the Pueblo I phase of the Anasazi.

❖ TSIN KLETSIN: (6600 ft) Also Tsin Łitsinih. Navajo: Tsin Łizhiní, "Black Wood Place" or "Charcoal Place." This ruin sits atop South Mesa, about seven miles south of Pueblo Bonito. The people who occupied it had a panoramic view in all directions. With at least 81 rectilinear rooms and five kivas, the site was constructed in a single phase, shortly after A.D. 1110. McElmo masonry style predominates (Flint and Flint 1987, 60). The National Park Service performed some stabilization work here in 1971 and 1981.

❖ UNA VIDA: (6200 ft) Navajo: Uncertain. Spanish translates to "One Life." Van Valkenburgh (1941, 33) thought this name possibly pertained to a "living stump of a tree," but Brugge discounts this. This north-bank ruin is closest to the Park Visitor Center, and sits about three miles upstream (southeast) of Pueblo Bonito. It contains at least 226 rectilinear rooms and eight kivas, constructed in four phases. Masonry Type I dominates in the first two phases (A.D. 860–909 and A.D. 910–959), Type III is predominant in the third phase (A.D. 1010–1059), and Type IV and McElmo dominate the fourth phase

(A.D. 1060–1109) (Flint and Flint 1987, 64). Excavations have been conducted here from the 1930s (University of New Mexico), through the 1960s (National Park Service) and 1979 (the Chaco Center).

✦ WIJIJI: (6400 ft) Navajo: Díwózhiishzhiin, "Black Greasewood" (Sarcobatus vermiculatus) (Young and Morgan 1987, 340). Also Kin Dootł'izhí, "Turquoise House" or "Blue House"; Díwózhiikin, "Greasewood House." This, the easternmost pueblo in Chaco Canyon, is on the north bank, approximately four and one-half miles upstream (southeast) of the mouth of Gallo Canyon. The site consists of at least 206 rectilinear rooms and two kivas, all built around A.D. 1110–15. Masonry Types III and IV predominate (Flint and Flint 1987, 68). Extensive stabilization work has been conducted by the National Park Service (1940, 1941, 1959, 1975, and 1978).

This ruin is important in Navajo mythology, and Van Valkenburgh (1941, 34–35) associated it with a legend concerning the origin of weaving:

Jiní. They tell. Once there was a Pueblo woman who was a Navajo slave. She lived at Turquoise House. While wandering about searching for food, she saw smoke coming out of the ground. Looking down into the hole from where the smoke was coming, she saw an old woman spinning. This was Spider Woman, and when she saw the woman's shadow cast over her, invited her to come down into her house. She saw that Spider Woman was weaving the first blanket. It was a full black blanket. On the next day, Spider Woman started another blanket. She made this one square and it was just as long as from her shoulder to the tip of her middle finger. This was called "Pretty Designed Blanket." On the third day Spider Woman wove another blanket with black figures on a white field. On the fourth morning the Pueblo woman returned to Spider Woman's home and asked for yellow, black and white cotton. Her loom was not like that of the Spider Woman, but like those used by the Navajo women of today. She made two blankets. Pueblo men watched her and then went home and copied.

After that, the Pueblo woman went back to the Spider Woman and learned how to make water jars, carrying-baskets and other woven things.

Then she returned to the Navajo camp and showed the Navajos how to weave these things.

Spider Woman told her always to leave a hole in the center of a blanket like in a spider's web, for if this was not done, it would bring the weaver bad luck.

All these things happened at Turquoise House in Chaco Canyon.

Wijiji also houses a feature of postulated archaeoastronomy. Behind the ruin, a staircase leads to a ledge on the canyon rim. A sunface is found on the cliff near the point where the winter solstice sun rises over a natural pillar of rock. Sunset some days sees the sun set in a natural cleft (Malville and Putnam 1989, 33).

Many other ruins are found in the park and still others exhibiting Chacoan characteristics have been recorded beyond the park's boundaries. These are collectively known as "Chacoan Outliers." A number of them are discussed separately in this volume.

Recent interpretations of the Chaco Phenomenon suggest a peak population in the canyon of about two thousand people (Frazier 1986, 185), a considerable reduction from the earliest estimates that Pueblo Bonito alone housed that many. Construction of the famous "Chaco Roads" probably began about A.D. 1050, and continued for roughly 65 years. The earliest appear to be those reaching southward toward Kin Ya'a (Kin Yaa'á). Northern extensions (toward Pierre's Ruin, Twin Angels, and Salmon) most likely were the latest to be built (Frazier 1986, 187). These are generally considered indicative of the Chaco people's connection to the distant Chacoan Outliers (Lekson et al. 1988, 8). The Chaco region figures in the Zuni migration narrative and is important to their Sword Swallower Society (Ferguson and Hart 1985, 126), as are Canyon de Chelly and Mesa Verde.

CHACO RIVER: (7000–5000 ft) McKinley County, NM. Also Chaco Wash. Navajo: Tséyaa Chahałheeł Ńlíní, "Flows Along in Darkness Under Rock." Colonel (Governor) Jose Antonio Vizcarra named this body "Agua de San Carlos" when he crossed it on June 26, 1823 (McNitt 1972, 57). A tributary of the San Juan River, heading in the barren flats 10 miles north of Star Lake Trading Post. It flows southwest, west, and northwest some 30 miles into Chaco Canyon, passing Pueblo Alto Trading Post and Pueblo Pintado en route. It drains the 20 miles of Chaco Canyon, and flows another 85 miles west, north, and west through the San Juan Basin, to merge with the San Juan River a mile south of U.S. Highway 550, two miles east of Shiprock.

Archaeologists have dated Navajo presence along the Chaco River since at least A.D. 1690 ± 80 years (Sessions and Williams 1979, 202). Newcomb (1964, 13–14) contends that in 1835, a party of Mexican ranchers and soldiers under Captain Hinojs was ambushed and soundly defeated by Navajos led by Narbona at the Big Bend of this river. However, Brugge (p.c. 1996) points out that nineteenth-century documentation places this battle at Narbona Pass.

Coyote and Tunicha washes are substantive tributaries of this normally dry river, but early Spanish maps paint a different picture. The Upper Chaco, east of the Big Bend and the convergence with Coyote Wash, was originally called Arroyo de San Carlos. From that point to the mouth of Tunicha Wash the channel was considered Coyote Wash, and from that juncture to the San Juan River, the stream was Tunicha Wash (Brugge 1965, 16–17).

CHACRA MESA: (7400–6550 ft) McKinley County, NM. Also Chaco Mesa, and Mesa Azul (McNitt 1972, 57). Navajo: Tségai, "White Rocks." This 31-mile-long sandstone mesa runs southeast to northwest and forms the southeast terminus of Chaco Canyon.

CHAMA: [DB] (8000 ft) Rio Arriba County, NM. Navajo: Either Tchaman, a corruption of Tewa language, Ts'á'ma, meaning "Wrestling Place" (Van Valkenburgh 1941, 36); or Ts'ímah, "Oof!" as when pushing a heavy object (Young and Morgan 1987, 742), though even this pronunciation is probably a corruption of the Tewa Ts'á'ma. A lumber and stock town at the junction of U.S. Highways 84 and 64 and New Mexico Highway 17, just nine miles south of the Colorado state line. Chama is in the valley of one of the upper branches of the Chama River, and

once was a station on the Denver & Rio Grande Railroad. The vestiges of this railroad are still active as the Cumbres and Toltec narrow-gauge tourist route between Chama and Antonito.

Chama was the headquarters and shipping point for the Edward Sargent interests and those of other large stock operators, who summered their flocks of sheep in the mountains of the vicinity and in adjacent Colorado, moving them in the fall across the Jicarilla Apache Reservation into the so-called "Checkerboard" area of the eastern Navajo country.

The vicinity is well known to the eastern Navajos, who were in the vicinity as early as A.D. 1600 (McNitt 1972, 10), and who have worked as herders for Anglo and Hispanic sheep men for many years. Battles with Navajos occurred in this region as early as 1702 (Reeve 1958, 214). Northeast of Chama stand the Chama Peaks, known to the Navajos as Ts'í'mah Dziil, "Chama Mountains." North of them is the high San Juan Range with elevations reaching over 13,000 ft.

Several features in the region are named for the Navajos. According to Van Valkenburgh, the Rio de Nabajoo, shown on the Dominguez-Escalante map of 1776, is the Navajo River of today, flowing west of Chama. (Others say this name refers to the San Juan River.) The 11,339-ft Navajo Peak, some 30 miles north of Chama near Juanita, Colorado, is shown on some of the old maps as Sierra de Nabahu, the northeast corner of the Provincia de Nabajoo. And, finally, another Navajo Peak rises just north of the juncture of the Rio Cebolla with the Chama River, about 11.5 miles northeast of Llaves.

CHECKERBOARD AREA: McKinley, San Juan, and Cibola counties, NM. Navajo: Uncertain. This name refers to a vast expanse of land (east of and contiguous to the New Mexico portion of the Navajo Reservation) in which alternating sections (square miles) of land were granted to the Santa Fe Railroad prior to the expansion of the reservation into this region (Leighton and Kluckhohn 1974, 129). The grants extend 40 miles both north and south away from the railroad tracks. Stretching almost from the Arizona–New Mexico line to the Rio Puerco of the East, the region includes much territory occupied by the Navajos prior to the June 1, 1868, establishment of the reservation (a small fraction of their previous domain). The Navajo Nation has since acquired some sections (square miles) by grant and purchase, and individual Navajos have acquired quarter-section tracts by federal allotment and by purchase. Other tracts have been sold to non-Indian interests.

Since the portion of this land that is privately owned (including those tracts owned by the Navajo Nation and individual Navajos) is not actually reservation land (which is held in trust by the U.S. government), legal jurisdiction has been confused in the checkerboard. The federal and Navajo Nation courts (and enforcement agencies) have traditionally had authority only over the reservation land as established by act of Congress or presidential executive order. State and county law enforcement had authority only in non-reservation tracts, so legal jurisdiction changed with land status every other square mile.

This problem was finally addressed during the early 1980s, when the Navajo Nation passed legislation expanding their police authority over the Navajo-owned (non-reservation) tracts, and the State Of New Mexico and the Navajo Nation entered into a "Joint Powers Agreement" giving each entity's law enforcement agencies authority to act within the other's jurisdiction—provided the Navajo policemen received training at the New Mexico State Police Academy in Santa Fe.

CHEECHILGEETHO TRADING POST: (6900 ft) McKinley County, NM. Navajo: Uncertain, but probably same as Chichiltah (Chéch'iltah). Curt Cronemeyer (sometimes spelled Kronemeyer or Kronemayer) opened this post in the early 1880s at the site of the community of the same name (now called Chichiltah), possibly in partnership with a man named Chambers, prior to moving to Allentown (McNitt 1962, 327).

CHICHILTAH: (6900 ft) McKinley County, NM. Also Cheechilgeetho, an Anglicized phonetic spelling of the Navajo name. Navajo: Chéch'iltah, "Among the Oaks," named after a Navajo who sold land to the USIS for a day school in what Van Valkenburgh described as "high rolling pine and oak clad country" eight miles west of New Mexico Highway 602 (the Gallup-Zuni highway), about 30 miles southwest of Gallup. A number of Anasazi ruins are found in the area. Cousins Trading Post was located a half mile to the east.

Curt Cronemeyer (sometimes spelled Kronemeyer or Kronemayer), a Dutchman, with a man named Chambers was the first to open a trading post in the region. Cronemeyer and Red McDonald were later murdered by Mexicans near Allentown, Arizona. Dan Dubois (1833–1925), a frontier character whom the Navajos called "Iron Shirt" (and who married Ross, the daughter of the Navajo chief Manuelito) homesteaded here in 1864. He was accepted by the Navajos due to his marriage to Ross, and his daughter was still living on his homestead some two miles from the day school in 1941. Chéch'il Łaní, "Many Oaks," the Navajo for whom the day school was named, was born on the trail to Fort Sumner in 1864.

CHIMNEY ROCK: (5950 ft) San Juan County, NM. Navajo: Uncertain; probably Tsé 'Íí'áhí, "Standing Rock." Just east of Eagle Nest Arroyo, nine miles northeast of Shiprock village. Not to be confused with the more famous location of an Anasazi ruin (and archaeoastronomy site) in southeastern Colorado.

CHINA SPRINGS TRADING POST: (6800 ft) McKinley County, NM. Navajo: K'aatání, "Many Arrows" (Young and Morgan 1987, 501). The English name derives from the fact that Chinese railroad laborers camped here in the 1880s (Brugge p.c. 1996). This trading post roughly six miles north of Gallup on U.S. Highway 666 was opened by Frank Mapel between 1906 and 1910, and closed prior to 1945 (Kelley 1977, 252–55; McNitt 1962, 334–36). Another post was operated here by Shanty Myers in the 1950s (Young p.c. 1995). Navajos were grazing livestock in this vicinity by 1861 (U.S. Indian Claims Commission n.d., vol. IV, 712–15), and in 1863, a patrol of Kit Carson's cavalry from Fort Defiance was ambushed here by Navajos. Trader Frank Lewis was killed by Navajos here on April 23, 1921.

CHUPADERO: (approx. 6500 ft) Cibola County, NM. Navajo: Uncertain. This community was probably little more than a hacienda during the time it served as Henry Dodge's Navajo Agency between 1850 and 1853. It is located between Pagaute and Cebolleta, on the southeast slope of Mount Taylor, ". . . perched high on a narrow shelf of the mountains" (McNitt 1972, 229). The Cibola National Forest map of the Mount Taylor Ranger District shows a "Rancho Chupadero" about three miles northwest of Pagaute and two miles southwest of Bibo. Navajo headman Sandoval visited the site frequently.

Dodge later moved the agency to Narbona (Washington) Pass, and even later it was moved to Chuska Valley, Laguna Negra (Black Lake), and Fort Defiance (McNitt 1972, 247).

CHURCH ROCK: [DB as Navajo Church] (6700 ft) McKinley County, NM. Also Navajo Church, Temple Rock. Navajo: Tsé 'Íí'áhí, "Standing Rock." Vaguely resembling a church with steeples, this rock spire of eroded red and white Wingate sandstone stands above the broken cliffs and mesas that rise some three miles north of I-40, roughly six miles east of Gallup. It was called Navajo Church as early as 1881 by Captain John Bourke, though the name likely predates his usage.

This rock is important to the Navajos in their Haneełnéehee (Coming Up Side Ceremony or Moving Upwardway). They tell the following story about it:

Jiní. Two birds made two bows and arrows. This was in Mancos Canyon. They were made from the fir and pine tree. They were made for killing Coyote. Coyote got possession of the arrows and held them against himself saying, "They can't kill me. Shoot me!" The birds told him to stand close—then a little farther for four times. On the fourth time, he got nearly 100 yards away. They stood still. When the birds got close, he jumped and dodged, but the arrows kept right after him.

He started to run to find a place to hide, but the arrows followed him. He ran faster and could hear them whistle behind him. He went around in a clock-wise circle four times. After that he ran north to the La Plata Mountains, then east to Blanca Peak, then south to Mount Taylor, and west to Hosta Butte. Then he went on west to

Navajo Church and crawled inside. The pine arrow stuck on the top and the fir arrow stuck under a ledge and stayed there. (Van Valkenburgh 1941, 104)

ALSO: (6700 ft) McKinley County, NM. Also (formerly) Wingate Navajo Village. Navajo: Kinłitsosinil: "Yellow Houses in Position" (Wilson 1995, 14). This chapter village is at the junction of I-40 frontage road (old U.S. Highway 66) and New Mexico Highway 566, six miles east of Gallup. It is named for the red and white sandstone formation about two miles to the northwest that resembles a multi-steepled church. Springstead Trading Post was opened about five miles north of the community in the late 1930s, and is still operational (Kelley 1977, 254). Carson Trading Post in this vicinity opened in the early 1940s, but closed prior to 1975 (Kelley 1977, 255–56).

The village was initially constructed at an AT&SF Railway siding to house Navajo workers at Fort Wingate Army Ordnance Depot during World War II. When it was deeded to the Navajo Nation (then the Navajo Tribe), the apartments were rented to Navajos and non-Navajos working nearby or in Gallup (Brugge p.c. 1996). Today the village is entirely Navajo. In the late 1980s the Navajo Nation constructed a "cluster" of some two dozen modern, pitched-roofed, stucco houses on the west side of New Mexico Highway 566, each owned by a Navajo family.

CHUSKA MOUNTAINS: [DB as Chuska Peak] (approx. 7500–9365 ft) McKinley and San Juan counties, NM, (and Apache County, AZ). Navajo: Ch'óshgai, "White Spruce," referring to the Chuskas specifically (Van Valkenburgh 1941, 39). The Chuskas are the major component of the 90-mile-long Chuska-Tunicha-Lukachukai Range snaking north along the New Mexico–Arizona line from New Mexico Highway 264. This entire range is referred to as Níłtsá Dził, "Rainy Mountain" (U.S. Indian Claims Commission n.d., vol. VI, xiii). McNitt (1973, 142–43) errs in suggesting that Chuska is an Americanization of the Spanish "Tunicha"—the closest the Spanish could come to spelling the Navajo Tó Ntsaa ("Abundant Water")—which some scholars suggest refers to the entire range. The mountain's highest point is just north of Narbona Pass (formerly Washington Pass); Chuska Peak (above Tohatchi) is six hundred feet lower at 8765 ft.

In the Navajo Blessing Chant stories, the Chuskas comprise the body of Yo'dí Dził ("Goods of Value Mountain"), a male anthropomorphic figure, of which Chuska Peak is the head. Beautiful Mountain is his feet and the Carrizos his lower extremities; Shiprock is a medicine pouch or bow that he carries (McPherson 1992, 21). This figure is the antithesis of a similar female figure known as Pollen Mountain, comprised of Navajo Mountain, Black Mesa, and other features.

Navajos occupied the Chuska Valley as early as A.D. 1750, and the mountains were a confirmed stronghold by 1796 (McNitt 1972, 35–36). The mountains were traversed by Governor Jose Antonio Vizcarra in 1823. Some important battles were fought by the Navajos against the Spanish, Mexican, and American militaries in and around the Chuskas.

CHUSKA PASS: [DB] (6400–8200 ft) McKinley County, NM. Navajo: Tsé Bii' Naayolí, translated by Van Valkenburgh as "Windy Trail through the Rocks," but is more accurately "Wind Blows about within the Rock" (Young and Morgan 1987, 729). This mountain pass over the southern end of the Chuska Mountains passes north and west of Tohatchi, between Chuska Peak and the Deza Bluffs. It crosses the Chuskas and terminates at the western end of Todilto Park, through the natural cut made by Tó Dildǫí Wash. Atop the Chuska Range (in the vicinity of the Tohatchi Lookout Tower, at an elevation near 8200 ft), the road forks, with the northern road heading back to the east toward Mexican Springs. The roads are not paved, and the pass is generally not negotiable in winter or in the rainy season.

CHUSKA PEAK. [DB] (8795 ft) McKinley County, NM. Navajo: Ch'óshgai, "White Spruce." This cone-shaped knob rises above the pine-clad top of the southeasternmost projection of the Chuska Mountains, some six miles northwest of Tohatchi, and is the tallest point of the southern Chuskas.

The U.S. Geological Survey map of 1882 shows this peak as Choiskai Peak, while other maps have listed it as Flat Top Peak (which may be a confusion with Twin Buttes, about eight miles to the west, or possibly even Zilditloi Peak, two miles northwest of the Twin Buttes).

Chuska Peak is an important sacred location to the Navajos. In 1935, Navajo medicine men objected to an Indian Forest Service plan to erect a fire tower on the peak's summit, so Tohatchi Lookout Tower was built at its present location atop another high point that is not sacred to the Navajos. (The vista from this high steel tower is sensational, with an unobstructed view of Mount Taylor about one hundred miles to the southeast; Fluted Rock projecting above the Defiance Plateau to the west; and Black Pinnacle to the north, standing out from the southwestward projection of the Tunicha Mountains.)

Chuska Peak figures prominently in Navajo mythology, particularly in the Tł'éé'jí Hatáál, or Night Chant; it serves as the head of Yo'dí Dził ("Goods of Value Mountain") (see Chuska Mountains).

CHUSKA VALLEY: (5500 ft) McKinley County, NM. Navajo: Uncertain, though the English name is a derivative of the Navajo Ch'óshgai, the name of the nearby mountains. This designation refers to that portion of the San Juan Basin at the foot of the Chuska Mountains, between the range and Chaco River.

It was in this valley that Spanish Governor Fernando Chacon met with Navajo headmen in May 1800 (McNitt 1972, 37).

CIBOLA MESA: (highest point 7568 ft) Rio Arriba County, NM. Navajo: Tsé Yik'áán Nahgóó, "Hogback to One Side" (U.S. Indian Claims Commission n.d., vol. VI, xx), "Windy Flattop Rock" (Kelley p.c. 1994). This mesa forms the southern boundary of Largo Canyon in the vicinity of that feature's shift to the name of Cañada Larga. It lies east of Crow Mesa and north of Lybrooks and Counselors. La Pajarita

Canyon and Rincon Largo flow out of Cibola Mesa into Largo Canyon.

CLY CANYON: (6400–6200 ft) San Juan County, NM. Navajo: Ha'aastséli, "Chipped Out One" (Kelley p.c. 1994), referring to a path or road chipped out of the rock. A two-mile-long northern tributary of Chaco Wash, entering approximately two miles upstream (southeast) of the mouth of Escavada Wash. This canyon contains four seeps, including "The Great Gambler's Spring," mentioned in chantways (Gabriel 1991, 263).

COAL CREEK: (6100–6000 ft) San Juan County, NM. Navajo: Uncertain. Tributary of De Na Zin (Déél Náázíní) Wash, east of Tanner Lake. Some references (Pearce 1965, 37, 167; AAA Indian Country map 1989) erroneously equate Coal Creek with De Na Zin Wash itself.

COAL MINE PASS. [DB] (7217 ft) McKinley County, NM. Navajo: Tséteel Naagai, "Wide Rock Coming Down White" (Young and Morgan 1987, 731). A pass through the southern reaches of the Chuska Mountains (described as the Defiance Mesa by Van Valkenburgh), located some 15 miles southwest of Chuska Peak and about six miles east of Fort Defiance.

This pass lies between the heads of Coal Mine Wash (to the west) and Black Spring Wash (to the east), approximately seven miles north of present-day New Mexico Highway 264, and provides a very rough shortcut between the Window Rock area and Mexican Springs. According to Van Valkenburgh, this route was followed by Major O. S. Shepherd and Captain H. B. Schroeder in 1859 and by other military parties.

COCHITI PUEBLO: (5,300 ft) (Population: 434) Sandoval County, NM. Navajo: Tó'gaa', meaning uncertain. Located at the foot of the southeasternmost extension of the Jemez Mountains, 31 miles north of Albuquerque, 14 miles northeast of I-25 on New Mexico Highway 22. The native name for the pueblo is Kotyete, "Stone Kiva" (Mays 1985, 17). One of seven Keresan pueblos (see also Zia, Santa Ana,

Santo Domingo, San Felipe, Laguna, and Acoma pueblos).

According to Bandelier (Lange and Riley 1966, 158–59), the Navajos feared the Cochitis and seldom visited the pueblo in the late 1800s. This may be due at least in part to an incident prior to 1822 in which a group of Navajos were invited to the pueblo for a treaty and then were attacked and killed (Benally et al. 1982, 94).

This village appears to have been founded about A.D. 1200, by people moving down from villages in Frijoles Canyon (New Mexico Office of Cultural Affairs 1992, 29). The Stone Lions atop the cliffs west of the pueblo is a shrine to many pueblos, including the Zuni (Ferguson and Hart 1985, 65).

CONTINENTAL DIVIDE (TRADING POST): (7200 ft) McKinley County, NM. Navajo: 'Ahideelk'id: "Hills Converge" (Young p.c. 1995). This small collection of roadside businesses and homes straddles I-40 where the continental divide crosses the highway 27 miles east of Gallup, five miles west of Thoreau. A trading post was opened here prior to 1950 (Kelley 1977, 255).

COOLIDGE: [DB] (7100 ft) McKinley County, NM. North of I-40, 27 miles east of Gallup. Navajo: Chíshí Nééz (Young and Morgan 1987, 272), "Tall Chiricahua Apache." Few locations in Indian country have had such an identity crisis as this one. It was first known as Bacon Springs, a name accepted at least by September 13, 1875. In 1881, when the AT&SF established a railroad camp on Billy Crane's ranch, the community became known as Crane's Station. But the name changed again a year later, in an effort to honor an AT&SF director, T. Jefferson Coolidge. When the population center changed to Gallup, the ghost town was known once again as Crane's Station. The AT&SF changed it once again, naming it for Admiral Dewey, hero of the Battle of Manila Bay. In 1900, the railroad renamed it Guam, apparently in recognition of the Guam Lumber and Trading Co., founded just 40 feet north of the tracks a year earlier by Hans Newman and a man named Johnson. Finally, a trader by the name of Berton I. Staples moved there in 1926 and re-established the name of Coolidge—but this time in honor of then President Calvin Coolidge. Between the early 1890s and 1930 there were four separate Perea Trading Posts in Coolidge.

In the 1940s, the community boasted a trading post (C. G. Newcomb) and pueblo-style guest ranch, constructed in 1923–24 of red sandstone taken from Anasazi ruins in the vicinity, and located on the north side of the upper Wingate Valley, backed by scenic red sandstone cliffs, on old U.S. Highway 66 about 18 miles east of Gallup. Objects collected from the same ruins as the building stones once lay in the former Wayside Museum (the first of its kind in the Southwest), but have since been relocated to the Gila Pueblo at Globe.

The hamlet has been "home away from home" to a variety of celebrities. Alma Wilmarth Tekes wrote "Mesa Land" here, and Malvina Hoffman, renowned sculptor and author of "Heads and Tails," spent her vacations at Coolidge. Gladys Reichard was based here when she wrote "Spider Woman" and studied Navajo ethnology; Charles Lummis (author of the "Land of Poco Tiempo" and other historical travel volumes), who described Coolidge in 1884 as the only town of one hundred people between Albuquerque and Winslow, Arizona (McNitt 1962, 232), lived at O'Linn's Trading Post (near Coolidge) in 1894. Gouverneur Morris, author of "We Three" and other works, resided here into the 1940s.

The Navajo chief Mariano and his followers lived in this region, eventually dispossessed by the former Civil War veteran William Crane (known to the Navajos as Hastiin Tł'ohí ["Mr. Hay"]), who established his hay ranch and stock operations in the 1870s, giving rise to the name Crane's Ranch or Spring. With the coming of the Atlantic and Pacific Railroad in 1881, Coolidge Station and village mushroomed at a point one mile northwest of Crane's Ranch.

Coolidge was the shipping point for Fort Wingate and its many soldiers. No fewer than 14 saloons sprang up catering to the riffraff that followed on the heels of the new railroad. Outlaws and Navajos openly purchased intoxicants. Eventually a series of killings resulted in the lynching

of seven outlaws a short distance from the present Coolidge by troops from Fort Wingate. With the development of Gallup, the town of Coolidge disappeared and all that remains of it today are the foundations of a few buildings.

The Atlantic and Pacific Railroad once threatened to level Coolidge with a construction gang over the theft of a wagonload of barrels of beer (Teller 1954, 216).

During the 1930s and 1940s, Casa del Navajo Trading Post was operated at Coolidge by Burton I. Staples. It was described as a "sort of pueblo style palace," constructed of stones scavenged from Anasazi ruins by Hans Nuemann years earlier. Staples served as the first president of the United Indian Traders Association. The post later was owned by the Newcomb family, and it burned in 1955 (Kelley 1985, 27).

COOLIDGE RUIN: (7180 ft) McKinley County, NM. Navajo: General area called Tsé 'Ałts'óózí Deez'á, "Narrow Rock Point," after a nearby geologic structure (Young p.c. 1995). A Chacoan great-house community on a ridge-top near Coolidge, on the north side of the Red Mesa Valley. It is 17 miles west-northwest of the better known Casamero great house. The site is comprised of two great kivas and two Bonito-phase house mounds. Dates to Pueblo I and early Pueblo II to Pueblo III.

COUNSELORS: [DB] (7000 ft) Sandoval County, NM. Navajo: Bilagáana Nééz, "Tall White Man." Named for trader Jim Counselor. A trading post situated on New Mexico Highway 44, 12 miles west of the junction of that road and New Mexico Highway 537, around 30 miles west of Cuba. By the mid-twentieth century, a sheep ranch and guest ranch were added to the settlement in the high wooded region west of the continental divide on New Mexico State Highway 44, 28 miles west of Cuba and at a midway point between Albuquerque and Farmington.

Prior to the Navajo acquisition of automobiles, this locale was the trading center for the Navajos living southwest of the Jicarilla Apache Reservation. Lying in the Dinétah, the locale also served as base for archaeological and historical investigations of the old Navajo country by the School of American Research, Columbia University, and the United States Indian Service. The region abounds in old Navajo sites, and many stone watchtowers are located at vantage points on mesa rims. Counselor Chapter House is located here.

COUNSELORS TRADING POST: (7000 ft) Sandoval County, NM. Navajo: See Counselors. Opened during the winter of 1922–23, by Jim Counselor.

COUSINS (TRADING POST): (7000 ft) McKinley County, NM. Navajo: Uncertain. Also known as Round House, according to Pearce (1965). Located 19 miles south of Gallup, 11 miles west of New Mexico Highway 602, near Chichiltah Boarding School. Cousins Trading Post was established here by Charles Cousins early in the century, and sold in 1925 to Charlie Davis (Richardson 1986, 282).

COYOTE CANYON: [DB] (6100 ft) McKinley County, NM. Navajo: Mą'ii Tééh Yítłizhí, "Where the Coyote Fell into Deep Water." Located on Highway N-9, 10 miles east of U.S. Highway 666, this deeply eroded canyon heads five miles south of Navajo Highway 9, cut by headwaters of Coyote Wash. A segment of Chacoan prehistoric road leads northward from this vicinity.

Coyote Wash continues north, joining Tohatchi Wash which, with Red Willow and Standing Rock washes, meets Chaco Wash at the Great Bend 30 miles north of Coyote Canyon Trading Post. The Chuska (or Choiska) Irrigation Project (USIS) irrigated some 235 acres midway between Coyote Canyon and Tohatchi.

Navajos say the name Coyote Canyon came from the story of a coyote that, while trying to drink from a sinkhole in the rock, fell in and could not get out.

The first trading post at Coyote Canyon was established by Charles Baker in 1909.

COYOTE CANYON TRADING POST: (6100 ft) McKinley County, NM. Located on a fork of Coyote Wash. George Washington Sampson—known as Hastiin Báí, "Gray Man"—established

this post in the 1890s. It was sold to Dan Dubois in 1902. Sampson also held posts at Sanders, Arizona (1883), Rock Spring (north of Gallup, 1887), Tohatchi (prior to 1892), Lukachukai, and Chilchinbito, Arizona (McNitt 1962, 251). Charles Baker held the post in 1909. (Van Valkenburgh mistakenly identifies Baker as the first trader.) James Brimhall expanded the post in 1919 (Noe 1992, 10). The locale later became home to Coyote Canyon Chapter House.

CROWNPOINT: [DB] (6943 ft) (Population: 2,108) McKinley County, NM. Navajo: T'ííst'óóz Ńdeeshgizh, "Narrow-Leafed Cottonwood Gap"; also T'iists'ózí, "Slender Cottonwood" (Young and Morgan 1987, 723). A government settlement located on New Mexico Highway 371, 24 miles north of Thoreau, at the junction of New Mexico Highway 371 and Navajo Highway 9. This chapter community includes public schools, a BIA boarding school, and an Indian Health Service medical center opened here in 1940, starting with a 65-bed hospital. Radio station KTGM operated from here in the 1940s, as did a U.S. Weather Bureau station, and the headquarters of the eastern division of the Civilian Conservation Corps–Indian Department. There was also a coal mine, and the Navajo Police maintain a substation here. Churches include a Christian Reformed mission. Traders included Crownpoint Trading Post (two separate posts between 1905 and 1915 [Kelley 1977, 253]) and E. B. Simm, trader. Traders Madison and McCoy also operated in the vicinity, between the late 1890s and 1920 (Kelley 1977, 252).

Crownpoint was founded in 1909 as the Pueblo Bonito Indian School, the sixth on the reservation, by its first agent, Samuel F. Stacher (see Chaco Canyon, Pueblo Bonito), whom Navajos called Nat'áanii Yázhí ("Little Boss"). Later it was known as the Eastern Navajo Agency until the opening of the Navajo Central Agency at Window Rock in 1935. It reverted to agency status in 1955, first as the Crownpoint subagency, a few years later as the Crownpoint Agency (Young p.c. 1995).

One of the most important Navajo figures of this region was Becenti, the son of Becenti Sani, who in 1868 met with the Navajo chiefs at Fort

Wingate to determine where the Navajo boundaries were to lie. Becenti, after many years of leadership and cooperation with the Indian Department, died in 1937 and was buried in the Gallup cemetery.

The hero's youngest brother goes to Crownpoint and Hosta Butte at the end of the Navajo Gun Shooter Red Antway Myth (Wyman 1965).

This name is also applied to a southerly-projecting mesa ridge overlooking Gallup, east of Heaton Canyon.

CRUMBLED HOUSE RUIN: (5880 ft) San Juan County, NM. Navajo: Kin Náázhoozhí, "Sliding House." Located near the base of the east slope of the Chuska Mountains, in the vicinity of Newcomb. Pottery analysis classifies this site as "Chuskan-Mesa Verde," occupied between A.D. 1150 and 1250. The site has two components. The "Upper House" is one of the most unusual of all the prehistoric ruins in Navajoland. Located on the extreme tip of a mesa point 30 meters above the surrounding plain, it has been dubbed "The Castle" by archaeologists. Thick walls along the mesa edge, tower kivas at each of the three corners, and a wall-backed trench (possibly a moat?) separating the structure from the main body of the mesa give it quite a medieval appearance. The structure contains 80 ground-floor and 24 upper-story rooms, in addition to the tower kivas. There is a large isolated kiva nearby.

The "Lower House," constructed on the steep mesa slope below the Upper House, contains approximately 150 rooms and up to 16 kivas. This rectangular structure was built in terraces, so that the upslope rooms are 20 meters above the lower rooms.

CRYSTAL: [DB] (7800 ft) San Juan County, NM. Old name, Cottonwood Pass. Navajo: Tó Niłts'ílí, "Clear Water" or "Sparkling Water." Trading post and community on Navajo Highway 32, five miles east of Navajo Highway 12 in the Chuska Mountains, at the west entrance to Narbona (Washington) Pass.

Government records show that the first trader at Crystal was Michael Donovan of Onondaga County, New York, who in 1884 established the post with Clarence Tooley and John H. Bowman (Navajo Agent 1884–85) as clerks. These early traders were followed by John B. Moore, who, according to his 1912 commercial brochure on Navajo weaving, with color plates, was one of the earliest traders to send Navajo wool away to be scoured, to grade the rugs, and to develop a mail order business in Navajo rugs.

That same brochure lists Moore's Special Grade (ER-20) as priced (according to size) from 90 cents to $1.00 per square foot. His second Tourist Grade (-TXX) rugs sold for $1.00 to $2.00 per pound, regardless of size. Moore also publicized one of his top weavers, a young woman called Łíjłbáhí Be'esdzáán (Gray Horse's Woman). Many of the rugs shown in this catalogue are strikingly similar to those of the Two Grey Hills type of today.

A reinforced concrete diversion dam in Cottonwood Wash (also called Simpson Wash and Crystal Creek) irrigated some 169 acres in 1941, divided into the upper and lower Crystal Projects (Van Valkenburgh 1941, 47).

CRYSTAL CREEK: (8900–7300 ft) San Juan County, NM, and Apache County, AZ. Also Simpson Creek. Navajo: Tó Niłts'ílí, "Clear Water" or "Sparkling Water." An intermittent stream in the Chuska Mountains, rising in Washington Pass and flowing west into Black Lake, north of Black Creek Valley. According to Granger (1960, 22), the stream following this path was named Simpson Creek by Herbert Gregory, in honor of Captain James Simpson, member of the first Anglo-American expedition to cross the Chuska and Lukachukai Mountains, in 1849–50.

This creek was once referred to as Rio Negro (McNitt 1972, 147), possibly because of the fact that it fed Laguna Negra (Black Lake).

CRYSTAL TRADING POST: (7800 ft) San Juan County, NM. Navajo: Uncertain, but probably the same as Crystal. Romulo Martinez was trading in Washington Pass in 1873. Ben Hyatt was trading in 1882–84, and Stephen Aldrich and Elias Clark were present in 1884. Clark joined Charles Hubbell (brother of Lorenzo) the next year, followed by Walter Fales in 1885, Michael Donovan in 1886, and Perry Williams in 1887.

Joe Reitz (who had earlier traded with Joe Wilkin and Elmer E. Whitehouse) opened a post on the present site in 1894 (James 1988, 45–46). They were bought out by John B. Moore during the winter of 1896–97 (McNitt 1962, 252).

Moore published a catalogue in 1911 that did much to promote sales of Navajo rugs world-wide. Moore sold the post to his manager, Jesse A. Molohon, in 1911, the post became part of the C. C. Manning company 1919–22, and Charlie Newcomb owned the post until 1936. Jim Collyer was owner until 1944, when he sold to Don Jenson, who held the post until 1981, when he sold to Charlie and Evelyn Andrews and moved to the Inscription House post (James 1988, 48). Jenson was responsible for developing the current Crystal rug (James 1988, 103).

CUBA: [DB] (6928 ft) (Population: 760) Sandoval County, NM. Also Nacimiento. Navajo: Na'azísí To'í, "Gopher Water." A village (formerly Spanish-American) on the Rio Puerco of the East, located in a grassy basin bounded on the east by the Nacimiento section of the Jemez Range and on the west by the high juniper- and pine-covered mesas that sweep westward to the continental divide. On New Mexico State Highway 44, 69 miles northwest of Bernalillo, at the junction of Highway 44 with New Mexico Highways 126 and 197.

Cuba is situated on the site of the old New Mexican community of Nacimiento (Spanish for "Nativity") shown on both banks of the Rio Puerco of the East on the Miera y Pacheco map of 1779. The village was part of the San Joaquin del Nacimiento land grant of 1769 for 36 families (Fugate and Fugate 1989). Miera y Pacheco labeled the village "Arruinadas por los enemigos," or "Ruined by the enemies." Navajo attacks had forced the abandonment in 1774, as they retaliated against the Spanish alliance with the Utes, in an apparent effort to force the Navajos out of the Puerco Valley (Brugge p.c. 1996).

The village was resettled by the McCay and Atencio families in 1879. The name Cuba was given to the settlement by a Spanish-American rancher and lumberman, Mariano Otero, about the turn of the century. It is now the center of a large agricultural and stock-raising countryside.

The largely Hispanic population began changing with the arrival of Anglo homesteaders in the 1920s. During the 1940s and 1950s, several dude ranches lay east of Cuba in the Jemez Mountains. Navajos from the Penistaja, Eagle Springs, and Torreon regions come here frequently to trade.

The region is part of the old Navajo habitat, and its Navajo name, Na'azísí To'í, was derived from Hastiin Na'azísí, an old Navajo chief who had a spring, To'í, where there were many gophers. The camp of the Navajo chief Bi'anesta'-nih (supposedly "Guardian" or "The One Who Looked Over Them," though Young was unable to decipher this) was six miles southeast of present Cuba at San Miguel. Seven miles west of Cuba, at Chihuili (Navajo: Tsé Łitso, "Yellow Rock"), the father of Santiago Ortiz, centenarian Navajo of Torreon (died 1938), once had a farm.

CUBERO: [DB] (6200 ft) Cibola County, NM. Navajo: Tsék'iz Tóhí, "Water in the Crevice." The Spanish name means "Cooper." An old New Mexican town located on the banks of a small wash in the mesa country south of Mount Taylor, some five miles north of I-40, 10 miles west of Laguna Pueblo. The old town was only a half-mile off the old U.S. Highway 66. Three miles north of Cubero and on the road to the Laguna village of Encinal is the isolated volcanic plug called Picacho Peak.

Founded in the late seventeenth century, the present village was settled in 1833 by Juan Chavez and 61 residents of Albuquerque (McNitt 1972, 72). Van Valkenburgh (1941, 48) has this old adobe and stone village named after the Spanish governor, Don Jose Cubero, but McNitt (1972, 72) suggests it was named after Don Pedro Rodriquez Cubero, governor from 1697 to 1703. It is shown as "Cubera" on the old Dominguez-Escalante map of 1776. In the eighteenth and early part of the nineteenth century, Cubero was a Spanish military outpost and trading center for the Navajos, and it served as the staging area for many miliary campaigns into Navajo country. As such, it was also the scene of several skirmishes with the Navajos (McNitt 1972, 423).

American troops were stationed at Cubero in 1846, and intermittently until 1851. On the

J. F. McComb map of 1860, it is Cubero, though newspaper accounts of the 1860s spelled it "Cuvero."

In his "Memoir of a Tour of Northern Mexico" in 1846–47, A. Wisizenus wrote of Cubero:

This (Cubero) being a frontier settlement, the people have greatly suffered from the incursions of the Navajos; occasionally they have been driven from their village to take refuge in the cliffs. The Navajos are not always hostile. They frequently visited the village on friendly terms, and probably, the inhabitants by trade with them, have made as much peace as war.

It was once the boast of these Indians that they only spare them to save themselves the trouble of planting corn and raising sheep. Last night two Navajos were in our camp at Laguna. They were from Caravajal's band, which is now far off, and were supposed to have been sent as spies. This man Caravajal . . . seems to be a man of great enterprise and cunning. It is said, that formerly, he was accustomed to hover over the settlements till, seeing a fair chance for pillage, he would communicate the fact to some band in the vicinity, prepared to impress the opportunity, then turning informer, put the Mexicans on the trail of the plunderers—claiming reward on both sides. (Quoted in Van Valkenburgh 1941, 48–49)

Caravajal was one of the Diné 'Ana'í (Enemy Navajos) of the region, a branch of the tribe commonly guiding punitive expeditions against the larger body of Navajos to the west. These people were, as Wisizenus described them, tricky, and they allied with whatever group offered them the best gain.

In March 1862, Fort Fauntleroy physician Finis Ewing Kavanaugh turned over the post's stores at Cubero to the Confederate Army. Serving under contract at $120 per month, Dr. Kavanaugh was an advocate of slavery (McNitt 1972, 423).

It was at Cubero in 1863 that Barboncito and the Navajos received the final ultimatum from Brigadier General James Carleton before the opening of the Navajo Wars. From Cubero in the 1880s came Big Lipped Mexican, who taught the Navajos at Ganado many of their refinements in silvercraft. And here, in 1932, died Jesus Alviso (also called Arviso, Albrizzo), old-time

interpreter of Fort Defiance and Fort Sumner during the 1860s.

CUDAI: [DB] (4800 ft) San Juan County, NM. Navajo: Gad 'Íí'áí, "Where a Juniper Tree Sticks Up" (Young and Morgan 1987, 369); also Kóyaaí (Van Valkenburgh 1941, 49), "The One Down Here" (Young p.c. 1995). Navajo farming and chapter area located on the south bank of the San Juan River, five miles west of Shiprock, across from Malpais Arroyo. Here six hundred acres of agricultural land are irrigated from a diversion from the San Juan River. This tract is known to have been irrigated by the Navajos as early as 1880, possibly much earlier. In 1905, its water supply came from San Juan Ditch No. 3, known as Cudai Canal.

DALTON PASS: [DB] (approx. 7000 ft) McKinley County, NM. Navajo: Náhodeeshgiizh, "Pass Coming Down" (sometimes Anglicized to "Nahodishgish." Also Łíí' Haa'nah, which Young (p.c. 1995) interprets as "Where the Horse Crawls Up." This pass drops off the north rim of the Mesa de los Lobos, down to the flat country that slopes north to the Chaco Wash, connecting the Mariano Lake region of Mesa de los Lobos with the Standing Rock country to the north. This used to be an old wagon road and horse trail used as the main route north to the San Juan River until the early 1900s; it is now superseded by the route over which U.S. Highway 666 passes. Site of Nahodishgish Chapter House.

DALTON PASS TRADING POST: [DB] (7375 ft) McKinley County, NM. Navajo: Uncertain, probably the same as the pass. Trading-post community on Mesa de los Lobos, five miles north of Mariano Lake on New Mexico Highway 566. Located at the head of the north-flowing canyon by the same name. The first trader in the region was Schillingberg Trading Post, which opened in the first decade of this century (Kelley 1977, 253).

DANOFFVILLE: [DB (map 17)] (7300 ft) McKinley County, NM. Navajo: Chííh Ntł'izí, "Hard Nose," the name they used for Sam Danoff, trader (Kelley p.c. 1994). (This same name was applied to nearby Pinehaven.) Abandoned trading post in western Zuni Mountains, about two miles west of Pinehaven, on Navajo Route 7082. See Pinedale.

DEFIANCE STATION TRADING POST:
[DB] (6200 ft) McKinley County, NM. Also Defiance. Navajo: Tsé Ńdeeshgiizh, "Gap in the Rock." A service station and trader on the now-defunct old Highway 66. It was located on the south side of the Rio Puerco of the West in the barren, treeless river valley eight miles west of Gallup. Twin Buttes is located a slight distance southeast. The trading post opened in 1881. Twelve years later, during the winter of 1893–94, trader D. M. Smith was killed here. The post closed by 1950 (Richardson 1986, 322; Kelley 1977, 251).

With the coming of the Atlantic and Pacific Railroad in 1882, Defiance Station superseded Fort Wingate Station, then called Sheridan, as the main shipping point for Fort Defiance. At the time a deep rutted road ran northward to a point near Rock Springs where it picked up the old Fort Defiance–Fort Wingate military road. Manuelito, then called Ferry Station, soon replaced Defiance Station until it in turn was replaced by Gallup.

Between Gallup and Defiance Station, and north of the highway in the sloping hills, several coal mines, the largest becoming Mentmore Mine, operated until the late 1980s.

DE-NA-ZIN WASH: (6300–5600 ft) San Juan County, NM. Navajo: Déél Nááziní, "Standing Crane," referring to a petroglyph site and surrounding area (Kelley p.c. 1994); one source spelled it Tiz Nat Zin. Heads in the San Juan Basin 15 miles north of Chaco Canyon. Flows southeast approximately 10 miles before joining the Chaco River, about five miles southeast of Bisti Trading Post. Also erroneously called Coal Creek in some literature (Pearce 1965, 37 and 167; AAA Indian Country map 1989). According to USGS maps, Coal Creek is actually tributary to De-Na-Zin from the southeast.

DEZA BLUFFS: (8000 ft) McKinley County, NM. Navajo: Deez'á, "Point," "Promontory" or "elongated ridge." The east face of the Chuska Mountains above and north of Tohatchi drops sharply toward the San Juan Basin, sloping down to U.S. Highway 666.

DINÉTAH: (5500–9000+ ft) San Juan and Rio Arriba counties, NM. Navajo: Dinétah, the old Navajoland, the area occupied by the Navajos during their earliest years in the Southwest—as early as A.D. 1550 (Roessel 1983b, 24) or even prior to A.D. 1500 (Reed and Reed 1992; Brown and Hancock 1992). There are some isolated and largely unsubstantiated tree-ring dates (from samples lacking the outside rings of growth, which indicate cutting date) elsewhere in Navajoland that suggest a possible earlier presence—including those found in the vicinity of Quemado, dating to the late 1300s (Roessel 1983b, 41; Correll 1976). But the Dinétah is generally accepted by Navajo traditionalists and non-Navajo archaeologists and historians alike as the Navajo's earliest southwestern habitation.

The definition of the Dinétah most often quoted in the literature has it stretching roughly from the continental divide on the east to the juncture of the San Juan River with Canyon Largo on the west, and from the southern edge of Canyon Largo on the south to just above the Colorado state line in the north (Schroeder 1963, 8). Brugge (p.c. 1996), however, notes that there are many definitions of the Dinétah, and suggests that Schroeder, as a government witness in the Navajo land claims case, was necessarily restrictive.

Roessel (1983b, 3, 90) presents a much broader area, based largely on Navajo land claims. While he defines it simply as including Blanco, Largo Carrizo, and Gobernador Canyons and their surrounding drainages in northeastern New Mexico, he goes on to suggest that it includes such important Navajo places as the La Plata Mountains (Dibé Ntsaa), Blanca Peak (Sisnaájiní), Hosta Butte ('Ak'iih Dah Nást'ání), Mount Taylor (Tsoodził, "Mountain Tongue") or Kinya'a Ruin (Kin Yaa'á), Shiprock (Tsé Bit'a'í), and Wide Belt Mesa (Sis Naateel). This is a far larger area indeed, and Brugge notes that it exceeds any definition of the Dinétah with which he is familiar.

In any case, the Dinétah is where the Navajo first contacted the Pueblo Indians, and it is where Spanish explorers in the region first encountered the Navajos. It is also the birthplace and home of Changing Woman ('Asdzą́ą́ Nádleehé—see Gobernador Knob and Huerfano Mesa).

In the seventeenth and eighteenth centuries, the Navajos spread southward and westward into the Chama Valley and Big Bead Mesa regions, though the current boundaries of their reservation are artificial, imposed upon them by the Treaty of 1868.

DINÉTAH PUEBLITOS: Within the region discussed above, the early Navajo material culture seems to concentrate in the Largo and Gobernador canyons (McNitt 1972, 4). Here, on Bureau of Land Management land, a large number of important early Navajo sites have been recorded and investigated. These ruins were built during the Gobernador phase of Navajo history. This period of great population movements and hostilities started with the Pueblo Revolt of 1680, in which the Spaniards were driven from the region. With the return of the Spanish in 1692, many Pueblo people fled their Rio Grande homes, some venturing westward into Navajo territory.

There is evidence that the Puebloans and the Navajos lived together here, probably intermarrying. The threat of attack by the Navajos' northern neighbors, the Utes, kept the sites in defensive locations, such as on mesa ridges and hilltops. The region was ultimately abandoned in the early 1750s, possibly hastened by a drought.

These ruins are all minor in stature, and Navajo names are unknown today, but the generic Navajo term "Kits'iilí" ("Shattered House") most likely applies to all of them. Similar structures were discovered in 1978–79 on the east escarpment of the Chuska Mountains (Linford 1982, 111–14), and Brugge notes their appearance on Mesa de los Lobos, as well as near Manuelito, Klagetoh, Ganado, and Nazlini in the 1760s.

The majority of the information on the sites listed below was gleaned from the Bureau of Land Management document "Pueblitos of the Dinétah" (n.d.).

✦ CROW CANYON PETROGLYPHS SITE: (6250 ft) San Juan County, NM. A collection of Navajo rock art located on the north wall of the juncture of Crow Canyon and Canyon Largo, just east of the Rio Arriba County line. Included are hundreds of animal, human, and ceremonial figures.

✦ CROW CANYON SITE: (6350 ft) Rio Arriba County, NM. This site on the first bench of the south wall of Crow Canyon consists of a single room with standing slab masonry walls atop a large boulder about a mile east of the Crow Canyon Petroglyphs Site.

✦ FRANCES RUIN: (6500 ft) Rio Arriba County, NM. Located on an unnamed western tributary of Frances Creek, approximately three miles southeast of the Frances Creek Arm of Navajo Reservoir. This is one of the largest pueblitos, with 40 rooms, a plaza, and a three-story tower situated on the edge of a cliff. The site contains intact roofs, loom fittings, mortar and plaster, semi-concealed entries, and Spanish-style hooded fireplaces.

✦ HOODED FIREPLACE SITE: (6250 ft) Rio Arriba County, NM. A mile and a half south of Canyon Largo School, this site is the south face of an unnamed minor western tributary of Canyon Largo, almost directly across from the mouth of Dogie Canyon, and a half-mile south of Largo School Ruin. This site contains six ground-floor rooms with some intact roofs. It is named for an unusually well-preserved Spanish-style hooded fireplace in the corner of one room. Nearby are two stone circles, which may have been foundations for hogans.

✦ LARGO SCHOOL RUIN: (6250 ft) Rio Arriba County, NM. Site located about a mile south of the Canyon Largo School, on the west wall of Largo Canyon (on the east face of Superior Mesa) across and a mile upstream from the mouth of Dogie Canyon. This site consists of several masonry rooms at the end of a sandstone bench above the river bed. Hooded Fireplace Site is on the same bench, a half mile south.

✤ SHAFT HOUSE RUIN: (6350 ft) Rio Arriba County, NM. A half mile upstream from Crow Canyon Site is Shaft House Ruin, situated on the opposite (north) face of Crow Canyon. This site was built at the top of a steep talus slope, against the sandstone cliff. There are two levels in the site, connected by a round masonry access tower (the "shaft"). The site contains 14 well-preserved rooms.

✤ SIMON RUIN: (6250 ft) San Juan County, NM. One of the northernmost recorded Gobernador-phase Navajo pueblitos, this site is located in Simon Canyon, about a half-mile upstream from that canyon's juncture with the San Juan River, some four miles downstream from Navajo Dam. A single room sits atop a gigantic boulder 20 feet high.

✤ SPLIT ROCK RUIN: (6550 ft) Rio Arriba County, NM. On the east bank of Canyon Largo, on the west end of Ensenada Mesa, between the mouths of Dogie (to the north) and Tapacito Canyons, less than a half-mile north of Tapacito Ruin. Four single-story rooms sit atop a 40-ft-high boulder, and there may have been a second story. The site commands an impressive view of the bench on which the boulder sits, the west side of Canyon Largo, and a long stretch of the canyon downstream (to the northwest).

✤ TAPACITO RUIN: (6550 ft) Rio Arriba County, NM. Like Split Rock Ruin, this site is situated on the east bank of Canyon Largo, on the north side of the mouth of Tapacito Canyon. It contains four well-preserved rooms, and has been dated to the A.D. 1690s, which makes it one of the earliest pueblitos recorded. Perhaps the site's biggest surprise is its "core and veneer" masonry, a style usually associated with prehistoric Chacoan sites dating to the Pueblo II and Pueblo III periods.

DIVIDE TRADING POST: [DB (map 12)] (approx. 6755 ft) McKinley County, NM. Richardson (1986, 246) credits James Damon, son of Anson C. Damon, with opening this post around 1940 and operating it for two years just east of

Window Rock, Arizona. However, Kelley (1977, 254) asserts a post existed here—just east of Window Rock—as early as 1921.

DOWA YALANI MOUNTAIN: (7100 ft) McKinley County, NM. Also Zuni Sacred Mountain, Corn Mountain, Thunder Mountain, Taaiyolone, Towayalani, and variations thereof. Navajo: Tséé'dóhdoon, "Rumbling Inside the Rock" (Young and Morgan 1987, 732); also Tsé Hooghan, "Rock House" (Kelley p.c. 1994). Located two miles southeast of Zuni Pueblo.

DULCE: [DB] (6800 ft) (Population: 2,438) Rio Arriba County, NM. Navajo: Beehai (Van Valkenburgh says Beehai Kééhbat'į), "Jicarilla Apache Home." Capital of the million-acre Jicarilla Apache Reservation. Located five miles south of the Colorado state line on U.S. Highway 64, this community is situated on a south fork of the Navajo River in a high mountain region of running streams, lakes, and grassy meadows bounded by ponderosa pine forests. The Denver & Rio Grande Railroad maintained a station here, and the U.S. Indian Service ran a cooperative trading post. The name Dulce is Spanish meaning "sweet," and derives from a spring in the area (Fugate and Fugate 1989, 183).

Dulce is well known to the eastern Navajos, particularly to those in the Counselor region, due to a long contact with the Jicarilla Apaches and the appreciable amount of government work they have received from this agency.

Most of the Jicarilla Apaches live in the mountainous region near Dulce in the north; the southern part of the reservation is used primarily for grazing.

The trading post at Dulce was for forty years the property of Emmett Wirt, pioneer trader and stockman of northern New Mexico.

DUSTY: (6400 ft) Socorro County, NM. Navajo: Tsé Hóteel (U.S. Indian Claims Commission n.d., vol. VI, xx), "Wide Rock." This ranching and mining community sits on New Mexico Highway 52 in the southwest corner of the county, near the site of the 1870s Ojo Caliente Indian Agency and cavalry post on Alamosa Creek.

Both Apache chiefs Victorio and Geronimo were once held here (Pearce 1965, 49).

DZIINTSAHAH: [DB] (6880 ft) San Juan County, NM. Navajo: Dził Ntsaaí, "Big Mountain." An extension of Cibola (or Blanco) Mesa, running along the San Juan River for 10 miles west of the mouth of Largo Canyon. It extends south to form the west margin of the Largo Canyon to its juncture with Jaques Canyon.

Dził Ntsaaí is sacred to the Navajos and is important in folklore. Many old Navajo sites are found along the rims and rincons of this mesa.

DZILDITLOI MOUNTAIN: (8400 ft) McKinley County, NM. Also Ziltigloi, Zilditloi Mountain. Navajo: Dził Ditł'ooí, "Fuzzy Mountain" or "Fluffy Mountain," although Gregory (1915, 155) thought it meant "Wooded Mountain" when he named it. Above and immediately east of the community of Navajo, and forming the southwest boundary of Todilto Park.

In the Gun Shooter Red Antway Myth, this elevation was attacked by supernaturals but protected by Thunder and Bear (Wyman 1965).

DZIL NDA KAI: (6070 ft) McKinley County, NM. Also Little Ear Mountain. Navajo: Dził Nda'akai, "Yeibichei Dance Hill" (Kelley p.c. 1994). Small sandstone bluff in the flats of Coyote Wash, a mile east of the wash, some four miles north of Navajo Route 9. A possible Chacoan prehistoric road lies in this vicinity (Gabriel 1991, 279).

EL MALPAIS (NATIONAL MONUMENT): (6550 ft) Cibola County, NM. Also El Malpais Lava Flow, San Mateo Lava Flow. Navajo: Yé'-iitsoh Bidił Niníyęęzhí, "Where Big God's Blood Coagulated" (Van Valkenburgh 1974, 15). One of the nation's newest national monuments, this one spotlights on El Malpais (Spanish: "The Badland"), the lava flows from volcanos in the San Mateo and Zuni Mountains. The flows extend from the Grants/Milan area south approximately 35 miles. Most lie between New Mexico Highway 53 (on the west) and New Mexico Highway 117 (on the east), an area four to six miles wide. The monument lies west of New Mexico Highway 117 between 10 and 31 miles south of I-40, extending west to the Ice Caves.

The Navajo name derives from that portion of the Navajo creation myth in which the Twin War Gods on Mount Taylor (Apache and Jim 1982, 12)—or the Zuni Mountains (WPA 1940b, 320)—killed Yé'iitso, "Big God," a monster. The lava flows are the coagulated blood of Yé'iitso. The legend holds that if the lava flows separated by the Rio San Jose ever grow together, Big God will live again (Van Valkenburgh 1974, 58).

Bandelier suggested Navajos had killed "many people" along the railroad right-of-way in the lava flow east of Grants (Lange and Riley 1966, 282).

EL MORRO NATIONAL MONUMENT: [DB] (6800–7000 ft) Cibola County, NM. Also Inscription Rock. Navajo: Tsék'i Na'asdzooí, "Rock that Has Marks (Writing) on It" (Young p.c. 1995); also Tséikiin, "Refuge Rock," more literally, "Rock Where there is Water and Food" (Young and Morgan 1987, 729). South of New Mexico Highway 53, 12 miles east of Ramah. Site of Inscription Rock. The Spanish "El Moro" refers to the big round promontory that rises 200 ft above the lava-strewn valley. In addition to the famous inscriptions, there is a major Anasazi ruin and a number of smaller ones located on the crown of the rock.

Spanish explorers named the rock and left over 50 inscriptions, the earliest dating from 1605 (or 1606). The eminent Soutwestern writer Charles Lumis noted an inscription dating as early as 1580 that is no longer visible (Lister and Lister 1983, 115). Hundreds of other inscriptions commemorate visits of missionaries, soldiers, immigrants, traders, and travelers. El Morro was a strategic point on the old Zuni-Acoma Trail. The cove on the east side afforded shelter for a whole company, where a deep pool was always full of fresh water.

The earliest inscription discernible today is that of Don Juan de Oñate, governor and colonizer of the Province of New Mexico and founder of Santa Fe. In 1605, on his return journey from the Gulf of California to New Mexico, he passed El Morro and left a record of his visit cut into the sandstone walls. Governor Manuel de Silva Nieto, who succeeded Oñate and conveyed the first Franciscan missionaries to the Zuni village of Hawikuh, left an inscription dated July 29, 1629, which reads in part:

> I am Captain-General of the provinces of New Mexico for the King, our Lord. Passed here on the return from the towns of Zuni on the 29th day of July of the year 1629, and put them at peace at their petition, they asking favor as vassals of his Majesty, and promising anew their obedience, all of which he did, with clemency, zeal, and prudence, as a most Christianlike (gentleman) extraordinary and gallant soldier of enduring and praised memory.

Three Zunis were killed here by Apaches in 1752 (Ferguson and Hart 1985, 60). Lieutenant J. H. Simpson and the artist R. H. Kern, though not the first Americans to see the rock, visited the place in 1849, and Simpson's report contains a lengthy description of the rock, together with Kern's invaluable sketches.

In addition to the inscriptions in Spanish and English, there are many Indian glyphs carved on the walls. Far above the inscriptions and reached today by a paved foot trail is a large Anasazi pueblo called "Atsina" (a Zuni word for "writing on the rock") occupied between A.D. 1200 and 1300, containing possibly a thousand rooms, and considered ancestral to the nearby Zuni Indians.

Inscription Rock and 240 acres of land were set aside as the El Morro National Monument by presidential proclamation in 1906.

ENCINAL: (6400 ft) Cibola County, NM. Also Encinel. Navajo uncertain. This Laguna colony lies in a valley between two mesas some four miles northeast of Cubero, and two miles east of Picacho Peak. The name Encinal is Spanish meaning "Oak Grove."

In 1744 (Van Valkenburgh 1941, 53), or 1745 (Reeve 1959), or 1748 (McNitt 1972, 27–28), or 1749 (Adams and Chavez 1956, 187), the Franciscan Fathers established a mission at this site for the Navajos, which failed after two years. The Navajos of the region departed for the Zuni Mountains, Chuska Valley, and Canyon de Chelly in the fall of 1816 (McNitt 1972, 47). They attacked sheep herder Juan de Dios Gallegos here on June 25, 1856 (McNitt 1972, 280).

A few Navajos live on the slopes of Mount Taylor some 10 miles northwest of Encinal.

ESCAVADA WASH: [DB] (7000–6200 ft) San Juan and Sandoval counties, NM. Navajo: Gah 'Adádí, "Where You can Block the Rabbit's Trail" (Van Valkenburgh 1941, 54) or "Rabbit Ambush" (Young and Morgan 1987, 369). A tributary of the Chaco River, heading about two miles southwest of Lybrook (on New Mexico Highway 44), formed by the convergence of Bitani Tsosi (Bit'ahniits'ósí) Wash and Deesh Bik' Anii'á Bitó (Béésh Bíyaa 'Anii'á Bitooh) Wash.

This channel is more extensive than Van Valkenburgh's estimated five-mile lengh. It travels 26 miles southwest and west to the Chaco River at the northwestern corner of Chaco National Historical Park, at Tó Bíla'í, "Water Fingers" (Van Valkenburgh 1941, 54; Young and Morgan 1987, 706), near what Van Valkenburgh refers to as "Roy Newton's camp" and Peñasco Blanco Ruin. Pearce's (1965, 34) description of "Choukai Wash" fits this channel, even though that publication also includes a separate listing for "Escarvada" (*sic*) Wash. According to Pearce, "Escarvada" may be a corruption of Spanish "excavada," derived from "excavar," which means to excavate, possibly relating to the many prehistoric ruins in the vicinity. Brugge (p.c. 1996) concurs with the derivation, but asserts the name actually refers to the fact that water can be found by excavating in the bed of the wash.

ESCONDIDO MOUNTAIN: (9869 ft) Catron County, NM. Navajo: K'ai'tsoh, "Big Willow" (Young and Morgan 1987, 501). Navajos have traditionally gathered wild plants on this mountain (U.S. Indian Claims Commission n.d., vol. IV, 712–15), and Navajo hogans with early dates are found on the mountain (Brugge p.c. 1996).

ESCRITO SPRING: (7000 ft) Rio Arriba County, NM. Navajo: Tódóó Hódik'ą́adi (Van Valkenburgh 1974, 12), "Slanted Water" (Kelley p.c. 1994), or "Where an Area Extending from the Water is Slanted" (Young p.c. 1995). Also "Spring from a High Place." Located near Lybrook on New Mexico Highway 44. The spring has Navajo clan associations, and there are many old Navajo sites in this vicinity.

ESPAÑOLA: [DB] (5589 ft) Rio Arriba County, NM. Navajo: Uncertain. This Hispanic farming community straddles the Rio Grande about 24 miles north of Santa Fe, and just south of the confluence of the Rio Grande and the Chama River. The town is situated on U.S. Highways 84 and 285. Navajos often traded at Española, though this has diminished in recent years.

FAJADA WASH: (6575–6150 ft) McKinley and San Juan counties, NM. Navajo: Uncertain. This wash heads in a series of ephemeral washes gathering a few miles north of Whitehorse, southeast of Pueblo Pintado. It flows northwest approximately 20 miles, merging with the Chaco Wash just east of Fajada Butte within the main body of the Chaco Culture National Historical Park. It has also been called Becenti Wash.

FARMINGTON: [DB] (5308 ft) (Population: 33,997) San Juan County, NM. Navajo: Tóta', "Between the Waters," referring to the fact that the community lies between the San Juan and Animas rivers. This agricultural, Indian trading, and oil refining center lies primarily north of the San Juan River.

Farmington was founded in the 1880s, and during its early days was the scene of many difficulties with the Navajos over land tenure. The northeast corner of the Navajo Reservation is two miles west of Farmington, and Navajos have lived on the south side of the San Juan River in this vicinity for many years, coming to Farmington to barter their products for the excellent fruits grown in the region. They now shop in the town quite regularly all year round.

The Navajo Methodist Mission School was operated by the Woman's Home Missionary Society beginning in 1890. Originally a grade school, it was developed into a vocational high school for a hundred Indian children by the 1940s. In 1941, Van Valkenburgh thought it important to note the presence of an Episcopal hospital on the south bank of the San Juan, the Christian Reformed Farmington Mission, and the Navajo Methodist Mission one mile west of the town.

In 1932, the Soil Conservation Service identified a possible Chacoan prehistoric road in the vicinity of the town (Gabriel 1991, 277). The town's population grew wildly during the 1950s, from 3,637 to 23,786, a sevenfold increase (Smith 1992, 163), due largely to the oil industry.

FENCED UP HORSE CANYON RUIN: (6900 ft) McKinley County, NM. Navajo: Possibly "Łíí Biná'ásht'ih, "Horse Enclosed in Fence." This Cibolan ruin dates to A.D. 1100–1250, and contains 16 separate roomblocks and a great kiva complex. It is located on the west side of Fenced Up Horse Canyon on the old Fort Wingate Munitions Depot military reservation. Situated 90 ft above the valley floor, the largest structure in the site, Casa Vibora contains 133 ground-floor rooms, 20 second-floor rooms, nine kivas, and a great kiva in association.

FENCE LAKE: (7000 ft) Cibola County, NM. Navajo: "Dibé 'Íijéé', "Sheep Ran Away" (Kelley p.c. 1994; U.S. Indian Claims Commission n.d., vol. VI, v); also Be'ekid Biná'ázt'i', "Fenced Lake," or "Lake Surrounded by a Fence." Situated 33 miles south of Zuni on New Mexico Highway 36, where that road makes a 90-degree turn to the east. This community was founded by Texan migrants fleeing the "dust bowl" drought in the 1930s, and was included (along with Ramah) in an anthropological study of multiculturalism under the guidance of Clyde Kluckhohn (Vogt and Albert 1970).

FIGUEREDO WASH: (7500–5900 ft) McKinley County, NM. Navajo: Uncertain. Spanish-surnamed creek bed heading in the eastern slopes of the Chuska Mountains west of Mexican Springs (Naakaii Bitó'). It flows easterly, south of Mexican Springs into the San Juan Basin, where it joins Coyote Wash some five miles north of Navajo Route 9 at a point 10 miles east of Tohatchi. (Granger [1960, 11] erroneously places this creek as partially in Arizona, when it actually comes no closer than nine miles to the state line.) It was named for Roque de Figueredo, a missionary to the Zuni Indians in 1629. A possible Chacoan prehistoric road segment along the wash is aligned with Mexican Springs (Gabriel 1991, 279).

FORD BUTTE: (6000 ft) San Juan County, NM. Navajo: Chézhiní, "Lava Rock" (Kelley p.c. 1994). This solitary lava "plug" sits a half-mile east of U.S. Highway 666, some 22 miles south of Shiprock village. It is almost directly across U.S. Highway 666 from Bennett Peak, a slightly larger butte of similar volcanic origin. The English name almost almost certainly commemorates someone named Ford, but just who remains uncertain.

FORT MARCY: (7000 ft) Santa Fe County, NM. Navajo: Uncertain, but probably referred to by the name given to Santa Fe: Yootó, "Bead Water." This post was built near the plaza in Santa Fe by Colonel Stephen Watts Kearny, U.S. Army, in 1846. Kearny erected a flagpole so large that "men walked 60 miles to see it." The fort served as military headquarters for New Mexico Territory and thus was the launch point of expeditions against the Navajos until most of its garrison was removed to Fort Union in 1851 (Frink 1968, 8–9). The fort had no water, so soldiers were housed in the town of Santa Fe, manning the fort in shifts or on call (Giese 1991, 7–8).

FORT SUMNER (OLD): [DB] (4025 ft) De Baca County, NM. Navajo: Hwéeldi, a corruption of the Spanish "fuerte," or "fort" (Van Valkenburgh 1941, 58). This deserted site is four miles south of U.S. Highway 60, three miles east of the present town of Fort Sumner in southeastern New Mexico. The fort was built in the Bosque Redondo (Spanish meaning "Round Grove") on the Pecos River in 1863 to house an Army contingent overseeing the Indian residents of a new reservation. Older Navajos called it T'iis Názbąs ("Cottonwood Circle," the same as Teec Nos Pos, Arizona).

The fort was situated just north of the confluence of the Pecos River with Alamogordo Creek, a locale visited by Captain Arellano of Coronado's 1541 Quivira expedition (Bolton 1949, 274), de Sosa in 1590 (Schroeder 1965, 72), the Rodriguez-Chamuscado expedition in 1581 (Chilton et al. 1984, 380), and by Espejo in 1583 (Schroeder 1965, 4).

After some 8,500 Navajos were removed from their homeland in 1863–64, they were force-marched on the infamous "Long Walk" to the Bosque Redondo on the Pecos River in east-central New Mexico. Here they were settled on a reservation 40 miles square, which they were to share with the Mescalero Apaches, under the watchful eyes of the troops at Fort Sumner. (The Apaches stayed until 1865 and decamped in one night.)

The Long Walk was devastating to the Navajos, and tales of cruelty on the part of their White guards persist today. It has been said that the trail to the Bosque Redondo reservation could be identified by the bodies strewn along the way. While many were the victims of brutality, even more were the unfortunate casualties of stupid oversights. For instance, the Army issued wheat flour to the Navajos, but did not give any instructions for cooking a substance so alien to the Indians, and many died of dysentery after eating flour mixed with water (Mangum 1991, 403).

The Navajos tried to farm the alkaline soil from the irrigation system laid out by Army officers, but each year brought greater failure and a mounting death rate. Desertions (escapes) were numerous, and graft by military and civil agents robbed the Navajos of government supplies. Conditions became so deplorable that in the spring of 1868, General W. T. Sherman and Colonel Francis Tappan, Indian Peace Commissioners, were sent to Fort Sumner and there drafted the Navajo Treaty of June 1, 1868. Within one month, the Navajos were on their way home. No old Navajo forgets Hwéeldi and the four years spent in far eastern New Mexico. Many of that generation even calculated their age from the date of return.

While at the Bosque, Navajos lived a rigidly controlled life. Article 6 of the treaty sending them to the Bosque read: "Any adult Indian who shall be found absent from his or her village between the hours of 7 o'clock pm and 5 o'clock am in winter, and between 8 o'clock pm and

4 o'clock am in summer, shall be imprisoned" (Brader 1990, 126).

The home of Lucien B. Maxwell, in which famed bandit Billy the Kid was killed on July 18, 1881, served as the Army officers' billet during the Navajo incarceration. Deluvina Maxwell, the woman who first entered the dark room where the dead or dying Billy lay, was an Indian slave girl who claimed to be a Navajo from Canyon de Chelly, sold to Lucien Maxwell by Apache captors (Keleher 1962, 73, 74n).

On June 6, 1868, the Navajo return to their homeland was nearly cancelled when renegades fled the reservation and killed six Whites on Twelve Mile Creek (12 miles from the post). The Army pursued these fugitives with the help of the Navajo headmen from the reservation, and all were killed or captured near Apache Springs (Thompson 1976, 156). The planned Navajo release of June 18 took place as scheduled.

The fort (with the exception of the cemetery) was officially turned over to the Department of the Interior on February 24, 1871, though the reservation had been transferred back on October 31, 1867.

Today it is a large grassy field with few visible remnants of the original fort.

FORT UNION: (6847 ft) San Miguel County, NM. Navajo: Uncertain. Founded in 1851 to guard the Santa Fe Trail, this post on the western edge of the Great Plains near Las Vegas, New Mexico, was constructed of pine logs (Giese 1991, 7–8). The fort became the focal point of the military forays into Navajo country in 1851, when Fort Marcy's garrison was reduced and Fort Defiance opened (Frink 1968, 8–9).

FORT WINGATE: [DB] (7000 ft) McKinley County, NM. Navajo: Shash Bitoo, "Bear Spring." Also Bear Springs, Big Bear Spring. Situated three miles south of I-40, 12 miles east of Gallup, this site of the old military fort (and now a boarding school, farming, mining, and ranching community) has a colorful history. The Navajos had known of the fine spring in the vicinity for quite some time before the arrival of the Whites. The Spanish name for the region, Ojo del Oso, came from the Navajo name. In 1821–

22, and again in 1836, both long before the military post was established, Navajos were killed in this vicinity by Spanish soldiers (Ferguson and Hart 1985, 60–61).

The name Fort Wingate has referred to a total of four southwestern posts. There were actually two Fort Wingates—referred to as "Old" and "New"—in New Mexico. To confuse matters even more, the second fort was assigned "Wingate" as its third name. It had previously been known as Fort Fauntleroy and Fort Lyon. A third installation garrisoned at Cebolleta (some 30 miles northeast of Old Fort Wingate) between 1846 and 1851 has sometimes been confused in the literature with the "old" Fort Wingate (Van Arsdale 1971). Further complication arises in the fact that Fort Wise, a post in southern Colorado, also previously bore the names Fort Fauntleroy and Fort Wingate (Frazer 1972, 41–42).

Old Fort Wingate was established at Ojo del Gallo (Spanish, meaning "Chicken Spring"), three miles south of present-day Grants, on October 22, 1862. It was named for Captain (Brevet Major) Benjamin Wingate, 5th U.S. Infantry, who had previously served at Fort Fauntleroy some 50 miles to the west at Bear Springs. Wingate died on February 21, 1862, of wounds received from Confederate soldiers on June 1, 1861, in the Battle of Valverde on the southern Rio Grande (Frazer 1972, 108; Mangum 1991, 396).

Navajos called this post Béésh Dáádílkał, "Iron Door," and it was one of the few western forts surrounded by a stockade. Plans for the fort called for 4,340 feet of eight-foot-high wooden stockade, which required over a million feet of lumber. The post also incorporated 9,317 feet of foot-thick, eight-foot-high adobe walls. Much of these materials were salvaged from the previously abandoned Fort Lyon (formerly known as Fort Fauntleroy and later, when reoccupied, to be named "New" Fort Wingate) at Bear Springs (Mangum 1991, 398).

Old Fort Wingate was first garrisoned by Companies D and G, First Dragoons, and it served as Kit Carson's headquarters in rounding up the Navajos in 1863–64. Navajo chieftain Manuelito surrendered at the post, effectively ending the Navajo War (Mangum 1991, 410). The post was ordered abandoned in 1868, and the name was transferred to the previously abandoned Fort Lyon at Bear Spring.

Fort Lyon was situated at the foot of the northwestern end of the Zuni Mountains, overlooking the Wingate Valley just three miles south of present I-40. It had originally been established on August 31, 1860, as Fort Fauntleroy, with seven officers and 240 enlisted men of Companies C, E, F, and K, 5th U.S. Infantry, "126 miles west and a little north of Albuquerque, and 40 miles southeast of Fort Defiance" (McNitt 1972, 392n). It was named for department commander Colonel Thomas T. Fauntleroy, 1st U.S. Dragoons. Fauntleroy, however, left the Army at the outbreak of the Civil War to join the Confederacy, so the post's name was changed to Fort Lyon on September 25, 1861. This name honored Union Brigadier General Nathanial Lyon, killed at the Battle of Wilson's Creek, Missouri, on August 10, 1861.

The Union Army, being mauled by the Confederates, found soldiers in short supply, so regular Army troops were withdrawn from Fort Lyon in August and September 1861, to head east. They were replaced with New Mexico militia until the fort was closed about two months later (McNitt 1972, 421; Frazer 1972, 108).

During their tenure, the Fort Fauntleroy Massacre (the post's new name had not yet caught on) was one of the most infamous events to occur at either fort. In August 1861, many Navajos had gathered at the fort for rations and a council with their new agent, Ramon Luna. A festive atmosphere was enjoyed by all, and Luna and special agent John Ward agreed to meet with the Navajos again in 40 days. Some five hundred Navajos remained in the vicinity of the post and a series of horse races started on September 10. Three days later, a race went sour when a Navajo named Pistol Bullet raced his horse against one owned by the post surgeon. Pistol Bullet lost control of his mount and lost the race. The Navajos accused the Whites of cutting his bridle rein, and pandemonium broke loose. A dozen Navajos were killed by small arms and cannon fire; there were no White casualties.

Colonel Manuel Chavez, the commandant and known hater of Navajos, was accused by Navajos and his own subordinates of precipitating the hostilities and overreacting, causing the unnecessary deaths. He was temporarily relieved of command, but never placed on trial (McNitt 1972, 421–28, 427n–28n), and the post was closed.

When the Navajos returned to their homeland in the summer of 1868, Old Fort Wingate was too far away from the newly established reservation for adequate guard duty, so, on July 25, 1868, the fort was abandoned and its name transferred to what had been Fort Lyon. This post became commonly known as "New" Fort Wingate, or Fort Wingate II.

According to 'Ayóó Ániłnézii ("Very Tall Man"), a Navajo traditionalist in the 1930s, the Navajo name (Shash Bitoo) originated in the following incident:

> Many years ago when the Navajos were raiding on the New Mexicans, the war parties used to stop at Bear Spring. There was always a bear near the springs, and Hastiin Nihoobáa-nii, a Navajo warrior of the Nihoobáanii Dine'é Clan, stopped there on his second raid, and again saw a bear. Hoping to gain success, he cast offerings into the spring—which was located south and west of the present school and was sacred to the Navajos. Nihoobáa-nii's raid was successful and on his return from the Rio Grande he named the spring Shashbitoo. This was long over one old man's life ago. (Van Valkenburgh 1941, 59)

Hastiin Nihoobáa-nii remains an obscure figure, but Brugge (p.c. 1996) suggests that perhaps he took part in the war of 1774–75.

New Fort Wingate's future location was shown as Ojo del Oso (Spanish for "Bear Spring") on the Miera y Pacheco maps of 1779, and seems to have been of common usage by then. The Treaty of Bear Springs was signed there between Narbona, Zarcillas Largo, and other Navajo chiefs and Colonel Alexander Doniphan of the 3rd Missouri Volunteers of the United States Army in 1846, and it was a regular stopping place on the military road between Albuquerque and Fort Defiance in the years 1851–54. In 1863, after the closure of Fort Lyon, the location was an express station for use during the Navajo War. It served as one of the stops for the Navajos traveling to Fort Sumner, though no military post existed at the springs at the time.

By an executive order of 1870, the 10-mile-square military reservation of 1860 was expanded to one hundred square miles, and in 1881 it was enlarged again, to 130 square miles, to include certain timber resources. In 1911, after the military post was decommissioned, the entire Fort Wingate reserve became a part of the Zuni National Forest but remained under the control of the War Department for military purposes. Troops continued to be stationed there until 1912.

One of the most interesting military figures connected with Fort Wingate was Dr. Washington Matthews, called Hataałii Nééz, "Tall Medicine Man," by the Navajos. As surgeon at Fort Wingate 1880–84 and 1894–95, he became an outstanding authority on Navajo culture. His many publications remain standard references in scientific literature on Navajo ethnology.

Victorio, the chief of the Warm Springs band of the Chiricahua Apaches, and members of his band were interned at Fort Wingate in 1880 and later returned to their country by Agent Thomas V. Keam. Some of them, however, led by an Apache sub-chief called Loco, stayed in the Navajo country and left descendants in the Chíshí Dine'é (Chiricahua Apache) Clan of the Navajo—a number of whom still live in the vicinity of Fort Wingate.

During the Poncho Villa uprisings in Mexico, Fort Wingate was used to intern refugees from northern Mexico (WPA 1940b, 322). A number died here, and their graves can be seen in the cemetery a half-mile east of the school. The Southwestern Range and Sheep Breeding Laboratory (U.S. Department of the Interior and U.S. Department of Agriculture) was installed three miles south of the depot, and became a district headquarters for the National Forest Service.

In 1925 the Indian Department (later Bureau of Indian Affairs) took over the buildings and an area around Fort Wingate under a lease from the War Department. The barracks and officers' quarters were turned into dormitories and residences for Indian students and their instructors. The original name, Charles H. Burke Vocational School and Hospital, was changed in 1937 to the Wingate Vocational High School. In 1941 it had an enrollment of five hundred pupils, predominantly Navajo. The curriculum stressed academic training and vocational work (adapted to preparation for living in the Navajo country) along with Navajo arts and crafts.

The Zunis used to acquire soapstone in the vicinity of the fort for making fetishes (Ferguson and Hart 1985, 129).

Today few of the old Army buildings remain standing; all are condemned. A more modern complex of government buildings is comprised of Wingate High School and Wingate Elementary School, BIA boarding schools.

FORT WINGATE ARMY DEPOT: (6800 ft) McKinley County, NM. Navajo: Same as Fort Wingate. U.S. Army munitions storage depot three miles west of the erstwhile New Fort Wingate. The storage of munitions began here as a Magazine Area right after World War I (WPA 1940b, 322). Over 46,000,000 pounds of TNT were stored here until the stock was sold to England, the last of it just one month before the Japanese attack on Pearl Harbor. The post expanded tremendously during World War II, and served as a storage depot until it closed in January 1993. As late as 1997, highly unstable munitions were still being removed from the bunkers with occasional accidental explosions. A large number of Navajos were employed at the depot during its heyday. (See also Church Rock.)

FORT WINGATE TRADING POST: (approx. 7000 ft) McKinley County, NM. Also Wingate Trading Post. Navajo: Same as Fort Wingate. This post began as a combination military sutler and Indian trader. The first trader was Willi Spiegelberg, appointed on July 8, 1868, the first officially sanctioned trader to the Navajos—though he was off-reservation and thus did not need a license. His brother Lehman was the first to receive a license to trade on the reservation, on August 28 of that year, trading at Fort Defiance eight years prior to Congress's formal creation of the position of civilian post traders. Willi and Lehman were two of the German Jewish Spiegelberg Brothers (the others being Jacob, Levi, and Emanual), whose importation and wholesale and retail empire stretched from New York City to Santa Fe.

Spiegelberg left in March of 1869, leaving the

post (which, like the "fort," was really no more than a collection of tents) to one John L. Waters. Henry Reed was licensed to trade there from 1872 to 1877, employing a young Lorenzo Hubbell, who would become a giant in the Navajo trading industry. Lambert Hopkins took over in 1877, but was bankrupt by 1882 (McNitt 1962, 80, 83n, 142n, 164–65). A post was operated here by Richard White in the 1930s and 1940s, and the Merrill family ran it through the middle 1990s—though it shifted its emphasis to restaurant and convenience store.

FOUR CORNERS: [DB] (4800 ft) San Juan County, NM., Apache County, AZ., San Juan County, UT., and Montezuma County, CO. Navajo: Tsé 'Íí'áhí, "Rock Spire" (Young and Morgan 1987, 730). A Navajo Tribal Monument has been erected at the only point in the United States where four states (New Mexico, Colorado, Utah, and Arizona) and two Indian reservations (Navajo and Ute Mountain) come together. On U.S. Highway 160, six miles northeast of Teec Nos Pos, Arizona. A trading post that was operated here by Wilken and Whitecraft in 1910 is now abandoned (see Four Corners Trading Post).

The benchmark was set in 1875, and a small cement boundary marker was installed in 1912. The Four Corners Monument was established by the Navajo Nation in 1964.

This location is not without its controversy. A 1925 survey proved the original 1868 survey of the 37th Parallel was in error, placing the boundary between New Mexico and Colorado and between Arizona and Utah some one hundred yards too far south. The courts ruled that the original boundaries would stand, but this created a problem between the Navajos and Utes. The U.S. treaty with the Navajos gave them land north to the 37th Parallel, while the treaty with the Utes gave them land south to the New Mexico–Colorado state line. Thus, a strip of land a hundred yards wide and 25 miles long remains contested by both tribes, with no solution in sight (Fugate and Fugate 1989, 177–78).

FOUR CORNERS TRADING POST: (4800 ft) Navajo: Uncertain, probably the same as Four Corners. This post was operated at the conver-

gence of the four states about 1910, by Wilken and Whitecraft (Van Valkenburgh 1941, 60). It had been abandoned by the time of Van Valkenburgh's writing.

FRUITLAND: [DB] (5100 ft) San Juan County, NM. Navajo: Bááh Díílid, "Burned Bread" (Van Valkenburgh 1941, 60); also Niinah Nízaad or Nenahnezad, "Long Upgrade" (Young and Morgan 1987, 669). This Mormon farming community and Navajo trading center is located on the north bank of the San Juan River, 18 miles east of Shiprock, and 11 miles west of Farmington, on U.S. Highway 550 (and formerly on the Denver & Rio Grande Western Railroad). Trading concerns in the vicinity have included Albert Farnsworth (see Fruitland Trading Post), Southside Trading Post, Fruitland Trading Co., Joe Hatch, Hatch & Ashcroft, and Ray Foutz.

The name Bááh Díílid was derived from Navajo observation of a Mormon burning a batch of bread. Early maps show this location as Burnham, a name bestowed in 1877–78 to honor Mormon Bishop Luther C. Burnham. The name Fruitland was selected to advertise the agricultural enterprise (WPA 1940b, 178–79).

The vicinity was first settled by the Mormon families of Benjamin T. Boice and Jeremiah Hatch, in 1878. The population was swelled in 1903 by the arrival of many Mormons displaced when their enclave at Tuba City was annexed to the reservation in a western extension of its boundaries. In 1892 the mesa south of Fruitland was recommended as an agricultural experiment irrigation project for the Navajos along the San Juan River. Immediately south of this is the vast Navajo Indian Irrigation Project (NIIP).

The Fruitland Ditch, built between 1933 and 1935, was the largest irrigation project of its time on the reservation. Unfortunately, inept government leadership led to chaos and failure of the project (Bailey and Bailey 1986, 204).

FRUITLAND PROJECT. Navajo: Niinah Nízaad, "Long Upgrade." This agricultural project was a precursor of the Navajo Indian Irrigation Project (NIIP). Located on the south side of the San Juan River, the Fruitland Project began as a narrow strip running some 16 miles from the dam (two miles west of Farmington) westward along the south river bank to near the Hogback. It consists of small farm tracts asigned to Navajo farmers who have individual rights to them as long as they plant regularly.

The first irrigation ditch in the vicinity was the Costiano Ditch, dug before 1880. The heading of this Navajo ditch was one mile south of the present San Juan River bridge at Farmington. During the 1880s, it irrigated some one hundred acres of Navajo farmland. When the Executive Order of 1880 added this section to the Navajo Reservation, White squatters refused to move off the lands. Violence was averted only by troops sent from Fort Lewis, Colorado, to eject them.

Cornfield's Ditch, as the Costiano Ditch was later known, supplied the lower agricultural area until 1939, when it was replaced by the New Fruitland Canal. This Indian Irrigation Service project, made possible by federal grants, was completed in 1939 and served some 1,400 acres of agricultural land. Under the Indian Service policy of conservation and development of Navajo resources, the lands under this canal were allotted to Navajos without livestock.

FRUITLAND TRADING POST: (5100 ft) San Juan Co., NM. Navajo: Uncertain. Opened in 1884, by Mormon Albert Farnsworth.

GALLEGOS CANYON AND GALLEGOS MESA: [DB] (6200–5400 ft) San Juan County, NM. Navajo: "Teeł Sikaad," "Clump of Cattails" (Young and Morgan 1987, 705). The ephemeral tributary canyon to the San Juan River heads five miles south of Huerfano Mesa, and flows northwest 30 miles to join the San Juan River approximately five miles east of Farmington. Gallegos Trading Post was located 10 miles southeast of Farmington, and the Navajo name comes from a small cienega in the vicinity of that trading post. Near the trading post is the site of the old Carlisle Cattle Company's ranch headquarters. In the 1870s, cowboys of this English-owned company engaged in a murderous fight with Mexican sheep men, and they were constantly embroiled with the Navajos over range and water rights.

Van Valkenburgh noted that, at least prior to

the 1940s, some maps called the Gallegos "Ojo Amarilla Wash," but this name refers to another wash some 10 miles to the west (though it does not flow into Chaco Wash as Van Valkenburgh contended). The east fork of the Gallegos runs past Carson Trading Post.

Navajo presence in the Gallegos Mesa area has been dated by archaeologists to as early as A.D. 1690 ± 80 years (Sessions and Williams 1979, 202). The first trading post was opened here some 30 years ago by an Englishman named Dick Simpson. The wash flows through the "Checkerboard Area," where alternate parcels are Indian land. Some Navajos live along the wash on allotted lands and an occasional White homesteader is found eking out a precarious existence on the waterless rolling hills that border the Gallegos.

GALLEGOS TRADING POST: (5783 ft) San Juan County, NM. Navajo: Uncertain, probably the same as Gallegos Wash. This post opened prior to 1910 (Kelley 1977, 252). Van Valkenburgh (1941, 61) lists it as being located about 10 miles southeast of Farmington in 1941.

GALLINAS: [DB as Gallina] (3600 ft) Rio Arriba County, NM. Navajo: Dził Deez'á, "Upper Ending of the Mountains." A Spanish-American settlement located on the south side of the Gallinas Creek in a picturesque country backed on the south by the northern extension of the Jemez Mountains. The village is situated on New Mexico Highway 96, seven miles east of its junction with New Mexico Highway 95. Four miles east of the Rio Gallina, one mile south of the Rio Capulin. Gallinas is Spanish meaning "Chickens."

Across the creek and north of the sheer red sandstone escarpments lie Capulin Peak and Cajita Blanca Ridge. There are many archaeological ruins in the region. Once an old Navajo hunting territory.

Navajo traditionalists consider this old Tewa Indian country the origin of the Tábąąhá Dine'é (Beside the Water Clan) of the Navajos. It is said that before they joined the Navajos they moved westward from the Gallinas via Stinking Lake to the San Juan River. It is interesting to note that Tó Łigaii (White Water), the Navajo name for Gallinas Creek, is similar to the Tewa designation.

GALLO CANYON: (6200–6000 ft) McKinley County, NM. Navajo: Tłohchin Nááholyé, "Wild Onions" (Franciscan Fathers 1910, 133), more accurately "Another Place Named Onions" (Young p.c. 1995). Also Ndíshchíí' Haazt'i', "Pine Trees Extend up in a Slender Line" (Young and Morgan 1987, 613). This tributary of Chaco Wash rises on North Mesa in the main body of the National Cultural Park and flows south to Chaco Canyon between Wijiji and Una Vida Ruins.

GALLUP: [DB] (6506 ft) (Population: 19,154) McKinley County, NM. Navajo: Na'nízhoozhí, "Spanned Across." Old Navajo name: T'iis Tsoh Sikaad (U.S. Indian Claims Commission n.d., vol. VI, xv), "Big Cottonwood Sits" (Young p.c. 1995). This town is located in the rock-rimmed valley of the Rio Puerco of the West at the junction of I-40 (formerly U.S. Highway 66) and U.S. Highway 666, 21 miles east of the Arizona state line. Wholesale distribution point for art and crafts and major tourist center (particularly in mid-August at the time of the Inter-Tribal Indian Ceremonial). The Burlington Northern Santa Fe Railway passes through the town, and Gallup is one of only three New Mexico stops for Amtrak passenger service. The Santa Fe Railroad used to maintain a station, roundhouse, shops, etc. in Gallup, but these dwindled over the years until virtually all railroad personnel (some three hundred families) were transferred to Belen and to Winslow, Arizona, in the late 1980s.

Gallup has been known for brick manufacturing, uranium mining (until the late 1970s), and coal mining (until the late 1980s). Offices for the Soil Conservation Service were located here, along with a Bureau of Indian Affairs regional office.

The Gallup region was the scene of numerous clashes between the Navajos and the U.S. Army prior to the Navajo relocation of 1863–64. One of these, in the summer of 1863, was described by an old Navajo:

We found out that more soldiers were being sent to Fort Wingate near Bear Springs. Some Navajos

had been there and had spied on them. A band collected at Many Arrows (China Springs, four miles north of Gallup). They hid behind the rocks—all in a line and not far apart. A troop of soldiers came up the road, and the Navajos all shot at once. Cháali Sání shot the soldier captain right in the middle of the back of the neck and the bullet came out through his eye. Other soldiers which we called Naago 'Adiłdoní [Those Who Shoot From the Side], were shot down. Some got away on their horses. The Navajos chased them and got some horses. Cháali Sání, who was the leader of the Navajos did not get any. (Van Valkenburgh 1941, 62)

Author's Note: Other names for American soldiers were Bijaa' Yee Njahí ("Those Who Sleep on their Ears"), Bigod Doodilí ("Scorched Their Kneecaps"), Sha Bidiiłchii ("Sunburnt"), Táa'ji' Adeez'ahí (Something Extends Out at the Forehead"—so called after the shape of the military caps of the Civil War era). (Names are from Van Valkenburgh 1941, 62; translations corrected by Young p.c. 1995).

The Atlantic and Pacific Railroad reached the vicinity of Gallup in the fall of 1881. The discovery of coal and shallow water encouraged the railroad to start operations to mine coal at Mineral Springs (see Gallup Hogback). Early in 1882 a station was established at the present site of Gallup and named after David Gallup, the Comptroller of the Frisco Railway (associated with the Atlantic and Pacific during the building of the transcontinental railroad).

During the early days, Gallup and the surrounding villages were rip-roaring settlements. Eastman wrote the Commissioner of Indian Affairs on February 14, 1882:

I have hitherto governed these people through persuasion, and now all but a few heed my advice, but there is a condition of affairs at the four stations, viz. Bacon Springs or Coolidge, Gallup, Defiance Station and Defiance (formerly Sheridan) in the vicinity of Fort Wingate as is referred to in the Acting Governor Cosper's report to the President on the 9th instant, on conditions in southern Arizona. Bunco men and desperados collected there, including three or four hundred employees at the coal mines who are employed at the stations mentioned above. Two days since four men were killed at Crane's Station—or Coolidge as it is called. (Van Valkenburgh 1941, 63)

The evolution of Gallup beyond the railroad station and mining camp stage (populated largely by desperate characters) began after 1890, when traders on the reservation began opening outlets in Gallup in order to offer the Indian goods to the increasing numbers of travelers through the area. Clinton M. Cotton, formerly a partner of Don Lorenzo Hubbell of Ganado, was one of the first wholesalers to establish a business in Gallup. In 1890, there were fewer than 10 Navajo traders. The number increased until by 1941 there were over two hundred firms doing business in various parts of the Navajo area, and then it declined to fewer than 30 by the middle 1990s (Linthicum 1997, B1).

In 1941, Gallup's wholesalers handled nearly a quarter of a million dollars of Indian arts and crafts products per year. Today the figure is in the tens of millions. It has been estimated that 60 percent of Gallup's business is derived from Navajo, Zuni, and federal sources, and the remainder comes mainly from tourist trade (which is fed by the commerce of Indian arts). The town's population of 20,000 is estimated to swell to over 50,000 on weekends when Navajos and Zunis come to town.

The town continues a rocky relationship with the Navajo (and Zuni) tribes, as it houses dozens of liquor outlets that contribute to a severe addiction epidemic among the local Native Americans. It also plays host to two hospitals (one an Indian Health Service facility) and several addiction/mental health providers.

Gallup has been made world-famous by the annual Inter-Tribal Indian Ceremonial, held in the community every year since 1922 (except 1975). The defunct United Indian Traders Association flourished in the town between 1931 and 1950, as an effort to police an industry often permeated with fraud (imported and machine-made products labeled "Indian made").

GALLUP HOGBACK: [DB] (7000 ft) McKinley County, NM. Navajo: 'Alnaashii Háálíní, interpreted by Young (p.c. 1995) as "Water Flows Out (springs) on Opposite Sides." Also Tsé Ałtch'i' Naak'ání, "Converging Hogbacks"

(Young and Morgan 1987, 728). This high ridge, also known as the Nutria Monocline, is created by a geological formation called a monocline (a tilting of rock strata resulting in one edge jutting skyward). This one runs from the north bank of Ramah Reservoir in the south, through the Zuni Mountains to the eastern end of White Cliffs Mesa, a length of some 30 miles. It is most striking where it cuts through the far eastern end of the city of Gallup.

Old Route 66, the Rio Puerco of the West, and the Burlington Northern Santa Fe Railway pass through a natural break in the ridge approximately two miles south of the man-made cut through the ridge through which I-40 passes. The formation in this region is spotted with numerous pits and shafts from abandoned coal and uranium mines, especially in the vicinity of Gallup. (Local legend has it that one can get a full year's maximum recommended dosage of radiation just driving through this cut.)

In the 1850s the natural pass through the Hogback was known as Puertocito, or Little Gate (McComb's map of 1860), and in 1857 Lieutenant Edwin Beale stopped here with Uncle Sam's camels.

Ben Wittick called the hogback the "Stone Wall" in titling an 1890 photograph taken near Nutria (Ferguson and Hart 1985, 91).

GAMERCO: (6750 ft) McKinley County, NM. Navajo: "Łigai 'Íí'áhí, "White Thing Sticking Up" (Kelley p.c. 1994), a reference to the magnificent smokestack from the old coal mine that still stands in the community. Two miles north of Gallup, west of U.S. Highway 666. Established in 1920, named for the Gallup American Coal Company. Post office from 1923 to the present. The population in 1940 reached 1,221 people. Coal mines sent shafts four hundred feet deep, and horizontal tunnels held 30 miles of underground track.

The mines eventually died out, but open-pit or strip mines replaced them in the 1960s and 1970s.

GA'NGI DAI: Exact location uncertain. Catron County, NM. This is an Apache phrase, Géengii Dził, referring to a mountain, but with uncertain etymology. Due to the similarity in the Navajo and Apache languages, the Navajo name may be similar, yet the meaning is uncertain. This low peak about 15 miles north of Quemado was a source of Navajo plant and herb medicine (Van Valkenburgh 1974, 12).

THE GEYSER: (approx. 4800 ft) Valencia County, NM. Navajo: Tó' 'Ałchiní, "Wild Water." This spring eight miles south of Correo was important in the Navajo Blessingway Chant. Water from here was once carried to Blanca Peak for a ceremony (Van Valkenburgh 1974, 12, 66).

GOBERNADOR CANYON AND CREEK: (6400–5700 ft) Rio Arriba and San Juan counties, NM. Navajo: Uncertain. This 22-mile-long canyon is a tributary of the San Juan River, running southeast to northwest. It joins the San Juan at a point five miles west of Navajo Dam and Reservoir. The path of Gobernador Creek mostly parallels the route of U.S. Highway 64 east to Navajo City, then New Mexico Highway 539 for three miles before diverging into a deeper channel.

The canyon was traversed by Roque Madrid's expedition following their battle with Navajos in La Jara Canyon on August 11, 1705.

GOBERNADOR KNOB: [DB] (7100 ft) Rio Arriba County, NM. Navajo: Ch'óol'į'í, "Fir Mountain." (Young notes that this is a "folk etymology" and that the true meaning is unclear. The ceremonial name is Ntł'iz Dziil, "Hard Goods Mountain" (Young and Morgan 1987, 296). This rounded, cone-shaped pinnacle rises above the broken mesas sloping west from the continental divide toward Canyon Largo, between Cereza Canyon (on the south) and Munoz Canyon (on the north), some five miles west of the Jicarilla Apache Reservation, and about seven miles south of the community of Gobernador (trading post and post office).

Gobernador Knob is one of the sacred mountains of the Navajos interior to their homeland, and can be seen as a small cone from great distances to the west. In the vicinity of the knob, archaeological investigations since the 1930s have identified a number of old Navajo remains, and the region is a part of the Dinétah or Old Navajo

Country. Some 75 years ago Dr. Alfred V. Kidder of the Phillips-Andover Academy investigated what he believed to have been refuge sites of Puebloans fleeing Spanish vengeance during the troubled years following the Pueblo Revolt of 1680.

The Navajos have many traditions relating to Gobernador Knob, including this "condensation of one" related by Van Valkenburgh (1941, 66):

Jiní. Times were bad. Everywhere there were Enemy Monsters who killed and ate people. One day a rain cloud came to rest on Gobernador Knob. Gradually it enveloped the mountain until on the fourth day it completely covered it.

'Átsé Hastiin (First Man), seeing this from Huerfano Mountain told 'Átsé 'Asdzáán (First Woman) knew that something unusual was happening on Gobernador Knob. He went there to look things over and sang a Blessing Song as he went.

When he reached Gobernador Knob, he heard a baby cry. He found this baby lying with its head toward the west and its feet toward the east. Its cradle was made from two short rainbows. Across the baby's chest and feet lay the red beams of the rising sun. Arched over its face was another short rainbow. Four blankets covered the baby. One was black, another was blue, another was yellow and the fourth was a white cloud. Along both sides there was a row of loops made of lightning and through these sunbeams laced back and forth.

Not knowing what to do with the fastenings, First Man took the babe back to Huerfano Mountain to First Woman. He told her that he had found the baby in the darkness and rain on Gobernador Knob.

They heard the call of Haashch'é'éłti'í ("Talking God"), as he came. They heard the call of Haashch'é'ohaagan ("Growling God"), as he came. Talking God clapped his hands over his mouth and then struck them together saying something important had happened. The baby was what the Holy People had been wishing for. Talking God placed the child on the ground and with one pull of the strings, the lacings came free.

"This is my daughter," said the First Woman. First Man said the same. The days passed—they were the same as years—and when two years had passed, the girl sat up. She was then dressed in white shell. She walked for two days, and in three days, she danced. On the tenth day, she was named. She was called Yoołgai 'Adszááń (White Shell Woman). Thus the benevolent goddess was brought to the Navajos by the Holy People from Gobernador Knob. (White Shell Woman is also known as Changing Woman.)

The Diné Habitiin, "Navajo Trail Up," mentioned in the Navajo Beadway Story of the Navajo clans, is located west of Gobernador Knob. West of this trail and on the mesa above the trail is Ta'neeszah, the place where the Ta'neeszahnii (Tangle People Clan) of the Navajos are reputed to have lived at one time. It is claimed by Blanco Canyon Navajos that remnants of the old hogans and a "braided" wood fence were still in evidence in the 1940s. Indeed, there are many ruins in the area, some possibly early Navajo.

In 1705, Roque Madrid's expedition marched a short distance through this canyon south of Magdena Butte and Santos Peak (Hendricks and Wilson 1996, 80) between their second and third battles with Navajos. (See Los Peñoles and Largo Canyon.)

GOODS OF VALUE MOUNTAIN: Navajo: Yo'dí Dził, "Goods of Value Mountain." This feature of Navajo mythology is comprised of the mountains of the eastern Navajo reservation. It is a male figure, with the Chuska Mountains comprising the body and Chuska Peak the head. The Carrizo Mountains form the legs and Beautiful Mountain the feet. Shiprock is a medicine pouch or bow the figure carries. This formation is mirrored by a female figure known as Pollen Mountain, formed by Navajo Mountain, Black Mesa, and other features (McPherson 1992, 21).

GRANTS: [DB] (6470 ft) Cibola County, NM. Navajo: 'Anaa'task'ai'i, which Van Valkenburgh interpreted as "With Her Legs Spread." Young (p.c. 1995) suggests it is a garbled version of Naatooh Sik'ai'í (Young and Morgan 1987, 601) and refers to an Isleta Indian prostitute. Nestled between Horace Mesa on the east (foothills of the San Mateo Mountains) and Black Mesa on the northwest, the village is situated on the Rio San Jose and north of I-40, 60 miles east of Gallup, 75 miles west of Albuquerque.

The community was formerly a station for the Santa Fe Railroad. Limited logging takes place in the nearby Zuni Mountains, a mere vestige of the former industry. Cattle and sheep raising and dry land farming are of growing importance. Mining activities include pumice, flurospar, and coal, and, until the 1980s, especially uranium.

The earliest event described in the Grants vicinity is known as the Comanche Massacre. Before Europeans entered the region, a group of Navajos planting corn at the mouth of present Bluewater Canyon had posted sentinels about a mile from the corn field. These sentinels were attacked by a band of Comanches who stole all of their horses. The alarm was sounded and the main camp set out in immediate pursuit. The only water hole available to the Comanches (whom the Navajos call Naałání, "Many Enemies") was a spring that came out of the Malpais near present Grants. The Navajos made a shortcut to the spring and watched from behind rocks while the Comanches killed and ate one of the stolen horses. They then attacked, killing all the Comanches.

The earliest White settler at Grants was Don Jesus Blea who lived there prior to the Civil War. His home, still standing in the 1940s, was the oldest building in Grants. The town was first called Grants Camp after the Grants Brothers, railroad contractors, during the building of the Atlantic and Pacific Railroad. In 1872, the community was called Alamitos (Spanish, "Little Cottonwoods") (WPA 1940b, 320–21). The family of Don Ramon Baca moved into the village in 1873. Uranium was found in the vicinity of Grants in the 1950s.

Another community, Milan, grew adjacent to and west of Grants, and the two have grown together into a single line of homes and businesses. This mining town incorporated in 1957, and was named for an early Hispanic settler, Salvador Milan.

GUADALUPE CANYON: [DB] (8200–6900 ft) McKinley and Sandoval counties, NM. Navajo: Tséyi' Hayázhí "Little Rock Canyon." A four-mile-long canyon on the northeastern face of the

Cebolleta Mountains, flowing eastward into the Rio Puerco of the East near the Hispanic community of Guadalupe. This area is important in Navajo ceremonialism and archaeology. The region between Cebolleta and Cabezon Peak was listed by the Spanish as one of four major concentrations of Navajos in 1800, the other three being Chaco Canyon/Chacra Mesa, the Chuska Mountains/Chuska Valley, and Canyon de Chelly (McNitt 1972, 36n).

On the slopes that run into Guadalupe Canyon from the north and south are many old Navajo hogans. These are the "orthodox" or early Navajo 'ałch'i' 'adeez'áhi, "forked-stick joined together (hogan)," possibly dating from the mid-eighteenth century.

HARD GROUND CANYON AND FLATS:
(7020–6950 ft) McKinley County, NM. Navajo: Ni' Hotł'izí, "Hard Ground" (Kelley p.c. 1994). Small, flat valley and connected canyon some five miles west of the Kerr McGee Church Rock Uranium Mine at the north end of New Mexico Highway 566. A small number of Navajo homesteads dot the valley floor, though grazing looks to be scarce.

HAYNES: [DB] (approx. 6500 ft) Rio Arriba
and San Juan counties, NM. Also Haynes Ranch. Navajo: Uncertain. Doc Haynes's ranch and store opened just prior to 1910 and closed before 1931 (Kelley 1977, 253–54), but the exact location of the remains of this trading post is disputed by several major sources. Van Valkenburgh states that they are at the mouth of a small rincon of Haynes Canyon—through which New Mexico Highway 55 (now Highway 44) passed—five miles northeast of Counselors. Brugge (p.c. 1996) relates that he visited the stone ruins of a trading post reported to have been operated by a medical doctor from the midwest (named Haynes) in very nearly this location. This doctor apparently did not practice medicine here.

Pearce (1965, 69, 79), on the other hand, lists the location of "Haynes" as being in San Juan County, 50 miles southeast of Farmington and 10 miles north of Kinnebito. This location fits with that given by McNitt (1962, 302), which lists W. B. Haines's (*sic*) Trading Post as being in the Gallegos Canyon region. These descriptions would fit with the Haynes shown on the 1926 Southern California Automobile Club map, lying in the mouth of Cañada Largo, some five miles due north of Counselors (on New Mexico Highway 44). Perhaps two posts so named existed.

HAYSTACK: (approx. 7200 ft) McKinley
County, NM. Navajo: Kin Łigaií, "White House" (Kelley p.c. 1994). (The same name is applied to nearby Prewitt.) This chapter house is located east of New Mexico Highway 605 some 10 miles north of Grants.

HAYSTACK MOUNTAIN: [AAA] (7833 ft)
Cibola County, NM. Navajo: Kits'iil Yaa'á, "Towering Ruin," after a Chacoan outlier ruin; also Dził Łichíí', "Red Mountain" (Brugge p.c. 1996). Some apply this name to a steep-walled red sandstone mesa approximately three miles east of Prewitt. However, see also Old Crater.

HAYSTACK RUIN: (6980 ft) McKinley
County, NM. Navajo: Kits'iil Yaa'á, "Towering Ruin" (Young p.c. 1995). This site consists of three Chacoan great-kiva complexes in the valley near the foot of Haystack Mountain, some 15 miles northwest of Grants. One of the complexes dates to late Pueblo II–early Pueblo III, the second to Pueblo II, and the third to Late Pueblo I–early Pueblo II. A nearby reservoir may be Anasazi, renovated by Navajos in 1960, the dam possibly being reused as an antelope trap (Gabriel 1991, 269).

HEART ROCK: (6970 ft) McKinley County,
NM. Navajo: Uncertain. Sandstone formation some 200 ft high on the flat plains north of Mesa de los Lobos, seven miles east of Crownpoint. Presumably the location of Heart Rock Trading Post, opened between 1946 and 1950, and closed by 1955 (Kelley 1977, 255).

HERRERA MESA: (6400 ft) Sandoval County,
NM. Navajo: Uncertain. This mesa is part of the eastern slope of the larger Mesa Chivato, the major upland formation northeast of the San Mateo Mountains. Herrera Mesa lies west of Canada del Ojo, just north of the Bernalillo County line,

and a couple of miles east of the junction of the Sandoval/Bernalillo line with the Cibola County line.

It was here that Sandoval, a Diné 'Ana'í headman, died after he was thrown from and kicked by a horse in February 1859 (McNitt 1972, 363).

HOGBACK: [DB, NMPN] (6200 ft) San Juan County, NM. Navajo: Tsé Kíniitíní, meaning "Leaning Rock," and Tsétaak'áán, "Rock Extending into Water"; or Tsétaak'á, "Rock Ledge Slants into Water" (Young and Morgan 1987, 731). This 18-mile-long, vaguely S-shaped monocline is of Mesa Verde sandstone, and is similar in appearance to the Gallup Hogback. It begins 14 miles southwest of Shiprock, near Bennett Peak, and five miles east of U.S. Highway 666, and travels north through Waterflow, in the vicinity of the Chimney Rock Oil Lease.

In 1894 the Navajos constructed an early irrigation system—known as the Hogback Ditch—at the point where the San Juan River bisects the Hogback. It irrigated some 75 acres. In 1941 the subsequent system irrigated 3,500 acres of agricultural land on the north bank of the San Juan River, constituting the largest functioning irrigation project in the Navajo country. That system later gave birth to the Bureau of Indian Affairs Navajo Indian Irrigation Project (NIIP, managed by the Navajo Agricultural Products Industries, or NAPI). This massive undertaking was initiated in the late 1960s, and will eventually irrigate 110,000 acres.

In 1941, the Midwest Oil Company maintained a long-term lease in the region where the Hogback intersects the Chaco River. The BIA operated a coal mine in the monocline some 20 miles southeast of Shiprock.

HOGBACK TRADING POST: (5000 ft) San Juan County, NM. Navajo: Uncertain, presumably the same as the geologic formation. Located on U.S. Highway 64 just north of the San Juan River, where the highway cuts through a pass in the hogback (a couple of miles west of Waterflow, and one hundred yards outside the eastern boundary of the Navajo Reservation). This post was established by Hank Hull at least by September 1871. Hull sold out to his nephew, Harry Baldwin, in 1900. Joe Tanner purchased the post from Baldwin in 1916, but sold it a year later to Wilfred Wheeler and Albert Hugh Lee. Wheeler became sole owner in 1918, and the post has since remained in the Wheeler family.

HOSPAH: [NMPN] (7050 ft) McKinley County, NM. Navajo: Haazbaa', a woman's war name in Navajo (Kelley p.c. 1994). A small community on New Mexico Highway 509 in the San Juan Basin. Situated about 35 miles northeast of Thoreau, and five miles south of Whitehorse (which is located on Navajo Route 9 at the point where that east-west road turns north toward Pueblo Pintado).

HOSTA BUTTE: [DB, NMPN] (8620 ft) McKinley County. Navajo: 'Ak'iih Nást'ání, "Mountain that Sits on Top of Another Mountain." This broad sandstone butte rises at the south of the eastern end of Mesa de los Lobos, two and one-half miles north of New Mexico Highway 371, some four miles west of Smith Lake. (Van Valkenburgh's location was erroneous.) This landmark appears to be the southern terminus of the prehistoric Chacoan South Road, which travels north toward Chaco Canyon (Gabriel 1991, 114).

According to Van Valkenburgh, the present name dates back to 1877, and was given by W. J. Jackson in honor of a Jemez Indian who guided Colonel John Washington's expedition through the country in 1849. The United States Geological Survey map of 1886 shows it as Mesa Butte.

Hosta Butte is a Navajo sacred peak that can be seen for many miles from the north and east. It is said by medicine men to be the home of Hadahoniye' 'Ashkii (Mirage Stone Boy) and Hadahoniye' 'At'ééd (Mirage Stone Girl) (Apache and Jim 1982, 6), and to be fastened to the sky with "mirage stone," Hadahoniye' (aragonite), surrounded by dark clouds (k'os diłhił) and male rain (níłtsá bika ft). Hosta Butte is mentioned in the Night and Blessingway Ceremonies. The vicinity is attacked by supernaturals in the Red Antway Myth, and Hero's youngest brother goes to Hosta Butte at the end of the Gun Shooter Red Antway Myth (Wyman 1965).

HUERFANITO: [DB, NMPN] (7000 ft) San Juan County, NM. Also El Huerfanito. Navajo: Dził Ná'oodiłí Chilí, a diminutive of Dził Ná'oodiłii (see Huerfano Mountain). A small sandstone mesa similar in appearance to Huerfano Mountain, and located 10 miles northeast of that mountain, three miles west of Blanco Canyon on the west side of Blanco Canyon. This landform is often confused in the literature with nearby Angel Peak, the location of a state recreation area.

HUERFANO MESA: [DB, NMPN] (7470 ft) San Juan County, NM. Also Huerfano Mountain, El Huerfano. Navajo: Dził Ná'oodiłii, "People Encircling Around Mountain," referring to a legend in which people moved around the mountain (Young and Morgan 1987, 360). A sacred name is Nłiz Dził, "Mountain of Precious Stones" (Franciscan Fathers 1910, 136–37). This large, isolated mesa is situated 25 miles south of Bloomfield, a mile northeast of New Mexico Highway 44. The old Huerfano Trading Post lies between the highway and the southern tip of the mesa, in the vicinity of Dził Ná'oodiłii (BIA) School. (Van Valkenburgh suggested the remains of two posts lay south of the mesa.)

The mesa is steep-walled and angular, one arm extending east, the other south, and is topped with four cupolalike sandstone crags. It dominates the country south of the San Juan River for 40 miles, and can be seen from the Chuska Mountains, 50 miles to the west. By 1941, it had been ascended by relatively few White men (Van Valkenburgh 1941, 76). Traditional Navajos frown upon efforts to climb it, preferring that only their medicine men climb to the top, but since Van Valkenburgh's writing, the mesa has been crowned by a veritable fence of radio and microwave towers—an affront to Navajos, and placed there without their consent.

Huerfano is one of the three sacred mountains interior to the traditional Navajo homeland (see also Hosta Butte and Gobernador Knob), and is said to be suspended from the sky with sunbeams. It is reputed to be the home of Yódí 'Ashkii (Goods of Value Boy), and Yódí 'At'ééd (Goods of Value Girl), as well as one of the homes of 'Átsé Hastiin (First Man) and 'Átsé 'Asdzáán (First Woman). Navajo mythology tells that in the beginning it was decorated with pollen, rugs, hides, cloth, and male rain. It was also the scene of First Girl's puberty rites and is mentioned in the Blessingway (Van Valkenburgh 1974) and Coyoteway myths (Luckert 1979).

In 1967, the Bureau of Land Management (earlier responsible for the microwave towers), proposed to make a recreation area of the east wing, complete with picnic tables. Navajo singers protested, and the Navajo Tribe sent historian Dave Brugge to investigate. His report enabled Edward O. Plummer of the tribe to negotiate a land exchange with BLM, returning the east wing to the tribe. While the Navajos did not get all that they hoped, the east wing is now a sort of "sacred wilderness" accessible only to Navajo singers and those accompanied by singers (Brugge p.c. 1996).

The mesa and surrounding area was the scene of a bitter protest by Navajos in 1992 to prevent a Farmington firm from establishing an asbestos dump on private land about seven miles north of the mesa beneath the "line-of-sight" between Huerfano and Gobernador Knob. (The line-of-sight is said to have led First Man to the infant Changing Woman in Navajo mythology). The company eventually withdrew its proposal.

HUERFANO TRADING POST: (6800 ft) San Juan County, NM. Navajo: Uncertain, though likely the same as the mesa. Located 25 miles south of Bloomfield and 11 miles northwest of Nageezi on New Mexico Highway 44. Kelley (1977, 253) lists this post as opening prior to 1916, but McNitt (1962, 303) asserts that Stokes Carson founded it around 1920. The Carsons donated the land on which the Huerfano chapter house was built.

ICE CAVE: (8000 ft) Cibola County, NM. Navajo: Dibé Hooghan, "Sheep Hogan" (Young and Morgan 1987, 312). This cave at the foot of Bandera Volcano is in El Malpais lava beds south of Grants. The temperature hovers just below freezing in the "cave" (which is really a collapsed horizontal volcanic tube), preserving a wall of green-tinted ice.

ISLETA PUEBLO: [DB, NMPN] (4900 ft) (Population: 1,703) Bernalillo County, NM. Navajo: Naatooho, "River Enemy" (Young and Morgan 1987, 601); Bandelier recorded this as Na'ta (Lange and Riley 1966, 330). A Tiwa village spanning both banks of the Rio Grande 14 miles south of Albuquerque on U.S. Highway 85 and I-25, whose original name is "Tsugwevaga," meaning "Kicking Flint," after a running game involving a piece of flint kicked by the participants (Pearce 1965, 75). The Spanish name "Isleta" means "Island," and refers to the fact that the pueblo was located on an island in the Rio Grande at the time of first European contact in 1540, by Captain Hernando de Alvarado. It was reported in 1581 that the village had 1,500 inhabitants; in 1941 the population was 1,183.

The first Spanish mission here was built in 1613, dedicated to patron Saint Anthony. About 1675, Isleta received people from the Tewa pueblos of Quarai and Tajique (both since deserted) and other pueblos east of the Rio Grande. Isleta did not take part in the Pueblo Revolt of 1680 (perhaps because of a large contingent of Spanish soldiers garrisoned there), but when Governor Otermin and 250 soldiers attempted a reconquest a year later, he took 350 Isleta "captives" (539 according to Van Valkenburgh) with him on his retreat to El Paso. These were given land south of El Paso, founding Isleta del Sur— South Isleta. (Van Valkenburgh suggests that the inhabitants of Isleta del Sur were only 119 who escaped from the 539.) Those left behind when Otermin took his prisoners south abandoned the Isleta, possibly moving to the Hopi villages and not returning until 1718.

Diego de Vargas, hero of the Reconquest of 1692, found the village in ruins—possibly destroyed by other pueblo Indians indignant over Isleta's failure to join the hostilities of the Pueblo Revolt. The pueblo was rebuilt and settled by three hundred returnees from Isleta del Sur and the mission was rebuilt, though now dedicated to Saint Augustine.

In 1742, a pair of Spanish friars escorted some 80 Isletan families back to the pueblo from the land of the Hopis, where they had fled following the Pueblo Revolt of 1680. They brought with them Hopi wives and half-Hopi children, and Hopi customs (New Mexico Office of Cultural Affairs 1991, 45). It was possibly at this time that Oraibi Hill was named (this being a distinctly Hopi name). A village was created here (and called by the same name) by residents of Laguna Pueblo who fled religious strife there between 1878 and 1881 (Ellis 1979a, 354).

In 1940 the community was split over religious rifts (having to do with succession of caciques or governors) dating back to 1896, and a "revolution raged for seven years" (Ellis 1979a, 362–63).

Navajos were traditional enemies of Isleta and figure extensively in Isleta witchcraft. Anthropologist Elsie Clews Parsons contended that there were Navajo scalps in Isleta kivas in the 1940s, and these are most likely still present. In those days, the Nakafur, "Captive Dance," took place every Saturday night at Isleta. This ceremony was reminiscent of the days when the Navajos raided Isleta. The pueblo allied with Sandia Pueblo and the New Mexicans during the Navajo War of 1863–64. Army troops under Captain William P. Walton observed a scalp dance at Isleta with the scalps of three Navajos accused of kidnapping and killing some women and children in November 1846. The Navajos had been chased and killed by soldiers (McNitt 1972, 102).

Isleta is the site of the famous "resurfacing Padre." Fray Juan Jose Padilla died in 1756 of an unidentified illness, and was buried beneath the church floor. His casket and perfectly preserved body have resurfaced at least three times (1826, 1889, and 1962). After the last incident, it was buried beneath a six-inch slab of concrete.

IYANBITO: [DB] (7000 ft) McKinley County, NM. Navajo: 'Ayánii Bitó', "Buffalo Spring." This Navajo community is located at the foot of the red sandstone cliffs three miles north of I-40, and seven miles east of Church Rock. It formerly housed a BIA day school in the 1940s, and now includes a chapter house. Kelley (1977, 255) has identified a Buffalo Springs Trading Post that may have been located here from the late 1940s until the late 1950s.

The name 'Ayánii Bitó' is of recent origin, having been given after imported buffalos for an early Gallup ceremonial were watered nearby. Previously the name was Tł'ízí Łigai, "White Goat," after the English Goat Ranch operated here in the 1880s by an English "remittance man." An older name was Naakaii Haayáhí, "Mexican's Ascent," after a trail a Mexican ascended through the cove that opens at the site of the old day school.

JACQUES CANYON: [DB] (7600–7300 ft) Rio Arriba County, NM. Navajo: Tsékooh, a descriptive term for a lesser rock canyon. The Anglo name comes from Candalero Jaques, a Navajo who owned allotments here in the 1940s. (There is evidence the Navajo name has been applied to different canyons through time, as Van Valkenburgh noted a tributary to Blanco Canyon, two miles upstream, by the same name.) As shown on current maps, this shallow tributary of Canyon Largo actually heads four miles east of Lindrith and joins Canyon Largo two miles west of that community. Van Valkenburgh names a spring at the junction of the two canyons Tó Diłhił ("Dark Water"), and notes that a relatively new seep in the west bank of Canyon Blanco now bears the same name.

A group of Navajos known as the Blanco Canyon Navajos settled in this shallow canyon flanked on the south by Dził Ntsaa ("Big Mountain"). These relatively isolated people were the descendants of a Navajo man and his two wives who moved away from the tribal block some 70 years ago.

The canyon is on the main route used every autumn by White sheep men transferring their sheep from their Colorado ranges to winter in the Checkerboard area of the Navajo country.

Across the canyon rise the sheer walls of Cibola Mesa as it narrows down to end at Salt Point. A trail leads up the cliff from Tó Diłhił to the top of the mesa, and in the winter the Navajos take their sheep up the trail to get snow. Many old ruins of unknown origin are found on the mesa top.

JEMEZ HOT SPRINGS: [DB, NMPN] (6250 ft) Sandoval County, NM. Navajo: Nearest Navajo name is Mą'ii Deeshgiizh, "Coyote Pass," located some three miles to the south. Mineral springs and ruins of the Jemez pueblo of Guisewa and Mission of San Diego de Jemez. The springs are situated in a deep canyon on the southwestern section of the Jemez Mountains, nine miles north of Jemez Pueblo on New Mexico Highway 4. There are many other ruins in the locality, including Kwastijukwa, "Place of the Rock Pine Locust." Guisewa was deserted before the Pueblo Revolt of 1680.

JEMEZ MOUNTAINS: [DB, NMPN] (6550–11,254 ft) Sandoval, Rio Arriba, and Santa Fe counties, NM. Navajo: Dził Łizhinii or Dziłizhiin, "Black Appearing Mountains"; also Aniłt'ánii Dził, "Corn Beetle Mountain" (U.S. Indian Claims Commission n.d., vol. VI, i; spelling corrections by Young, p.c. 1995). This heavily wooded mountain range straddles the boundary between the Rocky Mountain Province and the Basin and Range Province. The range runs some 45 miles between the junction of the Rio Grande and Jemez Creek on the south and Los Alamos on the north. On the east it is bounded by the Rio Grande Valley, and on the west lies the upper Rio Puerco of the East. These mountains are of volcanic origin, which distinguishes them from both the Rocky Mountains and the basin-and-range mountains. Valle Grande, a broad valley west of Los Alamos, is the result of a tremendous volcanic explosion.

The San Pedro Mountains, the Nacimiento Mountains, and Cejita Blanca Range are all physically a part of the Jemez Range, dominated by 11,254-ft Redondo Peak west of Los Alamos.

The Jemez Mountains are well known to the Navajos. Pelado Peak, called Dził Dijool, "Round Mountain" or "Globular Mountain" (Young p.c. 1995—though Van Valkenburgh translated this as "Big Buttocks Place"), was a favored hunting ground of the old-time Navajos, and is one of several promontories hypothesized as being the Navajo sacred mountain of the east (Matthews 1897; O'Brian 1956). (See also Pelado Peak, Wheeler Peak, Blanca Peak.) Pedernal

Peak is known as Noolyínii ("Obsidian"—but generally any flaking material).

Pajarito Peak is called Tł'iish Jik'áhí ("Grinding Snakes"), and is an important place in the Navajo Wind Chant stories. Cejita Blanca Ridge is known as Bistah ("Among the Adobes"). According to the Rounded Man Red Antway Myth, the first home of the Ant People was in the Jemez Mountains (Wyman 1965). In the Navajo creation myth, Déélgééd ("Horned Monster") was killed by the Twin War Gods in the Jemez Mountains (Benally et al. 1982, 16).

Through the entire Jemez Range there were old Navajo hunting and raiding trails as well as camp sites: Yé'ii Bikék'eh ("Yei's Footprints") at Piedra Lumbre, and Táála Hooghan ("Flat-topped Hogan") are well known old Navajo camps and fields. Under the name Dził Łizhin, they are mentioned in the Navajo Ghostway tradition of the Male Branch of Shootingway (Haile 1947, 170; Haile 1950, 54).

JEMEZ PUEBLO: [DB, NMPN] (5575 ft) (Population: 1,783) Sandoval County, NM. Navajo: Mąʼii Deeshgiizh, "Coyote Pass," (misinterpreted by Matthews [1897, 158] as "Wolf Pass"), named for a gap eight miles north of the current village. This Towa pueblo (related only to the now-abandoned Pecos Pueblo, situated about 30 miles to the east, at the southern end of the Sangre de Cristo Range) is located on the east bank of Rio San Jose at the southern end of the Jemez Mountains. It is situated on New Mexico Highway 4, 45 miles north of the junction of that road with New Mexico Highway 44. The name Jemez is from the Towa "Hay Mish," meaning "the people." Towa is a branch of the Kiowa-Tanoan language family (Sando 1979, 418).

The present site of the pueblo was established after many movements of the Jemez people in the region, many precipitated by the Navajos, whom they called Wangsave, Towa translating to "Jemez-Apaches." Navajo raids and difficulties with the Spanish nearly depopulated Jemez in the latter part of the sixteenth century. It is known that by the Pueblo Revolt of 1680 there were three villages (Asti'olakwa, Guisewa, and Patoqua). After the Reconquest of 1692, the old village was rebuilt on Jemez Creek, and is the present village of Jemez (Fugate and Fugate 1989, 195).

In 1541, Pedro de Castañeda, chronicler for Francisco Vásquez de Coronado, wrote of seven Jemez pueblos in the vicinity of Jemez Hot Springs (Aguas Calientes). Mission San José de Guise was founded in 1622 (New Mexico Office of Cultural Affairs 1991, 46). In 1639, Fray Diego de San Lucas was killed during a Navajo attack on the pueblo. Between 1644 and 1647, Governor of New Spain Luis Arguello hanged 29 Jemez leaders after the pueblo allied itself with the Navajos and killed Diego Martinez Naranjo, a Spaniard. In 1662, Fray Miguel Sacristán hanged himself at the pueblo, and during the Pueblo Revolt of 1680, Fray Juan de Jesus Matador was killed by the pueblo's occupants.

Following the Reconquest of 1692, the Jemez were less than totally supportive of the Spanish and their allies—the Keresan pueblos of Zia and Santa Ana. Over the next two years, the people of Jemez raided these two nearby villages, eventually killing four Zia men. This led to a punitive expedition of 120 Spanish soldiers and auxiliaries from Zia, San Felipe, and Santa Ana, led by de Vargas. A battle on the mesa above the pueblo led to the deaths of 84 Jemez people and the capture of 361. Legend states that during the battle, a likeness of San Diego appeared on a cliff from which many people were leaping to their deaths; all leapers landed on their feet with no harm after the appearance. Today a likeness still exists on the red sandstone cliff above Jemez Hot Springs.

On June 4, 1696, another friar, Francisco de Jesus, was killed at Jemez, which led to another battle (this one in San Diego Canyon) in which 28 to 40 Indians were killed (including eight Acomas who had allied themselves with the Jemez). After this only a portion of the Jemez people returned to the pueblo; many sought their ancestral homeland in the northwest (Canyon Largo or "Stone Canyon" to the Jemez), or went to live among the Navajos and Hopis to the west. (Some went as far as the White Mountain Apache country to the southwest in Arizona.)

Most eventually returned to Jemez, although some stayed with the Navajo (Sando 1979, 418–29). They even formed a new clan, Mą'ii Deeshgiizhinii, within that tribe. Matthews (1897, 145) says the village from which these people originated was called Klogi (Tłogi, the Navajo name for Zia Pueblo), but it was situated where Jemez Pueblo now stands. Brugge (p.c. 1996) suggests that Matthews was mistaken in this, as the Tłogi clan with which he is familiar is descended from Zia Pueblo.

Many Jemez refugees settled at Hopi First Mesa. Between 1730 and 1734 a drought drove them eastward to Canyon de Chelly where they met with other Mą'ii Deeshgiizhii who had previously joined the Navajos.

Navajos attacked Jemez Pueblo on June 8, 1708; in March 1714; in 1796; 1826 through 1829; 1833 and 1835 (McNitt 1972, 22, 25, 36, 70, 72–73). Spruce Baird, the first Indian agent to the Navajos, established his agency at Jemez in 1852. The village was the staging area for many incursions into Navajo country throughout the Spanish, Mexican, and American periods. In January of 1824, and again in 1839 and December 1851, peace talks between the Navajos and New Mexicans were held at Jemez (Benally et al. 1982, 94). In 1838, people abandoning Pecos Pueblo to the southeast moved into Jemez (New Mexico Office of Cultural Affairs 1991, 46).

In 1863–64, the Jemez sheltered Navajos fleeing the U.S. Army (under Kit Carson), refusing to surrender them until the pueblo was surrounded by the Army (Brugge p.c. 1996).

Anthropologist Adolph F. Bandelier (1890–92) stated that

> Jemez is more than half Navajo, and one of their leading men, whom unsophisticated worshipers are not wont to admire as typical and genuine pueblo, the Nazlo, was Navajo by birth, education, and inclination. We ought to consider, for instance, the Indians of Zuni have married with, and plentifully absorbed Navajo, Tegua (Tewa) and Jemez blood.

Today there is a close friendship between the Navajos of Torreon and the Jemez, their eastern neighbors and relatives. Traditionally many Navajos would travel to Jemez on feast days to trade, and regularly Jemez traders traveled through the Navajo country trading vegetables and fruits for sheep, blankets, and silver.

JEWETT: (5100 ft) San Juan County, NM. Navajo: Uncertain. This community was located in the Jewett Valley, west of Fruitland (Stribling 1986, 42, 83) and had its own post office from 1884 to 1907 (Pearce 1965, 76). The first mission boarding school on the Navajo Reservation was located here, in this community near Fruitland. It later became the Methodist Mission School (Bailey and Bailey 1986, 168). Jewett had its own post office from 1884 to 1907. See also Waterflow.

JICARILLA APACHE RESERVATION: (7000+ ft) Sandoval and Rio Arriba counties, NM. Navajo: Beehaí, "Always Winter People." This tribe of Apacheans is now situated on a reservation located in north-central New Mexico near the Colorado state line. The agency is at Dulce. The language spoken is Jicarilla Apache of Athapaskan stock, and is very similar to Navajo.

The former habitat of the Jicarilla was in central and eastern New Mexico and southern Colorado in an area bounded by the Canadian, the Arkansas, and the Chama rivers, and the region of Mora. There were two main divisions, or bands, of the tribe. The eastern was known as the Cooxgaen, or Plains People, called the "Llanero" in contemporary literature. They ranged east of the Rio Grande, having their favorite retreat in the Sangre de Cristo Range north of Taos. The other division lived west of the Rio Grande and called themselves Shaindeh, or Sand People. In Spanish and early American literature they were known as the Ollero.

The Jicarillas were the only Apaches to join in the Pueblo Revolt of 1680, aiding the Taos Indians in ridding northern New Mexico of Spanish settlers and missionaries (Gunnerson 1974, 100, as noted in Tiller 1983, 447). During the 1700s, the Jicarillas greatly feared their neighbors to the east, the Comanches, who had obtained guns from the French to the north, while the Spanish forbade supplying the Apaches with firearms.

The Jicarilla under Chief Chatto were subdued in military campaigns conducted by Lieutenant Colonel Philip St. George Cook and Lieutenant Davidson in 1854. They were placed on the nucleus of their present reservation in 1873, the agency at Dulce established in 1900.

Until the 1930s, the Jicarilla were dying at an alarming rate from tuberculosis and conditions of abject poverty. A program of rehabilitation, both physical and economic, was inaugurated by the Indian Department (later BIA) with the support of Emmett Wirt, pioneer trader. Since the 1940s, the Jicarilla have been increasing in population. They are a relatively wealthy tribe, deriving revenues from oil and gas and from taxes they impose on mining. They recently outbid the State of New Mexico to purchase an extensive and valuable Chama Ranch property. All sheep and wool sales are managed through the Jicarilla Apache Cooperative Store established in 1937. They are essentially stockmen, having little interest in agriculture. Arts and crafts are not considerable, but there is some work in basketry, beading, and tanning, and there has been a recent revival of Jicarilla micaceous pottery (Brugge p.c. 1996).

JONES RANCH: (7000 ft) McKinley County, NM. Navajo: Gahyázhí, "Little Rabbit" (Austin and Lynch 1983, 36), or Jééhkał, "Deafness" (Brugge p.c. 1996). This small BIA day school community is south of Gallup, 14 miles from New Mexico Highway 602 on Navajo Route 7048. A trading post was opened here during the late 1890s, closing during the later 1950s (Kelley 1977, 152, 155).

KIMBETO (TRADING POST): [DB, NMPN] (6500 ft) San Juan County, NM. Also Kimbito, Kinbeto, Kinebito Kinbito, Kinnebito. Navajo: Giní Bit'ohí, "Sparrowhawk's Nest." A trading post on the sandy north bank of Kimbeto Wash and New Mexico Highway 56, approximately four miles southeast of Nageezi (which is located at the junction of New Mexico Highways 44 and 56). The original post was half a mile north of the present location (Brugge p.c. 1996). Pearce (1965, 79) described the location as 10 miles south of Haynes. In the 1930s, the USIS con-

structed a sheep dip here, and nearby Anasazi pueblo ruins made the locus a popular stop for archaeologists and other tourists.

The site was named by the Navajos after circular Anasazi ruins situated north of the Kinbito Wash. This ruin figures in the story of Nááhwíiłbįįhí (the Gambler from the Bead Chant), which tells how the Navajos obtained their sheep. Paleontological expeditions of the American Museum of Natural History made their headquarters at Kimbeto while excavating for fossils in the eroded badlands of the vicinity in the 1930s.

The trading post, better known as Kimbito or Kinnebito, was in operation by 1901 and was closed by 1975 (Kelley 1977, 253). Brugge (1986, 55) notes that John Arrington claimed to have opened the post in 1915, but documentation of various traders' involvement with the post dates to 1901. Between 1914 and 1920 it was operated by an Anglo named Shorty Woody. The post was robbed twice (by Anglos) between 1914 and 1938.

KIMBETO WASH: (7000–6200 ft) San Juan County, NM. Also Kinbito Wash or Kinnebito Wash. Navajo: Same as Kimbeto. 16-mile-long tributary of Escavada Wash, heading east of New Mexico Highway 44 about two miles south of Nageezi. Joins Escavada Wash three miles upstream from that wash's confluence with the Chaco River.

KIM-ME-NI-OLI VALLEY: (6200 ft) San Juan County, NM. Navajo: Kin Binááyołí, "House the Wind Blows Around" (Young p.c. 1995). Immediately south of Yellow Point Valley, this broad plain is 18 miles north of Crownpoint, and is bisected by New Mexico Highway 371. It is named for the Chacoan outlier ruin (Kini Bineola) described below.

KIM-ME-NI-OLI WASH: [USGS-2] (6200 ft) San Juan County, NM. Navajo: Same as Kim-Me-Ni-Oli Valley. Drainage of the valley of the same name.

KIN BINEOLA RUIN: [MSLN] (6060 ft) McKinley County, NM. Also Kimenola, Kin

Binola, Kin Binioli, Kinbiniyol. Navajo: Kin Binááyołí, "House Around Which the Wind Blows" or Kin Bii'Naayolí, "House in Which the Wind Blows" (translations by Young, p.c. 1995). A massive E-shaped Chacoan great-house community on the Chacoan Yellow Point Road, between Coyote Canyon and the Great Bend of the Chaco River. The ruin contains 245 rectilinear rooms (including at least 106 on the ground floor, 58 on the second, and 34 third-floor rooms) and 10 round rooms (including two tower kivas). Core and veneer Chacoan masonry is evident (Flint and Flint 1989, 51–53; Gabriel 1991, 258–60).

KIN HOCHO'I: McKinley County, NM. Navajo: Kin Hóchxǫ́ǫ́'í, "Ugly House" (Young p.c. 1995). A Chacoan great-house community near the point where the Rio Puerco of the West crosses into Arizona. Bonito-style architecture is evident, along with probable great kiva. Four possible prehistoric roads emanate from the vicinity (Gabriel 1991, 278–79).

KIN INDIAN RUIN: San Juan County, NM. Navajo: Uncertain; the name is a combination of Navajo Kin, "house," and English "Indian." This Chacoan great-house community is some three miles north of Pueblo Alto on the Chacoan Great North Road. The site dates to A.D. 1000, with four to six single-story rectangular rooms and one round room (Gabriel 1991, 238–39).

KIN KLIZHIN RUIN: [MSLN] (6080 ft) San Juan County, NM. Navajo: Kin Łizhiní, "Black House." It is a Chacoan great-house community on the west side of Kin Klizhin Wash, four miles east of Lake Valley. Dating to A.D. 1080–90, it consists of as many as 17 single-story rectilinear rooms and eight possibly two-story rooms, with up to five round rooms, including one tower kiva. Construction is Chacoan core and veneer architecture (Gabriel 1991, 258–59; Flint and Flint 1989, 55–57). This locale is mentioned in the Hailway legend.

KIN NIZHONI RUIN: [MSLN] (6900–7000 ft) McKinley County, NM. Navajo: Kin Nizhóní, "Beautiful House." A pair of mesa-top, multi-story Chacoan great-house structures overlooking San Mateo Creek approximately 10 miles northwest of the San Mateo Mountains, and 10 miles east of Haystack Ruin. The site dates to A.D. 950, with 14 rectilinear and round rooms. Some 86 domiciliary structures lie within two square miles, two of which are great-kiva complexes. Prehistoric roads lead from Kin Nizhoni to both San Mateo and El Rito Chacoan great-house ruins (Gabriel 1991, 268–69).

KIN YA'A RUIN: [MSLN] (6780 ft) McKinley County, NM. Also Kin Yai (WPA 1940b, 333). Navajo: Kin Yaa'á, "Towering House" (the same name as the home of Rainboy's parents in the Hailway origin legend, and the home of Kin Yaa'áanii, one of the four original Navajo clans). This Chacoan great-house community sits in a broad valley three miles southeast of Crownpoint, and dates to A.D. 1087–1106. It contains approximately 42 rectilinear rooms—at least 26 on the ground floor and nine second-story rooms—a third story, and a four-story tower kiva. Four additional round rooms lie within the ruin, and two great kivas lie two hundred yards to the northwest. Within four square miles of Kin Ya'a are 104 other ruins, and a probable prehistoric road passes to the southeast (Flint and Flint 1989, 59–61; Gabriel 1991, 248–51).

KIRTLAND: [NMPN] (5150 ft) (Population: 3,552) San Juan County, NM. Navajo: Dághaa' Łichíí', "Red Mustache" (Kelley p.c. 1994; Young p.c. 1995). Small farming community 10 miles west of Farmington on the north bank of the San Juan River. Situated approximately one mile east of Fruitland.

An Army column led by Lieutenant Robert Ransom visited this vicinity on November 17, 1853—long before there was a settlement here (McNitt 1972, 230).

KIT CARSON'S CAVE: [DB] (6800 ft) McKinley County, NM. Navajo: Tsé'áhálzhiní, "Black Rock Cave" (Young and Morgan 1987, 730). More a rock shelter (a hollow in the side of the sandstone cliff) than a cave, this feature is located just off New Mexico Highway 566, a few miles north of the Navajo community of Church

Rock. (Van Valkenburgh mislocated this feature three miles south of U.S. Highway 66.) The cave is named after Colonel Christopher "Kit" Carson, leader of the 1863–64 "scorched-earth" campaign that finally subdued the Navajos. Local tradition has Colonel Carson using the cave as a stopover. While it is not impossible that the cave and the spring in the inner recess were used by Carson's troops, no official record of his visit there has as yet been discovered.

LAGUNA PUEBLO: [DB] (5800 ft) (Population: 3,731) Cibola County, NM. Navajo: Tó Łání, "Much Water," referring to the lake (originally a beaver pond) at which the pueblo was originally constructed, just north of present-day I-40, about 40 miles west of Albuquerque (and the Rio Grande). Keresan name: Kawiaka, "Laguna Pueblo" (Ellis 1979b, 438–49). The Spanish name, Laguna (or, more properly, San José de la Laguna), refers to the lake as well. The pond disappeared when the beaver dam washed away in 1855.

The main village is situated on the Rio San José (earlier called the Rio Cubero), a tributary of the Rio Puerco of the East, 25 miles to the east. The pueblo is Keresan linguistically (as are nearby Acoma and the Rio Grande pueblos of Zia, Santa Ana, San Felipe, Santo Domingo, and Cochiti). The Laguna people now reside in six villages in addition to Old Laguna: Seama, Mesita, Encinal, Paguate, Paraje, and New Laguna.

Historians date the origin of this latecomer to between 1697 and 1699 (Ellis 1979b, 438). It is believed to have been peopled by refugees from the Spanish Reconquest of 1692 who fled Cochiti, Cieneguilla, Santo Domingo, and Jemez in 1697, along with some people from Acoma Pueblo. Some scholars believe there is some Plains Indian heritage at the pueblo as well (New Mexico Office of Cultural Affairs 1991, 48). The Spanish name was conferred upon the pueblo by New Spain Governor Cubero on July 4, 1699.

In the Hodge translation of the Benavides Memorial presented at the court of King Carlos of Spain in 1730, we find this footnote: "It was visited by Governor Don Pedro Rodriguez on July 4, 1699, when the natives of the new settlement declared their allegiance, and the town was named San José de Laguna, from a lagoon that formerly existed west of the pueblo, and by that name it has ever since been known."

In the early 1870s Laguna was sharply divided over religious quarrels. The native hierarchy crumbled into two factions, the pro-American "Progressives" and the anti-American "Conservatives." The latter moved out of the original pueblo, Punyana, to the village of Mesita, though some went to Isleta Pueblo, staying there instead of proceeding to Sandia Pueblo as they originally planned. The lands given the Laguna at Isleta were called Oraibi, possibly after the name of a nearby hill (Ellis 1979b, 354). Old Laguna became rapidly depopulated and the former farming communities of Casa Blanca (Seama), Encinal, Santa Ana, Paraje, Paguate, and Tsisma became permanent villages.

The pueblo was raided by Navajos in 1796 and 1851. A scalp dance over four Navajo scalps was observed at Laguna by Army Lieutenant Colonel Congreve Jackson in October 1848 (McNitt 1972, 36, 196, 104).

Laguna has been gradually changing from its original pueblo cluster to a scattered village of modern, individual adobe-stucco houses. Atop the hill above the old village sits the old church of San José de Laguna, which opens its doors during the feast days of San Jose held annually in September.

The Navajo name Tó Łání refers to the people of Laguna as well as the physical location, unless they are grouped with the people of Acoma Pueblo, when they are called Haa'kohnii. During the feast days of San Jose in September, numbers of Navajos come to Laguna from great distances.

Although the Navajos were largely peaceful following their return from the Bosque Redondo in 1868, George H. Pradt, a surveyor of the Navajo Reservation in 1869, helped organize Laguna volunteers against raiding Navajos and Apaches in 1882 (Lange and Riley 1966, 394n).

LAGUNA PUEBLO TRADING POST: (5800 ft) Cibola County, NM. Navajo: Uncertain, but probably the same as the pueblo. This post was operated by Simon Bibo in 1873.

LA JARA: [DB] (7100 ft) Sandoval County, NM. Navajo: K'ai' Ch'íneeltł'ǫ́, "Willows Extending Out Tangled" (Van Valkenburgh 1941, 85; Young p.c. 1995). A small Hispanic community on New Mexico Highway 96, in the flat swale country some two miles north of the junction of that road with New Mexico Highway 44, near Cuba. The Spanish "La Jara" means "the willow."

This village is very close to the remains of the old San José de la Laguna, where refugees from Jemez Pueblo fled and settled during the seventeenth century. The Navajo and Spanish names refer to a long willow-lined swale between La Jara and Cuba.

LA JARA CANYON: (7800–6200 ft) Sandoval County, NM. Navajo: Uncertain, probably the same as the name of La Jara village above. This 40-mile-long canyon is north of Gobernador Canyon. It flows east to west, heading some 10 miles south of Dulce and merging with the San Juan River about seven miles northeast of Navajo Dam. It was visited by Roque Madrid's 1705 expedition. Madrid's first combat with Navajos took place near the junction of La Jara and La Fragua canyons on August 11, 1705, during which many Navajo "*milpas*" (fields of maize) were burned (Hendricks and Wilson 1996, 24, 76).

LAKE VALLEY: (5900 ft) San Juan County, NM. Also Juan's Lake. Navajo: Be'ek'id Łigaií, "Small White Lake." The name refers to what most maps show as Juan's Lake, but applies to the region immediately east of Lake Valley Chapter (Rogers 1990, 128) in Yellow Point Valley, about 20 miles north of Crownpoint. A USIS day school was located here on the banks of a shallow, ephemeral lake surrounded by low mesas and sparsely covered grasslands.

This chapter community is in the "Checkerboard Area." In this vicinity, the railroad grant gave every odd-numbered section (square mile) of land to the railroad; even-numbered sections so vary in ownership, with land exchanges, sales, approvals and cancellations of allotments, and so forth that the original pattern of ownership is quite confused (Brugge p.c. 1996). Most of the land around Juan's Lake is now in trust status,

some being allotted land, and some withdrawn from public domain for the BIA school. There are even a few state school sections. Along the road between Lake Valley and Crownpoint and just outside the eastern line of the Navajo Reservation lie a number of White-owned cattle ranches checkerboarded among Indian allotments and public domain. Van Valkenburgh (1941, 86) mentioned a Delawoshih (Navajo) family having operated large herds in this region for many years.

LAKE VALLEY RUIN: (5900 ft) Navajo: Kin Łání, "Many Houses." Several prehistoric, kivaless, single-story houses and middens with Chacoan core and veneer masonry, located in the plain west of Chaco Canyon. The complex dates to Early Pueblo II–Early Pueblo III (Gabriel 1991, 257–58).

LA PLATA RIVER: (10,800–5200 ft) Montezuma County, CO, and San Juan County, NM. Navajo: Tsé Dogoi Nlini, "Flowing Over Projecting Rock" (Franciscan Fathers 1910, 133). Rises in the La Plata Mountains of southeastern Colorado, 35 miles north of the New Mexico state line, at the western foot of 12,511-ft Snowstorm Peak (four miles east of 13,225-ft Hesperus Mountain). Tributary to the San Juan River some 19 miles south of the Colorado line, three miles west of Farmington. Possibly named in 1765 by Juan Rivera, who traversed the region in search of gold and silver. ("Plata" is Spanish for "silver.")

LARGO CANYON AND CREEK: [DB] (6600–5550 ft) Rio Arriba County, NM. Also Cañon Largo, Cañada Largo, Canyon Largo. Navajo: Various names (translations by Young p.c. 1995). The upper canyon (shown as Cañada Larga on the USGS Aztec 1:250,000 map) is known as 'Ahidazdiigaii, "Where Treeless Vales Come Together," while the lower canyon (Largo Canyon on the map) is called Tsííd Bii' Tó, "Spring in the Coals." The mouth of the canyon, at Blanco, is called Taahóóteel, "Broad Strip Extends to Water." The Franciscan Fathers list another name, Taahóóteel Ńlíní ("Stream in a Broad Strip that Extends to the River"), for the whole canyon system. Early Spanish documents refer to this canyon as Cañada Grande Larga (Reeve 1956, 303).

This 35-mile-long, rugged canyon system of Largo Creek played a central role in early Navajo history. Including that section the USGS maps identify as Cañada Largo, this network begins near the continental divide just east of New Mexico Highway 44, close to the southern Jicarilla Apache boundary. Fed by several substantial arroyos (including Blanco Creek), Largo Creek is tributary to the San Juan River at Blanco, 10 miles east of Bloomfield.

Largo Canyon is one of the main silt feeders of the San Juan River, this great drainage being fed by the western slopes of the continental divide for some 50 miles before entering the San Juan River.

Roque Madrid's expedition passed through a portion of the canyon, and fought their third and final battle with Navajos near its junction with Tapacito Creek on August 14, 1705. As with the battle at Los Peñoles, the Navajos held the high ground and fended off Spanish attacks until Madrid, while pretending to parley for peace, sent his Pueblo auxiliaries up Tapacito Creek to attack the Navajos from behind. The ruse was successful, and the Navajos were driven from the field. An unknown number of Navajos died, while Madrid lost one Indian auxiliary (Hendricks and Wilson 1996, 31–33, 84–85).

Cañon Largo later became the most important route for Indians and Whites from the Rio Grande to the upper San Juan River. Captain J. F. McComb passed through the canyon in 1859. In 1941, Van Valkenburgh described the wagon road as impassable in bad weather. Today it is graded and graveled, but still treacherous when wet. There are a number of White ranches in the rincons of the Largo, and many prehistoric and historic Indian sites, some of them watchtowers, along the canyon rims. Some in the section of the canyon between Trubey's and Haynes Canyon have been identified as being old Navajo, dating from the eighteenth century, when Navajos were joined by Jemez and other Pueblo Indians fleeing the return of the Spanish Reconquest following the Pueblo Revolt of 1680. The merging of cultures created an everlasting impact on the Navajos.

At least one Navajo pueblito ruin (known as LA 2298), located on a bench above the north bank, just north of the mouth of Tapicito Creek, has provided tree-ring dates clustering around 1690 and 1694, among the earliest for Navajo sites. Hendricks and Wilson (1996, 85), however, argue that the structure was almost certainly not present during the battle fought there by Madrid's force in 1705.

LA VENTANA: [DB] (6561 ft) Sandoval County, NM. Navajo: 'Iishtááh Dził (Van Valkenburgh 1941, 87), "Flying Mountain," referring to Cache Mountain. However, Young (p.c. 1995) was unable to decipher the word "'Iishtááh." A small ranching and mining community situated on the banks of the east fork of the Rio Puerco, on the western slope of the Jemez Range (in the Nacimiento Mountains). It is located across the Rio Puerco of the East from New Mexico Highway 44, some 50 miles northwest of Bernalillo. About all that remained by the early 1990s was an old store.

The Spanish name means "Window," referring to a stone archway that looked like a window. It was reportedly pulled down by cowboys many years ago (Young p.c. 1995). The community maintained a post office 1927–32.

The Dominguez-Escalante map of 1776 shows Ventana Mesas, which probably included La Ventana Mesa, San Luis Mesa, and Mesa Portales to the north. Ventana Mesa lies to the south of the old village. Some eight miles south, near Ojo Espiritu Santu (Holy Ghost Spring; see Jemez Mountains) was the old Navajo farm of Táala Hooghan ("Flat-topped Hogan"). The Ojo de Espíritu Santo, located some 15 miles south of La Ventana, was a regular stopping place for Navajos who traveled every fall to the dances at Jemez and Zia. Navajo hunters used to cache food by a spring on a small mesa immediately north of the village.

LINDRITH: (7200 ft) Rio Arriba County, NM. Navajo: Uncertain. Trading community located at the end of New Mexico Highway 95, 20 miles northwest of Cuba. Situated adjacent to Cañada Jacques (which is tributary to Cañada Larga). According to Pearce (1965, 88), the community was named for Lindrith Cordell, stepson of the first postmaster in 1915.

LITTLE WATER: (5600 ft) San Juan County, NM. Navajo: Uncertain, but most likely Tó 'Áłts'íísí, "Little Water." Trading location on U.S. Highway 666 at Sanostee Wash, 24 miles south of the village of Shiprock.

ALSO: (7000 ft) McKinley County, NM. Navajo: Tó 'Áłts'íísí, "Little Water" (Kelley p.c. 1994). A chapter house located on Navajo Route 48, approximately five miles southeast of Crownpoint, about halfway between Crownpoint and Borrego Pass.

LONG LAKE: (9000 ft) McKinley and San Juan counties, NM. Navajo: Be'ek'id Hóneez, "Long Lake." This small lake sits in a natural basin atop the ponderosa pine–covered Chuska Mountains on the San Juan/McKinley County line, four miles south of Narbona Pass (formerly Washington Pass).

Measuring approximately three hundred by seven hundred feet, this lake is the largest natural body of water on the Navajo Reservation, and is fed by melting snows and springs. Nearby are Whiskey Lake and a number of smaller lakes and ponds. Many Navajos from the eastern benches of the Chuska Mountains camp in this vicinity in the summer owing to the abundant water and forage for their sheep. Heavy snows drive them out in November.

LOS PEÑOLES: (approx. 7000 ft) Sandoval County, NM. Navajo: Uncertain. This Spanish term was applied by Roque Madrid in 1705 to two 500-ft peaks about a mile south of Muñoz Canyon, and approximately a half-mile distant from one another. The taller, Magdalena Butte, lies to the east of the smaller Santos peak. The former is nearly a quarter of a mile long, while the latter is topped by a flat region no more than three-quarters of an acre in area.

On the slopes of Santos Peak, Roque Madrid's

expedition fought their second battle with Navajos in as many days on August 12, 1705. The Navajos held the crest of the peak, which the Spaniards failed to scale, so the battle was a tactical victory for the Navajos, although their fields and homes were destroyed and a number were killed and wounded. The Spaniards suffered only five wounded. From this point, Madrid led his troops south across Ensenada Mesa toward Cañon Largo.

LOS PINOS RIVER: (8000–7200 ft) San Juan County, NM. Also known as Rio Los Pinos, Rio Los Piños. Navajo: Bíina, Navajo pronunciation of the Spanish "pinos" ("pines") (Kelley p.c. 1994). A 38-mile-long tributary of the San Juan River at Navajo Reservoir, this river enters New Mexico from Colorado, where it heads at Vallecito Reservoir, some 25 miles north of the New Mexico state line.

The juncture of this river with the San Juan River, called Tó 'Aheedlí ("Water Flows in a Circle"), is especially important to the Navajos, and is likely the location described by Newcomb (1964, 27–28) as Tóhí Ha Glee ("Meeting of the Waters"), the location of the "Shining Sands" where Navajo medicine men would read the "Page of Prophecy" in 1850, 1868, and 1929. Young (p.c. 1995) suggests the proper etymology is actually Tó Hahadleeh, "Water Well."

This point is now under the waters of Navajo Lake.

LYBROOK: [DB] (6950 ft) Rio Arriba County, NM. Also Lybrooks. Navajo: Tó Náálíní, "Water Running Down." Trading center located between Blanco and Largo canyons on New Mexico Highway 44 (17 miles west of the junction of that road with New Mexico Highway 537) grew out of the large stone and log house that was the center of the Lybrook Ranch. It is located at the gap in the southern end of Cibola Mesa, dividing Blanco and Largo canyons. It is home to Escrito Trading Post, a Giant Industries petroleum refinery, and Bannon Energy, Inc. Van Valkenburgh noted many Navajo campsites in the vicinity in 1941, and about four miles south of here is an important Navajo citadel site on a high crag commanding the entire Chaco Canyon region (Mc-Nitt 1962, 303).

In this general vicinity of Cibola Mesa and its various spurs there are many old Navajo defensive sites with watchtowers and breastworks in association with hogans. Some of those situated on crags have the notched log ladders still *in situ*. According to tree-ring data these hogans date from A.D. 1720 to 1760 and seem to have been occupied by Navajos and refugees from the Rio Grande and Acoma pueblos. Van Valkenburgh suggests the local Navajos called these towers Tsé Łani, "Many Stones," but Young (p.c. 1995) notes that watchtowers are called Bii'dóó'-adéest'įį' ("Watching Goes on from Inside It"), or Bighą́ą́'doo 'Adéest'įį' ("Watching Goes on from on Top of It").

LYBROOKS TRADING POST: (6950 ft) Rio Arriba County, NM. Navajo: See Lybrooks. In the early 1920s, Bill Lybrook (a nephew of R. J. Reynolds, the tobacco magnate) built a massive stone house and trading post at the location soon to assume the trader's name. He had the help of Jim Counselor, who had worked for Doc Haynes in 1919, and who built his own post (see Counselors) a few miles south of Lybrook's in the winter of 1931–32 (McNitt 1962, 303n).

MANUELITO: [DB] (6100 ft) McKinley County, NM. Navajo: Kin Hóchxǫ'í, "Ugly House," referring to an Anasazi pueblo ruin sitting atop the mesa immediately west of the village. Settlement 17 miles southwest of Gallup on old Highway 66 (now a frontage road for I-40) and the AT&SF Railway. The English (actually Spanish) name commemorates the famous Navajo chief. A post office was established here in 1881. It was also a station on the AT&SF. Ruins of an old Star Mail Route stage station lie one mile to the southwest. A Catholic mission is the largest concern in the community. Many Anasazi ruins dot the surrounding mesas.

Originally known as Cook's Ranch, the location assumed importance with the coming of the Atlantic and Pacific Railroad in 1881 as a railroad and telegraph station, post office, and railhead for Fort Defiance, some 28 miles north. The rail-road named the stop Ferry Station. In 1882 S. E. Aldrich established the community's first trading post. In 1884, Aldrich became a partner of Henry Chee Dodge (son of Chee Dodge, first chairman of the Navajo Tribal Council) in the Round Rock Trading Post, and with Archibald Sweetland of Tsailie Creek.

The Navajos tell of hunting mountain sheep on the second sandstone point west of Manuelito. They say, "These sheep were impossible to trap and never hesitated in jumping over a cliff. They didn't get hurt—they just put down their heads and rebounded from their big horns."

Trader Mike Kirk established the Museum of Indian Arts and Crafts here, but this facililty no long exists.

MANUELITO CANYON: [DB] (6500–6100 ft) McKinley County, NM. Navajo: Kinyaa Tó Deezliní, "Stream of Water Begins Under a House." This six-mile-long canyon in the cedar-covered mesas of Wingate sandstone stretches north from Manuelito (and the Rio Puerco and I-40), to Manuelito Springs.

The Navajo name originated from a spring that flowed from under the house of a Navajo named Naaljįįd ("Crippled") (Van Valkenburgh 1941, 89). The (Spanish) name Manuelito honors Navajo headman Manuelito.

The old freighting trail through Manuelito Canyon was once the main route between Ferry Station (Manuelito) and Fort Defiance. Over this trail, which went north through Oak Springs and Black Creek Valley, New Mexican oxen drivers Anson C. Damon and Samuel Day, Sr., and other teaming contractors brought mail and supplies to Fort Defiance in the 1880s.

It was in Manuelito's Canyon that Chach'oshneez, better known in history as Delagidito, of the Diné 'Ana'í, ("Enemy Navajos" of the Cebolleta region), warned the local Navajos against a New Mexican ambush at St. Michaels, Arizona.

MANUELITO SPRINGS: [DB] Also Manuelito's Spring and Manuelito Spring. (5900 ft) McKinley County, NM. Navajo: Ch'il Haajiní, "Weeds Extend Out (or Up) Black" (translation by Young p.c. 1995). This location is in the flats 14 miles east of Tohatchi in the San Juan Basin, roughly halfway between Mesa de los Lobos and the "big bend" of the Chaco River. This is reputed by Van Valkenburgh to be the location where Navajo Chief Manuelito lived and died. One of the earliest trading posts on the reservation opened in this vicinity in the late 1870s, but had closed by 1885 (Kelley 1977, 251).

The spring, located near the southeastern corner of the Navajo Reservation as established under the Treaty of 1868, is named after Manuelito, whose Navajo name was Hastiin Ch'il Haajiní ("Mr. Weeds Extend Out [or Up] Black"—from the old name of this spring).

Manuelito was born about 1818 and died at Manuelito's Spring in 1893. He married one of the daughters of Narbona—known to the Navajos as Hastiin Naat'áanii ("Mr. Chief")—a chief of the Navajos until 1849 (when he was killed by Colonel Washington's troops near Crozier). With the death in 1879 of the Navajo head chief Barboncito, Manuelito and Ganado Mucho became the two leading chiefs of the Navajos. Ganado Mucho was the chief of the western bands, and Manuelito's sway was in the east. Manuelito was the fourth signer of the Treaty of 1868 at Fort Sumner.

In 1872, Manuelito was appointed chief of the 200-man Navajo cavalry—actually policemen—that had been organized by Thomas V. Keam, then acting as Special Agent at Fort Defiance. This organization failed, due to the lack of government financial support.

In 1876 Manuelito went to Washington, where he talked to President Grant about Navajo land problems. In 1880, he went with Captain Frank T. Bennett to Santa Fe to take part in a reception given for President Rutherford B. Hayes.

He remained the active head of the Navajo tribe until 1884, when, according to Van Valkenburgh (1941, 910), he fell out of favor with his people over his increasing use of spirits, and his receiving many favors from various agents. The earliest windmills and wagons, given in the form of annuities, had been issued to Manuelito and other favored headmen who were expected to promote "civilization" and set a "good example" for their tribesmen. The annuities period of the Treaty of 1868 expired in 1878, and no more were issued after that date. Goods issued later were either in return for services rendered or were outright welfare, such as when weather destroyed crops or killed livestock (Brugge p.c. 1996).

Manuelito was the first chief to allow his children to be sent away from the Navajo country to school. Unfortunately, one of his sons died at Carlisle, Pennsylvania, in 1883 and Manuelito summarily demanded that the other son be returned to the reservation. This had a dampening effect on the Indian Service and missionary ambitions for sending young Navajos away to school off the reservation.

Manuelito's great interest lay in the return of old tribal lands to his people. He died in 1893 at Manuelito's Spring, when a case of measles developed into pneumonia after treatments in a sweat lodge and generous use of whiskey.

A report of First Lieutenant W. C. Brown, while making a water survey of the Navajo Reservation in 1892, gives a contemporary picture of Manuelito Springs at that time:

> Learning that the agent contemplated a visit to the camp of Manuelito, (former) chief of the Navajos on September 28, I accompanied him. Here I found the largest collection of Indian farms seen on the trip, the camp and farms extending over an area about a mile long by ¼ mile wide, with about 10 to 20 families, according to the season.
>
> Manuelito's Springs, at his permanent house, were next visited and here were found a series of mud springs. They were evidently very old and permanent springs. (Van Valkenburgh 1941, 92)

This location should not be confused with one located six miles north of Manuelito, at the head of Manuelito Canyon. The stream from that spring is tributary to the Rio Puerco of the West at the community of Manuelito.

MANUELITO TRADING POST: (6100 ft) McKinley County, NM. Navajo: See Manuelito. This post was opened 12 miles west of Gallup in 1882 by S. E. Aldrich, who two years later became a partner of Henry Chee Dodge in the Round Rock Trading Post, and also joined with Archibald Sweetland at Tsaile Creek. In 1941 the proprietor was Mike Kirk of Gallup (Van Valkenburgh 1941, 90). It closed between 1960 and 1965 (Kelley 1977, 255).

MANY ARROWS WASH: (6700 ft) McKinley County, NM. Navajo: K'aa Łání, "Many Arrows." This minor tributary of Burned Death Wash merges with the latter two miles south of Yah Ta Hey. This is in the vicinity of the old China Springs, which was the scene of Navajo ambushes on Army columns en route to Fort Defiance. The name is likely related to these attacks.

MANY WATERS: (6400 ft) McKinley County, NM. Navajo: Tó Łání, "Many Waters." This small Navajo community is approximately eight miles east of Standing Rock. The area is liberally strewn with ephemeral washes and arroyos.

MARATA: [DB] (approx. 6500–7500 ft) Cibola, Socorro, or McKinley County, NM. Navajo: Uncertain. Zuni: Mak'yata. This name refers to the area south of Zuni, and includes the Zuni Salt Lake and Atarque. Van Valkenburgh (1941, 92) refers to the region as a "historical Anasazi province located in general region south of Zuni, and in western Socorro and Valencia (now Cibola) Counties, New Mexico." This area is formerly a habitat of northern bands of the Chiricahua Apaches. A number of Navajo place names refer to the area—such as the Salt Lake and Atarque—which is also a former Navajo antelope and deer hunting ground.

Father Marcos de Niza, on his way to Cibola in July of 1539, learned from an old Zuni, then living with the Piman tribes in southern Arizona, of the provinces of Acus, Marata, and Totonteac. Acus has since been identified as Acoma, Totonteac as Tusayan (old Spanish name for the Hopi country), and Marata as a group of pueblos called by the Zunis Mak'yata or Matyata.

The Navajo clan of Nihoobáanii Dine'é (Gray Streak Ending People) is reputed to have originated from one of the Anasazi pueblos of this region, deserted during the early sixteenth century, or even perhaps in the late fifteenth century (Brugge p.c. 1996).

MARIANO LAKE: [DB] (7200 ft) McKinley County, NM. Navajo: Be'ekid Hóteelí, "Wide Lake." This lake and chapter community are located near the center of Lobo Valley, the long,

east-west dale south of Mesa de los Lobos. A day school was established here by the USIS.

The lake is semi-artificial, filling an improved natural sink high in the thickly wooded section of the mesa. some 20 miles northeast of Fort Wingate. This was a demonstration area for the Soil Conservation Service, with 7,005 acres under irrigation. Trading posts have included Mariano Lake Trading Post and Dee Westbrook Trading Post.

McComb's map of 1860 shows the site of Mariano Lake simply as "Pool." The present name dating from about 1885 is given in honor of Mariano, Hastiin Łitsoiits'ósí, ("Mr. Slim Yellow Man"), headman of the Fort Wingate vicinity between 1870 and 1890. It was Mariano who first dammed the sink fed by seasonal runoff in the 1870s. Old Navajos tell that he and his men carried the clay in cowhides to construct the dam.

Brugge (1972, 10–11) found Navajo defensive sites, dating to the 1760s, in the vicinity of this lake.

MARIANO LAKE TRADING POST: (7200 ft) McKinley County, NM. Navajo: See Mariano Lake. This post was founded between 1886 and 1890 (Kelley 1977, 252). Charlie Wiedemeyer operated it around 1908 (McNitt 1962, 282n), and another man, named Westbrook, ran it in the late 1930s (Kelley 1977, 254). In 1990, Merle and Rosella Moore, who had owned the post for over 20 years, sold out and moved to Borrego Pass. Mariano Lake Trading Post closed within two years thereafter.

MARIANO'S STORE: (approx. 6500 ft) McKinley County, NM. This post was located near the prehistoric Chacoan ruin Pueblo Pintado, and it appears to have been constructed about 1906 by a New Mexican named Mariano. He was given permission by Navajo headman "Mr. Slim" to build near a well in Chaco Wash, along an old wagon road, using materials scavenged from the nearby ruin. The post was short-lived, and Mr. Slim apparently moved into the abandoned facility and added corrals, a shed, and a blacksmith shop. Mr. Slim died from drinking poisoned whiskey, and the buildings were abandoned in 1918 (Kelley 1985, 22–24; Brugge 1979).

McCARTY'S: (6890 ft) Cibola County, NM. Navajo: Gad Sikaad Tsékooh, "Juniper Sits Canyon" (translation by Young, p.c. 1995). A trading village on the Acoma Reservation. It is situated along the Burlington Northern Santa Fe Railway and the Rio San Jose, about a mile south of I-40, and approximately 10 miles east of Grants. The English name is for a contractor whose AT&SF construction camp was here. The community was first named McCarty's, but the name was later changed to Santa Maria de Acoma, then changed back to McCarty's (WPA 1940b, 320).

McGAFFEY: (7900 ft) McKinley County, NM. Navajo: Uncertain. This small summer community is 10 miles south of I-40 on New Mexico Highway 400. It is named after A. B. McGaffey of Albuquerque, who joined W. S. Horabin (on the departure of Horabin's partner, Al Wetherill) in a trading venture in Thoreau until 1913. They ran a sawmill at McGaffey in 1906, and a railroad spur ran into the Zuni Mountains to connect to the sawmill. There was a post office here from 1919 to 1944. The pond at this site, McGaffey Lake, is a favorite fishing spot for local Navajos and non-Navajos alike, and offers ice fishing in the winter.

MENTMORE: (6300 ft) McKinley County, NM. Navajo: Uncertain. A small former coal-mining community, now a suburb of Gallup, located one mile north of I-40, on Gallup's west end (listed by Pearce as five miles west of Gallup). Post office from 1917. Also once the site of a Baptist mission and a BIA day school. The community offers stark contrasts between the old and the new, with traditional Navajo hogans widely dispersed around the more modern suburban streets and ranch-style homes largely occupied by non-Navajos.

MESA BUTTE: (8005 ft) McKinley County, NM. Navajo: Dził Diné Łichíí' (U.S. Indian Claims Commission n.d., vol. VI, vi), "Red Man Mountain" (Young p.c. 1995, in which he noted that this is an odd name). A flat butte atop the dramatic sandstone cliffs that form the northern boundary of Wingate Valley. It sits

about 13 miles north of I-40, and six miles northwest of Iyanbito.

MESA DE LOS LOBOS: [DB] (7000–8000 ft generally; highest point 8748 ft); McKinley County, NM. Also Lobo Mesa. Navajo: No general name, but called by the Navajos from the north by the general descriptive term "Dził," or "Mountain."

This feature is the higher, northern extremity of the long mesa formation that separates the valley of the Rio Puerco (of the West) from the San Juan Basin to the north. The name of the mesa goes back to the McComb map of 1860.

In a canyon of this mesa on October 1, 1858, troops under Captains Andrew J. Lindsay and George McLane battled Cayetano's band of Navajos. Two privates (Paulman and Neugent) were killed, along with seven Navajos. Sergeant John Thompson and several Navajos were wounded (McNitt 1972, 344–45).

The brown sandstone of Mesa de los Lobos sits atop the much more spectacular red sandstone for which the Navajo Reservation is known. This was called Wingate sandstone, originally named for these red cliffs forming the northern boundary of the Wingate Valley (Dutton 1885). Ironically, after the name was applied, testing determined that the closest outcropping of the true Wingate layer is some 60 miles to the north, along the northeastern edge of the Chuska Mountains (Baars 1995, 56–58).

MESA QUARTADO: (6000–7000 ft) San Juan County, NM. Also Harris Mesa. Navajo: Dził Ntsaaí, "Big Mountain." This large mesa is situated six miles southeast of Blanco, between the San Juan River and Canyon Largo. It is important to Navajo clan traditions (Van Valkenburgh 1974, 30).

MESA SANTA RITA: [DB] (7200 ft) McKinley County, NM. Navajo: Níhoobá, "Horizontal Gray Streak" (Young p.c. 1995), though Van Valkenburgh mistakenly interprets this as "Gray Streak Ends." This ridge immediately north of the Zuni Salt Lake is said to be the origin of the Nahoobaanii ("Gray Streak Ends People") Clan of the Navajos. The ridge sheers off on the south side from a sloping rise from the north, and the south side appears like a horizontal gray streak from the Salt Lake.

Navajos traditionally gathered wild plants on this mesa (U.S. Indian Claims Commission n.d., vol. IV, 712–15).

MESA TIERRA RUIN: (6080 ft) San Juan County, NM. Navajo: T'iis Ch'ínílí, "Cottonwood Outflow" (Young p.c. 1995), referring to the general area. This fortified mesa-top Chacoan great-house site sits 90 ft above the surrounding plain, and contains 35 rectangular rooms and as many as 10 kivas. Occupied A.D. 1100–1325, the site has strong Mesa Verdean traits.

MESITA: [DB] (5650 ft) Cibola County, NM. Navajo: Tsé Ch'ééchii', "Red Rocks Pointing Out Horizontally." This is a village of Laguna Pueblo, a mile north of I-40 on the Rio San Jose, four miles southeast of Laguna Pueblo.

As in Laguna, the language is Keresan. The Spanish name means "Small Mesa," referring to Mesita Negra, a small hill a mile west of the pueblo. Mesita is a recent pueblo built during the division of the Laguna population due to the formation of conservative and progressive factions over the introduction of White culture and religion. The conservatives, who wished to retain the crumbling native hierarchy, abandoned the old pueblo, moving to Mesita and Isleta. One mile east of Mesita is the ruin of the old stage station built near the old New Mexican town of El Rito. This station was on the Kansas City and Stockton Route of 1859.

MEXICAN SPRINGS: [DB] (6500 ft) (Population: 242) McKinley County, NM. Also Nakaibito. Navajo: Naakaii Bitó', "Mexican's Water." Old name: Naakaii Chííhí Bitó', "Long Nosed Mexican's Water." This trading, chapter, and government community is located on the flats at the foot of the Chuska Mountains, five miles west of U.S. Highway 666, about three miles north of the intersection of that highway with Navajo Route 9 (to Crownpoint).

A Navajo Experiment Station (Division of Research, Soil Conservation Service of the USDA) was opened in 1934 under the auspices of the old

Soil Erosion Service (USDI), the first demonstration area to be established on the Navajo Reservation. The site was chosen by H. H. Bennett and other officials of the national soil conservation movement. The station area ranges in elevation from 8000 ft on its ponderosa pine–covered borders on the crest of the Chuska Mountains, down to 6500 ft in the badly eroded flats and hillocks of its eastern boundary near Coyote Canyon. The variety of climatic and soil conditions in this small area has made it possible to develop solid conservation practices applicable to all conditions in the Navajo area.

In the spring of 1939, a group of Navajos at Mexican Springs took over the Mexican Springs Trading Post, turning it into a cooperative venture with an outside (White) manager.

MEXICAN SPRINGS TRADING POST: (6500 ft) McKinley County, NM. See Mexican Springs. This post was operated by Edward Vanderwagen around the turn of the century (McNitt 1962, 242), though Kelley 1977, 254) suggests it was not opened until after 1916.

MITTEN ROCK: (6300 ft) San Juan County, NM. Navajo: Tsé Digóní "Pock-marked Rock" (Kelley p.c. 1994). This sandstone formation is located five miles east of the Arizona state line, 10 miles southwest of Shiprock Pinnacle.

MOGOLLON BALDY: (10,778 ft) Catron County, NM. Navajo: Noodah Haas'aí, "Yucca Slope" (Van Valkenburgh 1974) or "Yuccas Extend Up Out in a Line" (Young and Morgan 1987, 677). Brugge (p.c. 1996), however, notes that "noodah" refers to the agave, not the yucca, and says that the long-standing error in interpretation needs to be corrected. This peak, the highest in the Mogollon Range of southwestern New Mexico, is some 15 miles southeast of the village of Mogollon. It is one of the main Blessingway mountains.

MOQUINO: (6800 ft) Cibola County, NM. Navajo: Uncertain. This small village is located two miles southeast of Cebolleta and two miles north of Paguate. Most likely it was named for Miguel Moquino, who claimed land in the area.

Colonel Congreve Jackson and Company G, First Dragoons, camped at this Mexican village in September and October 1846 (McNitt 1972, 105–6).

MOUNT TAYLOR: [DB] (11,301 ft) Cibola County, NM. Also San Mateo Mountain, San Mateo Peak, Cebolleta Mountains. Navajo: Tsoodził, "Mountain Tongue" (Franciscan Fathers 1910, 136) or "Tongue Mountain" (Young p.c. 1995, who notes that the etymology is as uncertain as the origin, a ceremonial name with an obscure origin). Sacred terminology: Dootł'izhii Dziil, "Turquoise Mountain" or "Blue Bead Mountain." The name Mount Taylor generally refers to the highest peak in the San Mateo Mountains, 10 miles north of I-40, about 15 miles northeast of Grants. Formerly called Seboyeta Mountain (Spanish for "Little Onion"). The English name commemorates Zachary Taylor, the twelfth President of the United States and Army general of Mexican War fame. It was the center of the Diné 'Ana'í occupation of Navajos. When Colonel Alexander W. Doniphan's column traversed these mountains in November 1847, they were referred to as the Sierra Madre (Hughes 1962, 183).

The mountain is visible from points in the Navajo country as far west as Chuska Peak, one hundred miles away. Projecting to the south and northeast from Mount Taylor are large lava flows forming mesas that sheer off from their forested tops in irregular and ragged escarpments. The peak retains snows until late in the spring.

Navajos refer to Mount Taylor as their sacred mountain of the south, and use it to indicate the southern boundary of their old country. It is said in the creation myth that First Man placed turquoise in this mountain, covered it with blue sky, and fastened it to the sky with a great stone knife (McPherson 1992, 15). Its symbolic color is blue or turquoise, and it is referred to in other mythology as the Turquoise Mountain. It is decorated with dark mist, female rain, and all species of animals and birds. It is the home of Dootł'izhii 'Ashkii (Turquoise Boy) and Naadá'áłtsoii 'At'ééd (Yellow Corn Girl). It is also said to be the home of one of the Haasch'é'ooghaan, beings that defy etymology

(Van Valkenburgh 1941, 102). Mount Taylor is important in the Blessing Side ceremonies and the 'Anaa'jí (Enemyway Ceremony). Navajo mythology considers the mountain female, along with Hesperus Peak (the sacred mountain of the north). Blanca Peak and the San Francisco Peaks, sacred mountains of the east and west, are considered male (Luckert 1977, 51). Two other sacred mountains internal to Navajoland are Gobernador Knob and Huerfano Peak.

Mount Taylor, legends say, was once the home of Yé'iitsoh ("Giant Yé'ii"), chief of the Enemy Gods, but it does not have the sacred significance of the other sacred mountains of the cardinal directions. The Twin War Gods killed Yé'iitsoh here (Benally et al. 1982, 15), his blood running down and coagulating into the Malpais lava flows around Grants. This prominence also figures in the Navajo Mountain Chant (Powell 1887, 415).

This mountain is also sacred to the Zunis, especially the Medicine and Big Fire Societies (Ferguson and Hart 1985, 126).

MUDDY WATER RUIN: (6750 ft) McKinley County, NM. Navajo: Hashtł'ish Bii' Kits'iil, meaning "Ruin in the Mud." This site is comprised of three Bonito-Phase great houses on the northern margin of Dutton Plateau, west of Crownpoint. With these structures is a single great kiva. One great house is Pueblo II, while the other two date to early Pueblo III. At least 46 roomblocks (255 rooms and six kivas) lie within a square mile of Muddy Water, and a major Chacoan road passes through the site (Gabriel 1991, 270).

NAGEEZI (TRADING POST): (6950 ft) San Juan County, NM. Navajo: Naayízí, "Squash" (the vegetable) (Kelley p.c. 1994). Trading post and chapter house on New Mexico Highway 44, 26 miles south of Bloomfield. Post office from 1941. The trading post was opened by Jim Brimhall around 1920 (McNitt 1962, 303).

NAMBÉ PUEBLO: (6775 ft) (Population: 1,402) Santa Fe County, NM. Navajo: Uncertain. Located at the foot of the west slope of the Sangre de Cristo Mountains, 15 miles north of Santa

Fe. The pueblo is situated on the Pojoaque River and New Mexico Highway 4, five miles east of U.S. Highway 285 and 15 miles north of Santa Fe. The language spoken is Tewa. Nambé is a Spanish rendition of two Tewa words: "nan" meaning "earth" and "be" meaning "round."

The first European visit was by Gaspar Castaño de Sosa in 1591. The Franciscans built a mission here in the early 1600s, which was destroyed by a storm; its priests were then killed in the Pueblo Revolt of 1680. The church was rebuilt in 1729, and was destroyed by lightning in 1909. Its replacement lasted until the 1960s; the present structure was constructed in 1975. A Navajo captive was baptized here in 1824 (Correll 1968, July 27).

NARBONA PASS: [DB] (8800 ft) San Juan County, NM. Also Washington Pass, Cottonwood Pass. Navajo: Sǫ' Silá "Twin Stars" (Franciscan Fathers 1910, 134); Béésh Łichí'í Bigiizh, which Van Valkenburgh interpreted as "Red Metal Pass" or "Copper Pass," referring to the metallic formations in the pass. However, Brugge (p.c. 1996) points out that "Béésh" can also refer to chert or flint, which is probabaly the original impetus for the name (the pass is the source of Washington Pass chert used as far back as Anasazi times for chipped stone tools); and that Sǫ' Silá actually refers to the Sonsola Buttes to the west in Arizona.

This passage separates the Chuska Mountains on the south from the Tunicha Mountains on the north, between Sheep Springs and Crystal, and is traversed by New Mexico Highway 134 and Navajo Route 32.

In 1993, the U.S. Geological Survey was successfully petitioned by members of the Navajo Nation to change the name of Washington Pass to Narbona Pass, honoring Navajo Headman Narbona (Hastiin Naat'áanii, "Mr. Chief"). The previous name was bestowed in 1859, on the map made by Captain McComb, honoring Lieutenant Colonel John M. Washington, the military governor of New Mexico in 1848–49. Washington traversed the pass as he led an expedition against the Navajos in 1849. His route led him down the eastern face of the Tunicha Mountains near Two Grey Hills and westward over the pass.

According to older Navajos, Navajo warriors skirted the flanks of Washington's soldiers, stopping at a spring near the summit. The soldiers missed the camp and walled up the spring before moving on westward. The stones were still visible in 1941, and the Navajos today consider the spring a minor shrine, depositing fragments of white shell, turquoise, abalone shell, and jet into it as offerings for rain.

Mexican Colonel (Governor) Jose Antonio Vizcarra crossed the Chuska Mountains through this pass on his wide-ranging expedition of 1823 (McNitt 1972, 58). Blas de Hinojos led an expedition into a Navajo ambush in this pass in 1835. Hinojos and several others were killed by Navajos (McNitt 1972, 73–74, 120).

Captain Henry Lafayette Dodge established the second Navajo agency at the eastern mouth of the pass, having moved there from Chupadero. Ruins of the agency are still visible in the pass. Also on the east slope, near the summit, there is a sheer lava crag, called "Sun Resting." Nearby is a tsé ninájihí, a pile of rocks and twigs upon which traveling Navajos add further rocks and twigs as offerings to the success of their journeys. Owl Spring, developed during the 1930s, lies beside the roadbed, also on the eastern slope.

The name Cottonwood Pass, shown on some maps, is incorrect. First Navajo Tribal Council Chairman Chee Dodge stated that that name refers to another pass east of Narbona Pass. Dodge also asserted that that canyon was named after some Navajos observed a party of Whites cutting a trail for their wagons through a dense copse of willows and cottonwoods.

The region of Narbona Pass is known to produce numerous bear, and is a prime deer-hunting area, although Van Valkenburgh notes that by 1941 they were a rarity. Wild turkey also declined almost overnight in the last decade of the 1800s. Chee Dodge told that they migrated to the San Francisco Mountains (!) following a particularly harsh winter (possibly the winter of 1892). They have made a modest comeback. The pass is blanketed with aspen, spruce, and dense thickets of Gambel oak and ponderosa pine. One of the few stands of birch in these mountains is found along Cottonwood Creek, which flows from the west side.

Curiously, Van Valkenburgh fails to note the most significant historical fact concerning this pass: the death of Narbona, Navajo headman, in the vicinity. Washington's troops had summoned Narbona and other Navajo leaders to a council near the pass, but when a soldier tried to claim an Indian horse as one stolen days earlier, shooting erupted and Narbona was killed.

It is fitting that the name of Colonel Washington be erased from this Navajo landmark deep within their own country. It is also fitting that it be replaced with the name of one of the earliest Navajo leaders to combat the encroachment of the Whites into Navajoland, Narbona. Yet, naming a place after a person is a break with Navajo tradition, as such an act may bring unwanted attention to his spirit, and saying his name aloud is likely to attract that spirit—something traditional Navajos dread.

It also seems ironic that the name chosen should be the name Spaniards applied to this chieftain, but Martin Link (p.c. 1997), who played a role in getting the name changed, has related to me (p.c. 1997) that the selection of Narbona's Hispanic name was a compromise between the various chapters that had to approve the petition to USGS.

NASCHITTI: [DB] (5950 ft) (Population: 323) McKinley County, NM. Also Drolet's Naschiti. Navajo: Nahashch'idí, "Badger." Established by Tom Bryan and Charlie Verden in 1880–81, the trading post located here is one of the oldest posts on the east side of the Chuska Mountains. The chapter community is located on present-day U.S. Highway 666, 16 miles south of Newcomb and 42 miles north of Gallup. The name is a derivative of Nahashch'idí Bito', "Badger Springs," which surface on the south fork of Salt Springs Wash, near the present store. In the 1940s, this community was known for its silversmiths, including one woman.

NASCHITTI TRADING POST: (5950 ft) McKinley County, NM. Also Naschiti Trading Post. Navajo: Bíchį́į́h Digiz, "Crooked Nose," referring to trader Thomas C. Bryan's flat, twisted nose. This post was established by Bryan and Charlie Verden in 1880–81, as one of the first

posts on the eastern slopes of the Chuska Mountains. C. C. Manning of Gallup purchased the post in 1902, employing Charlie Newcomb as manager. (See Newcomb Trading Post.) (McNitt 1962, 303–4)

NAVAJO: (7200 ft) (Population: 1,985) McKinley County, NM. Navajo: Ni'iijíní, "Place where Sawing is Done" (Wilson 1995, 39). A relatively new community on Navajo 12, 11 miles north of Fort Defiance and at the southern tip of Red Lake, where Navajo 12 crosses the Tohadildonen Wash. Griswold's Store (trading post) was here from the early 1970s (Kelley 1977, 256) until the mid-1980s, when it moved to Tsé Bonito.

In 1858, a temporary military post was established here, probably by Lieutenant Colonel Dixon Stansbury Miles. It was called Valley Camp (Giese 1991, 5).

In 1962, a new state-of-the-art sawmill was constructed here replacing the one at Sawmill, Arizona (Aberle 1983, 468). The mill was closed in the mid-1990s, as traditional Navajos and environmentalists successfully protested the cutting of timber on the reservation.

NAVAJO CHURCH TRADING POST: Exact location uncertain. McKinley County, NM. Navajo: Uncertain. Charlie Fredericks opened this post in the late 1800s (McNitt 1962, 233). It may be that this is the precursor to the Outlaw Trading Post at Red Rock State Park, located at the foot of Church Rock.

NAVAJO (NAVAHO) CITY: (6450 ft) San Juan County, NM. Navajo: Uncertain. This tiny community is located in Gobernador Canyon, at the junction of U.S. Highway 64 and New Mexico Highway 539, approximately 12 miles east of Bloomfield. The spelling Navaho City is English, while the Navajos, by a proclamation of the tribal council, have adopted the Spanish spelling, "Navajo."

NAVAJO DAM: (7200 ft) San Juan County, NM. Navajo: Dá'deestł'in, "Dam." This dam blocks the San Juan River 25 miles east of Aztec. The Bureau of Reclamation started construction in 1958; completion was in 1962. At the time of its construction, it was the second largest earth-filled dam in the United States.

NAVAJO INDIAN IRRIGATION PROJECT (NIIP):

(6200 ft) San Juan County, NM. Navajo: Dá'ak'eh Ntsaa: "The Big Farm." This vast, federally sponsored agricultural project on Gallegos Mesa in the San Juan Basin was authorized on June 13, 1962. The project lies between New Mexico Highway 44 on the east and Chaco River on the west, and extends some 40 miles south of the San Juan River.

The project calls for 216,843 acres, of which 110,630 will be irrigated. Only 40,343 of the acres are within the Navajo Reservation; the remaining 176,000 acres have been—or will be—purchased by the Navajo Nation. The irrigated acreage is divided into 11 10,000-acre plots, not all of which are contiguous. Irrigation on Block I was started in 1975 (Vogler 1993, 1–3). The irrigation will require 508,000 acre-feet of water per year, and the project will potentially employ 4,400 Navajos (Aberle 1983, 644–46). By the end of 1998, some 50,000 acres were being watered.

NAVAJO LAKE:

(7200 ft) San Juan County, NM. Also Navajo Reservoir. Navajo: Uncertain. This 35-mile-long, 110,000-acre lake was created some 18 miles east of Aztec by the closing of Navajo Dam on the San Juan River in 1962. A New Mexico state park and recreation area surround the lake.

The lake covers Tó 'Aheedłí (Young and Morgan 1987, 706) or Tóalnaazli Tó Bil Dahsk'id (Benally et al. 1982, 4), "Place Where the Waters Crossed" (though Young asserts this is undecipherable), referring to the juncture of the San Juan and the Los Pinos Rivers. The site was a highly sacred location to the Navajos, especially to medicine men—as are the junctures of the San Juan and Colorado rivers and the San Juan with Mancos Creek. Here ripples in the sand were "read" by medicine men. Such readings reportedly predicted both the Bosque Redondo internment of the Navajos and the Navajo livestock reduction (McPherson 1992, 33).

McPherson (1988, 25) asserts that the location of Navajo emergence from the fourth world into the present one was near present Navajo Dam, but Brugge (p.c. 1996) refutes this.

NAVAJO PEAK:

(7200 ft) Rio Arriba County, NM. Navajo: Uncertain. This peak is located on the northeast bank of the juncture of the Rio Chama and the Rio Cebolla. Its name is significant, as it suggests historic Navajo presence in this area.

NAVAJO RIVER:

(10,400–6380 ft) Rio Arriba County, NM; Archuleta County, CO. Navajo: Uncertain. This stream rises in the San Juan Mountains some 20 miles east of Pagosa Springs, Colorado. It travels a southwesterly course for 25 miles, passing into New Mexico about five miles north of Lumberton. It travels another 15 miles in New Mexico, passing within a mile of Dulce, before crossing the Colorado line again and merging with the San Juan River at Juanita, Colorado, approximately two miles north of the New Mexico state line.

This is one of the northeasternmost features to bear the name "Navajo," and it may be an indicator of the northeastern extent of Navajo territory. This river was crossed by Roque Madrid in 1705 on his historic push through Navajo country that resulted in three confrontations with the Diné.

NAVAJO TRAIL:

(approx. 6000 ft) San Juan County, NM. Navajo: Diné Habitiin, "Navajo Trail Going Upward." At the confluence of Compañero and Largo canyons, near Salt Point, this location is important to Navajo clan traditions (Van Valkenburgh 1974, 30).

NAVATA:

(6800 ft) McKinley County, NM. Navajo: Uncertain. Now abandoned (though new businesses have begun to spring up in the vicinity), this trading point was on U.S. Highway 666 four miles north of Gallup, halfway between Gallup and Yah Ta Hey.

NEHANEZAD:

(5100 ft) San Juan County, NM. Navajo: Niinah Nízaad, "Long Upgrade" (Young and Morgan 1987, 669). Chapter community on the southern margin of Fruitland, about halfway between Farmington and Shiprock.

NEWCOMB: [DB] (5850 ft) (Population: 388) San Juan County, NM. Also Blue Mesa Trading Post, Crozier Trading Post, Nava, and Newcomb's. Navajo: Bis Deez'áhí, "Clay Point." This trading post and school community is located 60 miles north of Gallup, on the south bank of Captain Tom Wash and on U.S. Highway 666. (Although many sources referred to this location by the above English names, careful research has shown that each was actually a different location for the main trading post in this region, all within a couple of miles of one another.) The mesa behind the trading post, called Blue Mesa, led to the post itself often being referred to as Blue Mesa Trading Post (Newcomb 1966).

Newcomb is distinguished for its Two Grey Hills Navajo rugs, developed by trader Arthur J. Newcomb, who may have picked up the designs from J. B. Moore while trading at Crystal. These finely woven rugs in natural grays, whites, browns, and blacks have characteristic geometrical designs and run to elaborate borders. (Early photographs of the rugs of J. B. Moore, who traded at Crystal from the 1890s until 1912, show a great similarity to the present Two Grey Hills type.)

A renowned medicine man, Hastiin Klah (Tł'ah) lived in the Newcomb vicinity before his death in 1937. He was a weaver of rare, but well known, sandpainting blankets and the subject of a book by Franc Newcomb (1964). There is an agricultural area on Captain Tom Wash, containing some six hundred acres, divided into Upper and Lower projects.

A feature known as the Anthill, located near Nava, is important to the Navajo Mothway myth (Haile 1978, 64).

NEWCOMB TRADING POST: (6,000 ft) San Juan County, NM. Navajo: Bis Dootł'izh Deez'áhí, "Blue Clay Point" (Young p.c. 1995), though Newcomb (1966, 9, 75) preferred "Trader at Blue Point." John Oliver built a post just south of Captain Tom Wash in 1904, which White men called "Crozier," after a Captain Tom Crozier (U.S. Army). Crozier had led troops on a reconnaissance through the area in 1846. According to McNitt (1962, 304), Oliver sold the post to Charles Nelson in 1911, and the post came to be known as "Nelson's Trading Post," or simply "Nelsons." In 1913–14, McNitt asserts, Arthur J. Newcomb purchased the post and changed the name to "Nava," though McNitt states that some older maps refer to the location as "Drolet's" (or Drolet's Trading Post), after J. M. Drolet (a subsequent owner) or "Newcomb's" after Charlie Newcomb.

However, McNitt's scenario may be in error. The 1929 "Automobile Club of Southern California Automobile Road Map of The Indian Country" (which evolved into the currently popular and annually revised "AAA Guide to Indian Country") identifies and pinpoints four separate locations for Crozier, Nava, Newcomb, and Drolet's. The map places both Crozier and Nava on the south side of the road from Newcomb to Toadlena, and Drolet's is shown on U.S. Highway 666, about 16 miles south of Newcomb.

The post was also known as Blue Mesa Trading Post (Newcomb 1966, 9, 15); it burned to the ground in 1936 and was rebuilt.

NEW LAGUNA: (5900 ft) Cibola County, NM. Navajo: Uncertain. This is a modern village three miles west of Old Laguna, the traditional pueblo village, and 26 miles southeast of Grants. It is situated on the Rio San Jose and the Burlington Northern Santa Fe, about three-quarters of a mile north of I-40.

NUTRIA, UPPER AND LOWER: [DB] (6800 ft) McKinley County, NM. Also Las Nutrias and Nutrioso. Navajo: Tsé Dijíhí, "Rock Starts to Extend Along Black" (Young p.c. 1995). The same name applies to the lake. Zuni: Ts'iakwin, "Seed Place; Planting Place." The Spanish name "Nutria" means "Otter." These two small Zuni farming villages sit on Rio Nutria (north branch of the Zuni River) in the Zuni Mountains, 23 miles northeast of Zuni.

Formerly occupied only during planting and harvesting, these communities are now permanent villages, with many Navajos living immediately to the north. During the latter part of the nineteenth century the Navajos were prone to impose on the people at Nutria. Van Valkenburgh

(1941, 108) contends that Pinto, the Navajo head-man of the region, actually waged warfare on the Zunis, though Brugge (p.c. 1996) suggests that this was more a matter of intertribal boundary disputes.

The best known Anasazi ruin in the Nutria Valley is the Village of the Great Kivas, some seven miles southwest of Lower Nutria, on the north side of Nutria Creek. This large ruin, occupied between A.D. 1000 and 1030, was excavated in the summer of 1930 by Dr. Frank H. H. Roberts, Archaeologist of the Bureau of American Ethnology.

The land around Nutria was given to Zuni Pueblo by the Spanish crown but was contested by the Navajos until their removal to the Bosque Redondo from 1864 to 1868 (Lange and Riley 1970, 56). A trading post operated here in the 1930s (Ferguson and Hart 1985, 96).

A series of four man-made reservoirs along Rio Nutria, three to five miles downstream from the village of Lower Nutria, are called collectively Nutria Lakes, offering fishing for Navajos and non-Navajos.

OAK CREEK: (7800–7300 ft) McKinley County, NM. Navajo: Chéch'il Bii' Tó, "Spring in the Oaks" (Young p.c. 1995). Only five miles long, this creek is tributary to Squirrel Springs Wash in Todilto Park, north of Twin Buttes.

OJO ALAMO TRADING POST: (approx. 6400 ft) San Juan County, NM. Navajo: Uncertain. This was one of several trading posts operated by the Hyde Exploring Expedition between 1898 and 1903 (the others were located at Chaco Canyon, Farmington, Thoreau, Tiz-Na-Tzin, Largo, and Raton Springs, and on the Escavada Wash). John Wetherill managed the Ojo Alamo post (McNitt 1962, 84, 234), which was located about 10 miles south of Carson Trading Post and about 20 miles north of Chaco Canyon (Thomas 1978, 253). The post closed by 1921 (Kelley 1977, 254).

OJO CALIENTE: [DB] (6400 ft) Cibola County, NM. Navajo: Tó Sido, "Hot Water" (U.S. Indian Claims Commission n.d., vol. VI,

xvii). Zuni: 'I'iapwainakwin, "Place Whence Flow Hot Waters." Small Zuni farming village located about 13 miles southeast of Zuni, in the vicinity of Hawiku and at least 30 other prehistoric ruins. It is located on the southernmost boundary of the Zuni Reservation, just inside the Cibola County line.

Two Navajos were killed here by Zunis in 1865 (Ferguson and Hart 1985, 61), when most Navajos had been removed to the Bosque Redondo. In February 1844, Spaniards attacked the Navajo rancheria here, killing 19 Navajos and capturing 19. They also took 1,600 sheep and 200 other livestock (Correll 1968, February).

OJO ENCINO: [DB] (6700 ft) McKinley County, NM. Navajo: Chéch'iizh Bii' Tó, "Spring in the Rough Rocks," from a number of fallen sandstone pinnacles around the fine springs seeping out of a barren sandstone cove above one of the upper branches of the Torreon Wash (some nine miles northeast of Star Lake). Also Chéch'il Dah Lichí'í, "Red Oak Up at an Elevation" (Young and Morgan 1987, 271).

These springs, first developed for a dipping vat, were on the allotment of an old Navajo woman named "Old Lady Salvador Toledo." Robert (Bob) Smith, of Star Lake, formerly had a trading post here from about 1916 until the late 1920s (Kelley 1977, 254). Some miles west is Ojo Alamo, a treeless region of rolling hills and badlands, cut by sandy washes lined with a few cottonwoods, with some excellent grazing land and corn fields.

OLD CRATER: [DB] (7831 ft) Cibola County, NM. Navajo: Nááʼaghání, "Eyes That Kill" (Young p.c. 1995). A low, rounded volcanic dike standing isolated from the eastern end of the red Wingate sandstone cliffs that rise near Gallup some 50 miles west. Located about 10 miles north of Bluewater, this crater is also known as Haystack Mountain, where Paddy Martinez first discovered uranium in 1950. However, see also Haystack Mountain.

The crater is reputed to be the place where Déélgééd—the guard for Yé'iitsoh ("Big God," chief of Enemy Gods)—fled after Yé'iitsoh was killed south of Mount Taylor by Naayéé Neizghání (Killer of Monsters) and Tóbájíshchíní (Born from Water), the Navajos' Twin War Gods.

OLD OTERO RANCH: [DB] (6800 ft) Rio Arriba County, NM. Navajo: Uncertain. Now abandoned, this ranch was located on the Jicarilla Apache Reservation. Van Valkenburgh's description coincides with the 1929 Automobile Club of Southern California automobile road map locus called simply "Otero," which lies on Jicarilla Route 7 near the juncture of Cañada Larga and Cañada de los Ojitos (approximately 10 miles northeast of Counselors).

Located on a cienega by a fine spring on the banks of one of the main arroyos feeding into Largo Canyon, the ranch served as a fence-rider and stockman's headquarters on the Jicarilla Apache Indian Reservation. A large number of old hogan remains in the vicinity indicate that it was once an early Navajo habitat as well. Older Anasazi campsites are also found in the vicinity.

This point is shown on the McComb map of 1860 as Ojo Amarilla, a known location on early Indian and military trails. The remains of the old stone ranch buildings of the Otero family can still be found. In the latter part of the eighteenth century this Spanish-American family ran sheep into the Navajo country as far west as Tohatchi.

OLIO TRADING POST: [DB] (4900 ft) San Juan County, NM. Navajo: Uncertain. This post was built by John Moss around 1880 on the San Juan River across from Waterflow. The name means "hodgepodge," or "mixture," and was chosen by Moss to illustrate the many cultures of the area: Mormon, gentile, Navajo, Ute, etc. (McNitt 1962, 293). The community hosted a post office from 1884 to 1903. According to Pearce (1965, 113) the post office then moved to Kirtland. Pearce also lists Olio as a precursor to Fruitland. (See also Kirtland and Fruitland, which is two miles from Kirtland.)

Located on the lower terrace of the San Juan River across from Waterflow, Olio is the former headquarters of J. F. Coolidge, civil engineer and one of the owners of the Coolidge Ditch, which

irrigated lands on the south side of the San Juan River. Olio appears on U.S. Geological Survey maps in 1885. The lands and the ditch were later turned over to the Navajos.

OTIS TRADING POST: Exact location uncertain. San Juan County, NM. Navajo: Uncertain. According to Pearce (1965, 115), this was the site of a trading post established in 1919 and named for the founder. It does not appear on contemporary maps, and the exact location remains unknown to this author. It may be the Otis shown by the Automobile Club of Southern California's 1929 map of Indian Country at the approximate location of Nageezi Trading Post on New Mexico Highway 44, between Counselors and Huerfano.

OUTLAW TRADING POST: (6750 ft) McKinley County, NM. Navajo: Uncertain. This post was established between 1881 and 1885 (Kelley 1977, 251). Once operated by Edward Vanderwagen, it was later acquired by the Richards brothers, who sold it, along with a half-section of land, to the Inter-Tribal Indian Ceremonial Association of Gallup in 1975.

When the City of Gallup, the Inter-Tribal Indian Ceremonial Association, and the Gallup Lions Club formed a Joint Powers agreement and approached the state of New Mexico for funding to build a multi-use facility here, the land and buildings subsequently became part of Red Rock State Park, a facility managed by the City of Gallup. The trading post was managed by the Inter-Tribal Indian Ceremonial Association until the late 1970s, when it was deeded to the City of Gallup in lieu of back rent for the facility at which the annual ceremonial is held. Joe Richards continued to serve as postmaster until the late 1980s.

PAGUATE: [DB] (6200 ft) (Population: 492) Cibola County, NM. Navajo: K'ish Ch'ínít'i', "Black Alders Extending out Horizontally in a Line" (Young and Morgan 1987, 511). A Laguna Pueblo colony, formerly a summer camp named for Antonio Paguat, a Mexican from whom the Laguna Indians purchased the land on which it is situated. The community is located on the southeast slope of the Seboyeta (Cebolleta) Mountains, seven miles north of Old Laguna on New Mexico Highway 279. The community has hosted its own post office intermittently from 1905 to the present, and has grown only a little from its 1940 population of four hundred.

As in Laguna, the language spoken here is Keresan. Paguate, once a farming community, eventually developed into the proportions of a pueblo. Old Navajos say they used to trade woven belts with the people of Paguate in the middle of the nineteenth century. A Navajo raid near Paguate in 1863 resulted in the deaths of two Lagunas.

A treaty between Mexico and the Navajos, negotiated here on February 2, 1823, required an exchange of captives, conversion of Navajos to Catholicism, and settlement of Navajos in pueblo-like villages (Correll 1968, February).

Today the village is the site of the inoperative Anaconda Jackpile Mine, once the world's largest open-pit uranium mine, closed in 1981 (Fugate and Fugate 1989, 363).

PAJARITO PEAK: (8200 ft) Sandoval County, NM. Navajo: Tł'iish Jik'áhí, "Grinding Snakes." This elevation at the southern end of the Nacimiento Mountains (some 12 miles northwest of San Ysidro) is important in the Navajo Windway Ceremony, and is a source of white clay used in various ceremonies (Van Valkenburgh 1974, 48).

PARAJE: (6000 ft) (Population: 622) Cibola County, NM. Navajo: Uncertain. A Laguna village located one mile north of I-40 on New Mexico Highway 124, at the junction of that road with New Mexico Highway 23. Also situated on the Rio San Jose, Paraje started out as a summer farming camp.

PECOS PUEBLO: (6900 ft) San Miguel County, NM. Navajo: Uncertain. This community was established about A.D. 1100 by Indians from Rio Grande pueblos. Its residents called it Cicuye. The first European visitors were Coronado's expedition of 1542. The Mission of Nuestra Señora de Los Angeles de Porcinucula was es-

tablished in the early seventeenth century—probably between 1619 and 1634 (Adams and Chavez 1956, 209)—and partially destroyed in the Pueblo Revolt of 1680. Raids from Plains Indians and smallpox decimated the population, and in 1838 the last 17 residents moved to Jemez Pueblo.

On December 23, 1864, the Santa Fe New Mexican reported that the bodies of 15 Navajos who starved to death on the Long Walk to the Bosque Redondo lay unburied at Pecos ruins for five to six weeks (La Farge 1959, 28). Reports such as this helped bring about the transfer of Colonel Edwin Canby and the end of his Bosque Redondo experiment, allowing the Navajos to return to their homeland.

PEDERNAL MESA: (9862 ft) Rio Arriba County, NM. Navajo: Uncertain. This abrupt mesa rising some 1400 ft above the surrounding landscape has been suggested as one of many possible promontories the Navajos call Sisnaajiní, most often translated as "(Woman's) Belt Extending Down Black." Young (p.c. 1995), however, notes that the name most likely stems from *tsis*, Navajo for "mountain," rather than *sis*, Navajo for "belt."

Sisnaajiní refers to the Navajo sacred mountain of the east (Bennett 1990, 3, 8). Pedernal Mesa, however, is one of the least likely candidates for the sacred mountain (see also Blanca Peak, in Colorado, and Wheeler and Pelado Peaks in New Mexico).

PELADO PEAK: (11,260 ft) Sandoval County, NM. Navajo: Dził Dijool, "Round (ball-shaped) Mountain." Also possibly Sisnaajiní (or Tsisnaajin, or Tsisnaajinii with a dozen other spellings), if this feature is the Navajo sacred mountain of the east (Matthews 1897; O'Brian 1956). (See Pedernal Mesa for translations.) This peak, 15 miles northeast of Jemez Pueblo, is one of the highest in the Jemez Mountains, and is sacred to the Zia, Jemez, Santa Ana, San Felipe, Santo Domingo, Cochiti, and northern Tewa pueblos (Ellis 1974, 157), and has been suggested as the Navajo sacred mountain of the east.

The exact location of the Navajo sacred mountain of the east has been the object of much study, as each scholar seems to find informants with different locations in mind. However, most authorities today agree that it is Blanca Peak in Colorado, and not Pelado Peak.

The four sacred mountains mark the four cardinal directions and were once considered boundaries of Navajo range. The other three mountains are more firmly known: Mount Hesperus (Colorado) in the north, Mount Taylor (New Mexico) in the south, and the San Francisco Peaks (Arizona) in the west. Gobernador Knob, Hosta Butte, and Huerfano Peak are three promontories internal to Navajoland that are also sacred.

PEÑA BLANCA: (5250 ft) Sandoval County, NM. Navajo: Uncertain. This tiny community some three miles south of Cochiti Pueblo was attacked by Navajos on August 26, 1851. A single New Mexican girl was killed (McNitt 1972, 198n).

PEÑA BLANCO ARROYO: (5500–5300 ft) San Juan County, NM. Also Theodore Wash. Navajo: Uncertain. A five-mile-long tributary of the Chaco River, flowing northeast into the Chaco four miles north of the confluence of that channel with Captain Tom Wash and Brimhall Wash. This arroyo is formed by the confluence of Tó Bii' Hask'idí ("Moved in the Water") Wash (from the south) and Tó Niłchxoní ("Stinking Water") Wash (from the north).

This wash was traversed by Major Henry Lane Kendrick's First Dragoons, Third Infantry, and Second Artillery in August 1853.

PENISTAJA: [DB as Penastaja] (6650 ft) Sandoval County, NM. Navajo: Bíniishdáhí, "Where I Sat Leaning Against It" (translation by Young p.c. 1995). This scattered farming and stockraising community is spread out over the rolling hills of the continental divide, on New Mexico Highway 197, some 14 miles southwest of Cuba. The location given by Van Valkenburgh coincides only roughly with an existing community by the same name. Pearce's (1965, 119) description of Penastaja coincides roughly with both. Pearce defines the name as Spanish for rocky formations nearby (peña meaning "boulder").

However, the Spanish and Navajo names sound much alike, and it is likely that one is a mimicry of the other (regardless of which came first).

The community of homesteaders was established in 1920 by World War I veterans. A trading post was established about the same time (Kelley 1977, 254), run by J. L. Ballard in the 1940s. Land ownership in the region is a mixture of White and Navajo, though the country previously was held by the Navajos.

This region, partly within the Navajo Eastern Extension (now called the Navajo Checkerboard Area), has a few excellent springs, one adjacent to the Penistaja post office and store. One of the finest springs in the region, 'Atsá Bitó, "Eagle Spring," is located some eight miles west of Penistaja on an Indian allotment.

PESCADO: [DB] (6750 ft) McKinley County, NM. Also Pescado Springs. Navajo: Táala Hótsaii, "Large Flattopped Area." Zuni: Heshotatsinakwin, "Place of Glyphs." The Spanish name "Pescado" means "fish," and refers to small fish in the spring-fed reservoir and streams. A small Zuni farming village scattered along the banks of a south fork of the Zuni River, some 13 miles east of Zuni. High forested mesas tower above the village to the north and south, and springs are found near the village, forming a reservoir with the help of a U.S. Indian Irrigation Service dam. An Anasazi ruin lies about two hundred yards east of the present community.

Old American maps show this site as Piscado (sic) Spring, Ojo del Piscado, and Piscad. The Zuni name refers to pictographs found on the walls of the ancient Anasazi village.

Pescado Spring served as an important watering place on the Indian, Spanish, and early American trails. In 1846, Navajos attacked this village. When warriors from Halona'wa came to their aid, a larger force of Navajos attacked Halona'wa. That village was successfully defended by women and children until their warriors could return (Ferguson and Hart 1985, 60). The spring was an important stopping place on the route laid out by Captain Willis in 1863 for the opening of Arizona Territory. Lieutenant Simpson, in his journal of the Washington

Expedition of 1849, mentions a nameless American trader operating at this place.

On August 30, 1851, Colonel Edwin Vose Sumner's column was hit here by Navajos who stole all but two of their mules. The mules were recovered the next day.

Pescado marks the southeastern corner agreed upon in peace negotiations held at Fort Defiance on December 25, 1858, between Herro Delgadito and other Navajo chiefs with Colonel B. L. E. Bonneville (Military Commander of New Mexico), and James Collins, Indian Superintendent for the territory. An eastern boundary was agreed upon, to run from Piscado Springs at the head of the Zuni River, to Bear Springs (present Fort Wingate) and from there to the ruins of the Escondido on the Chaco River (possibly the ruins of the present Chaco Culture National Historical Park), thence to the juncture of the Chaco and San Juan Rivers. However, this treaty was never ratified by Congress, so the reservation never took effect (McNitt 1972, 194–95, 362).

PICURIS PUEBLO: (7500 ft) (Population: 1,882) Taos County, NM. Navajo: Uncertain. Situated on the Rio Pueblo on the west slope of the Sangre de Cristo Mountains, about 18 miles south of Taos Pueblo. This is one of two Northern Tiwa pueblos (the other is Taos), and it is closely related linguistically to the Southern Tiwa pueblos of Sandia and Isleta. Archaeologists say the pueblo has been in place since the middle of the thirteenth century. Excavations during the 1960s at Pot Creek Ruin near Picuris suggest that Picuris was occupied by at least A.D. 1250 (New Mexico Office of Cultural Affairs 1991, 66).

The first recorded European contact was with the Gaspar Castaño de Sosa expedition of 1591. By 1620 Spanish missionaries had arrived and forced the occupants of Picuris to build the Mission of San Lorenzo. This church was ruled by Fray Martin de Arvide, a harsh believer in taxation to the point of starvation.

Picuris warriors were known to join other pueblos and the Spaniards in raids on the Navajos during the seventeenth century. Spanish Governor Don Bernardo Lopez de Mendizabal once purchased two Navajo captives from Picuris in the 1660s in exchange for cattle.

In 1680, Luis Tupato, governor of Picuris, was instrumental in the planning and leading of the Pueblo Revolt. About 20 Spaniards were killed and the mission destroyed at Picuris. Following the return and "peaceful" reconquest by de Vargas, Picuris revolted twice more—in 1694 and 1696. Following the final revolt the Picuris Indians abandoned the pueblo and lived on the plains with Apachean groups for 10 years, returning—at about one-tenth their previous strength—in 1706. At least one Navajo was baptized here in October 1837, and again in October 1857 (Correll 1968, October). The first serious impact of American culture on the pueblo was when the United States opened a day school in 1899.

PIERRE'S RUIN: Exact location withheld. San Juan County, NM. Navajo: Beesh Schichii, "Flint Striking Stones," (though Young is dubious; this doesn't sound like a Navajo word). This Chacoan great house sits on the Great North Road, 112 miles north of Pueblo Alto. Built about A.D. 1060 (50 years after the road was formalized), it appears to be the only structure on Great North Road that may have been occupied. The locale was reportedly used as a hideout by Navajos during the Bosque Redondo Period (Gabriel 1991, 107, 111).

PINEDALE: [DB] (7000 ft) McKinley County, NM. Navajo: Tó Bééhwíisganí, "Place that is Dry Around Water" (Young and Morgan 1987, 706). This trading and chapter community and BIA school is located in the high pine- and piñon-covered mesa country six miles northwest of Mariano Lake in Lobo Valley, the broad east-west dale at the southern foot of Mesa de los Lobos. Navajos were grazing livestock in this vicinity as early as 1802 (U.S. Indian Claims Commission n.d., vol. IV, 712–15). The day school is one of the oldest in the Navajo area, having been established in the 1910s. At one time, Jacob C. Morgan, present chairman of the Navajo Tribal Council and missionary, was in charge of the school.

PINEDALE TRADING POST: (7000 ft) McKinley County, NM. Navajo: See Pinedale. This post opened prior to 1910 (Kelley 1977, 253), and was once owned by the Foutz brothers (McNitt 1962, 300n).

PINEHAVEN: [DB] (7300 ft) McKinley County, NM. Also Danoff, Danoffville, McKittrick. Navajo: Chííh Ntł'izí, "Hard Nose," referring to the countenance of the trader. This small trading community is located in the well-watered and timbered slopes of the Zuni Mountains five miles east of New Mexico Highway 602 (formerly 32), 15 miles south of Gallup. It was known in the 1940s as "Cowboy Chapter House" (Van Valkenburgh 1941, 115).

Navajo settlement of the region seems to have begun after the return of the tribe from Fort Sumner in 1868, one of the first Navajos to settle being Cha'a. Earlier, the vicinity was a staging area for Navajo raids on the Zunis. Old Pinto (see Nutria), whose activities kept the Indian Department embroiled in the 1880 and 1890s, still lived near Pinehaven in 1941, though he was substantially more pacific than in his younger days.

PINEHAVEN TRADING POST: (7300 ft) McKinley County, NM. Navajo: See Pinedale. Between 1900 (Van Valkenburgh 1941, 115) and 1913 (McNitt 1962, 233–34), Hans Neuman founded this post near the Box S Ranch. The Danoff brothers, Russian-Jewish immigrants, operated a post and post office here beginning around 1915, giving their name to the vicinity, though some called it "McKittrick," after Charley McKittrick, who operated a post on the Box S Ranch near the present post. The Box S formerly spread out over much of the region.

PIÑON SPRINGS TRADING POST: Exact location uncertain. McKinley County, NM. Navajo: Uncertain. Located between Gallup and Zuni, this post was purchased by Lorenzo Hubbell about 1918, when he learned that the "Mexicans" operating it previously had been selling liquor to the Indians. Hubbell promptly smashed the still and destroyed its contents. Edward Vanderwagen operated the store for

Hubbell for a short time thereafter. Hubbell sold the post around 1925. The post was one that used "seco," or tokens, for money, a tactic to keep Indians trading at the same location (McNitt 1962, 205–6, 206n, 242).

POJOAQUE PUEBLO: (5905 ft) (Population: 2,556) Santa Fe County, NM. Navajo: Uncertain. This small Tewa village is related linguistically to Nambe, San Ildefonso, Santa Clara, San Juan, and Tesuque pueblos. It is located 16 miles north of Santa Fe, on the Pojoaque River, a tributary of the Rio Grande. It is the least "pueblo-like" village, conducting no ceremonies, and having no cacique (the last died in 1900). It has always been one of the smallest Tewa villages.

As with all the Rio Grande Pueblos, Pojoaque's ancestors were in the area by A.D. 900, with the community probably initiated in the 1300s with the influx of Tewas into the region. The pueblo probably saw first European contact in the mid-sixteenth century, and its inhabitants took an active role in the Pueblo Revolt of 1680. For this they suffered greatly during the Reconquest, and subsequently lost great chunks of its fertile land through the years. By 1712, only 79 people lived at Pojoaque, and early in the twentieth century, it was described as being abandoned. Those occupying the pueblo since it was resettled in 1934 are a mixture of Tewas, Tiwas, and Hispanic (Lambert 1979, 324–29). The Spanish name Pojoaque is probably borrowed from the Tewa "posuwaege," meaning "drink-water place," although Pearce (1965, 124) quotes a resident of the pueblo as describing the name as a corruption of "povi age," Santa Clara for "place where the flowers grow along the stream."

The population of the pueblo was very hard hit by the 1918 influenza epidemic. This was the first pueblo to elect a female governor (New Mexico Office of Cultural Affairs 1991, 67).

PREWITT: (6900 ft) McKinley County, NM. Also Baca. Navajo: Kin Łigaaí, "White House" (Young and Morgan 1987, 496). Fifteen miles west of Grants/Milan on I-40, this small community grew near a railroad switching station called Baca, around a trading post opened after World

War I by Robert C. Prewitt (Noe 1992, 6–7). Kelley (1977, 252) cites a post in the vicinity in the very late 1890s (which closed down in the mid-1960s), and notes that Zuni Mountain Trading Post opened in the vicinity in the early 1940s.

PUEBLO ALTO (TRADING POST): [DB as Setzer's Store)] (6542 ft) McKinley County, NM. Navajo: Tsédáá'tóhí, "Spring on the Edge of a Rock" (Young and Morgan 1987, 729). Located under a shaley rim 14 miles northeast of Chaco Canyon, six miles north of Pueblo Pintado, this post was opened on Indian allotment land by Pennsylvanian Ralph Tucker about 1915. It was called "Tucker's Store." The Navajo name applies more to the region as a whole than just to the post. Tucker himself was known by the Navajos as Jeeshóó', "Buzzard," in apparent reference to the man's bald pate and prominent nose (although the Indians had apparently convinced Tucker the name meant "American Eagle").

This post was only about four miles east of the slightly older Mariano's Store, and consisted of a store building, stock corral, and storage cellar excavated into the slope of the canyon behind the store (Kelley 1985, 24).

The post was partially burned in 1916, when two Navajos killed the younger brother of Bob Smith, later a trader at nearby Star Lake. Tucker rebuilt it but died soon after. His widow sold it to Ed Sargent (a sheep operator from Chama) and Bob Smith, who hired Lester Setzer as manager. Later they sold it to Arthur Tanner, who moved it ten miles east and renamed it Pueblo Alto Trading Post (McNitt 1962, 331n–332n). Today the post, really a convenience store, is located on New Mexico Highway 197, four miles east of Pueblo Pintado.

PUEBLO BONITO TRADING POST: (6200 ft) San Juan County, NM. Navajo: Kinteel, "Wide House," or Tsé Bíyaa 'Aníí'áhí, "Supporting Rock Wall" (Kelley p.c. 1994; Young p.c. 1995). This trading post was conceived by Richard Wetherill and financed by the Hyde Expedition. It was constructed by Richard's brothers Al and Clayton and Orian Buck in October 1897. It was built against the north wall of Pueblo Bonito ruin, and was operated by Buck until

Richard Wetherill arrived the following May. Probably more in an effort to perpetuate year-round excavations at Chaco Canyon—and Pueblo Bonito in particular—Richard filed a homestead on the land that included Bonito, Chetro Ketl, and Pueblo del Arroyo, naming the claim Triangle Bar Triangle Ranch. He continued to manage the post as well as excavate—though possibly illegally—in the ruins.

On June 22, 1910, shortly after he'd sold the store, Richard was shot and killed by a Navajo named Chiisch'ilí Biye' (commonly written as Chiscilling-Begay) at the big turn of Rincón del Camino. Bad blood seems to have existed between the two for some time. At his trial, Biyé claimed that Wetherill was stealing some of his livestock, and that the shooting was self-defense. Nonetheless, he was convicted of voluntary manslaughter and served four years in the New Mexico State Penitentiary in Santa Fe. He died of natural causes in 1950 (McNitt 1966).

PUEBLO PINTADO: [DB] (6480 ft) McKinley County, NM. Navajo: Kinteel, "Wide House." This trading point on Navajo Route 9, just north of the "big bend" of New Mexico Highway 197, is some 60 miles northeast of Thoreau, and 12 miles northwest of Starr Lake. The chapter community is named for the ruins of a Chacoan "Great House," located approximately one and one-half miles north of the Pueblo Pintado Boarding School (nine miles east-southeast of Chaco Canyon). This 161-room pueblo was constructed just after A.D. 1060 (Flint and Flint 1989, 67–70). A trading post was erected here between 1910 and 1915 (Kelley 1977, 254).

PUEBLO PINTADO RUIN: (6520 ft) McKinley County, NM. Also Pueblo Colorado, Pueblo Montezuma, Pueblo Grande (and, erroneously, Pueblo Alto). Navajo: Kinteel, "Wide House," or Kinteel Ch'ínílíní, "Wide House Outflow" (Young and Morgan 1987, 496). This same name is also applied to the Aztec West great house. This ruin is named in the Navajo Excessway, Waterway, and Shootingway, and is the starting point of Beadway.

This Chacoan great-house community—with a Mesa Verdean reoccupation—is located three

miles west of the Pueblo Pintado Boarding
School, overlooking the Chaco River a mile and
a half northwest of the Pueblo Pintado Boarding
School. Dating to A.D. 1060, it contains 161 rectilinear rooms (including many that are two- and
three-story) in an "L" shape. Two single-story
wings connect the larger roomblocks to an enclosed plaza in near "D" shape. The complex
contains 14 to 16 round rooms, and is surrounded
by a village of 14 houses totaling 116 rooms and
19 pithouses or kivas. A great kiva lies near the
southwest corner. The site exhibits core and veneer Chacoan masonry, and a prehistoric road
extends from the southwest corner to Chaco
Canyon.

In historic literature, the site has also been
called Kin Kale (Grand House), Pueblo de Montezuma, Pueblo Ratones, Pueblo Colorado, and
Pueblo Grande (Gabriel 1991, 266; Flint and Flint
1989, 67–69). Colonel (Governor) Jose Antonio
Vizcarra referred to the ruin as Pueblo Raton
(Rat Village) when he passed by in 1823. By
1941, the name Pueblo Pintado had been restored.

Pueblo Pintado rises some 25 ft above the
crown of a small knoll, with three stories in
one section, and two wings measuring 228 and
174 feet. There are about a dozen other Anasazi
ruins of smaller size within a mile of the main
structure.

The ruin is important to the tales of the Navajo
Tsé Ńjíkiní, "Honey Combed Rock People"
Clan. Navajo traditions on clan development in-
clude Pueblo Pintado:

Jiní. Fourteen years after the Hashk'ąą Hadzohó
Dine'é, "Yucca Fruit Strung Out in a Line People,"
came to join the nuclear Navajo clans, the tribe
moved to Pueblo Pintado. It was deserted then.
They spread out and camped there at night. Their
many camp fires attracted the attention of some
wanderers on Chacra Mesa.

On the next morning, the strangers came down
to see who the numerous people were who had
made the camp fires. When asked from whence
they came, the wanderers said that they came from
Nihoobá, south of Zuni. [Note that Young and
Morgan 1987, 630, locate Nihoobá between
Torreon and Mount Taylor.] They had been driven
from their country by enemies. The Navajos called
them Nihoobáanii ["Gray Line Ending People"].

They made their camp with the Nihoobáanii
Dine'é and the Dził Ná'oodiłnii Dine'é [people
of the place called "Mountain that People Go
Around"—see Huerfano Mountain]. These people
then became members of the Navajo tribe. (Van
Valkenburgh 1941, 117)

PUYE: [DB] (7054 ft) Santa Fe County, NM.
Navajo: Uncertain. These ancient Anasazi pueblo
and cliff dwellings are located on the Parajito
Plateau (on the east slope of the Jemez Moun-
tains), west of Santa Clara Pueblo, north of Ban-
delier National Monument. They are situated on
New Mexico Highway 5, 11 miles southwest of
Española.

The residents of Santa Clara Pueblo (Tewa linguistic stock) claim Puye as their ancestral
home. Dr. Edgar Lee Hewitt and the School of
American Research conducted excavations here
in 1907. Later, it became a part of the Bandelier
National Monument.

Near Puye are other ruins from which Dr.
Hewitt believed the name Navajo may have
derived. On the basis of information secured at
Santa Clara Pueblo, he explained:

On the next mesa, and in the adjacent valley south
of Puye are three small pueblos, one on the mesa
rim, and two in the valley, those being the only
valley pueblos of any size in the region.

There is a lack of certainty in Tewa tradition
with reference to these ruins, but from most reliable information obtainable, I now believe that
these together constituted the settlement of
Navahu (Navaho, Navahuge); place of cultivated
fields; Nava; field; hu: place.

There is a ruin known to the Tewa Indians as
Navahu, this being, they claimed, the ancient
name of the village. I infer that these fields are
not only of the people of Navahu, but the more
populous settlements beyond the great mesa to
the north. The Tewa Indians assert that the Navahu
refers to large and cultivated lands. This suggests
an identity with Navajo, which Fray Alonso de
Benivides, in his Memorial of New Mexico published in 1630, applied to that Apache Nation
(Apaches de Nabajo) then living to the west of
the Rio Grande beyond the section mentioned.
Speaking of these people, Benavides says, "But
these (Apaches) of Navajo are very great farmers

(Laboradores), for that is what Navajo signifies, 'great planted fields (Sementeras Grandes).'" (Hewitt 1906, 193)

Van Valkenburgh (1941, 119) notes that the Spanish word "navaja," so similar to "Navajo," means razor, clasp knife, folding knife. He also points out that the Spanish "navajó" refers to a drinking pool for cattle or a morass, and that there is a town in the southern part of the state of Sonora, Mexico, which is called Navajoa. But he fails to note that Navajó is stressed on the last syllable, and Navaja is stressed on the next to last, while Navajo is stressed on the first syllable. There remains some question as to the Tewa meaning of the word "Navahu," since some informants state that it means to take away from the fields, rather than planting them.

PYRAMID ROCK: (7480 ft) McKinley County, NM. Navajo: Tsé Chííhí, "Nose Rock" (Wilson 1995, 45). This 1000-ft promontory sits atop the west end of the red sandstone mesa, about five miles east of Gallup.

QUEMADO: (6890 ft) Catron County, NM. Navajo: Tó Háálį́, "Flowing Spring" (U.S. Indian Claims Commission n.d., vol. VI, xvi), or "Water Flows Up Out" (Young p.c. 1995). This small ranching community on Largas Mangas Creek is situated on U.S. Highway 60, at its junction with New Mexico Highways 36 and 601. It was founded in 1880 when Jose Antonio Padilla moved from Belen, and called the place Rito Quemado, "Burned Creek." The Spanish name referred either to burned rabbit bush on either side of the creek, or to the scorched appearance of the volcanic soil (Fugate and Fugate 1989, 394–95). The name later became simply Quemado. The village has had a post office since 1886. Between 1951 and 1963, during investigations for Navajo land claims cases, tree-ring dates were obtained from Navajo-looking structures in this region dating to as early as A.D. 1350. However, other samples from the same structures dated to the mid-seventeenth century (Roessel 1983b, 31–34), and the earliest dates could have come from logs scavenged from other (possibly non-Navajo) sites.

QUINI: See Zuni. (Variable elevation) McKinley County, NM. Navajo: Uncertain. This is one of five names that Juan de Oñate used to refer to the region of Zuni, which also apparently included the Pueblo of Acoma (spelled Aquima). The other names, besides Zuni, were Comi, Xala, and Tsuni (Eggan 1979, 252).

RAMAH: [DB] (6950 ft) (Population: approx. 1,000, of whom 194 are Navajo) Cibola County, NM. Formerly Seveyo (Cebolla, Spanish for "Onions"). Navajo: Tł'ohchiní, "Wild Onions" (Allium palmeri). This Mormon farming community straddles New Mexico Highway 53, eight miles east of El Morro National Monument and 13 miles east of the junction of New Mexico Highways 53 and 602 (formerly Highway 32). A small (population in 1941 was 300) Mormon farming community located in a wide green valley on a south fork of the upper Zuni River, surrounded by scenic mesa country breaking from the southeastern slopes of the Zuni Mountains.

This village was founded in 1876 by Mormons following the orders of Brigham Young. The village's first post office came 10 years later. Local farmers (a Mormon stake house is located here) grow small grains, vegetables, alfalfa, and fruit. The town is the Navajo trading center for the Ramah Navajos (Tl'ohchin Dine'e or "Wild Onion People"). Day schools are operated by Gallup-McKinley County Schools. Several trading posts have operated in the vicinity, including Red and White; Ramah; Bond Brothers, opened between 1916 and 1920, and Lambson, opened between 1931 and 1935, both closing before 1950 (Kelley 1977, 254–55); and Ashcroft Trading Post.

The first Mormon missionaries in the region were sent to Zuni in 1876, forming a colony at the foot of the Zuni Mountains some five miles west of the present village. In 1877, the colony was nearly wiped out by smallpox, and was largely abandoned by 1880 (Noe 1992, 117–18). Bishop Joseph Tietjen and one Pitkin, Mormon missionaries, left the town of Sunset with their families and settled at Seboyeta, some three miles north of the present townsite, and gave it the name Navajo. It was changed to Ramah (pronounced *Ray*-ma, the name of a hill where sacred records are stored, according to the Book of Mormon) because another village was already named Navajo.

Other families from the decaying Sunset soon joined them and a dam was built across Seboyeta Canyon, one mile east of Ramah. The impounded waters of Ramah Lake gave the Navajos permanent water storage. In 1915, the population was augmented by the arrival of five families from the Mexican Mormon colonies of Chuchupa, Colonia, and Naco in the state of Chihuahua, brought north by unsettled political conditions in Mexico. During the 1920s a number of Texan ranchers moved into the area (Vogt and Albert 1970, 47).

Van Valkenburgh identified three trading posts operating in Ramah in 1941: Ramah Trading Post, Bond Brothers Trading Post, and Red and White Trading Post. Ashcroft Trading Post was 14 miles south of Ramah at the same time.

RAMAH NAVAJO RESERVATION: (approx. 7000 ft) Cibola and McKinley counties, NM. Navajo: See Ramah. This isolated section of the Navajo Reservation lies mostly south of New Mexico Highway 53, in the vicinity of Ramah, and El Morro National Monument. The reservation is roughly 25 miles north-south by 15 miles east-west. Its chapter house and compound sit on Navajo Route 125, about six miles south of El Morro.

RAMAH TRADING POST: (approx. 6950 ft) Cibola County, NM. Navajo: See Ramah. Opened by 1890 (Kelley 1977, 251), this was one of three posts listed by Van Valkenburgh (1941, 120) as operating in Ramah in 1941. The others were Red and White Trading Post and Bond Brothers Trading Post. Ashcroft Trading Post was 14 miles south of Ramah at the same time.

RATON SPRINGS: [DB] (7980 ft) McKinley County, NM. Navajo: Tó Dích'íí, "Bitter Water." This locality does not appear on current maps, but Van Valkenburgh's coordinates ("one mile north of the Crownpoint-to-Star Lake road, some five miles west of Star Lake") place it in the vicinity of Pueblo Pintado.

The springs were an important Navajo watering place, and there is a twelfth-century Anasazi ruin—which appears more Mesa Verdean than Chacoan—standing on the canyon rim immediately east of the springs. This was also once an important stopping place on the old Farmington-Albuquerque wagon road. A trading store and road house were operated at the springs many years ago by the Montoya Brothers of Bernalillo. The spring was improved in 1933.

RATON SPRINGS TRADING POST: (7980 ft) McKinley County, NM. Navajo: Uncertain, but probably the same as Raton Springs. This post was one of several operated by the Hyde Exploring Expedition during their excavations at Chaco Canyon between 1898 and 1903 (McNitt 1962, 84).

RATTLESNAKE: [DB] (5200 ft) San Juan County, NM. Navajo: Siláo 'Atiin, "Soldier Road," "Soldier Trail." Van Valkenburgh places this oil pumping station eight miles south of Shiprock Pinnacle, although it is actually located in the rolling plains north of that landmark. A trading post existed here from the early 1940s until the early 1960s (Kelley 1977, 255).

Here, beside Shiprock Wash, is a small oil field (4,800 acres) opened in 1923 by the Continental Oil Company (Conoco), producing some five hundred barrels of high-gravity crude oil daily by 1941. The contract with the Navajo Nation called for the Navajos to receive $3,000,000 plus a 12.5 percent royalty on oil produced. For some unknown reason, a small bonus of $1,000 was also paid at the time.

In 1926, the Tribal Council signed an agreement that extended the lease indefinitely, making it possible for the oil company or its successors to operate as long as oil and gas are available. A pipeline connected the field with a small refinery at Farmington. The wells also supply a limited amount of natural gas for use in government establishments on the reservation.

RED BUTTE: (7675 ft) McKinley County, NM. Navajo: Tsézhin 'Íí'áhí, "Black Rock Spire" (Van Valkenburgh 1974, 14). This feature is located on the north face of Mesa de los Lobos, overlooking the San Juan Basin some two miles northeast of Borrego Pass.

RED LAKE: (7100 ft) McKinley County, NM. Navajo: Be'ek'id Halchíí, "Red Lake." A small reservoir on the New Mexico–Arizona state line, at the north end of Black Creek Valley and 14 miles north of Fort Defiance on Navajo Route 12. A chapter house is located near the lake, and a trading post was opened here in the early 1960s (Kelley 1977, 255).

Northeast of the lake is a locality the Navajos call Water Pops, which is the home of Water Monster in the Navajo Gun Shooter Red Antway Myth. This vicinity is protected by Thunder and Bear when it is attacked by supernaturals in the myth (Wyman 1965). The locale is important in the Big Starway Ceremony; it was home of a very large snake (Van Valkenburgh 1974, 171).

RED MOUNTAIN: (6935 ft) McKinley County, NM. Navajo: Dził Łichíí', "Red Mountain." This mesa is located two miles south of Fajada Wash, some seven miles east of the graded portion of New Mexico Highway 57 that heads into Chaco Canyon. This is a location of Windway chants (Van Valkenburgh 1974, 47).

RED ROCK: (6800 ft) McKinley County, NM. Navajo: Tsé Łichíí' Dah 'Azkání, "Red Rock Mesa" (Young and Morgan 1987, 730). Pearce (1965, 131) mislocates this Navajo chapter community as being southeast of Fort Wingate, when actually it is situated eight miles south of Gallup, less than a mile west of Highway 602.

RED ROCK STATE PARK: (6750 ft) McKinley County, NM. Navajo: Tsé 'Ast'ees, "Cooking Rocks." Located six miles east of Gallup, and one mile north of I-40, this multi-use facility includes an outdoor arena seating 6,500; an amphitheater; a convention center with kitchen, dining room, conference rooms, and auditorium; the Red Rock Museum; two campgrounds; and a trading post. Construction on the park began in 1975, when its location was selected as the replacement for downtown Gallup's Lyons Park, then home of the annual Inter-Tribal Indian Cer-

emonial. The old park had been condemned for the construction of I-40.

The Inter-Tribal Indian Ceremonial Association deeded half the square mile on which the park is situated to the state, along with its option to purchase the second half. The facilities were built by the state. The state then promptly leased the entire facility to the City of Gallup for 15 years at $1 per year, and the park was governed by a Joint Powers Commission comprised of representatives of the city, the Ceremonial, and the Gallup Lions Club. Because the facility was meant to serve a broad number of functions, it never quite fit the needs of the Ceremonial Association that brought it about. In 1990, the facility was deeded by the state to the City of Gallup.

REHOBOTH: [DB] (6700 ft) McKinley County, NM. Navajo: Tséyaaniichii', "Termination of Red Streak of Rock" (Young and Morgan 1987, 732). The settlement is located immediately south of I-40 at the present eastern city limits of Gallup. It was established under the direction of Rehoboth's first missionary, the late L. P. Brink. The English name was taken from a biblical source (Genesis 26:22). A school was founded here by the Board of Missions of the Christian Reformed Church in 1903. A hospital was established in 1910. The hospital was merged with one run by the county in 1984, but the school and mission remain.

Situated in a valley running north from the foothills of the Zuni Mountains east of the Gallup Hogback, the boarding school soon accepted non-boarding students as well, reaching a capacity of 120 students in 1941. Dr. R. H. Pousma, superintendent and resident physician in the 1940s, authored a book of Navajo stories, "He Who Always Wins" (1934).

RINCON LARGO: [DB] (7000–6400 ft) Rio Arriba County, NM. Navajo: No specific name, but general descriptive term, Tsékooh, "Rock Canyon," is used. A tributary of Largo Canyon, this cove or rincon—with tributary rincons—heads in Cibola Mesa four miles northwest of Lybrooks. It runs northeast for approximately nine miles, joining Largo Canyon approximately 10 miles due north of Counselors.

A ranch operated by Mariano Otero in 1941 was formerly owned by Sam Lybrook and Jim Counselor of trading fame. Many old Navajo sites and watchtowers overlook the canyon from prominent mesa points on either side of the rincon.

In his 1788 report to Jacobo Ugarte de la Loyola, the Commander General of the Internal Provinces Governor Fernaldo de la Concha described watchtowers that were evident in the general region, though not necessarily the ones in the Rincon Largo:

> The excellent footing upon which we find ourselves at present with the Navajo nation demands that most prudent steps be taken in order that we may accomplish their conversion and settlement into Pueblos in the environs of the province, increasing its [the Spanish] forces by such means.
>
> The need which they have to protect it is well known to them, for from the abandonment of my campaign up to the present time, they have built ten rock towers within their encampments to safeguard their women and families for the continuous invasion of the Gilenos (Gila Apaches). (As quoted in Van Valkenburgh 1941, 123)

Watchtowers and hogan sites were pointed out in the spring of 1936 by Jim and Ann Counselor, traders and stock-owners of Counselors. These have since yielded valuable data on early Navajo history. Tree rings from timbers used in the sites date between A.D. 1730 and 1750. Glyphs of all descriptions are found in association with the numerous ruins. Some of the more spectacular of these are found in Mud Lake Rincon, a small cove off the Rincon Largo. They are similar to those observed in Canyon de Chelly and other locations in the present Navajo habitat.

Henry Chee Dodge identifies this area as a refuge of the Pueblos during the eighteenth and nineteenth centuries. It is deep in the Dinétah (the Old Navajo Country), the region occupied by the Navajos before they moved west to make the center of their activities in Canyon de Chelly.

RIO GRANDE: (12,000–0 ft) Hindsdale, Mineral, Rio Grande Alamosa, Conejos, and Castilla counties, CO, and Taos, Rio Arriba, Sandoval, Bernalillo, Valencia, Socorro, Sierra, and Dona Ana counties, NM, and international border between Texas and Mexico. Navajo: Naakaai Bitooh, "Mexican River" (Young p.c. 1995). This river was important to the Navajos due to the presence of pueblos and Hispanic villages. The Navajos generally consider this to be a female river, "tooh ba'ááá" (Young and Morgan 1987, 708).

RIO NUTRIA: (8100–6600 ft) McKinley County, NM. Navajo: See Nutria, Upper and Lower. Located in the southern Zuni Mountains and tributary to the Rio Pescado near the junction of New Mexico Highways 602 and 53, this stream heads six miles southeast of McGaffey, with a lesser fork originating at McGaffey.

RIO PESCADO: (7800–6600 ft) McKinley County, NM. Navajo: See Pescado. This river is the lifeblood of the Zuni settlements, coursing east to west through the southern periphery of the Zuni Mountains. It flows into Black Rock Reservoir, about four miles east of Zuni Pueblo. The stream that emerges from that reservoir is called Zuni River.

RIO PUERCO (OF THE EAST): (approx. 8000–4600 ft) Sandoval, Bernalillo, Valencia, and Socorro counties, NM. Navajo: Nasisitge, possibly a rendering of Na'azísí Tó, "Gopher Water" (Young p.c. 1995). This river heads some five miles northeast of Cuba, and flows into the Rio Grande at Bernardo, approximately midway between Belen and Socorro. It is the second longest tributary of the Rio Grande (Widdison 1959, 248–84), and, early in the American period, this was the only tributary of the Rio Grande that did not run dry before merging with the larger river (Greg 1967, 133).

Navajos ranged freely throughout the watershed of the Rio Puerco of the East prior to the Bosque Redondo period, and even after they returned, some settled in this region rather than within the boundaries of the reservation.

RIO PUERCO (OF THE WEST): (8000–5075 ft) McKinley County, NM. Also Puerco River of the West. Navajo: Uncertain, possibly Béésh Bitiin Tó, "Railroad Water" (Bennett p.c. 1993), alluding to the Burlington Northern Santa Fe railroad tracks that follow the river from east of Gallup to the river's juncture with the Little Colorado near Holbrook, Arizona. This broad—though largely dry—water course runs east to west along the same route as I-40 (and the railroad). It heads on the south slope of Mesa de Los Lobos at the approximate point where the continental divide crosses the mesa, and runs west through Gallup and into Arizona, where it is tributary to the Little Colorado River at Holbrook. Pearce (1965, 135) erroneously suggests that "of the West" is not applied to the river until it crosses the Arizona state line.

RIO SAN JOSÉ: (approx. 6550–5250 ft) Cibola and Valencia counties, NM. Navajo: Tooh Biką'í, "Male River" (Matthews 1897, 297). This stream is formed by the merging of Bluewater Creek and San Mateo Wash, about four miles west of Grants. It wanders along the southern periphery of the San Mateo Mountains for nearly 60 miles before joining the Rio Puerco of the East about 10 miles south of I-40 and two miles east of New Mexico Highway 60.

Camp San José, where Colonel Congreve Jackson's Company G, First Dragoons, moved from Moquino in October 1846, was along this stream (McNitt 1972, 105–6). Lieutenant A. W. Whipple's 1853–54 expedition surveying for a rail route traveled along the stream. Whipple (Foreman 1941, 120) noted that portions of the stream at that time were named Rio de Gallo, Rio de la Laguna, and Rio Rita, seemingly after settlements along its banks.

The confluence of this river with the Rio Puerco of the East was named Los Quelites ("greens") by early Spanish explorers (Brugge 1965, 16–17).

RIVER JUNCTION: (7200 ft) Rio Arriba County, NM. Navajo: Tó 'Aheedlí, "Water Flows In a Circle" (Young p.c. 1995). One of the most sacred of places to the Navajo, the convergence of the Los Pinos (Piños) and San Juan rivers is a traditional medicine location, and home of the Hero Twins (Twin War Gods). This locus figures prominently in the Blessingway traditions and the Nightway ceremonies. It is the original home of the Navajo Tó 'Aheedlíinii, "Water Flows To-

gether People" Clan. Numerous Navajo petroglyphs in the vicinity were attributed to the Hero Twins (Van Valkenburgh 1974, 142–50).

This location is now under the waters of Navajo Lake. (See also Los Pinos River, San Juan River, Navajo Dam, and Navajo Lake.)

ROCK SPRINGS: [DB] (6600 ft) McKinley County, NM. Navajo: Chéch'ízhí, "Rough Rock"; more recently, Tséyaató, "Spring Under the Rock." This ranch site—and historic landmark—is located in the rolling hill country eight miles northwest of Gallup, and two miles south of New Mexico Highway 264.

The ranch includes the buildings of an old trading post located on the 1850s military trail between Fort Wingate and Fort Defiance. This trail left the Rio Puerco of the West at Mineral Springs over the site of present Gallup and then turned north to China Springs. From there it went west to Rock Springs, and crossed the rolling hills to the Haystacks at present Tse Bonito, near Window Rock, Arizona. It then crossed Black Creek and continued upstream past Black Rock. In 1882, this road was intercepted by a new road from Defiance Station on the AT&SF (now the Burlington Northern Santa Fe), eight miles west of Gallup, providing Fort Defiance with direct access to the rail line.

Captain John G. Bourke, military officer and writer on travel and Indian lore, described a trip to Fort Defiance made on Sunday, April 24, 1881:

We had a lovely day for our journey and a very good team of mules. For the first twelve miles there was not much to notice but the titanic blocks of sandstone piled up into great hills, one of most peculiar being the spire called Navajo Church, a landmark distinguishable for a number of miles in every direction.

The ranch at Mineral Springs [apparently Hopkins Ranch; see Gallup Hogback] (ferrigenous), twelve miles from Wingate furnished our relay which had been sent out of the post the day previous—twenty-five miles from Wingate rested our team for an hour while we lunched. Erected a monument of a beef can and two beer bottles to commemorate our occupancy of the country and resumed our course (due west), thirty miles from Wingate came to a singular formation of sandstone called the Haystacks, where there are three immense boulders of sandstone two hundred feet above ground and named in accordance with their shape. In from these, there is a "natural bridge," a stone archway, spanned by a chord of not less than seventy-five feet horizontal, with a "rise" of nearly two hundred feet [see Window Rock].

Our proximity to the Navajo Agency was indicated by an occasional corral of stone. At an abandoned "hogan"—on the summit of a favorably situated hill, we were shown by Colonel Bennett [Captain Frank Tracy Bennett] the decayed fence of brushwood formerly enclosing the "antelope run" made by these Indians for hemming in antelope and deer.

Old Fort Defiance, ten miles across the Arizona line, was reached at sundown. (Van Valkenburgh 1941, 124–25)

A Navajo presence has made itself known in the vicinity, and a chapter house has been established not too far from the old ranch.

ROCK SPRINGS TRADING POST: (6600 ft) McKinley County, NM. Navajo: Sometimes referred to by the name of trader George Washington Sampson, called Hastiin Báí ("Gray Man"), who established the post in 1887. He also owned posts at Lukachukai, Sanders, and Chilchinbito, Arizona, and at Tohatchi and Coyote Canyon in New Mexico (McNitt 1962, 251). The post closed in the late 1930s (Kelley 1977, 254).

ROCKY POINT (TRADING POST): [DB] (6450 ft) McKinley County, NM. Navajo: Chézhin Ditł'ooí, "Fuzzy Traprock." Located on a rocky mesa projection south of I-40 and on the south bank of the Valley of the Rio Puerco of the West, this site is nine miles west of Gallup, across from Defiance Station. According to Van Valkenburgh, the post was operated by a Mexican and his mother, called 'Asdzaan Sidah ("Woman Sits"), the first traders in this region. They apparently paid high prices for Navajo wool (as much as 50 cents per pound), drawing Navajos from great distances. Kelley (1977, 252, 255) suggests an opening date of about 1900 for the post, and a closing date of around 1950.

The Navajo name derives from a volcanic plug

a mile south of Rocky Point. Old-timers say that in times when their enemies were hunting them Navajos would hide in the valley behind that rock and subsist on wild foods. A short distance to the south is Biyáázh ("Her Offspring"), a favorite hunting place for the Navajos. To the west, in the head of a small cove, is a spring with the appetizing name of Dibé Bichaan Bii' Tó, "Spring in the Sheep Manure."

SALMON RUIN: (5400 ft) San Juan County, NM. Navajo: Kin Dootł'izhí, "Blue House." This feature appears in the Navajo Enemyway, Blessingway, Waterway, and Beautyway (the same name is applied to Wijiji in Chaco Canyon). A Chacoan great-house community, or "outlier," this ruin is located on a bench above the valley floor of the north bank of the San Juan River two miles west of Bloomfield. It dates to A.D. 1088–1263, and contains at least 183 rectilinear rooms and 18 round rooms in a shallow U-shape. A great kiva lies in the plaza. As at Aztec Ruin, Type II Chacoan masonry occurs here long after its apparent demise at Chaco Canyon. A prehistoric road may run from the opposite bank of the San Juan River toward Kutz Canyon (Gabriel 1991, 233, 236; Flint and Flint 1989, 71–73).

Salmon was built and occupied by Chacoans, who abandoned it about A.D. 1150. It was then reoccupied and partially rebuilt by Mesa Verdeans around A.D. 1210. Forty years later, some 50 children and one adult female died in a fire when a kiva roof on which they were standing collapsed (Ferguson and Rohn 1987, 159–61).

The name Salmon came from a nineteenth-century homesteader, George Salmon, on whose land the ruin was discovered.

SALT CREEK: [DB (map 4)] (6500–4900 ft) San Juan County, NM. Also Salt Creek Wash. Navajo: Tó Dík'óózh Bikooh, "Salt Water Canyon." The upper reaches are labeled Salt Water Canyon on USGS maps.

This tributary of the San Juan River northeast of Shiprock and south of Mancos Creek is important in the Navajo Emergence myths, which place Navajo ancestors in this vicinity (Van Valkenburgh 1974, 135).

SALT POINT: [DB] (6740 ft) San Juan County, NM. Navajo: 'Áshįįh Nááʼá, "Descending Line of Salt." This name refers to the mesa that lies between Largo and Blanco canyons at their juncture. It is traditionally associated with Navajo Salt Woman (Van Valkenburgh 1974, 30).

Ruins of Anasazi and old Navajo origins lie on the alluvial tongue below this high point, the northernmost extension of the Cibola Mesa. Long ago, the Navajos used to gather saline minerals from the lenses or pockets in the sandstone stratum that is exposed at Salt Point.

The crossing of the Blanco Canyon below these sites is treacherous in flood season (May through September) because of the quicksand and steep sandy approaches.

SALT WASH: (5800–5400 ft) San Juan County, NM. Navajo: Uncertain. This tributary of Little Shiprock Wash heads in the east opening of Red Rock Valley, flowing northeast about five miles before joining the larger stream.

This vicinity was traversed by Major Electus Backus's second column of three companies of infantry and a company of Mounted Riflemen in November 1858, on their way to Canyon de Chelly (McNitt 1972, 353).

SAN ANTONE: [DB] (7478 ft) McKinley County, NM. Navajo: Tó Łitso, "Yellow Water." Formerly a range headquarters for the Indian Service range riders and a mission station (Christian Reformed) situated at the foot of San Antone Hill, six miles northeast of Thoreau, where New Mexico Highway 371 skirts the east end of Mesa de los Lobos.

With its excellent spring, San Antone was the site of one of the earliest New Mexican cattle and sheep ranches in the Navajo country, occupied as early as 1858. A squad of New Mexico Volunteers, stationed here during the Navajo War in 1863–64, acted as a guard on a section of the military road between old Fort Wingate and Fort Defiance.

Immediately southeast of San Antone is a large spur of reddish sandstone whose fluted sides flare out. Navajos call this Woman's Skirt. Nearby is Naasilá ("It Lies on Its Side" or "Hori-zontal Line"), where, in the old days, Navajo warriors stopped to procure earthen pigments to paint themselves before making forays on the Rio Grande Valley.

SANDIA MOUNTAINS: [DB] (10,678 ft at highest point) Bernalillo County, NM. Navajo: Dził Nááyisí, "Mountain that Revolves." This massive mountain range—with its sheer western face—runs generally north-south immediately east of Albuquerque, and extends from Tijeras Pass (and I-40) 15 miles north to Placitas. (The mountains immediately south of Tijeras Canyon are not part of the Sandias, they are the Manzano Mountains.) "Sandia" means "watermelon" in Spanish, and reportedly refers to the color of the range at sunset. However, a more likely explanation is that the mountains were named for San Diaz (Saint Diaz).

These are the southern sacred mountains of the Tewa Indians and are revered as sacred by the Keres and the Zunis (Van Valkenburgh 1941, 132). Before 1864, the deep canyons and high peaks of the Sandias were the base of operations for Navajo forays on the Rio Grande settlements.

A contingent of Diné 'Ana'í (Enemy Navajos) may have lived in the Sandias under the half-breed Francisco Baca, around 1826, where they were plagued by Zuni raiders (McNitt 1972, 70).

On their winter 1864–65 journey to the Bosque Redondo (Fort Sumner), Navajos skirted the southern edge of the mountain, passing through Tijeras Canyon. As closely as can be determined from the hazy memory of aged informants, the captive Navajos crossed the Rio Grande at Isleta and Albuquerque, and passed through Tijeras Canyon to Canyon Blanco and the Pecos River. Here they turned southward to Fort Sumner.

The Zunis call these mountains Chis Biya Yalanne and consider them the place of origin of their Big Fire Society. They are also a shrine for the Shua:que Society (Ferguson and Hart 1985, 125).

SANDIA PUEBLO: [DB] (5050 ft) (Population: 3,971) Bernalillo County, NM. Navajo: Kin Łigaaí, "White House," or, less often, Kin Noodǫ́ǫ́z, "Striped House." The name "Sandia" is Spanish for "watermelon," which was first applied to the Sandia Mountains to the east of the pueblo (supposedly because of their shape and color at sunset). The Sandians call their village "napiad," which means "at the dusty place." This pueblo now sports a casino. In 1941, the population of this Southern Tiwa Pueblo was only 138. Situated on the east bank of the Rio Grande about 12 miles north of Albuquerque between U.S. Highway 85 and I-40. According to archaeological evidence, the present reservation has been occupied continuously since at least A.D. 1300. However, the exact location of the pueblo itself at the time of European contact—A.D. 1540—is in doubt. This village was particularly vulnerable to attacks from the Navajos, Apaches, and Comanches, and, as of the mid-1870s, Navajos in general were still considered enemies. It was first identified at its current location in 1617, when it was made the seat of the mission of San Francisco (Bandelier 1890–92, 3, 220).

Sandia's population participated in the Pueblo Revolt of 1680, and the pueblo was burned by New Mexico Governor Antonio de Otermin on his flight from Santa Fe. A year later, in 1681, Otermin burned the pueblo a second time during his fruitless attempt at reconquest. Between 1688 and 1692, at least three additional attempts at reconquest found the village abandoned. There is considerable speculation as to where the Sandias went, and tribal tradition holds that they never left (Brandt 1979, 343–50). Most prevalent is the unsubstantiated tradition that they fled to Hopi, settling the village of Payupkihe on Second Mesa. In any case, it wasn't until 1733 that a group from Isleta petitioned the New Mexico governor to resettle the abandoned site.

Permission was denied, and reoccupation did not occur until 1748, when Fray Menchero obtained permission to settle a group of 350 converted Hopi Indians at Sandia. (Van Valkenburgh asserts that the year was 1742, the number of returnees was 441, and they were brought back by Fathers Delgado and Pino.) A second settlement was in evidence by 1760. While in Hopi country, they are supposed to have built the pueblo of Payupkihe, whose ruins are to be found on Second Mesa about one mile north of Shipaulovi.

The residents of Sandia allied with the Isletas against the Navajos in 1863–64. By 1910 the population had declined to less than one hundred, but it rebounded in the next quarter-century.

With its widely dispersed homes, this pueblo bears little resemblance to the traditional ("Taos-style") pueblo. However, Sandia retains a heavy emphasis on its religious ceremonies, with many sacred shrines located in the Sandia Mountains.

SAN FELIPE PUEBLO: [DB] (5200 ft) (Population: 1,557) Sandoval County, NM. Navajo: Tsédáá'kin, interpreted by Young and Morgan (1987, 729) as "House on the Edge of a Cliff" (though some interpret it as "Houses between the Rocks," which is actually Tséta'kin). Also Séí Bee Hooghan, "Sand Houses" (Franciscan Fathers 1910, 135); and Dibe Łizhiní, "Black Sheep" (Young and Morgan 1987, 312). A Keresan village located 12 miles upstream from Bernalillo, at the foot of Santa Ana Mesa and on the west bank of the Rio Grande, six miles upstream from the juncture of that river with the Jemez River. The pueblo—or similar, nearby antecedents—has been occupied since the late fourteenth century. When Francisco Vasquez de Coronado passed through in 1540, two villages were identified: "Castil de Arvil" on the west bank of the Rio and "Castilblanco" on the east. Two pueblos were also noted by Juan de Oñate in 1598.

The village was given a mission around A.D. 1600. San Felipe joined in the Pueblo Revolt of 1680, killing and/or driving out all Spanish settlers. When Antonio de Otermin tried his ill-fated reconquest of 1681, the residents fled to Horn Mesa, southwest of Cochiti Canyon, along with the residents of Cochiti, Taos, San Marcos, Santo Domingo, and Picuris pueblos. After returning to the pueblo with Diego de Vargas's successful reconquest of 1692, the people of San Felipe suffered attacks from other pueblos for remaining friendly to the Spaniards (Strong 1979a, 390–97). The pueblo was rather isolated and appears seldom in the reports of government or travelers into the twentieth century, though it is known to have had two stories during the 1800s and the 1941 population was 654.

The name is derived from the Spanish mission

at the village. The Keresan name is "Katishtya," the meaning of which is lost to the ages (Mays 1985, 53).

Among the Navajo, this pueblo is reputed to be the original home of the Dibé Łizhiní, "Black Sheep" Clan of the Navajo, who are said to have come from an old San Felipe pueblo called Dibé Łizhin. Another ancient pueblo, Séí Bee Hooghan is associated by some informants. Language: Keres.

Before the arrival of the Spaniards, the ancestors of San Felipe and Cochiti formed a single group. Because what Van Valkenburgh calls "the aggression of the Tewas" caused a rift, the San Felipes split off and went down the Rio Grande, and the Cochiti moved to Potrero Viejo. It was in this general vicinity that Coronado found the San Felipe at a village called Katishtya.

When Diego de Vargas came to reconquer New Mexico in 1692, the San Felipes again fled to the Potrero, but were induced by the Spaniards to return to their pueblo. In 1693, de Vargas found them at the northern end of Black Mesa, west of the present site of their pueblo.

Soon after the opening of the eighteenth century, when they no longer needed a defensive site, the San Felipes deserted the mesa and erected the present village. Today the village is among the most conservative of the Pueblos.

SAN FIDEL: [DB] (6069 ft) Cibola County, NM. Navajo: Dził Łeeshch'ihí (Van Valkenburgh 1941, 134), "Ash Mountain" (Young p.c. 1995; expressing surprise at Van Valkenburgh's suggestion that the term refers to blood on a Navajo). A small Indian-Hispanic village located on New Mexico Highway 124 five miles northeast of McCarty's, and an equal distance west of Cubero. First settled in 1868 by Baltazar Jaramillo. The community was first named for the patron saint of Acoma Pueblo, "La Vega de San Jose," but was changed to Ballejos (family name) before the name San Fidel (for Saint Faithful, Saint Fidelis, or Saint Fidharleus) was adopted (Pearce 1965, 144). (Van Valkenburgh suggests that the village was established by and named for the father of John Fidel, an Albuquerque hotel owner, about 1905.)

Navajos tell that some years before they were removed to Fort Sumner, a band of their people had raided the Rio Grande settlements and were returning with their plunder when a Mexican posse caught up with them at the round mountain a few miles southeast of present San Fidel. A fight ensued in which a Navajo was killed and the New Mexicans regained their stock. The village was home to Diné 'Ána'í leader Francisco Baca, a half-breed Navajo, in 1825 (McNitt 1972, 70–71).

SAN ILDEFONSO PUEBLO: [DB] (5500 ft) (Population: 447) Santa Fe County, NM. Navajo: Tséta'kin, "House Between the Cliffs." A Tewa village, San Ildefonso is located 29 miles north of Santa Fe on the east bank of the Rio Grande, on New Mexico Highway 4. The population claims descent from Mesa Verde, having migrated to the Pajarito Plateau around A.D. 1300, establishing the villages of Potsuwi (also known as Otowi) and Tsankawi before settling at the present site (Edelman 1979, 312). The village was the headquarters of a Spanish expedition led by Francisco Leyva de Bonilla in 1593. The first mission was built around 1617, with Santa Clara and San Juan Pueblos as visitas.

At the time of the Pueblo Revolt of 1680, San Ildefonso was the largest of all Tewa villages, and the population took an active role in the revolt. These people then fortified themselves atop Black Mesa and resisted de Vargas' reconquest until 1694, two years longer than the other Tewa villages. Two years later, the last armed Pueblo resistance against the Spaniards (Spicer 1962, 165) took place at San Ildefonso, whereupon the villagers once again took refuge on Black Mesa.

This pueblo was the least receptive to Christianity, destroying the first mission in the revolt and its replacement in the attempted revolt of 1696. Christian practices were not really accepted until the middle 1800s. The name stems from the first mission, though the Tewa name is "poxoge," meaning "where the water runs through."

Navajo raids on the pueblo were recorded in March 1705, 1713, and October 1849 (McNitt 1972, 19, 24, 155).

Today, there is very little contact between San Ildefonso and the Navajos, though there was some in the early history of the pueblo. San Ildefonso was the home of Maria Martinez, the famed potter, and in 1941 the population was 114.

SAN JUAN PUEBLO: [DB] (5500 ft) (Population: 5,209) Taos County, NM. Navajo: Kin Łichíí, "Red House," referring to ancient San Juan; a more recent name is Kin Łigaaí, "White House." The northernmost of the Tewa pueblos, San Juan is located four miles north of the confluence of Chama River and the Rio Grande, on the east bank of the Rio Grande. Tewa tradition states that the San Juan people came from the north, settling in San Juan (and the other Rio Grande Tewa pueblos) about A.D. 1300. Prior to the sixteenth century, the ancestors of San Juan occupied and abandoned at least three pueblos. The Tewa name is simply "Ohke," the meaning of which is unknown. (Alfonso Ortiz, a Tewa himself, emphatically points out that this name is *not* the same as "óhkê," meaning "hard grinding stone.")

The first European contact was by a food-seeking party from the Francisco Vasquez de Coronado expedition of 1541 (Hammond and Rey 1940, 244, 259, as quoted in Ortiz 1979, 280). Gaspar Castaño de Sosa visited in 1591, and Juan de Oñate arrived in 1598, establishing on the west bank of the Rio Grande the first "permanent" Spanish settlement in New Mexico (Ortiz 1979, 280). It was the site of a previously existing village called Yúngé. Here Oñate established the first provisional government of New Mexico, naming the capital "San Juan de los Caballeros" ("Saint John of the Gentlemen"). The Indians soon relinquished the pueblo to the Spanish and moved to the east side of the Rio Grande. Under intense pressure from the Navajos, the Spanish settlement was abandoned before 1610.

San Juan participated in the Pueblo Revolt of 1680, and was again subjugated in the Reconquest of 1692. Navajos raided the pueblo in March 1705 (McNitt 1972, 19).

From old San Juan, possibly on the west side of the river, came the ancestors of the Kin Łichíí'nii (Red House clan) of the Navajos. Adolph Bandelier (1892) recorded the following San Juan story relating to the Navajos:

Finally it was agreed that a bridge should be built across the Rio Grande, and the official wizards went to work and constructed it by laying a long feather of a parrot over the stream from one side, and the long feather of a magpie from the other. As soon as the plumes met in the middle of the river, people began to cross over this remarkable bridge; but bad sorcerers caused the delicate structure to turn over, and many people fell into the river where they were instantly turned into fishes. For this reason, the Navajos, Apaches, and some of the Pueblos refuse to eat fish to this day.

SAN LUIS: [DB] (6350 ft) Sandoval County, NM. Also Dominguez. Navajo: Tsé'yaa Tséteelí, possibly "Lying Face Down Under the Wide Rock" (translation from Young p.c. 1995). This tiny Hispanic farming community is situated in rolling mesa country on the east side of the Rio Puerco of the East on New Mexico Highway 279, nine miles west of New Mexico Highway 44, and about 20 miles due west of Jemez Pueblo.

The scissors-like crossing of roads here gives the settlement its earliest name, Las Tijeras. Father George Juillard named the village San Luis in the 1890s. During Van Valkenburgh's time, locals began to refer to the town as Dominguez, after a prominent local family. Navajos from Torreon traded here at times.

SAN MATEO: (7200 ft) Cibola County, NM. Navajo: Haltso, "The Meadow." Small community at the northeast foot of Mount Taylor. The community was founded either in 1835 by Colonel Manuel Chavez (who discovered the location returning to Seboyeta after a battle with the Navajos), or it was founded 20 years later by Ramon A. Baca, Chavez's half-brother. The region was well known to the Diné 'Ána'í (Enemy Navajos) of the Cebolleta region.

SAN MATEO PEAK: (10,141 ft) Socorro County, NM. Also Mount Withington. Navajo: Tsé Naaha'bith, which Van Valkenburgh (1974, 15) translates as "Overhanging Rock Ledge," but which Young (p.c. 1995) cannot confirm. This is the highest point in the San Mateo range west of Socorro. The peak is the point of origin of the Tsé Nahabiłnii ("Overhanging Rock Ledge People") Clan (Van Valkenburgh 1974, 15).

Young (p.c. 1995) notes that Nahabił may be an obsolete word long forgotten, though it is a clan name.

It is important not to confuse this peak with Mount Taylor (Navajo sacred Mountain of the South); each is situated in a range named the San Mateo Mountains, and each is sometimes known as San Mateo Peak.

SANOSTEE: [DB] (6000 ft) San Juan County, NM. Also known as Sanastee. Navajo: Tsé 'Ałnáozt'i'í, "Overlapping Rocks" (translation by Kelley p.c. 1994). This name was applied by non-Navajos to a nearby location. Also Tó Yaagaii, "Water Rises in a White Column," referring to a now inactive artesian well that used to geyser (Young and Morgan 1987, 708). This trading community is located on Sanostee Wash, on the eastern slope of the Tunicha Mountains 20 miles south of Shiprock, and eight miles west of U.S. Highway 666.

Tocito and Sanostee washes, heading in the Tunicha Mountains, join to form the Peña Blanca, which in turn joins the northward flowing Chaco Wash some 20 miles south of the San Juan River. The name Peña Blanca comes from a large expanse of smooth white rock that lies on the north side of Beautiful Mountain.

Lieutenant W. C. Brown of the U.S. Army resource survey of the Navajo country visited farms in the Sanostee region in 1892 and inspected the Indian irrigation system on Sanostee Wash. Today there are several areas irrigated out of this wash between Beautiful Mountain and the juncture with the Peña Blanca.

Some 12 miles southwest of Sanostee is an abandoned sawmill established in 1907 to cut lumber for the Shiprock and Toadlena schools. The Sanostee BIA boarding school has been closed, and is in the process of being torn down. The ruins give the impression of a bombed-out, evacuated community. A couple dozen new government-subsidized houses have been built east of the school, while at least as many government-owned houses, once occupied by teachers, now stand empty, boarded up and/or vandalized. A day-school sits in the middle of the ruined boarding school complex.

SANOSTEE TRADING POST: (6000 ft) San Juan County, NM. Navajo: See Sanostee. This post was built by Will Evans in 1899, for Joseph Wilken. In 1905, Frank Noel purchased it. Still later it became a Foutz Brothers enterprise.

While Noel owned it, the post played an important role in the Beautiful Mountain Uprising. In this colorful escapade of autumn 1913, the followers of Bi-Joshii, an old Navajo medicine man, resisted Superintendent Shelton's edict against plural marriages by freeing from the Fort Defiance jail three wives of Bi-Joshii's son, Hataałii Yázhí, "Little Medicine Man." Going into hiding on Beautiful Mountain, they defied all efforts to dislodge them for two months. No less than four troops of cavalry (261 men armed with three hundred rounds of ammunition each) were dispatched from Fort Robinson to Gallup by train, and then to Beautiful Mountain by horseback under General Hugh L. Scott to confront the 12 or so men with Bi-Joshii. Negotiations between Bi-Joshii, Scott, and Fr. Anselm Weber (from St. Michaels) took place at Noel's Sanostee post, leading to the surrender of Bi-Joshii on Thanksgiving Day, November 27, 1913. Bi-Joshii was the last of the renegades to surrender, telling General Scott, "But I am not afraid of you!" (McNitt 1962, 347–58).

This incident marked the last time U.S. Army troops were called out against American Indians.

SANOSTEE WASH: (8400–5500 ft) San Juan County, NM. Navajo: See Sanostee. This intermittent stream heads in the Chuska Mountains a few miles southeast of Roof Butte, then flows east 21 miles, passing south of Beautiful Mountain, just north of Sanostee, and through Little Water, before joining Tocito Wash about six miles upstream from that wash's confluence with the Chaco River.

According to Newcomb (1964, 67), Slim Woman's family hid from Ute raiders in a canyon of this arroyo during the period of the American Civil War. The Utes burned the Navajos' hogans and killed their sheep.

SAN RAFAEL: [DB] (6450 ft) Cibola County, NM. Navajo: Tó Sido, "Hot Water." This small, largely Hispanic farming community is located on New Mexico Highway 53 four miles south of Grants, in a well-watered basin of the east slope of the Zuni Mountains on the western margin of the Malpais. It has had its own post office intermittently since 1881. In 1863 New Mexicans broke the Navajo Treaty of 1835 by attacking and destroying Navajo homes in this vicinity (Benally et al. 1982, 96). It was the site of the first Fort Wingate.

This place was shown as Ojo del Gallo (Spanish, meaning "Rooster Spring") on the Dominguez-Escalante map of 1776, and as Hay Camp in 1860 on the McComb map.

The Ojo del Gallo took on historic significance in January 1863, with the plans for military action against the Navajos. Lieutenant Colonel J. Francisco Chaves, with the First New Mexico Volunteers, established (Old) Fort Wingate, naming it after Lieutenant Benjamin Wingate, who had been killed at the Battle of Valverde in 1861 by Confederate troops. The square parade ground, surrounded by sod, log, and rubble buildings, became the base of Captain Rafael Chacon's raids against the eastern Navajos.

In 1864, when 8,500 Navajos were being moved to Fort Sumner on the Pecos River in east-central New Mexico, Old Fort Wingate became one of the four concentration and forwarding depots. The others were at Fort Defiance, Fort Fauntleroy—near Bear Springs, and later named Fort Lyon and still later (New) Fort Wingate—and Camp Florilla, near present Kinlichee.

Ojo del Gallo had long been the eastern point of departure for emigrant and military parties over the Zuni Mountains to Inscription Rock (El Morro) and Zuni country. In 1892, Major G. B. Willis and Colonel Chaves examined and reported to the War Department on a new road to Fort Whipple. After the removal of the Navajos, much of the travel from the east passed through Ojo del Gallo or old Fort Wingate to the west.

When Old Fort Wingate was abandoned as a military post in 1868, the village of San Rafael grew up around the Ojo del Gallo. Only a few outlines of the stone foundations of the old buildings are still visible. A local guide stated that some years ago the sods from the upper parts of the structures of the old fort had been removed from the fields. Aside from the scattered rubble of the old fort, only the grave of the post chaplain, Father Chavez, lies in the San Rafael village cemetery (Van Valkenburgh 1941, 136).

This location was visited by the Twin War Gods of the Emergence story of the Navajo creation legend (Matthews 1897, 114).

SAN RAFAEL CANYON: (6200 ft) Rio Arriba County, NM. Navajo Ta'neezah, "Tangled" (Young p.c. 1995), mistakenly translated as "(Fence) Poles Strung Out," by Van Valkenburgh (1974, 15). This tributary of Gobernador Canyon (merging with the latter nine miles southeast of its confluence with the San Juan River) is the point of origin of the Navajo Ta'neeszahnii ("People of the Tangle") clan.

SANTA ANA PUEBLO: [DB] (5250 ft) (Population: 476) Sandoval County, NM. Navajo: Dahmi, Santa Anans' name for themselves. This Keresan village is situated on the Jemez River, 10 miles northeast of Bernalillo and seven miles downstream from its closest neighbor, Zia Pueblo (also Keresan). Though the ancestors of the pueblo's population were in the region earlier, moving from site to site, the present village of Santa Ana is known to have been occupied since the late sixteenth century. The old pueblo was located on the north bank of the Rio San Jose some 10 miles northeast of Bernalillo, but was abandoned prior to the Spanish conquest.

Another village was settled on Black Mesa between present Santa Ana and San Felipe pueblos. The first clearly documented Spanish visit to the pueblo was that of Juan de Oñate's colonization expedition of 1598. In July of that year, the pueblo—and the others—submitted to the King of Spain at Santo Domingo. A Spanish mission was established in the pueblo, but at the outbreak of the Pueblo Revolt of 1680, in which the village participated, no priest was there. The residents fled to the Jemez Mountains when Otermin attempted his reconquest of 1682. In 1687, Governor Pedro Renos stormed Santa Ana and burned it. The erstwhile residents were found on a mesa known as Cerro Colorado by Diego de Vargas in 1692, and he persuaded them to move to the vicinity of their former village, where they live today. They later allied with the Spaniards against other tribes and pueblos. The population was decimated by a smallpox epidemic in 1779–81 (Strong 1979b, 398–406), and as late as 1941 numbered only 267.

Warriors from this pueblo joined the Concha expedition against the Gila and Mimbres Apaches on August 22, 1788, an expedition joined by Navajo auxiliaries along the way. The Santa Anans also joined Colonel John Washington's expedition against the Navajos in 1849— the American incursion that led to the death of Navajo headman Narbona (McNitt 1972).

Presently the old pueblo is occupied only during ceremonial times (Fugate and Fugate 1989). The rest of the year, the inhabitants live at the farming community on the Jemez River.

SANTA CLARA PUEBLO: [DB] (5600 ft) (Population: 1,156) Santa Fe County, NM. Navajo: Naashashí, "Bear Enemies" (same as Hano Pueblo in Arizona); and T'iisyaa Kin, "House Under the Cottonwoods." This Tewa village is located on the west bank of the Rio Grande at its confluence with Santa Clara Creek, some 39 miles north of Santa Fe. The Santa Clarans have a tradition that they moved from southern Colorado to the vicinity of Pecos Pueblo, then back across the Rio Grande to the pumice cliffs of Puye in a 740-room pueblo with a great community house (New Mexico Office of Cultural Affairs 1991, 78) before settling at their present site.

The village was visited by Francisco Vasquez de Coronado in 1540. Juan de Oñate began forcing Christianity on its occupants in 1598. The pueblo's first mission and monastery were established by Father Alonso de Benavides between 1622 and 1629. Navajos traveled an ancient trail down the east slope of the Jemez Mountains to Santa Clara, and Father Benavides is known to have baptized certain Navajos here in 1626 (Van Valkenburgh 1941, 137).

The oppressive, coercive measures were relaxed somewhat following de Vargas's reconquest 12 years after the Pueblo Revolt of 1680 (in which a contingent of soldiers was killed at the pueblo and the mission burned). However, the Santa Clarans revolted again in 1694, and were finally forced into submission in 1696. Rather than return to their homes, many Santa Clarans joined with some people from San Ildefonso and fled to Zuni and the Hopi mesas farther west. The population in 1941 was 444. There is very little present-day contact with the Navajos.

Santa Clara was raided by Navajos in March 1705, and in February, four years later (McNitt 1972, 22).

SANTA FE: [DB] (7000 ft) (Population: 55,859) Santa Fe County, NM. Navajo: Yootó, "Bead Water." Refers to the Santa Fe River from the Tewa name. The capital city of New Mexico is located in the western foothills of the Sangre de Cristo Mountains about 60 miles north of Albuquerque on I-25. The community was founded in 1610 as the capital of the Province of New Mexico, by Don Pedro de Peralta, and named "The City of Holy Faith of St. Francis of Assisi." The town was abandoned during the Pueblo Revolt of 1680, though many of the refugees returned in 1692–93 with Don Diego de Vargas.

The first Americans entered the area about 1820, as traders violating dictates from Mexico City. The city (and the state of New Mexico) became part of the United States when General Stephen W. Kearny marched in on August 18, 1846. A U.S. post office was established three years later.

Until the 1940s and 1950s, when the population hovered around 15,000 people, the city was a center for the weaving of Spanish-American textiles and wood-carving. It has gradually become better known as a retail center for Indian goods. It is a Mecca for tourists, artists, and writers. Among its more substantial facilities are the Museum of New Mexico, the Laboratory of Anthropology, School of American Research, Saint Francis Art Museum Historical Society, the Wheelwright Museum of Indian Culture (originally the Church of Navajo Religion), and the Institute of American Indian Art. Palace of the Governors (housing the Museum of New Mexico's major exhibits) was built 1601–14; Saint Francis Cathedral was constructed 1711–14 (though it remains unfinished, as it began to sink into the ground before the towers were completed). Santa Fe is home to the oldest house in the United States, built prior to 1636; and Guadalupe Church was built in the early 1800s. Fort Marcy (built in 1846) was the source of many of the U.S. Army expeditions into Navajo country prior to the establishment of Forts Wingate and Defiance.

The Institute of American Indian Arts (formerly the Santa Fe Indian School [USIS]) is one of the most prestigious of all Indian institutions of higher learning in the arts. It grew out of a BIA boarding school opened in 1891 (Bailey and Bailey 1986, 168).

The city sits atop at least two major puebloan ruins. In 1680 the governor, Capitan General Don Antonio Otermin, fighting the Pueblos in rebellion, was driven out of Santa Fe and the province for 13 years. When Don Diego de Vargas reconquered New Mexico in 1692–93, he found some Tano living in Santa Fe.

From the beginning of Spanish contacts, all Navajo business with the Spanish government was conducted in Santa Fe—even while Diné continued to raid just beyond the city limits.

Santa Fe remained under the crown of Spain until the Mexican Revolution in 1821, when it became a part of Mexico. It was the western terminus of the famous Santa Fe Trail as well as the northern terminus of the Chihuahua Trail out of Old Mexico. In 1837, it was the scene of a revolt of the outlanders, called Los Chimayosos, from Rio Arriba to the north. The United States took control in 1846 under General Stephen Watts Kearny. The Stars and Bars of the Confederacy flew over Santa Fe under General Sibley for a short time during the Civil War.

SANTO DOMINGO PUEBLO: [DB] (5200 ft) (Population: 2,866) Sandoval County, NM. Navajo: Tó Hajiiloh, "People Draw Up Water" (Young and Morgan 1987, 706). This village is one of eight of Keresan language stock (see also Jemez, Santa Ana, Zia, Cochiti, San Felipe, Laguna, and Acoma pueblos). Santo Domingo is located on the west bank of the Rio Grande, 21 miles upstream from Albuquerque, and is reached by taking New Mexico 22 West off I-25.

According to Keres tradition, the earliest location of the Santo Domingans was Potrero de la Cañada Quemada, from which they moved successively to two villages—both named Gipuy. The earlier pueblo of Gipuy stood on the banks of the Arroyo de Galisteo some four miles east of present Santo Domingo. Floods drove out the inhabitants. The second Gipuy, occupied when Oñate visited in 1592, was also ravaged by floods (together with another pueblo on the banks of the Rio Grande) in 1607, 1700, and 1885. Around 1770, the present pueblo was erected and given the name Kiva.

Santo Domingo was the site of a historic gathering of pueblo leaders to meet with Juan de Oñate in 1598. In 1680, the village joined in the Pueblo Revolt. In 1692 the leaders surrendered to de Vargas, but then fled into the Jemez Mountains. De Vargas defeated them in 1694, killing 90 warriors. Survivors joined with refugees from Cochiti and fled to the pueblo of Cienaguilla (now abandoned). By 1696 this enclave had also been beaten by de Vargas, and most Santo Domingans returned to the pueblo—although some escaped to the Acoma region to the Pueblo of Laguna. The Spanish name refers to Saint Domingo, while the local dialect calls the pueblo "tyiwa," meaning unknown. Early Spanish documents refer to it as "Gigue" or "Quigui." Another name commonly attributed to Santo Domingo is "Guipui" (Guipuy), which actually refers to the abandoned prehistoric pueblo about four miles east of the present village (Lange 1979b, 388). In 1941 the population was 920 persons.

Second to Jemez, Santo Domingo is the most important of the Rio Grande pueblos in respect to the volume of trade done with the Navajos, who came to Santo Domingo for turquoise, shell bead necklaces, mosaic turquoise, coral, and jet. According to Van Valkenburgh (1941, 132–33), Santo Domingans also traveled the Navajo country in pairs to trade their crafts for Navajo blankets that were later peddled in the streets of Santa Fe and Albuquerque. Some Santo Domingo pottery reached the Navajo country and was used by medicine men as containers for medicine. Navajos say they got the idea of setting turquoise in silver from a Navajo smith named Black Mustache, "who had a woman at Santo Domingo in 1885." When on the Rio Grande, Navajos often visit Santo Domingo to see old trading friends.

Treaties between the Spaniards and Pueblos and the Navajos were signed here in March 1841 and March 1844. Santo Domingo warriors joined Captain Henry Lafayette Dodge's militia against the Navajos in 1849. The pueblo was raided by Navajos that same year. In July 1851, some three hundred Comanches camped outside the pueblo on their way to raid the Navajos (McNitt 1972, 86, 88–90, 155, 186).

SAN YSIDRO: (5600 ft) Sandoval County, NM. Navajo: Uncertain. This Hispanic village was settled in 1699 by a group led by Juan Trujillo and was named after Saint Isadore the Farmer (Pearce 1965, 151). The community is located at the juncture of New Mexico Highways 44 and 4, some 23 miles north of Bernalillo.

Navajo unrest was noted in this vicinity in 1818. A surrender of Navajo prisoners to the Mexicans took place here in October 1848, and a military post was established in September two years later by Brevet Colonel John Munro. In a Navajo raid on June 8, 1856, one villager was wounded and three cattle were stolen. The village became a staging area for expeditions to Navajoland. (McNitt 1972, 47, 156, 158, 278n, 351, 391, 393)

SATAN PASS: [DB] (7450 ft) McKinley County, NM. Also Satan's Pass, Devil's Pass. Navajo: Hahodeeshtł'izhí, "Blue All the Way Up," referring to the canyon's blue-gray mud. New Mexico Highway 371 passes through this steep-walled, rugged sandstone canyon in the northeast extremity of Mesa de los Lobos on its route between Thoreau and Crownpoint. The pass lies 16 miles north of the former and eight miles south of the latter.

Old Navajos tell that their trail through this pass was known to early New Mexican travelers as the Cañon del Infierno ("Hell Canyon"), probably because of its rugged, seasonally impassable terrain.

SCHIELINGBURO TRADING POST: [DB] (6450 ft) McKinley County, NM. Navajo:

Uncertain. An abandoned trading post in the flats south of Many Waters, six miles northwest of Crownpoint.

SEAMA: (6400 ft) Cibola County, NM. Navajo: Uncertain. This Laguna Indian village is located at the confluence of the Rio San José and Cañada Cruz, two miles south of Flower Mountain and I-40. Early name was Cañada de la Cruz, meaning "Canyon of the Cross" in Spanish. The present name means "Door" in Laguna dialect Keres. It refers to the fact that the community is a pass to the canyon. Seama had its own post office from 1905 to 1932.

The Zunis gather clay here for making white paint (Ferguson and Hart 1985, 127).

SECTION 8 RUIN: (6740 ft) McKinley County, NM. Navajo: Kits'iil Dah Yisk'id, "Hill Ruin." Less than a mile northwest of Muddy Water Ruin, this Chacoan ruin, dating from A.D. 1050–1125, consists of a rectangular house structure with two blocked-in kivas, and the masonry is core and veneer.

SEVEN LAKES: [DB] (6600 ft) McKinley County, NM. Also Faris Ranch. Navajo: Tsosts'-id Be'ak'íd, "Seven Lakes." Early Spanish documents refer to this region as Siete Lagunas ("Seven Lakes") (Brugge 1965, 16–17). This trading post is located in the region of a series of small lakes in the rolling, virtually treeless country about 17 miles northeast of Crownpoint, at the juncture of New Mexico Highway 57 and Navajo Route 9 (where Highway 57 turns north—and turns to dirt—to enter Chaco Canyon). The Jerry Faris Ranch was located at the road fork in the 1940s. The Marvin Jacobs, Kelsey Presley, and Pitt Ranches were nearby, and Brece-Pruett holdings lay to the south. Seven Lakes Oil Field is some 15 miles southeast. A trading post was opened here around 1900 and lasted until the late 1930s (Kelley 1977, 252, 254). A new post by this name has opened at the juncture of New Mexico Highway 57 and Navajo Route 9 and is still in operation.

This locale was on the main route followed by many military campaigns from Jemez to the Navajo rancherias in the Chuska Valley. In 1849

Colonel John Washington used the route for his expedition that led to the death of Navajo headman Narbona (McNitt 1972, 176n).

Old Navajos and New Mexicans tell that many years ago, large flocks of sheep came here from the Otero Ranch and from Nacimiento (present-day Cuba) for water and range.

An oil boom that started here in 1909 was a contributory factor in President Taft's 1911 Executive Order No. 1284, canceling President Theodore Roosevelt's 1908 Executive Order No. 1000, which had established the Pueblo Bonito Reservation for the Navajos. This area was to have adjoined the eastern line of the present Navajo Reservation and extended it for 50 miles east to the Jicarilla Apache reservation's western line.

In 1906, White stock operators from the Chama River Valley (100 miles to the northeast) began to enter the country and eventually established themselves on this valuable winter range country, maintaining ownership after much of the region was returned to Indian use in a checkerboard pattern by executive orders between 1911 and 1917 (Correll and Dehiya 1979, 24–29). The WPA guide to New Mexico (1940b, 334) listed the community as a single family settlement in the 1930s.

SHEEP SPRINGS: [DB] (5900 ft) San Juan County, NM. Navajo: Tooh Haltsooí, "Spring in the Meadow" (Van Valkenburgh 1941, 142); also Tó Haltsooí, "Water in the Meadow" (Young and Morgan 1987, 707), and Dibé Bitooh, "Sheep Spring" (Newcomb 1964, 80). Charles Newcomb established a trading post near the springs in 1912. Called Taylor Trading Post in 1941, this chapter community now boasts a Navajo housing development. It is situated at the foot of the barren eastern foothills of the Chuska Mountains, at the junction of U.S. Highway 666 and New Mexico Highway 134 (the road through Narbona Pass—formerly Washington Pass—also designated Navajo Route 32). It is one of many posts once owned by Foutz and Sons.

Some 10 miles to the southwest, on a bench of the Chuska Mountains, Captain Reid and a small command held council with Narbona and the Navajo chiefs in 1847. Only the wisdom of Nar-

bona saved Reid and his men from the fury of Narbona's wife and other Navajos (see Two Grey Hills).

The springs, located nearly one and one-half miles west of the trading post, were visited by First Lieutenant W. C. Brown in 1892, who reported them as a well-known camping site. Several stone and adobe homes were standing at the time, and the local Navajos had built two small tanks for catching runoff. The remains of the buildings were still standing in 1941.

The Navajos of this region spend their winters on the lower benches of the Chuska Mountains and the flats that slope east to the Big Bend of the Chaco. They summer in the high pine- and aspen-covered Chuskas. Some 60 years ago, these seasonal shifts covered more territory, some outfits moving as far as 75 miles east to the continental divide country. Descendants of Sheep Springs Navajos now live permanently in the eastern portion of their old range.

SHEEP SPRINGS TRADING POST: (5900 ft) San Juan County, NM. Navajo: See Sheep Springs. This post was founded in 1912 by Charles Newcomb; it was later one of twenty posts once owned by the Foutz brothers.

SHIPROCK (COMMUNITY): [DB] (4965 ft) (Population: 7,687) San Juan County, NM. Navajo: Naat'áani Nééz, "Tall Boss"; also Tooh, "River" (in reference to the San Juan River). The largest Navajo community in New Mexico, Shiprock is located on the San Juan River 95 miles north of Gallup at the junction of U.S. Highways 666 and 64. Starting as a cluster of ranches and farms on the north bank of the San Juan prior to 1884, it was called "Needles" (James 1988, 33), and was little more than a verdant meadow when Agent Miller was killed by the Indians in the cottonwoods and willows in 1873. In 1903, the U.S. Indian Service opened a northern Navajo agency here. It was originally called San Juan Agency, but later became known as Shiprock Agency (after the nearby pinnacle).

The community was headquarters for Land Management District No. 12, when farming was begun with 3,005 acres under irrigation by the U.S. Indian Irrigation Service (USIIS). It is the location of Northern Navajo Fair, held early in October. Franciscan and Christian Reformed churches moved in early on, and traders have included the Shiprock Trading Company and Bruce M. Bernard (both opening just after 1900), Bond (opening in the late 1920s), Manning Brothers (opening in the late 1950s) (Kelley 1977, 253–54), and B and B Trading Co. A garage and a hotel were important facilities in the 1940s.

Shiprock was founded September 11, 1903, as the San Juan (agricultural) School and Agency. The school became the third boarding school on the reservation in 1907 (Bailey and Bailey 1986, 169). Superintendent William T. Shelton, from whom the name Naat'áani Nééz originated, opened the school and administrative agency for the northern Navajos with a staff of three White and three Navajo employees.

The settlement was laid out originally on land belonging to a Navajo named Tsenayabegay. According to one of Shelton's reports, Indians had been irrigating here for many years, and there were 275 Navajo farms under some 25 ditches drawing water between Shiprock and Farmington. Shelton immediately pushed an agricultural program, improved and extended the irrigation system, developed a fine dairy herd, initiated the Shiprock Fair, built a sawmill near Sanostee, and opened a coal mine in the Shiprock Hogback. Shelton was a stern disciplinarian and ruthless in his prosecution of moral lapses. He is to this day respected throughout the region for his staunch championship of the Navajos and for his efforts in adding the Utah-Colorado extension to the reservation.

The first buildings in Shiprock were constructed of logs and adobe. These were largely replaced by brick after the disastrous flood of 1912. A bridge was built to replace Jimmy the Boatman's ferry in 1909. A new concrete bridge was completed in 1938.

Shiprock was the site of a large uranium mill until the mid 1970s (Moon 1992, 175–85), and serves as a chapter seat.

SHIPROCK PINNACLE: [DB] (7178 ft) San Juan County, NM. Also The Needle, Wilson Peak (Gregory 1915, 154). Navajo: Tsé Bit'a'í, "Winged Rock" or "Wings of Rock." This 1800-ft-high volcanic plug is situated in the high plains country 13 miles southwest of Shiprock, at a point eight miles west of U.S. Highway 666 and six miles south of New Mexico Highway 504. High volcanic trap-dikes run north and south of the main spire. It has been ascribed ceremonial significance through several Navajo legends. However, more than one author (Franciscan Fathers 1910; Wheelwright 1942) points out that the earliest treatments of Navajo ceremonialism do not mention the peak or its myths; thus any ceremonial significance may be of recent origin rather than based in antiquity.

The pinnacle, visible for many miles in all directions, and which, from some angles, is said to resemble a full-rigged sailing schooner, was called The Needle by Captain J. F. McComb in 1860. The name Shiprock apparently came into use in the 1870s as indicated by the U.S. Geological Survey Maps. The pinnacle was first scaled in October of 1939, by climbers from the Sierra Club of California. Navajos resent such invasion of their sacred places, as illustrated in the following myth:

A long time ago they tell that the Navajos were hard pressed by the enemy. One night their medicine men prayed for the deliverance of their tribe. Their prayers were heard by the Gods. The earth rose, lifting the Navajos, and it moved like a great wave into the east. It settled where Shiprock now stands. This is the way they escaped from their enemies. After this, the Navajos lived on the rock, only coming down to plant their fields and get water.

They tell that for some time all went well. One day during a storm, and while the men were at work in the fields, the trail up the rock was split off by lightning and only a sheer cliff was left. The women and children and old men on top starved to death. Their bodies are still up there. Therefore, the Navajos do not wish any one to try to climb Shiprock for fear they might stir up the ch'įįdii (ghosts), or rob their corpses. (Van Valkenburgh 1941, 144)

According to Van Valkenburgh, Shiprock is associated with a number of Navajo ceremonies, including the Bead Chant; and the Naayee'ee Ceremony (for dispelling evil monsters) has a story of a large bird called Tsé Nináhálééh ("It

Puts People Down on a Rock—as Eagles do when eating their prey"—see Roof Butte, Arizona) (translation by Young p.c. 1995). It also appears in stories from the Enemy Side ceremony. The pinnacle is also said to be either a medicine pouch or a bow carried by the mythological Goods of Value Mountain, in which the Chuska Mountains comprise the body and Chuska Peak the head. The Carrizo Mountains are this male figure's legs, and Beautiful Mountain his feet (McPherson 1992, 21). The pinnacle is also the scene of Monster Slayer legends. After Monster Slayer destroyed Déélgééd at Red Mesa, he went to Shiprock and killed two adult Tsé Nináhálééh, and dispersed two young ones as an eagle and an owl. It is also mentioned in the Navajo Mountain Chant (Powell 1887, 388).

Medicine men used to climb to a point called Lightning Struck Tree on the highest reaches until the rock was profaned by the 1939 Sierra Club climb (McPherson 1992, 34–35). Shiprock's English name gave rise to a White man's myth in the first half of this century: that the Navajos once lived on the Pacific Coast and so named the rock when they came into the Southwest.

There are a number of Anasazi sites of undetermined association and date in the open country west of Shiprock, and the first oil on the reservation was discovered in the San Juan Basin near the pinnacle (Kelly 1963, 12). Oil was discovered in this vicinity in 1921, and helium was pumped in the 1940s (Leighton and Kluckhohn 1974, 122).

SHIPROCK TRADING POST: (approx. 4965 ft) San Juan County, NM. Navajo: See Shiprock community. In 1872 this location was first scouted by Thomas Keams, as the Indian Service hoped to open a sub-agency here. (This did not materialize until September 11, 1903.) In 1909, Agent W. T. Shelton began the Shiprock Fair during the first week of October. The first trading post here was established by Robert Baker, who sold out to Bruce Bernard in 1909. Bernard held on to the post until 1952. Another post was built in 1911 by Walker and Hubbell; this was sold to Will Evans two years later. Evans sold the post to the Jacks Brothers in 1948, and Russell Foutz purchased it in 1954. Ed Foutz became the owner

in 1972, and was still operating the post in 1990 (James 1988, 32–34).

SIMPSON: (approx. 6200 ft) San Juan County, NM. Navajo: See Carson Trading Post. This community is listed by Pearce (1965, 156) as being six miles west of New Mexico Highway 44, 17 miles south of Bloomfield. It does not appear on modern maps, but Pearce's description places it in the vicinity of Carson Trading Post in Gallegos Canyon.

SIMPSON CREEK: (8900–7250 ft) San Juan County, NM. Navajo: Uncertain. Like Simpson, this locus does not appear on modern maps, but Pearce (1965, 156) locates it 12 miles south of Farmington near Gallegos Canyon, and attributes the name to Lieutenant J. H. Simpson, U.S. Army. Granger (1960, 22) describes the course of a stream by this name as that followed by Crystal Creek in the Chuska Mountains—rising in New Mexico and flowing west into Arizona—on current maps.

SKUNK SPRINGS RUIN: (5820 ft) San Juan County, NM. Navajo: Kin Łizhin, "Black House." This mesa-top Chacoan great-house community lies near the foot of the east slope of the Chuska Mountains, just southwest of Newcomb Ruin. It dates to A.D. 850–950, with later remodeling around A.D. 1050–1250. The site contains three great kivas—one Pueblo II and two Pueblo III—in one complex. There are 56 rectangular rooms in the great house. Two of the kivas lie in the plaza. A Chacoan prehistoric road passes nearby (Gabriel 1991, 274).

Navajos call the spring giving the ruin its name Gólízhibito', "Skunk Water," with an older name of Looka, "Cane" (U.S. Indian Claims Commission n.d., vol. VI, viii, x).

SMITH LAKE: [DB] (7500 ft); McKinley County, NM. Also Smith's Lake. Navajo: Tsin Názbas, "Circle of Trees (or Poles)" (Young and Morgan 1987, 738). This small chapter community is located 10 miles north of Thoreau, on New Mexico Highway 371 (just south of Satan Pass). A trading post opened on this ephemeral lake in the first decade of this century (Kelley 1977, 253) was once owned by Foutz and Sons and was accompanied at first by the Seventh Day Adventist Lake Grove mission.

The site and tule-covered lake were named after J. C. Smith, a trader who operated in this region some 80 years ago. In 1938, the property was purchased by the Roman Catholic Church for a school and monastery. Now the site is a public school, with a small teacherage and a new Navajo housing development.

SOCORRO: [DB] (4519 ft) (Population: 9600) Socorro County, NM. Navajo: Sighóla, Navajo pronunciation of the Spanish (Young and Morgan 1987, 686). The Spanish means "Assistance," named for Nuestra Señora del Socorro, Our Lady of Assistance. Located on the west bank of the Rio Grande, the community straddles I-40, 77 miles south of Albuquerque. In 1941, the population was 2,058.

A Piro pueblo once occupied the site of Socorro. It was given its name by Oñate in 1598 and became the Mission of Nuestra Señora del Socorro in 1626. Its population was six hundred persons at the outbreak of the Pueblo Rebellion of 1680. Most of the population were friendly to the Spaniards, and afterwards a new village, still extant, and bearing the name of Socorro del Sur, was founded some 16 miles down the Rio Grande from El Paso, Texas.

The region around Socorro was once a favored region for Navajo raids, as attested by the letter files of Fort Defiance as well as early newspaper accounts in the Rio Abajo News. One old raiding trail struck the Rio Grande some 20 miles north of Socorro, swinging northward along the flanks of the Manzano and Sandia Mountains. In October 1832, Navajos raided the Mexican Army here, stealing horses (Benally et al. 1982, 96).

During favorable years the Navajos would range through the piñon forests extending from the Magdalena Mountains (south of the town of Magdalena) westward to Pie Town near the New Mexico–Arizona state line. A portion of this region became the Alamo Navajo Reservation.

Navajos attacked the village of Sabinal, some 30 miles north of Socorro, in May 1823, killing eight Mexicans in a single raid. Socorro itself was struck in June 1835, and in October 1846,

one hundred Navajos attacked the village of Polvadera, 10 miles north of Socorro. All the hamlet's livestock was driven off (McNitt 1972, 56, 100). The Civil War Valverde Battlefield is located 20 miles south of Socorro.

SOUTHWESTERN RANGE AND SHEEP BREEDING LAB: [DB] (7000 ft) McKinley County, NM. Navajo: Lók'a'ch'égai, "Reeds Coming Out." Van Valkenburgh's locational description for this facility—three miles west of Fort Wingate (community) and six miles south of I-40—fits with a "laboratory" shown on USGS maps; however, this would place it within the boundaries of the military reservation for Fort Wingate Munitions Depot, which it was not.

This was a cooperative establishment of the Office of Indian Affairs (precursor of the BIA), the Bureau of Animal Industry, and the Soil Conservation Service, geared toward increasing the wool production of Navajo sheep and improving the quality of wool for Navajo weaving.

The Navajos had acquired sheep almost from the time of European contact, helping themselves to Spanish (and later Mexican) flocks in the seventeenth, eighteenth, and nineteenth centuries. Their accumulated flocks numbered in the tens of thousands. The Navajo breed of sheep (the "Churro") produced an excellent wool for the weaving of clothing, blankets, and bedding, and fair mutton. But the animals were small and the fleeces light in weight, and, under American jurisdiction, efforts were undertaken prior to 1880 to improve the sheep by the introduction of rams from adjacent states.

There was no uniformity in the improvement efforts and the old "Churro" sheep had almost disappeared by the 1940s. Their place was being taken by a mixed fine-wool type poorly adapted to the environment and to the weaving needs of the Navajos. The slight increase in production secured over the entire reservation was more than offset by a reduction in the quality of weaving wool that threatened the future of hand-weaving craft.

In 1934, the Southwestern Range and Sheep Breeding Laboratory was established in response to an exhaustive survey concerning sheep in Navajo economics. The site chosen for the research station was near the former site of the Milk Ranch at West Spring in the rolling foothills of the northern Zuni Mountains. The facility consisted of a number of pueblo-style buildings constructed of sandstone in 1935. About one thousand head of experimental sheep were maintained on an adjacent range.

Today, the facility has become a U.S. Forest Service work station for the Cibola National Forest, and many of the unneeded original buildings are falling into ruin.

(WALTER) STALLINGS TRADING POST: (5050 ft) San Juan County, NM. Navajo: Ch'íídii Łichíí, "Red Devil," (same as Waterflow). One of two trading posts listed by Van Valkenburgh (1941, 170) as being at Waterflow in 1941. (The other was Valley Trading Post; Hogback Trading Post is seven miles west of Waterflow.) According to Van Valkenburgh, the Navajo name was a reference to trader Walter Stallings.

STANDING ROCK: [DB] (6300 ft) McKinley County, NM. Navajo: Tsé 'Íí'áhí, "Standing Rock" (literally, "Rock Extending [or Pointing] Up"). A tiny community near a low sandstone crag in a shallow basin 14 miles west of Crownpoint on Navajo Route 9 at Standing Rock Wash. The community, with a trading post, boarding school, and chapter house, was named for the the crag.

In the 1850s, this region was once under the leadership of the elder Dilwoshí ("Shouter"). This location is mentioned in the Navajo Mountain Chant as Tsé Ceza, "Rock Standing Up" (Powell 1887), but is most likely Tsé Deez'á, "Rock Point" (Young p.c. 1995). The southeastern corner of the Navajo Reservation as defined in 1939 lies five miles south of Standing Rock.

STANDING ROCK TRADING POST: (6300 ft) McKinley County, NM. This post was established by 1925 (Kelley 1977, 254), later closed and reopened in 1975.

STAR LAKE TRADING POST: [DB as Estrella] (6450 ft) McKinley County, NM. Also known as Estrella (Spanish for "Star") and Starr Lake. Navajo: Chéch'il Dah Łichíí', "Red Oak."

This very small community is located in the upper Chaco drainage about 55 miles northeast of Crownpoint. It is approximately halfway between Pueblo Pintado and Torreon, on New Mexico Highway 197. Albert Starr opened a trading post here in the late 1890s. In 1913, Starr sold the post to George and Albert Blake, who in turn sold it to Richard Franklin in 1917–18. Ed Sargent, of Pueblo Alto Trading Post, purchased it during the 1920s, and encouraged local Navajos to grow as much corn as they could so he could buy it for winter stock feed after most of his herd was killed in the blizzard of 1931 (Kelley 1985, 25). It was operated by R. G. Smith in the 1940s. The community also hosts a Christian Reformed mission.

The locale was picked because of a shallow tank nearby, which is still visible in the topography of the rolling, mostly barren landscape. A homesteader's community was once located a few miles westward, but it failed after a brief existence because of the region's non-agricultural character.

The post was lately owned by a son of Art Tanner, who earlier had purchased the Pueblo Alto post. It went out of business in 1963 (Kelley 1985, 25).

STINKING LAKE: [DB] (7102 ft) Rio Arriba County, NM. Also known as Burford Lake, Buford Lake. Navajo: Tó Ndoots'ósí, "Slim Water Between the Ridges." This mountain lake is located in the high mesa country of the continental divide, just inside the Jicarilla Apache Reservation's eastern boundary, about nine miles west of El Vado Lake. It is reached via Jicarilla Route 16, 11 miles east of New Mexico Highway 537.

This is one of the lakes shown as Las Tres Lagunas de la Trinidad on the Dominguez-Escalante map of 1776. The northernmost of these lakes, now called Horse Lake, is shown on the McComb map of 1860 as Laguna de Caballeros. The middle lake is called Boulder Lake and the southern one Buford—or, more commonly, Stinking Lake.

Stinking Lake is one of the traditional stopping places mentioned in the Navajo migration tradition of the Tábąąhá ("The Shore People")

Clan when they came west from the Rio Grande and Gallinas Valleys to join the Diné. The Jicarilla Apache hold their Annual Bear Dance in the fall of the year near Horse Lake. The Navajos call this lake Łį́į́' Bito' ("Horse Lake"). Stone or Boulder Lake is called Tó Dilkohi, "Nauseating Water" (though Young disputes the existence of such a word). With such unappetizing names, it is a wonder the Navajos utilized these lakes at all.

SUANEE: [DB as "Suwanee"] (approx. 5600 ft) Valencia County, NM. Also Los Cerros, Correro, Swannee, San Jose. Navajo: K'aalógii Dziil, "Butterfly Mountain," taken from a barren, rugged mountain some three miles south of Suanee, where the Navajos obtain their sacred Hadahoniye' Łigai (mirage stone), the banded calcareous aragonite.

This switching station for the Santa Fe Railroad is located five miles south of I-40, 30 miles east of Laguna Pueblo. According to Pearce (1965, 161) it was first called San Jose, for the Rio San Jose, but because there was another station on the line with this name, it was changed in 1902 to Suanee. A post office opened here in 1914 was called "Correo" (Spanish for "Mail").

The post office and store here were once on the old Route 66. The road to Puertocito on the Alamo Navajo Reservation leaves here in a southward direction.

SULPHUR SPRINGS: [DB] (approx. 5600 ft) San Juan County, NM. Navajo: Séí Ha'atiin, "Sand Trail Up Out" (Young and Morgan 1987, 684); Van Valkenburgh (1941, 153) translates as "Sun Coming Out." Also Tó Dík'ǫ́ǫ́zh, "Alkaline Water." Van Valkenburgh locates this place in the barren, broken flats east of the Tunicha Mountains, four miles north of Nava (Newcomb), and immediately east of U.S. Highway 666 in the vicinity of Bennett Peak. It does not show on current maps. The spring is the site of an old camping and resting place. A trading post here was licensed to Allison F. Miller in 1888 and operated until 1892 by Stephen A. Booten. In 1933, the Indian Irrigation Service developed the spring and built a concrete catch-basin.

ALSO: (8200 ft) Sandoval County, NM. Navajo: Uncertain, possibly Tó Dík'ǫ́ǫ́zh, "Alkaline Water." A hot spring located in the Jemez Mountains, 21 miles north of Jemez Pueblo and two miles north of the "big bend" in New Mexico Highway 4 (and four miles northeast of Redondo Peak, the highest point in the Jemez Mountains). The Towa name for this place is "pat-yo-shool-oonu," meaning "place of the boiling water." It is not to be confused with Jemez Hot Springs to the south.

SULPHUR SPRINGS TRADING POST: (approx. 5600 ft) San Juan County, NM. Navajo: See Sulphur Springs. This post was opened by Allison F. Miller near Ford Butte in 1888. After only a year, Miller sold out to Stephen A. Booten, who operated the post until May 1891, when it was abandoned.

TABLE MESA: (5859 ft) San Juan County, NM. Navajo: Bis Dah 'Azká, "Adobe Mesa" or "Clay Mesa" (Navajo Place Names Project p.c. 1994). This imposing landform lies west of and adjacent to U.S. Highway 666, some 15 miles south of Shiprock. This may be the area in which Navajos first used coal as a fuel in the 1890s (Bailey and Bailey 1986, 161). The discovery of oil here in the 1920s led to black-topping of the road between Shiprock and Gallup (later to become U.S. Highway 666), with the oil company providing the materials and the U.S. government providing the labor.

TANNER LAKE TRADING POST: (approx. 6000 ft) San Juan County, NM. Also Tanner. Navajo: Uncertain. This post was situated about 30 miles downstream from Star Lake Trading Post on De Na Zin Wash (also called Coal Mine Wash), a tributary of the Chaco River, approximately 32 miles south of Farmington, and about seven miles north of Tsaya. It consisted of a three-room store, a dam and irrigation ditch, and a large structure rumored (erroneously) to have been field headquarters for a contingent of Black cavalry soldiers. The post was run by Ruel Tanner (of the Tanner trading family) between 1935 and 1946 (Kelley 1985, 25–26). The post is now abandoned.

TAOS: (6952 ft) (Population: 4,055) Taos County, NM. Navajo: The same as Taos Pueblo. This community is located 70 miles north of Santa Fe, and a couple of miles southwest of Taos Pueblo, at the junction of New Mexico Highways 68, 240, and 522, with U.S. Highway 64. The first Spanish settlement was a mission built by Fray Pedro de Miranda in 1617. The early name for the community was "Fernando de Taos," after settler Don Fernando de Chavez, whose family was killed in the Pueblo Revolt of 1680. The name was changed by the U.S. post office (opened in 1852) in 1885 for the sake of simplicity.

The community was the site of the first agency for the Moache Ute Indians from 1854 to 1859, with Colonel Christopher "Kit" Carson serving as agent (McNitt 1972, 354n). Many of the military and militia campaigns against the Navajos throughout the White era were staged at Taos. Carson led the 1863–64 campaign into Navajo country that finally subdued the Navajos. He lived out his final years at Taos and is buried there.

Artists discovered the settlement as early as the 1890s, and the community has seen several "booms" of art-based tourism popularity. The first waves of artists and writers hit Taos in the first decade of this century. A second period of popularity came after World War II, and the third from the mid-1960s to the mid-1970s. The artists popularized Taos as they portrayed their Taoseño subjects in idyllic cultural paraphernalia and settings. In actuality, such portrayals resulted in a tourism industry that depended on under-development of the region in other negative socioeconomic measures.

Arrows for the Navajo Male Branch of Shootingway were made from reeds obtained either at Taos or at Oraibi, Arizona (Haile 1947, 18).

TAOS PUEBLO: [DB] (7900 ft) (Population: 1,187) Taos County, NM. Navajo: Tówoł, "Gurgling Water." The village's name in Tiwa is either "Tua-tah" meaning "Our Village," or "Tu-o-ta," meaning "Red Willow Place." The meaning and origin of the word "Taos" is unknown.

This Indian community lies 70 miles north of Santa Fe, two miles north of the town of Taos, on the west slope of the Sangre de Cristo Mountains. Prehistoric habitation sites in the vicinity of this Tiwa village date as early as A.D. 1000–1200, though the Taoseños have refused to allow excavations in close proximity to the still-occupied pueblo. It is generally accepted that these people of Kiowa-Tanoan linguistic stock migrated into the region from the north. Some continued their migration to the east, ending in Oklahoma, and became the Kiowas. Others became the various Tiwa, Tewa, and Northern Tiwa groups of the mountainous regions of northern New Mexico (Bodine 1979, 257–59).

The first European contact came when Captain Hernando de Alvarado visited in 1540 and named the site "Braba." Juan de Oñate followed in 1598, changing the name to Taos. Much of the plotting of the great Pueblo Revolt of 1680 took place in the kivas of Taos, led by the San Juan Pueblo medicine man Popé, living surreptitiously at Taos. Two priests and several Spanish civilians were killed and the mission burned on August 10, when the revolt finally erupted. Eight years of intermittent fighting followed de Vargas's reconquest of 1692, the peak of which was in 1695, when 26 Spaniards were killed. The pueblo was abandoned briefly following this incident.

This was an important trading center for surrounding tribes. Conflict frequently erupted here with the warlike nomadic tribes, including the Utes and Navajos. Taos is generally considered the northeastern limit of Navajo influence (McNitt 1972, 6). Utes often served as guides for Taos raids on the Navajos, especially those led by the Whites (in 1705, 1788, 1836, and 1846) (McNitt 1972, 18, 20, 33, 76, 113), and Hodge (1907) suggested that there had been a fair amount of intermarriage between the Taoseños and the Utes, as the culture of the pueblo shows many Ute traits, including headdresses and hairbraid. In 1700, Navajo chiefs signed a peace treaty with the Spanish at Taos. The vicinity is a source of reeds necessary for certain Navajo ceremonies (Van Valkenburgh 1974, 22).

In 1847, just a year after America wrested the Southwest from Mexico, Charles Bent (the territory's first civilian governor) and several companions were killed in an uprising at Taos. A contingent of 320 avenging American soldiers used cannon to demolish the Mission of San Geronimo, in which the Taoseños had barricaded themselves. One hundred fifty Indians were killed. The population of Taos remained quite peaceful until 1912, when troops were once again called out to quiet a threatened uprising in reaction to continuous White encroachment upon the Indians' land.

TAYLOR TRADING POST: (5900 ft) San Juan County, NM. Navajo: Uncertain. This post is described by Van Valkenburgh as being at Sheep Springs in 1941. This may or may not be the same as Sheep Springs Trading Post.

TEEC NI DI TSO WASH: (5800–5350 ft) San Juan County, NM. Navajo: T'iis Niditso, "Yellow Starts to Extend Downward" (Young p.c. 1995). This five-mile-long, normally dry creek is tributary to the Chaco River approximately four miles southwest of Burnham Trading Post.

TEKAPO: (6100 ft) McKinley County, NM. Navajo: Uncertain. This is a former trading point six miles west of Zuni Pueblo, two miles south of New Mexico Highway 53.

TESUQUE PUEBLO: [DB] (5700 ft) (Population: 1,498) Santa Fe County, NM. Navajo: Tł'oh Łikizhí, "Spotted Grass." Tewa: Tesuge, "Structure at a narrow Place." Another Tewa village, like Nambé, San Ildefonso, Santa Clara, and San Juan (and Pojoaque). Tesuque is located seven miles north of Santa Fe on U.S. Highway 285. It has been occupied since 1694. The original village—location uncertain—was abandoned shortly after the Pueblo Revolt of 1680.

The long-range prehistory of the pueblo likely parallels that of its sister villages, with the ancestral populace arriving in the region about A.D. 1300. Here the Spaniards established the Mission of San Lorenzo, which was destroyed (and the priest, Fray Juan Bautista Pio, killed) in the Pueblo Revolt of 1680. Two Tesuqueans, Nicolas Catua and Pedro Omtua, were runners sent to alert other pueblo leaders of the schedule of the revolt. When they were betrayed and captured by the Spanish, the Tesuque leadership moved the revolt up by several days, and it seems likely that the first bloodshed was at Tesuque (Edelman and Ortiz 1979, 332–33).

The people gradually accepted Catholicism after de Vargas's reconquest of 1692, as the church relaxed its opposition to indigenous religious practices.

The Tesuqueans and Navajos have generally had very little contact with one another, except that the Tesuqueans served as auxiliaries in raids against the Navajos (McNitt 1972, 61).

THO'HEDLIH: [DB] (6095 ft) Rio Arriba County, NM. Navajo: Tó 'Aheedłį, "Water Flows in a Circle." This Navajo sacred place is located at the mouth of a box canyon below high, forested mesas a mile below the confluence of the San Juan and Los Pinos rivers (now largely under the waters of Navajo Lake).

Some Navajo medicine men believe this is where the story of the Night Chant starts, and it is the source of the Navajo Tó 'Aheedlíinii ("The Water Flows In a Circle") Clan.

Before the filling of Navajo Reservoir, the Los Pinos River left a brown streak on the north side of its confluence with the San Juan. The clear waters of the San Juan left a greenish streak on the opposite bank. A Hispanic farm occupied the delta between the two rivers.

At Tó Aheedłį, there was a large rock in the middle of the stream that the Navajos say was never covered by floods. They believe footprints of Naayéé' Neizghání (Slayer of Alien Monsters) could be seen on the rock. However, in the high waters of the flood of 1912, during which the waters here rose 12 feet above normal, the rock that was never covered was covered and washed away. Petroglyphs on the south bank of the river canyon, attributed to Naayéé' Neizghání and Tóbájíshchíní ("Born for Water"), were covered with large slabs of rock that fell during landslides caused by the flood.

THOREAU: [DB] (7172 ft) McKinley County, NM. Navajo: Dlǫ́'áyázhí, "Little Prairie Dogs." This largely Mormon village lies 32 miles east of Gallup on I-40.

Old maps show the location immediately east of Thoreau as "Navajo" and "Campbell's Pass." The site of the town was laid out soon after the arrival of the Atlantic and Pacific Railroad in 1881. A sawmill was built the same year, and the village was known as "Mitchell," after its owners, Austin and William Mitchell, who hailed from Cadillac, Michigan. To found the town, they purchased 314,668 acres from the Atlantic and Pacific Railroad at $2 per acre (Teller 1954, 220). The name Thoreau may have been applied by the Mitchell brothers in 1890 (Noe 1992, 13–14). According to Van Valkenburgh, however, the site was purchased by the Hyde brothers (financiers of the Hyde Exploring Expeditions to Chaco Canyon) in the 1890s—after the sawmill ceased operations—and renamed for the naturalist and author Henry David Thoreau. The Hydes used the site as a freight point for Navajo art and crafts and for the plunder of the Indian ruins they were excavating in Chaco Canyon.

Around 1900, Herman Switzer encouraged a local trader to produce enough Navajo silver jewelry for commercial distribution by the Fred Harvey Company on trains and in the ubiquitous Harvey Houses along the tracks. Largo, a student of the well-known Mexican silversmith Big Lips (of Cubero and Ganado), was the leading smith during this period. Trading posts here have included Thoreau Mercantile (founded in the early 1880s and surviving until about 1970), Red Arrow Trading Post (opened just prior to 1900), and Lewis Trading (opened in the late 1940s) (Kelley 1977, 251–55).

When U.S. Highway 66 was rerouted a mile south of Thoreau in 1937, the town lost much of its livelihood. Navajo trading and stock shipping kept the village alive during the 1940s. Later, mining—especially of uranium—was the mainstay of the community, but this died out in the early 1980s.

(THE) THUMB: (6000 ft) San Juan County, NM. Tsé Bitsii', "Rock's Hair." This 200-ft-high spire is located about a mile southeast of Red Rock, Arizona. Black God scraped the hair off a buckskin here in the Navajo hunter tradition. This feature is also known as Tsé Bináookahí ("Rock that People Dance Around") and was the site of an annual Yeibichei dance (Luckert 1975, 44).

TIERRA AMARILLA: [DB] (6800 ft) Rio Arriba County, NM. Navajo:Łitsooí, "Yellow Place." The county seat, Tierra Amarilla is located 71 miles northwest of Española, on U.S. Highway 84, at the juncture of that road with U.S. Highway 64 and New Mexico Highways 531 and 162. The Spanish name means "Yellow Earth." Interestingly, the Tewa name for the place has the same meaning. The first townsite was in 1832, under the name Las Nutrias. The community rated a post office beginning in 1866.

A deposit of yellow clay in the vicinity gives the village its name. For years the Rio Grande pueblos have come here to get this yellow pigment for ceremonial purposes as well as for stuccoing their homes. It was an important stopping place on the old trading trail between the Rio Grande Valley and California.

In September 1866, three Mexican shepherds were killed, along with Weeminuche Ute chief Cabeza Blanca, in a battle involving Mexicans, Navajos, and Utes (McPherson 1988, 14). Army Major Albert Pfeiffer determined that the combined Navajo-Ute war party departed to the Dolores River in Colorado, then to the La Sal Mountains and the region of the Bears Ears in Utah.

TINAJA: (7400 ft) Valencia County, NM. Navajo: Uncertain. The site of a "walk-in" well next to an Indian ruin in a circular depression in the lava, this place is located three miles north of New Mexico Highway 53, three miles east of El Morro National Monument. The village was founded in 1865 as a frontier rancheria. Two sheep families came in 1869 and called the community San Lorenzo. Two more families arrived in 1870.

TIZ NA TZIN TRADING POST: (6000 ft) Navajo: Uncertain, possibly Teec Náshjin: "Black Cottonwood Circle." This post was located on Coal Creek Wash between Tsaya and Bisti. Tiz Na Tzin was one of the oldest posts on the reservation, opened by "Old Man" Swires about 1880. Swires operated it until 1895. Win Wetherill operated the post for the Hyde Exploring Expedition between 1898 and 1903. The post was abandoned with the demise of the expedition, but was rebuilt shortly after by Harvey Shawver of Farmington, who later sold it to Bert McJunkins. It ceased to operate around 1920 (Kelley 1977, 254; McNitt 1962, 339n–340n).

TOADLENA: [DB] (7172 ft) San Juan County, NM. Navajo, Tó Háálį́, "Water Flows Up." Located on the eastern slopes of the Chuska Mountains, in the vicinity of numerous springs, this trading post and BIA school community is located 13 miles west of U.S. Highway 666, 60 miles north of Gallup. Though the Navajos had settled here many years earlier, the post office came in 1917. A Mrs. Cole, a missionary at Toadlena around the turn of the century, served as a doctor to the traders and the Navajos along the eastern slope of the Chuskas (McNitt 162, 340–41). In the 1930s, there was a USIS hospital here.

The boarding school, the seventh on the reservation, was established in 1913 under the supervision of Agent W. T. Shelton, on land purchased for $600 from a Navajo known as "One Eyed Medicine Man."

Nearby was a Navajo dam and canal predating 1880. The Wetherill brothers rebuilt it in 1904 and called it Wetherill Canal. It did not meet their needs and was abandoned shortly thereafter. However, Navajos repaired it and it was still in use in 1941.

TOADLENA TRADING POST: (7172 ft) San Juan County, NM. Navajo: See Toadlena. This post was built in 1909 by Merritt and Bob Smith. Shortly thereafter it was bought by George Bloomfield (McNitt 1962, 259–61). In 1926, Smith purchased Aneth Trading Post in Utah from Dick Simpson. George Bloomfield and the Toadlena Post, along with Ed Davies and the Two Grey Hills Trading Post, were largely responsible for the development of the Two Grey Hills–style Navajo rug.

TO BILA'I: (6100 ft) San Juan County, NM. Navajo: Tó Bíla'í, "Water Fingers" (Young and Morgan 1987, 706). This is the confluence of Chaco River and Escavada Wash east of Chaco Canyon.

TO BIL HASK IDI WASH: (8000–5700 ft) San Juan County, NM. Navajo: Tó Bił Hask'idí, "Water with a Mound" (Young p.c. 1995) or "Earth Dam" (Kelley p.c. 1994). This wash heads in the Chuska Mountains north of Toadlena and flows northeast, joining Tóniil 'Aho'nii ("Sound of Something Passing Through Water Out of Sight") Wash two miles west of U.S. Highway 666, two miles southwest of Bennett Peak.

TOCITO TRADING POST: (6700 ft) San Juan County, NM. Navajo: Tó Sido, "Hot Water." This trading post is located 10 miles north of Newcomb, three miles west of U.S. Highway 666. Jess Foutz and Sante Bowen founded the post in 1913, first trading out of a hogan. Thanks to a feud between Frank Noel of Sanostee Trading Post and Superintendent Shelton, this post was licensed only seven miles southeast of the Sanostee post and cut that store's business in half (McNitt 1962, 358).

TO DIL HII WASH: (9000–5600 ft) San Juan County, NM. Navajo: Tó Diłhił, "Dark Water" (Kelley p.c. 1994), also translated as "Whiskey Creek." Heading in the Chuska Mountains southwest of Toadlena, this intermittent stream flows northeast through Toadlena and into Captain Tom's Wash at Newcomb.

TODILTO PARK: [DB] (7400 ft) McKinley County, NM. Navajo: Tó Dildǫ', "Popping Water" or "Roaring Water" (Young and Morgan 1987, 706). This broad, sandy valley lies west of the Chuska Mountains, north of Twin Buttes, and east of Split Mesa. The valley is washed by Oak Creek, Squirrel Springs Wash, Little Water Creek, and Bowl Canyon Creek, all draining into Tohdildonen Wash, which in turn feeds into Black Creek, just below Red Lake.

Before heavy flooding of the early 1880s, this valley—then called Laguna Negra (Black Lake)—was a verdant spot with a large natural body of water and marshy swales and swamps. The floods destroyed the earthen barrier at the lower and western end of the basin, releasing the impounded waters and lowering the water table. A masonry dam was built in the 1930s to divert the waters of Todilto into Red Lake.

The basin, hemmed in by broken brick-red Wingate sandstone cliffs, was once a famed Navajo rendezvous. In 1854, Captain Henry Lafayette Dodge (Bi'éé' Łchíí, "Red Shirt"), then resident Navajo agent, held his first general council with the Navajos at Todilto.

TOGOYE LAKE: (7000 ft) McKinley County, NM. Navajo: Probably Tóyéé, "Scarce Water" (Kelley p.c. 1994). A small lake in the highlands south of the Zuni Mountains, located nine miles due west of El Morro National Monument and six miles south of Ramah, both located on New Mexico Highway 53.

TOHADILDONEN WASH: (7600–7200 ft) McKinley County, NM. Navajo: Tó Dildǫ', "Popping Water" (Young and Morgan 1987, 706). A tributary to Black Creek just south of Red Lake, this arroyo drains Todilto Park.

TOHATCHI: [DB] (6300 ft) (Population: 661) McKinley County, NM. Navajo: Tó Haach'i', "Water is Dug Out with One's Hand" (Young and Morgan 1947, 284). Young (p.c. 1995) relates that though the wash may look dry in summer, one can scoop out sand by hand and quickly find the hole filled with water.

Starting as a trading post in 1890, this chapter settlement is located at the mouth of Tohatchi Canyon, at the foot of Deza Bluffs and Chuska Peak, and 24 miles north of Gallup on U.S. Highway 666. An Indian Service boarding school was opened in 1895, and the community today includes public schools, a few businesses, and many homes. Across the highway is an El Paso Natural Gas pumping station. The village was first named Little Water (WPA 1940b, 338).

The community hosted a BIA boarding school, a USIS hospital, Catholic and Christian Reformed churches, and a trading post run in 1941 by Albert Arnold. Chuska Trading Post opened in the mid-1960s (Kelley 1977). The first boarding school on the reservation was built here in 1900 (Bailey and Bailey 1986, 109), but was preceded by a day-school built in 1895. Called Little Water, this school was only the second on the reservation.

A number of Anasazi pithouses are known in the vicinity of the community.

TOHATCHI FLATS: (6560–6050 ft) McKinley County, NM. Navajo: Basneyaah, translation uncertain; possibly Bis Niiyah, "Clay (or adobe) Storage Pit" (Young p.c. 1995). The southwest extension of the Chuska Valley (in turn part of the San Juan Basin) which begins at Tohlakai in the south and flows gently downhill to the north to Tohatchi. It is bounded on the east by Mesa de los Lobos, and on the west by the southernmost Chuska Mountains.

TOHATCHI TRADING POST: (6300 ft) McKinley County, NM. Navajo: See Tohatchi. George Washington Sampson (Hastiin Bái, "Gray Man") opened this post in 1890. His first post had been at Sanders, Arizona, seven years earlier. In 1887 he operated a post at Rock Springs north of Gallup. He sold Tohatchi in 1892 to Percy A. Craig. Later posts operated by Sampson included Tolakai and Coyote Canyon in New Mexico, and Lukachukai and Chilchinbito in Arizona.

TOHATCHI WASH: (6100–5900 ft) McKinley County, NM. Pearce (1965, 167) erroneously places this dry channel in the location of Teec Nos Pos Wash in the extreme northwestern corner of San Juan County. While no Tohatchi Wash appears on current maps, Van Valkenburgh's Gallup Quadrangle map shows Figueredo Wash as much shorter than current maps, becoming "Tohatchi Wash" just east of U.S. Highway 666.

TOH LA KAI RUIN: (6450 ft) McKinley County, NM. Navajo: Báhástł'áh, meaning "Against the Cliff Wall" (Gabriel 1991, 279) or an interior recess (or corner) on either side of a hogan door (Young and Morgan 1987, 145). An L-shaped Chacoan great-house community with a Bonito-style house of up to 31 rectangular rooms and two round rooms. A Basketmaker III village lies nearby, as does a great kiva. A possible Chacoan prehistoric road leads toward Grey Ridge Community, another Chacoan "outlier."

TOLAKAI: [DB] (6550 ft) McKinley County, NM. Also Tohlakai, Toh La Kai, Tohgaii, Tuye Spring. Navajo: Tó Łigaaí Háálíní, "White Water Coming Out," and Tóyéé', "Scarce Water" (referring to the danger of sinking in a bog surrounding the spring at times). This locale is not included on today's maps. A trading post on U.S. Highway 666 some nine miles north of Gallup. George Washington Sampson opened this post in 1890, the same year he opened his Tohatchi Trading Post. He also owned several other posts in New Mexico and Arizona (McNitt 1962, 351). (See Tohatchi Trading Post.)

Navajos say that the Zunis used to come here to dig for kaolin clay, which they use in ceremonials. The name reflects the whitish, kaolin-laden water seeping from the springs at the rear of the old trading post.

TOMÉ: (5000 ft) Valencia County, NM. This farming community 25 miles south of Albuquerque on the Rio Grande was founded prior to the Pueblo Revolt of 1680, and appears to have been named for Tomé Dominguez de Mendoza, maese de campo to Governor Otermin (Pearce 1965, 167).

On December 3, 1840, two Mexicans killed by Navajos were buried here. General Kearny's column of seven hundred mounted troops passed through the village in September 1846. Navajos raided the village immediately behind him, killing a Mexican man (McNitt 1972, 97).

TO NIL EHONI WASH: (7800– 5600 ft) San Juan County, NM. Navajo: Toniil 'Aha'nii, "Sound of Something Passing through Water Out of Sight," or possibly Tó Niłchxoní, "Stinking Water" (Kelley p.c. 1994). With headwaters in the Chuska Mountains south of Tocito Wash and north of To-bil-nask-idi Wash, this ephemeral stream is tributary to Peña Blanca Arroyo approximately two miles south of Ford Butte where the channel is crossed by U.S. Highway 666.

TORREON: [DB] (6370 ft) Sandoval County, NM. Also Dolion. Navajo: Ya'niilzhiin, "Black (Dark) Pinnacle Above the Horizon." Also Na'neelzhiin ("Black Spots Extend Across"), referring to a line of old boundary markers (Young and Morgan 1987, 750). A very small chapter community centering around a school on New Mexico Highway 197, 25 miles southeast of Pueblo Pintado at the mouth of Piñon Canyon

(Vicente Arroyo). The name Torreon is Spanish for a fortified tower, and is often applied to a combined tower and dwelling. It is an apparent reference to one or more of the numerous "fortified" Navajo sites in the region. Kidder (1920, 322–29) asserted that Navajos lived in this area prior to 1800.

Local Navajos say that the Navajo name is derived from the view of Cabezon Peak some 20 miles to the southeast. The day school here, while it was run by the BIA Navajo Service, was the easternmost school in the system, being one hundred miles east of Window Rock, Arizona. The school is now a Sandoval County, school.

Colonel (Governor) Jose Antonio Vizcarra passed through this vicinity in 1823 (McNitt 1972, 65), and Torreon used to lie on the most reliable all-season road to Chaco Canyon (though the construction of New Mexico Highway 371 from Thoreau and New Mexico Highway 509 from Grants now provides more direct access to the canyon from I-40).

The economy of the Navajos in the Torreon area is mostly agriculture and stock-raising. The most common language in the area is Spanish, and most Navajos here speak this as well as their own language, conducting considerable trade with San Luis and Cabezon. They also maintain close contacts with Jemez, Santa Ana, and Zia pueblos. A trading post was established here prior to 1920 (Kelley 1977, 254).

TRUBEY'S: [DB] (approx. 6000 ft) Rio Arriba County, NM. Also Truby's. Navajo: Uncertain. The exact location of this trading post is problematical, as it no longer appears on current maps. Van Valkenburgh locates it 17 miles northeast of Counselors, while McNitt's (1962, 6–7) map shows it northwest of Counselors. McNitt describes the location as at the juncture of Trubey's Canyon and Canyon Largo on Cibola Mesa, while Hendricks and Wilson (1996, 84) identify a Truby Ranch on the south bank of Largo Canyon at its juncture with Tapacito Creek.

This post was founded by Henry Trubey (for whom the canyon was named); he operated it with his brother John (McNitt 1962, 303). Another post, owned by "a settler named Rogers," was at this same location as early as 1886 (Kelley 1977, 251). Trubey's closed about 1960. The region is sprinkled liberally with eighteenth-century Navajo sites and Navajo watchtowers.

During the Navajo Wars of 1863–64, this remote region was used extensively as a refuge from the Army. To the east, across the wide, sandy bed of Largo Canyon, is a region once known as the "Lapis," which Van Valkenburgh suggests is corrupted Spanish for "Rogers," the name of a White settler who operated a small trading post for the Navajos and Jicarilla Apaches in the 1880s. However, the Spanish word for "pencil" is lapí, with nearly identical pronunciation.

TSAYA CANYON: (6100–5900 ft) San Juan County, NM. Navajo: Tséyaa Chahałłeeł, "Dark (Shadow) Under the Rock" (Kelley p.c. 1994; Young p.c. 1995). This six-mile-long canyon joins the Chaco River from the north, across from the Chaco's juncture with Yellow Point Valley.

TSAYA TO: (6600 ft) McKinley County, NM. Navajo: Tséyaa Tó, "Rock Spring" (not to be confused with the historic trading post and chapter house eight miles to the northeast, known by their English name of Rock Springs). Tsayatoh is a small community centered around a chapter house between Mentmore and Black Hat.

TSAYA TRADING POST: [DB] (5900 ft) San Juan County, NM. Navajo: Tséyaa, "Under the Rocks." Located on New Mexico Highway 371, 10 miles north of Crownpoint, this trading post is on the north bank of the Chaco River at the mouth of Tsaya Canyon. (Van Valkenburgh places the location some 12 miles northwest of Pueblo Bonito in Chaco Canyon—either an error, or an indication that the post changed locations.) The trading post was most likely built by H. L. Haines during or prior to 1887. It was run by Harvey Sawyer from 1906 until it was sold to the Blake brothers in 1910. Roy Burnham purchased it (actually a rebuilt post) from the Blake brothers in 1918 (McNitt 1962, 74 and note). Be'ek'id Łizhiní (Black Lake), situated one mile south of the store, has been identified by

some Navajo medicine men as one of the stopping places in the wanderings of the early Navajo clans. Old (eighteenth and nineteenth century) Navajo campsites are found in the area, and numerous paleontological specimens are found in the sandstones and shales, which are of the Eocene geological period.

TSÉ BINÁÁYOŁÍ: (6560 ft) McKinley County, NM. Navajo: "Rock Wind Blows Around" (Wilson 1995, 48). This rock is on the southwest margin of Ya Tah Hey, and is named for the way breezes seem to swirl around it.

TSÉ BONITO: (6700 ft) McKinley County, NM. Navajo: Tsé Biníí'tóhí, "Spring Midway up the Rock," or Tsé Bííni'Tó, "Spring on the Face of the Rock" (Correll and Watson 1974, 133; Young p.c. 1995). The Anglicized "Tse Bonito" is often misinterpreted as "Pretty Rocks," a mixture of Navajo (Tsé) and Spanish (Bonito). This commercial suburb of Window Rock, Arizona, straddles the New Mexico–Arizona state line on Arizona and New Mexico Highways 264. Included are several national chain restaurants, gas stations, a bank and a credit union, a motel, the Navajo Nation Museum and Navajo Nation Zoo, Navajo Arts and Crafts Enterprise, and a shopping center complete with movie theater. Most commonly, however that portion lying in Arizona is considered part of Window Rock.

TSÉ BONITO TRADING POST: (7000 ft) McKinley County, NM. Navajo: See Tse Bonito. This trading post was built by Lewis Sabin in 1932. He sold it to missionary Rev. Howard Clark in 1957 (McNitt 1962, 232).

TSISNAATEEL: Exact location uncertain. San Juan County, NM. Navajo: "Wide Hill Descending Broad" (Young and Morgan 1987, 738). This wide mesa is east of Huerfano.

TUCKER'S STORE: See Pueblo Alto (Trading Post).

TUNICHA MOUNTAINS: (9512 ft at Matthews Peak, the highest point) San Juan County, NM. Navajo: Tó Ntsaa, "Much Water." A higher uplift in the western Chuska Mountains, this range is 10 miles southeast of Beautiful Mountain. Most of the range lies in Arizona. The name most likely reflects the heavy precipitation at the higher elevations (in comparison to the surrounding desert).

TUNSTA WASH: (7800–5650 ft) San Juan County, NM. Also Tunicha Creek. Navajo: Tó Ntsaa, "Much Water." Heading in the Chuska Mountains in the vicinity of Washington Pass, this usually dry creek runs northeast for approximately 16 miles before merging with Captain Tom Wash about five miles southeast of Newcomb. The stream has been named for the mountain range of the same name (see Tunicha Mountains).

A north fork of this channel was followed by Colonel John Washington's column in 1849. They encountered a large prehistoric ruin in the vicinity of present-day Two Grey Hills prior to their council with Navajos that erupted into bloodshed and the death of Navajo headman Narbona. Major Electus Backus traversed the creek in November 1858, five or six miles south of Bennett Peak, and Brevet Major Oliver Shepherd searched the vicinity for Cayetano's and/or Armijo's bands of Navajos eleven months later (McNitt 1972, 143, 347, 376).

From 1853 to 1868, the U.S. Army maintained a post, Tuni Cha, near the juncture of this wash with Captain Tom Wash, near Henry Dodge's Navajo agency. In 1855, Dodge reported the Navajos in this region had planted some four thousand acres of crops (Giese 1991, 5).

TURLEY: [DB] (5700 ft) San Juan County, NM. Navajo: Nashdóí Bighan, "Wildcat's House." A small trading post on the south bank of the San Juan River, eight miles upstream from Blanco. It was named for the first postmaster, Urna B. Turley. The post office ran from 1906 to 1941. In 1908, engineer J. Turley applied to the New Mexico State Engineer for water storage rights on the San Juan River, in preparation for an apparent major irrigation project. In 1917, the application was cancelled. In 1937, suit was brought in District Court to compel the State Engineer to restore the previous priority right. The case went before the New Mexico Supreme Court, with cloudy results.

Van Valkenburgh noted that there was, at the time of his writing, a slim chance that a dam was to be built on the San Juan about four miles upstream from Turley. The Navajo Tribe had a considerable interest in seeing this dam built, as they would have claim to some of the water impounded. The dam was actually constructed closer to a dozen miles upstream, the resulting impoundment named Navajo Reservoir.

The region south of Turley is part of the Navajo Dinétah, or Old Navajo Country. Turley Mesa, which lies immediately south of the settlement, is called Tsé Bíyaah ("Under the Rock") by the Navajos, and is mentioned in the clan migration traditions. Directly across the San Juan River is 'Azee Łich'íí' ("Red Medicine"), a promontory from which Navajo medicine men used to obtain a certain medicine. A wash running west of this point is called 'Azee' Łichíí' Bikooh ("Red Medicine Wash").

TUYE SPRING: [DB] (approx. 6800 ft) Also Togay, Togai, Toghaii, Tohgaii, Toyé. Navajo: Tóyéé', "Hazardous Water," referring to the sinking bog that surrounds the spring at times. This bubbling mud spring is located 16 miles southeast of Tohatchi, which places it in the vicinity of Coal Mine Spring on modern maps.

Tuye Spring is of historical interest to the Navajos. In March 1861, José Manuel Sanchez, leader of 52 citizens from Abiquiu, was killed here by Navajos (McNitt 1972, 418–19). It was once an important rendezvous for both the Becenti and Arviso "outfits." Old hogan sites abound, and it was once a landmark by which the Navajos designated the southeastern corner of the Treaty Reservation of 1868.

First Lieutenant W. C. Brown visited Tuye during his 1892 water survey of the Navajo Reservation. He described it as ". . . a collection of mud springs which covers about an acre of ground and is quite alkaline. The mud of these springs boils up, flows over and dries, forming mounds a foot or more above the surface" (Brown and others 1892, as quoted in Van Valkenburgh).

The first known trader at this location was

Tuye Springs Trading Post, though its history is cloudy. According to McNitt (1962, 249n), James Bennett (of Houck, Arizona) and Volney P. Edie opened this post in June 1889, under the name "Chaco Trading Company." Van Valkenburgh asserts that Edie established the post in 1884, selling it to Bennett in 1889, who—apparently after his stint at Zuni—was at Lupton in 1941. Kelley (1977, 251) says it was in operation by 1885, Edie selling out the same year, and the post closing in 1892 when Bennett, by then the sole owner, moved to Zuni.

TWIN BUTTES: (6450 ft) McKinley County, NM. Navajo: Tsé'in Desgizh, "Capped Rock" (Van Valkenburgh 1974, 15); Tsin Deeshgizh, "Forked Wood, or Tsé Ńdeeshgiizh, "Rock Gap." This Twin Buttes is located four miles southwest of Gallup, half a mile south of I-40, and one mile south of Mentmore. This is possibly the site of "Campos los Pasos," Colonel Canby's camp of November 30, 1860 (McNitt 1972, 405). These formations figure in the Navajo Windway Ceremony and served as a stopping place for Salt Woman on her way south to her home at Zuni Salt Lake (Van Valkenburgh 1974, 72). They have recently been heavily mined as a gravel pit, and no longer appear as two buttes.

Another pair of features bearing the same name (also called Twin Cones) rises to 8546 ft above the Manuelito Plateau, four miles east of Black Creek Valley and two miles southeast of Zilditloi Mountain.

TWIN LAKES: [DB] (6500 ft) McKinley County, NM. Navajo: Bahastł'ah, "Rounded Inner Corner" (Van Valkenburgh 1941, 166), literally referring to a recess on each side of a hogan door used for storage (Young and Morgan 1987, 145). Also Tsé Náhádzoh "Rock with a Line (Drawn) around It" (Young and Morgan 1987, 730) or Tséhahadzoh, "Area Bounded by a Circle of Rocks" (Wilson 1995, 65). A defunct trading post (which closed during the late 1980s), chapter house, and public grammar school make up this community, situated on the long sloping plain that drains the southeastern slopes of the Chuska Mountains (called Defiance Mesa by Van Valkenburgh), 11 miles north of Gallup on U.S.

Highway 666. The English name refers to two ephemeral ponds in the vicinity.

TWIN LAKES TRADING POST: (6500 ft) McKinley County, NM. Navajo: See Twin Lakes. Owned by the family of Tom Lee, a Navajo, and one-time New Mexico State Senator. Lee passed away in 1985, and, though the post closed, an arts and crafts business was continued by his widow, Emma.

TWO GREY HILLS: [DB] (5900 ft) San Juan County, NM. Also Crozier. Navajo: Bis Dah Łitso, "Yellow Clay at an Elevation," (Van Valkenburgh 1941, 166; Young p.c. 1995), referring to two Mesa Verde sandstone crags nearby. This was erroneously translated by Pearce (1965, 173) as "Two Yellow Adobes." One of the most famous of the Navajo trading centers, this one is noted for its distinctive natural-hued Navajo rugs. The chapter community is located 11 miles east of Newcomb on the Toadlena road (three and a half miles south of Navajo Route 19). Early maps (prior to 1900) show the location as "Crozier."

A great many prehistoric Anasazi and early Navajo sites are found on the mesas in this vicinity, many of which were discovered by Charles Bernheimer and Earl Morris in the 1930s. One mesa lying east of Two Grey Hills and west of Nava (Newcomb), was named Cemetery Ridge because of the large number of burials uncovered.

Narbona (Hastiin Naat'áanii), an influential chief of the Navajos, was killed near Two Grey Hills by Colonel John Washington's troops in 1849 (see Narbona Pass).

TWO GREY HILLS TRADING POST: (5900 ft) San Juan County, NM. Navajo: See Two Grey Hills. The trading post was founded near the old Dutch Reformed Church mission. The history of this post is among the best documented. Joe Wilkin (of Crystal, only a year earlier) and brothers Frank and Henry Noel established this post in 1897. Frank sold out to another brother, H. B. Noel, in 1900. Win Wetherill purchased the post in 1902, and sold it to Joe Reitz (a former partner of Wilkin) two years later. An Englishman by the name of Ed Davies purchased a share of the post and later bought Reitz out. Vic Walker owned the structures in 1938, taking Walter Scribner as a partner in 1941. Willard and Marie Leighton purchased it in 1948. Derold Stock became a partner in 1972, but sold his interest back to Marie Leighton in 1981. Les Wilson purchased the post in 1987 (James 1988, 52–56).

The Noels were instrumental in originating the Two Grey Hills style of rug, showing the Navajo weavers pictures of Persian rugs and publishing brochures and small catalogs to push the resulting rugs back east. This is now one of the most famous and best recognized styles of rugs exemplifying the Navajo weavings.

VALLECITO: (8000 ft) Rio Arriba County, NM. Navajo: Uncertain. This farming and ranching community between Española and Abiquiu was founded in 1776.

On May 3, 1858, five Navajos attacked the grazing camp of Ramon Martin here, killing him, and carrying away five boys and all livestock. Three of the boys were later returned (McNitt 1972, 218).

VALLE GRANDE: (8550 ft) Sandoval County, NM. Navajo: Uncertain. This broad, high meadow is part of the Caldera, a massive, collapsed volcanic cone that dominates the mountains of northern New Mexico. Colonel (Governor) Jose Antonio Vizcarra returned from his 1823 expedition into Navajo country through this meadow, having killed 33 Navajos (including at least eight women), and five Paiutes mistaken for Navajos (McNitt 1972, 65). The Valle served as a conduit for Navajo raids into New Mexico, and in June 1856 two Navajos were killed here by New Mexicans (McNitt 1972, 278).

VALLEY TRADING POST: (5050 ft) San Juan County, NM. Navajo: Uncertain. This post was opened between 1936 and 1940 (Kelley 1977, 254), and is one of two listed by Van Valkenburgh at Waterflow. (The other is Walter Stallings Trading Post.)

VANDERWAGEN: (7000 ft) McKinley County, NM. Also "Vander Wagen." Navajo: Tsé Yaayí, "Space Under the Rock" (Young p.c. 1995). A

trading post on New Mexico Highway 602, 19 miles south of Gallup. It was first called White Water, but the name was changed in 1949 for the new post office. The English name is for Andrew Vander Wagen, a missionary of the Christian Reformed Church who arrived in 1897.

VENUS' NEEDLE: [DB (map 12)] (7200 ft at the base) McKinley County, NM. Navajo: Tsé Łichíí' 'Íí'áhí, "Red Rock Spire." A thin stone spire located in Todilto Park, about three miles east of Red Lake. The English name was applied by Gregory (1915, 155).

WATERFLOW: [DB] (5050 ft) San Juan County, NM. Navajo: Ch'įįdii Łichíí, "Red Devil," referring to the trader present in 1941, Walter Stallings. This small Anglo trading and farming community is located on the north bank of the San Juan River, 13 miles east of Shiprock, and six miles west of Fruitland. Warren Trading Co. was opened here in the early 1950s (Kelley 1977, 155).

Near the present village of Waterflow, there was once a farming settlement called Jewett. During the 1890s and early twentieth century, a government farmer and matron were stationed here. In 1893, Mrs. Mary Whyte and Miss Mary Eldridge, financed by the Cambridge Indian League of Massachusetts, started a farming project for the local Navajos. They worked for several years developing an irrigation system and operated a school and mission. Both Whites and Indians opposed them, the former because of difficulties over land and water tenure and the latter due to the introduction of intoxicants. In 1893, troops from Fort Wingate were required because of these difficulties. Navajos were removed to the south bank of the San Juan in 1910.

Two trading posts existed here. The first opened during the late 1930s, the second during the early 1950s (Kelley 1977, 254–55).

(DEE) WESTBROOK TRADING POST: (7200 ft) McKinley County, NM. Navajo: Uncertain. This post was listed by Van Valkenburgh as one of two (see also Mariano Lake Trading Post) serving the local populace at Mariano Lake in 1941.

WHEELER PEAK: (13,160) Taos County, NM. Navajo: Uncertain. One of the elevations suggested as the Navajo sacred mountain of the east (Sleight 1950, 390; Bennett 1990, 3, 8), though the most commonly accepted theories postulate that the eastern sacred mountain, called Sisnaajiní ("Descending Black Belt") is really Blanca Peak in Colorado.

The four sacred mountains mark the four cardinal directions and were once considered boundaries of Navajo range. The other three mountains are more firmly known: Mount Hesperus (Colorado) in the north, Mount Taylor (New Mexico) in the south, and the San Francisco Peaks (Arizona) in the west. Gobernador Knob and Huerfano Peak are two promontories internal to Navajoland that are also sacred.

WHITE CLIFFS: (7350 ft) McKinley County, NM. Navajo: Tsaaniigai, "Sloping White Rock Extending Down" (Wilson 1995, 67). These cliffs northeast of Gallup contrast sharply in color and texture with the nearby red sandstone of cliffs along I-40.

WHITE HORSE: (7000 ft) McKinley County, NM. Also White Horse Lake. Navajo: Tó Hwiiłhíní, "Where the Water Killed One" (Young and Morgan 1987, 707); also Łíí Łigaii Bito', "White Horse Spring" (Kelley p.c. 1994). This community is situated at the junction of New Mexico Highway 509 and Navajo Route 9, 12 miles southwest of Pueblo Pintado. It is home to Whitehorse Lake Chapter House. Two trading posts have operated here: Buck (established between 1916 and 1920) and Rangel (opened in the early 1940s) (Kelley 1977, 254–55).

WHITE ROCK: (6635 ft) San Juan County, NM. Navajo: Tsé 'Ałch'i' Naagai, "White Rock Descending Together" (Young and Morgan 1987, 728). A rock formation four miles southeast of Red Rock, Arizona, just inside New Mexico. Located about two miles southeast of another distinctive formation known as The Thumb.

ALSO: [DB (as Stoney Butte), NMPN] (6000 ft) San Juan County, NM. Also Stoney Butte, a name applied by oil men working in the area. Navajo: Tsélgaii, "White Rock." This small chapter community is five miles west of Tsaya on New Mexico Highway 371, approximately 20 miles north of Crownpoint. It used to be at the terminus of the road north out of Crownpoint, but this road has long since been extended all the way to Farmington. The name apparently refers to a crumbling rocky mesa that dominates the rolling badlands south of the Chaco River in this region. Currently this is the site of a day school and a chapter house.

WHITE ROCK TRADING POST: (6635 ft) San Juan County, NM. Navajo: Same as White Rock community. This post was listed by Van Valkenburgh as being in service in 1941 at the Rock (or Stoney Butte) north of Crownpoint.

WHITE WATER TRADING POST: Exact location uncertain. McKinley County, NM. Also Tolakai. Navajo, Tó Łigaaí Háálíní, "Where White Water Flows Up Out" (Young and Morgan 1987, 707). Kelley (1977, 252) lists this post, some twenty miles south of Gallup, as being established prior to 1890. McNitt suggests it was built by Charlie Cousins in 1909. Cousins sold it in 1925 to Charlie Davis, when Cousins moved south, closer to Zuni. The post was one of the twenty or so owned by Foutz and Sons (McNitt 1962, 282n, 300n).

WIDE BELT MESA: [DB] (7200–7450 ft) Sandoval County, NM. Also Sisnathyel Mesa. Navajo: Sis Naateel, "Descending Wide Belt." Located 18 miles west of Cuba, and 10 miles east of Counselors, this landform is shown on most maps under its Navajo name.

This landmark once defined the northwest perimeter of the land the Navajos claimed as their own. It is part of the Dinétah, or Old Navajo Country. Though it now lies within the Jicarilla Apache Reservation, many old sites in the vicinity are of Navajo origin. An archaeological survey of the sites in the region by Malcolm Farmer included a description of a "semipit" (semi-subterranean) forked-stick hogan, which local Navajo informants told Farmer was constructed long ago for a sing (Navajo

Ceremony). Utes and Mexicans forced the Navajos to abandon the structure.

According to some traditional legends, Navajos obtained their first sheep and horses through an attack on a Spanish caravan on Wide Belt Mesa. The mesa also plays an important role in a number of rite-myths. In the Blessingway story it is called the home of Tséghádi'ñdínii 'Ashkii (Rock Crystal Boy) and Tséghádi'ñdínii 'At'ééd (Rock Crystal Girl).

WILDCAT TRADING POST: (approx. 7000 ft) McKinley County, NM. Navajo: Náshdóí B'áán, "Wildcat's Den" (Young p.c. 1995); also Tł'ízíchoołchíí', having to do with a goat. Possibly named for a nearby spring, this post appears to have been built by one Gib Graham in 1945. The Graham family was from the Zuni area, and carried a tough reputation. Gib's son "Hooch" ran a store at Torreon, east of Star Lake Trading Post, for a time, until he was killed by a local Navajo. Gib sold the Wildcat post in 1949 and fled to Mexico to avoid U.S. federal charges of irregular trading practices. The post burned, was repaired, then razed by a road-paving crew (Kelley 1985, 28). Young (p.c. 1995) recalls Gib having a ranch in Chihuahua, Mexico.

WINGATE VALLEY: (7000–6500 ft) McKinley County, NM. Navajo: Uncertain. This broad, gently sloping valley lies between the distinctive red cliffs north of I-40 (on the north) and the Zuni Mountains, and extends from Gallup east some 15 miles, to the vicinity of Jamestown, though some discussions have the valley extend all the way east to the vicinity of Blue Water. Within this valley are Ojo del Oso—Bear Spring—a stopping place for Navajo war parties for generations, and the site of (new) Fort Wingate, from whence came the current name of the valley.

Major Henry Lane Kendrick surveyed a trail through this meadow in 1852 (McNitt 1972, 217–18) as a new supply route to Fort Defiance, cutting 38 miles off the old route through Zuni. A year later, Lieutenant A. W. Whipple apparently labeled the valley Campbell's Pass (Foreman 1941, 154 and map insert).

YA TAH HEY: (6700 ft) McKinley County, NM. Navajo: Yá'át'é'héi, "Hello," also, "T'áá Bíích'-íídii, "Devilish Person" or "Go-getter," referring to trader J. B. Tanner (Wilson 1995, 71). A trading post and bedroom community eight miles north of Gallup at the junction of U.S. Highway 666 and New Mexico Highway 264. The renowned J. B. Tanner Trading Company closed here in 1990.

Another major post (T & R Market) was established halfway between Ya Tah Hey and Gallup in the early 1970s (Kelley 1977, 256). Wells from Ya Tah Hey provide all Gallup's water supply (Noe 1992, 90).

ZIA PUEBLO: [DB] (5400 ft) (Population: 637) Sandoval County, NM. Navajo: Tl'ógí, "Hairy Ones" (Young and Morgan 1987, 727), the name of a Navajo clan as well. The Zia name for their pueblo is "Tsiya," the meaning of which has been lost. This Keresan village is located 20 miles northwest of Bernalillo on New Mexico Highway 44. The early ancestors of Zia came from the Chaco region about A.D. 400. Six pueblo ruins in the Jemez vicinity are associated with Zia; five of these were occupied into the sixteenth to eighteenth centuries. These may be the five Zian pueblos referred to as the "Punames" by Antonio de Espejo in 1583.

The first Spanish contact was 42 years earlier by Captain Juan Jaramillo of the Coronado expedition of 1541. In that year, Castaneda, chronicler for the expedition, mentioned only one village. The Zians participated in the Pueblo Revolt of 1680, but did not resist Otermín's attempted reconquest the following year. However, they were overwhelmed anyway and the large pueblo of "Old Zia"—with eight plazas and over one thousand two- and three-story houses (Hoebel 1979, 408, quoting Espejo 1916, 181–82)—was completely destroyed by Domingo Jironza Petriz (or Domingo Cruzate, according to Fugate and Fugate 1989, 200) in 1689. This was just a year after the occupants had resisted an invasion by Pedro Reneras de Posada.

The surviving Zians were instructed by Diego de Vargas, upon his successful reconquest of 1692, to build a new pueblo on the ruins of the old one. They aided the Spaniards in their campaigns against other pueblos and the Navajos from 1692 through 1696. The Zians' policy of friendship with the Spaniards was especially hard on neighboring pueblos, such as Jemez and Cochiti. The pueblo's population was decimated in the nineteenth century by internal strife over witchcraft.

Although the pueblo was the target of many Navajo incursions in early years, there was considerable trade contact between Zia and the continental-divide Navajos in the first half of the twentieth century.

The pueblo was the rendezvous site for the Spanish expedition of 1675 into Navajo country. Zia warriors joined expeditions in 1705 and July 1786. A peace treaty was signed with the Navajos here on October 22, 1822. The pueblo was raided by Navajos in 1833, and provided auxiliaries for Colonel John Washington's 1849 expedition that resulted in the death of Navajo headman Narbona (McNitt 1972, 18, 21, 33, 54, 72).

ZUNI MOUNTAINS: (7800–9256 ft) McKinley and Cibola counties, NM. Navajo: Dził Łání, "Many Mountains" (at western end); and Shashkin, "Bear's Home" (south of Thoreau) (U.S. Indian Claims Commission n.d., vol. VI, vi and viii). Broken highland region stretching from Gallup and New Mexico Highway 602 east to Grants, and from I-40 on the north to New Mexico Highway 53 on the south.

Alcalde José Ortiz of Laguna Pueblo led an expedition of 12 men into these mountains against the Navajos in 1818 (McNitt 1972, 48). Lieutenant A. W. Whipple's command traversed the range in 1853, though they were then referred to as the Sierra Madre (Foreman 1941, 131 and map insert).

Mount Sedgewick, at 9256 ft, is the highest point in the Zuni Mountains. The origin of the English name is also uncertain, though there is speculation (Robinson 1994, 1930) that the peak was named after Civil War Major General John Sedgewick, commander of the Union VI Corps. Sedgewick was killed by a Confederate sniper on May 8, 1864, in the Wilderness Battle (a prelude to the Battle of Spotsylvania, Virginia). He is said to have just brushed off warnings from his troops, declaring that the snipers "couldn't hit an elephant at this distance," when a bullet to the brain knocked him off his horse (Catton 1960, 455). He had earlier proven himself at Antietam, Chancellorsville, Gettysburg, and Fredericksburg, and Ulysses S. Grant considered Sedgewick "worth a division" of troops (Ward 1990, 295).

ZUNI PUEBLO: [DB] (6575 ft) (Population: 5,857) McKinley County, NM. Navajo: Naasht'ézhí, "Marked About with Charcoal" (Young and Morgan 1987, 594), referring to black paint around the eyes of Zuni warriors, or possibly referring to an old house at Zuni that may have had a black streak around it. Located 43 miles south of Gallup, on New Mexico Highway 53, some 17 miles east of the Arizona state line. This pueblo had a population of 2,220 in 1940. The name Cuni was first used by Francisco Sanchez Chamuscado in 1580, and Antonio de Espejo used the name Zuni in 1583. These two names appear to derive from a Spanish corruption of the Keresan word "Su'nyitsa," the meaning of which has been lost.

Prehistoric occupation of the Zuni–El Morro region dates back to 5000 B.C., when hunter-gatherer groups moved into the region. With the introduction of farming about A.D. 400, the occupants began to settle into small, permanent villages, the dawn of the pueblo culture. Changes in their construction methods and the advent of kivas in the area suggest contact with the people of Chaco Canyon about A.D. 1000. The region may have hosted as many as seven thousand people at this time. At the time of earliest European contact in 1540, Zunis occupied six villages: Hawikku, Kechiba:wa, Kyaki:ma, Mats'a:kya, Kwa'kina, and Halona:wa (present Zuni Pueblo).

Fray Marcos de Niza headed a Spanish exploratory expedition into the region in 1639, in search of gold and silver. His Moorish slave, Estevanico, while on a scouting mission, was the first European to lay eyes on the Zuni villages, inexplicably sending de Niza a message suggesting unbelievable riches at Zuni. The Moor did not live to see his leader's disappointment, as he was killed by the Zunis at Hawikku, after making himself exceedingly unwelcome. De Niza, seeing the villages only from afar, carried Estevanico's lie back to Mexico City, claiming to have seen the Seven Cities of Cibola, filled with riches. The following year, Francisco Coronado led the largest army the New World had yet seen against the Zunis and defeated them. The Zunis retreated to the top of Dowa Yalani, their sacred mountain.

Following a half-century of peaceful privacy, the Zunis were again visited by Spaniards under the command of Juan de Oñate in 1598, with no apparent violence. Father Andres Corchado was sent that year to be Zuni's first missionary. In 1629, the Catholic Church built Franciscan missions at Halona:wa and Hawikku. These first attempts at "saving" the Zunis led to the death of Fray Letrado at Hawikku in 1632, and the missions were abandoned and not re-established until 1640. In the Pueblo Revolt of 1680, the churches at Halona:wa and Hawikku were destroyed and the priests killed by the Zunis, whereupon they once again fled to the top of Dowa Yalani. In 1772, another friar at Hawikku was killed by raiding Apaches.

The present village was built atop Halona:wa in 1692, and things seem to have remained rather peaceful, except for a war with the Hopis between 1705 and 1715. Mormons sent missionaries to Zuni in 1875 (McPherson 1988, 24).

When Navajos appeared on the scene, they were known to the Zunis as "Apachu." They seemingly became instant "traditional" enemies, though a good deal of trade was carried on between the two tribes. The pueblo was attacked by Navajos or Apaches in 1658. Spanish Governor Narbona's winter campaign of 1804–5, launched from Zuni, narrowly averted disaster when they marched into a blizzard. The Zunis allied themselves with anyone willing to fight the Navajos, and happily took part in the 1805 Mexican massacre of Navajos in Canyon del Muerto (see Massacre Cave). A treaty between Zunis and Navajos was signed at the pueblo under American guard on November 26, 1846. Navajo raids resumed in January 1850 and April 1851.

A smallpox epidemic struck the pueblo in the winter of 1854. Apaches raided in October 1856 and January 1857. This raid had a profound effect on the Navajos, because a victim of the raid was Navajo Agent Henry Dodge, a friend of the Navajos who had also married into the tribe.

Navajos raided the pueblo in November 1857, August 1859, and again during the winter of 1860 as reprisals for Major Oliver Shepherd's Chuska campaign (with Zuni auxiliaries) of 1859 (McNitt 1972). Zuni guide service proved highly valuable in Colonel Kit Carson's final Navajo subjugation campaign in 1863–64.

When the Navajos returned to their homeland in 1868 after four years exile at Fort Sumner, they resumed their harassment of the Zunis. In 1882, Frank Hamilton Cushing, an anthropologist who had become Priest of the Bow Warrior Society, led a punitive expedition of Zunis to kill Navajo stock for encroaching on Zuni land. (There is considerable speculation as to whether or not Cushing fulfilled the Zuni requirement of killing a Navajo in order to become a member of the Bow Warrior Society.)

The dam across the Zuni River at Black Rock was constructed by the Indian Service shortly after 1870. The Zunis had their own agent at Black Rock until July 1, 1935, when all the pueblos were consolidated under the United Pueblo Agency. At that time, Black Rock boasted a subagency, a school, and an Indian Service hospital.

Today the Zuni economy is based on agriculture, livestock, and arts and crafts, with a healthy infusion of U.S. government subsidy. The population is the largest of any pueblo.

Modern astronomical practices at Zuni have led to archaeoastronomical interpretations of certain features at such prehistoric remains as Chaco Canyon and Hovenweep (Young 1983).

Several trading concerns have been based at Zuni over the years. Graham Trading Post operated here in the early 1880s; C. G. Wallace Trading Post was open from the early 1880s until the mid-1960s; Vanderwagen operated a post here prior to 1900; and Sabin R. Wallace ran a post from 1906 to 1910.

❖ HALONA:WA: (6250 ft) Cibola County, NM. Navajo: Uncertain. Also Halona, Holona. One of the six protohistoric Zuni villages occupied at the time of Spanish contact. The village has a violent history. Zunis killed three Spaniards here in 1703; two years later they joined a Spanish expedition against the Navajos. The next year, Hopis attacked and killed three Zunis. Apaches killed a dozen Zunis here in 1708, and the Zunis killed four Spaniards in 1709. Things were relatively peaceful over the next six decades, though Apaches killed a pair of Zunis in 1728, until a party of 50 Apaches killed six Zunis in 1771. A larger party of some three hundred Apaches attacked the village for a full day in 1807, killing a single Zuni and making off with six hundred sheep. A party of 20 Apaches killed four Zunis two years later, and the Zunis killed three Navajos here in 1837.

In 1846 a singular incident occurred when Navajos attacked the nearby Zuni farming village of Pescado. When warriors from Halona:wa rushed to the aid of Pescado, a larger force of Navajos lying in wait attacked Halona:wa. However, the Zuni women and children successfully defended the village.

Several more Navajo skirmishes occurred in 1850–51, and Coyotero Apaches raided twice in 1856 (aided in the second instance by Mogollon Apaches), killing a total of 11 Zunis.

In the fall of 1857, a Navajo woman was killed when Navajos raided Zuni corn fields. More Navajos were killed in 1863, and a combined force of Zunis and Americans killed 21 Navajos in 1865 (Ferguson and Hart 1985, 59–61). A portion of this village is incorporated into the current village of Zuni (Ferguson and Hart 1985, 132).

✤ HAWIKUH: (approx. 6250 ft) McKinley County, NM. Navajo: Uncertain. Also Abacus. Navajo: No known Navajo name. One of the six Zuni villages occupied at the time of European contact in 1540. Hawikuh was located in the Zuni River Valley some 13 miles southwest of modern Zuni Pueblo, near Ojo Caliente. It was here that Fray de Niza's Moorish guide, Estevanico, was killed by the Zunis. De Niza saw this and other Zuni villages only from a distance, but returned to Mexico City with tales of having seen the Seven Cities of Cibola, spurring more intrusions into the region.

Hawikuh was one of the most important Zuni pueblos when it was stormed by Coronado on July 7, 1540. He named it Granada after subjugating the population. Between 1629 and 1632, the Franciscans built a mission here. In February of 1632, the mission was burned and Fray Francisco Letrada and a fellow priest were killed by the Zunis. Forty years later, on August 7, 1670, the priest at the rebuilt mission—Pedro de Avila—was killed by Apaches or Navajos, and the mission again destroyed. De Avila's body was recovered the next day by Father Juan Galdo, the priest at Halona (present-day Zuni). The mission was likely abandoned for a time (Hodge 1937), but Zuni tradition holds that a missionary at Hawikuh at the time of the Pueblo Revolt of 1680 escaped the martyrdom experienced by the priest at Halona:wa, and was adopted into the Zuni tribe (Dominguez 1956, 197). In any case, the mission was finally destroyed in the Revolt of 1680.

The ruin of Hawikuh was excavated by Dr. Frederick W. Hodge under the auspices of the Museum of the American Indian, Heye Foundation, between 1917 and 1923.

✤ KWAKINA: Exact location withheld. McKinley County, NM. Navajo: Uncertain. One of the six Zuni villages occupied at the time of European contact in 1540. It was located on Rio Pescado a few miles downstream from present Zuni Pueblo.

✤ MATSAKI: Exact location withheld. McKinley County, NM. Also Matsakaya. Navajo: Uncertain. This is one of the six Zuni villages occupied at the time of first European contact. It is located at the foot of Dowa Yalani, a few miles southeast of present Zuni Pueblo.

ZUNI RIVER: (6500–5367 ft) McKinley County, NM, and Apache County, AZ. Navajo: Abestoh, "Lost Spring" (U.S. Indian Claims Commission n.d., vol. VI, i), though Young (p.c. 1995) asserts that this is not a Navajo word, and suggests it is possibly 'Abétó, "Hidden Spring." This stream drains from Black Rock Reservoir, four miles southwest of the confluence of the Rio Pescado and the Rio Nutria. It is tributary to the

Little Colorado River 70 miles downstream, 10 miles southeast of Petrified Forest National Park.

ZUNI ROAD: Bernalillo, Cibola, and McKinley counties, NM. Navajo: Uncertain. This was one of several routes into Navajo country followed by civilian traders and military expeditions for generations. The road led from Albuquerque through Laguna Pueblo to Ojo del Gallo (near present Grants), then to El Morro and on to Zuni. This route was taken by Major Walker's Santa Fe Battalion in 1847, and again by Colonel John Washington's column on their return from the Chuska Mountain/Canyon de Chelly expedition of 1849 (McNitt 1972, 152).

The other major routes into Navajo country were (1) the Wingate Valley Road, Albuquerque to Ojo del Oso (Fort Wingate) through Laguna and the Wingate Valley; (2) the Jemez–Chuska Valley Road, via Seven Lakes and the lower Chuska Valley; (3) the Chaco-Chuska route, from the middle Rio Grande to the Chuska Mountains via Chaco Canyon and Chacra Mesa; (4) the Jemez–San Juan route, via Cabezon, the upper Puerco Valley, and Huerfano Mesa; and (5) the Abiquiu-San Juan route, from the northern Rio Grande through the Canyon Largo region (McNitt 1972, 176n).

ZUNI SALT LAKE: (6500 ft) Catron County, NM. Also Salt Lake or Laguna Salina. Navajo: 'Ashį́į́h, "Salt." Located on New Mexico High-way 601, 20 miles south of Fence Lake, this lake bed once supplied salt for Indians and stockmen of the region, and was the site of the Curtis Salt Co. This locus is sacred to the Zuni Indians.

Indians of the region had collected salt here for centuries when it was first noted by Captain Far-fan of Oñate's 1598 expedition. Zuni Salt Lake was once a commerce center of sorts, with its own post office from 1902 to 1940.

Zunis and many other tribes, including Navajos, obtained salt here from the earliest times. A possible Chacoan prehistoric road in the vicinity was documented by Fray Marcos de Niza in 1540 (Gabriel 1991, 280). Hodge states that salt from this lake has been found in cliff ruins as far as two hundred miles to the north. It is perhaps Tsehakha ("Salt Gathering Place"), in Navajo mythology—said to be the home of 'Ashį́į́h 'Asdzą́ą́ (Salt Woman). The Navajo Dibé Binitch'ijí ("Sheep Windway Ceremony") termi-nates here; and chosen Navajos came here to get salinous mud to place on the lips of dancers in the now extinct Naachid.

The lake was patrolled by Major Henry Lane Kendrick's troops looking for Navajo Agent Henry Dodge in December 1855. (It was later determined that Dodge had been captured and killed by Apaches.) Major Oliver T. Shepherd passed the lake in September 1859 during a sys-tematic, two-column survey of Navajo country, ordered by Colonel Benjamin Bonneville (Mc-Nitt 1972, 287–91, 370).

7

UTAH LOCATIONS

ABAJO MOUNTAINS: (11,360 ft) San Juan County, UT. Also Blue Mountains. Navajo: Dził Ditł'ooí, "Fuzzy Mountain" (U.S. Indian Claims Commission n.d., vol. VI, vi). These high, steep mountains five miles east of Monticello include Abajo Peak (11,360 ft), Mount Linaeus (10,959 ft) and Blue Mountain (11,209 ft). Mount Linaeus is called Nát'ohdziil, "Tobacco Mountain," by the Navajos (Austin and Lynch 1983, 24). A local name during the early twentieth century was Shay Mountain (Van Cott 1990, 1).

These mountains were badly overgrazed by Mormon stock in the 1870s. The first survey was completed in 1873. Utes from this region were considered a bad influence on northern Navajos, so by the mid-1880s a company of soldiers was stationed in the area. In June and July 1884, Utes were blamed for the loss of 150 horses and 750 cattle in the region (McPherson 1988, 55, 57).

The Abajos are important to the Navajo Ghostway tradition of the Male Shootingway (Haile 1950, 125). Both Navajos and Zunis (Ferguson and Hart 1985, 132) hunted in these mountains.

ANETH: (4550 ft) San Juan County, UT. Navajo: T'áá Bíích'įįdii, "One Who Barely Gets Along," referring to the early trader who was so feeble he appeared barely able to take another step. Located on Utah Highway 262, at the juncture of McElmo Creek and the San Juan River in extreme southeastern Utah (just nine miles west of the Colorado state line). The community hosts a day school and a trading post.

The region known as the Aneth Strip was affixed to the Navajo Indian Reservation by an executive order of 1905 and by an Act of Congress in March 1933. It had been a part of the Navajo habitat since prior to the Long Walk to Fort Sumner. Mitchell and Daugherty were traders in the region in the 1860s, when the area was the scene of many difficulties between the incoming White settlers and the Paiutes, Navajos, and Utes who were already there.

Around 1904 a nondenominational mission was operated here by Howard Antes; it was abandoned in 1906. That same year—and for some years following—an "Additional Farmer" working under the Shiprock or San Juan Agency was stationed here. With the destruction of much of the farming lands by the San Juan River floods of 1912, this position was abolished.

On October 29, 1907, Superintendent Shelton dispatched Captain H. O. Willard and two troops of the 5th U.S. Cavalry from Fort Wingate, New Mexico, to arrest Be'álílii near here (Benally et al. 1982, 157). Be'álílii and a number of followers, in a near re-enactment of the 1893 Black Horse incident at Round Rock, were resisting the forced relocation of Indian children into government boarding schools. Following a brief encounter near Aneth, in which two Navajos were apparently killed, Be'álílii and eight of his followers were arrested. These men were sentenced—without trial—to two to 10 years hard labor. However, the Indian Rights Association protested the affair and the men were released from Fort Huachuca, Arizona, in March 1909 (James 1988, 39–41; McNitt 1962, 339–45).

Henry L. Mitchell was issuing passes to Navajos to graze on Mormon-controlled range in this area in 1883 (McPherson 1988, 52). (Henry was the father of Ernest Mitchell, for whom Mitchell Butte and Mitchell Mesa in Monument Valley are named.) The community was founded about this time, and in 1886 was known as Holyoak, after one of its early settlers. The name was changed to Anseth after 1900 (etymology un-known), and later to Aneth for the trader (Van Cott 1990, 8).

Author's Note: These two names are so similar, and misspelling of place names was so common during this era, that the author suspects Van Cott's description of their evolution may be in error. Anseth may simply be a misspelling of Aneth.

In 1956, oil was struck near Aneth, adding a fabulous $34.5 million to the Navajo tribal trea-sury that year alone. In 1978, the oil companies (Texaco, Superior, Continental, and Phillips) and the tribal government became the targets of a protest led by the Council for Navajo Liberation, closing all oil operations in the region for 17 days. The council sought renegotiation of oil leases and more emphasis on local needs. Oil companies agreed to many improvements for the Navajos, including reclamation of the areas dam-aged by oil activities and preservation of cultural resources (Iverson 1981, 68, 187–88).

The community has hosted a number of mer-cantiles, including Aneth Trading Post (see be-low), Spencer's (early 1880s to early 1890s), Ames and Scott's (late 1890s) and Hayes' (opened 1904) (Kelley 1977, 151, 156).

ANETH TRADING POST: (4550 ft) San Juan County, UT. Navajo: See Aneth. This post was first called Riverview. It was located on the north bank of the San Juan River, near the mouth of McElmo Creek, by Owen Edgar Noland in 1885 (McPherson 1992, 112). Sometime after 1889, the post was run by Pete and Herman Guillet. Pur-chased by Englishman Dick Simpson in 1921, it was sold five years later to Bob Smith—formerly of Toadlena Trading Post in New Mexico. The name Aneth is purported to commemorate a trader, but it is uncertain when one by this name ran the post.

In 1911, Superintendent William T. Shipley in-voked a little-used point of the Indian trade act that allowed him to fine unlicensed traders $500 and confiscate their goods, when Reverend Howard R. Antes, of a small Methodist mission in the region, took over the trading post tem-porarily for the trader who was to travel for sev-eral months. Antes and his wife were evicted from the reservation, and lost 116 sheep to confis-cation, along with other goods obtained in "ille-gal trade" (McNitt 1962, 47n). The post was at one time part of the Foutz and Sons trading empire.

In the fall of 1907, a Navajo headman named Byalilli (Be'álílii), who had defied the govern-ment's enrolling of Navajo children in boarding schools, was arrested near here by two com-panies of cavalry from Fort Wingate, New Mexico. (See Aneth for additional details of this incident.)

ARCHES NATIONAL MONUMENT: (4500 ft) Grand County, UT. Navajo: Uncertain. Cattle-men entered this region by 1870, but the big "dis-covery" was by Alexander Ringhoffer, a 1922 prospector. The national monument was estab-lished in 1929, and enlarged in 1938. The first car entered the monument in 1936, driven by renowned Navajo trader Harry Goulding. The entrance road was bulldozed along Goulding's pioneered route the following year (WPA 1941b, 450).

(THE) BEARS EARS: (9058 ft) San Juan County, UT. Navajo: Shashjaa', "Bear's Ears" (Van Valkenburgh 1974). Early Spanish records refer to this rock formation located at the south end of the Manti–La Sal National Forest (near the juncture of South Long Point and Maverick Point) as Orejas del Oso ("Bear's Ears") (Van Cott 1990, 25). It is approximately five miles east of Natural Bridges National Monument, and four miles north of Utah Highway 95. The formation is actually two peaks, reaching 9059 and 8508 ft in elevation.

Navajo tradition holds that this feature and Douglas Mesa and all points in between form a pathway for the gods (McPherson 1992, 29). It is also one of the most powerful symbols of protec-tion and the battle of good versus evil. The for-mation is considered to be the dismembered head of Changing Bear Woman in that legend of the Upward Reachingway Chant of the Evilway Cer-emony (McPherson 1992, 35–37).

The Bears Ears is a historically important lo-cation as well, as it was until the early 1990s the site of the earliest dated hogan ring north of the San Juan River (in White Canyon). It is the birthplace of Manuelito's brother K'aayéelii ("Quiver Man") about 1901 (Benally et al. 1982, 98), and several Navajo families took refuge in Naa'-hootso ("Enemy Pasture") near Kigalia Spring during the Navajo War of 1863–64 (McPherson 1992, 39; translations by Young p.c. 1995).

A party of Navajos, Utes, and Paiutes from this vicinity attacked New Mexicans in the Tierra Amarilla, New Mexico, region in 1866, when most Navajos were incarcerated at the Bosque Redondo (McPherson 1988, 14). This was also a major trading location for Navajos and Utes (McPherson 1988, 16). See also Montezuma Creek.

BLANDING: (5865 ft) San Juan County, UT. Navajo: Uncertain. This community is located on Utah Highway 47, 22 miles southwest of Monticello, at the north end of White Mesa. Blanding is an important commercial center for Navajos of southern Utah.

Settled in 1905, by 1915 this was the largest town between Moab and Arizona. It was first named Grayson, but in 1915 an eastern tycoon named Thomas W. Bicknell offered a thousand-volume library to any town in Utah named after him. The towns of Grayson and Thurber competed for this jackpot, and ended up compromising. Thurber became Bicknell and Grayson became Blanding, after Grayson's wife. They split the library (WPA 1941b, 434).

BLUE MOUNTAIN: (11,209 ft) San Juan County, UT. Navajo: Dził Dił̉ooí, "Fuzzy Mountain." This female peak in the Abajo Mountains is located five miles west of Monticello, and is a source of medicinal plants for the Navajos (McPherson 1992, 22). The Abajos were often referred to as the Blue Mountains.

BLUFF: (4465 ft) San Juan County, UT. Navajo: Tsél̉gaii Deez'á, "White Rock Point" (Franciscan Fathers 1910, 130). This small town is located on Utah Highway 47, at the convergence of Cottonwood Wash and the San Juan River, at the south end of Tank Mesa. Benjamin Albert Wetherill (1987, 205) noted that in 1895 the community experienced a flash flood of Cottonwood Creek, and the entire town was subjected to a four-foot layer of sand and debris. Prehistoric roads—differing from the straight-line roads associated with the Chacoan system—have been identified in this vicinity (Gabriel 1991, 276).

A rock formation called "the Navajo Twins," sacred to the Navajos, lies in nearby Cow Canyon (McPherson 1992, 32).

The region was first explored by the renowned Mormon missionary-explorer, Jacob Hamblin, in 1879, on his way to the Hopi Mesas. The community was founded in April 1880. It sits in an area used as a refuge by Navajos during the period when most of them were shipped off to the Bosque Redondo (1864–68). Amasa Barton, a trader at Rincon, outside Bluff, was killed on June 9, 1887, by Navajos who plundered the post. A week later, 60 Navajos threatened the 15 Mormon families at Bluff, but they were dissuaded by threats of bringing in the cavalry (McPherson 1988, 74).

BOUNDARY BUTTE: (5438 ft) San Juan County, UT. Navajo: Gahjaa, "Rabbit Ears." A 200-ft butte on Nokaito (Naakaiitó) Bench at the Arizona state line. This landform is located midway between Mexican Water, Arizona, and Red Mesa, Arizona, a couple of miles north of U.S. Highway 160. The 543-ft-high butte marked the northwestern corner of the original Navajo Reservation as defined by the Treaty of 1868.

BRYCE CANYON NATIONAL PARK: (8000–9000 ft) Garfield and Kane counties, UT. Navajo: Uncertain. Paiute: Unka tempe-wa-wina-pock-ich, "Red Rocks Standing Like Men in a Bowl-Shaped Canyon." A Paiute legend states that Bryce was a town built for coyote people—birds, animals, lizards and human-looking. They spent too much time beautifying, so Coyote destroyed their paints and turned the people to stone.

The first permanent settler to the region was Ebenezer Bryce, who once uttered the immortal words, "Well, it's a hell of a place to lose a cow!" The park was established in 1928, and was enlarged to 32,240 acres in 1931 (WPA 1941b, 457).

CHA CANYON: (8000–3600 ft) San Juan County, UT. Navajo: Chaa', "Beaver" (Franciscan Fathers 1910, 156). A nine-mile-long tributary of the San Juan River Arm of Lake Powell, flowing north from the northern flank of Navajo Mountain across the Rainbow Plateau, entering the lake some five straight-line miles (as opposed to river miles) upstream (east) of the confluence with the Colorado River Arm of the lake.

CIRCLE VALLEY: (6100 ft) Piute County, UT. Navajo: Uncertain. The name is descriptive. This valley lies east of the Circleville Mountains, just north of the Garfield County line on the Sevier River. Circleville lies at the center of the valley, which was settled in 1864 when Brigham Young called for 50 families from Sanpete County under Orson Hyde and William Anderson (Van Cott 1990, 79).

In December 1873, four Navajos were stranded in the valley by a snowstorm after bartering with Utes for a cow. Whites led by a man named Mc-Carty attacked them, killing three and wounding the fourth. The Navajos erroneously blamed Mormons for the attack, and reservation officials did nothing to correct their misconception (McPherson 1988, 31).

COMB RIDGE: (approx. 5000 ft) San Juan County, UT, and Apache and Navajo counties, AZ. Navajo: Tséyík'áán, "Overthrust Rock" (Kelley p.c. 1994), or "Hogback" (Young p.c. 1995). This extensive red "sharkstooth" ridge runs from the southeastern margin of Monument Valley (five miles east of Kayenta, Arizona) to the northeast, skirting the eastern periphery of Monument Valley. It curves to a northward path before entering the state of Utah, crossing the San Juan River at the mouth of Chinle Wash. From here it continues due north to the southern boundary of the Manti–La Sal National Forest—roughly 10 miles east of the Bears Ears, and 10 miles west of Blanding. The ridge is 70 miles in length, and in places presents as much as an 800-ft drop to the west.

This formation was an obstacle to the Hole in the Rock expedition of 1879 until they skirted it (Van Cott 1990, 88).

COMB WASH: (7000–4400 ft) San Juan County, UT. Navajo: Nagashi Bicho (*sic*),

"Mountain Sheep's Trail" (U.S. Indian Claims Commission n.d., vol. VI, xii), but the Navajo translation of this English phrase would actually be Tsétah Dibé Bitiin, and Young (p.c. 1995) disputes "Nagashi" as a Navajo word. This stream heads on the southeast tip of Milk Ranch Ridge, near the northern tip of Comb Ridge. It parallels the west face of Comb Ridge some 30 miles south, where it joins the San Juan River about 10 miles southwest of Bluff, two miles north of the mouth of Chinle Wash.

That portion nearest Mexican Hat is called Bi-cho'adahditiin, "Mountain Sheep's Testicle Trail Down," which Young fleshes out as Bicho' ("its/his scrotum and testes"), Adah ("downward from a height"), and ditiin ("a trail starts").

COPPER CANYON: (4800–3600 ft) San Juan County, UT. Navajo: Tsékooh Béésh Łichíí, "Copper Canyon" (Kelley p.c. 1994). A tributary of the San Juan River Arm of Lake Powell, two miles west of Monitor Butte. Approximately 15 miles long, it is formed by the convergence of East Copper Canyon and West Copper Canyon between Nokai and Hoskinnini mesas. This canyon was prospected for copper, gold, and silver during the late 1800s (Van Cott 1990, 90).

COTTONWOOD WASH: (7800–3800 ft) San Juan County, UT. Navajo: T'iis Bikooh, "Cottonwood Wash" (U.S. Indian Claims Commission n.d., vol. VI, xiv). This 45-mile-long (in terms of linear rather than river miles) tributary of the San Juan River rises south of Round Mountain in the Manti–La Sal National Forest. It flows southeast, passing west of Black Steer Knoll approximately eight miles northwest of Blanding. From here it flows east of Black Mesa, traversing Tank Mesa and entering the San Juan a mile or so southwest of Bluff.

This is the channel in which Richard Wetherill in October 1893 discovered the first remains of a culture predating the Cliff Dwellers. The culture was later named Basketmaker, due to the abundance of remains of baskets and other woven goods. Wetherill thought their region was bounded on the east by Cottonwood Wash, on the north by Elk Mountain, and on the south by Canyon de Chelly (McNitt 1966, 64–69).

COW CANYON: (5000–900 ft) Kane County, UT. Navajo: Uncertain. A tributary of the Escalante River, merging with that body from the east at the same point as Fence Canyon, some 10 miles upstream of the confluence of the Escalante with the Colorado River Arm of Lake Powell. Layers in the Navajo Twins (a rock formation in the canyon) represent the sacred materials (shell, turquoise, abalone, jet, eagle, and turkey feathers, mountain tobacco, etc.) that comprise a k'eet'áán, or prayer stick (McPherson 1992, 31). The canyon was named for wild cattle in earlier days (Van Cott 1990, 94).

CROSSING OF THE FATHERS: (3600 ft) Kane and San Juan counties, UT. Also Ute Ford. Navajo: Tódáá' N'deetiin, "River Ford," or, literally, "Trail Across at the Brink of the Water" (Young and Morgan 1987, 706). A ford of the Colorado River 14 miles upstream from the mouth of Navajo Canyon. This is the point where the Dominguez-Escalante Expedition of 1776 crossed the Colorado River on their return journey to Santa Fe, after having visited the region of the Great Salt Lake in their unsuccessful attempt at finding a passage to the California colonies.

At a point now beneath the waters of Lake Powell, some 26 miles downstream (southwest) of the mouth of the San Juan River, the 13 weak and starving members of the expedition crossed on November 7—in water that was merely waist deep—after searching for nearly a week for a crossing described to them by the Paiutes. (The ford described was actually some 40 miles downstream.) After the party hacked steps into the sandstone cliff walls with their axes, Felipe and Juan Domingo—untrusted runaway genizaro servants from Abiquiu, who had joined the expedition two weeks after it left Santa Fe—were the first to cross.

Today only vestiges of the crossing can be seen in Dominguez Butte on the south bank (named for Francisco Atanasio Dominguez, the head of all Franciscan missions in the Rio Grande region of New Spain and the senior of the two Franciscan Fathers on the expedition), between Face and Labyrinth canyons, and on Padre Butte, emerging from the waters of the lake a couple of miles north of Dominguez Butte.

Padre Butte and Padre Bay (now inundating the mouth of Padre Canyon) were both named for the friars leading the expedition.

The location was part of the Ute War Trail, the only ancient trail through the Navajo Mountain country. The ford was used by the Mormons of Jacob Hamblin's missionary and trading trip to the Moqui (Hopi) villages in 1858 and again in 1859 and 1862, and Richardson (1986, 88) suggests the steps carved in the stone were actually carved by Jacob Hamblin's men in 1858–59 rather than by the members of the Dominguez-Escalante Expedition.

Between 1870 and 1880 the Mormons from southern Utah dynamited the rock approaches to the crossing, for the ford was a favorite crossing for Navajos and Utes on their horse raids on the Mormon settlements (Van Valkenburgh 1941, 46).

DESHA CREEK: (5600–3600 ft) San Juan County, UT. Also Desh Canyon. Navajo: Deez'á, "Ridge" (Young and Morgan 1987, 311). A tributary of the San Juan River Arm of Lake Powell rising on the east slope of Navajo Begay Peak of Navajo Mountain. It flows north for seven miles, entering Lake Powell across from Wilson Creek.

DEVIL CANYON: (7000–5150 ft) San Juan County, UT. Navajo: Ch'įįdii Bikooh, "Evil Spirit Canyon" (U.S. Indian Claims Commission n.d., vol. VI, iv). A western tributary of Montezuma Canyon, Devil rises near Utah Highway 47, midway between Monticello and Blanding. It flows southeast 12 miles, merging with Montezuma a mile below the mouth of Coal Bed Canyon. This canyon is known to flood quickly when heavy rains strike its upper reaches (Van Cott 1990, 109).

DOUGLAS MESA: (5990 ft) San Juan County, UT. Navajo: Tsé Bił Deez'áhígíí (*sic*) (U.S. Indian Claims Commission n.d., vol. VI, xviii), translation uncertain. This broad, generally flat upland lies southeast of the San Juan River at the west end of a series of switchbacks called the Goosenecks.

Navajo tradition holds that this feature and the Bears Ears—and all points in between—form a pathway for the gods (McPherson 1992, 29).

Van Cott (1990:114) states that the English name is for James Douglas, a prospector who, in a fit of frustration, killed himself by jumping off the San Juan River Bridge at Mexican Hat in 1929. He had found gold on a sandbar in the river in 1909, but a rise in the river prevented him from working it. However, Van Valkenburgh (1941, 97) claims that it was named after William Boone Douglas of the U.S. Geological Survey.

DUNN'S TRADING POST: San Juan County, UT. Navajo: Uncertain. The exact location is uncertain, but this post was on Navajo Mountain, in the vicinity of Rainbow Bridge, in the 1940s.

ESCALANTE RIVER: (5773–3800 ft) Navajo: Uncertain. This major river follows an extremely tortuous, winding course from its headwaters on the Aquarius Plateau a few miles northeast of Escalante to its confluence with the Colorado River Arm of Lake Powell, some 10 miles upstream (north) of the mouth of the San Juan River. This river was named for Friar Silvestre Velez de Escalante, co-leader of the Dominguez-Escalante Expedition of 1776 (Cerquone 1976, 17; Martin 1989, 114).

This is considered one of the most crooked rivers in the United States, covering only 14 linear miles in a stretch of 35 river miles. It was named by John Wesley Powell's survey expedition, honoring the Spanish explorer—who never entered the region (Van Cott 1990, 131).

FORBIDDING CANYON: (4000–3600 ft) San Juan County, UT. Also Forbidden Canyon. Navajo: 'Ałtįį 'Ál'į́ Bikooh, "Canyon Where Bows are Made" (U.S. Indian Claims Commission n.d., vol. VI, i). This canyon marks the last five miles of Aztec Creek as it empties into Lake Powell. It forms the eastern boundary of Cummings Mesa, and a small tributary to the east shelters Rainbow Bridge National Monument.

(THE) GAP: (5400 ft) San Juan County, UT. Navajo: Uncertain. The pass between Oljeto Mesa (to the northwest) and Hat Rock, in which the trading/tourist community of Gouldings is situated.

THE GOOSENECKS: (5000 ft) San Juan County, UT. Navajo: Uncertain, but translates to "The One who Crawls with her Body," referring to Big Snake, who created the deep, twisting canyons (McPherson 1992, 26–27). A 30-mile stretch of extreme twists, turns, and switchbacks in the course of the San Juan River in deeply eroded canyons between Mexican Hat (on the east), and Johns Canyon.

It takes six river miles to travel one mile in this region (WPA 1941b, 440). Previously, this area was known as "The Twist" (Van Cott 1990, 158). This rugged, barren vicinity was visited by an Army contingent under Major Henry Lane Kendrick in August 1853 (McNitt 1972, 235).

GOTHIC CREEK: (5000–4400 ft) San Juan County, UT. Navajo: Uncertain. A 20-mile-long dry wash flowing north from the northern foot of Boundary Butte. Skirting the west margin of Casa del Eco Mesa, it merges with the San Juan River from the south, opposite the community of Bluff.

McNitt (1972, 354) mistakenly identifies this channel as a tributary of Walker Creek. It was named by Major Electus Backus in November 1858, due to the nature of the sandstone formations in the vicinity.

GOULDINGS (TRADING POST): (5192 ft) San Juan County, UT. Also Gouldings. Navajo: Tségiizh, "Rock Gap." Small trading and tourism center in Monument Valley, situated on the north slope of Hat Rock, on the northwestern margin of Monument Valley. Founded by Harry Goulding in October 1925, it was some two hundred miles north of the AT&SF Railway at Flagstaff, Arizona, and claimed the distinction of being "the White habitation most distant from a railroad in the U.S." (Van Valkenburgh 1941, 67).

The trading post was built on a "school section" of land set aside from the Paiute Strip land added to the Navajo Reservation in 1933. The land was officially sold to Goulding in 1937, 12 years after he founded the business (Moon 1992, 36). The site is now occupied by a major motel/lodge, trading post, museum, and a hospital (the land for the latter donated by Goulding).

Harry Goulding was personally responsible for bringing the motion picture industry to Monument Valley. He traveled to Hollywood in 1938, visiting United Artists Studios with large photos of the valley's landscape and monuments. When told no one of importance at the studio would see him, he threatened to camp in the lobby, sleeping bag and all. A studio official consented to see him and was so impressed that trucks from the studio beat Goulding to Flagstaff, Arizona, on their way to the valley.

The Seventh Day Adventist Hospital operated out of a trailer in 1941, when the government hospital closed due to World War II. A clinic was built in the 1940s out of lumber from a replica of old Tucson, the movie set of *She Wore a Yellow Ribbon*. These buildings had been turned over to the tribe, who sold the materials to the church. The hospital was expanded to 15 beds in the 1960s, and is located in Rock Door Canyon (Moon 1992, 206).

According to Navajo mythology, this location is the hearth of a giant hogan that is Monument Valley. Sentinel and Gray Whiskers Mesa form the doorposts (McPherson 1992, 29).

GRAND GULCH: (6800–4000 ft) San Juan County, UT. Navajo: Uncertain. This extensive network of deep, steep canyons heads on Grand Gulch Plateau south of Natural Bridges National Monument, and flows south for six miles. At the mouth of Kane Gulch, it veers southwest, then west, then northwest for another 12 miles before another 90-degree bend to the southwest. It flows 12 more linear (as opposed to river) miles into the San Juan River from the north some five miles upstream (east) of the mouth of Oljeto Wash.

Hastiin Biyááł ("Wealthy Man"), a northern Navajo headman, was born in Grand Gulch about 1832 (Benally et al. 1982, 99).

This formation is not to be confused with the Grand Gulch rising near the foot of Swap Mesa in Capitol Reef National Park.

HALCHITA: (4400 ft) San Juan County, UT. Navajo: Halchíítah, "Among the Red Areas" (Young and Morgan 1987, 409). A small school

community on the bench above the San Juan River, opposite Mexican Hat. (The same name is applied to the Painted Desert in Arizona.)

HALGAITO WASH: (5400–4200 ft) San Juan County, UT. Also Hogaitoh Wash. Navajo: Halgai Tó, "Plains Water" (Kelley p.c. 1994). This northernmost tributary of Gypsum Creek heads some three miles north of Douglas Wash in northern Monument Valley. It flows southeast, then northeast a total of 15 miles before merging with Gypsum Wash two miles south of Mexican Hat.

HATCH TRADING POST: (4800 ft) San Juan County, UT. Navajo: Uncertain. This historic trading post is located on the west bank of Montezuma Canyon, at the foot of Alkali Mesa and the confluence of Alkali Canyon. The location is about three miles south of the mouth of Cross Canyon.

HENRY MOUNTAINS: (11,522 ft) Garfield County, UT. Navajo: Dził Bizhi 'Adani, "Nameless Mountains" (U.S. Indian Claims Commission n.d., vol. VI, vi). Martin Link (p.c. 1997) stated that during the old Navajo land claims investigations, the researchers knew when they had come to the end of Navajo country when they encountered features called "Nameless" or "No Name." These mountains are located west of the Colorado River and south of the Fremont and Dirty Devil rivers. The highest peaks are Mount Ellen in the northwest (11,522 ft) and Mount Pennell (11,320 ft) and Mount Hillers (10,650 ft) in the southeast.

Given the Navajo name, it is interesting to note that the men of John Wesley Powell's first expedition down the Colorado called these mountains the "Unknown Mountains." On the second expedition, they named them for the secretary of the Smithsonian Institution, Joseph Henry. The mountains first appeared on maps in 1869 (Van Cott 1990, 183).

HOLE IN THE WALL: (4500 ft) Kane County, UT. Also Hole in Rock. Navajo: Uncertain. Steep drop to the Colorado River Arm of Lake Powell (formerly to the Colorado River), located on the north bank between Llewellyn Gulch (on the south) and the Escalante River, across from Cottonwood Gulch.

In 1880, Mormon colonists heading to Bluff on the unexplored route were snowed in atop the plateau. A four-foot gap was widened and a trail was blasted down the cliff face. It took two weeks to accomplish (WPA 1941b, 436).

HOVENWEEP NATIONAL MONUMENT: (5275 ft) San Juan County, UT, and Montezuma County, CO. Navajo: Kits'iilí, "Broken Down Houses," a generic term referring to ruins collectively. Ute: Hovenweep, "Deserted Valley." This region was traversed by the Spanish exploration of Dominguez and Escalante in 1776, and they encountered one of the ruins. The region was first mapped by William H. Jackson of the 1874 Hayden Survey. The national monument was established in 1923 by presidential proclamation. It consists of four separate groups of ruins in canyons and sage plains (WPA 1941b, 496).

There are few (if any) references to Hovenweep and Navajos in the literature, but given the monument's proximity to Ismay and Hatch Trading Posts, Aneth, and the San Juan River, Navajos certainly were cognizant of this region—even in times of antiquity. At the very least, they would have hunted in the area, or passed through it on their way to the mountains north of the monument.

The monument's series of isolated groups of ruins clustered about canyon heads on Cajon Mesa dates to A.D. 1100–1300 (though Unit Type House at Square Tower Ruins Group may date as early as A.D. 900). An archaeological survey in 1974 identified a single possible Basketmaker II site (A.D. 500), three probable Basketmaker III sites (A.D. 500–700), 19 small Pueblo I sites (A.D. 700–900), 194 Pueblo II sites (A.D. 900–1150), and 318 Pueblo III sites (A.D. 1150–1270), in 4,665 acres.

Prior to A.D. 1200, the occupants of the region were scattered, isolated. All major ruins groups date to Pueblo III and they appear to cluster on the rims of the canyon cliffs (though most of the cliffs are under 20 ft in height, and thus are not

nearly as dramatic as those at nearby Mesa Verde, Chaco Canyon, or Canyon de Chelly). Some ruins contain cliffside units as well as the clifftop structures. An unusual aspect of the ruins is the presence of towers, some square, some round. These "castles" seem to have been constructed about A.D. 1200, and all the ruins seem to have been abandoned a hundred years later. The structures are somewhat unique to Anasazi ruins in that they are constructed on very rough, irregular terrain, with walls traversing and incorporating huge boulders and outcrops. The occupants of the sites constructed and maintained extensive water control systems, with dams, canals, and reservoirs (Brody 1990, 127).

Some scholars consider the ruins of Hovenweep to possess some of the best documented and least controversial of the Anasazi "light and shadow calendars" (Malville and Putnam 1989, 39), though they are most likely "predictive" in nature (Frazier 1986, 199). Navajo names have not been determined for any of the ruins.

❖ CAJON RUINS GROUP: Six miles southwest of Hovenweep Castle, this ruins group is the southernmost (and lowest in elevation). At least four separate structures are clustered around a side canyon of Cajon Mesa. One structure contains nine rooms. A tower displays three portholes in the western wall. At summer-solstice sunset, light passes through two of them (Malville and Putnam 1989, 42).

❖ CUTTHROAT CASTLE RUINS GROUP: This group consists of two circular towers and a multi-room "castle." This is the only group in the monument not clustered around a canyon head. It is the northeasternmost and highest group, lying in the piñon/juniper forest.

❖ HACKBERRY RUINS GROUP: This group was named for the vegetation surrounding it. The medium-sized Pueblo III village may have been as large as Mesa Verde's Cliff Palace in a pattern similar to Holly and Horseshoe Ruins Groups, with rim-top roomblocks and below-rim dams and channels. Several rooms were two-story (Ferguson and Rohn 1987, 146–48).

✤ HOLLY RUINS GROUP: At Holly House, petroglyph spirals appear on boulders in a natural corridor in the canyon. Considered a possible "sun calendar" (Williamson 1983, 111; Frazier 1986, 200), they are "differentially lighted" by a "sundagger" of light at the spring equinox and at sunrise of summer solstice (Malville and Putnam 1989, 44).

✤ HORSESHOE RUINS GROUP: This village includes D-shaped Holly House on the canyon rim and a small cliff dwelling below. A dam on the canyon rim created a reservoir in a pattern similar to that at Holly Ruins Group (Ferguson and Rohn 1987, 146).

✤ HOVENWEEP CASTLE: named for its resemblance to a medieval European castle, this ruin contains a D-shaped tower and multiple rooms, constructed of double and triple course masonry. One rectangular room is called the "sun room," attached to the south side of the tower. At summer-solstice sunset a beam of light passes through a porthole and shines on the lintel of the door to an eastern room. At winter-solstice sunset a sunbeam passes through another porthole to the top of a doorway in the north wall leading to the tower (Malville and Putnam 1989, 40–41).

✤ SQUARE TOWER RUINS GROUP: Includes Square Tower, Hovenweep Castle, Hovenweep House, and Talus Pueblo Ruin, along with the monument headquarters. Clustered about Little Ruin Canyon, this is possibly the most extensive ruins group in the monument, with nine known structures and others extending nearly all the way across the canyon. Archaeoastronomical features are evident at Square Tower House and Unit Type House (so named because it is exemplary of the "resident unit") where wall ports look toward the summer and winter solstices.

✤ UNIT TYPE HOUSE: Located several hundred yards east of Hovenweep Castle, this is a ruin of six rooms and a kiva. Four portholes penetrate an intact wall of an eastern room. The winter-solstice sunrise sends a ray of light through one porthole to the room's northwest corner. At summer solstice, light passes through another porthole to the room's southwest corner (Malville and Putnam 1989, 41–42).

KAIPAROWITS PLATEAU: (7000–6000 ft) Kane County, UT. Also Wild Horse Mesa. Navajo: Tsé Ndoolzhah, "Rock Descending Jagged" (same as Wild Horse Mesa), referring to the point projecting down toward the juncture of the Colorado and San Juan rivers; also Dził Binii' Łigaii, "White Faced Mountains" (U.S. Indian Claims Commission n.d., vol. VI, vi). Paiute: Kaiparowitz, possibly meaning "Big Mountain's Little Brother" (Van Cott 1990, 211). A large uplift southeast of the Escalante Mountains and northwest of the Colorado River, made famous by western novelist Zane Grey. It is drained by Wahweap and Last Chance creeks. It is bounded on the east by Fiftymile Mountain and the Straight Cliffs (also known as the Escalante Rim).

This isolated, wild, rugged country was a favorite source of wild horses for the Navajos. The approach to the mesa from the south—prior to bridges and dams built in this century—was by two fords of the Colorado River. The first was a notoriously tedious trail from Navajo Mountain that first crosses the San Juan River, then follows the old Mormon Trail though Hole-in-the-Rock. The second was called "Crossing of the Fathers," following its use by the Dominguez-Escalante Expedition of 1776.

Everett Ruess, a Los Angeles artist, gained renown by becoming lost in this region and never found. The area was explored in 1929 by anthropologist Dr. Clyde Kluckhohn.

LAKE POWELL: (3711 ft at high water) San Juan and Kane counties, UT, Coconino County, AZ. Navajo: Tólá Dah Siyíní, "Large Body of Water at an Elevation" (Wilson 1995, 31). This enormous, man-made lake fills the former Glen Canyon and many side canyons at and below the confluence of the Colorado and San Juan rivers. To the Navajos, the confluence of these two rivers is To 'Ahidiidlíní, "Water Come Together," the point where the (male) San Juan River "mounts" the (female) Colorado River—a very sacred location (Luckert 1977, 24, 44–45).

Named for John Wesley Powell, one-armed

scientist and Civil War veteran who led the first Colorado River float with eight men in four wooden boats in 1869. Three million people annually visit the national recreation area (authorized in 1972). The surface of the lake is never to be allowed to drop below 1083 ft above sea level. The lake has nearly two thousand miles of shoreline, equal to the Pacific Coast between San Diego and Seattle. It peaked at 3707 ft above sea level on July 14, 1983. (See also Page, Arizona, Glen Canyon, Glen Canyon Dam.)

The lake contains 27,000,000 acre-feet of water, and took 17 years to rise 560 feet. It covers the equivalent of 252 square miles, reaching 186 miles up the Colorado River and 75 miles up the San Juan River in 1980 (Martin 1989).

The lake was extremely controversial among naturalists when the dam was constructed, because of the deep and beautiful canyons it inundated, and long-range plans to dam the Grand Canyon itself. But little discussion concerned the Navajo sacred sites to be inundated.

LA SAL MOUNTAINS: Grand and San Juan counties, UT. Navajo: Dził 'Ashdlaii, "Five Peaks" (U.S. Indian Claims Commission n.d., vol. VI, vi). This range, the second highest in Utah, parallels the Utah-Colorado line roughly halfway between Monticello on the south and Interstate Highway 70 on the north, and lies immediately north of the Utah community of La Sal on Utah Highway 46. The highest points are Mount Tomasaki (12,271 ft), Mount Ness (12,311 ft), and Mount Peale (12,721 ft). As with Blue Mountain, the Navajos acknowledge this is Ute country, but they consider the mountains a source of medicinal plants.

A party of Navajos, Utes, and Paiutes traveled through this range on their return to the Bears Ears after attacking New Mexicans at Tierra Amarilla, New Mexico, in September 1866 (McPherson 1988, 14). These mountains were badly overgrazed by Mormon stockmen in the late nineteenth century. The Dominguez-Escalante Expedition of 1776 named the mountains La Sal (Spanish for "The Salt") for salt deposits in the area. They were also once called the Elk Mountains (Van Cott 1990, 217), though by whom is not certain.

LIME RIDGE: (5000 ft) San Juan County, UT. Navajo: Uncertain. A steep north-south incline crossing the east end of the Valley of the Gods (north of the San Juan River) a mile or so east of Lime Creek. Navajos say that in a large trapezoidal boulder along this ridge, children disobedient to Johonaa'ei (Sun Bearer) are trapped. A pair of two-horned snakes live here guarding the eastern boundary of Navajoland (McPherson 1992, 25).

LONE MOUNTAIN: (4970 ft) San Juan County, UT. Navajo: T'áá Sahdii Dah 'Azkání, "Separate Mesa," or "Mesa Apart" (Young and Morgan 1987, 722). This mountain is located across the San Juan River from the community of Aneth. The name seems to stem from the fact that it is actually a small promontory separated from the main body of a larger mesa extending to the west.

MANCOS MESA: (5512 ft) San Juan County, UT. Navajo: Uncertain. This sizable mesa rests atop the elevated plateau west of the Red Cliffs, north and east of Cedar Canyon, south of the Colorado River. Named for Mancos Jim, a Paiute sub-chief killed by Whites near Bluff in 1923 (Van Cott 1990, 243).

McCRACKEN CANYON: (5150–4500 ft) San Juan County, UT. Navajo: Tsé Chizhi, "Rough Rock" (U.S. Indian Claims Commission n.d., vol. VI, xiv); actually translated as "Wooded Rock" (Young and Morgan 1987). On McCracken Mesa, this northern tributary of the San Juan River is between Recapture Creek on the west and Montezuma Creek on the east.

MCCRACKEN MESA: (5200 ft) San Juan County, UT. Navajo: 'Asaa' Si'á, "Pot Sitting" (U.S. Indian Claims Commission n.d., vol. VI, i). Flat highland north of the San Juan River, bounded on the west by Recapture Creek and on the east by Montezuma and Alkali Canyons.

MEXICAN HAT: [DB] (4150 ft) (Population: 259) San Juan County, UT. Navajo: Ch'ah Łizhin, "Black Hat" (Van Valkenburgh 1941, 97); Naakaii Ch'ah, "Mexican Hat" (Young and Morgan 1987, 945). A small community on the San Juan River at the east end of the Goosenecks, where the suspension bridge on Utah Highway 47 first crossed the river in 1909 (near the mouth of Gypsum Creek, some 30 miles southwest of Bluff). The community is named for a rock formation, a few miles north of the San Juan River, that resembles a Mexican sombrero resting upside down atop a spire of sandstone. The community was first known as Goodridge, after E. L. Goodridge, a prospector in the region in 1882. Goodridge was the first to boat down the San Juan River in his search for gold. Instead, he found oil in 1882, and founded the settlement and named it for himself.

The country here is rough and broken by many drainages into the San Juan. A trading post was opened here by Nevill on the north side of the river between 1906 and 1910, according to Kelley (1977, 253). The formation for which the location is named was a mile and a half northwest of Nevill's. Five miles downstream are the famed Goosenecks of the San Juan River, great scalloping curves cut through the badlands and terraces of crumbly shales. Flat-bottomed boats that used to float down the San Juan River from Mexican Hat have largely been replaced by rubber rafts. Some Navajos live south of the river along Gypsum Wash and others reside on Douglas Mesa.

Neither the community nor the rock formation have much significance in Navajo history or mythology. The region, however, is known for the presence of Big Snake, a powerful supernatural being, and a nearby butte is called Dził Náhineests'ee', "Mountain that is Coiled Up." This rounded formation has the appearance of a series of coils very much like the pattern of a coiled bullsnake. The region is dangerous to those who do not show proper respect to these beliefs (McPherson 1992, 25).

In 1892–93, a gold rush brought nearly two thousand prospectors to Mexican Hat (WPA 1941b, 441). The town was the site of uranium milling between World War II and the 1980s (Moon 1992, 175–85).

MONTEZUMA CREEK: (8600–4300 ft) San Juan County, UT. Navajo: Díwózhii Bikooh (U.S. Indian Claims Commission n.d., vol. VI,

vi), translated as "Greasewood Canyon" by Young (p.c. 1995). This 55-mile-long stream rises on the northeast flank of 11,360-ft Abajo Peak, some seven miles east of Blanding. The stream flows east, past Monticello, then turns south, flowing through Montezuma Canyon and entering the San Juan River approximately 11 miles downstream (northwest) of the mouth of McElmo Creek at Aneth.

Like the Bears Ears, this was a major trading region for Utes and Navajos (McPherson 1988, 15). Utes traded buckskins, buckskin clothing, elk hides, buffalo robes, saddlebags, horses, beaded bags, beaver skins, buffalo tails (for rattles), and pitch (for ceremonial whistles and baskets). Navajos traded woven blankets, silver, and agricultural produce (McPherson 1988, 16).

ALSO: (4550 ft) (Population: 345) San Juan County, UT. Navajo: Uncertain. This trading center sits on the north bank of the San Juan River and Utah Highway 163, a couple of miles west of the junction of that highway with Navajo Route 35 and Utah Highway 262. Here there are schools and Aneth Natural Gas Plant. Sunrise Trading Post, established between 1916 and 1920 (Kelley 1977, 254), is now closed. The bridge spanning the San Juan River here was dedicated on December 7, 1958 (Correll 1968, November).

This community was first known as Fort Montezuma, established by Peter Shirts, who for some reason believed Aztec leader Montezuma was captured and killed near here (see Recapture Creek) (McPherson 1988, 41; Van Cott 1990, 256).

MONUMENT VALLEY: [DB] (4800–5700 ft), San Juan County, UT, and Navajo County, AZ. Navajo: Tsé Bii' Ndzisgaii, "Stretches of Treeless Areas" or "Clearings Among the Rocks" (Young and Morgan 1987, 729). Straddling the Arizona-Utah state line about 20 miles north of Kayenta, Arizona, this vast expanse of desert highland measures some 20 by 30 miles (about one hundred square miles of which is now a Navajo tribal park), and contains some of the most astonishing—and, thanks to western-genre motion pictures, some of the most familiar—natural geological formations in the world. These include Mitchell and Spearhead mesas, Merrick, Mitchell, and The Mittens buttes, and Mystery Valley—sheer, isolated mesas and sandstone pillars of various sizes and shapes. Though the majority of the park is in Arizona, the entrance is in Utah.

The valley floor is actually higher in elevation than the southwestern perimeter, near Monument Pass, and the northern boundary, the San Juan River at Mexican Hat. Many of the monuments loom 1000 ft above the valley floor. Gouldings, the famed trading post/guest ranch, is located a mile northwest of the main road at Monument Pass. The lowest point in the valley is in Gypsum Valley, and the highest (excluding the monument crests) is Monument Pass (Klinck 1984, 120).

This fantastic landscape was formed by geologic and environmental activity that began 25 million years ago, during the Cenozoic era. The entire region was under a vast inland sea that receded, leaving beds of sand compacted into stone some hundreds of feet thick. While the receding waters (and rain since then) may have affected some of the general topography, the great monuments for which the valley is noted today were formed by wind, driving minuscule grains of sand in a relentless sculpting of the landscape.

Monument Valley is a part of the old Paiute Strip and was the original northwest corner of the Treaty Reservation of 1868, prior to which it was a Paiute habitat shared with western Navajos. The western and northern part of the region was annexed to the Navajo Reservation by an executive order of 1884. A portion later was restored to public domain, but again became the property of the Navajos by Act of Congress in 1934. Today, its population is almost totally Navajo, with some Paiutes married to Navajos.

In December 1879, or January 1880, two prospectors, Ernest Mitchell and James Merrick (Fletcher 1977, 68) were killed in the northern portion of the valley. Navajos, Utes, and Paiutes all blamed one another, though it seems Paiutes were the most likely culprits. Separated, each prospector died at the foot of a different sandstone monument that would later bear his name—Mitchell Butte and Merrick Butte.

In another story with many parallels, two prospectors named Sam Walcott and James Mc-

Nally were killed in 1884, south of the valley near Agathla Peak (El Capitan), by Hashké Neiniihí Biye' (commonly spelled Hoskinini Begay) Dinéts'ós'ósí. A military expedition accompanied by the Navajo agent, John Bowman, and his interpreter, Henry Chee Dodge, went to Monument Valley. All of the killers, with the exception of Hashké Neiniihí Biye', were apprehended. Unfortunately, his father, Hashké Neiniihí, the headman of the region, was imprisoned for some time for his son's misdeed (Van Valkenburgh 1941, 101).

Navajo mythology considers this region a giant hogan, with Gouldings as its fireplace and Sentinel and Gray Whiskers mesas being doorposts.

Many Anasazi ruins are found in Monument Valley, most of them small. In the 1930s, the Rainbow Bridge–Monument Valley expeditions conducted considerable research in the valley. Monument Valley Tribal Park contains 30,000 acres and was established by the Navajo Tribal Council on July 11, 1958.

In October 1925, a White man and his wife, Harry and "Mike" Goulding, arrived in the valley and claimed a stake, giving rise to Goulding's Trading Post (Moon 1992, 11). Harry was personally responsible for bringing the motion-picture industry to the valley.

Some of the landmarks of the valley for which Navajo names and/or historic/ceremonial information has been recorded include the following:

❖ CLY BUTTE: (5789 ft) Navajo County, AZ. Navajo: Possibly Tł'aa'í, "Left Handed." This sandstone feature of Monument Valley is located near the extreme northeastern corner of Navajo County. It is two miles southeast of Merrick Butte, a mile west of Spearhead Mesa, and immediately east of the slightly larger Elephant Butte. The name honors an old Navajo headman named Cly (Tł'aa'í), who died in 1934 and is supposedly buried at the foot of the butte (Klinck 1984, 117–18). The name Cly now appears as a Navajo surname.

❖ EAGLE MESA: (6200 ft) San Juan County, UT. Navajo: Uncertain. Also known as Eagle Rock Mesa. This mesa, rising some 800 ft above the floor of Monument Valley, lies two miles west of Saddleback and five miles north of Sentinel Mesa. According to Navajo mythology, this is where spirits go after death (McPherson 1992, 29).

✦ GRAY WHISKERS BUTTE: (5800 ft) Navajo County, AZ. Navajo: Dághaa' Łibáí or Bidághaa' Łibáí, "Gray Whiskers." This formation is located on the terrace forming the west slope of Mitchell Mesa. In Navajo mythology it is a doorpost of the giant hogan formed by Monument Valley. The other doorpost is Sentinel Mesa (McPherson 1992, 29).

✦ GYPSUM CREEK: (5600–4200 ft) San Juan County, UT, and Navajo and Apache counties, AZ. Navajo: Uncertain. A 25-mile-long dry wash heading in the vicinity of Sand Springs north of Hunts Mesa in Monument Valley. It flows northeast and north into Utah, merging with the San Juan River at Mexican Hat. This channel was named by John Wesley Powell's party of 1869, when they discovered a large deposit of gypsum in a canyon of the river (Van Cott 1990, 171).

✦ HOLE-IN-THE-ROCK MESA: (5800 ft) Navajo County, AZ. Navajo: Tségháhoodzání, "Perforated Rock." This mesa is actually a tributary of Hunt's Mesa, between Yeibichei Mesa and Triangle Mesa.

✦ MERRICK BUTTE: (4800 ft) Navajo County, AZ. Navajo: Uncertain. Named for James Merrick, partner of Ernest Mitchell (Correll 1971, 151; Crampton 1983, 123), for whom Mitchell Butte was named. This pair of ex-soldiers turned prospectors was killed in Monument Valley in December 1879 or January 1880, presumably by Utes or Paiutes. Each is said to have died near the butte now carrying his name.

Merrick has also been identified as *Charles* Merrick (McPherson 1988, 14) and James *Merritt* (McPherson 1988, 41–43). For more details, see Mitchell Butte, below.

✦ MITCHELL BUTTE: (6382 ft) Navajo County, AZ. Navajo: Tsé Ntsaa, "Big Rock" (Jett p.c. 1999). This sandstone feature of Monument

Valley is located in the far northeast corner of the Arizona portion of the valley, a mile northwest of Mitchell Mesa and a mile south of the Utah state line.

The butte was named for Ernest Mitchell, a prospector who intruded into the vicinity with James Merrick in 1879 (see Merrick Butte). These two "explorers" had trespassed into the Navajo realm in search of gold and silver, and had recently visited the mining district in southern Colorado to gain financial backing on the basis of silver ore samples they had collected from the Monument Valley region (Correll 1971, 151). Despite a warning from Navajos that they had been observed and would be killed if they returned to the valley, they returned (Klinck 1984, 30). Both were indeed killed during the expedition, but by Utes (Brugge 1964, 151–60) or Paiutes (Gillmore and Wetherill 1934, 96) rather than Navajos. Mitchell was shot as he emerged from a mine in the vicinity of this butte, and Merrick, fleeing on horseback, was shot at the foot of Merrick Butte a few miles distant.

Author's Note: There is considerable confusion in the literature over this incident. McPherson (1988) identifies this second individual both as *Charles* Merrick (p. 17) and James *Merritt* (pp. 41–42). Elizabeth Compton Hegemann (1963, 351), trading in the vicinity for years, claimed that Navajo Hoskinini Begay confessed to her at Shonto Trading Post that he and Klee Lagai Begay (Łííłai Biye', "Son of White Horse") killed Mitchell by accident while struggling over a new rifle of Mitchell's that Hoskinini Begay wanted to see. She suggests that the blame was shifted to the Paiutes by John and and Louisa Wetherill, who were friends of Hoskinini Begay and his father, chief Hoskinini, and who were known to dislike the Paiutes anyway. However, Hegemann apparently has the Mitchell-Merrick incident confused with the 1884 killing of two other prospectors, elderly Samuel Walcott and his younger partner, James McNally (Correll 1971, 159).

✦ MITCHELL MESA: (6371 ft) Navajo County, AZ. Navajo: Uncertain. An elongated formation immediately north of Wetherill Mesa in Monument Valley. The formation is really two broad, flat mesas joined by a narrow neck. Named after Ernest Mitchell (see Mitchell Mesa).

✤ MITTEN BUTTES: (6229 ft) Navajo County, AZ. Navajo: ʼÁlá Tsoh, "Big Hands" (Jett p.c. 1999). Two sandstone buttes, East Mitten and West Mitten, tower nearly 1000 ft above the valley floor in the extreme northern Arizona portion of Monument Valley. (Klinck [1984] refers to them as North Mitten and South Mitten, and his frontispiece map places the North Mitten in Utah.) East Mitten Butte is two miles northeast of Merrick Butte, and West Mitten Butte is one mile northwest. Navajo tradition holds that these formations are hands the deities left behind as a sign that the gods will return someday (McPherson 1992, 31). Granger (1960, 245) ascribes religious significance to these buttes.

✤ MYSTERY VALLEY: (5500 ft) Navajo County, AZ. Navajo: Tsé Bii' Ndzisgaii, "Treeless or Clearing Among the Rocks" (Young p.c. 1995). Though this name actually refers only to the southwest margin of Monument Valley, northeast of Wetherill Mesa, it is often applied to Monument Valley in its entirety. "Swirling, softly rounded sandstone wind sculptures, cascading and colliding, and overlapping like an enormous geologic souffle" (Cheek 1992, 46–53) characterize this feature. These frozen dunes are 50–100 ft high, broken by numerous slot canyons. Two major petroglyph sites are found in the valley, one at House of Many Hands, a three-room Anasazi ruin said to be haunted by Anasazi.

✤ NAATANI TSO: (6000 ft) San Juan County, UT. Navajo: Naat'áaniitsoh, "Big Leader." This spire is just northeast of the series of three that make up the formation known as "The Castle," and was probably once part of a continuation of elevated land connecting the Castle and Saddleback Butte.

✤ RAIN GOD MESA: (6000 ft) Navajo County, AZ. Navajo: Uncertain. This sizable, roughly oval mesa lies across the northern entrance to Tsé Biyi', between Spearpoint Mesa and the north end of Wetherill Mesa. This monolith was once known as Squaw Dance Mesa (Klinck 1984, frontispiece).

✤ SENTINEL MESA: (6350 ft) San Juan County, UT. Navajo: Tsé Awéé Yałtélí, "Rock holding a Baby" (Jett p.c. 1997). Six miles east of Goulding, and three miles south of Saddleback Butte and Eagle Mesa. In Navajo mythology, this mesa forms a doorpost (the other is Gray Whiskers Mesa) of a giant hogan that is Monument Valley (McPherson 1992, 29).

✤ TOTEM POLE ROCK: [DB (map 2)] (5600 ft) Navajo County, AZ. Navajo: Tsé Ts'óózi, "Slim Rock" (Jett p.c. 1999). A tall, columnar, sandstone spire, the northernmost of the Yeibichei Formation at the north end of Yeibichei Mesa (south of Gypsum Wash). Navajo tradition holds that this feature is a frozen Yei.

✤ TSE BIYI: (5300 ft) Navajo County, AZ. Also Tsay Begi. Navajo: Tsé Biyi, "Rock Canyon." A broad, flat valley within Monument Valley lies east of Wetherill Mesa and southeast of Mitchell Mesa.

✤ TSE BIYI YAZZI: (5300 ft) Navajo County, AZ. Also Tsay Begi Yazzi. Navajo: Tsé Biyi Yázhí, "Little Rock Canyon." A narrow valley in Monument Valley, lying immediately east of Yeibichei Mesa.

✤ YEI BICHEI FORMATION: (5600 ft) Navajo County, AZ. Navajo: Ye'ii Bicheii, Grandfather of the Ye'ii; the impersonator of Haashch'ééłti'í in the Night Chant, leader of the Yé'ii impersonators (Young and Morgan 1987, 756.) This series of sandstone spires at the north end of Yeibichei Mesa looks like a procession of Navajo Yé'ii (deity) figures. The northernmost figure is the Totem Pole.

MOUNTAIN MEADOWS: (1,737 ft) Washington County, UT. Navajo: Uncertain. This location is one of infamy in Mormon history, the scene of a massacre of Missouri emigrants headed toward California in 1857. Locals blamed Indians, but the blame finally came to rest on Mormons incensed by callous bragging by the wagoneers that they had played a role in the death of church founder Joseph Smith and the ouster of the Mormons from Missouri and Illinois in 1844. John D. Lee, founder of Lee's Ferry in Arizona, was a major player in this event.

A party of Indians killed three Mormons here in 1873. According to McPherson (1988, 16), this was possibly the same band of Paiutes and Navajos who attacked a group of miners near Needle Rock in Colorado about the same time.

NAAKAI CANYON: (6000–3600 ft) San Juan County, UT. Navajo: Naakai Kíhoniiłkaad, possibly meaning "Mexican Sloping Down" (Austin and Lynch 1983, 24). This steep-walled canyon is a southern tributary to the San Juan River on the west side of Naakai Mesa.

NASJA CREEK: (6000–3600 ft) San Juan County, UT. Navajo: Né'éshjaa', "The Owl" (Gregory 1915, 152). A tributary of the San Juan River Arm of Lake Powell, south of the second-to-last southerly gooseneck upstream from the Colorado River. It heads on the north slope of Navajo Mountain and flows into the lake at the same point as Bald Rock Canyon.

NASJA MESA: (4400 ft) San Juan County, UT. Navajo: See Nasja Creek. This landmark lies on the south bank of Lake Powell's main body and on the southwest bank of the San Juan River arm of the lake. It is bounded on the east by Nasja Creek and Bald Rock Canyon.

NATURAL BRIDGES NATIONAL MONUMENT: (6500 ft) San Juan County, UT. Navajo: Uncertain. Cass Hite visited this vicinity in the 1880s. In 1895 cattlemen Emory Knowles and James Scorup visited. It became a national monument in 1908 (WPA 1941b, 501). While the author unearthed no stories of Navajo activities in this region per se, it lies between such well-known Navajo enclaves as Bluff and the Bears Ears, and thus must have been frequented by the Diné.

NAVAJO MOUNTAIN: [DB] (10,388 ft) San Juan County, UT, Navajo County, AZ. Also Sierra Panoche (McNitt 1972:371) Navajo: Naat-sis'áán, said by Van Valkenburgh to refer to the head of the sacred female and pollen range of Navajo mythology. Young (p.c. 1995), however, asserts that this name actually defies analysis. Leighton and Kluckhohn (1947, 139) conjecture that the traditional, nonreligious Navajo name meant "Enemy Hiding Place," indicating it was in Paiute territory.

This high, rounded mountain straddles the Utah-Arizona state line, with most of it—including the highest peak—lying in Utah. It is situated east of Aztec Creek and south of the confluence of the San Juan and Colorado River arms of Lake Powell, some 90 miles north of Tuba City, Arizona, and 40 miles south of the Colorado River. It is the predominating landmark in western Navajo country. The Spanish Sierra Panoche means "Corn Mountain." John Wesley Powell first named it Mount Seneca Howland, after a member of his 1869 expedition, killed by parties unknown when he and two other men left the expedition part way through the canyon; the term Navajo Mountain was coined by Almon Thompson (Van Cott 1990, 270). Today, a chapter community named Navajo Mountain sits on the east slope of the mountain.

Author's Note: At first, the deaths of Seneca and his companions were blamed on the Shivwitz Indians (Powell 1895, 323), but an 1883 letter from William Leany (a resident of Harrisburg) to John Steele (of Toquerville) suggests that Mormons led by Eli N. Pace (a son-in-law of John D. Lee) killed the men in the Toquerville church ward (Anderson 1993, C7).

The mountain was visited by Antonio de Espejo's troops in 1583 (Richardson 1986); it was Espejo who labeled Sierra Panoche. That name is shown on McComb's map of 1860. In 1856, Major J. S. Simpson at Fort Defiance received information from friendly Paiutes that the Mormons had invited Navajos, Utes, and Mohaves to a council at Navajo Mountain. At this meeting, it was reported, arms were distributed to the Indians, and the United States government and its military represented as natural enemies of the Indians.

This region was a stronghold for Navajos as early as the first Spanish incursions into Navajoland. Headmen Hashké Neiniihii and Spane

Shank led refugees in the area during the Navajo Wars and the Bosque Redondo period (McPherson 1988, 9, 25). A wagon road to the foot of the mountain was not completed until 1925 (Leighton and Kluckhohn 1974, 143).

Van Valkenburgh suggests that during the Navajo Wars (1863–64), Navajo Mountain was used by the Army as a heliograph station, and beams were reflected over a series of mirrors to Fluted Rock and other points. Brugge (p.c. 1996), however, points out that the heliograph (signal mirror) had not been invented at this time.

This isolated dome dominating the horizon of the western Navajo country is regarded as sacred by the Navajos. They tell in their Blessing Side stories that Navajo Mountain represents the head of the female and pollen figure of Navajoland, called Tádídíín Dził ("Pollen Mountain") or Ni'go 'Asdzáán ("Earth Woman") (Luckert 1977, 5). This anthropomorphic formation includes Black Mesa as her body, and Balakai Mesa as her feet. Comb Ridge is one arm, and a monocline near Marsh Pass is the other. Tuba Butte and Agathla Peak are her breasts (McPherson 1992, 21).

Navajo Mountain is also a home of the Bear People of the Rounded Man Antway Myth (Wyman 1965), and figures prominently in the Navajo Coyoteway myth (Luckert 1979). T'áá'neiyá (Place of Raising) and Béésh Bee Hooghaní (Flint Hogan), two Navajo sacred places, sit atop the mountain.

Traditional Navajos are reluctant to climb above the lower elevations of the mountain and fear underground rumblings that are reported on the west slopes. Until the 1940s, very few Navajos would go north of the mountain into the broken country between there and the Colorado River, while Paiutes would regularly travel this section with no fear.

The only stand of limber pine (Pinus flexilis) in the Navajo country is found on Navajo Mountain. Rainbow Lodge and Trading Post on the south slope conducted business from the early 1920s until the mid-1950s (Kelley 1977, 254), and was formerly owned by the late Arizona Senator Barry Goldwater. This was only 50 straight-line miles from Gouldings, but 100 miles by road (Moon 1992, 104–5).

Rumors of silver being discovered on Navajo Mountain circulated in the 1860s, but the riches never materialized (McPherson 1988, 87).

NAVAJO MOUNTAIN TRADING POST: (6000 ft) San Juan County, UT. Navajo: See Navajo Mountain. Located in a side canyon of Piute Canyon, on the southeast slope of Navajo Mountain, four miles east of the highest peak. The post was opened between 1931 and 1935 (Kelley 1977, 254). This was also the site of a USIS day school that today is a public day school.

NESKAHI WASH: (6300–3600 ft) San Juan County, UT. Navajo: Neesk'áhí, named for Hastiin Neesk'áhí, "Old Man Fatty" (Kelley p.c. 1994). This minor tributary of the San Juan River Arm of Lake Powell heads on Piute Mesa near Thumb Rock. It flows northeast into the lake south of the Great Bend, east of Piute Creek.

NEVILLE TRADING POST: (4400 ft) San Juan County, UT. Navajo: Uncertain. This establishment was listed by Van Valkenburgh (1941, 97) as being on the north side of the San Juan River at Mexican Hat in 1941, and may have been known by the same name as that community.

NOKAI CANYON: [USGS] (7000–3600 ft) San Juan County, UT, Navajo County, AZ. Navajo: Naakaii, "Mexican." An extensive canyon network on the west flank of Nokai Mesa, heading in the steep broken canyons between Zilnez Mesa (on the west) and Skeleton Mesa in Arizona. It flows north 14 miles to the Utah state line, and another 15 miles to the San Juan River arm of Lake Powell. It enters the lake between Piute Mesa (on the west) and Nokai Mesa.

NOKAI DOME: (6045 ft) San Juan County, UT. Navajo: Naakaii, "Mexican." Rough, broken hilly mesa on the north bank of the San Juan River arm of Lake Powell, immediately west of Johnnies Hole and Castle Creek and across from the mouth of Nokai Canyon.

NOKAI MESA: [USGS] (6200 ft) San Juan County, UT, Navajo County, AZ. Navajo: Naakaii, "Mexican." A broad, broken upland between Nokai Canyon (on the west) and West Fork Copper Canyon, this mesa runs north-south approximately 25 miles. The north end of the mesa is capped by No Man's Mesa as it approaches the San Juan River arm of Lake Powell.

NOKAITO BENCH: (5000 ft) San Juan County, UT. Navajo: Naakaiitó, "Mexican Spring." The slightly elevated plain running north-south between Chinle Wash (on the west) and Gothic Creek. It extends from the juncture of Walker Creek and Chinle Wash in the south to the San Juan River in the north.

OLJETO: (4838 ft) San Juan County, UT. Also Oljaytoh, Moonlight. Navajo: 'Ooljéé'tó, "Moonwater." This chapter community and small agricultural area is located on Oljeto (Moonlight) Wash, at the northwest foot of Oljeto Mesa—on the western perimeter of Monument Valley about 25 miles northwest of Kayenta, Arizona. Water seeps out of the arroyo here and runs past Oljeto to drop into the San Juan River some seven miles east of Piute (Paiute) Farms. A trading post was established here by John and Louisa Wetherill and Clyde Coleville in 1906, near the camp of regional Navajo chief Hoskinini ("Handing Out War,"), actually Hashké Neiniihí (literally "The One Who Distributed Them [Sheep] Angrily Demanding that They Be Accepted"). They apparently did so with some peril to their lives, as they were the only Whites in the region. In 1910, John and Louisa Wetherill—who had moved to the region from Chaco Canyon—opened a post in Kayenta, thirty miles to the south, whose post office they boasted was the farthest distant from a railroad of any in the United States (McNitt 1962, 270–1).

Joseph Heffernan (son of Civil War General James J. Heffernan) built a new store here in 1921. (He also had posts at Aneth, Four Corners, and McElmo.) Heffernan died in 1925, and Harry Goulding of Goulding's had to go to Kayenta, Arizona, to get boards for a temporary coffin, in order to "get him out to where we could get a coffin" (Moon 1992, 25–26). The original trading post is now a Utah state historical site, amid a small community of a chapter house and homes.

OLJETO WASH: (5600–3600 ft) San Juan County, UT, Navajo County, AZ. Navajo: See Oljeto. This tributary of the San Juan River rises in a steep-walled, rugged canyon (tributary of Adahchijiyahi Canyon) on the northern end of Tyende Mesa in Arizona. It flows north 12 miles to the Utah state line, then another 20 linear (as opposed to river) miles past Oljeto Trading Post to join the San Juan five miles downstream (southwest) of the mouth of Grand Gulch.

PADRE BAY: (3600 ft) Kane County, UT. Navajo: Uncertain. Formerly Padre Canyon, this major bay of Lake Powell lies between Ramana Mesa (on the west) and Last Chance Bay. The bay is in what used to be Padre Canyon, and is named for the Crossing of the Fathers, the location at which Fathers Dominguez and Escalante crossed the Colorado River in 1776. The crossing is now under several hundred feet of water in the bay.

PANGUITCH: (6666 ft) Garfield County, UT. Navajo: Uncertain. The name is Paiute for "Water" or "Fish" (Van Cott 1990, 286). It was while visiting one of his wives in this little Mormon hamlet that John D. Lee was finally arrested for his involvement in the Mountain Meadows Massacre, after nearly 20 years of self-imposed exile at Lonely Dell—better known as Lee's Ferry, Arizona (McNitt 1962, 97–106). The community was settled in 1866 with the name "Fairview," but eventually drew its current name from the river on which it is situated and a nearby lake. In 1871, the Indian troubles led to evacuation of the town.

PIUTE CANYON: [DB, AP] (6800–650 ft) San Juan County, UT, and Navajo County, AZ. Also Paiute and Piute Creek. Navajo: Tsékooh, a common descriptive term for any rock canyon. The upper crossing is called Bá'azhchíní ("The One Who Gave Birth for Him," or "The Mother of His Child"). The middle crossing is known as Nastl'ah ("Long Box Canyon"), and the lower crossing is called Tiis naat'i ("Hanging Cotton-wood"). The bed of Piute Creek heads on the Shonto Plateau in northern Arizona, 20 miles northeast of Navajo Mountain, and runs 30 miles north to the San Juan River, the last 12 miles being in Utah. Beaver were still found at the mouth of the canyon in the 1940s.

This deep, rugged, and scenic canyon of red sandstone is the home of numerous Navajo and a few Piute summer farmers. According to local tradition, two Hopi women fleeing a drought were taken as slaves by prominent Navajos in the late 1890s and married into this band. In 1823, soldiers of Vizcarra's campaign reached this vicinity (Benally et al. 1982, 98).

The Paiutes are gradually becoming indistin-guishable from the Navajos, as these people have generally followed Navajo material culture in their mode of life. It was one of these people, Na'ahjaa Highe, who led John Wetherill and Byron Cummings to discover Rainbow Bridge.

According to Moon (1992, 107), this name was formerly applied to the location now known as Piute Farms, and Van Cott (1990, 297) described the canyon as the traditional boundary between the Navajos and the Paiutes.

PIUTE FARMS: [USGS] (3600 ft) San Juan County, UT. Also Paiute Canyon, Paiute Farms, Piute Parks (Van Valkenburgh 1941), Navajo Crossing, Clay Hill Crossing, and White Clay Crossing. Navajo: Báyóodzin Bikéyah, "Piute Fields." This relatively flat, desert farming area lies on the south bank of the San Juan River—at the mouth of Piute Farms Wash—about 45 miles upstream (east) of the confluence of the San Juan and Colorado rivers.

Once an old Piute farming area, this land at the San Juan River crossing (named Navajo Cross-ing on McComb's map of 1860) was later taken over by the Navajos. In 1912, the unusually high waters of the San Juan tore out a major amount of soil and waterlogged what was left. The tract is now deserted and overgrown by dense thickets of willows and many pools and marshy spots are found.

Many prospect holes dating back to the 1830s can be found in the vicinity. Around 1914, the region saw extensive drilling for oil.

Moon (1992, 107) says this location was formerly called Paiute (Piute) Canyon.

PIUTE MESA: [USGS] (6332 ft) San Juan County, UT, Navajo County, AZ. Navajo: Deez'á, "It extends" (Austin and Lynch 1983, 23). A long, narrow, high country running north-south between Zilnez (Dziłnééz) Mesa (south) and the Great Bend region of the San Juan River (north). It is bounded on the east by Nokai Canyon, and on the west by Piute Creek. Ap-proximately half the mesa's 10-mile length lies in Arizona.

In 1993, a Flagstaff corporation installed a state-of-the-art wind/solar-generated windmill to pump water to a 50,000-gallon storage tank on this mesa. The pump is fueled by the sun when the wind is still. This system replaces the Navajo Mountain Chapter's 30-year-old windmill at a cost of $17,000.

PIUTE STRIP: (approx. 4400–5700 ft) San Juan County, UT. Navajo: Uncertain. This strip of land between the San Juan River (on the north) and the Arizona state line (on the south) was added to the Navajo Reservation, along with land extending south to the northern boundary of the "Moqui" (Hopi) Reservation, by President Chester A. Arthur's executive order on May 17, 1884. It was removed to public domain by Presi-dent Benjamin Harrison's Executive Order of November 19, 1892 (Moon says by order of Inte-rior Secretary Albert B. Fall) to accommodate area developers. It was finally restored to the Navajo Reservation in 1933 (Correll and Dehiya 1978, 15–17).

PONCHO HOUSE: [DB] (4600 ft) San Juan County, UT. Navajo: Tséyaakin, "House Under the Rocks." This large, late Mesa Verde–type Anasazi cliff ruin is located in a large shallow cave on the west bank of Chinle Wash, some 10 miles south of that stream's juncture with the San Juan River. The English name derives from "a very unusual shirt made of four panels sewn to-gether, comprising the front, back and sleeves, with a slit for the head—much like a Mexican serape or poncho" (McGregor 1965, 341).

Poncho House was one of the first cliff pueblos

to be reported by W. H. Jackson, the photographer of the Hayden Survey in 1875. It was visited by Dr. S. J. Guernsey in the 1920s and by the Rainbow Bridge–Monument Valley Expedition in 1935. The cliff dwelling also has underlying strata of earlier phases of Anasazi culture.

RAINBOW BRIDGE (NATIONAL MONUMENT): [DB] (4000 ft) San Juan County, UT. Also Rainbow Bridge, Rainbow Natural Bridge. Navajo: Tsé'naa Na'ní'áhí, "Rock Span Across," Nageelid Na'nízoozhi, "Hole in the Rock Shaped like a Rainbow" (WPA 1941b, 508), and Nááts'íílid Na'nízhoozhí, "Rainbow Extends Across." Young (p.c. 1995) believes this latter name was applied by non-Navajos, possibly as erroneous translation, because Na'nízhoozhí refers to a bridge built by placing planks side by side. All names refer to a broad, arched, natural stone bridge located in Bridge Canyon, an east fork of Forbidding Canyon, some four miles upstream from the main channel of the San Juan River Arm of Lake Powell. This site is of religious significance to the Utes, Paiutes, and Navajos.

The bridge is situated 12 miles northwest of the heights of Navajo Mountain in broken and deep canyon country of extreme southern Utah. Rainbow Lodge, named after the span and run by Bill Wilson, was located on Navajo Mountain, and used to be the main starting point for 14-mile overland trips to the canyon and the bridge. It is now far easier to reach the bridge, presently a national monument, via boat on Lake Powell. National monument status was conferred by President Taft in 1910, setting aside 160 acres and providing for construction of a small dam to protect the feature.

The existence of this famed rock span arching over Bridge Canyon on its northwest meandering course to the San Juan River was known to the Paiutes and Navajos long before its "discovery" by Whites. William Boone Douglas, acting on information given him by a Paiute Indian, attempted to reach the bridge in November of 1908, but failed. It is possible that White beaver trappers may have seen the bridge in the nineteenth century, for it is known that Billy Mitchell, Fred Smith, W. C. Seifert, Hermann

Wolf, and other trappers worked the region (see Wolf Crossing). John Wetherill established a remote trading post in the vicinity in 1906, and the first Whites known for certain to have visited the bridge were Wetherill, Dr. Byron Cummings, and "Mr. Douglas" in September 1909. They were guided there by Nasja Begay and an unnamed Paiute. President Theodore Roosevelt visited the span in 1913 (WPA 1941b, 508).

Bridge Creek has cut a zigzag path through the salmon-red Navajo sandstone. No one knows how long ago one meander bored a hole through the sandstone, changing the stream's course. (The ancient bed of Bridge Creek can be seen to the northeast of the flying buttresses of the bridge.) Frost, rain, wind, and sun enlarged the hole. The span is truly colossal, measuring 309 feet high and 278 feet across (National Park Service 1926, 52), and the nation's capitol building in Washington, D.C. (as it stood in the 1920s) would fit beneath it.

Navajo mythology holds that the rainbow is an arch of two beings (male and female), frozen in place. From it come rainbows, clouds, and moisture for the reservation. Supernaturals traveled over the frozen rainbow. Sadly, excessive tourism has defiled the bridge and its canyon to the point that ceremonies are no longer performed there (McPherson 1992, 32).

The natural bridge's national monument status was used by environmentalists (led by the Sierra Club) to fight for several years the impending construction of Glen Canyon Dam. They pointed out that the resulting flood waters of Lake Powell would inundate Bridge Canyon and damage the National Monument—a violation of federal law. In order to appease the environmentalists, the federal government promised to build backwater dams preventing the waters from entering the canyon. (To further mollify the environmentalists, the feds further pledged to give up plans for a dam in Echo Park, on the Green River, a tributary of the Colorado. Nearly three hundred river miles upstream from Rainbow Bridge, this dam would have inundated Dinosaur National Monument on the Utah-Colorado state line.) With these concessions from the government, the Sierra Club, which had led the environmental opposition, actually gave tacit approval to Glen

Canyon Dam and the creation of Lake Powell in the fall of 1954.

However, protection of Rainbow Bridge evaporated in August 1956, when Interior Secretary Stuart Udall determined that the backwater dams would damage the site of the natural bridge more than the floodwaters. In June 1963, impounded waters intruded beneath the arch (Martin 1989, 9, 63–64, 240), and the subsequent influx of visitors has resulted in scores of insensitive tourists annually desecrating the Navajo, Ute, and Paiute sacred landmark by climbing upon it and passing beneath the arch.

Navajos credit Blind Salt clansmen with the initial discovery of the arch (Luckert 1977, 9), while rounding up horses. Possibly a member of Hoskinini's band, who never went to the Bosque Redondo.

In Echo Canyon (a tributary of Rainbow Canyon) there is a natural similar bridge known as Talking Rock, another site that is sacred to the Navajos (Luckert 1977, 16–17).

RECAPTURE CREEK: (9000–4000 ft) San Juan County, UT. Navajo: Dził Ditł'oo'í Bikooh, "Fuzzy Mountain Creek" (U.S. Indian Claims Commission n.d., vol. VI, vi). This stream rises on the southern slope of the Abajo Mountains, and flows south 35 miles. It is crossed by Utah Highway 47 four miles west of Blanding, and skirts to the east of White Mesa. It drains Bluff Bench and enters the San Juan River five miles east of Bluff.

This creek was named about 1877 by a man named Peter Shirts, who, for some reason, believed that the Aztec emperor Montezuma had escaped his Spanish captors in Mexico and was recaptured here (WPA 1941b, 34).

RED MESA: (5500 ft) San Juan County, UT. Navajo: Łíchíí Dah Azkání, "Red Mesa" (Kelley p.c. 1994). While the community of Red Mesa is located in Arizona at the junction of U.S. Highway 160 and Navajo Route 35, the Navajo chapter house is located in Utah, seven miles to the north on Navajo Route 35.

RED MESA TRADING POST: (approx. 5000 ft) San Juan County, UT. Navajo: Probably the same as the community and chapter. This post was opened by Gladwell Richardson in 1926 about seven miles north of the Utah state line on Navajo Route 35, near the present chapter house.

THUMB ROCK: (6515 ft) San Juan County, UT. Navajo: Tsé Íí'áhí, "Standing Rock," literally "Rock Extending (or Pointing) Up," though some translate it in this instance as "Thumb Rock." This small promontory sits atop Piute Mesa.

TSITAH WASH: (5400–550 ft) San Juan County, UT, and Apache County, AZ. Navajo: Tsiitah, "Among the Hair" (Young and Morgan 1987, 741). A dry wash east of White Mesa south of the San Juan River, intersecting the San Juan circa five miles upstream (southeast) of Aneth.

WHITE MESA VILLAGE: (5200 ft) San Juan County, UT. Navajo: Uncertain. A small Navajo village on the western arm of the V-shaped White Mesa, some eight miles south of the San Juan River and Utah Highway 262. It is 14 miles west of the Colorado state line.

WHITE ROCK VILLAGE: (approx. 4800 ft) San Juan County, UT. Navajo: Uncertain. A small Navajo community located on Navajo Route 35, five miles south of the San Juan River and the junction of Navajo Route 35 and Utah Highways 163 and 262.

WILLOW CREEK: (4350–3800 ft) Kane County, UT. Navajo: Uncertain. This tributary of the Escalante River heads at the foot of the Straight Cliffs of the Kaiparowits Plateau. It flows east about six miles into the Escalante six miles downstream (south) of the mouth of Coyote Creek. Benjamin Albert Wetherill and Alice Eastman (later Wetherill) traveled extensively along this stream in 1895, while Alice, a botanist, collected 475 specimens representing 162 varieties, including 19 that were new and mostly rare (Wetherill 1987, 213).

References

Aberle, David F. 1982. *The Peyote religion among the Navaho*. Chicago: University of Chicago Press.

———. 1983. Navajo economic development. In *Handbook of North American Indians,* vol. 10: *Southwest,* edited by Alfonso Ortiz. Washington: Smithsonian Institution.

Adair, John. 1944. *The Navajo and Pueblo silversmiths*. Norman: University of Oklahoma Press.

Adams, Eleanor B., and Fray Angelico Chavez. 1956. *The missions of New Mexico, 1776: A description by Fray Francisco Atanasio Dominguez with other contemporary documents*. Albuquerque: University of New Mexico Press (reprint).

Allen, T. D. 1963. *Navajos have five fingers*. Norman: University of Oklahoma Press.

Ambrose, James E. 1975. Plant resources of Canyon de Chelly National Monument. Manuscript, Western Archeological Center, Tucson.

Anderson, Bruce A. 1987. Wupatki National Monument: Exploring into prehistory. In *Exploration: Wupatki and Walnut Canyon. New perspectives in history, prehistory, rock art*, edited by David Grant Noble, 13–20. Santa Fe: School of American Research.

Anderson, Joseph K., and Susan E. Bearden. 1992. Data recovery at nine archaeological sites at Antelope Point, Coconino County, AZ. *Navajo Nation Papers in Anthropology* 27. Window Rock: Navajo Nation Archaeology Department.

Anderson, Vern. 1993. Did Mormons kill 3 explorers? Indians blamed in deaths of Powell's men. *Albuquerque Journal,* Nov. 28, 1993, C7.

Apache, Judy, and Rex Lee Jim. 1982. *Between sacred mountains*. Chinle, AZ: Rockpoint Community School.

Arnon, Nancy S., and W. W. Hill. 1979. Santa Clara Pueblo. In *Handbook of North American Indians,* vol. 9: *Southwest,* edited by Alfonso Ortiz, 296–307. Washington: Smithsonian Institution.

Austin, Martha, and Regina Lynch. 1983. *Saad Ahaah Sinil*. Dual Language, a Navajo-English Dictionary. Revised Edition. Edited by Martha Austin and Regina Lynch. Revisions by Regina Lynch. Chinle, AZ: Rough Rock Press.

Ayres, Mary C. 1931. History of Fort Lewis, Colorado. *The Colorado Magazine* 8 (3): 81–92. Denver: State Historical Society of Colorado.

Babbitt, James E. 1986. Trading posts along the Little Colorado River. *Plateau* 57 (3): 2–9.

Bailey, Garrick, and Roberta Glenn Bailey. 1986. *A history of the Navajos: The reservation years*. Santa Fe: School of American Research Press.

Bailey, Lynn R. 1964a. The long walk. A history of the Navajo Wars, 1846–68. *Great West and Indian Series* 26. Los Angeles: Westernlore Press.

———. 1964b. *The Navajo reconnaissance. A military exploration of the Navajo country in 1859 by Captain Joseph G. Walker and Major O. L. Shepherd*. Los Angeles: Westernlore Press.

———. 1966. *Indian slave trade in the southwest*. Los Angeles: Westernlore Press.

———. 1970. *Bosque Redondo. An American concentration camp*. Los Angeles: Socio-Technical Books.

Bandelier, Adolph F. 1890–1892. Final report of investigations among the Indians of the Southwestern United States, 1880–1885. Cambridge: *Papers of the Archaeological Institute of America, American Series,* 3–4, Parts 1–2.

Baars, Donald L. 1995. *Navajo country. A geology and natural history of the Four Corners region*. Albuquerque: University of New Mexico Press.

Basso, Keith H. 1996. *Wisdom sits in places*. Albuquerque: University of New Mexico Press.

Benally, Clyde, Andrew Wiget, John R. Alley, and Gary Blake. 1982. *Dineji Nakee Naahane. A Ute Navajo history*. Monticello, UT: San Juan School District.

Benavides, Fray Alonso de. 1630. *The memorial of Fray Alonso de Benavides*. Translated by C. E. Ayer; annotated by F. W. Hodge and C. F. Lummis. Chicago, privately printed, 1916.

Bennett, Noel, editor, and Tiana Bighorse. 1990. *Bighorse the warrior*. Tucson: University of Arizona Press.

Bingham, Sam, and Janet Bingham, editors. 1982. *Between sacred mountains: Navajo stories and lessons from the land*. Chinle, AZ: Rock Point Community School.

Blue, Martha. 1986. A view from the bullpen: A Navajo ken of traders and trading posts. *Plateau* 57 (3): 10–18.

Boaz, Franz. 1901–7. The Eskimo of Baffin Land and Hudson Bay. *Bulletin of the American Museum of Natural History* 15. New York.

Bodine, John J. 1979. Taos Pueblo. In *Handbook of North American Indians,* vol. 9: *Southwest,* edited by Alfonso Ortiz, 255–67. Washington: Smithsonian Institution.

Bohrer, Versilla L. 1972. The diffusion and utilization of cotton north of Mexico. Manuscript, Western Archeological Center, Tucson.

Bolton, Herbert E. 1949. *Coronado: Knight of pueblo and plains.* 1974 reprint, Albuquerque: University of New Mexico Press.

———. 1951. *Pageant in the wilderness*. Salt Lake City: Utah Historical Society.

Bradley, Zorro A. 1973. *Canyon de Chelly: The story of its ruins and people*. Washington: U.S. Department of the Interior, National Park Service, Office of Publications.

Brady, L. F. 1960. Dinosaur tracks from the Navajo and Wingate sandstones. *Plateau* 32 (4): 81–82.

Brandt, Elizabeth A. 1979. Sandia Pueblo. In *Handbook of North American Indians,* vol. 9: *Southwest,* edited by Alfonso Ortiz, 343–50. Washington: Smithsonian Institution.

Brew, J. O. 1979. Hopi prehistory and history to 1850. In *Handbook of North American Indians,* vol. 9: *Southwest,* edited by Alfonso Ortiz, 514–24. Washington: Smithsonian Institution.

Broder, Patricia Janice. 1990. *Shadows on glass: The Indian world of Ben Wittick.* Savage, MD: Rowman & Littlefield Publishers, Inc.

Brody, J. J. 1990. *The Anasazi.* New York: Rizzoli.

Brown, Donald N. 1979. Picuris Pueblo. In *Handbook of North American Indians,* vol. 9: *Southwest,* edited by Alfonso Ortiz, 268–77. Washington: Smithsonian Institution.

Brown, Gary. 1996. The protohistoric transition in the San Juan region. In *The archaeology of Navajo origins,* 47–70. Salt Lake City: University of Utah Press.

Brown, Gary M., and Patricia M. Hancock. 1992. The Dinetah phase in the La Plata Valley. In *Cultural diversity and adaptation: The Archaic, Anasazi and Navajo occupation of the Upper San Juan Basin,* 69–90. Cultural Resource Series No. 9. Santa Fe: Bureau of Land Management.

Brown, W. C., Gurovitz, and Supplee. 1892. "Certain reports on the condition of the Navajo Indian country." Washington: Ex. Doc. No. 68, 52nd Congress, 2nd Session.

Brugge, David M. 1964. Vizcarra's Navajo campaign of 1823. *Arizona and the West* 6 (3): 223–44.

———. 1965. Long ago in Navajoland. *Navajo Tribal Museum Series* 6. Window Rock.

———. 1972. The Navajo exodus. Archaeological Society of New Mexico Newsletter 2 (4, supplement), Las Cruces.

———. 1983. Navajo prehistory and history to 1850. In *Handbook of North American Indians,* vol. 10: *Southwest,* edited by Alfonso Ortiz, 489–501. Washington: Smithsonian Institution.

———. 1986. *Tsegai: An archeological ethnohistory of the Chaco region.* Washington: National Park Service.

———. 1993. *Hubbell Trading Post National Historic Site.* Tucson: Southwest Parks and Monuments Association.

Brundige-Baker, Joan. 1986. Restoration and preservation of historic trading posts. *Plateau* 57 (3): 26–31.

Bulow, Ernie. 1991. *Navajo taboos.* Gallup: Buffalo Medicine Books.

Bureau of Land Management. n.d. Pueblitos of the Dinetah. BLM-NM-GI-89-0029-4340. Washington: United States Department of the Interior.

Carlson, John B. 1983. Romancing the stone or moonshine on the sun dagger. Albuquerque: *Papers of the Maxwell Museum of Anthropology* 2: 77–88.

Carlson, John B., and W. James Judge. 1983. Astronomy and ceremony in the southwest. Albuquerque: *Papers of the Maxwell Museum of Anthropology* 2.

Carroll, Charles H. 1982. An ethnographic investigation of sites and locations of cultural significance to the Navajo people to be affected by PNM's Four Corners to Ambrosia to Pajarito 500 kv transmission project. Albuquerque: Public Service Company of New Mexico.

———. 1983. Ute mountain land exchange ethnographic study. Albuquerque: Public Service Company of New Mexico.

Catton, Bruce. 1960. *The American Heritage picture history of the Civil War.* New York: American Heritage Publishing Company, Bonanza Books.

Cerquone, Joseph. 1976. *In behalf of light: The Dominguez and Escalante expedition of 1776.* Denver: Dominguez and Escalante Expedition, Inc.

Chapin, Frederick H. 1892. *The land of the cliff dwellers.* Boston: Massachusetts Apalachian Club.

Cheek, Lawrence W. 1992. Mystery Valley—haunt of the Anasazi. *Arizona Highways* 68: 46–53.

Chilton, Lance, Katherine Chilton, Polly de Arango, James Dudley, Nancy Neary, and Patricia Stelzner. 1984. *New Mexico. A new guide to the colorful state.* Albuquerque: University of New Mexico Press.

Cirillo, Dexter. 1992. *Southwestern Indian jewelry.* New York: Abbeville Press.

Clemmer, Richard O. 1979. Hopi history, 1940–1970. In Handbook of North American Indians, vol. 9: *Southwest,* edited by Alfonso Ortiz, 533–38. Washington: Smithsonian Institution.

Colton, Harold S. 1939. Prehistoric culture units and their relationships in northern Arizona. *Museum of Northern Arizona Bulletin* 17. Flagstaff.

———. 1947. *Black sand: Prehistory in northern Arizona.* Albuquerque: University of New Mexico Press.

———. 1956. Names at Wupatki. *Plateau* 29 (1): 22–24.

Colton, Harold S., and Frank C. Baxter. 1932. Days in the Painted Desert and the San Francisco Mountains: A guide. *Northern Arizona Society of Science and Art Bulletin* 2. Flagstaff: Museum of Northern Arizona.

Connelly, John C. 1979. Hopi social organization. In *Handbook of North American Indians,* vol 9: *Southwest,* edited by Alfonso Ortiz, 539–53. Washington: Smithsonian Institution.

Cordell, Linda S. 1979. Prehistory: Eastern Anasazi. In *Handbook of North American Indians,* vol. 9: *Southwest,* edited by Alfonso Ortiz, 131–51. Washington: Smithsonian Institution.

———. 1984. *Prehistory of the southwest.* A volume in the New World Archaeological Record Series. A School of American Research Book. Boston: Academic Press, Inc., Harcourt, Brace, Jovanovich.

Correll, J. Lee. 1968. *Diné Bahaani'go Binaaltsoos Bik'ehgo Náhidízí.* Historical calendar of the Navajo people published to commemorate the 100th anniversary of the signing of the treaty of June 1, 1868. Window Rock, AZ: Navajo Tribal Museum.

———. 1971. Navajo frontiers in Utah and troublous times in Monument Valley. *Utah Historical Quarterly* 39 (2): 145–61.

———. 1976. *Through white men's eyes: A contribution to Navajo history.* Vol. I. Window Rock: Navajo Heritage Center.

Correll, J. Lee, and Alfred Dehiya. 1978. *Anatomy of the Navajo Indian reservation: How it grew.* Window Rock: Navajo Times Publishing Co.

Correll, J. Lee, and Editha L. Watson. 1974. *Welcome to the land of the Navajo: A book of information about the Navajo Indians.* Fourth Edition. Window Rock, AZ: Museum and Research Department, Navajo Tribe.

Courlander, Harold. 1982. *Hopi voices: Recollections, traditions and narratives of the Hopi Indians.* Albuquerque: University of New Mexico Press.

Crampton, C. Gregory. 1983. *Standing up country: The canyon lands of Utah and Arizona.* Salt Lake City: Gibbs M. Smith, Inc., Peregrine Smith Books.

Curtis, Edward S. 1922. *The Hopi.* Vol. 12 of *The North American Indian.* Reprint, New York and London: Johnson Reprint Co., 1970.

Dawson, Frank J. 1954. *Place names in Colorado: Why 700 communities were so named, 150 of Spanish or Indian origin.* Denver: Golden Bell Press.

Dockstaader, Frederick J. 1979. Hopi history, 1850–1940. In *Handbook of North American Indians,* vol. 9: *Southwest,* edited by Alfonso Ortiz, 524–52. Washington: Smithsonian Institution.

Dominguez, Fray Francisco Atanasio. 1956. *The missions of New Mexico.* Translated and annotated by Eleanor B. Adams and Fray Angelico Chavez. Albuquerque: University of New Mexico Press.

Downer, Alan S. 1990. Life on the reservation and historic preservation. In Preservation on the reservation: Native Americans, Native American lands and archaeology. *Navajo Nation Papers in Anthropology* 26: 201–4. Window Rock: Navajo Nation Archaeology Department and Navajo Nation Historic Preservation Department.

Dutton, C. E. 1885. Mount Taylor and the Zuni Plateau. *United States Geological Survey, 6th Annual Report,* 105–98.

Dyk, Walter. 1966. *Son of Old Man Hat: A Navajo Autobiography.* Lincoln: Bison Books, University of Nebraska Press.

Early, Frank Lee. 1976. Chaco Canyon. A study guide. *Museum Study Series* 2. Littleton, CO: Museum of Anthopology, Arapahoe Community College.

Edelman, Sandra A. 1979. San Ildefonso Pueblo. In *Handbook of North American Indians,* vol. 9: *Southwest,* edited by Alfonso Ortiz, 308–16. Washington: Smithsonian Institution.

Edelman, Sandra A., and Alfonso Ortiz. 1979. Tesuque Pueblo. In *Handbook of North American Indians,* vol. 9: *Southwest,* edited by Alfonso Ortiz, 330–35. Washington: Smithsonian Institution.

Eggan, Fred. 1979. Pueblos: Introduction. In *Handbook of North American Indians,* vol. 9: *South-*

west, edited by Alfonso Ortiz, 224–35. Washington: Smithsonian Institution.

Eggan, Fred, and T. N. Pandey. 1979. Zuni history, 1850–1979. In *Handbook of North American Indians,* vol. 9: *Southwest,* edited by Alfonso Ortiz, 474–81. Washington: Smithsonian Institution.

Eickemeyer, Carl. 1900. *Over the great Navajo trail.* New York: J. J. Little Company.

Eiseman, Fred B., Jr. 1959. The Hopi salt trail. *Plateau* 32 (2): 25, 32.

Ellis, Florence Hawley. 1974. *Navajo Indians I: An anthropological study of the Navajo Indians.* New York: Garland Publications.

———. 1979a. Isleta Pueblo. In *Handbook of North American Indians,* vol. 9: *Southwest,* edited by Alfonso Ortiz, 351–65. Washington: Smithsonian Institution.

———. 1979b. Laguna Pueblo. In *Handbook of North American Indians,* vol. 9: *Southwest,* edited by Alfonso Ortiz, 438–49. Washington: Smithsonian Institution.

Espinosa, Gilberto, translator. 1933. *A history of New Mexico, by Gaspar Perez de Villagra, Alcola 1610.* Los Angeles: The Quivira Society. Reprinted in 1962, Chicago: The Rio Grande Press.

Fall, Patricia L., James A. McDonald, and Pamela C. Magers. 1981. The Canyon del Muerto survey project: Anasazi and Navajo archeology in northeastern Arizona. *Publications in Anthropology* 15. Tucson: National Park Service Western Archeological Center.

Farella, John R. 1984. *The Main Stalk.* Tucson: University of Arizona Press.

Faris, James C. 1990. *The Nightway: A history and a history of documentation of a Navajo ceremonial.* Albuquerque: University of New Mexico Press.

Farmer, Malcolm A. 1954. An early visit to Canyon de Chelly, Arizona. *Plateau* 26 (4): 124–25.

Fassett, J. E., and J. S. Hinds. 1971. Geology and fuel reservoirs of the Fruitland Formation and Kirtland shale of the San Juan Basin, New Mexico and Colorado. Washington: *U.S. Geological Survey Paper* 676 (as quoted in Marshall, Stein, Loos, and Novotny 1979).

Ferguson, T. J., and E. Richard Hart. 1985. *A Zuni atlas.* Norman: University of Oklahoma Press.

Ferguson, William M., and Arthur H. Rohn. 1987. *Anasazi ruins of the southwest in color.* Albuquerque: University of New Mexico Press.

Fewkes, Jesse W. 1895. Preliminary account of an expedition to the cliff villages of the Red Rock country and the Tusayan ruins of Sikyatki and Awatobi, Arizona, in 1895. *Smithsonian Institution Annual Report,* 51–40.

Flint, Richard, and Shirley Cushing Flint. 1987. *A pocket guide to Chaco Canyon architecture.* Albuquerque: Century Graphics/Printing.

———. 1989. *Chacoesque: Chaco-like Great Pueblo architecture outside Chaco Canyon.* Albuquerque: Century Graphics/Printing.

———. 1991. *A field guide to Mesa Verde architecture.* Albuquerque: Century Graphics/Printing.

Foreman, Grant. 1941. *A pathfinder in the southwest: The itinerary of Lieutenant A. W. Whipple during his explorations for a railway route from Fort Smith to Los Angeles in the years 1853–54.* Chicago: Rio Grande Press.

Franciscan Fathers. 1910. *An ethnographic dictionary of the Navajo language.* St. Michaels, AZ: St. Michaels Press.

Frazer, Robert W. 1972. *Forts of the west: Military forts and presidios and posts commonly called forts west of the Mississippi River to 1898.* Norman: University of Oklahoma Press.

Frazier, Kendrick. 1986. *People of Chaco. A canyon and its culture.* New York: W. W. Norton and Co.

Frink, Maurice. 1968. *Fort Defiance and the Navajos.* Boulder: Fred Pruett.

Fugate, Francis L., and Roberta B. Fugate. 1989. *Roadside history of New Mexico.* Missoula: Mountain Press Publishing Co.

Gabriel, Kathryn. 1991. *Roads to Center Place: A cultural atlas of Chaco Canyon and the Anasazi.* Boulder: Johnson Books.

Garcia-Mason, Velma. 1979. Acoma Pueblo. In *Handbook of North American Indians,* vol. 9: *Southwest,* edited by Alfonso Ortiz, 450–66. Washington: Smithsonian Institution.

Giese, Dale F. 1991. *Echoes of Bugle: Forts of New Mexico.* Silver City, NM: Self-published.

Gill, Sam D. 1983. Navajo views of their origin. In *Handbook of North American Indians,* vol. 10: *Southwest,* edited by Alfonso Ortiz, 502–5. Washington: Smithsonian Institution.

Gillmore, Frances, and Louisa Wade Wetherill. 1934. *Traders to the Navajo: The story of the Wetherills of Kayenta.* Reprint, Albuquerque: University of New Mexico Press, 1953.

Gladwell, Richardson. 1986. *Navajo traders.* Tucson: University of Arizona Press.

Goodman, James M. 1982. *The Navajo atlas.* Norman: University of Oklahoma Press.

Goodman, Linda J., and Daisy F. Levine. 1990. The mines of the Cerrillos District, New Mexico: Myths and realities. *El Palacio* 96 (1): 22–37.

Granger, Byrd H. 1960. *Will C. Barnes' Arizona place names.* Revised and enlarged edition of 1935 publication by Will C. Barnes. Tucson: University of Arizona Press.

Greg, Josiah. 1967. *Commerce of the prairies.* Lincoln: University of Nebraska Press.

Gregory, Herbert E. 1915. The Navajo country, a geographic and hydrological reconnaissance of parts of Arizona, New Mexico and Utah. Washington: *U.S. Geological Survey Professional Paper* 93.

Gumerman, George J. 1970. Black Mesa: Survey and excavation in northeastern Arizona, 1968. Prescott College Press Studies in Anthropology 2. Prescott, AZ: Prescott College Press.

Gumerman, George J., Deborah Westfall, and Carol S. Weed. 1972. Archaeological investigations on Black Mesa. The 1969–1970 seasons. Prescott College Studies in Anthropology 4.

Gunnerson, Dolores A. 1974. *The Jicarilla Apaches: A Study in Survival.* DeKalb: Northern Illinois University Press.

Guterson, Ben. 1994. The vanishing trading post: Reservation landmarks struggle to survive. *New Mexico Magazine* 72, no. 8 (August).

Haile, Father Berard. 1938a. Origin legend of the Navajo Enemy Way. New Haven: *Yale Publications in Anthropology* 17.

———. 1938b. Navajo chantways and ceremonials. American Anthropologist 40(4): 639–52.

———. 1947. *Prayer stick cutting in a five night Navajo ceremonial of the male branch of Shootingway.* Chicago: University of Chicago Press.

———. 1950. *Legend of the Ghostway, ritual in the male branch of Shootingway.* St. Michaels, AZ: St. Michaels Press.

———. 1978. *Love magic and the butterfly people: The Slim Curley version of the Ajilee and Mothway myths.* Flagstaff: Musuem of Northern Arizona.

Hammond, George P., and Agapito Rey, editors and translators. 1940. *Narratives of the Coronado expedition, 1540–1542.* Albuquerque: University of New Mexico Press.

———. 1966. *The rediscovery of New Mexico, 1580–1594.* Coronado Historical Series 3. Albuquerque: University of New Mexico Press.

Harrington, John P. 1945. Note on the names Moqui and Hopi. *American Anthropologist* 47 (1): 177–78.

Harris, Arthur H., James Schoenwetter, and A. H. Warren. 1967. An archaeological survey of the Chuska Valley and the Chaco Plateau, Part I: Natural Science Studies. *Museum of New Mexico Research Records* No. 4. Santa Fe.

Hartman, Russel P., and Jan Musial. 1987. *Navajo pottery: tradition and innovations.* Flagstaff, AZ: Northland Press.

Haskell, J. Loring. 1987. *Southern Athapaskan migration, A.D. 200–1750.* Tsaile, AZ: Navajo Community College.

Hazen-Hammond, Susan. 1993. Antoine Leroux: The frontier guide history forgot. *Arizona Highways* 69 (7): 34–37.

Hegemann, Elizabeth Compton. 1963. *Navajo trading days.* Albuquerque: University of New Mexico Press.

Hendricks, Rick, and John P. Wilson. 1996. *The Navajos in 1705: Roque Madrid's campaign journal.* Albuquerque: University of New Mexico Press.

Hewitt, Edgar L. 1906. Origin of the name Navajo. *American Anthropologist,* n.s., 8: 193.

Hilleson, K. 1988. *Route 66 revisited. A wanderer's guide to New Mexico.* Vol. II of *Albuquerque to the Arizona Border.* Albuquerque: D. Nakii Enterprises.

Hodge, Frederick W. 1910. The handbook of the American Indian. *Bureau of American Ethnology* 30 (2 volumes).

———. 1937. *The history of Hawikuh.* Los Angeles: Southwest Museum.

Hoebel, E. Adamson. 1979. Zia Pueblo. In *Handbook of North American Indians,* vol. 9: *Southwest,* edited by Alfonso Ortiz, 407–17. Washington: Smithsonian Institution.

Hoffman, Virginia, and Broderick H. Johnson. 1970. *Navajo biographies.* Rough Rock, AZ: Dine, Inc., and the Board of Education, Rough Rock Demonstration School.

Houser, Nicholas P. 1979. Tigua Pueblo. In *Handbook of North American Indians,* vol. 9: *Southwest,* edited by Alfonso Ortiz, 336–42. Washington: Smithsonian Institution.

Hughes, John T. 1962. *Doniphan's expedition: An account of the U.S. Army operations in the great American southwest.* Chicago: Rio Grande Press. First published in 1848 by J. A. and U. P. James, Cincinnati.

Iverson, Peter. 1981. *The Navajo nation.* Albuquerque: University of New Mexico Press.

James, Charles D. 1976. Historic Navajo studies in northeastern Arizona. *Museum of Northern Arizona Research Paper 1.* Flagstaff: Museum of Northern Arizona.

James, George W. 1917. *Arizona the wonderland.* Boston: Page.

James, H. L. 1988. *Rugs and posts.* West Chester, PA: Schiffer Publishing, Ltd.

James, Harry C. 1974. *Pages from Hopi history.* Tucson: University of Arizona Press.

Jenkins, Myra Ellen, and Ward Alan Minge. 1974.

Record of Navajo Activities affecting the Acoma-Laguna area, 1746–1910. In *Navajo Indians*, vol. II, 95–324. New York: Garland Publishing Co.

Jett, Stephen C. n.d. Place names in Canyon de Chelly. Unpublished 1995 manuscript used by permission of the author.

Jett, Stephen C., editor. 1974. The destruction of Navajo orchards in 1864: Captain John Thompson's report. *Arizona and the West* 16 (4): 365–78.

Johnston, Denis F. 1982. Trends in Navaho population and education 1870–1955. Appendix A in *The Peyeote religion among the Navaho*, by David F. Aberle, second edition, 357–75. Chicago: University of Chicago Press.

Jones, Oakah L., Jr. 1966. *Pueblo warriors and the Spanish conquest*. Norman: University of Oklahoma Press.

Judd, Neil M. 1964. The architecture of Pueblo Bonito. *Smithsonian Miscellaneous Collections* 147 (1). Washington: Smithsonian Institution.

Julyan, Robert H. *Place Names of New Mexico.* Albuquerque: University of New Mexico Press.

Keleher, William A. 1952. *Turmoil in New Mexico, 1846–1868*. Santa Fe: Rydal Press.

———. 1962. *The fabulous frontier*. Albuquerque: University of New Mexico Press.

Kelley, Klara Bonsack. 1977. Commercial Networks in the Navajo-Hopi-Zuni Region. Ph.D. diss., University of New Mexico.

———. 1985. Ethnoarchaeology of Navajo trading posts. *The Kiva* 51 (1): 19–37.

Kelley, Klara Bonsack, and Harris Francis. 1994. *Navajo sacred places*. Bloomington and Indianapolis: Indiana University Press.

Kelly, Lawrence C. 1963. The Navajo Indians: Land and Oil. *New Mexico Historical Review* 38 (1): 1–28.

———. 1967. Where was Fort Canby? New Mexico Historical Review 40 (1): 49–62.

Kidder, Alfred V. 1920. Ruins of the historic period in upper San Juan Valley, NM. *American Anthropologist* 22.

Klesert, Anthony L. 1979. Black Mesa culture history and research design. In *Excavations on Black Mesa, 1978: A descriptive report,* edited by Anthony L. Klesert and Shirley Powell, 27–54. Southern Illinois University at Carbondale. Center for Archaeological Investigations Research Paper 8.

Klinck, Richard C. 1984. *Land of room enough and time enough*. Salt Lake City: Gibbs M. Smith Inc., Peregrine Smith Books. Reprint of 1953 original.

Kluckhohn, Clyde M. 1927. *To the foot of the rainbow*. New York: Century and Co.

———. 1944. *Navajo witchcraft*. Cambridge: Peabody Museum of Archaeology and Ethnology. Reprinted by Beacon Press, Boston, 1967.

———. 1967. *To the foot of the rainbow: The beautiful Four Corners country*. Glorieta, NM: The Rio Grande Press. Reprint of 1927 original, Century Co., New York.

Kluckhohn, Clyde, and Dorothea Leighton. 1962. *The Navajo*. New York: American Museum of Natural History, Doubleday and Co.

Kluckhohn, Clyde, and Leland C. Wyman. 1940. An introduction to Navaho chant practice. *Memoirs of the American Anthropological Association* 53.

La Farge, Oliver. 1959. *Santa Fe: The autobiography of a southwestern town*. Norman: University of Oklahoma Press.

Lambert, Marjorie F. 1979. Pojoaque Pueblo. In *Handbook of North American Indians,* vol. 9: *Southwest,* edited by Alfonso Ortiz, 324–30. Washington: Smithsonian Institution.

Lange, Charles H. 1979a. Cochiti Pueblo. In *Handbook of North American Indians,* vol. 9: *Southwest,* edited by Alfonso Ortiz, 366–78. Washington: Smithsonian Institution.

———. 1979b. Santo Domingo Pueblo. In *Handbook of North American Indians,* vol. 9: *Southwest,* edited by Alfonso Ortiz, 379–89. Washington: Smithsonian Institution.

Lange, Charles H., and Carroll L. Riley, editors. 1966. *The southwestern journals of Adolf F. Bandelier. 1880–1882*. Albuquerque: University of New Mexico Press.

———. 1970. *The southwestern journals of Adolf F. Bandelier. 1883–1884*. Albuquerque: University of New Mexico Press.

Lavender, David. 1954. *Bent's fort*. Lincoln: University of Nebraska Press.

———. 1980. *The southwest*. Albuquerque: University of New Mexico Press.

Leighton, Dorothea, and Clyde Kluckhohn. 1974. *Children of the people: The Navajo individual and his development*. New York: Octagon Books. Reprint of 1947 edition.

Lekson, Stephen H., Thomas C. Windes, John R. Stein, and W. James Judge. 1988. The Chaco Canyon community. *Scientific American* 259 (1): 100–109.

Leslie, Lewis Burt, editor. 1929. *Uncle Sam's camels: The journal of May Humphreys Stacey supplemented by the report of Edward Fitzgerald Beale (1857–1858)*. Cambridge: Harvard University Press. 1970 Rio Grande Press, Inc. Reprint.

Linford, Laurance D. 1982. Settlement and land use patterns in the forest highlands of the Navajo Nation. In Archaeological survey in the forest highlands of the Defiance Plateau and Chuska Mountains, Navajo Nation, by Laurance D. Linford and Teri Cleeland. Window Rock: *Navajo Nation Papers in Anthropology*, No. 6.

Linford, Laurance D., editor. 1982. Kayenta Anasazi archaeology on central Black Mesa, northeastern Arizona: The Piñor Project. Window Rock: *Navajo Nation Papers in Anthropology,* No. 10.

Link, Martin. 1993. Navajo two-dimensional art: A product of a centuries old tradition. *Inter-Tribal America Magazine.*

Linthicum, Leslie. 1997. A century of trading. Trading post stays true to its roots. Albuquerque Journal, August 3, 1997, Section B (Dimension): 1, 8.

Lister, Robert H., and Florence C. Lister. 1983. *Those who came before: Southwestern archeology in the national park system.* Globe, AZ: Southwest Parks and Monuments Association.

Locke, Raymond F. 1992. *The book of the Navajo.* Los Angeles: Mankind Publishing Co. Fifth edition.

Lomatuway'ma, Michael, Lorena Lomatuway'ma, and Sidney Namingha, Jr. 1993. *Hopi ruin legends.* Compiled and edited by Ekkehart Malotki. Flagstaff: Northern Arizona University Press.

Long, Paul V., Jr. 1960. Archaeology of the Curtain Cliff Site. *Plateau* 33 (1): 17–18.

———. 1992. *Big eyes: The southwestern photographs of Simeon Schwemberger.* Albquerque: University of New Mexico Press.

Luckert, Karl. 1975. *Navajo hunter tradition.* Tucson: University of Arizona Press.

———. 1977. Navajo Mountain and the Rainbow Bridge religion. *American Tribal Religions* 1. Flagstaff: Museum of Northern Arizona.

———. 1978. *A Navajo bringing home ceremony: The Claus Chee Sonny version of Deerway: Ajilee.* Flagstaff: Museum of Northern Arizona.

———. 1979. *Coyoteway: A Navajo Holyway ceremonial.* Tucson: University of Arizona Press.

Malville, J. McKim, and Claudia Putnam. 1989. *Prehistoric astronomy in the southwest.* Boulder: Johnson Publishing Company.

Mangum, Neil C. 1991. Old Fort Wingate in the Navajo war. *New Mexico Historical Review* 66 (4) 392–412.

Marsh, Charles S. 1982. *People of the shining mountains.* Boulder: Pruett Publishing Co.

Marshall, Michael P., John R. Stein, Richard W. Loos, and Judith E. Novotny. 1979. *Anasazi communities of the San Juan Basin.* Public Service Company of New Mexico and the New Mexico Historic Preservation Bureau, Planning Division, Department of Finance and Administration of the State of New Mexico.

Martin, Russell. 1989. *A story that stands like a dam: Glen Canyon and the struggle for the soul of the west.* New York: Henry Holt and Co.

Matson, Dan S., and Albert H. Schroeder. 1957. Cordero's description of the Apache, 1796. New Mexico Historical Review 32 (4): 335–56.

Matthews, Washington. 1897. Navajo legends. *American Folklore Society, Memoir No. 5.*

Mays, Buddy. 1982. *Ancient cities of the southwest.* San Francisco: Chronicle Books.

———. 1985. *Indian villages of the southwest.* San Francisco: Chronicle Books.

McDonald, James A. 1976. An archeological assessment of Canyon de Chelly National Monument. Tucson: *Western Archeological Center Papers in Anthropology* 5.

McGregor, John C. 1965. *Southwestern archaeology.* Urbana: University of Illinois Press.

McNitt, Frank. 1962. *The Indian traders.* Norman: University of Oklahoma Press.

———. 1966. *Richard Wetherill: Anasazi.* Albuquerque: University of New Mexico Press. Revised edition.

———. 1972. *Navajo wars.* Albuquerque: University of New Mexico Press.

McPherson, Robert S. 1988. *The northern Navajo frontier, 1860–1900: expansion through adversity.* Albuquerque: University of New Mexico Press.

———. 1992. *Sacred land, sacred view: Navajo perceptions of the Four Corners region.* Provo, UT: Charles Redd Center for Western Studies, Brigham Young University. Salt Lake City: Signature Books.

Mercurio, Gian, and Maxymilian L. Peschel. 1991. *Mesa Verde. A complete guide.* Cortez, CO: Lonewolf Publishing.

Miksa, Elizabeth. 1992. Geology of Antelope Point. Appendix A in Data Recovery at Nine Archaeological Sites at Antelope Point, Coconino County, AZ, by Joseph K. Anderson and Susan Bearden. *Navajo Nation Papers in Anthropology* 27. Window Rock: Navajo Nation Archaeology Department.

Miller, William C. 1955. Two possible astronomical pictographs found in northern Arizona. *Plateau* 27 (4) 6–12.

Mindeleff, Cosmos. 1891. Traditional history of Tusayan. In A study of Pueblo architecture: Tusayan and Cibola, edited by Victor Mindeleff, 3–228. Bureau of American Ethnology, Eighth Annual Report for the years 1886–87. Washington: Smithsonian Institution.

Moon, Samuel. 1992. *Tall sheep: Harry Goulding, Monument Valley trader.* Norman: University of Oklahoma Press.

Moore, J. B. 1987. A Collection of Catalogues Published at Crystal Trading Post 1903–1911. J. B. Moore, United States Licensed Indian Trader. Albuquerque: Avanyu Publishing, Inc.

Morris, Don P. 1986. *Archeological investigations at Antelope House.* Washington: National Park Service.

Morse, Frances. 1992. House of the Badlands: North America's first catacombs. *Inter-Tribal America Magazine*, 34–37.

Murphy, Lawrence R. 1973. Cantonment Burgwin, New Mexico, 1852–60. *Arizona and the West* 15 (1): 5–26.

National Park Service. 1926. *Glimpses of our national monuments*. Washington: Government Printing Office.

Newberry, J. S. 1859. Geology of the banks of the San Juan. In *Exploring expedition from Santa Fe to the junction of the Grand and Green rivers*. Washington: U.S. Government Printing Office.

Newcomb, Franc J. 1964. *Hasteen Klan. Navajo medicine man and sandpainter*. Norman: University of Oklahoma Press.

———. 1966. *Navajo neighbors*. Norman: University of Oklahoma Press.

New Mexico Office of Cultural Affairs. 1991. *New Mexico cultural resources directory: The complete guide to arts, history and community events*. Santa Fe: Musuem of New Mexico Press.

Noble, David Grant. 1981. *Ancient ruins of the southwest: An archaeological guide*. Flagstaff: Northland Publishing Co.

Noe, Sally. 1992. *66 sights on Route 66: A guide to Gallup, New Mexico, McKinley County and Indian country*. Gallup: Gallup Downtown Development Group.

———. 1993. Pawn: A Gallup tradition. *Inter-Tribal America Magazine*, 30–34.

O'Brian, Aileen. 1956. The Dineh: Origin myths of the Navajo Indians. *Bureau of American Ethnology Bulletin* 163.

Ormes, Robert, and the Colorado Mountain Club. 1970. *Guide to the Colorado mountains*. Chicago: Sage Books, The Swallow Press, Inc.

O'Rourke, Paul M. 1980. Frontier in transition. A history of southwestern Colorado. *Cultural Resource Series* 10. Denver: Bureau of Land Management, Colorado State Office.

Ortiz, Alfonso. 1979. San Juan Pueblo. In *Handbook of North American Indians,* vol. 9: *Southwest,* edited by Alfonso Ortiz, 278–95. Washington: Smithsonian Institution.

Oxford University. 1989. *Oxford dictionary of the English language*, vol. VII. Oxford: Clarendon Press.

Pearce, T. M. 1965. *New Mexico place names: A geographical dictionary*. Albuquerque: University of New Mexico Press.

Pilles, Peter J., Jr. 1987. The Sinagua: Ancient people of the Flagstaff region. In *Exploration: Wupatki and Walnut Canyon. new perspectives on history, prehistory, rock art*, edited by David Grant Noble, 2–12. Santa Fe: School of American Research.

Plog, Fred. 1979. Prehistory: Western Anasazi. In *Handbook of North American Indians,* vol. 9: *Southwest,* edited by Alfonso Ortiz, 108–30. Washington: Smithsonian Institution.

Pousma, R. H. 1934. *He who always wins*. Grand Rapids: Wm. B. Eerdmans Publishing Co.

Powell, J. W. 1887. *The Mountain Chant: A Navajo ceremony*. Fifth Annual Report of the Bureau of Ethnology to the Secretary of the Smithsonian Institution 1883–84. Washington. (Reprinted 1970 by Rio Grande Press, Glorieta, NM.)

———. 1895. *Canyons of the Colorado*. New York: Flood and Vincent. (Reprinted 1961 by Dover Publications, New York.)

Preston, Douglas. 1992. *Cities of gold. A journey across the American southwest in pursuit of Coronado*. New York: Simon and Schuster.

Preston, Robert A., and Ann L. Preston. 1983. Evidence for calendric function at 19 prehistoric sites in Arizona. In Astronomy and ceremony in the southwest, edited by John B. Carlson and W. James Judge, 191–204. Albuquerque: *Papers of the Maxwell Museum of Anthropology* 2.

Reed, Lori Stephens, and Paul F. Reed. 1992. The protohistoric Navajo: Implications of interaction, exchange and alliance formation with eastern and western pueblos. In *Cultural diversity and adaptation: The Archaic, Anasazi and Navajo occupation of the Upper San Juan Basin*. Cultural Resource Series No. 9, 91–104. Santa Fe: Bureau of Land Management.

Reed, Paul F. 1992. Upland adaptations in lower Glen Canyon during the archaic and pueblo periods. Archaeological data recovery at 20 sites along the Antelope Point Road (Route N22B) near Page, AZ. *Navajo Nation Papers in Anthropology* 28. Window Rock: Navajo Nation Archaeology Department.

Reeve, Frank D. 1956. Early Navajo geography. *New Mexico Historical Review* 31 (3): 290–309.

———. 1958. Navajo-Spanish wars, 1686–1720. *New Mexico Historical Review* 33 (2): 205–31.

———. 1959. The Navajo-Spanish peace, 1720s–1770s. *New Mexico Historical Review* 34 (1): 8–40.

———. 1974. The Navajo Indians. In *Navajo Indians*, vol. II, 235–335. New York: Garland Publishing Co.

Reichard, Gladys A. 1974. *Navajo religion: A study of symbolism*. Princeton University Press. (As reproduced by the University of Arizona Press, 1983.)

Richardson, Gladwell. 1986. *Navajo traders*. Tucson: University of Arizona Press.

Roberts, Alexandra. 1987. The Wupatki Navajos: An historical sketch. In *Exploration: Wupatki and*

Walnut Canyon. New Perspectives on History, Prehistory, Rock Art, 28–35. Santa Fe: School of American Research.

———. 1990. Navajo ethnohistory and archeology. In *The Wupatki archeological inventory survey final report,* edited by Bruce Anderson, 6.1–6.115. Santa Fe: Southwest Regional Offices, National Park Service.

Roberts, Frank H. H. 1929. Shabik'eschee village, a late Basketmaker site in the Chaco Canyon, New Mexico. *Bureau of American Ethnology, Bulletin* 92. Washington: Smithsonian Institution.

Roberts, Willow. 1987. *Stokes Carson: Twentieth-century trading on the Navajo reservation.* Albuquerque: University of New Mexico Press.

Robinson, Skerry. 1994. *El Malpais, Mount Taylor and the Zuni Mountains: A hiking guide and history.* Albuquerque: University of New Mexico Press, Coyote Books.

Roessel, Robert A., Jr. 1983a. Navajo history, 1850–1923. In *Handbook of North American Indians,* vol. 10: *Southwest,* edited by Alfonso Ortiz, 506–523. Washington: Smithsonian Institution.

———. 1983b. *Dinetah: Navajo History, vol. II.* Rough Rock, AZ: Navajo Curriculum Center and Rough Rock Demonstration School.

Roessel, Ruth. 1983. Navajo arts and crafts. In *Handbook of North American Indians,* vol. 10: *Southwest,* edited by Alfonso Ortiz, 592–604. Washington: Smithsonian Institution.

Roessel, Ruth, and Broderick H. Johnson. 1974. *Navajo livestock reduction: A national disgrace.* Tsaile, AZ: Navajo Community College Press.

Rogers, Larry. 1990. *Chapter images: 1989.* Window Rock: Navajo Nation Division of Community Development.

Sando, Joe S. 1979. Jemez Pueblo. In *Handbook of North American Indians,* vol. 9: *Southwest,* edited by Alfonso Ortiz, 418–29. Washington: Smithsonian Institution.

Schaafsma, Curtis F. 1996. Ethnic identity and proto-historic archaeological sites in northwestern New Mexico: Implications for reconstructions of Navajo and Ute history. In *The archaeology of Navajo origins,* 19–46. Salt Lake City: University of Utah Press.

Schaafsma, Polly. 1987. Rock art of Wupatki: Pots, textiles, glyphs. In *Exploration: Wupatki and Walnut Canyon: New perspectives on history, prehistory, rock art,* 21–27. Santa Fe: School of American Research.

Schmedding, Joseph. 1974. *Cowboy and Indian trader.* Albuquerque: University of New Mexico Press. Original edition, Caldwell, ID: Caxton Printers, Ltd., 1951.

Schroeder, Albert H. 1961. Puerco Ruin excavations,
Petrified Forest National Monument, Arizona. *Plateau* 33 (4): 93–104.

———. 1963. Navajo and Apache relationships west of the Rio Grande. *El Palacio* 70: 5–21.

———. 1965. *A colony on the move: Gaspar Castano de Sosa's journal: 1590–1591.* Santa Fe: School of American Research.

———. 1979a. Pueblos abandoned in historic times. In *Handbook of North American Indians,* vol. 9: *Southwest,* edited by Alfonso Ortiz, 236–54. Washington: Smithsonian Institution.

———. 1979b. Pecos Pueblo. In *Handbook of North American Indians,* vol. 9: *Southwest,* edited by Alfonso Ortiz, 430–37. Washington: Smithsonian Institution.

Schwartz, Douglas W. 1983. Havasupai. In *Handbook of North American Indians,* vol. 10: *Southwest,* edited by Alfonso Ortiz, 13–24. Washington: Smithsonian Institution.

Sessions, Steven E., and Wayne W. Williams. 1979. Navajo settlement. In The Archaeology of Southwest Gallegos Mesa: The EPCC Survey Project. *Navajo Nation Papers in Anthropology* 1. Steven E. Sessions, editor. Window Rock, AZ: Navajo Nation Cultural Resource Management Program.

Sleight, Frederick W. 1950. Navajo Sacred Mountain of the East—A Controversy. *El Palacio* 58 (12).

Smith, Duane A. 1992. *Rocky mountain boom town: A history of Durango, CO.* Niwot, CO: University of Colorado Press. First printed in 1980, revised in 1986 and 1992.

Sofaer, Anna P., and Rolf M. Sinclair. 1983. Astronomical markings at three sites on Fajada Butte. In Astronomy and ceremony in the southwest, edited by John B. Carlson and W. James Judge, 43–72. Albuquerque: *Papers of the Maxwell Musuem of Anthropology.*

Southwest Parks and Monuments Association. 1989. Motoring Guide to the North Rim of Canyon de Chelly. Pamphlet. Tucson.

———. 1991. Motoring Guide to the South Rim of Canyon de Chelly. Pamphlet. Tucson.

Spencer, Katherine. 1957. Mythology and values: An analysis of Navajo Chantway myths. *Memoirs of the American Folklore Society* 48. Philadelphia.

Spencer, Virginia E., and Stephen C. Jett. 1971. Navajo dwellings of rural Black Creek Valley in Arizona and New Mexico. *Plateau* 43 (4): 159–73.

Spicer, Edward H. 1962. *Cycles of conquest: The impact of Spain, Mexico and the United States on the Indians of the southwest, 1533–1960.* Tucson: University of Arizona Press.

Spiers, Randall H. 1979. Nambe Pueblo. In *Handbook of North American Indians,* vol. 9: *Southwest,* edited by Alfonso Ortiz, 317–23. Washington: Smithsonian Institution.

Spurr, Kimberley. 1993. NAGPRA and archaeology on Black Mesa, Arizona. Navajo Nation Archaeology Department: Navajo Nation Papers in Anthropology No. 30.

Steen, Charlie R. 1966. Excavations at Tse ta'a, Canyon de Chelly National Monument. *National Park Service Archeological Series* 9.

Stirling, Betty. 1961. *Mission to the Navajo*. Mountain View, CA: Pacific Press Publishing Associates.

Stribling, C. K. 1986. New Mexico, A county series: vol. IV, San Juan. Truth or Consequences, NM: The Talking Boy.

Strong, Pauline Turner. 1979a. San Felipe Pueblo. In *Handbook of North American Indians,* vol. 9: *Southwest,* edited by Alfonso Ortiz, 390–97. Washington: Smithsonian Institution.

———. 1979b. Santa Ana Pueblo. In *Handbook of North American Indians,* vol. 9: *Southwest,* edited by Alfonso Ortiz, 398–406. Washington: Smithsonian Institution.

Tedlock, Dennis. 1979. Zuni religion and world view. In *Handbook of North American Indians,* vol. 9: *Southwest,* edited by Alfonso Ortiz, 499–508. Washington: Smithsonian Institution.

Teller, Irving. 1954. Coolidge and Thoreau: Forgotten frontier towns. *New Mexico Historical Review* 29 (3): 210–23.

Thomas, D. H. 1978. *The southwestern Indian detours.* The Story of the Fred Harvey/Santa Fe Railway Experiment in "Detourism." Phoenix: Hunter Publishing Co.

Thompson, Gerald. 1976. *The Army and the Navajo: The Bosque Redondo reservation experiment, 1863–1868.* Tucson: University of Arizona Press.

Thybony, Scott. 1987. *Fire and stone: A road guide to Wupatki and Sunset Crater national monuments.* Tucson: Southwest Parks and Monuments Association.

———. 1988. *Walnut Canyon National Monument.* Tucson: Southwest Parks and Monuments Association.

Tiller, Veronica E. 1983. Jicarilla Apache. In *Handbook of North American Indians,* vol. 10: *Southwest,* edited by Alfonso Ortiz, 440–62. Washington: Smithsonian Institution.

Towner, Ronald H., and Jeffrey S. Dean. 1992. LA 2298: The oldest pueblito revisited. *The Kiva* 57 (4): 315–29.

Trimble, Marshall. 1986. *Roadside history of Arizona.* Roadside History Series. Missoula: Mountain Press Publishing Company.

Turner, Christy G., III. 1960. Mystery canyon survey: San Juan County, Utah, 1959. *Plateau* 32 (4): 73–81.

Turner, Ronald F. 1996. *The archaeology of Navajo origins.* Salt Lake City: University of Utah Press.

U.S. Indian Claims Commission. n.d. "Proposed Findings of Fact in Behalf of the Navajo Tribe of Indians in the Area of Overall Navajo Claim" (Docket 229). Vol. I, Findings 1–12; vol. II, Findings 13–14; vol. III, Findings 15–17; vol. IV, Findings 18–19; vol. V, Findings 20–22; vol. VI, Appendices (Appendix A-1, Alphabetical Index of Navajo Place Names Relative to the Navajo Land Claim).

U.S. National Commission on Libraries and Information Service. 1992. Pathways to excellence. Improving library and information services for Native American peoples. Summary Report.

Van Arsdale, Perry C. 1971. Pioneer New Mexico. Limited Edition Map. Self-published.

Van Cott, John W. 1990. *Utah place names.* Salt Lake City: University of Utah Press.

Van Valkenburgh, Richard F. 1938. *A short history of the Navajo people.* Window Rock: U.S. Department of the Interior Navajo Service.

———. 1941. Diné Bikéyah ("Navajo's Land"). 197-page typed, mimeographed, Office of Indian Affairs document. Window Rock, AZ.

———. 1974. *Navajo sacred places.* First Report presented before the Indian Claims Commission, Docket No. 229, Plaintiff Exhibit No. 687. New York: Garland Publishing Co. Inc.

Van Valkenburgh, Richard F., and Frank O. Walker. 1945. Old place names in Navajo country. *Master Key,* vol. XIX, No. 3, 89–94.

Velez de Escalante, Silvestre. 1976. *The Dominguez-Escalante journal. Their expedition through Utah, Arizona and New Mexico in 1776.* Edited by Fray Angelico Chavez and Ted J. Warner. Provo: Brigham Young University Press.

Vogler, Lawrence E. 1993. The Navajo Indian irrigation project. Chapter One in Daa'ak'eh Nitsaa: An Overview of the Cultural Resources of the Navajo Nation Indian Irrigation Project, Northwestern New Mexico, by Lawrence E. Vogler, Kristin Langenfeld, and Dennis Gilpin. *Navajo Nation Papers in Anthropology* 29. Window Rock: Navajo Nation Archaeology Department.

Vogt, Evon Z. 1961. Navajo. In *Perspectives in American Indian cultural change*, edited by Edward H. Spicer. Chicago: University of Chicago Press.

Vogt, Evon Z., and Ethel M. Albert, eds. 1970. *The People of Rimrock: A study of values in five cultures.* New York: Atheneum.

Voth, Henry R. 1905. *The traditions of the Hopi.* Field Columbian Museum 96, Anthropological Series 8.

Ward, Al E., Emily K. Abbink, and John R. Stein. 1977. Ethnohistorical and chronological basis of the Navajo material culture. In *Settlement and subsistence along the lower Chaco River*, edited by Charles A. Reher, 217–76. Albuquerque: University of New Mexico Press.

Ward, Geoffrey C. (with Ric Burns and Ken Burns). 1990. *The Civil War: An illustrated history.* New York: Borzoi Books, Alfred A. Knopf.

Waters, Frank. 1963. *Book of the Hopi.* New York: Viking Press.

Watson, Edith L. 1964. *Navajo sacred places.* Window Rock: Navajo Tribal Museum.

Wetherill, Benjamin Alfred. 1987. *The Wetherills of Mesa Verde.* Edited and annotated by Maurine S. Fletcher. Lincoln and London: University of Nebraska Press.

Wendorf, Fred. 1951. Archaeological investigations in petrified forest: Twin Butte site, a preliminary report. *Plateau* 24 (2): 77–83.

Wheelwright, Mary C. 1942. Creation myth. The story of the emergence. By Hosteen Uclah, recorded by Mary C. Wheelwright. *Navajo Religion Series* 1. Santa Fe: Museum of Navajo Ceremonial Art.

Widdison, Jerold Gwayn. 1959. Historical geography of the middle Rio Grande Valley. *New Mexico Historical Review* 34 (3): 248–84.

Williams, Jerry I., and Paul E. McAllister. 1979. *New Mexico in maps.* Albuquerque: University of New Mexico, Technology Application Center, Institute for Applied Research Services.

Williams, Lester L. 1989. *C. N. Cotton and his Navajo blankets.* Albuquerque: Avanyu Publishing Company.

Williamson, Ray A. 1983. Light, shadow, ritual and astronomy in Anasazi structures. In Astronomy and ceremony in the southwest, edited by John B. Carlson and W. James Judge, 99–120. Albuquerque: *Papers of the Maxwell Museum of Anthropology* 2.

———. 1987. *Living the sky: The cosmos of the American Indian.* Norman: University of Oklahoma Press.

Wilson, Alan, with Gene Dennison, Navajo Consultant. 1995. *Navajo place names: An observer's guide.* Guilford, CT: Audio Forum, Jeffrey Norton Publishers.

Witherspoon, Gary. 1977. *Language and art in the Navajo universe.* Ann Arbor: University of Michigan Press.

———. 1983a. Navajo social organization. In *Handbook of North American Indians,* vol. 10: *Southwest,* edited by Alfonso Ortiz, 524–35. Washington: Smithsonian Institution.

———. 1983b. Language and reality in Navajo world view. In *Handbook of North American Indians,* vol. 10: *Southwest,* edited by Alfonso Ortiz, 570–78. Washington: Smithsonian Institution.

Wood, John J., Walter Vanette, and Michael J. Andrews. 1979. *Sheep is life: A sociocultural assessment of the livestock reduction program in the Navajo-Hopi joint use area.* Flagstaff: Northern Arizona University Anthropology Paper No. 1.

Woodbury, Richard B. 1979. Zuni prehistory and history to 1850. In *Handbook of North American Indians,* vol. 9: *Southwest,* edited by Alfonso Ortiz, 467–73. Washington: Smithsonian Institution.

Worcester, Donald E. 1951. The Navajo during the Spanish regime. *New Mexico Historical Review* 26: 101–18.

WPA (Work Projects Administration, Writer's Program). 1940a. *Arizona. A guide to the Grand Canyon state.* Revised 1960 by Joseph Miller. New York: Hastings House.

———. 1940b. *New Mexico. A guide to the colorful state.* New York: Hastings House.

———. 1941a. *Colorado. A guide to the highest state.* New York: Hastings House.

———. 1941b. *Utah. A guide to the state.* New York: Hastings House.

Wyman, Leland C. 1957. *Beautyway: A Navajo ceremonial.* Told by Singer Man; Father Berard Haile, trans. (Bollingen Series J3). New York: Pantheon Books.

1962. *Windways of the Navajo.* Colorado Springs: Taylor Museum.

———. 1965. *Red Antway of the Navajo.* Santa Fe: Museum of Navajo Ceremonial Art.

———. 1975. *The Mountainway of the Navajo.* Tucson: University of Arizona Press.

———. 1983. Navajo ceremonial system. In *Handbook of North American Indians,* vol. 10: *Southwest,* edited by Alfonso Ortiz, 536–57. Washington: Smithsonian Institution.

Wyman, Leland C., and Clyde Kluckhohn. 1938. Navajo classification of their song ceremonials. *Memoirs of the American Anthropological Association* 50.

Yazzie, Ethalou, editor. 1971. *Navajo history.* Rough Rock, AZ: Rough Rock Demonstration School.

Young, M. Jane. 1983. The nature of the evidence: Archaeoastronomy in the prehistoric southwest. In Astronomy and ceremony in the southwest, edited by John B. Carlson and W. James Judge, 169–89. Albuquerque: *Papers of the Maxwell Museum of Anthropology* 2.

Young, Robert W. 1961. The Navajo yearbook. 1951–1961, A decade of progress. *Report No. viii.*

Window Rock, AZ: Department of the Interior, Bureau of Indian Affairs, Navajo Area Office.

———. 1972. The rise of the Navajo tribe. In *Plural societies in the southwest*, edited by Edward M. Spicer and Raymond H. Thompson, 167–238. Albuquerque: University of New Mexico Press.

Young, Robert W., and William Morgan. 1947. Navajo place names in Gallup, New Mexico. *El Palacio* 57 (12): 238–85.

———. 1987. *The Navajo language. A grammar and colloquial dictionary*. Albuquerque: University of New Mexico Press.

Zeilik, Michael. 1983. Anticipation in ceremony: The readiness is all. In Astronomy and ceremony in the southwest, edited by John B. Carlson and W. James Judge, 25–41. Albuqerque: *Papers of the Maxwell Museum of Anthropology 2*.

Zolbrod, Paul G. 1984. *Diné Bahane', The Navajo creation story*. Albuquerque: University of New Mexico Press.

A NOTE ON PERSONAL COMMUNICATIONS (P.C.) REFERENCES

Throughout this volume there are references identified as "p.c." ("personal communication"). These refer to instances where the information was provided to the author by an individual through conversation and/or written materials. Descriptions of these communications follow:

Bennett, p.c. 1993: Kay Bennett, noted Navajo performer and author, provided conversational information on several Navajo place names.

Brugge, p.c. 1996: David Brugge, retired archaeologist and Navajo historian for the National Park Service, reviewed approximately 80 percent of the seventh draft of the manuscript. His input was invaluable in discovering many typographical errors as well as errors in transcription from the author's notes to the written page. He also added a substantial amount of new information concerning historical people, events, and places.

Clah, p.c. 1994: Dennis Clah, a Navajo civil engineer with the Bureau of Indian Affairs Branch of Roads, provided maps and conversational information on the Navajo translations and meanings of several Navajo places.

Jett, p.c. 1999: Steve Jett, in addition to sharing from his unpublished manuscript on Canyon de Chelly (cited above), also provided an eleventh-hour list of Monument Valley names and translations.

Kelley p.c. 1994: Klara Kelley, then a contractor to the Navajo Nation Office of Historic Preservation, reviewed much of the fourth draft of the manuscript, and also searched for the Navajo translations to a sizable list of place names.

Link p.c. 1993 and 1997: Martin Link, former Navajo Tribal Archaeologist and Tribal Museum Director, and currently publisher of the Indian Trader newspaper, was able to provide information on some obscure topics, thanks to his extensive knowledge of things Navajo, as well as his continual networking on and around the reservation.

Malone p.c. 1988 and 1997: I first became acquainted with Bill Malone when he ran Piñon Trading Post and my archaeological crew purchased supplies from him in 1979 and 1980. We have held many conversations about Navajo weaving and silversmithing, and Navajo places. It was after he took over at Hubbell Trading Post that I obtained the data included in this volume.

Navajo Place Names Project p.c. 1994. Clay Slate and Lydia Fasthorse Begay of the Navajo Place Names Project met with me at their offices at Diné College in Shiprock in the fall of 1994. They showed me a video presentation of Navajo elders discussing—in Navajo—little-known sacred places on the reservation. Clay and Lydia provided some unpublished project papers that contained a few place names, but cautioned me that those discussed by the elders were not for publication. I have abided by their wishes.

Young, p.c. 1995: Professor Robert Young reviewed the sixth draft of the manuscript in the summer of 1995. His written comments were extensive, his scrutiny intensive. While his primary focus was on the translations and interpretations of Navajo words and the proper spelling thereof (including all the requisite diacriticals), he also was able to provide considerable historical and political information.

Index

Author's note: This volume is an inventory of places. Accordingly, the index includes only places, and not the people and/or events associated with them. (To include these would have meant virtually repeating the entire manuscript.) To the best of my ability, all places within the text have been listed alphabetically herein, and page numbers included for all pages on which the place appears.

If a place appears as an entry in the text, the page number on which that entry appears is listed in bold type. All other page numbers refer to "mentions in passing."

English translations of Navajo names appear in quotations, just as they do in the text. (If the Navajo translation happens to be the same as the common English name, the name will appear twice in the index—once with quotations and once without.)

Glottal stops (') are treated as the first letter of the alphabet, preceding even the letter "A."

Thus, 'Abétó will precede Abajo. However, in order to simplify a search, Navajo words beginning with an apostrophe are listed in the index under the first vowel following the apostrophe. This means that instead of listing all the Navajo words beginning with apostrophes at the beginning of the index, those beginning with 'A- are included at the beginning of the A's, those beginning with 'I- are included with the I's, and so forth.

Many place names represent more than one place. I have, to the best of my ability, indicated such in this index, by identifying state, county or other identifiers for such places. In cases where a name indicates both a feature and a community, the community is indicated by the initials of the state in which the community lies.

Other than the glottal stop, the presence of diacriticals (such as the accents) does not affect the location of the word in the listing; they are simply listed alphabetically.

'Aba'tó
'Abestoh (see Zuni River)
'Abétó (see Zuni River), 283
'Ada'ooldoní (Canyon de Chelly), 47
'Adáá Dik'á, 124
'Adáá' Hwiidzoh, 150
'Adáá'dilkóóh, 124
'Adáágíi Łichi'i, 173
'Adah 'Ahodoonilí, 61
'Adah Ch'íjíyáhí, 33
'Adahiilí, 84
'Adahiilíní, 84
'Adah Hosh Łání, 110
'Adeií Tó, 143
'Aghaałá, 33
'Ah Ba Deel Hadisa, 72
'Ahidiidłi, 114

'Ahidiidlíní, 55
'Ahidazdiigaii, 227
'Ahideelk'id, 195
'Ahidiidlí, 114
'Ahihodiiteel, 178
'Ahoyoolts'ił, 98, 115
'Ak'ehal'í, 57
'Ak'i Dah Nást'ání, 201
'Ak'iih Dah Nast'ání, 201
'Ak'iih Nást'ání, 218
'Alnaashii Ha'atiin, 59
'Alnaashii Háálíní, 214
'Alnaashii Ha'atiin Hayázhí, 55
'Ałtíí Ál'í Bikooh, 290
'Ałníi'gi, 147
'Ałtíí Jik'áshí, 114
'Ałts'óózí Deezz'á, 196
'Anaa' Sin Yił Haayáhí, 50

'Anaa'task'ai'i, 216
'Anaasází Bikin, 150
'Anaasází Bikooh, 162
'Anaasází Habitiin, 57
'Anabi'ání, 178
'Ane'étséyi', 55
'Aniłt'ánii Dził, 221
'Asaa' Si'á, 294
'Asaats'iil, 112
'Ásaayi', 172, 178
'Asdzání Ayáásh Bitooh, 117
'Asdzání Bitł'aa' Bikooh, 117
'Asdzání Habitiin, 47
'Asdzání Taah Yíyá, 66
'Asdząą Łigaaí Habitiin, 55
'Asdząą Łigaaí Kits'iilí, 55
'Asdząąts'ósí, 34
'Asga Dah Sitání, 57, 60

'Ashį́įh, 95, 284
'Áshįįh Bikooh Yázhí, 105
'Áshįįh Łibáhí, 170
'Áshįįh Náá'á, 254
'Ashiih Nabitiin, 127
'Ashíshjíízh Sikaad Ha'atiin, 63
'Ashíshjíízh Sikaad Nástl'ah, 63
'Ata'adeez'a, 55
'Ata'deez'á Hayázhí, 58
'Ata' Ha'atiin, 62
'Ata' Ha'atiin Nástl'ah, 62
'Atíin Honítzaa, 62
'Atsá Bitó, 243
'Atsé Hooghan, 46
'Awéé Haazhilizhí, 56
'Awéé Hajiloh, 57
'Ayahkin, 90
'Ayahkinii, 87
'Ayánii Bitó', 220
'Azee Łich'íí', 276
'Azee' Dích'ií', 129
'Azéé' Díílid, 179
'Azee' Łichíí' Bikooh, 276
'Azhei, 52
'Azhííh Naachii', 159
"(A) Broad Strip of Land (Valley) Extends to the River", 177
"(A) Crowd is returning with Feathers", 151
Abacus (see Hawiku), 283
Abajo Mountains (also Blue Mountains), **285**
Abajo Peak, 285
"Abalone Shell Mountain", 128
Abiquiu, NM, 7, 9 (Table 5), 11, **169**, 278, 289
Abiquiu–San Juan route, 284
"Abundant Water", 193
Ackmen Trading, 25
Acoma Pueblo, **169–70**: peaceful relations of with Spaniards, 6; Navajo raids at, 11; as possible oldest continuously occupied North American community, 94; refugees from flee to Lybrooks area, 230
Acomita, NM **170**, 170
Acus, 170, 232
Adahchijiyahi Canyon, **33**
Adamana, AZ, 73
"Adobe Mesa", 268
"Adobe Spire", 36
Adultery Dune, **45**
"Adultery Sand", 45
"Against the Cliff Wall", 273

Agassiz Peak, 128–29
Agate House Ruin, **33**, 119
Agathla Peak, **33**, 34, 70, 296, 300
"Agave Slope", 146
Agua Azul (see Bluewater), 178
Agua de San Carlos, 190
Agua Salada, 183–84
Agua Sal Creek, **33**
Agua Vibora, 119
Ahshislepah Wash, **170**
Alamo, NM (also Puertocito, Field), **170–71**
Alamo Navajo Reservation, 170, 266
Albuquerque, NM, 9(Table 5), **171**: Albuquerque to Fort Whipple Star Mail Route, 66; residents settle Cubero, NM, 199; road to Fort Defiance, 209; citizen A. B. McGaffey opens sawmill at McGaffey, NM, 233; Navajo goods peddled in streets, 261; Albuquerque–Zuni Road, Albuquerque–Wingate Valley Road, 284
Alcatraz Prison, 88, 94
Algert, 41
Algert, C. H., Trading Co., 25, **171**
"Alien Ancestor's House", 150
"Alkaline Water", 268
"Alkaline Water Coming Out", 164
Allegro Mountain, **171–72**
Allen Canyon, 121
Allentown, AZ, **34**, 192
Allentown Ruin, **34**
Alsada Canyon, 121
"Always Beaten Up's Spring", 50
"Always Winter People", 223
Ambrosia Lake, **172**
Ames and Scott's Trading, 286
Amity, AZ, 132
"Among the Adobe Formations", 176
"Among the Adobes", 222
"Among the Cliff Edges", 139
"Among the Hair", 304
"Among the Oaks", 192
"Among the Rabbit Brush" (Chrysothamnus naneosus var. graveolens), 71
"Among the Red Areas": 118 (Painted Desert); 291 (Halchita, UT)

"Anasazi House", 150
"Anasazi Trail", 57
Anderson Mesa (and Point), **34**
Aneth, UT, 135, 162, **285**, 301
Aneth Strip, 285
Aneth Trading Post, 25, 272, **286**
Angel Peak (also Angel's Peak), **172**, 219
"Angry Warrior", 95
"Animals fall into Deep Water", 100
Animas City, CO, **151**, 156
Animas River, 155, 156, **172**
"Another Place Named Onions", 213
Anseth (see Aneth, UT), 285
"Antelope Ascending Trail", 34
Antelope House, 43, **57**, 60
"Antelope Lookout", 172, 175 (Becenti Chapter)
Antelope Lookout Mesa, **172**
Antelope Pass, **34**
"Antelope Refuge", 134
"Antelope Spring", 34: Jeddito, AZ, 99
Antelope Springs Trading Post, 26, **34**
Antelope Trail, 57
Anzac, **172**
"Archery Rock", 48
Arches National Monument, **286**
"Area Bounded by a Circle of Rocks", 11, 277
"Area in One's Back Between the Shoulder Blades", 73
"Area Tapers at the Base", 36 (Bitsiuitsos), 150 (near Yale Point)
"Area that Extends Out Yellow and Green", 126
Arizona, **34**
"Armpit", 114
Arnold, Albert, Trading Post, 25
Arroyo de Carrizo, 85, 107
Arroyo de los Algodones, 112
Arroyo de los Pilares, 72
Arroyo de Moqui, 121
Asaayi Lake, **172**
"Ascending Lamb Trail", 178
"Ascending Wagon Road", 71
Ashcroft Trading Post, 26, 248
"Ash Mountain", 256
Asti'olakwa, 222
Aspen Canyon, **52**
"Aspen Trail", 52

"Aspen Trail Up Out", 52
Atarque, **173**, 232
Atarque Trading Co., 173
"At Flows Repeatedly Rockside",
45
Atsina, 205
"At the Base of a Cliff", 36
"At the Boat", 103
"At the Place of the (Bell) Peals",
171
Awatovi, **89**, 92
Azansosi Mesa, **34**, 130
Aztec, NM, **173**
Aztec Creek, 290
Aztec Ruin, 172, **173**, 189, 253

B and B Trading Co. (B & B
Trading), 26, 264
Ba'ádíwei, 41
Bá'azhchíní, 301
Baa'oogeedí, 145
Bááh Díílid, 211
Bááh Háálí, 179
Báálók'aa'í, 34
Baashzhinii Dziil, 157
Babbitt and Roberts Trading Post,
34
Babbitt's Trading Post, 26, 100
"Baby Is Customarily Hoisted Up
(with a Rope)", 57
Baby Pee(d) Trail, **56**
Baby Rocks, **34**, 75
"Baby Rocks", 34
Baby Rocks Trading Post, 25, 34
Baby Trail, 57
Baca, NM, 245
"Back Canyon", 55
"Back of Deer", 39
"Back of in Between The Rocks",
55
Baakavi, 93
Bacavi (also Bacabi, Bakabi), AZ,
93
Bacon Springs, 195, 213
Bacon Springs Trading Post, 26
"Badger", 237
Badger Butte, 87
Badger Springs, 237
Bad Land, The, 204
Bad Trail, **62**
Bad Trail Cove, 46
"Bad Trail Up", 62
Báhástł'áh, 273: Twin Lakes, NM,
277
Balakai (also Salahkai, Balukai)

Mesa, 33, **34**, 64, 70, 91, 127,
300
Balakai Point, 35
Balanced Rock, **56**
Balcomb, Spencer, Trader, 26, 127
"Bald Mountain", 150
"Balding Mountain", 150
Ballard Trading Co., 26
Ballejos, 256
Banded Mountain, 157
Bandera Volcano, 219
Bandolier National Monument,
247
Barber Peak, **174**
Bare Rock Trail, **56**
Barringer Crater, 110, 42
Basneyaah, 273
Bat Canyon, **54**
Bat Rock, 54
Bat Woman Ruin, 115
Báyóodzin Bikéyah (see Piute
Farms), 302
Báyóodzin Bikéyah, 120
Be'ek'id 'Ahoodzání, 119
Be'ek'id Di'níní, 35
Be'ek'id Halchíí', 122
Be'ek'id Halchíídéé', 36
Be'ek'id Halgaa, 53
Be'ek'id Halzhiní, 37
Be'ek'id Halehu Dee, 36
Be'ek'id Hatsoh, 35, 67
Be'ek'id Hóneez, 229
Be'ek'id Hoteel, 113
Be'ek'id Hóteelí, 232
Be'ek'id Łigaií, 227, 275
Be'ek'id Łizhiní, 275
Be'ekid Biná'ázt'i', 206
"Bead Water", 207, 260
Bear Canyon, 52
"Bear House", 122
"Bear People", 89
"Bear Spring" (see Fort Wingate),
208
Bear Springs, **35**, 79, 244
"Bear Springs", 35
Bear's Ears, The, 95, 155, 271,
286, 289, 294, 295
"Bear's Ears", 286
"Bear's Home", 281
"Beaver", 287
Beaver Creek, 159
"Beaver Rincon", 66
"Beautiful Canyon", 78
"Beautiful House", 225
Beautiful Mountain, 9(Table 5),

64, **174–75**, 181 (Casafuerte),
194, 216, 258, 365
"Beautiful Town" (from the
Spanish), 188
Becenti, **175**
Becenti Springs Trading, 26, 175
Beclabito (also Biklabito), **175**
Beclabito Trading Post, 26, **176**
Bee Burrow Ruin, **175**
Bee'eldííldahsinil, 171
Béégashii Bito', 35, 72
Béégashii Nit'ání, 34
Béégashii Siziní Kits'iil, 58
Beehai: 203 (Dulce); 223 (Jicarilla
Apache Reservation)
Beehai Kééhbat'í, 203
"Beehive House", 50
Beehive Ruin, **50**
Beehive Trail, 50
Béésh Bee Hooghaní, 300
Béésh Bitiin Tó, 251
Béésh Bíyaa 'Anii'á Bitooh,
205
Béésh Dich'ízhii, 72
Béésh Łichí'í Bigiizh, 236
Beesh Schichii, 244
Béésh Sinil, 148
Bééxh Wahaaldaas, 143
Begashibito Wash, **35**
Bekihatso Lake, **35**
Bekihatso Wash, **35**
Belen, NM, 132, 213
Bell Trading Post, 26
Bennet-Turner Trading Post, 26
Bennett Peak, **175–76**
Bernalillo, NM, **176**
Bernard, Bruce M., Trading, 26
Betatakin Canyon, 115
Betatakin Ruin, 114, **115**
Betatakin Trading Post (see
Shonto Trading Post), 26, 131
"Between the Waters", 206
"Beveled Cactus", 34
Bi'keesh Wash, **36**
Bibo, 26, **176**, 182
Bíchjj Digiz, 237
Bicho'adahditiin, 288
Bickel's Trading Post, 26
Bicknell, UT, 287
Bidáá' Ha'azt'i', 83
Bidáá Hatsoh, 135
Bidághaa' Łibáí, 297
Bidahochi (also Bitahooii), 26, **35**
Bidahóóchii', 35, 111 (Mitten
Peak)

"Big Bead", 176, 179
Big Bead Mesa (also Cerro Calisto), **176**, 202
"Big Boulder Hill", 91, 92
"Big Bridge", 108
"Big Buttocks Place", 221
"Big Canyon", 43 (Canyon De Chelly), 83 (Grand Canyon), 155 (Dolores River)
"Big Canyon Among the Rocks", 43
Big Cave, **59**
Big Cave Gap, **60**
Big Cottonwood Canyon, **55**
"Big Cottonwood Sits", 213
Big Cottonwood Trail, 55
"Big Cottonwood Tree", 170
"Big Cottonwood Tree Sitting Between the Two Walls of the Canyon", 179
"Big Dam", 118
"Big Farm, The", 238
Big Flow Canyon, **62**
Bigháá'doo 'Adéést'įį, 230
Bigháá Háada'alwo'ó Ha'atiin, 47
"Big-headed", 179
Bighorn Cave Ruin, **46**
"Bighorn Sheep Ambush", 60
"Bighorn Sheep Ambush Cove", 60
"Bighorn Sheep Among the Rocks", 46
"Big It Flows Downward Area Cove", 62
"Big It Flows Downward Area Trail Up Out", 63
"Big Lake", 35, 67
"Big Leader", 298
"Big Leggings", 169
Big Mountain, 35, 105, 204, 221: 177 (near Blanco, NM); 233 (Mesa Quartado)
"Big Mountain Sheep", 157
Big Mountain Trading Post, 26, **35**, 97, 108
"Big Rim", 135
"Big Rock" (Canyon De Chelly), 59 (in Canyon De Chelly), 189 (in Chaco Canyon)
"Big Rock Hill", 92
"Big Rock Ledge", 103
Big Rock Hill, **176**
"Big Rock Point", 123
"Big Sheep", 153, 156, 162
"Big Snake's House", 40

"Big Space Under Rock (Cave)", 59, 60
"Big Space Under Rock Gap", 60
"Big Span", 118
"Big Spring", 171
"Big Stars Strung Out", 132
Big Water, **176**
"Big Water", 107, 142, 176
"Big Water Place", 35
"Big Water's Spring", 181
"Big Willow", 205
"Big Yei Went Up and Out", 60
"Big Yei's Wash" (Canyon De Chelly), 60
Bii'dóó'adéést'įį, 230
Bíina, 156, 229
Bikooh Dootłish Canyon, 112
Bikooh Hatsoh, 155
Bikooh Hodootłizh, 41
Bikooh Ntsaa Ahkee, 83
Bilagáana Nééz, 196
Bill Williams Mountain, **36**
Billy Crane's Ranch, 195
Bíniishdáhí, 243
Bird Head Rock (Canyon De Chelly), **63**
"Bird's Face" (Canyon De Chelly), 63
"Bird's Face Trail Up Out", 63
"Bird Springs", 36
Bird Spring, **36**
Bis'ii Ah Wash, **36**
Bis Dah 'Azká, 268
Bis Dah Łitso, 277
Bis Deez'áhí, 239
Bis Dootł'izhí Deez'áhí (also Bis Dootł'izh Deez'áhí), 125, 239
Bis Dootł'izh Ndeeshgiizh, 41
Bis 'Íí'á, 36
Bis Niiyah (also Basneyaah), 273
Bistah, 222
Bistahí, 176
Bisti (Badlands), **176**
Bisti Trading Post, 26, 175, **176**
Bit'ahniits'ósí, 205
Bitahooche Butte, 98
Bitahooche Trading Post, 98
Bitát'ahkin, 114, 115
Bitát'ah Dzígai, 108
Bitł'ááh Bit'o', 175
Bits'ádi, 172
Bits'iis Nineezí, 163
Bits'iis Nteelí, 163
Bitsihuitsos, **36**

Bitsįįh Hwiits'os, 36, 150 (near Yale Point)
"Bitter Medicine Butte", 129
"Bitter Spring", 36
Bitter Springs, **36**
Bitter Springs Trading Post, 26, 36
"Bitter Water", 33 (Agua Sal Creek), 249 (Raton Springs)
Biyáázh, 253
Bíyah 'Anii'ahí, 188
"Black Alder", 65
"Black Alders Extending out Horizontally in a Line", 241
"Black Appearing Mountains", 221
Black Canyon, **36**
"Black Cottonwood Circle", 271
Black Creek, **36**, 39 (Blackhorse Wash), 252
Black Creek Canyon, **37**, 115 (Oak Springs)
Black Creek Valley, 10, **36**, 147
"Black Downward Rock", 190
Black Falls, **294**
Black Falls Trading Post, **37**
"Black Greasewood" (Sarcobatus vermiculatus), 190
"Black Hat", 294
Blackhorse Wash, **37**
"Black House", 225, 265 (Skunk Springs Ruin, NM)
Black Lake, 10, **37**; Navajo Agency at, 193; and Navajo Clan Migrations, 275
"Blake Lake", 37, 275
Black Mesa or "Black Streak Mountain", 2, 8(Table 4), 9(Table 5), **38–39**: as Navajo stronghold, 12; as part of Pollen Mountain, 33, 34, 64, 70, 300; Dinnebito Wash on, 74; Hopi Mesas emanate from, 87; Marsh Pass on north of, 108; Moenkopi Wash on, 112; Mexican trading expedition to, 120; Polacca Wash on, 121
Black Mesa Trading Post, 26, 39
Black Mountain, 38, **39**, 97, 130
"Black Mountain, The", 76
Black Mountain Trading Post (also Black Mountain Store), 26, **39**, 82
"Black Mountain Peak", 35
"Black Mountain Sloping Down", 165

Black Mountain Wash, 68

Black Pinnacle, **39**, 138, 274

"Black (Dark) Pinnacle Above the Horizon", 274

Black Point, **39**

"Black Reeds in the Distance", 101

Black Rock, **40** (near Fort Defiance); 51 (near Canyon De Chelly); 52; **177** (near Zuni); 282

"Black Rock", 177

Black Rock Butte, 40

Black Rock Canyon, 55, **57**

"Black Rock Cave", 225

"Black Rock Coming Down", 175

"Black Rock Coming Down" (Bennett Peak), 175

"Black Rock Coming Down" (Cabezon Peak), 180

"Black Rock Cove", 58

"Black Rock in a Blue Area", 42

Black Rock Navajo Fortress (also Fortress Rock), 58

Black Rock Plateau, 40

Black Rock Rincon, 52 (In Canyon De Chelly), 180 (near Cabezon)

"Black Rock Spire", 249

Black Rock Trail, **52**

Black Rock Trail Canyon, **52**

"Black Rock Trail Up Out", 52

"Black Rock Trail Up Out Cove", 52

"Black Rock Waterfall", 37

"Black Salt", 40

"Black Saltpeter", 37

Black Salt Trading Post, 26, **40**, 139

Black Salt Valley, 37, **40**

"Black Sheep", 255

Black Soil Wash, **40**

"Black Soil Water", 40

"Black Speck Mountain", 35, 105

Black Speck Mountain, 35

"Black Spots Extend Across", 234

"Black Streak of Wood", 146

"Black Wood Place", 189

"Black Wool", 33

Blade Rock, **46**

Blanca Peak (also Blanco Peak), Sacred Mountain of the East, 21, 128, **151–52**, 235, 242–43, 279: in Coming Up Side Ceremony or Moving Upward

Way, 193; possibly included in Dinétah, 201; water carried to for Ceremony, 215; and other possible choices for Sacred Mountain of the East, 221

Blanco, NM, **177**

Blanco Canyon (and Blanco Wash), **177**, 216, 221, 254

Blanco Trading Post, 26, **177**, 177

Blanding, UT, 165, **287**

"Blasted Away Upward", 47

"Blasted Out Downward (From a Height)", 47

"Blasted Through Rock", 47

"Blisters of Water Here and There at an Elevation", 137

Bloomfield, NM, 163, **178**

"Blue Adobe Gap", 41

"Blue All the Way Up", 262

"Blue Area in the Lava Flow or Traprock", 42

"Blue Bead Mountain", 235

"Bluebird Mountain" (Cerro Berro), 183

"Bluebird Mountain", 183

"Blue Bull That Stands", 59

Blue Canyon, 8(Table 4), **41**, 112, 141

"Blue Canyon", 41, 112

Blue Canyon Trading Post, 26, **41**, 42

Blue Cave Pictograph, **59**

"Blue Clay Point", 125, 239

Blue Gap, **41**

"Blue House", 165: 190 (Wijiji Ruin), 253 (Salmon Ruin)

"Blue Land Goes Into River", 172

Blue Mesa, **178**: 184 (Chaco Canyon, from the Spanish)

Blue Mesa Trading Post (see Newcomb), 178, 239

Blue Moon Bench, 41, 103, 135

Blue Mountain (see also Abajo Mountains), 285, **287**

Blue Mountain (also Blue Mountains), 285

Blue Peaks, 87

Blue Spring, 95

Bluewater, NM, **178**

Bluewater Lake, 178

Bluff, UT, 24, 112, **287**

Bluff Trading, 26

Bodaway Mesa, **41**, 82

Boehm's Trading Post, 26

"Bog Hole", 141

Bowl Canyon Creek, 272

Bond Trading, 26

Bond Brothers Trading Post, 26, 248

Bond Trading Company, 26

Bonito Canyon, **41**

Bonito Creek, 40, 41, 42

Booming Rock, 85

Borderlands Trading Post, 26, 148, 232

Borrego Pass Trading Post, 26, **178**

Bosque Redondo: Pre-Bosque Redondo hiatus activities, 34, 45, 46, 47, 78–79, 110, 113, 118, 251; journey to Bosque Redondo, 12, 13, 38, 62, 77, 78–79, 131, 242, 254; strongholds during hiatus, 95, 100, 240, 244, 300, 304; activities at Bosque Redondo, 14, 207–8, 287; escapes from Bosque Redondo, 171, 180; predicted at Tó Aheedłi, 238; return from Bosque Redondo, 2, 45, 78–79, 150, 251

Boulder Lake (see Stinking Lake), 267

Boundary Butte, **267**

Bowdish Canyon, **153**

Bowl Canyon Creek, **178**

"Bow Smoother", 114

Box S Ranch, **178–79**, 245

Boyle's Trading Post, 26

"Bread Flows Up and Out", 179

Bread Springs, **179**

Breast Butte, 87

"Breezes Blow Out from Between the Rocks", 86, 148

Bridge Across, 95

"Bridge Across Parallel Place", 57

Bridge Canyon (and Creek), 303

"Bridged House", 178

Bridge Trail, **57**

Brigham, 99

Brigham's Lake, 101

Brimhall Trading Post (also Brimhall, Brimhall Wash Trading Post), 26, **179**

"Broad Strip of Land (Valley) Extends to the River, A", 177

"Broad Strip Extends to Water", 227

"Broken Down House", 143

"Broken Down Houses", 292

"Broken Pottery House", 101, 102
Brook Creek (see Tsaile Creek), 138
Bryce Canyon National Park, **287**
Bubbling Spring, 49
Bubbling Water Spring, 49
Buck Trading, 26, 279
Buckskin Ears (Bat) Rock, 54
"Buckskin Ears (Bat) Wash", 54
"Buckskin Ears (Bat) Trail", 54
Buckskin Mountains, 100
Buell Park (Bule Park), **42**
Buell Mountain, 122
Burford Lake (also Buford Lake) (see Stinking Lake), 267
"Buffalo Spring", 220
Buffalo Springs Trading Post, 26, 221
"Building in which the Wind Blows About", 187
"Building that Gradually Slid Down", 49
Bunched Feathers, **51**
"Burned Area", 155
"Burned Bread", 211
"Burned Creek" (from the Spanish), 248
"Burned Death", 179
Burned Death Wash, **179**, 232
"Burned Post", 186
"Burned Water", 179
Burned Water Canyon, **179**
Burnham, **179**
Burnham's Trading Post, 26, 127, **179**
"Burnt Corn", 42
Burnt Corn Wash, 39, **42**, 72
Burnt Piñon, 72
"Burnt Post", 186
Burnt Water, **42**
"Burnt Water", 42
Burnt Water Trading Post, 42
Burro Springs, **42**, 112
"Burro Spring", 42
"Butterfly" (from the Hopi), 90
Butterfly Cave, **56**
"Butterfly Mountain", 183 (Cerro Berro), 268 (Suannee)
"Butterfly Ruin" (from the Zuni), 146

C. N. Cotton Trading Co., 96
Cabezon, **179–80**, 274, 284 (on Jemez–San Juan Rte.)
Cabezon Peak (also El Cabezon,

Cerro Cabezon), 172, 179, **189**, 217, 274
Cache Mountain, **180**, 228
Cahone Trading, 26
Cajon Ruins Group, **292**
Calites Canyon, 8(Table 4), 36
"Camel" (or "Hunchback [God]"), 53
Cameron Trading Post, 26, **42**
Cames Canyon (also Kaimes Canyon), **180**
Campañero Canyon (see Cereza Canyon), 183
Campbell's Pass, 270, 280
Camp Florilla, 259
"Campos Los Pasos" (see Twin Buttes in NM), 277
Camp San José, 252
"Cane", 265
Cantonment Burgwin, **181**
Cantonment La Plata, 156
"Canyon", 43
"Canyon Across from Rock Struck by Lightning", 49
"Canyon Below Wild Cherry Spring", 50
Canyon Bonito, 9(Table 5)
Canyon De Chelly (National Monument), 7(Table 3), 8(Table 4), 9(Table 5), **43–63**: Washington's 1849 expedition to, 10; as Bosque Redondo Stronghold, 12; specifically included in new reservation, 13; Chinle at mouth of, 67; American troops visit to in 1848, 68; battles fought at, 79, 121; in Hopi migration stories, 88, 90; Mexican trading expedition to, 120; Ute raiders to, 165; Navajos push westward to, 180, 251; Lt. Narbona's attack on, 182; in Zuni migration narrative, 190, and Encinal, 205; major Navajo concentration in 1800 at, 217; refugees from Jemez at, 223; visited by Major Backus, 254; ruins of compared to Hovenweep, 292
Canyon Del Muerto (Canyon De Chelly), 43, **55–63**: Lt. Narbona's attack upon, 182; Zunis in attack upon, 282
Canyon Diablo, **63**, 104, 133, 137, 149

Canyon Diablo Trading Post, 26, 63, **64**
"Canyon of High Rock", 53
Canyon of the Dead Man, 55
Canyon of the Dead People, 61
Canyon Largo (see Largo Canyon)
Canyon Padre, **64**
"Canyon Where Bows Are Made", 290
Canyoncito Bonito (also Cañoncito Bonito), 10, 42
Cañada Grande Larga, 228
Cañada Larga (also Cañon Largo, Cañada Largo, Canyon Largo), 7(Table 3), 217
Cañon Bonito, 78
Cañon Del Infierno (see Satan Pass), 262
Cañon De Trigo, 142
Cañon Trigo, 55
Cañoncito, 10, **180–81**
"Capped Rock", 277
"Captain, The", 33
"Captains, The", 51
Captain Tom Wash, 181, **239**, **272**
Carrizo, 183
Carrizo Canyon (see Cereza Canyon), 183
Carrizo Mountains, 2, 6, 9(Table 5), **64–65**, 67, 123, 134, 175, 194, 216, 265: visited by Capt. Walker, 72
Carson Trading Post (also Carsons) (San Juan County, NM), 25, 26, 177, **181**, 265
Carson Trading Post (McKinley County, NM), 26, 193
Casa Blanca (see Seama), 226
Casa Chiquita, **185**
Casa Del Rio Ruin, **181**
Casa Malpais Ruin, 132
Casa Rinconada, 166, **185**
Casafuerte, 5, 7(Table 3), 174, **181**
Casamero Lake, **181–82**
Castil De Arvil, 255
Castilblanco, 255
Castle Butte, **65**, 87
Castle Butte Trading Post, 26, 65
Cat Face, **56**
Cataract Canyon, 85
"Cat's Head", 56
Cave of the Bones, 61
CDC, 86, 48

Cebolleta (also Seboyeta), 3, 5, 6, 7, 10, 96, 126, **182**

Cebolleta Mountains, 180, 181 (possibly Casafuerte), 217, 257

Cebolletita, **182**

"Cedar Bark Descending Red", 159

Cedar Point (Trading), 26

Cedar Ridge, **65**, 121

Cedar Ridge Trading Post, 26, **65**, 102

Cedar Springs Trading Post, 26, **65**, 97

"Cedars in an Undulating Line", 159, 166

Cejita Blanca Range, 221

Cejita Blanca Ridge, 221, 222

Cemetery Ridge, 277

Cereza Canyon (also Carrizo Canyon, Campañero Canyon), **182**

Cerrillos, **183**

"Cerro Alto", 150, 173

Cerro Berro, **183**

Cerro Cabezon, 180, 183

Cerro Calisto (see Big Bead Mesa), 176

Cerro Chato, 184

Cerro Elevado, 33

Ch'ah Łizhin, 294

Ch'al Sitą́, 50

Ch'áyaí, 114

Ch'į́įdii, 67

Ch'į́įdii Bikooh, 289

Ch'íídii Łichíí, 267, 278

Ch'il Haajini, 230

Ch'ínílį́, 44, 67, 143 (Walker Creek)

Ch'izhóó, 66

Ch'odáá' haatz'i', 60

Ch'odáá' haatz'i' Ha'atiin, 60

Ch'óol'į́'í, 153, 215

Ch'óshgai, 193, 194

Ch'óyaató Bikooh, 42

Cha Canyon, **287–78**

Chá'oł, 68, 114

Chaa', 287

Chaa'istł'ah, 66

"Chaca", 183

Chaco Canyon, 9(Table 5), **183–90**: and Zuni Sword Swallower Clan migration, 63; Lorenzo Hubbell at, 96; abandonment of, 114; astroarcheaological features of as similar to

Yellow Jacket, 166; residents of take refuge at Keams Canyon, 180; as possibly Casafuerte, 181; Hyde Expedition to, 240; Chaco architecture at Salmon Ruin, 253; possible ancestors of Zia Pueblo, 280; evidence of contact with Zuni in A.D. 1000, 281; archeoastronomy at, 282; on Chaco-Chuska route, 284

Chaco Culture National Historical Park, 183

Chaco Mesa (see Chacra Mesa), 191

Chaco River (also Chaco Wash, Rio Chaco), 144, **190–91**

"Chaco Trading Company", 24, 277

Chaco-Chuska Route, 284

Chacoli, 183

(El) Chacolin, 184

Chacra Mesa (also Chaco Mesa, Blue Mesa), 8(Table 4), 183–84, 189, **191**, 217, 247: on Chaco-Chuska Rte., 284

Chaistla Butte, **66**

Chama, **191**

Chama Mountains (and Peaks), 191

Chama River, 9(Table 5)

Chama Valley, 7(Table 3), 202

Chambers, **66**

Chambers Ruin, **66**

Chambers Trading Post, 26

Chaol Canyon, 114

Charcoal Cliff, **62**

"Charcoal Mark on Rock", 62

"Charcoal Place", 189

Charley Day Spring, **66**

Chato, 128

Chaves Pass, 88, 150

Chaves Pass Ruin, **66**

Chavez Trading Post, 26

Chéch'iizh Bii' Tó, 240

Chéch'il Bii' Tó, 240

Chéch'il Dah Lichí'í, 240, 267

Chéch'il Dah Lichíí (Star Lake Trading Post), 267

Chéch'iltah, 192

Chéch'ízhí, 252

Checkerboard Area, 181, **191–92**, 212, 221, 227, 243

Cheechilgeetho Trading Post, 26, **192**

Chéh'ilyaa, 107

Chelle, 184

Chetro Ketl (also Rain Pueblo, Chettro Kettl, Cheto Kette), **185–86**, 246

Chevlon Butte, **67**

Chézhin Deez'áhí, 39, 126, 138 (Tsaile Peak)

Chézhin (or Tzézhin) Dikǫǫhí, 74

Chézhin Ditł'ooí, 253

Chézhín Náshjiní, 109

Chézhiní (also Tsézhiní): 39 (Black Pinnacle); 40 (Black Rock near Ft. Defiance); 207 (Ford Butte)

Chichiltah (also Cheechilgeetho), **192**

Chichiltah Trading Post, 66

Chicken Spring (from the Spanish), 208

Chico Arroyo, 179

Chihuili, 199

Chíí'a Ha'atiin, 52

Chííh Hajíítseełí, 52

Chííh Hajíítseełí Nástłah, 52

Chííh Ntł'izí, 200

Chííh Tó, 127

Chííhłigai, 136

Chiihtó, 77

Chį́į́h Ntł'izí, 200, 245

Chiiłchin Bii'Tó (or Tsiiłchin Bii'Tó), 67

Chilchinbito, AZ, **67**, 77, 128, 197, 253, 273

Chilchinbito Canyon, 37

Chilchinbito Trading Post, 26, **67**

Chimney Butte, 87

Chimney Rock, **154** (in Archuleta County, Co), **192** (near Farmington, NM)

China Springs Trading Post, 27, **192**, 232, 252

Chinde Mesa, **67**

Chinle (Chinlee, Chin Lee, Tsinlee), AZ, 24, 39, **44**, 47, 67, 138 (Diné College)

Chinle to Ft. Defiance Road, 68, 79, 82, 97

Chinle Valley, 2, 5, 9(Table 5), 38, 39, 101, 125

Chinle Valley Store, 68

Chinle Valley Trading Post, 27

Chinle Wash (also Chinle Creek), 44, 67, **68**, 110 (at Mexican Water), 124

"Chipped Out One", 195
Chiquito Colorado, 105
Chíshí Nééz, 195
Ch'ó Haazt'i', 60
Ch'ó Łání, 54
Choal Canyon (sometimes Chaol), **68**
Choiska Peak, 194
Choke Cherries Spread out Canyon, **53**
"Chokecherry (Bushes) Are Standing Spread out Wash", 53
"Chokecherry (Bush) Is Spread out Spring", 49
"Chokecherry (Bush) Is Standing Spread out Cove", 49
Chooh Dínéeshzheé, 72
Chooyíní Dah Sidáhí, 45
Chooyíní Sitání, 45
Chukai Wash, 205
"Chunks of Earth Sticking up Alone", 118
Chupadero, 10, **192–93**, 236
Church Rock (also Navajo Church, Temple Rock), 122, **193**
Chusca, 184
Chuska Mountains, 1, 8(Table 4), 9(Table 5), **193–94**, 202, 216, 265: and Chaco-Chuska Rte., 284
Chuska Pass, **194**
Chuska Peak, 64, 175, 193, **194**, 216, 235, 265
Chuska Trading Post, 27, 273
Chuska-tunicha-lukachukai Ranges, 38, 193
Chuska Valley, 7(Table 3), 8(Table 4), 9(Table 5), 193 (Navajo agency in), **194**, 262
Cibola Mesa, **194–95**
Cicuye, 242
Ciénega Amarilla, 9(Table 5), **69**, 73, 126, 128
Cienega Amarilla (Trading), 27
Cienega De Maria, 126
Cienega Juanico, 144
Cieneguilla, 226, 261
Cieneguilla Chiquita, 37
Cienega Negra, 37, 144, 145
Circle Valley, **288**
"Circular House", 185, 187
"Circular Mountains" (as erroneous interpretation), 64
"Circle of Pine Trees", 186
"Circle of Trees (or Poles)", 265

Clay Hill Crossing (see Piute Farms), 302
"Clay Mesa", 268
"Clay Point", 239
"Clay (or Adobe) Storage Pit", 273
"Clear Water" (Crystal), 198
"Clear Water" (Crystal Creek), 198
"Clearings Among the Rocks" (also "Stretches of Treeless Areas"), 295
Cliff Palace, 160
"Close to the Red Rock", 124
"Clump of Cattails", 212
Cly Butte, **296**
Cly Canyon, 188, **195**
Coal Creek, **195**
"Coal Mine", 69
Coal Mine Canyon, **69**
Coal Mine Mesa, **69**
Coal Mine Mesa (Trading), 27, 69
Coal Mine Pass, **195**
"Coal Spring Canyon", 177
Cochiti Pueblo, **195**, 226, 242, 255, 261, 281
Coconino Point (and Plateau), 69, 84–85
Cold Spring, **70**
"Cold Water Flows Up", 70
"Collected Tallows", 155
Colorado River, 1, **70**, 83, 85, 105, 111, 163, 293
Coma'a Spring, **70**
Comb Ridge, 33, 34, **70**
Comb Ridge (near Monument Valley), **288**, 300
Comb Wash, **288**
Concho, **71**
"Confluence, The", 55
"Confluence up Extending Rock", 46
Congolomerate Wash, **45**
"Conical Sands Female", 145
"Conical Sands Male", 145
Conley, Favella and Sharp Trading Post, 27
Continental Divide (Trading Post), 27, **195**
"Converging Hogbacks", 214
"Cooking Rocks", 250
Coolidge, NM, 73, **195–96**, 213
Coolidge-Perea (Trading), 27
Coolidge Ruin, **196**
Coon, A. C., Trading Post, 27, 127
Coon Butte (Coon Mountain), 110
"Cooper", 199

Copper Canyon, **288**
"Copper Canyon", 288
"Copper Pass", 236
Coppermine, **71**
Coppermine (Trading), 27, 71
Corona de Geganta, 174
"Corn Beetle Mountain", 221
Corn Creek Wash, 38
Corn Rock, 92
"A Corner Where a Small Stubby Cactus with Interlocking Thorns Grows", 71
Cornfields, **71**
Cornfields Trading Post, 27, **71**
Corn Mountain: 128 (San Francisco Peaks); 203 (Dowa Yalani); 299 (Navajo Mountain)
Cornered House, 185
Correo (also Correro), 268
Cortez, CO, **154–55**
Cosnino Wash, 86
Cottonwood, 127
Cottonwood Canyon, **45**
Cottonwood Circle, 207
"Cottonwood Outflow", 234
Cottonwood Pass (see Crystal, NM), 236
"Cottonwood Spring", 136
Cottonwood Tank, **71**
Cottonwood (Trading), 27
"Cottonwood Tree Lying Down", 71
Cottonwood Wash, **71**, 127
Cottonwood Wash (tributary of San Juan River in UT), **288**
"Cottonwood Wash", 288
"Cottonwood Water", 135
"Cottonwoods in a Circle", 135
Counselors, **196**
Counselors Trading Post, 27, **197**, 230, 250
Cousins (Trading Post), 27, **192**
Cove, **71**
Cove (Trading), 27, 71
Cove Mesa, **72**
"Covered Antelope", 67
"Covered Well", 39
"Cove (Where) Douglas Firs Extend Up Out in a Line (To the Rim)", 60
"Cove Where Sand Is Repeatedly Blown", 46
"Cove Where Cottonwoods Stretch Across in a Line", 45
Cow Canyon, 287, **289**

"Cow Spring", 72
Cow Springs Trading Post, 27, **72**
"Cow's Water", 35
Coyote Box Canyon, 53, 55
Coyote Canyon, 54, 128, **197**, 234, 253, 273
"Coyote Canyon", 27, **197**
Coyote Canyon Trading Post, 27, **197**
"Coyote Fell into Deep Water", 179
"Coyote Pass" (Jemez Pueblo), 222
"Coyote Pass", 221
Coyote Spring, 89, 95, 112
"Coyote's Tracks Trail Up Out", 47
Coyote Trail, 47, 55
"Coyote Trail Up Out", 55
Coyote Wash, 191
Coyote Wash Canyon (Canyon De Chelly), **53**, 55
Crack-in-the-Rock Ruin, 37
Crack-in-the Rock Trail, 58
"Crane Mountains", 163
Crane's Station, 27, 195
"Creek Connection", 72
Cronmeyer, Hoske Trading Post, 27, 96, 127
"Crooked Nose", 186, 237
Cross Canyon, **74**
Cross Canyon Trading Post, 27, **72**
"Cross Canyon Trail", 59
Crossing of the Fathers (also Ute Ford), 84, 104, 114, **289**, 293
Crow Canyon, **153**
"Crow Canyon", 153
Crow Canyon Petroglyphs Site (Dinétah), **202**
Crow Canyon Site (Dinétah), **202**
Crow Trail, **45**
Crown Rock, **73**
Crownpoint, NM, 24, 25, 138 (Diné College), **197**
Crownpoint (Trading), 27, 197
Crozier (see Two Grey Hills), 231, 277
Crozier Trading Post (see Newcomb), 27, 239
Crumbled House Ruin, **198**
"Crumbling Well", 98
Crystal, NM, **198**, 236, 277
Crystal Creek, 37
Crystal Creek (also Simpson Creek), 36, 51, **198**, 265

Crystal Trading Post, 24, 25, 27, **198**
Cuba (also Nacimiento), **199**
Cubero (also Cubera), 7, 9(Table 5), **199**, 271
Cudai, **200**
"Curved Traprock", 57
"Cut Upward", 169
Cutthroat Castle Ruins Group, **292**

Dá'deestł'in: 83 (Glen Canyon Dam); 237 (Navajo Reservoir Dam)
Da'deestł'in Hótsaa, 118
Dá'ák'eh Haláni, 108
Dá'ak'eh Ntsaa, 238
Daadílí, 171
Dághaa' Łibái, 297
Dághaa' Łichíí', 225
Dah Dą'ąstsélí, 47
Dahmi, 259
Dalton Pass, **200**
Dalton Pass Trading Post, 27, **200**
"Dam", 237
"Dam at the Place Where the Rock Slants into the Water", 82
"Damaged-Arm's Land", 46
"Dangling Ladder", 54
"Dangling Ladder Trail Up Out", 60
Danoff (also Danoffville, McKittrick) (see Pinehaven), 245
Danoffville (Trading), 27, **200**, 245
"Dark Mountain", 130
"Dark (Shadow) under the Rock", 275
"Dark Water": 144 (Whiskey Creek); 177 (Blanco Canyon); 221 (Jacques Canyon); 272 (To Dil Hii Wash)
"Darkness under the Rock Stream", 184
"Date Mountains", 130, 165
Day's Chinle Trading Post, 24, 27, 67, **73**
Day's, Sam, Trading Post, 27, 83, 126
De Chelly Wash, 68
Dead Wash, **73**
Deadman Flat, **73**
Deadman's Flat, 76
"Deafness", 224
Debebikid Lake, **73**
Déél Náázíní, 201

"Deep Rock Canyon", 141
Deer Springs, 4
Deesh Bik' Anii'á Bitó", 205
Deeshgizh, 74
Deestsiin Bikooh, 154
Deez'á, 302
Deez'á (Piute Mesa), 302
Defiance Plateau, 2, 9(Table 5), 36, 68, **73**, 78–79, 82
Defiance Station Trading Post (also Defiance), 27, **201**, 213, 252, 253
De-na-zin Wash, **201**
Del Muerto Wash, 68
Denihootso, 75
Dennehotso Canyon, 75
"Descending Black Belt (or Mountain)", 153, 279
"Descending Line of Salt", 254
"Descending Wide Belt", 279
Desert Viewpoint, **73**, 87
Desha Creek (also Desh Canyon), **289**
Deshgish Butte, **74**, 87
Devil Canyon, **289**
Devil's Pass (see Satan Pass), 262
"Devilish Person", 280
Deez'á, 201
Deza Bluffs, **201**
Diamond Fields, **74**
Dibé Be'ek'id, 73, 78
Dibé Bichaan Bii' Tó, 253
Dibé Bighanteelí, 78
Dibé Bitooh, 263
Dibé Dáád, 60
Dibé Dáád Nástlah, 60
Dibé Dah Shijé'é, 130
Dibé Dah Sitiní, 87
Dibé Habitiin, 54
Dibé Hooghan, 219
Dibé 'Íijéé', 206
Dibé Łání, 108
Dibé Łizhiní, 255
Dibé Ntsaa, 153, 156, 162
Dibé Ntsaa (La Plata Mountains), 157, 201
Dibé Yázhí Habitiin, 178
Dinen Jikahn, 87
Dibéntsaa Tsétah, 46
Dích'íító, 36
Didzé Łání Ha'aatiin, 59
Didzé Łání Nástłah, 48, 49, 59
Didzé Sikaad, 50
Didzé Sikaad Bikooh, 53
Didzé Sikaad Tó, 49

Didzétsoh Łání Bikooh, 165
Diichiłí Dziil, 128
Dilcon (also Dilkon), **74**
Dilcon Trading Post, 27, **74**
Diné Bito', 74
Diné Habitiin, 216, 238
Diné Habitiin, 238
Dineh Mesa (also Dinne Mesa, Diné Mesa), 136
Dinetah: as earliest Navajo sites north of San Juan River, 3; Navajos pushed from by Utes, 63; Blanco part of, 177; Counselors part of, 196; **201–2**, Gobernador Knob within, 215; Rincon largo included in, 251; Turley included in, 276; Wide Belt Mesa included in, 279
Dinétah Pueblitos, **202**
Dinnebito, **74**, 94, 97
Dinnebito Trading Post, 27, **74**, 108
Dinnebito Wash, 38, **74**
Dinnehotso (also Dennehotso and Dennehatso), 8(Table 4), 34, **75**, 139,
Dinnehotso Canyon, **75**
Dinnehotso Trading Post, 27, **75**
Dinosaur Canyon, **75**
Divide Trading Post, 27, **203**
Díwózhii Bii' Tó, 75, 85, 107
Díwózhii Bikooh, 161, 295
Díwózhiikin, 190
Díwózhiishzhiin, 190
Dleesh Łigai, 145
Dleesh Ndigaií, 34
Dló'áyázhí, 270
Dog Rock, **46**
"Dog Rock", 46
Do Ha Hi Biton, **75**
Dolion (see Torreon), 274
Dólii Dził (Cerro Berro), 183
Dólii Dził, 183
Dolores, CO, **155**
Dolores River, **155**, 160, 271
Dominguez, 180
Doney Mountain, **75**
Doney Park, 76
Donovan's Trading Post, 27
Doo Hahí Bito', 128, 75
Dook'o'osłííd, 128, 153
Dóola Dootl'izh Sizínígí, 59
Dooyá Ndeeshgizh, 60
Dot Klish Canyon, 40
Dootł'izh, 41

Dootł'izhii Dziil, 153, 235
"Douglas Firs Extend Up Out In a Line (To the Rim)", 60
Douglas Mesa, 286, **289–90**, 295
Dowa Yalani Mountain (also Zuni Sacred Mountain, Corn Mountain, Thunder Mountain, Taaiyolone, Towayalani), **202**, 281, 282
Dowoshiebito Canyon, **76**
"Dreadful", 137
Drolet's (see Naschitti), 237
Drolet's Trading Post, 27
Dropped Out Mountain, 180
Dry Hide Hanging Up, 57, **60**
Dulce, **203**, 223
Dunn Mercantile Trading Company, 27, **76**, 132
Dunn's Trading Post, 27, **290**
Durango, CO, **155**, 156
Dusty, **203**
Dzaanééz Habitin, 52
Dzaanééz Habitiin Nástł'ah, 52
Dziintsahah, **204**
Dzil Nda Kai (also Little Ear Mountain), **204**
Dzil Tusayan Butte, 77
Dzilditloi Mountain (also Ziltigloi, Zilditloi Mountain), **204**
Dził, 73, 233
Dził 'Ashdlaii, 294
Dził Ba'áádi, 102
Dził Béét'óód, 150
Dził Bét'ood, 150
Dził Bii'Haldzisí, 109
Dził Bílátah Łitsooí, 134
Dził Binii' Łigaii (Kaiparowitz Plateau), 293
Dził Binii' Łigaii, 162
Dził Bíni' Hólóonii, 157
Dził Bizhi 'Adani, 291
Dził Dashzhinii, **76**
Dził Dah Si'ání, 77
Dził Dah Neeztínii, 124
Dził Dah Zhin, 105
Dził Deez'á, 150, 242
Dził Dijool, 221, 242
Dził Diné Łichíí', 233
Dził Diłhił, 130
Dził Ditł'a', 122
Dził Ditł'ooí, **204**
Dził Ditł'ooí (Abajo Mountains, UT), 285, 287
Dził Ditł'oo'í Bikooh, 303

Dził Ghá'niłts'įįlii, 128
Dził Łání, 281
Dził Łeeshch'ihí, 256
Dził Łibáí, 41, 69, 84
Dził Łibáí Bikooh, 85
Dził Łichíí', 75 (Doney Mountain), 250
Dził Łichíí', 217
Dził Łigaii, 162, 165, 217
Dził Łizhin (Jemez Mountains), 221
Dził Łizhinii, 221
Dził Ná'oodiłí Chílí, 219
Dził Ná'oodiłíchílí, 153
Dził Ná'oodiłii, 219
Dził Naajiní, 165
Dził Nááyisí, 254
Dził Náhineests'ee', 295
Dził Náhooziłii, 64
Dził Nda'akai, 204
Dził Nééz, 117, 173
Dził Nnééz, 150
Dził Ntsaaí, 35, 204 (Dzintsahah), 233
Dził Tusyan Butte, 77
Dzilghá'í Bikéyah, 146
Dziłk'i Hózhónii, 174
Dziłłátahzhiní, 35
Dziłíjiin, 38, 39
Dziłizhiin, 221
Dziłyi, 65

'E'é'ni' Be'adááad, 46
Eagle Crag, **76**
Eagle Mesa (also Eagle Rock Mesa), **296–97**
"Eagle Springs", 199, 243
"Eagle Traps", 94
"Earth Dam", 272
"Earth Hollow", 42
"Earth Hollow Hill", 42
"Earth Woman", 300
"Earth's Center", 147
East Fork Dinnebito Wash, **76**
Echo Cave, **55**
Echo Cliffs, **76**, 82, 85
"Echo of Thunder", 138
Echo Trading Post, 27, **76**
Eduardo Wash, 177
Egloffstein Butte, **76**, 87
Eighteen Miles Spring Trading Post, 27, **76**
El Cabezon (see Cabezon Peak), 179
El Cabezon De Los Montoias, 179

El Capitan, 33 (Agathla Peak); 77; 188 (Pueblo Alto)
El Disierto Pintado, 118
El Juegador, 188
El Malpais National Monument, 31, **204**, 235
El Morro (National Monument) (also Inscription Rock), 4, 8(Table 4), **204–5**, 284
El Morro (Trading), 27
El Vadito del Rio Chiquito Colorado, 126
Elden Pueblo, 130
Elden Spring, 130
"Elderly Man's Trail Up Out", 47
Elephant Butte, 87
Elephant Feet (Legs), 72, **76**
Elk Mountains, 294
"Elk Water" (Paiute), 118
Elongated Ridge, 201
Emigrant Springs, **77**
Empty House, 115
Empty Houses, 102
Enchanted Mesa, 170
Encinal (also Encinel), **205**, 225
"Enemy Bears", 89
"Enemy Hiding Place", 299
"Enemy Pasture", 287
"Enemy's Cave", 178
Ensenada Mesa, 229
Escalante River, **290**
Escavada (Trading), 27
Escavada Wash, **205**, 240
Escondido Mountain, **205**
Escrito Spring, **205**
Escrito (Trading), 27, 229
Escudilla Mountain, **77**
Española, **206**, 278
Estrella (Trading) (see Star Lake Trading Post), 27, 267
"Evil Spirit Canyon", 289
Ewell's Hay Camp, 37
"Extensive Mountain", 35
"Eyeglasses", 96
"Eyes Become None", 113
"Eyes That Kill", 240

Face Rock, **51**, 267
Fajada Butte (also Mesa Fahada, Mesa Fachada, Mesa Fajada), **186**
Fajada Wash, **206**
"Falling Flints", 144
"Family Members Rock", 54

Faris Ranch (see Seven Lakes), 262
Farmington, NM, 163, 179 (Road to Ft. Wingate); **206**, 240 (Hyde Trading Post); 249 (pipeline from Rattlesnake); 249 (Farmington to Albuquerque Road)
Far Spiral Canyon, **57**
"Far Spiral Cove", 57
Far View House, 160
"Father", 52
Father Rock, **52**
"Faultless Mountain", 128
"Fear", 132
"Feathers Bunched", 51
"Female Mountain", 102
Fence Lake, 172–73, **204**
"(Fence) Poles Strung Out", 259
Fenced up Horse Canyon Ruin, **206**
"Fenced Lake" (or "Lake Surrounded by a Fence"), 206
Ferry Station, 230
Field, 170
Figueredo Wash, **206–7**
Fingers, The, **77**
"Fingers of Water" (or "Fringed Water"), 100
Fir Lined Trail, **60**
"Fir Mountain", 215
Fir Tree Alcove, **60**
Fir Tree Canyon, **60**
"Fir Tree Spring Canyon", 42
Fir Tree Trail, 60
Fire Temple Ruin, 61
"First Home Place", 46
First Mesa, AZ, 52, **89–91**, 143, 223
First Ruin, **46**
Fish Point, 106
"Fish Spring", 106
"Fish Flow Out", 106
Five Butte, 67
"Five Peaks", 294
Flagstaff, AZ, **77**, 149, 150, 290
Flat Rock Refuge, **59**
Flattop Mesa with Trees, 96
Flattop Peak, 194
Flattop Ruin, 119
"Flat-Topped Hogan", 89, 134, 228
"Flat Topped House", 187
Flat Topped Mountain, 154
"Flat-Topped Round Area, 102
"Flattened Rock", 46

Flax River, 105
"Flint Hogan", 300
"Flint Striking Stones", 244
"Flowing Over Projecting Rock", 227
"Flowing Spring", 248
"Flow of the Fluted Rock", 53
"Flows Along in Darkness Under Rock", 190
"Flows from Red Lake", 36
"Fluffy Mountain", 204
Fluted Rock, 39, 54, **77**, 78, 194, 300
Flute Player Cave, **45**
Flying Butte, 87
"Flying Mountain", 228
Forbidding Canyon (also Forbidden Canyon), **290**
Ford Butte, **207**
Forest Lake, **78**
"Forest Lake", 78
Forestdale, AZ, 131
Fork Rock, **60**
"Forked Wood", 277
Fort, 78
Fort Apache, 126
Fort Canby (Defiance), 12, 40, 82, 122
Fort Defiance, AZ, 9(Table 5), **78–80**: establishment of in 1851, 10; Navajos bring body to, 11; post sutler trading with Navajos, 23; becomes a government town, 25; Chinle–Fort Defiance Road, 68; namesake of Defiance Plateau, 73; as Fort Canby; 82; Long Walk from, 86, 148, 259; commanded by Major Kendrick, 102; and Mexican trail, 108; soldiers of attack Manuelito, 121–22; A. C. Rudeau trading at, 125; and first written Navajo at, 127; W. M. Staggs Trading at, 132; Wheatfields grain for, 144; Navajo Agency at, 193; Jesus Arviso interpreting at, 200; Fort Defiance–Fort Wingate Road, 201, 252, 254; and Fort Union Garrison, 208; Albuquerque to Fort Defiance Road, 209; Speigleberg trading at, 210; Manuelito, NM, becomes railhead for, 230; Thomas Keams Navajo Agent at, 231; columns

of ambushed, 232; and 1858 peace negotiations, 244; and Beautiful Mountain Uprising, 258; word reaches of Mormons meeting to distribute weapons to Navajos, 299

Fort Defiance Trading Post, 27

Fort Fernando de Taos, 181

Fort Fauntleroy (see Fort Wingate), 79, 100, 108–9, 259

Fort Huachuca, AZ, 68, 285

Fort Lewis, **155–56**, 161

Fort Lyon (see Fort Wingate), 79, 156, 208–9

Fort Marcy, **207**, 208, 260

Fort Montezuma, 295

Fort Sumner (Old), **207–8**: Bosque Redondo at, 12, 79; Navajos prior to removal to, 71, 84, 130, 156, 185; Long Walk to, 86, 148, 154, 259; escapees from, 171, 180; friendlies interned at, 182; Jesus Arviso, interpreter at, 200; return from, 245, 282

Fort Union, 79, 207, **208**

Fort Whipple, 66, **80–81**, 86, 99, 115, 127, 259

Fort Wingate (also Bear Springs, Big Bear Spring), **208–10**: initially called Fort Fauntleroy, 11; Navajos return from the Bosque Redondo, 13; Caballo Mucho surrenders at, 38; soldiers of rescue miners in Carrizo Mountains, 65; Fort Defiance abandoned in favor of, 79; Fort Wingate–Fort Whipple Star Mail Route, 86; Hopis imprisoned at, 93; Washington Matthews physician at, 109; Fort Wingate–Fort Apache mail route, 126; troops of converge on Animas, CO., 156; Navajo-Ute peace treaty signed in 1868, 165; reservation boundaries defined, 175, 197–98; officers of, 178; and road to Farmington, 179; outlaws lynched by troops of, 196; bunco men and desperados in vicinity of, 213; and Bear Springs, 244; and trail to Fort Defiance, 252, 254; troops of to Waterflow in 1893, 278; and location of Wingate Valley,

280; troops of sent to Aneth, UT, 285

Fort Wingate, Old, 12, 99, 115, 208–9, 259

Fort Wise, 208

Fort Wingate Army Depot, 193, **210**, 266

Fort Wingate Station, 201

Fort Wingate Trading Post, 27, 210

Fortress Rock, 58

Forty Four (Trading), 27

Four Corners, 24, 162, 163, 184, **211**, 301

Four Corners Trading Post, 24, 27, **211**

Frances Ruin (Dinétah), **202**

Fraizer, Kuhn and Mcmahon Trading, 126

Frazier Trading Post (Many Farms and St. Michaels), 27, **81**, 108, 109, 126

Fremont Peak, 128–29

French Butte, **81**, 87

Frog Rock, **50**

"Frog Sits", 50

Fruitland, NM, 24, 171, **211**, 241

Fruitland Project, **211**

Fruitland Trading Co., 211

Fruitland Trading Post, 27, **211**

Fuerte (Spanish), 207

"Fuzzy Mountain", 122, 204, 285, 287

"Fuzzy Mountain Creek", 304

"Fuzzy Traprock", 253

Ga'ngi Dai, **214**

Gáagii Bikooh, 155

Gáagii Haayáhí, 45

Gaaní Bikéyah, 46

Gaawasóón, 179

Gad Bił Naalk'id, 100

Gad Dah Yisk'id, 117

Gad Deelzhah, 159, 166

Gad 'Íí'áí, 200

Gad Sikaad Tsékooh, 233

Gadtah Dahisk'id Bikooh, 64

Gah Adádí, 205

Gahjaa, 287

Gahyázhí, 224

Galisteo Basin, 89

Gallegos Canyon and Gallegos Mesa, **212**, 217

Gallegos Trading Post, 27, **212**

Gallinas, **212**, 267

Gallinas Creek, 212

Gallo Canyon (also Gio Canyon), **186**, 213

Gallup, NM, **213–14**: Indian hospital at, 80; C. N. Cotton trading at, 81; uranium mines at, 107; Beautiful Mountain Uprising charges dropped at, 175; and road to Santa Fe, 179; Fort Wingate Army Depot employees live at, 193; and population shift from Coolidge, 195

Gallup Hogback, **214**, 218, 250

Gamerco, **214**

"Gambler's House", 187

Ganado, AZ, 11, 67, **81–82**, 96–97, 120, 121, 125, 138 (Diné College), 202, 271

Ganado Lake, **82**, 196

Ganado Trading Post, 27, 81, **82**

Ganado Wash, **82**

Gap, The, **86**, 90, 290

"Gap in the Rock", 201

"Gapped Butte", 74

Gap Rock, **50**

Gap (Trading Post), 24, 27, **82**

Gap Trail, 45

Garces Mesa, **82**

Garcia's Trading Post, 27, **83**, 97

Garden of Angels, 172

Géengii Dził, 214

Geyser, The, **215**

Ghą́ą́' Ask'idii, 53

"Ghost (Or Spirit) Mesa", 67

Ghost Ranch Living Desert Museum, 169

Giant Track Canyon, **60**

Giant's Chair, 66, 112

Gibbs Peak, 157

Gigue (see Santo Domingo Pueblo), 261

Gila River, 8(Table 4)

Giní Bit'ohí, 224

Gio Canyon, 213

Gipuy (also Guipui) (see Santo Domingo Pueblo), 261

Gishí Bikéyah, 114

"Giving Out Anger", 95

Glen Canyon, 70, **83**, 293

Glen Canyon Dam, **83**, 114, 117, 163, N303

"Globular Mountain" ("Round Mountain"), 221

"Goat Became Emaciated", 62

Goat Ledge, **62**

Gobernador Canyon and Creek, 3, 202, **215**, 237

Gobernador Knob, 21, 128, 153, 183, 202, **215**, 219, 235, 243, 279

Gobernador Store, 28, 215

"Go-getter", 280

Gólízhibito', 265

Goma'a (Ute word), 70

Goods of Value Mountain (also Pollen Mountain), 175, 194, **216**, 265

"Goods of Value Mountain", 216

Góóhníinii, 85

The Goosenecks, 289, **290**, 294

"Gopher", 179

Gopher Canyon, **54**

"Gopher Spring", 54

"Gopher Water", 199, 251 (Rio Puerco of the East)

Gopher Water Ruin, **54**

Gothic Creek, **290**

Gothic Mesa (also Gothic Butte), 136, 143

Government Bridge, 42

Gouldings (Trading Post) (also Gouldings), 28, **290–91**, 296

Graham's (Trading), 28, 282

Grand Canyon, 1, 4, 12, 43, 70, **83–84**, 85, 294

Grand Falls, **84**

Grand Gulch, **291**

"Grand House", 247

Grand Junction, CO, **156**

Grants, NM, 107 (uranium mines), **216**

"Graven Rock", 189

"Gray Cottonwood Wash", 52

"Gray Man": 67 (Chilchinbito T. P.); 197 (Coyote Canyon T. P.)

Gray Mountain, 69, **84**, 120

"Gray Mountain", 69, 84

Gray Mountain, AZ, 85

Gray Mountain Trading Post, 28, 85

Gray Mountain Canyon, **85**

"Gray Mountain Canyon", 85

"Gray Mountain Wash", 41

"Gray Salt", 170

"Gray Spring" (from the Hopi), 93

"Grey Streak Ends" (see Mesa Santa Rita), 233

"Gray Streak Mountain", 102

"Gray Whiskers", 297

Gray Whiskers Butte, 291, 296, **297**

Greasewood (Lower), **85**

Greasewood Spring, 85

Greasewood (Lower) Trading Post, 28

Greasewood (Upper) Trading Post, 28, **85**

"Greasewood Arroyo", 161

"Greaswood Canyon", 295

Greasewood Creek, 107

"Greasewood House", 190

Great Gambler's Spring, The, 195

"Great House", 246

Green Cottonwood Canyon, **53**

"Green House", 165

"Green Place Between the Rocks", 41

Green Tableland, 159

"Grinding Snakes", 222, 242

Griswold's Trading Post, 28, 237

Groaning Lake, 35

"Groaning Lake", 35

Guadalupe, 184

Guadalupe Canyon, **216–17**

Guam, 195

Guisewa, 222

"Gurgling Water" , 269

Gypsum Creek, **297**

Gypsum Wash, 295

Gypsum Valley, 296

Ha Ho No Geh Canyon, 69, **85**

Hawhi Yalin Wash, 86

Ha'aastsélí, 195

Ha'ałtsédii Íí'áhí Ha'atiin, 47

Ha'asdoní, 47

Ha'ashgizh, 169

Ha'naa Na'ní'á, 95

Ha'thohih Spring, 50

Hááhonoojí, 69

Haak'oh, 169

Haashk'aan Silá Mesa, 10

Háásita', 73

Haaz'áí Habitiin, 49

Haaz'áí Łání, 58

Haaz'éí Dah Hidédlo'í Ha'atiin, 60

Haazbaa', 218

Haazéí Hidétání, 60

Haaz'éí Dah Hidétání Kit'siil, 54

Haaz'éí Nahíítání, 54

Habídí Bito'í, 56

"Hack Out Red Ochre Place", 52

"Hack Out Red Ochre Place Cove", 52

Hackberry Ruins Group (Hovenweep), **292**

Hahodeeshtł'izhí, 262

Hahoyíliní, 86

"Hairy Ones", 280

Hajíínáí, 157, 163

Hak'eelt'izh, 145

Halchíítah, 118, 291

Halchita, **291**

Halgai Tó, 291

Halgaito Wash, **20**

Halona:wa (also Halona, Holona), 281, **282**

Haltso, 257

Hama, 46

Hamblin Creek, 82, 85

Hamblin Ridge, **85**

Hanáádłį, 181

"Hanging Cottonwood", 302

"Hanging Ladder Fragmented House", 54

"Hanging Ladders Trail Up Out", 60

Hanging (Pole) Ladder Trail, **60**

Hano, **89**

Hanu, 89

"Hard Goods Mountain", 153, 215

Hard Ground Canyon and Flats, **217**

"Hard Ground", 217

"Hard Nose", 200, 245

Hard Rock, AZ, **85**

Harris Mesa (see Mesa Quartado), 233

Hasbitito Creek, **85**

Hasbídí Tó, 85

Hashtł'ish Bii' Kits'iil, 235

Hashké Neiniihi, 95

Hastiin Tl'ó Bitséyaa, 57

Hastoí Habitiin, 47

Hatch Trading Post, 28, **291**, 292

Hatsxil Hááyolí, 62

Havasupai Indian Reservation, **85**

Hawikuh (also Abacus), 204, 240, **289**

Hawikku, 281, 282

Hay Camp, 259

Hayes' Trading, 286

Haynes (also Haynes Ranch), 28, **217**, 228

Haynes, W. B., Trading Post, 217

Haystack, **217**

Haystack Butte, 87

Haystack Mountain, **240**
Haystack Ruin, **217**
Haystacks, The, **86**, 148
"Hazardous Water", 276
Hazéi Łání, 50
Haazneest'í'í, 62
"He Doesn't Obey", 57
"Head of One's Penis", 145
"Head Mountain", 112
Head Rock, **52**
Heart Butte Post, 28
Heart Rock, **217**
Heart Rock Trading Post, 28, 217
"He Distributed Them with Angry Insistence", 95
Helena Canyon, 108
Hell Canyon, 262
Hell's Gate, 42
"Hello", 280
Heller Trading Post, 28
Henry Mountains, **291**
Hermano Peak, 253
"Her Offspring", 165
Hennesey Buttes, 87
Herrera Mesa, **217–18**
Hesperus Peak (also Mount Hesperus), 21, 128, 153, **156**, 235, 242
"Hidden Spring", 283
"High Hill", 150
"High Town" (from Spanish), 187
"Hill Above a Basin", 42
"Hill Among Cedars Canyon", 64
"Hill Ruin", 262
"Hills Converge", 195
"Hill Slopes Down and Ends", 65
Hitaveli, 93
Hóchxǫ'í Ha'atiin, 46, 62
Hóchxǫ'í Ha'atiin Nàstł'ah, 46
Hodíílid, 154
Hodzhgani Wash 39, **86**
Hogaitoh Wash, 291
"Hogan Built over Water", 39
Hogback, **218**
"Hogback", 76, 108, 288
"Hogback to One Side", 194
Hogback Trading Post, 24, 28, **218**
Hol Hahayólí, 62
Holbrook, AZ, **86**, 105
Hole in the Wall (also Hole in Rock), **291–92**
Hole-in-the-rock Mesa, **297**
"Hole in the Rock Shaped like a Rainbow", 303

"Hole Spreading as Its Sides Continuously Crumble and Fall Away", 115
Holly Ruins Group (Hovenweep), **293**
Holyoak (see Aneth, UT), 285
"Holy Rock", 186
Holy Ghost Spring, 285
"Home", 183
Homolovi, 87, 88, 92
Honoojí, 69
Hooded Fireplace Site (Dinétah), **202**
Hoop and Pole Game Rock, **48**
Hopi Buttes, **87**
Hopi Mesas, 3, 5, 8(Table 4), 11, 38, 43, 63, 85, 95, 101, 146, 232, 260, 287, 289
Hopi Reservation, **87**
Hopi Salt Mine, **95**, 147
Hopi Villages, 4, 160, 220, 255
"Horsefly Creek", 107
Hovenweep Castle, **293**
Hovenweep National Monument, 165, 187, **292–93**: archeoastronomy in, 282
"Horizontal Gray Streak", 233
"Horizontal Line", 254
"Horizontal Red Point", 127
"Horse Enclosed in Fence", 206
Horse Lake (see Stinking Lake), 267
"Horse Lake", 267
Horse Rock, **50**
"Horse Rock", 50
"Horse Trail Going Up", 54
"Horsehead Crossing", 86
Horseshoe Ruins Group, **293**
Hosh Dik'ání, 34
Hosh Yishkhíízh, 179
Hoskininni Mesa, **86**
Hospah, **218**
Hosta Butte, 17, 193, 198, 201, **218–19**, 219, 243
Hot Na Na Wash, **95**
"Hot Spring", 115
"Hot Water", 240, 258, 272
Hotevilla, AZ, 88, **93–94**
Houck, AZ, **95**
Houck Trading Post, 28, **96**
Houck's Tank, **96**
"House Around Which the Wind Blows", 225
"House at the Water", 134
"House Between the Cliffs", 256

"House in the Ground", 187
"House in the Oaks", 117
House in the Rock Ruin, **50**
"House in the Sage", 98
"House in the Sagebrush", 115
"House in Which the Wind Blows", 225
House of Many Hands, 198
"House on a Rock Ledge", 114, 115
"House on the Edge of a Cliff", 255
"Houses Between the Rocks" (see San Felipe Pueblo), 255
"House the Wind Blows Around", 187, 224
"House under Goat Rock", 56
"House under the Cottonwoods", 86, 260
"House under the Rock", 61, 139
"House under the Rocks" (Poncho House Ruin), 302
"House with White Stripe Across", 47
"House Strung in a Circle", 92
Howell Mesa, 85, **96**
Hóyéé', 132, 137
Hubbell and Cotton Trading Post, 28, 97
Hubbell Trading Post, 24, 28, 81–82, **96–97**, 120
Hubbell's Chinle Trading Post, 28, 97
Huerfanito (also El Huerfanito), **219**
Huerfano Mesa (also Huerfano Mountain, El Huerfano), 4, 5, 128, 153, 202, **219**, 235, 243, 279: on Jemez–San Juan Rte., 284
Huerfano Trading Post, 28, 181, **219**
"Hunchback [God]" (or "Camel"), 53
Hungo Pavi (also Hungopavie), 186
"Huge Cottonwood Spreads Cove", 55
"Huge Cottonwood Trail Up Out", 55
Humphreys Peak, 128–29
Hunchback Rock, **45**
Hunter's Point, **97–98**
Hunter's Point Trading Post, 28, 98

Hwééldi, 207
Hyatt Trading Post, 28

'Iishtááh Dził, 228
Ice Cave, **219–20**
Ignacio, CO, **156–57**, 164
"In a Bowl", 172
"In the Bowl", 178
"In Between the Rocks", 139
Indian Wells, **98**, 133
Indian Wells Trading Post, 28, 98
Inscription House Ruin, **115**, 116
Inscription House (Trading Post),
28, **98**, 114, 115, 199
Inscription Rock (see El Morro
National Monument), 204, 259
"Inside Corner of the Traprock",
58
"Inside the Rock", 139
"Into the Black Rock it Starts to
Flow", 177
"Iron Lying Down", 148
Island Lake, **157**
Isleta Pueblo, **220**, 226, 254
Ismay Trading Post, 28, **157**, 166,
292
"It Extends", 302
"It Lies on its Side", 254
"It Flows Back Out", 73
"Its Back" (literally "Area in
One's Back Between the
Shoulder Blades"), 73
Ives Mesa, **98**
Iyanbito, **220–21**

Jaa'baní Bikooh, 54
Jaa'baní Habitiin, 54
Jacob's Well, **98–99**, 115
Jacques Canyon, **221**
Jádí Bí'h iikáál, 134
Jadí Bik'iilkaad (also Jadi
Bukiikaad), 67
Jádí Deíjechí, 57
Jádí Deíjeehí Kits'iilí, 57
Jádí Habitiin, 34, 59
Jádí Hádít'įįh, 172, 175
Jádító, 34, 99
"Jagged Area", 69
"Jagged Rock Extending
Upward", 75
"Jagged Sand Dune", 130
Janice Peak, 87
Jara Spring, 134
Jeddito (Jádító, Jadito, Jedito), 34,
99

Jeddito Trading Post, 28
Jeddito Mesa (also Jedito, Jadito),
99
Jedito Wash, **99**
Jeeh Deez'áhí, 106
Jééhkał, 224
Jemez–Chuska Valley Road, 284
Jemez Hot Springs, **221**, 222
Jemez Mountains, **221–22**, 242,
259, 260, 261, 268
Jemez Pueblo, 7(Table 3), 8(Table
4), 9(Table 5), **222–23**: Navajo
origin narratives about, 4;
Navajo raids on, 11; and Jemez
Clan Navajos, 43; trail to, 180;
and guide for Washington's
1949 expedition, 184; refugees
from help establish Laguna
Pueblo, 226; Navajos travel
to, 228; as most important Rio
Grande pueblo for Navajo
trading, 261; Seven Lakes on
the road to, 262; Torreon
Navajos maintain close contact
with, 274; hardships caused
at by Zia friendship with
Spaniards, 281
Jemez River, 184
Jemez–San Juan route, 284
"Jet Mountain", 157
Jewel Mountain, 128
Jewett, **223**
"Jicarilla Apache Home", 203
Jicarilla Apache Reservation, 191,
203, **223–24**, 267, 279
Jiłháli Bító, 50
Joint Use Area, 35, 38, **99**, 128
Jones Ranch, 28, **224**
Joppe, AZ, 131
Joseph City, 77, 86, **99**
Juan's Lake (also Lake Valley), 227
Junction, The, **55**
Junction Ruin, **47**
Junction Rock, 46
"Juniper Hill", 117
Juniper Ridge, **100**
"Juniper Sits Canyon", 223
"Juniper Slope", 100
"Jutting Rock–it Extends out to a
Point", 39

K'aa Łaní, 232
K'aabizhii, 71
K'aabizhiistł'ah, 71
K'aalógii Dził, 183, 268

K'aatání, 192
K'ai' Bii' Tó, 100
K'ai' Ch'íneeltł'ǫ, 227
K'aí' Naashchii' Bikooh, 176
K'ai' Si'ání, 134
K'ai'tsoh, 205
K'ii'aaha, 171
K'iiłtsoii, 162
K'iiłtsoiitah, 71
K'ish Ch'ínít'i', 241
K'iishzhinii, 65
Kah Bihghi Valley (Kah Bizhi or
Koh Bizhi), 123
Kaibab Plateau, 84, **100**
Kaibito, **100**
Kaibito Canyon, 114
Kaibito Plateau, 71, 82, 95, **100**,
112
Kaibito Trading Post, 28, **100**
Kaimes Canyon, 180
Kaiparowitz Plateau (also Wild
Horse Mesa), **293**
Kana'a Creek, **100**
Kanab, UT, 120
Karigan's Trading Post, 28, **100**
Kawaioukuh, **91**
Kayenta, AZ, 24, **100**, 102, 138,
139, 301
Keams Canyon, AZ, 24, 41, 71, 80,
87, 97, **101**
Keams Canyon Trading Post, 24,
28, **101**, 108
Kechiba:wa, 281
Keet Seel Canyon, **101–2**
Keet Siel, 114, **115**
Kendrick Peak, **102**
Kerley's Trading Posts, 28, 100,
102
Ketro Kete (see Chetro Ketl), 185
Kidziibahi, **102**
Kigalia Spring, 287
Kiisa'vi, 91
Kimbeto (Trading Post) (also
Kimbito, Kinbeto, Kinebito,
Kinbito, Kinnebito), 28, **224**
Kimbeto Wash (also Kinbito
Wash or Kinnebito Wash), **224**
Kim-me-ni-oli Valley, **224**
Kim-me-ni-oli Wash, **224**
Kin Benyola (also Kin Benayola),
187
Kin Bii Naayoli, 187,
Kin Binááyołí (Chacoan Outlier),
224–25
Kin Bineola Ruin (also Kimenola,

Kin Binola, Kin Binioli, Kinbiniyol), **224**

Kin Bii'Naayolí, 187, 224

Kin dah'lichi'i, 102

Kin Dah Łichí'í, 81

Kin Dootł'izh (Salmon Ruin), 253

Kin Dootł'izhí, 165, 190

"Kingdom of Hacus", 170

Kiníí Dah Shijaa', 46

Kin Hocho'i, 225

Kin Hóchxǫ́ǫ́'í, 225, 230

Kin Hóchxǫ́'í (Manuelito), 230

Kin Indian Ruin, **225**

Kin Kale, 247

Kin Kletso, **187**

Kin Klizhin Ruin, **225**

Kiníí' Na'ígai Ha'atiin, 46, 47

Kiníí' Na'ígai, 47

Kinlichee (Kin Lichee), 4, 81, **102**

Kinlichee Trading Post, 28

Kinlichee Wash, 40

Kin Łani: 115 (Betatikin Ruin); 155 (Durango, CO); 227 (Lake Valley Ruin)

Kin Łání Dook'o'osłííd Biyaagi, 77

Kin Łichíí, 257

Kin Łigaaí, 63 (Canyon Diablo), 111 (Moencopi), 115 (Navajo Springs), 217 (Haystack), 245 (Prewitt), 254, (Sandia Pueblo), 257 (San Juan Pueblo)

Kin Łitsoo'í, 187

Kinłitsosinil, 193

Kinłitsosinil, 193

Kin Łizhin, 265

Kin Łizhiní, 225

Kin Na'ní'á, 178

Kin Naadzíí, 50

Kin Náázhoozhí, 49, 198

Kin Nasbas (Chaco Canyon), **187**

Kin Názbas, 185, 187

Kin Názt'i, 92

Kin Nizhoni Ruin, **225**

Kin Nizhóní, 225

Kin Noodǫ́ǫ́z, 176, 254

Kin Yits'ill, 115

Kinleechee Creek, 82

Kinteel (also Kintiel), 146, 173, 187

Kinteel (Chaco Canyon), **187**, 246

Kinteel Ch'inílíní, 246

Kinteeldę́ę́' Ńlíní, 172

Kin Ya'a (also Kin Yaa'á), 201

Kinyaa Tó Deezliní, 230

Kiogi Pueblo, 4

Kin Ya'a Ruin (also Kin Yai), 190, 201, **225**

Kirtland, **225**, 241

Kit Carson's Cave, **225**

Kits'ill, 115, 128, 143

Kits'iil Dah Yisk'id, 262

Kits'iil Yaa'á, 217

Kits'iilí, 33 (Agate House Ruin), 34 (Allentown Ruiin), 66 (Chambers Ruin), 101 (Keet Seel Canyon), 102 (Kitsili Wash), 106 (Long House Ruin), 112 (Montezuma's Chair), 292, (Hovenweep)

Kit Sili Wash, **102**

Klagetoh (Trading Post), 28, **102**, 202

Klethla Valley (also Klethlana Valley), 9(Table 5), **103**

Knee Rock (from the Spanish), 125

Knees, the, (Ute Mountain), 165

Kodak House, 161

Kóyaaí, 200

Kuhn Trading Post, 28, 81, **103**, 109

Kutz Canyon, 253

Kwakina, **283**

Kwa'kina, 281

Kwastijukwa, 221

Kyaki:ma, 281

Kykotsmovi, 88, **94**

La Agua De San Carlos, 184

"Ladder Trail" (Canyon De Chelly), 49

"Lady Behind's Spring", 117

Lady White Trail, **55**

"Lady Is White's Trail Up Out", 55

Laguna Canyon (see Tsegi Canyon), 139

Laguna Creek (also Laguna Wash), 68, 100, **103**

Laguna De Caballeros, 267

Laguna Negra, 37, 193, 272

Laguna Pueblo, 6, 11, 170, 220, **226**, 234, 261, 281: on Zuni Road and Wingate Valley Road, 284

Laguna Pueblo Trading Post, 28, **226–27**

Laguna Salina (see Zuni Salt Lake), 283

La Jara, **227**

La Jara Canyon, 215, **227**

La Joya, 42

La Labor, 108

La Laguna Difunto Ambrosio, 172

Lake Powell, 2, 69, 70, 83, 114, 163, 289, **293–94**, 303

"Lake That Has a Hole in It", 119

"Lake Surrounded by a Fence", 206

Lake Valley (also Juan's Lake), **227**

Lake Valley Ruin, **227**

Lambson Trading Post, 28, 248

Lana Negra, 33

Land Where They Came Up", 157

"Lapis", 275

La Plata Mountains (also Sierra de le Plata, La Plata Range) (San Juan Mountains), **157**, 193, 201

La Plata River, 155, 156, 161, **227**

La Posita, 179

"Large Body of Water at an Elevation", 293

"Large Cottonwood Tree Where the Water Flows Out", 178

"Large Flattopped Area", 243

"Large Village" (from the Spanish), 146

Largo Canyon and Creek (also Cañon Largo, Cañada Largo, Canyon Largo), 3, 177, 202, 216, 222, **227–28**, 229: Hyde Expedition at, 240; on Abiquiu–San Juan Rte., 284

Largo School Ruin (Dinétah), 202

La Sal Mountains, **157**, 160, 271, 294

Las Nutrias, 271

Las Tijeras, 257

Las Tres Lagunas De La Trinidad, 267

"Last Spring", 147

"Late Game Trap (Obstacle)" (Canyon De Chelly), 46

"Lava Butte", 39, 138

"Lava Head", 138

"Lava Point", 126

"Lava Rock", 207

"Lava Rock Water Fall", 37

"Lava with Black Band Around It", 109

La Ventana, **228**

"Leaning Rock", 189, 218

Leche'e, **103**

Leche'e Rock, **103**
Leche'e Wash, **103**
Ledge Ruin (Canyon De Chelly), **56**
Lee's Ferry, AZ, 28, 83, **103–4**, **301**
Lee's Ferry (Trading), 28
Lee's Ferry Bridge, 114
"Left Handed", 296
"Lesser Rock Canyon", 114
Leroux Wash, **104**, 111
Leupp, 14, 64, 98, **104**
Leupp Trading Post, 28, **104**
Lewis Trading, 28, 271
Leyit Kin, **187**
"Life Without End", 70
"Lightning Struck Rock Cave", 48, 49
"Lightning Struck Tree", 265
Lime Ridge, **294**
Limestone Tanks, **105**
Linden, AZ, 131
Lindrith, NM, 28, **228–29**
"Line Carved Into the Rock", 139
"Line Extends to the River", 149
"Line of Cat Tails, A", 117
"Line of Houses Ledge", 56
"Line of Lava Extends Horizontally Outward, A", 87
"Line of Rock-niche Houses", 50
"Line on the Canyon's Edge", 139
"Line on the Rim", 150
Lingle, Washington and Thomas Trading Post (see Hubbell and Cotton Trading Post), 28
"Little Area Point Between", 58
Little Black Spot Mountain (Little Black Speck Mountain), 35, **105**
Little Colorado River, **105**: Black Falls on, 37; drainages on Black Mesa tributary to, 39; juncture with Colorado River, 41; and Albuquerque to Ft. Whipple Star Mail Route, 66; Lt. Sitgreaves surveys, 84; Joseph City on, 99; Leroux Wash tributary to, 104; through the Painted Desert, 118; and Navajo trading expedition, 120; Tolchico on, 137; Wupatki on, 150
Little Colorado River Gorge (also Little Colorado River Canyon), 41, 42, 85, 147
Little Cottonwoods (from Spanish), 216

Little Crossing of the Little Colorado River (from Spanish), 125
Little Door (from Spanish), 170
Little Ear Mountain, 204
Little Gate (from Spanish), 214
Little House, 185
Little (mountain) Pass (from Spanish), 170
Little Middle Mesa, **58**
Little Mustache's Trading Post, 28, **105**
"Little Onion", 182
"Little Oraibi", 111
"Little Prairie Dogs", 270
"Little Rabbit", 224
Little Red (from Spanish), 105
Little Red River (from Spanish), 105
"Little Rock Canyon", 216, 298
Little Round Rock, **105**, 131
"Little Round Rock", 105
Little Salt Canyon, **105**
"Little Salt Canyon", 105, 131
"Little Span Across", 42
Little Water, **229**, 273
"Little Water", 229
Little Water Creek, 272
Little Water Trading Post, 28
Little White Cone, 145
Little White House Canyon, **106**
Lizard Head Peak, 166
"Lizard Spring", 113
"Locoweed", 113
"Log Place Wash", 53
Lohali Point, **106**
Lók'a'ch'égai, 107, 266
Lók'a'deeshjin, 101
Lók'a'jígai, 106
Lók'aahnteel, 81, 96, 121
Lók'aaniteel Ch'ínílí, 82
Lolomai Point, **106**
"Lone Hogan", 86
"Lone House in the Desert", 86
Lone Mountain, 106, **294**
Lonely Dell, 301
"Long Box Canyon" (see Piute Canyon), 301
"Long Ear's (Mule's) Trail Up Out", 52
"Long Ear's (Mule's) Trail Up Out Cove", 52
Long House, **106**, 115, 139, 161
Long House Valley, **106**
Long Lake, **229**

"Long Lake", 229
"Long Mountain", 150
"Long Nosed Mexican's Water", 234
Long Trail, 62
"Long Trail Across Up Out Cove", 62
"Long Trail Up and Out", 62
"Long Upgrade", 211, 238
"Long Upgrade Gap", 169
Looka, 265
"Loop and Stick Game Rock", 48
Los Alamitos, 216
Los Algodones, 111
Los Cerros, 268
Los Gigantes Buttes, **106**
Los Peñoles, 216, 228, **229**
Los Peñalitos, 7(Table 3)
Los Pilares, 76
Los Pinos River (also Rio Los Pinos, Rio Los Piños), 3, 56, 163, **224**, 270
"Lost Spring", 147, 283
Low Mountain, **106**
Low Mountain Trading Post, 28
Lower Greasewood Trading Post, 28
Lower Sunrise Springs, 104
Lukachukai, AZ, **106**, 124, 128, 197, 253, 273
Lukachukai Mountains, 2, 61, 64, **107**, 123, 124: and Walker's Expedition, 71; Mexican Cry Mesa, 110; White Ash Streak Mountain, 145
Lukachukai Trading Post, 25, 28, **107**
Lukachukai Wash, 68, **107**, 124
Lululongturkui (Hopi), **107**
Lupton, AZ, **107–8**, 132, 277
Lybrook (also Lybrooks), NM, **229–30**
Lybrooks Trading Post, 28, **230**
"Lying Down Duck Rock", 45
"Lying Face Down Under the Wide Rock", 257
Łeets'aats'iil, 101, 112
Łeeyi' Kin, 187
Łeeyi'Kiní, 49
Łeeyi'tó, 102
Łeezh Łizhin Bitó, 40
Łeejin Haageed, 69
Łeets'aats'iil, 101, 112
Łeetsoii Bii'tó Ha'atiin, 47
Łíchíí, 103

Łíchíí Dah 'Azkání, 304
Łichíí' Deez'áhí, 127
Łíchíí Táá'á, 52
Łid Néigahí, 131
Łigaii Dah Azkání, 146
Łigai 'Íí'áhí, 214
Łíí Bináásht'ih, 206
Łį́į́' Bito' (see Stinking Lake), 267
Łį́į́' Haa'nah, 200
Łį́į́' Habitiin, 54
Łíí Łani, 103
Łíí Łigaii Bito', 279
Łitsooí, 271
Łizhiin Bikooh, 37
Łóó' Háálį́, 106

M'ii Tééh Yítłizhí, 179, 197
Mą́'ii' Aztł'iídi, 76
Mą́'ii Bikee Ha'atiin, 47
Mą́'ii Bikooh, 54
Mą́'ii Dah Siké, 172
Mą́'ii Deeshgiizh, 221, 222
Mą́'ii Ha'atiin, 55
Mą́'iilso Ch'nl, 45
Mą́'iito'í, 95
Madden Peak, 157
Madison & McCoy Trading Post, 28
Magdena Butte, 216, 229
"Makes a Turn Flowing", 116
"Makes Hunting Pipes", 53
"Male Water", 163
"Male River", 252
Mancos, CO, **157**
Mans Canyon, **157–58**, 161, 164, 193
Mancos Creek, **158**, 160, 163, 238
Mancos Creek Trading Post, 28, **158**
Mancos Mesa, **294**
Manning Brothers Trading Company, 29
Manson Mesa, 118
Manuelito, 202, **230**
Manuelito Canyon, **230**
Manuelito Springs (also Manuelito's Spring and Manuelito Spring), **230–31**
Manuelito Springs Trading Post, 29
Manuelito Trading Post, 29, **231**
"Many Arrows", 192, 232
Many Arrows Wash, **232**
"Many Berries Cove", 59
"Many Berries Trail Up Out", 59

"Many Big Berries (Peaches) Cove", 48
"Many Bodies of Water", 170
"Many Cacti (Coming) down from a Height", 110
Many Cherry Canyon, **59**
"Many Cherry Trail", 59
"Many Douglas Firs", 54
"Many Eagle Nests", 94
Many Farms, 9(Table 5), **108**
Many Farms Lake, 108
Many Farms (Trading), 29
"Many Fields", 108
"Many Horses", 103
"Many Houses", 115, 155, 227
"Many Houses below San Francisco Mountains", 77
Many Ladders Trail, 60
"Many Legged Hogan (Home)", 75
"Many Little Cottonwoods", 136
"Many Mountains", 281
Many Peaches Canyon, **48**, 165
"Many Peaches Canyon", 48 (in Canyon De Chelly), 165 (Trail Canyon)
"Many Rocks", 127
"Many Rock Pinnacles", 53
Many Sheep Valley, **108**
"Many Sheep Valley", 108
"Many Squirrels", 50
"Many Step Ladders (Trail)", 58
"Many Stones", 230
"Many Trees", 140
Many Waters, **232**
"Many Waters", 232
Many Waters Canyon, **54**
"Many Waters (Springs)", 54
Marata, **232**
Marble Canyon, 41, 70, 83, 97, **105**, 108
Marble Canyon Bridge, 14, 104, 114
Marble Canyon Trading Post, 29, **108**
Mariano Lake, NM, **232**
Mariano Lake Trading Post, 25, 29, **232**
Mariano's Store, 29, **232**
Mariano Wash, **158**
"Marked about with Charcoal", 281
Masipa Spring (Hopi), 93
Marsh Pass, 8(Table 4), 9(Table 5), 25, 103, **108**, 114, 139

Massacre Cave, **61–62**, 182, 282
Massacre Cave Trail, 62
Matsaki (also Matsakaya), 283
Mats'a:kya, 281
Matthews Peak, **109**
McCarty's, NM, 170, **233**
McClellan Tank, **109**
McCracken Canyon, **294**
McCracken Mesa, **294**
McCrary, Charles, Trading Post, 29
McElmo Creek, **158–59**, 165, 285
McElmo Trading Post, 29, **159**, 301
McGaffey, **233**
McKittrick (see Pinehaven), 245
McMahon Trading Post, 29, **81**, 109
"Meadow, The", 257
"Meadow in Between the Rocks", 78
"Meadow Between the Rocks Flows Out", 42
"Meadow Extends out Horizontally", 69
Meadows, The, 126
Meat Rock, **47**
"Meat Rock", 47
"Meeting of the Waters", 229
Menefee Mountain (and Peak), **159**
"Menstrual-blood-one (Hunchback) Is Lying Down", 45
"Menstrual-blood-one (Hunchback) Sitting at an Elevation", 45
Mentmore, **233**
Merrick Butte, **297**
Merrick Mesa, 296
"Mesa Apart", 294
Mesa Azul, 184
Mesa Butte, **233**
Mesa Cayatano, 174
Mesa Colorado, 123
Mesa De Los Lobos (also Lobo Mesa), 200, 202, **223**
Mesa De Las Vacas, 38
Mesa Fahada (also Mesa Fachada, Mesa Fajada) (see Fajada Butte), 186
Mesa Mountain (also Tank Mountain), **159**
Mesa Portales, 228
Mesa Prieta, 179

Mesa Quartado (also Harris Mesa), **233**
Mesa Redonda, **109–110**
Meteor Crater, **110**
Mesa Santa Rita, **233–34**
Mesa Tierra Ruin, **234**
Mesa Verde (National Park), 63, 139, 155, 157, **159–61**, 162, 166, 292: and Zuni Migration Narrative, 190
Mesita, 226, **234**
Mesita Negra, 234
"Mexican" (Nokai Canyon, Dome and Mesa), 300
Mexican Canyon, 71
"Mexican's Ascent", 221
Mexican Cry Mesa, 85, **110**, 145
Mexican Hat, 107, 288, 290, **292**, 295
"Mexican Hat", 294
Mexican Hat Trading Post, 29
"Mexican River", 251
"Mexican Sloping Down", 299
"Mexican Spring" (Naakaito Bench), 301
Mexican Springs (also Nakaibito), 195, **234**
Mexican Springs Trading Post, 29, **234**
"Mexican Trail Leading Up and Out", 63
"Mexicans Dug Shallow Wells", 110
"Mexicans Were Massacred", 73
Mexican Water, **110–11**, 143
"Mexican Water", 110, 143
Mexican Water Bridge, 110
Mexican Water Trading Post, 29, 110, **111**
"Mexican's Water", 234
"Middle House Sits at an Elevation", 46
Middle Crossing, 114, 301
Middle Trail Canyon, 55, **62**, 63
Middle Village, 90
Milan, NM, 216
Milk Ranch, 267
Mishongnovi, AZ, 87, **91**
Mission of San Diego De Jemez, 221
"Mister Weaver's under Rock", 57
Mitchell (see Thoreau), 270
Mitchell Butte, 285, 296, **297**
Mitchell Mesa, 285, 296, **297**
Mitten Peak, 87, **111**

Mitten Rock, 72, **234**
Mitten Buttes (also The Mittens, East Mitten, West Mitten), 296, **298**
Moccasin, AZ, 120
Mocking Bird Canyon, 186
Moenave (also Moe Ave), AZ, **111**
Moenkopi (Moencopi, Moncapi), AZ, 88, **111**
Moenkopi Wash (also Moencopi Wash), 38, 41, 86, **112**
Mogollon Baldy, 146, **234**
Mogollon Mountains, 96
Mogollon Rim, **112**
Montezuma's Chair, 87, **112**
Montezuma Creek, **295**
Montezuma Creek, UT, **295**
Montezuma Creek Trading Post, 29
Montezuma Valley (Tribal Park), **161–62**
Monument Canyon, 51, **53**
Monument Pass, 296
Monument Valley, 2, 33, 90, 98, 114, 288, 290, **295–98**
Monuments, The, 51, 107
"Moonwater", 301
Mooney, Bernard J., Trading Post (see Hubbell and Cotton Trading Post), 29
Moqui Buttes, 87, **112**
Moqui Canyon, **162**
Moquino, **234**
Moqui Wash, 121
"More than Three Utes Which Ride Along on Horses", 56
Mormon Lake, **113**
Mormon Trail, 109
Mósí Bitsiits'iin, 56
Moshangnovi, 91
"Mother Area", 46
"Mother of His Child, The" (see Piute Canyon), 301
Mother Cottonwood, **46**
Mount Elden, 130
Mount Ellen, 291
Mount Elous, 163
Mount Hesperus (see Hesperus Peak), 157, 162, 279
Mount Hillers, 291
Mount Linaeus, 285
Mount Moss, 157
Mount Nebo, 163
Mount Ness, 294
Mount Pannell, 291

Mount Peale, 294
Mount Sedgewick, 281
Mount Tomasaki, 294
Mount Taylor (also San Mateo Mountain, San Mateo Peak, Cebolleta Mountains), **235**: Spanish battle Querechos at, 5; as Navajo Sacred Mountain of the South, 21, 128, 153, 243, 279; and road to Santa Fe, 179; Yeii'tsoh's Blood (lava flow) ran north from, 180; seen from Chuska Peak, 194; possibly included in Dinétah, 201; Big Yei's Blood (lava flow) coagulated at base of, 204; Navajos living on, 205
Mount Withington, 257
"Mountain", 73
"Mountain Beautiful on Top", 174
Mountain Lion, 147
Mountain Meadows, 103, 111, 166, **298–99**, 301
"Mountain of Precious Stones", 219
"Mountain Sheep Lying down up at an Elevation", 87
"Mountain Sheep's Testicle Trail Down", 288
"Mountain Sheep's Trail" (see Comb Wash), 288
"Mountain Surrounded by Barren Soil", 150
"Mountain That Gropes Around", 64
"Mountain That Extends Black", 38
"Mountain That Has a Mind", 157
"Mountain That Is Coiled Up", 295
"Mountain That Lay Down", 124
"Mountain That Revolves", 254
"Mountain That Sits on Top of Another Mountain", 218
"Mountain That Sits up on an Elevation", 77
"Mountain Tongue", 235
"Mountain Which Appears Black", 38
"Mountain with a Basin in It", 109
"Mountaintoppers Land", 146
"Mourning Dove's Spring", 56
"Moved in the Water", 243
"Mr. Cane's Field", 114

"Much Fur", 33
"Much Water", 122, 226, 275
"Much Water Creek", 181
"Much Wool", 33
Muddy Water Ruin, **235**
Mule Canyon, **52**
Mule Trail, **52**
Mummy Cave, 43, 55, **61**
Mummy Cave Ruins, 61
Mummy House, 43, 61
Mystery Valley, 296, **298**

Na-ah-tah Canyon Trading Post, 108
Na'ashǫ'iito'í, 107, 113
Na-ah-tee, 97, 113
Na'azísí Nástł'ah, 54
Na'azísí Tó, 251
Na'azísí To'í, 199
Na'azizi, 179
Na'azízí Tó, 54
Na'iiníjé'é, 57
Na'neelzhiin, 274
Na'ní'á Hatsoh, 108, 114
Na'ní'á Hayázhí, 42
Na'ní'á Hótsaa, 118
Na'nízhoozhí, 213
Náá'á Djjh, 113
Náá'aghání, 240
Naa'azhníídee'é, 62
Naa'hootso, 287
Naabi'ání, 178
Naadą́ą́' Díílid, 42
Naadzįįł Haayáhí, 50
Nááhwíłbiihí Bikin, 187
Naahtee Canyon (also Na-ah-tee), **113**
Naahtee Canyon Trading Post, 29, **113**
Naak'a'k'éé'dílyéhé, 112
Naakaii 'Adáánání, 63
Naakaii 'Adáánání Ha'atiin, 63
Naakaii Bitó', 143, 234
Naakaai Bitooh, 251
Naakai Canyon, **299**
Naakaii Ch'ah, 294
Naakaii Chį́įhí Bitó' (see Mexican Springs), 234
Naakaii Haayáhí, 221
Naakaii Habitiin, 63
Naakai Hatsoh Ha'atiin, 63
Naakaii Hojííghání, 61,
Naakaii Jííghání, 73
Naakaii Kíhoniiłkaad, 299
Naakaii Sání, 96

Naakaii Tó, 110, 120
Naakaiitó, 120
Naakaii Tó Hadayiiznilí, 110
Náálí Hatsoh Nástł'ah, 62
Náálí Hatsoh Ha'atiin, 62
Naashashí, 89, 260
Naasht'ézhí, 281
Naasht'ézhí Haayáhí, 49
Naasilá, 254
Naat'áani Nééz, 263
Naat'áaniitsoh, 298
Naatani Tso, **298**
Naatooho, 220
Naatooh Sik'i'í, 216
Nááts'íílid Na'nízhoozhí (see Rainbow Bridge), 303
Naatsis'áán, 299
Naayízí, 235
Nacimiento, 199, 263
Nacimiento Mountains, 221
Na Daxas'ai, 146
Nageelid Na'nízoozhi, 303
Nageezi (Trading Post), 29, **235**, 241
Nagashi Bicho (see Comb Wash), 288
Nahashch'idí, 237
Nahaschchidí Bito', 237
Náhodeeshgiizh, 200
Nahodishgish, 200
Nahoditsʼǫ, 141
Nahoneeshjéél, 69, 85
Nák'ee Sinilí, 96
Nambé Pueblo, **235–36**, 245
"Nameless Mountains", 291
Narbona Pass (also Washington Pass, Cottonwood Pass), 8(Table 4), 9(Table 5), 10, 184, **236–37**, 263: (Hinojos-Narbona Battle), 190; Navajo Agency near, 193
"Narrow Canyon", 106
Narrow Canyon Trail, 62
Narrow Gate, 109
"Narrow Rock Canyon", 106
"Narrow Rock Point", 196
"Narrow Under the Rocks", 140
Naschitti (also Drolet's), **237**
Naschiti Trading Post, 24, 29, **237**
Nashbito, **113**
Náshdóí B'áán, 280
Nashdóí Bighan, 276
Náshdóíts'ǫ'í, 147
Nasisitge (possibly a rendering of Na'azísí Tó), 251

Nasja Creek, **299**
Nasja Mesa, **299**
Nástl'ah, 60
Nastl'ah (see Piute Canyon), 301
Nát'oh Dził, 84, 99
Nát'ohdziil, 285
Nát'ostse' Áljjgi, 53
Nát'oste' 'All'íní, 53
Nát'ostse' 'Ál'íní, 144
Natural Bridge, **113**
Natural Bridge Canyon, **113**
Natural Bridges National Monument, **299**
"Nauseating Water" (see Stinking Lake), 268
Nava (see Newcomb), 239
Navaho City, **237**
Navahu (Navaho, Navahuge), 247
Navajo, AZ, 115
Navajo, NM, **237**, 270
Navajo Army Depot, **113–14**
Navajo Bridge, **114**
Navajo Canyon, 84, 98, **114**, 149
Navajo Canyon (tributary of the Mancos River), **162**
Navajo Church, 193, 252
Navajo Church Trading Post, 29, **237**
Navajo Creek, 114, 115
Navajo Crossing (see Piute Farms), 302
Navajo Dam, **237–38**
Navajo Fortress, **58**
Navajo Fortress Gap, **58**
Navajo Fortress Trail, 58
Navajo Indian Irrigation Project, 211, **238**
Navajo Lake (also Navajo Reservoir), 163, **238**, 270
Navajo Mountain (also Sierra Panoche), 33, 34, 39, 64, 70, 78 (see from Fluted Rock), 95, 120, 165, 289, **299–300**: on trail to Kapairowitz Plateau, 293
Navajo Mountain Trading Post, 29, 122, **300**
Navajo National Monument, 98, 102, **114**, 139
Navajo Peak, **191** (NM), **239** (Utah)
Navajo River, 163, 191, **238**
"Navajo River", 163
"Navajo's Spring", 74
Navajo Springs, 99, **115**, **116** (near Ute Mountain)

Navajo Springs (Trading), 29
Navajo Trails (Trading), 29
Navajo Trail, **238**
"Navajo Trail Going Upward", 238
"Navajo Trail Up", 216
Navajo Twins, 287, 289
Navajo Watchtower, **161**
Navata, **238**
Navata (Trading), 29
Náyaaseęsí, 99
Nazlini, 97, **116**, 202
Názlíní, 116
Nazlini Canyon (also Nazlini
    Creek or Wash), 68, **116**
Nazlini Trading Post, 29, **116**
Ndeelk'id, 65
Ńdíshchíí' 'Ajisht'óóhí, 159
Ndíshchíí' Haazt'i', 213
Ndíshchíí' Haazt'i' Nástl'ah, 62
Ńdíshchíí' Názt'i', 186
Né'éshjaa', 299
Neal and Damon's (Trading), 29
Needle, The (see Shiprock
    Pinnacle), 264
Needle Rock, 166
"Needles", 263
Neesk'áhí, 300
Nehanezad, **238**
Neheyołí Nástł'ah, 46
Nehiagee, 129
Nelson's Trading Post, 29, 239
Nenahnezad, 211
Neskahi Wash, **300**
"Never Thaws on Top", 128, 153
Neville Trading Post, 29, **300**
Newberry Mesa, 174
Newcomb (also Blue Mesa
    Trading Post, Crozier Trading
    Post, Nava and Newcombs), 29,
    176, **239**
Newcomb Trading Post, 123, 178,
    239
New Laguna, 226, **239**
New Oraibi (Trading), 29, 94
Ni'ałníí'gó, 147
Ni'go 'Asdzáán, 300
Ni' Haldzis, 42
Ni'haldizis Dahisk'id, 42
Ni' Hotł'izí, 217
Ni'iijíhí, 129
Ni'iijíhí Hasání, 129
Ni'iijíní, 237
Níhoobá, 233, 247
Nihoyostsatse, 157
Niidzí, 116

Niinah Nízaad, 211, 238
Niiyahkinii, 90
Níłtsá Dził, 193
Nínánízaadí Ha'atiin Nástłah, 62
Nipple Butte, 87
Nitsin Canyon, 115, **116**
Nízaa'aliwozh Nástłah, 57
Nízaad Ha'atiin, 62
Nłiz Dził, 219
Nokai Canyon, **300**
Nokai Dome, **300**
Nokai Mesa, **301**
Nokaito Bench, **301**
Noland's Four Corners Store
    (Trading Post), 29, **162**
Noodah Haas'aí, 146, 234
Nóódá'a Łii' Bił Yikahigi, 56
Nóóda'í, 164
Nóóda'í Bito', 163
Nóódá'í Vi' Dziil, 159
Noodah Haas'ei, 146, 234
Noolyínii, 222
North Mesa, 183
"Nose Rock", 175, 248
"Not-go (Forbidden?) Gap", 60
"No Water Mesa", 136
Ntł'iz Dziil, 153, 215
Nłiz Dził, 219
Nutria Creek, 240
Nutria, Upper & Lower (also Las
    Nutrias and Nutrioso), **239–40**
Nutria Lakes, 240
Nutria Valley, 240

'Ooljéé'tó, 301
'Oozéí, 94
'Oozéí Biyashi, 94
'Oozéí Biyáshí, 94
'Oozéí Hayázhí, 111
Oak Creek, **240**, 272
Oak Creek Canyon, 39, **116–17**
Oak Grove (from Spanish), 205
Oak Springs (also Oak Spring),
    117
Obed, AZ, 99
"Obsidian", 222
Odzai, 94
"Offspring or Eagle Traps", 94
"Offspring of Many Bodies of
    Water", 170
"Offspring of Wild Onion
    Spring", 93
Ojo Alamo Trading Post, 29, **240**
Ojo Amarilla, 241
Ojo Amarilla Wash, 212

Ojo Caliente, 203, **240**
Ojo Del Gallo, 208, 259, 283
Ojo Del Oso, 8(Table 4), 9(Table
    5), 11, 208, 280
Ojo Encino, **240**
Ojo Encino (Trading), 24, 29
Ojo Espiritu Santu, 228
Ojos Calientes, 175
O'Leary Peak, **117**
"Old Age River", 163
Old Crater, **240–41**
Old Laguna, 226
"Old Mexican", 96
Old Otero Ranch, **241**
"Old Sawmill", 129
Old Taylor, AZ, 99
Olio Trading Post, 29, **241**
Oljeto (also Oljaytoh, Moonlight),
    29, 101, **301**
Oljeto Wash, **301**
Omer, AZ, 132
"One down Here, The", 200
One Life (from Spanish), 189
"One with Long Body", 163
"One with Wide Body", 163
"One Who Barely Gets Along",
    285
"One Who Crawls with Her Body,
    The", 290
"One Who Gave Birth for Him,
    The" (also "The Mother of His
    Child"), 301
"Oof!", 191
Oraibi, AZ, (also Oraivi, New
    Oraibi, Lower Oraibi), 42, 70,
    88, 93, **94–95**, 97, 111, 122, 142,
    170, 226
Oraibi Hill, 220
Oraibi Trading Post, 29, 108, **117**
Oraibi Wash, 42 (Burro Springs),
    85 (Hard Rock), **117**, 122 (Red
    Lake)
Orejas Del Oso, 286
Osborne and Walker Trading, 29,
    126
Otero, 241
Otter (from Spanish) 239
Otis (Trading Post), 29, **241**
Otis, E. E., Trading Post, 29
Otowi, 256
"Outflow Where Cottonwoods
    Extend Away in a Black Line",
    181
Outlaw Trading Post, 29, 237, **241**
"Outside Post", 175

"Overhanging Rock Ledge", 257
"Overlapping Layers", 56
"Overlapping Rocks", 258
"Overthrust Rock", 288
"Owl, The", 299

Padilla Mesa, **117**
Padre Bay, **301**
Page, AZ, 83, **118**
Pagosa Springs, CO, 256
Paguate, 226, **241**
Painted Desert, 2, 39, 105, 111, **118**
Paiute Strip, 98, 290
Pajarito Peak, 222, **242**
Panguitch, **301**
Paraje, 226, **242**
Paria Plateau, **118**
Parrot Peak, 157
Parking Lot Trail, 47
"Pass Coming Down", 200
Patoqua, 222
Payupki, 255
"Peach Orchard Spring", 101
"Pebble Outflow", 45
Pecos Pueblo, 4, 222, 223, **242**,
    260
Pecos River, 11, 79, 207, 254
Pedernal Mesa, 153, **242**
Pelado Peak, 153, 221, **242**
Peninsula, The, 58
Penistaja, 29, 199, **243**
Peña Blanca, **243**
Peña Blanco Arroyo (also
    Theodore Wash), **243**
Peñasco Blanco, **187**
Peñasco Blanco Ruin, 205
"People Draw Up Water", 261
"People Encircling Around
    Mountain", 153, 219
"People of the Kiva", 90
"People of the White Rock," 169
Perea Trading Posts, 29, 195
"Perforated Rock", 50, 147, 148,
    297
Pescado (also Pescado Springs),
    8(Table 4), **243**, 283
Petrified Forest National Park, 35,
    118–19
Petroglyph Rock, **45**
Picuris Pueblo, **244**, 255
Piedra Lumbre, 222
Piedra Mountains (San Juan
    Mountains), 161
Piedra Rodilla, 125
Pierre's Ruin, 190, **244**

"Pillars, The", 76
Pinedale, NM, 131
Pinedale, AZ, **244**
Pinedale Trading Post, 29, **245**
Pinehaven (also Danoff,
    Danoffville, McKittrick), **245**
Pinehaven Trading Post, **245**
Pine River (see Los Pinos River),
    29
"Pines in a Crescent Around the
    Canyon's Edge", 117
Pine Springs, 29, **119**
Pine Tree Canyon, **62**
Pinetop, AZ, 131
"Pine Trees Extend up in a
    Slender Line", 213
Piñon, AZ, 38, 97, **119–20**, 143
"Piñon", 68
"Piñon Canyon", 154
Piñon Springs Trading Post, 29,
    97, **245**
Piñon Trading Post, 29, **120**
Pipe Caves, **53**
Pipe Spring, **120**
"Pitch Point", 106
Piute (Paiute, Piute Strip, Paiute
    Strip), **120**, 296
Piute Canyon (also Paiute and
    Piute Creek), 121, **301–2**
Piute Farms (also Paiute Canyon,
    Paiute Farms, Piute Parks,
    Navajo Crossing, Clay Hill
    Crossing and White Clay
    Crossing), **302**
"Piute Fields" (see Piute Farms),
    302
"Piute Land", 120
Piute Mesa, **302**
Piute Strip, 165, **302**
"Place of the Black Man", 91
"Place of the Hills Ruins", 94
"Place of the Jointed Reed", 93
"Place of Emergence", 157, 163
"Place of the Antelope Notch", 66
"Place of a Rock Called Orai"
    (Hopi), 94
"Place of Raising", 300
"Place of Running Water" (Hopi),
    111
"Place of Snow on the Very Top"
    (Hopi), 128
"Place of the Gap" (Hopi), 90
"Place of the Mosquitos", 92
"Place of the Rock Pine Locust",
    221

"Place of the Water Rivulets",
    104, 140
"Place That Is Dry Around
    Water", 224
"Place Where Red Ochre Is
    Gathered", 52
"Place Where Sawing Is Done",
    237
"Place Where Stone Pipes Are
    Made", 53, 144
"Place Where the Waters
    Crossed", 238
"Plains Water", 291
"Pockets about (Gopher) Cove",
    54
"Pock-marked Rock", 234
"Point", 201
"Point Between Canyons", 55
Poison Ivy Canyon, **63**
"Poison Ivy Stands Spread out
    Cove", 63
"Poison Ivy Stands Spread out
    Trail Up Out," 63
Pojoaque Pueblo, **245**
Polacca, 29, 88, **90**
Polacca Wash, 38, **121**, 143
Polakaka, 90
Pollen Mountain, 64, 70, **121**, 175,
    194, 216
"Pollen Mountain", 33, 34
Polonta Mountains, 64
Polvadera, 266
Poncho House, 61, **301–2**
"Ponderosa Pines Extending Up
    Out in a Line Cove", 62
"Ponderosa Pines Extend up in a
    Line Trail Up Out," 62
"Ponderosa Rock Rim Crescent",
    36
"Popping Water", 272, 273
"Post Sticks into the Ground", 186
Postle's Ranch, 80
"Pot Sitting", 294
Pottery Sherds, 112
Potrero De La Cañada Quemada,
    261
Potrero Viejo, 256
Potsuwi, 256
Pouring down Rock, **45**
Poverty Butte, 137
Prayer Rock Canyon, 148
Prescott, AZ, 77, 80, 99
Preston Mesa, **121**
Prewitt (also Baca), 29, **245**
"Prominent White Cliffs", 130

"Promontory" (or "Elongated Ridge"), 201
"Propped Rock", 188, 189
Province of Tusayan (from Spanish), 88
Provincia de Nabajoo (Spanish), 191
Pueblo Alto, **187–88**
Pueblo Alto (Trading Post) (also Setzer's Store), 29, **246**, 267
Pueblo Bonito, 173, 183, **188**, 189, 246
Pueblo Bonito Trading Post, 29, 185, **245**
"Pueblo Canyon", 162
Pueblo Colorado (see Pueblo Pintado Ruin), 81, 102, 246
Pueblo Colorado Wash, 11, 79, 82, **121–22**
Pueblo Del Arroyo, **188–89**, 246
Pueblo Grande, 146
Pueblo Grande (see Pueblo Pintado Ruin), 246
Pueblo Montezuma (see Pueblo Pintado Ruin), 246
Pueblo Pintado, **246**
Pueblo Pintado Ruin (also Pueblo Colorado, Pueblo Montezuma, Pueblo Grande and, erroneously, Pueblo Alto), **246–47**
Pueblo Pintado Trading Post, 29, 232
Pueblo Ratones, 247
Puerco Ruin, 119
Puerta de las Lemitas, 109
Puerta Limita, 109
Puertocito, 170–71, 214, 268
Punyana, 226
Puye, **247**
Pyramid Rock, **248**

Quarai, 220
Quartzite Canyon, 42
Quchaptuvela, 90
Quelites, 37, 252
Quemado, **248**
Querino Canyon Trading Post, 30
Quigui (see Santo Domingo Pueblo), 261
Quini (see Zuni), **248**

"Rabbit", 70
"Rabbit Ears", 287
"Rabbit Ambush", 205
"Rabbit Brush", 162

Rabbit Ear Mountain, 87
Rabbit Mesa Trading Post, 30, **122**
Rabbit Mountain, 111
"Railroad Ends", 83
"Railroad Water", 251
Rainbow Bridge (National Monument) (also Rainbow Bridge, Rainbow Natural Bridge), 299, 302, **303–4**
"Rainbow Extends Across", 303
Rainbow Lodge (Trading), 30, 300
Rainbow Trail, **122**
Rain God Mesa, **298**
Rain Pueblo, 185
"Rainy Mountain", 193
Ramah, NM, 206, **248–49**
Ramah Navajo Reservation, **249**
Ramah Reservoir (or Lake), 214, 249
Ramah Trading Post, 30, 248, **249**
Rancheria De Gandules, 111
Rancho Chupadero, 193
Rangel Trading, 30, 279
Raton Springs, 240, **249**
Raton Springs Trading Post, 30, **249**
Rattlesnake, **249**
Rattlesnake Trading Post, 30
Recapture Creek, **303**
"Red", 54
Red Arrow Trading Post, 30, 271
Red and White Trading Post, 30, 271
"Red Area Rock Underside", 54
Red Butte, **249–50**
Red Clay Canyon, **52**
Red Clay Cave, **52**
"Red Clay Springs", 77
"Red Devil", 267
"Red Extends into Water", 52
"Red House", 257
"Red House in the Distance", 81, 102
Red Lake, 9(Table 5), **122**, 147, 237
"Red Lake", 36, 82, 122
Red Lake Trading Post, 30, 37, 64, **122**
Red Lake Trading Post (Coconino County, AZ), 30
Red Lake Trading Post (McKinley County, AZ), 30
"Red Man Mountain", 233
"Red Medicine", 276
"Red Medicine Wash", 276

Red Mesa, **123** (AZ), 265, **304** (UT)
"Red Mesa", 304
Red Mesa Trading Post, 30, **304**
"Red Metal (Copper) Pass", 236
Red Mountain, 217, **250**
"Red Mountain", 250
"Red Mustache", 225
"Red Oak", 267
"Red Oak up at an Elevation", 240
"Red Ochre Water", 127
Red Ochre Trail, 52
"Red Ochre Trail Up Out", 52
Redondo Peak, 211
Red Point, **221**
Red Rock, 9(Table 5), 175, **250**
"Red Rock", 103 (Leche'e Rock), 123 (Red Mesa), 173 (Atarque), 250 (Red Rock)
Red Rock Bridge (see Wittick Natural Arch), 148
"Red Rock Coming Down", 97
"Red Rock Extending out to a Point", 123
"Red Rock Going Around in a Circle", 97
"Red Rock Mesa", 123
Red Rock Point, **52**
"Red Rocks Pointing out Horizontally", 234
"Red Rock Slide", 35
"Red Rock Spire", 103, 278
"Red Rock Spreading Out", 173
"Red Rocks Standing Up", 173
Red Rock State Park, 237, 241, **250**
Red Rock Trading Post, 30, **123**
Red Rock Valley, 123, 181
Red Rock Wash, 72
"Red Streak Running Down", 134
"Red Streak Running into Water", 111
"Red Streaks Going Up", 35
Red Valley (also Red Rock Valley), **123**
Red Wash, 9(Table 5)
"Red Water Canyon", 105
"Red Water Wash" 137, 149
"Reeds at Elevation Water Outlet", 82
"Reeds Coming Out", 266
"Reeds Extend in a Black Line", 101
"Reeds Extend White", 107
"Reeds under the Rim", 34
Refuge Rock, **48**

"Refuge Rock", 204
"Refuge Mountain", 180
"Refused to Follow", 57
Rehoboth, **250**
"Ridge", 65
"Ridge That Runs out to a Point", 125
Rimmy Jim's (Trading), 30, 110
Rincon Largo, **250**
Rio Abajo, 171
Rio Chama, 3
Rio that pColorado Chiquito, 105
Rio Cubero, 226
Rio De Chelly (also Rio De Cheille, Rio De Chella), 68
Rio De Gallo, 252
Rio De Laguna, 252
Rio Del Lino, 105
Rio Del Muerto, 55
Rio De Los Pinos, 156, 163
Rio De Nabajoo, 191
Rio De Navajoo, 162
Rio Dolores (also Dolores River), 155
Rio Estrella, 145
Rio Grande, **251**: Spanish encounter Querechos at, 3; Navajos claim west bank of, 5; survivors of 1850s battle with Navajos escape to, 70; and Tewa refugees to western pueblos, 88, 89, 90; Mesa Verde descendents at, 160; and Abiquiu as buffer between Navajos and Rio Grande Pueblos, 169; Albuquerque on, 171; and refugees to Lybrook region, 230
Rio Grande Valley, 9(Table 5), 254
Rio Los Pinos (also Rio Los Piños), 252
Rio Nabajoe, 163
Rio Navajoo, 163
Rio Negro, 37, 198
Rio Nutria, 239, **251**
Rio Pescado, **259**
Rio Puerco (of the East), 8(Table 4), 37, 179, 180, 199, **251**
Rio Puerco (of the West) (also Puerco River of the West), 2, 107, 116, **251–52**
Rio San José, 37, 172, 226, **252**, 259
Rio San Juan, 163
"River", 263

"River Enemy", 220
"River Ford", 289
River Junction, **252**
Riverview Trading Post, 30, 162, 286
Riverward Knoll, 87
"Roaring Water", 272
Roberts' Trading Post, 30
"Rock Around Which Floating Took Place", 44
"Rock Around Which the Wind Blows", 52, 109
"Rock Canyon", 50, 250–51, 298
"Rock Canyon People Rolled Into", 149
"Rock Cleft", 139
"Rock Crossing", 37
"Rock Descending Jagged", 293
Rock Door Canyon, 291
"Rock Edge Ruin", 46, 55
"Rock Edge Wash", 53
Rock Extending into Water, **59**
"Rock Extending into Water", 48, 59, 218
"Rock Extending (or Pointing) Up", 267, 304
"Rock Extends in the Form of a Narrow Edge", 70
"Rock Fissure Trail Up Out", 58
"Rock Gap", 50 (in Canyon De Chelly), 277 (Twin Buttes), 290 (Gouldings)
"Rock Holding a Baby", 298
"Rock House", 203
"Rock in the Middle Crooked", 46
"Rock Is Broad (Flat)", 51
"Rock Ledge Slants into Water", 218
Rock Lying Out, **46**
"Rock Meadow Outflow", 42
Rock Mesa, **123**
"Rock Mesa", 123
"Rock Niche House", 136
"Rock Pass" (Angel Peak), 172
Rock Point, 67, **123–24**
"Rock Point" (see Standing Rock, NM), 267
Rock Point Trading Post, 30, **124**
"Rock Rim on Which There Are Lines Scratched", 139
"Rock's Father" (Canyon De Chelly), 52
"Rock's Hair", 271
"Rock's Head", 52
"Rocks Rolled Down", 149

"Rock's Writing, The", 46
Rockside Trail, 45
"Rock Sits", 56
"Rock Sits (in Place)", 48
"Rock Sits Spread Out", 52
"Rock Sits Spread Out at an Elevation", 46
"Rock Span Across", 113 (Natural Bridge), 303 (Rainbow Bridge)
"Rock Spire", 154 (Chimney Rock), 211 (Four Corners),
"Rock Spring", 275
Rock Springs, 128, 197, 201, **252**, 273
Rock Springs Trading Post, 30, **253**
"Rock Standing Up" (see Standing Rock, NM), 267
"Rock Starts to Extend Along Black", 239
Rock Struck by Lightning, **48**
"Rock Struck by Lightning", 48
"Rock Struck by Lightning Trail Up Out", 49
"Rock That Has Marks (Writing) on It", 204
"Rock That People Crawl Through Trail Up Out", 45
"Rock That People Dance Around", 271
Rock That People Turned Into, **53–54**
"Rock That People Turned Into", 54
"Rock That Water Flows Around", 53–54
"Rock-tip Gap", 58
"Rock Tip (Where) They Repeatedly 'Rubber Neck'", 48
"Rock That Extends Outward and Ends", 74
"Rock That People Crawl Through Trail Up Out", 45
Rock They Ran Into, **56**
"Rock They (the people) Turned Into", 45
"Rock Under which the Hoop and Pole Game is Played", 48
"Rock Under which Something Extends Supporting It", 188
"Rock Under which There Is an Echo", 55
"Rock Where there is Water and Food", 204
"Rock Wind Blows Around", 275

"Rock with a Face", 51
"Rock with a Hole in It", 139
"Rock with a Line (Drawn) Around It", 277
"Rocks in a Row", 108
"Rocks Jut Out", 106
Rocky Point, **124**
Rocky Point (Trading Post), 30, **253**
Roof Butte, 2, **124**, 264
"Rough Flintstone", 72
Rough Rock, AZ, 30, **124**
"Rough Rock", 124, 252, 294
"Rough Rocky Canyon", 69, 85
"Rough Spot", 69
Round Cave, **48**
Round Cave Ruin, **56**
"Rounded Inner Corner", 277
"Round Flat-topped Rock", 124
Round House (Trading), 30, 197
Round Mountain, 221
"Round (Ball-shaped) Mountain", 242
"Round Place Where a Sing Was Held", 102
Round Rock, AZ, **124**, 132, 135, 139, 285
"Round Rock", 72, 107
"Round Rock Extending Up Out Rock", 49
Round Rock Sticks Up, **49**
Round Rock Trading Post, **49**
"Round Stick Lying Down" (also Round Wood), 148
Round Top, 87
Round Top Trading Post, 30, 81–82, **125**
Round Valley (Trading), 126
Royal Arch, 60
Royal Natural Bridge (see Wittick Natural Arch), 148
Roy Newton's Camp, 205
Rubbish Ruin, 115
Rudeau, A. C., Trading Company, 30, **125**, 132
Ruin, A, 106
"Ruined House", 143
"Ruin in the Mud", 235
"Rumbling Inside the Rock", 203
"Running Water", 272

St. Johns, AZ, 81, **125–26**
St. Joseph, AZ, 77
St. Michaels, AZ, 103, **126–27**, 142

Sạ́ Bitooh, 163
Sa Kahn, 85
Sabinal, 266
Sacred Mountain Trading Post, 30, **127**
Sahdii Bisí, 118
Sahdii Hooghaní, 86
Sáí Biis Tóhí, 127
Sagebrush Spring, 102
Sage House Wash, 102
Salina (Salina Springs), **127**
Salina Springs Trading Post, 30, **127**
"Saline Water", 33
Salitre Negro, 37
Salmon Ruin, 190, **253**
"Salt", 95 (Hopi Salt Mine), 284 (Zuni Salt Mine)
Salt Creek (also Salt Creek Wash), 9(Table 5), **253**
"Salt Gathering Place" (see Zuni Salt Lake), 284
Salt Lake (see Zuni Salt Lake), 284
Salt Point, 177, **254**
Salt Springs, **127**
"Salt Trail", 127
Salt Trail Canyon, 25, **127**
Salt Wash, **254**
"Salt Water", 34
"Salt Water Canyon", 253
San Antone, **254**
San Antone Hill, 254
San Cristobal, 87
San Estevan De Acoma, 170
San Felipe Pueblo, 222, 226, 242, **255–56**, 261
San Fidel, NM, 170, **256**
San Francisco Peaks (and Mountains), 21, 39, 69, 84, 86, 92, **128–29**, 150, 153, 164, 235, 243, 279
San Gabriel Del Yunque, 5
San Ildefonso Pueblo, 245, **256–57**, 260
San José, 268
San José De La Laguna, 226, 227
San Juan, 126
San Juan Agency, 264
San Juan Basin, 2, 7(Table 3)
San Juan De Los Caballeros, 257
San Juan Mountains, 1, 7(Table 3), 160, **162–63**
San Juan Pueblo, 5, 245, 256, **257**, 269

San Juan River, 7(Table 3), 8(Table 4), 9(Table 5), **163–64**: as Colorado River watershed, 1; confluence of with Los Pinos River, 3; confluence of with Colorado River, 70; and clan migrations, 117; confluence of with Mancos Creek, 158; Utes living in upper drainage of, 164; and Navajos from Gallinas, 212; dammed, 238; Aneth, UT, on, 285; and oldest Navajo sites, 286; crossing of to Kapairowitz Plateau, 293
San Lorenzo, 271
San Luis (also Dominguez), **257**, 274
San Marcos, 255
San Mateo, **257**
San Mateo Lava Flow, 204
San Mateo Mountains, 176, 180, 204, 235
San Mateo Peak (also Mount Withington), 235, **257**
San Miguel, 199
San Miguel Lake, 157
San Pedro Mountains, 221
San Rafael, NM, 99, 172, **258–59**
San Rafael Canyon, **259**
San Ysidro, **262**
"Sand Floats Up Out", 66
"Sand Gap", 133
"Sand Houses", 255
"Sand Piled Against the Ridge", 129
"Sand Sage (Artemesia frigida)", 66
Sand Springs, **97**
Sand Springs Trading Post, 30
"Sand Trail Up Out", 268
Sanders, AZ, **127**, 197, 253
Sanders Ruin, **128**
Sanders Trading Post, 30, **128**
Sandia Mountains, 171, **254–55**, 266
Sandia Pueblo, 220, **254–55**
Sandoval Trading Company, 30
Saneneheck Rock, **127**
Sangre De Cristo Mountains, 153
Sanostee (also Sanastee), 175, **258**
Sanostee Trading Post, 30, 174, **258**, 272
Sanostee Wash, **258**
Santa Ana Pueblo, 222, 226, 242, **259–60**, 261, 274

Santa Ana (at Laguna Pueblo), 226
Santa Clara Pueblo, 89, 245, 247, 256, 260
Santa Fe, NM, 8(Table 4), 9(Table 5), **260–61**: headman Chapitone killed on route to for peace talks,10; three expeditions between 1758 and 1761 from; and road to Gallup, 179; Fort Marcy at, 207; Manuelito visits, 231; Otermin's flight from, 255; and Dominguez-Escalante Expedition, 289
Santa Fe River, 260
Santa Maria de Acoma, 233
Santa Rosa de Abiquiu, 169
Santo Domingo Pueblo, 9(Table 5), 10, 226, 242, 255, **261**
Santos Peak, 216, 229
Sastanha Mesa, **129**
Satan Pass (also Satan's Pass, Devil's Pass), **262**
Savino (also Sabino) Canyon, 54
"Sawery", 129
Sawmill, AZ, 73, **129**, 237
Sawmill Trading Post, 30, **129**
"Scaled Rock", 185
"Scalps", 104
"Scarce Water", 132 (Steamboat Canyon), 137 (Toyei), 273 (Togoye Lake, Tolakai, NM)
"Scattered Bones", 131
"Scented Reed Water", 67
Schielingburo Trading Post, 30, 200, **262**
Schmedding Trading Post, 106
Scorpion Rock, 45
Screen Cave, 60
Seama, NM, 226, **262**
Seba Delkai, **129**
Sebolleta (see Cebolleta), 248, 257
Seboyeta Mountains, 235
Second Mesa, 89, **91–92**, 255
Section 8 Ruin, **262**
Segeke Butte, 132
Segetoa Spring (Tsegito), **129**
Segi Canyon (see Tsegi Canyon), 139
Segihotsosi Canyon, **129**
Segi Mesas (Tsegi), **129**
Sehili (Tsaile) Trading Post, 30, 40
Séí 'Adiléhé, 45
Séí Bee Hooghan, 255

Séí Bídaagai, 129
Sei Deelzha, **130**
Séí Ha'atiin, 268
Séí Haha'eeł, 66, 141
Séí Heets'ósí Ba'áád, 145
Séí Heets'ósí Bikạ', 145
Séí Heeyołí, 46
Séí' Ndeeshgizh, 133
Seklagidsa Canyon, **130**
Sentinel Mesa, 291, 296, **298**
Sentinel Rock, **164**
"Separate Mesa" (also "Mesa Apart"), 294
"Series of Hills Going Down", 150
Setzer's Store, 30
Seven Cities of Cibola, 282, 283
Seven Figures Rock, 50
Seven Lakes (also Faris Ranch), **262–63**, 284
"Seven Lakes", 262
Seven Lakes Trading Post, 30
Seveyo, 248
Sevolleta, 183
Shą́ą́'tóhí, 50, 130–31
Sháá' Tóhí, 133
Sha'thohih Spring, 50
Shą́ą́' Ha'atiin, 50, 59
Sháá'tóhí, 50
Shabik'eschee Village, **189**
Shá Bik'e'eschí, 189
Shadow Mountain, **130**
Shaft House Ruin (Dinétah), 202
Sharkstooth, 157
"Shattered House", 33 (Agate House Ruin), 101 (Keetseel Canyon), 106 (Long House), 112 (Montezuma's Chair), 115 (Keet Seil), 128 (Sanders Ruin)
Shash Bighan, 122
Shash Bitoo, 35, 208
Shash Dits'iní, 39
Shashjaa', 286
Shashkin, 281
Shay Mountain, 285
Sheep Hill, **130**
"Sheep Hogan", 219
"Sheep Lake", 73, 78
Sheep Point, **60**
Sheep Point Canyon, **60**
"Sheep Ran Away", 206
Sheep Springs, 236, **263**, **270**
Sheep Springs Trading Post, 30, **263**, **270**
"Sheep Trail Going Up", 54
Sheridan, 201

Shį́į́k'eh, 107
Shining Pueblo (see Chetro Ketl) 185
"Shining Sands", 229
Shipaulovi (also Shipolovi, Sipaulovi, Shopaulovi), **92**
Shiprock (Community), NM, 2, 24, 25, 163, 174, **263–64**: Uranium Mines, 107, 175; Dinétah, 138
Shiprock Pinnacle (also The Needle, Wilson Peak), 64, 72, 175, 194, 201, **264**
Shiprock Trading Company, 264
Shiprock Trading Post, 30, 265
Shonto (Shato, Shanto), 130
Shirley Trading Post, 108
Shonto Spring, **130–31**
Shonto Trading Post, 30, **131**
Shonto Wash, **131**
Shooting Arrows in the Rock, **48**
"Shooting Arrows into the Rock", 48
"Shooting Pine", 159
"Shore House", 188
Short Creek, AZ, 120
Show Low, **131**
Shung-o-hu Pa Ovi, 92
Shungopa Spring, 93
Shungo Povi (also New Shungo Povi, Shungopavi, Shongopovi, Shongopavi), 88, 122, **192–93**,
Sichomavi, **90**
"Side Hill House", 115
"Sideways Rock Lies Elongated (at an Elevation)", 46
"Sideways Rock Lies Elongated's Ruin", 46
Sierra Blanca (also Sierra Blanco), 153
Sierra de Carrizo, 64
Sierra de Chegui, 64
Sierra de las Grullas, 163
Sierra de Nabahu, 191
Sierra de la Plata (see La Plata Mountains), 157, 163
Sierra del Datil, 160, 165
Sierra Madre, 235, 281
Sierra Napoc, 128
Sierra Panoche (see Navajo Mountain), 299
Siete Lagunas, 262
Sighóla (see Socorro), 266
Sikyatki, 90, **91**
Siláo 'Atiin, 249

Silver Lake, 157
Silver Mountains (from Spanish), 157, 163
Simon Ruin (Dinétah), **202**
Simpson, **265**
Simpson Creek, 198, **265**
Sisnaajiní, (Sisnaajinii, Tsisnaajin, Tsisnaajinii), 153, 201, 242, 279
Sis Naateel, 201, 279
Sisnathyel Mesa (see Wide Belt Mesa in NM), 279
Sitting God (Canyon De Chelly), **48**
Sitting Rock, **48** (in Canyon de Chelly), 107 (Lupton, AZ)
"Sitting Willow", 134
Skeleton Mesa, 102, 129, **131**
"Skinned Back" (Hopi) 93
Skunk Springs Ruin, **265**
"Skunk Water" 265
"Sky City", 170
"Slanted (Roof-shaped) Rim", 124
"Slanted Water", 205
"Slave Went up There Quick", 50
Sleeping Duck Rock, **46**
Sleeping Duck Ruin, 45
Sleeping Ute Mountain (see Ute Mountain), 160
"Slender Canyon", 129
"Slender Cottonwood", 197
Sliding Rock Ruin, 43, **49**
"Sliding House", 198
Sliding House Ruin, 49
Sliding off Rock, **48**
"Sliding off Rock", 48
Sliding Ruin, 49
"Slim Canyon Between the Rocks", 140
"Slim Rock", 298
"Slim Stream (Canyon)", 159
"Slim Water", 71
"Slim Water Canyon", 70, 159
"Slim Water Between the Ridges", 267
"Slim Woman", 34
"Sloping Down", 82
"Sloping White Rock Extending Down", 279
"Slow Man's Water", 75
"Small Trails Up Out Opposite Each Other", 55
Small Twin Trail Canyon, **54–55**
Small Twin Trails, 55
"Small White Lake", 227

Smith Butte, 87
Smith Lake (also Smith's Lake), NM, **265–66**
Smith Lake Trading Post, 30
Smoke Signal (Trading Post), 30, 106, **131**
"Smooth Area Rock Trail Up Out", 49
"Smooth Lava Rock", 74
"Smooth Rock", 74
Snake House, 115
Snider's Well, 167
Snowflake, AZ, 131
"Soaring Hill", 33
Socorro, NM, 8, **266**
Soda Spring (also Sulphur Spring), **164**
"Soldier Road" (also "Soldier Trail"), 249
Sonsola Buttes (also Sonsala Buttes), **131–32**, 236
"Something (the Railroad) Extends in a Line to Its Brink", 83
Sǫ Silá, 131, 236
Sǫ'tso Lá, 132
"Sound of Something Passing through Water Out of Sight", 272, 274
"Sour Water", 136, 181
Southern Ute Indian Reservation, **164**
South Mesa, 183
Southside Trading Post, 211
Southwestern Range and Sheep Breeding Lab, **266–67**
"Space under the Rock", 278
"Spaniards Massacred", 61
Spanish Expedition Mural, **58–59**
Spanish Trail, 63
"Spanned Across", 213
"Sparkling Water", 198
"Sparrowhawk's Nest", 224
"Speaking Rock", 51
Spearhead Mesa, 296
Speigelberg Trading Post, 30
Spencer's Trading Post, 30
"Spikey Rock at an Elevation, The", 53
Spider Rock, **51**
"Spider Rock", 51
Spiller Peak, 157
Spirit Lake, 157, 163
Split Rock Ruin (Dinétah), **202**
"Spotted Cactus", 179

"Spotted Grass", 270
"Spread among the Cottonwoods", 177
Spring Canyon, **49**, 112
Spring Canyon Trail, **49**
Springerville, AZ, **132**
Springer's Store, 132
"Spring from a High Place", 206
"Spring in the Coals", 177 (Blanco), 227 (Largo Canyon)
"Spring in the Forest", 129
"Spring in the Greasewood", 76, 85
"Spring in the Meadow", 263
"Spring in the Oaks", 240
"Spring in the Quaking Aspens", 71
"Spring in the Rock Niche", 142
"Spring in the Rough Rocks", 240
"Spring in the Sand", 127
"Spring in the Sheep Manure", 253
"Spring in the Sumacs (Rhus trilebata)", 67
"Spring in the Traprock", 40
"Spring in the Willows", 100
"Spring Midway up the Rock", 275
"Spring on the Edge of a Rock", 124, 246
"Spring on the Face of the Rock", 275
"Spring on the Sunny Side", 50 (in Canyon de Chelly), 130 (Shonto)
"Spring Underneath", 175
"Spring Under a Rock", 175
"Spring Under the Rock", 148, 252 (Rock Springs)
Spring Water, **56**
"Springy Rock", 116
Springstead Trading Post, 30, 193
Spruce Creek (see Tsaile Creek), 55, 72, 138
"Spruce Hill", 153
Square Butte, **132**
"Square Rock", 132
Square Tower Ruins Group, **293**
"Squash", 235
Squirrel Rock, **50**
Squirrel Springs Wash, 272
Staggs, W. M., Trading Co., 30, **132**
Stallings, Walter, Trading Post, 30, **267**

"Standing Cottonwood", 119
Standing Cow Ruin, **58**
"Standing Cow Ruin", 58
Standing Cow Trail, 58
"Standing Crane", 201
Standing Red Rocks, **132**
Standing Rock, 39 (Black Pinnacle), **59** (Wide Rock), **59** (up Extending Rock), **267** (Standing Rock, NM)
"Standing Rock", 154, (Chimney Rock 2 in CO), 164 (Sentinel Rock), 192 (near Farmington), 193 (Church Rock), 267 (Standing Rock, NM), 304 (Thumb Rock)
Standing Rock River, 163
Standing Rock Trading Post, 30, **267**
Standing Rock Wash, 179, 267
"Standing Tower", 73
"Standing Walnut Tree Trail Up Out", 47
Star Butte, 87
Star Lake Trading Post (also Estrella and Starr Lake), 24, 30, 240, 246, **267**
Star Mountain, **132**
"Stars Lying Down", 131
Stateline Trading Post, 30, 108, **132–33**
Steamboat Canyon, 9(Table 5), 67, **132–33**
Steamboat Canyon Trading Post, 30, **133**
Step House, 161
Stephen Butte, 87
"Stepped Rock Trail", 56
Stewart-Weid (Trading), 30, 126
"Stiff Dried Hide Lying up at an Elevation", **60**
Stinking Lake (also Burford Lake, Buford Lake), 212, **267–68**
Stinking Springs Mountains, 142
"Stinking Water", 243, 274
Stone Canyon, 222
"Stone Logs", 118
Stoney Butte (see White Rock), 279
Stover-Hubbell (Trading Post), 30
Streaked Rock, **48**
"Streaked Rock", 48
"Stream in a Broad Strip that Extends to the River", 227

"Stream in the Dark Under Rock", 184
Steam of the Cotton Fields (from Spanish), 112
"Stream of Water", 99
"Stream of Water Begins Under a House", 230
"Stretches of Treeless Areas" (also "Clearings Among the Rocks"), 295
"Striped House", 254
"Striped Houses", 176
"Stream in the Dark Under Rock", 184
"Striped Rock", 132
"Strip of Water Extending Away into the Distance", 144
"Strip of Water Extending Into Distance's Wash", 53
Suanee (also Suwanee, Los Cerros, Correro, Swannee, San Jose), **268**
"Subterranean House", 41
Sulphur Spring, 164
Sulphur Springs, **268**, (two NM locations—one in Sandoval County and one in San Juan County)
Sulphur Springs Trading Post, 30, **168**
"Summer Place", 107
"Sun Coming Out", 268
"Sun Is Engraved upon It", 189
Sunnyside Trail, 59
"Sun Resting", 236
Sunrise Springs, 98, **133**
Sunrise Springs Trading Post, 30, **133**
Sunrise Trading Post, 31, 104, **133**, 137, 295
Sunset, **134**, 148, 248
Sunset Crater National Monument, **134**, 150
Sunset Mountains (East and West), **134**
"Sunnyside Spring", 133
"Sunnyside Trail Up Out", 50, 59
Sunshine Spring, **50**
"Sunshine Water", 50 (Canyon De Chelly), 130–31 (Shonto)
Sunshine Trail, **50**
Sun Temple, **161**
"Supporting Rock Wall", 246

Swallow's Nest, 115
Swannee, 265
Sweetwater, 137
Sweetwater Trading Post, 31
"Sweet Water", 137

T & R Market, 31, 280
T'áá Bíích'íidii, 280
T'áá Bíích'íidii, 285
T'áá'neiyá, 300
T'áásahdii Dah 'Azkání, 106
T'áá Sahdii Dah 'Azkání, 106 (Lone Mountain in AZ), 294 (Lone Mountain in UT)
T'ánáánééł, 51
T'iis Bikooh, 288
T'iisbáí Bii' Tó, 71
T'iisbáí Ha'atiin, 52
T'iis Bitó, 136
T'iisbáí Bikooh, 52
T'iis Bikooh, 288
T'iis Ch'ínílí, 234
T'iis Eejin Ch'íní'lí, 181
T'iis 'Íí'áhí, 119
T'iis naat'i, 302
T'iis Nanít'i'í, 45
T'iis Názbas, 135
T'iis Niditso, 270
T'iis Ndiitsoí Nástł'ah, 53
T'iis Nééz 'Íí'á, 136
T'iis Nítsxaaz Ha'atiin, 55
T'iis Nitsxaaz Sikaad Nástłah, 55
T'iis Ntsaa Ch'éélí, 178
T'iis Sitání, 71
T'iistah Diiteelí, 177
T'ííst'óóz Ńdeeshgizh, 197
T'iists'ózí, 197
T'iistsoh, 170
T'iistsoh Sikaad, 179
T'iistsoh Sikaad Tséta, 179
T'iis Tsoh Sikaad, 213
T'iis Tó, 135
T'iisyaa Kin, 86 (Holbrook, AZ), 260 (Santa Clara Pueblo)
T'iis Yáázh Łání, 136
Ta'neesza, 216
Ta'neeszah, 216
Ta'neezah, 259 (San Rafael Canyon)
Taahóóteel, 227
Taahóóteel Ńlíní, 227
Taaiyolone (see Dowa Yalani Mountain), 203
Táala Hodijool, 102

Táala Hooghan, 134 (Talahogan Wash), 222 (Jemez Mountain Navajo campsite), 228 (Jemez Mountains)
Táala Hótsaii, 243
Táalakin, 187
Tábąąkiní, 188
Table Mesa, **268**
Ta Chee, **134**
Táchii', 134
Tádídíín Dziil, 121
Tádídíín Dził, 300
Táala Hooghan, 89
Tajique, 220
Talahogan Wash, **134**
Talking Rock, 304
"Tall Boss", 263
"Tall Chriricahua Apache", 195
"Tall Cottonwood Stands", 136
"Tall House Ruins" (from the Hopi), 150
"Tall Mountain", 150, 173
"Tall Mountains" (also "Tall Mountain"), 117
"Tall White Man", 196
"Tangled", 259
"Tangled Water", 104
Tank Mountain (see Mesa Mountain), 159
Tanner, J. B., Trading Co., 280
Tanner Crossing, 43, **134**
Tanner French Trail, 134
Tanner Springs, **134**
Tanner Lake Trading Post, 31, **268**
Tanner Trail, **135**
Taos, NM, 8, 181, **269**
Taos Pueblo, 4, 7(Table 3), 95, 154, **269–70**
Tapacito Creek, 228
Tapacito Ruin (Dinetah), **203**
Tapering Sandhill, 145
Tát'a Hatso, 103
Tatahatso, 103
Tathoysa Wash, **135**
Tatohatso Point, **135**
Tatohatso Wash, **135**
Taylor, AZ, 131
Taylor Spring, 66
Taylor Trading Post, 31, 263, **270**
Tazhii Habitiin, 59
Tchaman, 191
Téé'ndééh, 100, 142
Teec Náshjin, 271
Teec Ni Di Tso Wash, **270**

Teec Nos Pos (Tisnasbas), **135**, 273
Teec Nos Pos Trading Post, 31, 111, **135**
Tees Tso Sacad, 31
Teeł Ch'ínít'i', 117
Teeł Sikaad, 212
Tees Toh (Teas Toh), **135**
Tees Toh (Trading), 31
Tekapo, 31, 177, **270**
Temple Rock, 193
Tenny's Camp, 149
"Termination of Red Streak of Rock", 250
"Terrible", 132
Tes Nez Iha, **136**
Tes Yahz Łani, **136**
Tesbito Wash, **136**
Teshda'astani Creek, 135
Teshim Butte, 87, **136**
Tesuque Pueblo, 245, **270**
Teyebaakit Lake, 73
"There Is a White Stripe Across the Middle House Trail Up Out", 47
"Thief Rock", 127
"Thick Lips", 171
"Thin Flat One (Extends) into Rock (Canyon)", 46
"Things Fall into Deeper Water", 142
Things Flow Around the Stone, **44–45**
"Things Flow Around the Stone", 44, 45, 54 (Rock That People Turned Into)
Third Mesa, 89, **93–95**, 117
Tho'hedlih, **270**
Thoreau, 240, **270–71**
Thoreau Mercantile, 31, 270
Threatening Rock (also Leaning Rock), **189**
"Three Springs Come out of the Side of a Hill", 100
Three Turkey Canyon, **136**
Three Turkey Ruin (Three Turkey House), **136**
Thumb, The, **271**
Thumb Rock, **304**
"Thumb Rock", 304
Thunder Mountain (see Dowa Yalani Mountain), 203
Thurber, UT, 287
Tierra Amarilla, 155, **271**, 294:

attacks on by Navajos from Bears Ears, 287
Tillage, The (from the Spanish), 108
Tijeras Canyon, 254
Tinaja, **271**
Tinian Trading Post, 31
Tisnaabąąs Habitiin, 82
Tisnnasbas, 135
Tisyaakin, 31
Tiz Na Iah (Trading), 31
Tiz Na Zin, 201, 240
Tiz Na Tzin Trading Post, 31, **271–72**
Tłízhí Ninílganí, 62
Tł'ógí, 280
Tł'aa'í, 296
Tłahchíín, 155
Tłiish Bitsoo', 138
Tł'iish Jik'áhí, 222, 242
Tł'iishtsoh Bighan, 40
Tł'ízíchoołchíí, 280
Tł'ízí Łigai, 221
Tłízí Tsé Yaa Kin, 56
Tł'ohchiní (Ramah), 248
Tł'ohchintó, 93
Tł'ohchintó Biyáázh, 93
Tł'oh Łikizhí, 270
Tł'óo'di Tsin, 175
Tó 'Ádin Dah 'Azką́, 136
Tó 'Aheedlí, 163, 229, 238 (San Juan River and Los Pinos River junction), 252, 270 (Tho'hedlih, NM)
Tó 'Ahidiidlíní, 293
Tó 'Ałchiní, 215
Tó 'Áłts'íísí, 229
Tó Bééhwíisganí, 244
Tó Biká'í, 163
To Bila'i, **272**
Tó Bíla'í, (Chaco River and Escavada Wash), 205, 272
To Bil Hask Idi Wash, **272**
Tó Bił Hask'idí, 243, 272
Tó Dah Da'aztání, 136–37
Tó Dích'íí, 249
Tó Dínéeshzhee', 100
Tó Dik'óózh, 33 (Agua Sal Creek), 136 (Todakazh Spring), 268 (Sulpher Springs)
Tó Dík'óózh Bikooh, 253
Tó Dík'óózhí, 181
To Dil Hii Wash, **272**
Tó Díílid, 179

Tó Dildǫ' (Tohadildonen Wash), 272 (Todilto Park), 273

Tó Dilkohi (see Stinking Lake), 268

Tó Diłhił, 144 (Whiskey Creek), 221 (Jacques Canyon), 272 (To Dil Hii Wash)

Tó Diłhił Biih Yílį, 131

Tó Diłhił Bikooh, 53 (Canyon de Chelly), 177 (Blanco Canyon)

Tó Dootłizhi, 172

Tó Dzís'á, 144

Tó Dzís'á Bikooh, 53

Tó Há'naant'eetiin, 104

Tó Haach'i', 273

Tó Háálí, 248, (Quemado, NM), 272 (Toadlena, NM)

Tó Háálíní, 49

Tó Hahadleeh, 98, 229

Tó Hajiileehé, 180

Tó Hajiiloh, 261

Tó Haltsooí, 263

Tó Hasłeeh, 158

Tohatchi, 253

Tó Hwiiłhíní, 279

Tó K'ǫ́ǫzhí, 181

Tó Łání, 54 (in Canyon De Chelly), 122 (Tolani Lakes), 225 (Laguna Pueblo), 232 (Many Waters)

Tó Łání Biyáázh, 170

Tó Łigaaí, 212

Tó Łigaaí Háálíní (White Water Trading Post), 279

Tó Łigaaí Háálíní, 273

Tó Łikan, 137

Tó Łitso, 254

To Na Lin Mesa, 137

Tó Náálíní, 137, 229

Tó Naneesdizí, 104 (Leupp, AZ), 108 (Many Farms, AZ), 140 (Tuba City, AZ)

Tó Ndoots'ósí, 267

Tó Nehełįįh, 122

Tó Niłchxoní, 243, 274

To Nil Ehoni Wash, 274

Tó Niłts'ílí, 198

Tó Niłts'ílí (Crystal), 198

Tó Niłts'ílí (Crystal Creek), 198

Tó Ntsaa, 142, 193 (Tunicha Mountains), 275

Tó Nts'ósíkooh, 70, 158 (Mancos Canyon/Creek), 166

Tó Nts'ósí, 159

Tó Ntsaa, 276

Tó Ntsaa Bito', 181

Tó Sido, 115 (Navajo Springs), 172 (San Rafael), 240 (Ojo Caliente), 272 (Tocito Trading Post)

Tó Sik'az Háálíní, 70

Tó Yaagaii, 258

Tǫ́'gaa', 195

Toadlena, NM, 14, 272

Toadlena Trading Post, 31, 272, 286

"Toadstool", 113

Tóalnaazli Tó Bil Dahsk'id, 238

"Tobacco Mountain", 84, 100 (Kaibab Plateau), 285 (Abajo Mountains, UT)

Tocito Trading Post, 31, 272

Tódáá' N'deetiin, 104, 289

Todiiniishii, 99

Todilto Park, 272–73

Todilto Wash, 122

Todkonzh 'Adlii, 164

Todokazh Spring, 136

Tódóó Hódik'ąadi, 205

Togay (also Togai, Toghaii, Tohgaii) (see Tuye Spring), 276

Togoye Lake, 273

Toh Atin Mesa, 136

Toh Chin Lini Canyon (and Wash), 136

Toh Chin Lini Mesa, 136

Tohgaii, 273

Toh La Kai Ruin, 273

Toh'ko'ozhi, 181

Tohadildonen Wash, 272, 273

Thotchi, NM, 273

Tohatchi Flats, 273

Tohatchi Trading Post, 24, 31, 197, 273

Tohatchi Wash, 273

Tohdenstani Wash (also Todastani), 136

Tohgai Trading Post, 31

Tóhí Ha Glee, 229

Tók'i Hazbí'í, 39

Tólá Dah Siyíní, 293

Tolacon (Trading Post), 137

Tolakai (also Tohlakai, Toh La Kai, Tohgaii, Tuye Spring), 31, 273–74, 279

Tolakai (see White Water Trading Post), 279

Tolani Lake (Tolani Lakes), 122

Tolani (Trading), 31

Tolchaco, 98, 104

Tolchaco Trading Post, 137

Tólchí'íkooh, 137

Tolchico, 137

Tółchí'íkooh, 105, 149

Tomb of the Weaver, 57

Tomé, 274

Tonalea, 122

Tonalea Trading Post, 31

"Tongue Mountain", 153, 235

"Tongue of the Snake", 138

Toniil 'Aha'nii, 274

Tóniil Aho'nii Wash, 272

Tónits' Osíkooh, 70

Tooh, 163, 263

Tooh Biką'í, 252

Tooh Haltsooí, 262

Toojí' Hwiidzoh, 149

"Top of the Rock", 58

Topicito Arroyo, 7(Table 3)

Toreva, 92

Torreon (also Dolion), 9(Table 5), 31, 199, 223, 274, 280: refuge at Chaco, 180

Tóta', 206

Totem Pole Rock, 298

Tontnteac, 232

Tóts'ózí, 71

Tótsoh, 107, 171, 176

Totsoh Trading Post, 107

Tovar Mesa, 137

Towaoc, UT, 165

Towayalani (see Dowa Yalani Mountain), 203

Tower Butte, 137

"Towering House", 225

"Towering Ruin", 217

Tówoł, 269

Tóyéé (also Toyé), 272 and 276 (Togoye Lake), 132 (Steamboat Canyon), 137 (Toyei, AZ), 273 (Tolakai, NM)

Toyei, AZ, 137–38

"Trader at Blue Point", 239

"Trail Across at the Brink of the Water", 104, 289

"Trail Across Rock Rim", 46

"Trail Alongside Rock", 45

Trail Canyon, 165

"Trail Hacked Out (Notched) Downward at an Elevation", 47

"Trail the Mexicans Came Down", 61, 62, 63

Trail the Mexicans Came down Canyon, 63

"Trail Through the Rock", 46

"Trail Through the Rock Within Rock (or Rock Canyon)", 59

"Trails Up On Both Sides", 59

"Trail Up Out Between", 62

"Trail Up Out Between Cove", 62

"Trails Up Out Opposite Each Other (or on Opposite Sides)", 59

"Trail Went Up Out (Where the Douglas Fir Trees Extend Up Out in a Line to the Rim)", 60

"Trail Where the Enemy Walked Up", 50

Trail Where the Enemy Walked up Singing, **50**

"Trail Where the Fir Trees Reach the Canyon Rim", 59

"Traprock", 40 40, 122

"Traprock Point", 138

"Traprock Pointing Out" ("Traprock Jutting Out"), 39

"Traprock Sticking up", 175

"Tree Grove", 140

"Treeless or Clearing Among the Rocks", 298

"Trees Extended in a Line Up Its Side (slope)", 36

Tres Lagunas de la Trinidad (see Stinking Lake), 267

Trubey's (also Truby's), 31, 228, 274–75

Ts'á'ma (Tewa), 191

Ts'ah Biis Kin, 98, 115

Ts'íhootso, 69, 126 (St. Michaels, AZ), 142 (Two Story Trading Post)

Ts'ímah (also Ts'í'mah) (Tewa), 191

Tsa Ya Kin, **139**

Tsaaniigai, 279

Tsankawi, 256

Tsai Skizzi Rock, **139**

Tsaile (Sehili, Tsehili, Tse-a-lee, Tsalee), AZ, **138**

Tsaile Creek, 55, 72, **138**

Tsaile Lake, 55

Tsaile Peak (Tsaile Butte, Tsaile Pinnacle), 39, **138**

Tsaile Trading Post (also Tse-a-lee), 31, **138–39**, 231

Tsaile-Wheatfield Chapter, 138

Tsay Begi (see Tsé Biyi) 298

Tsay Begi Yazzi (see Tsé Biyi Yazzi), 298

Tséyaa Chahałeeł Ńlíní, 184

Tsaya Canyon, **275**

Tsaya To, **275**

Tsayatoh, 275

Tsaya Trading Post, 31, **275**

Tszhii Bikin, 136

Tsé'áántsoh, 59

Tsé'ázoołyi'í, 45

Tsé'in Desgizh, 277

Tsé 'Achííh, 175

Tsé 'áhálzhiní, 225

Tsé 'Ahéskéhé, 52

Tsé 'Ałch'i' Naagai, 279

Tsé 'Ałnáozt'i'í, 258

Tsé 'Ałtch'i' Naak'ání, 214

Tsé 'Ałts'óózí Deez'á, 196

Tsé 'Ani'įjhí, 127

Tsé 'Ast'ees, 250

Tsé 'Atsj', 47

Tsé 'Awéé, 34, 75

Tsé 'Awéé Yołtélí, 298

Tsé Bazhei, 52

Tsé Bidádi'ní'ání, 185

Tsé Bii' Naayolí, 194

Tsé Bii' Ndzisgaii (Mystery Valley), 295, 298

Tsé Biih Ńjíjahí, 56

Tsé Bik'e'eschí, 189

Tsé Bik'e'eshchíní, 46

Tsé Bił Deez'áhígíí (see Douglas Mesa), 289

Tsé Biná'áz'éí, 44

Tsé Biná'ázélí, 45, 54

Tsé Binááyołi, **275**

Tsé Bináookahí, 271

Tsé Bináyołí, 52 (Canyon de Chelly), 109 (Matthews Peak)

Tsé Binii'í, 51

Tsé Bííni' Tó, 275

Tsé Biníí'tóhí, 275

Tsé Bí'oos'ní'í, 48, 49 (Round Rock and Rock Struck by Lightning, both in Canyon de Chelly)

Tsé Bit'a'í, 201, 264

Tsé Bitłááh Hachíí, 54

Tsé Bitsii', 271

Tsé Bíyaa 'Aníí'áhí (also Tsé Bíyah 'Anii'ahi), 189

Tsé Bíyaah, 276

Tse Biyi (also Tsay Begi), **298**

Tsé Biyi Yázhí, 298

Tse Biyi Yazzi (also Tsay Begi Yazzi), **298**

Tsé Bó'oos'ni'í, 49

Tsé Bó'oos'ni'í Ha'atiin, 49

Tsé Bonito, NM, 78, 86, 147, 237, 252, **275**

Tsé Bonito Trading Post, 31, **275**

Tsé Ceza (see Standing Rock, NM), 267

Tsé Ch'ééchi', 234

Tsé ch'ídeelzhah, 106

Tsé Ch'nl, 45

Tsé Chííhí, 248

Tsé Chizhi, 294

Tse Chizzi Wash, 106, **139**

Tsé Dáá Bikooh, 53

Tsé Dah 'Askán, 123

Tsé Dah Seeshzhaaí, 53

Tsé Dah Sitłé'é, 46

Tsé De Ninít'i', 74

Tsé Deez'á, 39

Tsé Deez'á (see Standing Rock, NM), 267

Tsé Digóní, 234

Tsé Dijíhí, 239

Tsé Dik'ání, 132

Tsé Dijoolí, 107

Tsé Dilde'í, 85

Tsé Diyiní (also Tsé Diyilí), 186

Tsé Dogoi Nlini, 227

Tsé Ha'ałchíní, 54

Tsé Hadeesk'ihí, 56

Tsé Hadoolkǫ Ha'atiin, 49

Tsé Hons'ózí, 106

Tsé Hóteel, 203

Tsé Hooghan, 203

Tsé 'Íí'áhí, 45, 59, (Round Rock Sticks Up, near Standing Cow Ruin, and in Twin Trail Canyon, all three in Canyon de Chelly), 77 (The Fingers), 154 (Chimney Rock, near Pagosa Springs, CO), 164 (Sentinel Rock), 192 (Chimney Rock north of Shiprock, NM, and Chimney Rock near Farmington, NM), 193 (Church Rock, NM), 211 (Four Corners), 267 (Thumb Rock)

Tsé 'Íí'áhí Ahidiidlíní, 46

Tsé Jaa'abaní, 54

Tse Joshi Si'ani, 135

Tsé K'ééyoł, 52

Tsé K'izí, 139

Tsé Kíniitíní, 218

Tsé Lééchąą'í, 46

Tsé Łání, 127, 230

Tsé Łichíí, 173

Tsé Łichii Dah 'Azkání, 123 (Red Mesa), 250 (Red Rock)
Tsé Łichíí' Deez'áhí, 123
Tsé Łichii 'Ííá'ahí, 132
Tsé Łichíí 'Íí'áhí (Venus' Needle), 278
Tsé Łichíí Sikaadí, 173
Tsé Łįįlí, 50
Tsé Łitso, 99, 199
Tsé Na'ashjé'ii, 51
Tsé Ná'áz'élí, 53, 54
Tsé Naa (Dah) Sitání, 46
Tsé Naachii', 97
Tsé Naaha'bith, 257
Tsé Naajin, 174
Tsé Naajiin, 175 (Bennett Peak), 179 (Cabezon Peak)
Tsé Nááh Sitání Bikits'iilílíí, 46
Tsé Naal'ęęłí, Sitíní, 45
Tsé Naashchii, 97
Tsé Naashzhoojí, 48
Tsé Náhaaztání, 49
Tsé Náhádzoh, 277
Tsé Náhidéétéél, 46
Tsé Náhoolyélí, 53–54
Tsé Nahoot'ood, 116
Tsé Naní'áhí, 113
Tsé Nástánii, 118
Tsé Ndoolzhaaí, 75
Tsé Ndoolzhah, 293
Tsé Né'élzhíhí, 48
Tsé Nikání, 124
Tsé Nikání Yázhí, 105
Tsé Noodǫǫz, 132
Tsé Ntsaa Deez'áhí, 123
Tsé Ńdadzisdlí'í, 54
Tsé Ńdeeshgiizh, 201, 277
Tsé Ńdeshgizh, 50
Tsé Ńdeeshgiizh, 277
Tsé Si'ání, 48, 56 (Sitting Rock and Balanced Rock, both in Canyon de Chelly), 107 (Lupton, AZ)
Tsé Sitłé'é, 52
Tsé Skizzi Wash, 131
Tse Ta'a Ruin, **48**, 63
Tsé Táá'á (both in Canyon de Chelly), 48 (Tsé Táá'á Ruin), 59 (Rock Extending into Water)
Tsé Tééh Yik'ání, 82
Tsé Teelí, 176
Tsé Ts'óózi, 298
Tsé Yaayí, 278
Tsé Yík'áán, 70 (Comb Ridge), 76 (Echo Cliffs)

Tsé Yík'áán Nahgóó, 194
Tsé Zhin Hadooklizh, 42
Tsé'aantsoh, 59
Tsé'asdzáán, 124
Tsé ázoołyi'í, 45
Tsé'láá Ndzíts'o'í, 48
Tsé'naa Na'ní'áhí, 303
Tsé'níí' Kin Yít'eezhí, 56
Tsébąąh Nááliní, 45
Tsébąąhatiiní, 45
Tsébááłigai, 177
Tsébina'azalí, 45
Tsébitsii'í, 52
Tséch'ízhí, 124, 139
Tsédáá Hwiidzohí, 139
Tsedaa Hwiidezohi Peak, **139**
Tsédáá Na'atiin, 46
Tsédáá'kin, 255
Tsédaa'tohi, 124
Tsédáá'tóhí, 246
Tsédáá'tah, 139
Tsedaatah Canyon, **139**
Tsédáhí Kits'iilí, 47, 55
Tséé'dóhdoon, 203
Tsééhí Yílí (also Tsééhílí), 138
Tsééhílį, 138
Tsééhdikadí, 46
Tségai, 183, 191
Tsegahodzani Canyon, **139**
Tséghá'íldoní, 47
Tséghá'atiiní, 45
Tséghá'atiin Tséyi', 46
Tséghą́ą́', 58
Tseghodzani Canyon, 148
Tségháhoodzání, 50 (The Window), 139 (Tsegahodzani Canyon), 147 (Window Rock), 148 (Wittick Natural Arch), 297 (Hole in the Rock)
Tségháji'nahí, 45
Tséghi, 158
Tsegi Canyon, 88, 90, 114, 115, 130, **139**
Tsegi Trading Post, 25, 31
Tségiizh, 290
Tsegito, 9
Tseh So, **189**
Tseh Ya Kin Canyon, **61**
Tse-hada'eemaz, 149
Tséhahadzoh, 277
Tsehakha (see Zuni Salt Lake), 284
Tséhįįh Deezlį, 177
Tséhootsooí, 41
Tsehootsooí Ch'ínílí, 42

Tséikiin, 204
Tsék'i Na'asdzooí, 204
Tsék'i Na'asht'ézhí, 62
Tsék'iz Tóhí, 199
Tsékooh, 50 (Wild Cherry Canyon), 114 (Navajo Canyon), 184 (Chaco Canyon), 221 (Jacques Canyon), 250 (Rincon Largo), 301 (Piute Canyon)
Tsékooh Béésh Łichíí, 288
Tsékoo Hatso, 83
Tsélą́ą́ Ha'atiin, 58
Tsélą́ą́ Ndeshgizh, 58
Tsélą́ą́, Nteel, 58
Tsełchíí, 103
Tsełchíí 'Íí'áhí, 103
Tsełgai, 34
Tsełgaii, 279
Tsełgaii Deez'á, 287
Tsełgiizh, 290
Tsełgizhíí, 172
Tséndíłkéłí, 48
Tséneeyséél, 53
Tsénii Noǫtl'iizhíí, 46
Tsénikání, 71
Tséníí' Kiní, 136
Tséníí'tóhí, 142
Tsénteel (all in Canyon de Chelly), 47 (Meat Rock), 51 (Wide Rock), 59 (Flat Rock Refuge)
Tsénteel Bikooh, 53
Tsétaak'ą́, 218
Tsétaak'áán, 218
Tséta'ch'éech'í, 86, 148
Tsétah Dibé Nahashch'idí (see Comb Wash), 288
Tséta'kin, 256
Tséteel Naagai, 195
Tsétł'áán Ndíshchí'í, 36 (Black Creek Canyon), 117 (Oak Springs)
Tsétsek'id, 92
Tsétsoh, 59 (in Canyon de Chelly), 189 (in Chaco Canyon)
Tsétsohk'id, 91, 92
Tséttaak'ą́ą́gi Dá'deestł'inígíí, 82
Tsewaii, 87
Tséyaa, 275
Tséyaa 'Ałts'ózí, 140
Tséyaa Ch'ó 'Íí'áhí, 60
Tséyaa Chahałheeł Ńlíní, 190
Tséyaa Chahałheeł, 275
Tséyaa Hahwiiyoolí, 62
Tséyaa Hodiits'a'í, 55

Tséyaa Kin, 139
Tséyaa Nda'azhǫǫshí, 48
Tséyaa Tó, 275
Tséyaa Tóhí, 56, 154
Tséyaahatsoh Ndeeshgizh, 60
Tséyaakin, 61
Tséyaakin (Poncho House Ruin), 302
Tséyaakiní Ha'atiin, 61
Tséyaakiní Nástl'ah, 61
Tséyaaniichii', 250
Tséyaató, 252
Tséyaatóhí (near Window Rock), 148
Tséyaatóhí, 154
Tseye Ha Tsosi Canyon, 140
Tséyi', 43 (Canyon de Chelly), 83 (Glen Canyon), 114 (Navajo Canyon), 130 (Segi Mesas), 139 (Tsegi Canyon), 165 (Ute Mountain)
Tsé Yik'áán Nahgóó, 194
Tséyí Naakií Habitiin, 59
Tséyi' Etso, 43
Tséyi' Hats'ózí, 106, 129
Tséyi' Hayázhí, 216
Tséyi'Kin, 166
Tséyí'kiní Yit'eezh, 50
Tséyík'áán Comb Ridge (near Monument Valley), 288
Tséyt', 86
Tsézhin 'Adahiilínígíí, 37
Tsézhin Bii' Tó, 40
Tsézhin Dahiilínígíí, 37
Tsézhin Deez'áhí, 39 (Black Point), 125 (St. Johns, AZ)
Tsézhin Dilkǫǫh, 74
Tsézhin Ha'atiin, 52
Tsézhin Hdootł'izh, 42
Tsézhin 'Ií'áhí, 175 (Bennet Peak), 249 (Red Butte)
Tsézhin Tsiits'iiní, 138
Tsézhiní (Chézhiní), 39, 40, 5, 122, 177
Tsézhiní, 40 (Black Rock, near Ft. Defiance), 51 (in Canyon de Chelly), 122 (near Fort Defiance), 176 (near Zuni)
Tsézhíní Ha'atiin Nástłah, 52
Tsézhiní Nástłah, 57
Tsézhiní Yistł'ah, 52, 57
Tsídii Binii'í, 63
Tsídiito'í, 36
Tsigai Deez'áhí, 127
Tsíhidzo Biihílí', 53

Tsii' Dził, 112
Tsííd Bii' Tó, 177 (Blanco, NM, and Blanco Canyon), 227 (Largo Canyon)
Tsjjh Hidzoh Bikooh, 53
Tsiiłchin Bii'Tó (or Chiiłchin Bii'Tó), 67
Tsiitah, 304
Tsiizizí, 104
Tsin Béel'áhí, 36
Tsin Bił Dah 'Askání, 96
Tsin Dah Yiskid, 117
Tsin Deeshgizh, 277
Tsin Kíikaad, 131
Tsin Kletsin, 189
Tsin Lani Creek, 140
Tsín Łání, 140
Tsin Łeeh Yí'áhí, 186
Tsin Łitsinih, 189
Tsin Łizhiní, 189
Tsin Naajinii, 146
Tsin Názbąs, 148 (Winona, AZ), 265 (Smith Lake, NM)
Tsin Sikaad, 140
Tsinaa'eeł Dah Si'á, 103
Tsinaabáás Habitiin, 71
Tsinlee, 67
Tsinyaa Ńt'i'í, 105
Tsisma, 226
Tsisnaajin (also Tsisnaajinii) (see Sisnaajinii), 242
Tsisnaateel, 275
Tsitah Wash, 304
Tsiyi'í Be'ek'id, 78
Tsiyi'tóhí, 129
Tsoodził, 153, 201, 235
Tsosts'id Be'ak'íd, 262
Tuba Butte, 33, 34, 70, 140, 300
Tuba City, AZ, 140: Navajo-owned businesses at, 24; Havasupai farms north of, 86; Kerley.s Trading Post at, 102; uranium mines at, 107; and Tuba to Kayenta Road, 109; and Garcés Expedition, 111; Diné College at, 138; and displaced Mormons settle at Fruitland, NM, 171
Tuba Trading Company, 31, 142
Tucker's Store, 24, 31, 246, 275
"Tule Extending Out", 117
Tuni Cha, 276
Tunicha, 184
Tunicha Creek (see Tunsta Wash), 276

Tunicha Mountains, 2, 102, 142, 236, 275–76
Tunnel Canyon, 46
Tunnel Spring, 142
Tunnel Trail, 45
Tunsta Wash, 191
Turkey Cave, 115
Turkey Trail, 59
"Turkey's House", 136
"Turkey's Trail up Out", 59
Turley, 276
Turley Trading Post, 31
"Turning [Changing] Rock", 54
"Turquoise House", 190
"Turquoise Mountain", 153, 235
"Tusayan Province", 137
Tuye, 138
Tuye Spring (also Togay, Togai, Toghaii, Tohgaii, Toyé), 273, 276–77
Tuye Springs Trading Post, 31, 277
"Turtle Dove Spring", 85
Twelve Mile Creek, 208
Twin Angels, 190
Twin Buttes, 142
Twin Buttes, NM, 277
Twin Buttes Site, 119
Twin Caves, 115
Twin Ladder House, 54
Twin Lakes, 277
Twin Lakes Trading Post, 31, 277
Twin Rocks, 52
Twin Trail Canyon, 55, 59
"Twin Trail Canyon", 59
Twin Trail Ruin, 59
Twist, The, 290
"Twin Stars", 236
"Two Coyotes Seated at an Elevation", 172
Two Grey Hills (also Crozier), 9(Table 5), 175, 236, 263, 277
Two Grey Hills Trading Post, 24, 31, 111, 272, 277–78
Two Guns, AZ, 64
"Two Rocks Sit Together", 52
"(Two) Standing Red Rocks", 132
Two Story House, 161
Two Story Trading Post, 31, 142
"Two Yellow Adobes" (see Two Grey Hills), 277
Two Wells (Trading), 31
Tyende Creek, 37, 142
Tyende Mesa (Tyenda Mesa), 130, 142

"Ugly Canyon", 143
"Ugly House", 225, 230
    (Manuelito)
"Ugly Trail", 46
"Ugly Trail Up Out Canyon", 46
Una Vida, **189**
Uncompahgre Plateau, **165**
"Under Rock (Cave) House
    Cove", 61
"Under Rock (Cave) Water", 56
"Under Rock Standing Douglas
    Fir", 60
"Under the Oaks", 107
"Under the Rock", 276
"Under the Rocks", 275
"Under Trees Extending (as in a
    line)", 105
"Underground House", 90
Underground Houses, 90
"Underground People", 87
Unit Type House, **293**
"Unknown Mountains", 291
"Up-extending (Standing) Rock",
    49
Upper Canyon De Chelly, **51**
"Up to the Point of the Mesa", 90
"Up Well Flow", 86
"Upper Ending of the Meadow",
    75
"Upper Ending of the
    Mountains", 212
Upper Greasewood Trading Post,
    31
Upper Rock Point, 124
"Upper Spring", 143
Upper Sunrise Trading Post, 104
"Upward Projecting Rocks Strewn
    Along", 75
Ute Fight Mural, **56–57**
Ute Ford, 289
Ute Mountain (also Sleeping Ute
    Mountain), **165–66**
Ute Mountains, 159
Ute Peak, 165
Ute Raid Trail, 57
Ute Trading Company, 31, **166**
Ute War Trail, 289
"Utes' River", 163

Valencia, 7
Valle Grande, 8(Table 4), 221, **278**
Vallecito, **278**
Vallecito Reservoir, 229
Valley Camp, 237
Valley of the Gods, 294

Valley of the Red House, 96
Valley of the Widows, 123
Valley Trading Post, 31, 267, **278**
Valverde Battlefield, 259
Vanderwagen (also Vander
    Wagen), 31, **278**
"Vehicles Run to Its Top Trail Up
    Out", 47
Venus' Needle, **278**
Ventana Mesa, 228
Verde River, 66
Village of the Great Kivas, 240
Viper Water (from Spanish), 119
Volunteer, 114, **143**
Volz Crossing, 137
Volz Trading Post, 31, 63, **143**

"Wagon Trail Up Out", 82
"Waiting Water", 147
Walker Butte, **143**
Walker Creek, 9(Table 5), 68, 110
    (called Mexican Water), 130
    (Seklgidsa Canyon), **143**
"Wall with Lightning", 46
Wallace, C. G., Trading Post, 31,
    282
Wallace, Sabin R. (Trading), 31
Walnut, AZ, 148
Walnut Canyon (National
    Monument), **143**, **150**
Walnut Trail, 47
Walpi, AZ, **148**
"Warpath Cottonwoods", 135
Warren Trading Post (Navajo
    County, NM), 31, **143**
Warren Trading Post (San Juan
    County, NM), 31
"Wart Under the Eye", 99
"Watching Goes on from Inside
    It", 230
"Watching Goes on from On Top
    of It", 230
Washington Pass, 236
"Water", 163
"Water Come Together", 293
"Water Comes Like Fingers Out
    of a Hill", 137
"Water Dropping Down", 84
"Water Fingers", 205, 272
Waterflow, NM, **278**
"Water Flowing Out", 136
"Water Flows in a Circle", 163,
    229, 252, 270
"Water Flows Out (springs) on
    Opposite Sides", 214

"Water Flows and Collects", 122
"Water Flows Downward", 137
"Water Flows Up", 272
"Water Flows Up Out", 248
Waterhold Canyon, 40
"Water in the Crevice", 199
"Water in the Greasewood", 85
"Water in the Ground", 102
"Water in the Meadow", 263
"Water is Dark Colored Wash", 53
"Water is Dug Out with One's
    Hand", 273
"Water Outlet" 44, 67, 143
"Water Rises in a White Column",
    258
"Water Running Down", 229
"Water Stringing Out in Rivulets",
    108
"Water Under the Rock", 154
"Water Washes Around the
    Rock", 45
"(Water) Washing Out Sand", 141
"Water Well", 229
"Water with a Mound", 272
"Weeds Extend Out (or Up)
    Black", 230
Weidemyer's (Trading), 31
"Wending Red Willow Wash", 176
Wetherill and Coleville Trading
    Co., 100
Wepo Spring, **143**
Wepo Wash, **143**
"We Stand in a Row", 116
Westbrook, Dee, Trading Post, 31,
    232, **278**
Western Navajo Trading Post, 31,
    144
West Mesa, 183
Wetherill and Coleville Trading
    Post, 31, **144**
Wetherill Mesa, **166**
Wetherill Trading Post, 31
Wheat Canyon, 55
Wheatfields, 9(Table 5), 51, **144**
"Wheatfield Canyon", 144
Wheatfields Canyon, **53**
Wheatfields Creek, **143**
Wheatfield Lake, **144**
Wheeler Peak, 153, 221, 242, **279**
"Where a Baby Urinated on the
    Way Up", 56
"Where a Juniper Tree Sticks
    Up", 200
"Where an Area Extending from
    the Water is Slanted", 305

"Where a Person Walked over the Cliff", 33
"Where Big Enemy God's Blood Stopped Flowing", 172
"Where Big God's Blood Coagulated", 204
"Where Cotton is Cultivated", 112
"Where Coyote Farted", 76
"Where I Sat Leaning Against It", 243
"Where It Flows Into the Dark Water", 131
"Where It was Dug into", 145
"Where Mountain Range Begins", 150
"Where People Repeatedly Run Into the Rock (Cave?)", 56
"Where People Were Pushed Away Downward (from a Height)", 61
"Where Sheep Lie up at an Elevation", 130
"Where She Fell from the Cliff", 33
"Where Smoked Stones (Pipes) Are Made", 53
"Where Spaniards Descended Trail Up Out", 63
"Where Swift Ones (Antelope) Run Along", 57
"Where Swift Ones (Antelope) Run Along Ruin", 57
"Where the Bear Lived", 39
"Where the Boat Sits up at an Elevation", 103
"Where the Cows Grow Up", 34
"Where the Coyote Fell into Deep Water", 197
"(Where) the Crow Ascended", 45
"Where the Enemy (a Hopi woman) Walked up Singing", 50
"Where the God Sits", 48
"Where the Horse Crawls Up", 200
"Where the Mountain Went Out on Top", 124
Where the Rock is Marked, 46
"Where the Water Comes Up", 158
"Where the Water Enters a Box Canyon", 138
"Where the Water Killed One", 138

"Where the Wind Eddies Under Rock", 62
Where the Yei Went Up, 46
"Where They Flow Together", 114
"Where the Zuni Went Up", 49
"Where They Crossed Against the Current", 104
"Where They Sneaked Up", 62
"Where Treeless Vales Come Together", 227
"Where Two Fell Down", 62
"Where Two Wide Valleys Come Together", 178
"Where Water is Drawn Out One Quantity After Another", 98
"Where Water is Drawn Up Out", 180
"Where White Water Flows Up Out", 279
"Where Yeis Came Running Down", 47
"Where You can Block the Rabbit's Trail", 205
"Which Flows from the Wide Ruin", 172
Whipple Barracks, 80
Whippoorwill, 127
Whirlwind Cave, **62**
Whiskey Creek, 51, **144**
Whiskey Creek Canyon, **53**
Whiskey Lake, 233
"White Area Pond", 53
White Ash-Streak Mountain, 110, **145**
"White Clay", 145
White Clay Crossing (see Piute Farms), 302
"White Clay Point", 34
White Clay Wash, **145**
White Cliffs, 214, **279**
White Cone, 98, 133, **145**
White Cone Trading Post, 31, **145**
"White Faced Mountain", 162
"White Faced Mountains" (Kaiparowitz Plateau), 293
"White Goat", 221
White Horse, NM, (also White Horse Lake), **279**
White Horse Mesa, 100
"White Horse Spring", 279
"White House", 43 (in Canyon de Chelly), 63 (Canyon Diablo), 111 (Moenavi), 115 (Navajo Springs), 217 (Haystack), 245

(Prewitt), 254 (Sandia Pueblo), 258 (San Juan Pueblo)
White House Ruin, **47**
White House Trail, **47**
White Lady Fortress, **55**
White Mesa, 39, **146**
White Mesa, UT, **304**
White Mesa Trading Post, 32, **146**
"White Mountain", 165
White Mountains, 124, **146**, 154, 162 (San Juan Mountains), 165 (Ute Mountains)
White Mesa Village, UT, **304**
"White Mesa", 146
White Mesa Trading Post, **165**
"White Ochre", 136
White Reservoir Canyon, **53**
White Rock, **279**
"White Rock", 183, 279
White Rock Crag (Pinnacle or Boulder) (from Spanish), 187
"White Rocks", 191
White Rock (Trading), 31
White Rock Trading Post, 31
"White Rock Descending Together", 279
"White Rock-Edge", 177
"White Rock Point", 127, 187
"White Rock Point" (Bluff, UT), 287
White Rock Trading Post, **279**
White Rock Village, UT, **304**
"White Shell Mountain", 153
"White Smoke Marks", 131
White Spring, 132
"White Spruce", 193, 194
"White Streak on the Ledge", 108
"White Streak of Reeds Extends Horizontally Out", 107
"White Stripe Across its Middle", 47
"White Thing Sticking Up", 214
"White Water", 212, 278
"White Water Coming Out", 273
White Water Trading Post (also Tolakai), 31, **279**
"Whitish Red Ochre Canyon", 136
"Wide Band of Reeds up at an Elevation", 81, 96 (Hubbell Trading Post), 121 (Pueblo Colorado Wash)
Wide Belt Mesa (also Sisnathyel Mesa), 201, **279–80**
"Wide Hill Descending Broad", 275

"Wide House", 146 (Wide Ruin), 187 (Kinteel Ruin), 246 (Pueblo Bonito Trading Post)

"Wide House", 246 (both Pueblo Pintado, NM, and Pueblo Pintado Ruin)

"Wide House Outflow", 246

"Wide Lake", 113, 232

Wide Mesa, 40

Wide Rock, **51**, 54

"Wide Rock", 59 (Standing Rock in Canyon de Chelly), 176 (Big Rock Hill), 203 (Dusty, NM)

"Wide Rock Coming Down White", 195

"Wide Rock's Wash", 5

"Wide Rock-Tip", 58

"Wide Ruin", 173

Wide Ruin (Trading Post), 25, 32, **146–47**

"Wide Sheep Corral", 78

Wijiji, **190**

"Wildcat Guts", 147

Wildcat Peak, **147**

"Wildcat's Den", 280

"Wildcat's House", 276

Wildcat Trading Post, 32, **280**

Wild Cherry Canyon, **49**

Wild Cherry Ruin, **49**

"Wild Cherry Tree Sits", 50

Wild Horse Mesa (see Kaiparowitz Plateau), 293

"Wild Onions", 182, 213 (Gallo Canyon), 248 (Ramah)

"Wild Water", 215

Wilkin-Wyatt (Trading), 32, 126

Willow Creek, **304**

Willow Spring, 86, 117 (Oak Springs), **147**

Willow Springs Trading Post, 32, **147**

"Willows Extending Out Tangled", 227

Wilson Peak (see Shiprock Pinnacle), 264

Wilson Pueblo, 64

"Wind Blows about within the Rock", 194

Window, The, (also Window Arch), **50**

Window Rock, AZ, 24, 25, 80, 120, 138 (Diné College), **147–48**, 195, 197 (Navajo Central Agency)

"Windpipe Rock Interior", 45

Windpipe Trail, 45

"Wind-Swept Rock", 52

"Wind-swept Vulva" 62

"Windy Flattop Rock", 194

Windy Rock (East and West), **52**

"Windy Trail through the Rocks", 194

Wingate Trading Post (see Fort Wingate Trading Post), 32

Wingate Navajo Village, 193

Wingate Valley, 7, 9(Table 5), 196, **280**

Wingate Valley Road, 284

"Winged Rock", 264

"Wings of Rock", 264

Winona, AZ, **148**

Winslow, AZ, 42, 105, **148**, 196, 213

"With People Pushed Upward by Wind", 62

"With Her Legs Spread", 216

"Without Eyes", 114

Wittick Natural Arch, **148**

Wolf Crossing (Woolf's Crossing), 137, **149**

"Wolf Pass" (see Coyote Pass, Jemez Pueblo), 222

Wolf Trading Post, 32

Wolf's Crossing, 137

"Woman Is White's Ruin", 55

"Woman's Rock," 123

"(Woman's) Belt Extending Down Black", 242

"Woman's Derriere Canyon", 117

"Woman's Skirt", 254

"Woman's Trail" 47 (two locations in Canyon de Chelly)

"Woman Went Into Water", 66

"Wooded Mountain", 204

"Wooded Rock", 294

Woodruff Butte, **149–50**

Woodspring (Trading), 32

"Woody Hill", 117

"Wrestling Place", 191

Wupatki Basin, 84, 150

Wupatki National Monument, **150**

Yá'át'é'héi, 280

Ya'niilzhiin, 274

Yaa'íí'áhí, 73

Yaa Ndee'nil, 150

Yaaniilk'id, 65, 82 (Gap Trading Post)

Yale Point, **150**

Ya Tah Hey, **280**

Ya Tah Hey (Trading), 32

Yé'ii 'Adáájé'é'ii, 47

Ye'ii Bicheii, 298

Yé'ii Bicheii Habitiin, 47

Yé'ii Bikék'eh, 222

Yé'íí Dah Sidáí, 48

Yé'íí Dah Sidáhí, 48

Yé'ii Hadeeyáhí, 46

Yé'ii Shijéé', 48

Yé'iitsoh Bikooh, 60

Ye'iitsoh Bidił Niníyęęzh, 172

Yé'iitsoh Bidił Niníyęęzhí (El Malpais), 204

Yé'iitsoh Haayáhí, 60

Yeibichai Trail, 47

Yei Bichei Formation, **298**

"Yeibichai's Trail Up Out", 47

"Yeibichei Dance Hill", 204

Yeibichei Mesa, 298

"Yei Sits at an Elevation, The", 48

"Yei's Footprints", 222

"Yei Went Up and Out, The", 46

"Yellow Clay at an Elevation", 227

Yellow Clay Reservoir Trail, 47

"Yellow Coyote Wash", 45

"Yellow Dirt (Ochre) Water Inside Trail Up Out", 47

"Yellow-green Cottonwoods Extending Downward (in a Line) Cove", 53

"Yellow-green Streak that Extends Up and Ends", 75

"Yellow House", 91, 187

"Yellow House of the Firewood People", 91

"Yellow Houses in Position", 193

Yellow Jacket Canyon, **166**

Yellow Jacket Ruin, **166**

"Yellow Marsh", 69

"Yellow Meadow", 126, 142

"Yellow Place", 271

"Yellow Rock", 99, 199

"Yellow Rock Spring", 120

"Yellow Starts to Extend Downward", 270

"Yellow Topped Mountain", 134

"Yellow Water", 254

Yisdá Dziil, 180

Yo'dí Dził, 194, 216

Yódídzill, 64

Yoołgaii Dziil, 153

Yoo'tsoh, 176, 179

Yootó, 207, 260

Yon Dot Mountains, **150**

"Your Middle", 147

Yucca House National Monument, **166–67**

Yucca Mountain, 167

"Yucca Range", 146

"Yucca Slope", 234

"Yuccas Extend Up Out in a Line", 234

Yúngé, 257

Yunque Yunque, 5

Zia Pueblo, 7(Table 3), 170, 222, 228, 242, 274, **280–81**: trail to, 180

Zig Zag Cave, 46

"Zigzag Rock Niche", 46

Zilbetad Peak, **150**

Zillesa Mesa, **150**

Zilnez Mesa, **150**

Ziltahjini Mesa, 35

Ziltigloi Mountain (also Zilditloi Mountain) (see Dzilditloi Mountain), 204

Zuni-Acoma Trail, 204

Zuni Mountain Trading Post, 32

Zuni Mountains, 1, 107, 178, 204, 205, 216, 233, 259, **281**

Zuni Pueblo, 8(Table 4), 9(Table 9), **281**: first White contact at, 4; Navajo Agent Henry Lafayette Dodge disappears south of, 10; Washington's 1849 expedition through, 107; and Zuni-Chinle trade route, 146; Zunis from trade at Wide Ruin Trading Post, 146; Zarcillos Largos killed by Zunis, 146; influence at from Mesa Verde, 160; and migration narrative, 190; and importance of Stone Lions at Puye as Zuni shrine, 195; and Hawikuh, 204; and Jemez intermarriage, 223; Santa Clarans flee to, 260; Volnie trading at, 277; and mail route to Fort Defiance, 280

Zuni River, 84, 244, **283–84**

Zuni Road, **284**

Zuni Sacred Mountain (see Dowa Yalani Mountain), 203

Zuni Salt Lake (also Salt Lake, Laguna Salina), 232, 277, **283**

Zuni Trail, **49**